Slow Boats to China

Also available in the Picador Travel Classics series:

Gavin Young

Slow Boats to China

PICADOR

First published 1981 by Hutchinson & Co

This edition published 1995 by Picador
an imprint of Macmillan General Books
25 Eccleston Place, London SW1W 9NF
and Basingstoke

Associated companies throughout the world

ISBN 0 330 34128 6

1 3 5 7 9 8 6 4 2

A CIP catalogue record for this book is available from
the British Library

Phototypeset by Intype, London
Printed in Great Britain by
Mackays of Chatham plc, Chatham, Kent

This book is for my Mother and Father

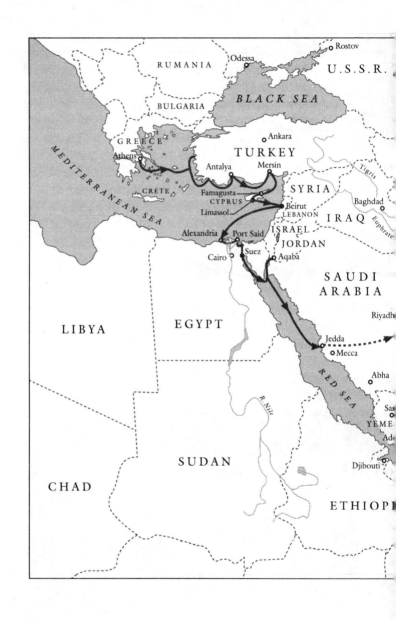

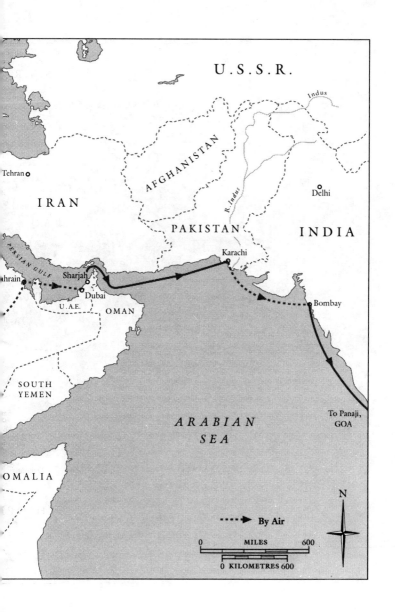

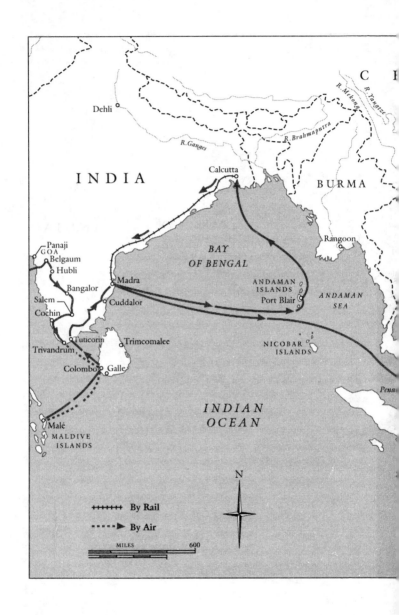

Dehli

INDIA

R.Ganges

Calcutta

BURMA

Rangoon

BAY
OF BENGAL

Panaji
GOA
Belgaum
Hubli
Bangalor
Salem
Cochin

Madra
Cuddalor

ANDAMAN
ISLANDS
Port Blair

ANDAMAN
SEA

Tuticorin
Trivandrum
Colombo
Galle

Trimcomalee

NICOBAR
ISLANDS

INDIAN
OCEAN

Malé
MALDIVE
ISLANDS

R.Mekong
R.Yangtse

C   F

R.Brahmaputra

Pena

N

+++++++ By Rail
- - - - ▶ By Air

MILES   600

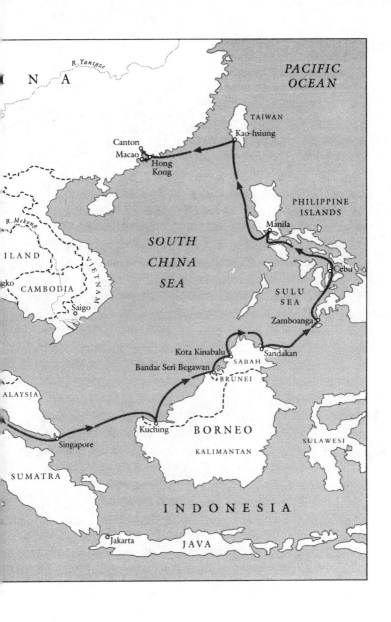

Acknowledgements

I owe many people a great debt of gratitude for helping me complete this adventure. I think my warm regard for most of them is to be found in the text, but an extra word is due to John and Glen Swire; to Captain Rashad of Alexandria, who saw me through the formidable obstacle of the Suez Canal; and to Tom Abraham, who smoothed my way to the mysterious Andaman Islands.

Donald Trelford, the editor of the *Observer*, and his associates Roger Harrison and Peter Crookston encouraged me and included some of what follows in the pages of the *Observer*'s colour supplement.

I have changed a personal name or two in the text and shifted the location of a couple of incidents to protect the people involved from possible political repercussions.

Finally, measureless thanks are due to Gritta Weil, my sea anchor in London, and to Roddy Bloomfield of Hutchinson.

Who hath desired the Sea? Her menaces swift as her
    mercies? . . .
Who hath desired the Sea? Her excellent loneliness rather
    than
The forecourts of kings.

> Rudyard Kipling, 'The Sea and the Hills'

Ah! These commercial interests – spoiling the finest life under
the sun. Why must the sea be used for trade – and for war as
well? . . . It would have been so much nicer just to sail about,
with here and there a port and a bit of land to stretch one's
legs on, buy a few books and get a change of cooking for a
while.

> Joseph Conrad, 'A Smile of Fortune'

Bir katredir ancak aldigum hep,
Derya yine durmada lebalep.
The things I've chosen are a drop, no more;
The undiminished sea still crowds the shore.

> Ziya Pasha

Contents

Prelude

I T WAS A SIMPLE idea: take a series of ships of many sizes and kinds; go where they lead for a few months; see what happens. It was an adaptation of the old idea of Running Away to Sea, a boyhood yearning bred of

> tales, marvellous tales
> Of ships and stars and isles where good men rest.

No doubt my dream of the sea was born during the long summers I spent as a child in what I still think of as the oldest-feeling, most soul-subduing and cosily creepy part of England, the part almost hidden between Britain's battered kneecap and shin. I mean, to be more exact, between Devon's Hartland Point and Cornwall's Fire Point Beacon above Boscastle, around the tiny harbour and old stone breakwater of Bude Haven. This is the Wreckers' Coast: a place of buzzards and seals and effigies of knights in dim, half-lost churches, where seas pound into cliffbound bays that have swallowed seamen from a hundred wrecked schooners and, in wartime, perhaps harboured German U-boats.

Once, poor Cornish children in these parts prayed, 'God save Father and Mother and zend a ship to shore vore mornin.' And on cold, rainy days there always seemed to me to be an aura here of doomed ships and silent watchers on terrible cliffs – an aura that survives today's asphalted roads and trailer parks. Yet in the summer sun it all looks quite different. Everything smiles on picnickers, surfers, flower gatherers and adventurous walkers with bird books, haversacks, sandwiches and hip flasks.

Under the sun, these cliffs give almost theatrically splendid views. South of Bude between Compass Point and Widemouth Bay's Black Rock (actually, the locals say, a Cornish giant eternally plaiting ropes sand), my grandmother years ago would jerkily brake the Austin two-seater and exclaim, 'What a lot of sea!' My grandmother's house stood back from the sea but on a rising slope of land, so that from my bedroom window I could see the gleam of the Atlantic Ocean over the rooftops of other houses. The attic of the gaunt and ugly Edwardian house smelled of damp floorboards, old suitcases and mouse droppings, but it was dark and large – ideal for hide-and-seek – and full of books, some of which had been my father's when he was a boy.

I spent hours up there delving into Robert Louis Stevenson, Jack London, Captain Marryat, R. M. Ballantyne and a Cornish writer of the 1920s called Crosbie Garstin who wrote exciting books about wreckers and smugglers on this very coast. Obsessed with the doings of Long John Silver or the Swiss Family Robinson, I was almost convinced that one clear day I would see on the horizon the Indies . . . tall ships . . . Hispaniola . . . Cathay. 'Fifteen men on a dead man's chest,' I would growl menacingly at my older sister, who would shrug and make herself scarce.

Even today, when I revisit Bude, this conviction sidles up to me like Blind Pew to Billy Bones. The cliffs there are as high as seven hundred and twenty feet, the waves relentlessly pound against them, larks and hawks move restlessly above, and the biggest gulls I've ever seen strut with eyes as cold as the sea below. The coastline here is a chain of tall headlands with names like Cow and Calf, Sharpnose Point, Wrangle Point, Longbeak, Dizzard. Their angry shapes and the prevailing westerly winds have done for dozens of ships, provoking the sailors' saying:

From Trevose Head to Hartland Light
Is a watery grave by day or night.

At the Falcon Inn in the old part of Bude, Desmond Gregory, the pub owner and a pillar of the hard-working Bude lifeboat team, lets off his signal rockets outside the pub if a boat is in trouble in the bay. Old photographs of spectacular wrecks adorn the walls of his bar; I have one of my own at home of the Austro-Hungarian barque *Capricorno*, her sails in tatters, her skipper drunk (so history books relate), being pounded to pieces by enormous seas below Compass Point in December 1900. Only two men were saved. In the picture, a solitary seaman stands on the doomed deck like Steerforth in *David Copperfield*.

Sailing ships regularly used Bude as a port of call up to 1936; I remember a locally famous ketch called *Ceres* and old bewhiskered sea captains strolling around the harbour.

All this contributed to my dream of adventure and sea travel that this book represents. It also gave me a sense of

the past, for Bude is ennobled by its cliffs, its thundering surf and its eerie hinterland. Even now, visiting the place after an interval of time, I am startled by the sheer *age* of the region. You can ramble for hours across headlands that run back forming broad, high land on which scattered farms seem settled hull down in wriggling lanes to escape the winter gales that have forced the trees to grow almost parallel to the earth. In long, deep valleys you come across small, ancient churches oddly far from any village, and smelling of flowers and grass. Huge trees loom over their tombstones, under stone canopies armoured effigies turn up stone toes, and fine old wooden pews are fighting erosion by age or the deathwatch beetle. On the gravestones the same names appear over and over, century after century: Mutton, Sleeman, Oke and Prust. Frequent Christian names here are Eli, Caleb, Joshua, Reuben. As a boy, I was particularly fond of a clifftop church at a village called Morwenstow because it had a ship's figurehead in its grave-yard, and because a once-famous and eccentric vicar is buried there. Parson Hawker ('Passon' was how the locals pronounced it) ate opium and wrote outrageous poetry

4

when he wasn't burying drowned sailors between 1834 and 1878. He was a practical joker, and one moonlit night he clambered on to a rock to impersonate a mermaid. In a book of the time, a Bude man was recorded as saying of this scene, 'Dressin' up in seaweed and not much else, and combin' his hair and zingin', till all the town went down to see 'un, they thought 'twas a merry maid [mermaid] sure enough.' Then the 'Passon' scared the daylights out of his audience by standing up on his rock and singing 'God Save the King'.

If a cloud covers the sun in this old region of England, you may feel suddenly uneasy. As a boy, I was sometimes glad to get back to the life of Bude's wide sandy beaches, where young men surfed, children's nannies helped to build sand castles, and hysterical dogs tried to dig their way to Australia. Kids with kites would shriek when their mother capsized in the shrimp pool ('Oh, Ma, you're showing all you've got!') while I sat by myself nursing my dream of far places among the long black lines of rock, knobbly with mussels and limpets, like arthritic fingers, running out into the booming surf.

Years passed before the dream achieved the least substance. This happened not long before my eighteenth birthday, when a school friend and I walked through the dead of a misty night to board a ship at a wharf in Fowey, a small Cornish river port. My friend's father had arranged with the shipowners for us to be signed on to a 500-ton coaster, the *Northgate*, out of Hull. A modest adventure, a short voyage up the English Channel to the Scheldt and Antwerp, but at that age it was as exciting as a round trip to Hispaniola and the Spanish Main.

We went down to Fowey in January, the month some

sailors refer to as 'between dog and wolf', and it was one of the wildest Januaries for years. The berthed ship seemed as dead as an icicle. I can still hear the ring of our hesitant heels on the freezing metal deck, our whispers in the dark, and at last the wavering cry of 'Who's there?' from the skylight, before the white, balding head of the ship's cook, a kind, brusque old man, emerged from the companionway.

I remember thinking that the *Northgate* seemed disconcertingly indifferent to our arrival. How could that be when we had dreamed about her for weeks? I didn't know then that a ship only wakes up and pays attention to those on board when she's at sea.

In the morning sunshine things seemed different, of course, not alarming at all. The captain was a friendly Yorkshireman, and the crew took our presence on board as a bit of a joke. We had signed on as 'deckie-learners', and I suppose we polished the brass and swabbed away the china clay that had clogged the decks during loading energetically enough to satisfy them.

A short trip, but it was the year of record gales in the Channel and we rode one of them out at anchor in a fleet of other ships off Dungeness on the Kentish coast. The *Northgate* was unduly long for her width and plunged about abominably − so abominably, in fact, that the captain and all his officers were seasick. A radio battery in the messroom broke loose, and its acid burned awkward holes in my corduroy trousers. I remember my relief at not being sick, and the captain's white face, and offering him a Capstan cigarette and my pride when he said, 'Thanks moochly, Gav.'

At Antwerp, although the city was still in ruins from the air raids in the war which had not long ended, we were allowed ashore escorted by Andie, a diminutive deckhand of about my age. In a deserted square near the bombed cathedral, Andie trotted confidently over to two tarts on a corner. He chose the taller of the two – at least a foot taller than himself. On the cathedral steps he had to stand one step above her, and for a moment he even lost his footing. Later he boasted, 'You've never seen that before,' and we had to admit we hadn't. He also boasted that he'd had syphilis and the quack had poured mercury up his penis. God knows if it was true; we'd have believed anything then.

That short trip marked me as much, perhaps, as the mercury marked Andie. For years I dreamed of taking a much longer sea journey, but travel and war reporting intervened. Only recently did the possibility occur, and by then it was almost too late.

Almost too late, that is, to find any ships. Working one's passage is difficult – impossible, perhaps – in these strict days of unions and unemployment. Passenger travel, as I was to discover, is moribund. Nevertheless, I set about finding out what would happen to someone who tried to port-hop to some far destination on the other side of the world. (The end of the line, I thought, could be a port in China – Canton, say; Canton would do.) Surely, it must be possible. How could sea travel be dead?

I could have taken a long cruise, but I ruled that out; I didn't want to travel long distances on a single ship. I wondered how travel agents would react to the sort of hop-skip-jump I had in mind, and when I tried a couple of them I found discouragement.

'It's impossible. Even for a single gent, it's utterly imposs-ible.' The middle-aged travel agent ran a finger delicately across his left eyebrow and organized a mouth that might, twenty years before, have been described as 'rosebud', into an apologetic smile. 'So my answer, I'm ever so sorry to tell you, is rather simple: "No can do." ' He lightly dabbed his lips with a handkerchief he took from his sleeve. He wore a puce knitted tie that looked like a hairnet.

He had been affability itself when I first came in, but when I told him what I wanted I saw at once that I was going to spoil his day.

'By sea? Oh, dearie me, that's a poser, that is. Well, let me just think. A single gent, from Europe to Macao, all on your own? I'm not even sure how I'd set about it. You're a dying breed, you lone travellers – you know that, I suppose. It's all groups now, you know. Frankly, on your own, you're more of a nuisance than anything.'

He looked me over without enthusiasm. 'A group, I'd know how to handle you. I mean, I can arrange a nice long tour for a *group* of old biddies, with exciting stopovers – well, *quite* exciting. But *you*? I might be flipping through those enormous shipping lists until the cows come home and still not have accommodated you in the way you fancy. Frankly, my time's limited and I must ask myself, is it worth spending it on this single gentleman? Nothing against you personally, of course.'

I rose to go.

'It's modern life,' he said. 'You've asked me for the utterly impossible, and my simple answer is: "No can do." '

His dismissive 'Cheeri-bye' followed me out.

At Thomas Cook's in Berkeley Street a sensible, much nicer man, Mr Bert Chattell, a former Cook's tour courier, was equally pessimistic.

'The trouble is, the traditional British sea routes to the Far East and across the Atlantic have disappeared because of rising prices and cheaper air travel. Prices – that's it in a nutshell. Now there's only P&O to Australia and New Zealand, and round the world now and again on a limited scale.

'I can't for the life of me think of any boat going south of the Med. Nothing springs to mind there. In the old days, of course, well. . . . There's Polish Ocean Lines, they go from Gdynia to Antwerp, and from there to Port Said, Singapore and Hong Kong, Japan and back again. But not, I think you'll find, on a schedule. You can never tell what delays there'll be.

'If someone came up to me and said, "Book me round the world now," I couldn't do it. Not on a *series* of ships, I mean.'

Not encouraging. But there must, I thought, be some way, however erratic, to travel by sea to Asia. I refused to believe it was impossible.

I telephoned the P&O Lines people in the City of London, but the news there was also depressing. P&O have cruise ships, they said, but nothing that would interest me.

A call to Swire & Sons, one of the biggest British trading and shipping companies in the Far East, brought an invitation from John Swire, head of the giant British group that includes, among much else, the China Navigation Company in Hong Kong. 'Come and lunch,' he said.

Swire's is big and grand. Grand enough and old enough to have accumulated traditions and a book or two of imperial history. Tycoon is a Japanese word (*taikun*). The Swires are tycoons. At Regis House (big but not grand) in the City near London Bridge, an elderly servant opened a door and said, 'For Mr John Swire? This way, if you please, sir.' Beautiful, meticulously constructed models of Swire

9

ships past and present stood along the walls in glass cases. A collection of old ship's bells lay in a row like the skulls of warriors in an African burial cave. I was looking at a bell inscribed with the name *Hupeh* and the date 1937 when John Swire, a towering, soldierly figure, came up. 'That's the old *Hupeh*, not the one we've got now,' he said. Several months later I sailed from Manila on the new *Hupeh* and thought back to this old bell.

'We have practically no cargo-passenger ships in the East,' John Swire said at lunch. Swire's cargo ships were still active between Hong Kong, Taiwan, China, Japan, the Pacific islands, Australia, New Guinea, the Philippines and Singapore, but air travel was taking over eastern passenger routes; the Swires themselves owned the airline Cathay Pacific. If only, he said, I had tried to do this ten years ago . . .

Nevertheless, he was helpful, willing to provide a safety net if he could. He would write to his offices throughout the East, asking his managers to look out for me and help where possible; I might need any help I could get if I was to avoid being stranded for weeks in some godforsaken place. Swire's also had an operation in the Gulf, he added – tugs working with offshore oil rigs, that sort of thing. Might be interesting.

Afterwards I walked out into King William Street and hurried past the quick-sandwich shops, the window full of telex appliances and the doors of Christian missionary societies, and took a tube to Green Park. In Cook's, kind Mr Chattell gave me a shipping list, the *ABC Shipping Guide*, and like a squirrel with a nut, I carried it home and devoured it.

About half of its pages was devoted to cruises: no good to me. The other half showed that people who wanted to move about between small collections of islands, or from one port to another one nearby, faced no problem. If you felt a burning desire to travel by sea between say, Gomera and Tenerife in the Canaries, you could easily do so; if a sudden impulse drove you to cross from Cape May, New Jersey, to Lewes Ferry, Delaware, the Delaware Bay Service was daily at your disposal for a small charge.

On other pages, long-distance round trips on large cargo-passenger ships were advertised. Farrell Lines, for example, would give you a round trip from the United States to South Africa and back again; the Moore-McCormack Lines would take you from New York to Cape Town to Dar es Salaam to Zanzibar and back every three weeks. Lykes Brothers Steamship Company would take you on a round trip to Japan. There were others, but none offered the flexibility I needed.

By now it was obvious that I must play the trip to Canton by ear. There was no point in relying on elusive dates and problematical itineraries of ships subject to whimsical change. I would take what came along the way, trusting to luck that any delay would not be horrendously long. I had taken leave of absence from the *Observer*, telling Donald Trelford, the editor, that the journey shouldn't take me much more than four months; that seemed a longish time as I pored over my maps in London. I would board any vessel moving in the right direction: a tanker, a freighter, a dhow, a junk – anything. Nothing that went too far at one time; that would reduce the number of ports of call – and I wanted to see a good number of ports.

I was embarking, in fact, on a game of traveller's

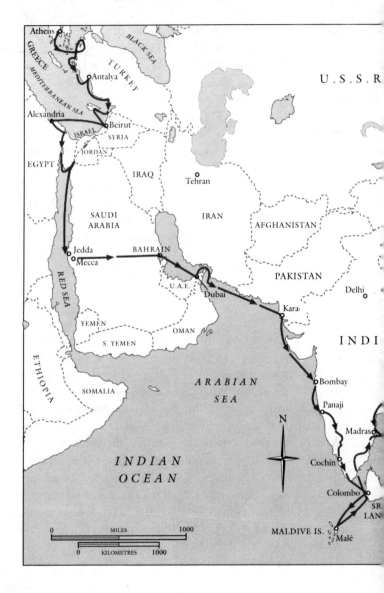

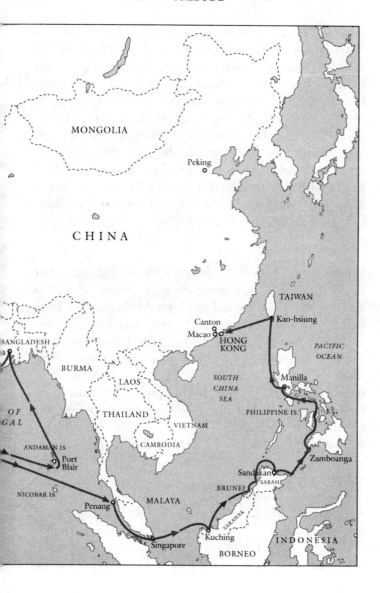

roulette. I bought a cheap atlas and marked with a ballpoint pen a number of ports either because I liked the sound of them or because I had been there before as a foreign correspondent: Smyrna, Alexandria, Port Said, Suez, Jedda, Dubai, Karachi, Bombay, Cochin, Colombo, Calcutta, Madras, Singapore, Brunei, Bangkok, Manila, Hong Kong, Macao, Canton. As an afterthought, though without much hope, I added the Andaman Islands, in the Bay of Bengal; the sombre vision of a tropical penal settlement and sudden and agonizing death from native poisoned darts had lodged in my mind since my first reading of Conan Doyle's Sherlock Holmes thriller *The Sign of Four*.

Where should I start? I went back to the lists again, but the decision was soon made. Not Rotterdam or Southampton; the Channel and the west Mediterranean were well known and well travelled. I would start in Europe, but as close to Asia as possible: Athens. Friends had told me of a steamer that shuttled passengers from Piraeus to the Greek island of Patmos, near Smyrna in Turkey-in-Asia. From there I could find my way slowly to the Suez Canal (even then the canal looked like a Becher's Brook, a first and formidable major hurdle).

That decided, I booked a flight to Athens and began to gather together the things I would need on a sea voyage of indeterminate length.

Notebooks, ballpoint pens and books were the first requirements. Conrad's *Under Western Eyes* and *Mirror of the Sea*, Ford Madox Ford's *Memories and Impressions*, a handful of thrillers, Joseph Heller's *Good as Gold*, *Vintage Wodehouse*. I was taking two cameras and I wanted to keep my money safe, so I bought a metal suitcase at some expense. It had a combination lock, and the salesman assured me it would take gelignite to open it if the lock was turned. It was heavy, so I took a light zip-fastened bag as well.

God knew where I would find myself from week to week, so I arranged with my bank to send money to certain places on my way where I could pick it up by producing my passport. I don't like travelling with bundles of notes or even large numbers of traveller's cheques. I bought a money belt, too, but in the end I used it only in the Sulu Sea, thinking that the pirates there might strip and search me without stopping to examine the back of the ordinary-looking belt. (The result of this subterfuge was that a number of banknotes were so damaged by salt water and sweat that for a long time in the Philippines I hesitated to try to pass them.)

It was going to be wet at sea and possibly cold, so I took my old green Grenfell anorak from Vietnam days. I had thick-soled, strong shoes and a pair of lighter ones to wear ashore. Medicines: I bought Septrin, Mexaform (for diarrhoea) and aspirin. I washed out my father's hip flask and filled it with Scotch. A newly acquired Polaroid camera was to prove almost as useful to me in breaking the ice with shy and hostile strangers as beads were to explorers of old.

I couldn't think of anything else.

At last I was ready for the traveller's roulette to begin, and drove to London airport to catch the Athens flight.

There is no better place than a crowded European airport on an August morning in which to say a tearless farewell to air travel for a few months. With its look of a tarted-up transit camp, London airport stifles euphoria at the best of times. Even so, I felt none of the elation you might expect in an adventurer departing for Eastern seas among crowds of August holidaymakers morosely contemplating the big boards announcing delays in their flights to Vienna, Rome and Lisbon.

I had spent a late last night – reluctant, when it came to it, to abandon friends for a seagoing mystery tour almost half across the world on unscheduled ships. In thirty years of travel I have seldom begun a long journey without the feeling that I shall never return, and this beginning was no exception.

I edged my way to the bar and ordered a small black coffee. 'Oh, and a Fernet Branca, please.'

'Brave man,' the barman said, and poured so generously that a small puddle of the dark-brown liquid formed around the base of the glass. I took his generosity as a good omen.

The Fernet Branca's bitter warmth raised my spirits a notch or two. Soon a precise English female voice on the loudspeaker system announced that the Athens flight would leave on time, and this helped as well. But it was a false prophecy. Another two hours went by before we were allowed to board and listen to the captain apologizing for the delay, caused, he said, by air-traffic congestion. And another hour before the arrival of plastic trays bearing the airline's 'paprika sauce' congealing on 'turkey escalopes' that retained the consistency of corrugated cardboard. The delays in the shipping world, I know now from experience, run into days or weeks, not hours, but only one out of the bizarre diversity of vessels I was to take on my long sea road to China produced food less appetizing than that airline meal between London and Athens.

I bought a cognac to wash away the taste and then the clear white Alps were below us. Later still, at last, the even clearer blue of Salamis Bay. Motorboats drew snowy trails among the islands and headlands basking in the warm sea. Seagulls wheeled and whitecaps flickered against the blue water – blue and white, the colours of the Greek flag. It was like a photograph on one of the postcards my fellow passengers would be sending home, whose recipients would sniff in disbelief at the unnaturalness of the colour reproduction. Here Europe ended; somewhere in the haze and glint of the eastern Mediterranean Sea, Europe and Asia came together. Beyond Athens airport the first of my ships waited for me; and, beyond that, Asia.

For the moment, Athens, much less Asia, was inaccessible beyond six long lines of passengers waiting for passport control. Evidently four jumbo jets had arrived at the same time.

A woman near me was saying, 'It's better at London airport, isn't it? Better organized, really.'

I went through customs behind two florid young Englishmen dressed in identical brown blazers with brass buttons who bantered, Bertie Wooster-fashion, in strong Yorkshire accents.

'To the yacht and straight into the sea, what?'

'Yeah. Second one in pays for the champagne.'

'Roger, old man.'

When I had reached the city centre and checked into a modest hotel on Mount Lyccabetos that someone had told me about, the receptionist told me I still had time to see Thomas Cook's before they closed. I wanted to make sure I could get on the next ship heading through the Greek islands to Patmos. I had been told that the hotel had a 'lovely view of the Acropolis', and I suppose that if I'd been a giraffe I might have spent some time peering at it around the corner of the hotel. My room, though perfectly comfortable, was gloomy and on the ground floor and looked out on to a busy construction site. 'It's the month for tourist groups,' the receptionist explained. It occurred to me that perhaps all the passenger ships were going to be full too, so I hurried to Cook's office in Constitution Square.

Cook's was oddly hard to find but, after an interlude of dodging through crowds of blond tourists in shorts, I found it in a corner of the square on the second floor of a tall modern building. A friendly Greek lady there told me that the next ship to sail in the direction I wanted would be the steamer *Alcheon*, a Greek passenger vessel leaving Piraeus the next day at two o'clock in the afternoon for her regular run through the Aegean. She will stop, as usual, the lady said, at the island of Mikonos, and reach Patmos in the middle of the following night. Eleven hours; it seemed worthwhile to book a cabin.

The Cook's lady blew her nose into a Kleenex, made a telephone call and reported, 'Tomorrow there's only one berth left. In a cabin with three other people.'

'Any way of knowing who they are?'

'No.'

It didn't matter. It was a stroke of luck that there was any berth at all. 'I'll take it.' At least it would be somewhere to lodge my ironclad suitcase. As I put my ticket and passport away, the Cook's lady said, 'I should board at one o'clock, if I were you.'

With my first steamship ticket in my pocket, there was time for a quiet evening in Athens. I had no intention of sightseeing; I had been to Athens several times before. I had pottered about the Parthenon and could remember enough nights filled with retsina, smashed plates and table-dancing to twanging *bouzoukis*, the Greek equivalent of the zither, in taverns full of apaches. Enough of that – at least until Cyprus. For someone about to walk the plank from Europe into Eastern seas, only the peace of Orfanides's beckoned with a wrinkled, ouzo-scented finger. But first I stopped at the bookstall of the Grande Bretagne Hotel and bought the Kümmerly and Frey map of Greece, the Geographia map of Turkey (which covers Syria, Cyprus and Lebanon too), some prickly-heat powder and half a dozen postcards. Then I strolled around the corner to old Orfanides's.

I say 'old' Orfanides. For whoever Orfanides is and whatever his age – let's hope he's still alive – he cannot be young. His bar, too, has the right kind of old dusty shelves, the right number of old dusty bottles around its walls, a marble-topped wooden bar inside at one end, and small tables at the opposite end and outside on the street. 'The Oldest Bar in Athens' is Orfanides's claim – 'Established in 1916'. The fan on a wall over the bar is massive and rusty and is probably one of the first revolving fans ever made, but it works. It is needed because it is unlikely that one's blood temperature will remain unaffected by the intake of alcohol made possible by the provision of a thick finger of ouzo for ten pence and a glass of Samos wine for twenty.

I took a table on the street and, when I had ordered ouzo, ice, a glass of water and a small plate of olives, I took my *Alcheon* ticket from my pocket and laid it carefully on the table next to the map of Greece. The rush of leaving England and friends, the many details I'd had to tidy up before leaving and the flight itself had all combined to smother any sense of what I was now embarked on. I wanted to brood on that first ticket. I wanted a reminder that I was going to China on slow boats, and that my destination was several months and thousands of miles away. I wanted to let the blissful thought seep into my head that, after nearly twenty years and fourteen wars, I was not embarking on one more harassing sprint for the *Observer*. In other words, I needed to slip into neutral, and Orfanides's was a good place for that. Once it had been a comforting place in an ugly time.

In 1967, when I was Paris correspondent of the *Observer*, a trio of colonels seized power in Greece. I knew what to expect from London and it soon came: a telephone call from the *Observer*'s foreign news editor. 'How about a trip to Athens?' he said.

The next day I had found the lobby of the Grande Bretagne crowded and chaotic. My friends Jo Menell and John Morgan with their BBC television crew were struggling with cameras, recording apparatus and miles of cable halfway in and halfway out of the glass-front doors. We had last met in the horrendous pandemonium of Vietnam the year before. Full-scale repression in Greece and mass graves of Greek and Turkish civilians in Cyprus were still in the future when I came upon Jo and John. At the time, the situation seemed mildly laughable but, in the days that followed, laughter died away, and the grim routine of revolution closed around the Greeks. Telephones whirred and clicked in a sinister way; friends vanished overnight.

That first evening, Jo, John and I went despondently to Orfanides's. The bar was full of equally despondent Greeks. Jo rapped the table and said ironically, 'Gavin, you're about to see the revival by the military of Greek democracy in its finest and purest form. Except that they'll probably institute the death penalty for everything from homosexuality to zither music. They'll have Socrates spinning in his grave.'

John and Jo had taken their camera into Orfanides's to see if the elderly Greek customers there were willing to discuss the colonels. They didn't expect that they would be, but neither the waiters nor the old gentlemen held it against Jo and John that they tried to film them. In the next few days we went there often, and one evening from Orfanides's terrace we watched soldiers, priests and men in double-breasted suits parading by to impress wavering Athenians and foreigners with their 'revolution' and its permanence.

Now, twelve years later, the colonels were in jail and in disgrace.

I ordered another ouzo, watched the ice turn it to milk, put my ticket away, and felt glad to be watching a different sort of parade: the promenade of August tourists. A decorous lot, by and large. The hippies seemed to have moved on. Perhaps I would catch up with them in Goa or Ceylon; perhaps they'd just grown up and settled down with mortgages and televised soap opera. Elderly English: men in panama hats, white-moustached; women in sensible, low-heeled shoes and head scarves. Americans in small, round straw hats. Schools of young German males in shorts so brief and tight you wondered where they found room to park their genitalia, and their pretty but big-bottomed girls; slip-slopping their sandalled feet, they went past Orfanides's to the grander Snack Bar, where a notice said in demotic German, *ein deutsch sprechen.*

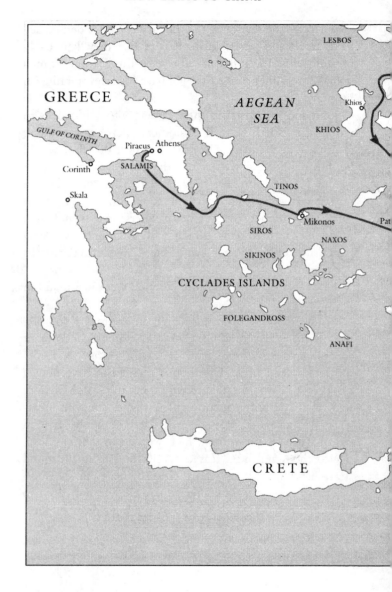

Betgama

Izmir

TURKEY

Ephesus
Kusadasi

MOS

Antalya

Bodrum

Marmaris

Finike

COS

Cuidus

Myra

RHODES

N

MEDITERRANEAN SEA

| 0 | MILES | 100 |

| 0 | KILOMETRES | 100 |

23

When darkness fell, I ate something in a small restaurant and then found a taxi. It was quite late enough. After all, I was leaving for China next day.

Part One

PIRAEUS TO JEDDA

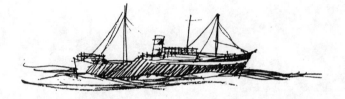

Chapter 4

Chapter One

THE FOLLOWING DAY, the Greek motor vessel *Alcheon*, alongside her pier in Piraeus, dribbled a soft ribbon of smoke from her sloping funnel and prepared to sail. 1.55 p.m.: the gangway would be hauled in soon; the passengers who were still boarding had cut it fine.

From an upper deck I looked at the sweep of Piraeus in the sunlight. A screen of medium-sized high-rise buildings of no distinction spread out against the bright hills of Attika. A line of cranes bent and swung their heads. Other vessels of Greece's big island passenger fleet awaited their turn to sail, their sirens impatiently mooing like cows sensing their release into a meadow: the *Kydon*; beyond her, the *Omyros* of Chios; next a torpedo-shaped yellow hydroplane with two fins, the *Flying Dolphin*; another gleam of orthodox white streamlining, the *Ariadne* . . .

Gloomy Northerners with heavy packs shuffled up the gangway, but the Greek passengers easily outnumbered the tourists. Solid island women swiftly commandeered benches on deck where they hauled off their shoes, exposing crimson toenails and varicosed and unshaven legs. Three frenzied Greek women had already pinned the young assistant purser in a doorway, buffeting him with bosoms that jostled each other like melons in black sacking. Having won their point, they petted him with shrugs and heavy sighs, as if enacting a grotesque parody of lovemaking. It seemed a more reasonable way of registering umbrage than the smouldering British way. I was about to be given a dose of the British treatment, and it increased my impatience for Asia.

Two elderly Britons stood near a companionway. He was pointing out landmarks ashore with a shooting stick. He had a white moustache and an open-necked shirt with a silk scarf worn like a cravat. His wife, who probed the air with long front teeth and had the swooping neck of a camel, turned to me. 'I was just saying to my husband it's exciting, isn't it, the last moment before sailing. Mysterious. Like entering the Tunnel of Love at a fun fair.' Her head jerked backwards and forwards as she spoke.

'Steady on, Maggie,' the husband said. He glanced at me with distaste, touching his scarf as if it were a talisman against the evil eye.

'We're doing a tour of the islands,' she said. 'First to Mikonos. We have old friends there with a lovely house. What about you?'

'I'm going to China,' I said, and saw at once that she thought I was being facetious.

'I see,' she said in a chilling voice. He took her arm and led her away, aiming his shooting stick at a power station as if it were the Parthenon. 'Uncalled for,' I heard her say.

What had upset her? Looking back now, I realize that I had no misunderstanding in the next seven months – not even with people who spoke no English – comparable to this ridiculous encounter with a fellow countrywoman on my first day at sea.

We sailed while I was learning from the young assistant purser some of the facts about the *Alcheon*.

'She's old,' he said. 'Thirty years old. But so *strong*.' He punched the bulkhead like a groom slapping a favourite horse. 'Eighteen miles an hour. Four-eight-zero-zero tons. Built Copenhagen. Named for a king – no, a queen. Maybe Queen Ingrid.'

Vibrations shook the deck, and I felt the ship sway. Steadily shrinking, the Greek customs officers on shore, immaculate in white shirts, belts and trousers, white shoes and caps, talking quietly together, watched us swinging out from the quay.

The captain, the four gold rings on his shoulder very bright, looked at the shore from the wing of the bridge; impassive, half Onassis, half Niarchos; white hair crinkled around a bald skull, tight curls at the back. The mirror surfaces of his dark glasses would now be reflecting a moving view of half-finished blocks of flats.

'Greek captains never will use a chart,' E. M. Forster wrote on a Mediterranean cruise eighty years ago. 'Although they sometimes do have one aboard, it is always locked up in a drawer; for as they truly say, it is nothing but paper and lines, which are not the least like the sea, and it's far better to trust to yourself, especially in parts where you have never been before.' As the Greeks combine instinct with caution, said Forster, progress is sometimes slow.

Such mockery was inappropriate to the hefty back of our captain, who now turned his curving nose and thick, firm lips toward the bay of Salamis. *His* drawer, one knew, was unlocked; *his* charts, with their beautifully engraved whirls of height and depth, intricate lines depicting bays and inlets, islands and headlands, were spread out on the chart-room table like works of art in an exhibition. Every line of them, it went without saying, was etched in his mind alongside all the instinct and caution we needed to get us to Patmos without bumping into something.

I lugged my bags below and found the cabin I was to share. Two lots of baggage stood just outside the door, but

the cabin was empty. I pushed my suitcase under a lower berth and put my anorak across it. The cabin had two washbasins and four metal bunks, two up, two down. It was hot.

I headed upstairs again, passing two middle-aged British couples wrestling with their bags at the open door of another four-berther. 'It's only for one night,' a man was saying. 'Quite hunky dory, really, don't you think, boys and girls?'

Later I saw the husbands carefully balancing cans of beer into the first-class lounge, where suffocating heat seemed to radiate from inappropriate deep armchairs covered with olive-drab material. The bar was cooler; fresh air came in through two large windows. Perhaps the heat in the lounge stifled holiday jollity in the British passengers. The British husbands came back at regular intervals to the bar, where I sat with my ouzo and Ford Madox Ford's *Memories and*

Impressions. Recognizing me as a fellow Briton, they treated me to the nod and twist of the lips that passes for a wry little smile north of the English Channel. 'Bit of a carry-on this, eh, old chap?' their silent message said. Perhaps my own absurd little smile spoke in the same idiom: 'Rather!'

As I saw when I went on deck, the *Alcheon* was probably doing her eighteen knots. The black–clad Greek ladies with varicose veins and elderly Greek men in straw hats and baggy grey trousers, shirt sleeves and braces had settled on the deck space like an occupying army. A solid youngish woman was shrieking with unbelievable volume at her husband, 'Ee? . . . Ee? . . . Ee?' It was as if someone were opening a rusty hinge an inch at a time.

We passed through the Cyclades, and my Kümmerly and Frey map showed me a spattering of islands I'd never heard of: Sifnos, Sikinos and Folegandros (a nice name); Tinos, Siros and Anafi. Are they all tourist traps in the summer? I peered at some of them through my old Leitz binoculars. At least I couldn't see any plastic beach huts. (The French export these vulgarities as cavalierly as Captain Cook transported smallpox to the South Seas. I'd even seen them in the remote mountain resorts of Iraqi Kurdistan.) Perhaps there are still a few Greek islands unviolated.

The islands sat in the sun, soaking heat into rock surfaces that were only occasionally marked by the white blobs of islanders' houses. This landscape is what you see from Spain to the immense knife-edge passes of Afghanistan, from Yugoslavia to Aden; in spring it is beautiful with small flowers, and at all times of the year the colours in the rock change as the light shifts. Moonlight can give the rock surfaces an illusion of snow. I wish I weren't conditioned to associate this kind of landscape with other memories: jet planes banking around headlands, skimming through valleys, bombing or rocketing, leaving behind them the roar of engines, plumes of smoke and mourning columns of refugees.

In the hot afternoon I went down to the empty cabin and slept.

When I awoke, the cabin was no longer empty: two men, both Greeks, were dozing. A large, oldish man lay in the berth above mine, fully clothed. From his throat issued a loud rattling and gargling. On the lower bunk opposite, a plump body sprawled on its back, corpse-white where it was not covered with thick black hair. It was nude except for a black jockstrap, over which a hand began to move restlessly. The cabin was as humid as a Turkish bath, and there was a bittersweet smell of underarms and feet. I wiped a trickle of sweat from my neck and hurried out to the upper air.

On the deck, passengers levelled their glasses shorewards. My Leitz binoculars were small, light and powerful, and they would fold into a pocket. I swung them about and found a seagull playing a game near the *Alcheon's* bows. It was a plump gull, and its head, back and the upper side of its wings were a muddy brown. Its game went like this. First, rise to twenty feet, moving parallel with and close to the ship. Next, hurl yourself down to within millimetres of the skin of the sea, and stay there, gently swaying on rigid wings, contouring the surface.

The gull seemed to be consciously challenging the bow

wave, which only had to rise two centimetres to turn it into a lump of feathers cartwheeling to destruction, just as Second World War Japanese kamikaze planes, shot down by American ships, cartwheeled and broke up in clouds of spray. Of course, the gull knew what it was doing. Whoever heard of a gull smashed by a wave? Gulls and dolphins like playing games with ships, and both seem to prefer an audience.

We passed barren island hillsides, Greek trawlers under power with sail-less masts, and the odd white island steamer.

In the evening darkness, the *Alcheon* dropped anchor off Mikonos three hundred yards from a stone jetty. Passengers who wanted to disembark gathered at the gangway to walk down to the small boats that would take them ashore. Among them were the Englishman with the shooting stick and the woman with the neck like a camel.

The rest of us went to the dining room. Over the lamb and salad, my dinner companion, a black-chinned, chubby man, told me cheerfully that he was a ship's barman on leave. His home, he said, was Kefallinia, an island off Greece's west coast, south of Corfu. He had been about quite a bit in different ships, and now was off to join one at the island of Cos, beyond Patmos, almost touching Turkey. When I told him I was heading for southern Turkey, he waved his fork, scattering drops of olive oil. 'I tell you. Izmir [Smyrna] no good, dirty. Mersin the same. *Very* dirty. From there, where do you go?'

'Perhaps Haifa. Perhaps Beirut. Perhaps Alexandria.'

'Haifa dirty.' He dismissed Haifa with his fork. 'Only good place Jerusalem.' He slopped retsina into both our glasses and beckoned to our waiter for more. 'But Haifa better than Alexandria. In Alexandria, ha, they want to kill

33

you.' He leaned toward me earnestly. 'Ye-e-s. I mean it. They kill sailors for their money. In Alex, I tell you, big crowds of bad peoples come to the ships. Why? Because they have nothing to eat, they are always starving. And they smell so bad in Alexandria.'

He sat back as the retsina came and poured more of it into our glasses. 'But, most important, they kill for money.' He looked at me, smiling sadly. 'You don't believe me.'

I had been in Alexandria several times without noticing exceptional smells. Nor had I noticed the inhabitants of that ancient and balmy city engaged in killing for money, although they can manage a spectacular riot. Still, the Greek barman was a happy companion. I wondered if he knew that three decades ago Alexandria was practically a Greek city, and I didn't mention the Greek poet of Alexandria, Constantine Cavafy. Later I looked up Cavafy's poem 'On Board Ship'; aboard the *Alcheon* it seemed appropriate:

> Of course it is like him, this little
> Drawing of him in pencil.
> Quickly done, on the deck of the ship;
> An enchanting afternoon.
> The Ionian ocean all around us . . .
>
> Out of Time. All these things are very old –
> The sketch, and the ship, and the afternoon.

After dinner we went to the ship's little bar; he'd be at home there. 'Screwdriver,' he cried joyfully, and in five minutes threw back two double vodkas mixed with fizzy Sunripe Orange, wincing at the bitterness of the orange taste.

'I make first-class screwdriver.' A professional was speaking. 'These are not screwdrivers, but nearly.' He jerked his chin at the barman, who responded with a thumb's-up sign and brought the same again: a screwdriver for him and for me a Metaxa brandy. We kept each other company until we reached Patmos, and I was sorry to say goodbye.

The *Alcheon* crept into the waters of Patmos at about midnight, and tied up at the stone quay of the small and only port, Skala, a crescent of low white buildings, cafés, a police station, one or two small hotels, tourist shops and tavernas. A hill rises steeply behind the town and stops in a spread of lights against the stars; the following morning I saw above me a monastery walled like a fortress and more white houses. From there, I discovered later, you can see almost the entire island of Patmos.

On the quay a company of grey-haired Greek women in black who had been eagerly awaiting the *Alcheon's* arrival now advanced like gendarmes to the foot of the gangway. The barman had told me to expect them. They were the landladies of Skala, come, like buyers in a slave market, to fill their empty rooms from the pool of arrivals. About thirty of us spilled awkwardly down the ramp into their arms.

I dropped my metal suitcase on the quayside with a thump and waited to be gathered up. At once a small but stocky lady in black appeared at my elbow.

'Room? Room?' she screamed into my face.

'Yes, room. Big room.'

'Come,' she ordered. I took up my suitcase and prepared to follow her. That had been simple, I thought. But she didn't move.

'How many friends?' She peered around me as if she

expected to find several people roped behind me like Alpine climbers.

'I have no friends.' The pathos of the remark struck me as I uttered it, but there was no corresponding pity in her voice, only disbelief.

'No friends?' She had never heard of such a thing. Everyone arrives in Patmos with friends. Suddenly her face was rigid with disappointment or suspicion. A single long hair thrust out quivering toward me from a mole on her cheek like a locust's antenna sensing trouble. Just then a party of young Germans came toward us, round-shouldered under huge knapsacks.

The hair from the mole excitedly tested the air near the four straw-coloured beards. 'Four persons?' She smiled at them.

'Ja, ja.' They smiled back. Four men to fill her rooms; that was more like it. She was radiant. All history might have conspired to deliver this quartet into her hands. Her back was turned to me by now like a slammed door. 'Come,' she said, and the little group moved away into the darkness.

All over the quay the same thing was happening. Groups of passengers in shorts were humping baggage single file after the triumphant landladies, like African porters behind white hunters on safari. Soon I was left alone under the puzzled gaze of those who had stayed on board, and who were now leaning on the *Alcheon's* rail staring curiously down at a man standing by a metal suitcase. A man who wore trousers, not shorts. A man alone in the middle of the night. A man, evidently, without friends.

Allez! This would not do. I gathered up my luggage and with feigned jauntiness followed the disappearing throng. I could see 'Police' written on a board near a cluster of lights. Perhaps I could rent a police cell for the night. But when I got there the police station was closed and its windows dark.

At that moment a voice fluted behind me. 'Nice room? Here wait,' and I turned to see a small boy cycling away around the side of the building. Presently a woman appeared in the circle of lights, a white-haired woman of the kind you read about in improbable books of travel – the good-hearted local woman who keeps the ideal pension, bright, clean, well aired and not too expensive; the woman with a face as bright and clean as her house, which is an old, white-painted house with blue shutters; a house ideally situated near the post office, the shipping agent's office, a taverna and the sea.

She stood in the light with the boy on the bicycle who had summoned her, and smiled and beckoned me to follow her. When we turned the corner of the Ionian Popular Bank of Greece, she led me through a gate in a low wall, and I looked up and saw the pension of my dreams: an old, newly painted white house with tall shutters the colour of the blue in the Greek flag.

Chapter Two

NEXT MORNING THE sun shone cheerfully on the empty quay, where at midnight I had left m.v. *Alcheon* (née *Queen Ingrid*), my first ship. I strolled around the little port and bought a guidebook to Patmos. Then I found a tree outside a café and sat under it.

'The name Patmos,' I read in the guidebook, 'as it is generally believed, derives from the word Latmos, which is the name of a mountain of Caria, a country situated across the island in Asia Minor where the Goddess Diana was particularly adored. . . . It is said that the mythological hero Oreste pursued by the Erinnyes [the Furies] because he killed his mother Clytemnestra, took shelter in Patmos.'

Apparently there had once been a temple to Apollo here, and another to Bacchus. 'Under the domination of the Romans, the island of Patmos falled [sic] to decline. It was abandoned and used as an exile place.'

I flapped the guidebook at the wasps that competed for my breakfast jam.

Skala, fresh and newly whitewashed in the sun, was peaceful except in the café behind me, where some youths had already begun to take turns playing the jukebox. Along the waterfront: Orion Hotel, tourist shops, cafés, fishermen unravelling acres of netting from boats tied up along the quay. At the dying of August, the bustle of tourists, mainly pink-faced young men and girls in shorts and T-shirts, with bouncing long hair, still hurried back and forth, although in Patmos there's nothing to hurry for, except perhaps a love affair or an illness. The girls' braless breasts wobbled about under their T-shirts like hot-water bottles under a sheet.

I bashed a couple of wasps with the guidebook. They fell to the ground, buzzed about on their backs for a while, and then flew back to the jam. Aegean wasps must be bred for endurance. I propped the guidebook against my coffee cup and read, 'In the year 96 of the new christian age the Evangelist St Jean the Theologue was banished in Patmos. This is the reason that the island of Patmos became the centre of the Orthodox Religion and moreover it got famous.' St John's Monastery was the walled fortress-like building I had seen rearing up against the skyline behind the port, built in 1088 and daringly sited on the very spot where un-Christian rites had once enlivened the worship of Diana. It must have had quite a reputation then. In its own way, it had no doubt 'got famous' long before the Christian era.

I might not see much of Patmos, for I wanted to move on to Turkey with a minimum of delay. Beautiful and peaceful though the island obviously was, a day or two here would be more than enough for someone bound for China.

Abandoning the jam to the wasps, I strolled past MIDAS – FINE JEWELLERS to the shipping agent's office on the waterfront. A number of young tourists were sitting or standing there asking about ways to go home; holidays were nearly over. Some of them were clearly anxious, because a noticeboard propped against a wall of the office said, 'The ship to Cos today is cancelled.'

First things first: I needed another ship. I had to take into account the delays I anticipated between Turkey and Cyprus, or Turkey and the Suez Canal – particularly *at* the Suez Canal.

I asked the photogenic Greek whom I took to be the manager of the agency about boats to Samos.

'Wednesday and Friday to Samos and Turkey,' he said. 'The ship is named the *Samos Express*.' This would mean three days on Patmos; bad for my patience, but it couldn't be helped. I couldn't swim to Samos and I was meant to be travelling on water.

'I'd like to book a passage for Wednesday,' I said.

'It is not allowed to reserve today. The harbour authorities are very strict. Perhaps the ship will be too full.'

'That's why I want to book now.'

'Sorry. The authorities will not allow it. Come Wednesday at eleven o'clock.'

At least I had the perfect place to stay. The Greek landlady who had temporarily adopted me at midnight had led me up some steps to the first floor of her white house with blue shutters, through a small hallway, through another door and into a large room with a high beamed ceiling. It had two big old-fashioned wooden beds, a scrubbed wooden floor and white walls. A framed studio photograph of a young man in naval uniform on a chest of drawers matched another of a young soldier with much the same cast of features. They had been taken a long time ago; the uniforms were of the Second World War. '*Adelphoi?*' – I wasn't sure how close that was to 'brothers' or to the Greek pronunciation. Close enough, evidently: the old woman nodded and smiled at me.

She showed me a bathroom at the top of the stairs and a notice behind the door that said, '350 drachmas a day. To include water and soap.' Just over four pounds. It was my turn to nod and smile at her.

The bedroom had an interesting feature. Over each

headboard hung an elaborately framed picture. At first sight, from the writing under them I took them to be Greek, but I soon saw that they were Russian and well pre-Soviet. One was a double close-up portrait of the last czar, Nicholas, in imperial robes, crown and medals, and the czarina, blank-faced and also in full imperial fig. The other showed a densely crowded square in Moscow or St Petersburg at the climax of a grand parade. The czar on a white horse was easily identifiable in the centre of rank upon rank of infantrymen. His hand was raised to salute a glittering phalanx of mounted officers, gorgeous in plumes, helmets and uniforms that might have come from the Hollywood wardrobe of *The Prisoner of Zenda*. In the distance was a pale queenly head and shoulders at the window of a coach.

1894. I could read the date but not the Cyrillic writing that would have told me whether I was looking at Nicholas's wedding, his coronation parade, or something else. The pictures were obviously much prized by my landlady and her family; I could tell this from the large new frames and the fact that they occupied pride of place in what I soon saw was the biggest room in the house.

Everything in the room was simple and well cared for. I was glad I wasn't a party of four Germans, and I had a feeling that my landlady was, too. Perhaps that was why she hadn't joined in the crush at the ship.

I filled the succeeding days easily enough. There wasn't much to Skala, but it was pleasant to stroll in. Ships came and went from Piraeus and other islands, including the one to Cos, each arrival creating an atmosphere of minor carnival – and a stampede of hopeful landladies to the dockside.

★   ★   ★

While waiting for the *Samos Express*, I was thrown violently into the past. It was curious. I was reading what Ford Madox Ford, in his *Memories and Impressions*, recollected about international terrorists at the turn of the century:

> In the nineties in England – as indeed in the United States, France, Germany, Spain and Italy, and subter-raneously in Russia . . . there were Anarchists . . . Irish Fenians, and Russian Nihilists.
>
> The outrages in London and the North of England were mostly committed by Fenians. Their idea was to terrorise England into granting freedom to Ireland. They dynamited successfully or unsuccessfully, underground railways, theatres, the Houses of Parliament and docks.

In Russia, nihilists assassinated czars and members of the imperial family, generals, superior officials. I thought of the picture over the bed: the czar and his officers saluting each other on parade. Targets, one and all. Elsewhere, anarchists murdered President Carnot of France, and some-one blew up the Prefecture of Police in Paris; naturally, several innocent people were killed.

Political terror is repulsive food for thought – rank with madness, ruin and destruction. To eviscerate a family for the sake of a dream . . .

I sat with Ford's book and time on my hands on the big old bedstead in that sunny room in Skala and saw some mementos I had left behind in Europe more vividly than anything around me.

I saw two brightly coloured dancing figures about an inch and a half high. They stand on the window ledge of my flat in Paris, and their pale little faces peer through the curtains. They are garishly painted and dressed in traditional Khmer (Cambodian) costumes made from scraps of red and black brocade-like material in which the gold thread sparkles against the light. Each figure has one leg raised and both hands stretched above its gold headdress in the ritual contortion of Khmer dancing. They wear little painted smiles and stand on small square bases of wood, on the bottom of which are small squares of paper cut from a school exercise book. On one square is written: Kem Sokha, student of Lycée Bungkak. And on the other: Pheth Mouny, Buddhist student of Lycée, Phnom Penh.

They are presents given to me by an eighteen-year-old student and her brother in Phnom Penh not long before the Khmer Rouge armies of Pol Pot entered the city. I had known them for two or three years. They took me sightseeing, and then I met their family in an unpretentious house in a suburb. Their father was a clerk in a ministry. They were studying hard at the Faculty of Medicine despite the war that had already carried off several of their friends.

They invited me to a dance that their fellow students were giving to celebrate some local festival. It was the last time I saw them, only a few months before the fall of Phnom Penh and the beginning of the Great Cambodian Death. A few months later Pol Pot began the purging of the cities, towns and villages he had planned with his cronies in Paris cafés years before: the population driven into the countryside – the sick, the old, the dying, no exceptions. Utter destruction in the service of a dream: the regeneration of Cambodian man.

As the students danced in Phnom Penh under coloured lights, cannon fire sounded close across the river and flares trickled down the sky. 'You should leave here,' I said, 'and go to Bangkok. Just for a holiday. See how things turn out.'

'Oh, we have exams,' they said. 'Very important exams. Our father would never forgive us.'

I bought the brother a beer, and when, as Asian faces do, his turned red with alcohol, I tried again. 'Just go to Bangkok for a while. Just see how things will be.'

'*Oh, non,*' he said. '*Mon père ne nous permettrait jamais!*'

'Please, excuse,' his sister said as we parted. 'These are for souvenirs. Until you come back.' She handed me a small box made of bamboo strips; inside lay the two dancing dolls.

A month or two later she wrote me a letter and I opened it in Paris. 'Things here are not normal, less calm. . . . It is difficult to live. Do you think next year it will still be possible to go to school?. . . . Oh, how hard it is!'

Things are not normal, less calm. . . . By the time of her writing, Pol Pot's rockets were falling in a regular stream on to the city. How far could these children of a doomed land go in dedication to their exams? They were like children playing with sand castles in the path of a tidal wave. I don't suppose they ever received my last urgent letter telling them to run – *run* – for the Thai border. 'Take a bus or a train if there is such a thing by now. Walk, crawl, if necessary. By any means possible leave the country. I beg you. *Exams are dead! Save yourselves.*' I underlined the last words several times.

I don't think they can be alive. Thousands of Cambodian refugees reached Thailand, but there is no sign of either of them, so I suppose they died of starvation or from the exhaustion of hard labour. Or perhaps of machete blows for disobeying the Organization of Pol Pot.

At any rate, all that is left is a letter in my drawer, a

44

photograph of a happy brother and sister posing beside a stone lion in a Phnom Penh garden, and the two dancing dolls on my windowsill, waving their hands, smiling their tiny painted smiles and staring with blind eyes at the Paris boulevard outside. In Cambodia the experiment in the regeneration of man is over.

My second morning in Patmos I had breakfasted and fought the wasps with no more success than Don Quixote battling his windmill, when a large steamer entered the bay. Through my binoculars I read *Odysseus* on her bow and lazily watched her draw alongside.

To my surprise, I recognized the first man to appear at the head of her gangway. A tall, elderly, professorial figure, evoking, even in the inappropriate eastern Mediterranean sunlight, memories of warm sherry in cold wet England, deep armchairs and tall austere windows overlooking the carefully mown lawns of Trinity College, Oxford; and the sound of my own uncertain voice reading uncertain essays on Stubbs's *Charters*, mortmain and nisi prius. Michael Maclagan, Oxford don, medieval historian and Portcullis Pursuivant at the College of Arms in London, looked greyer, but stepped spryly ashore. I closed Ford's *Memories* and waved, and Michael waved back and came over with his wife. They sat down and had a drink.

Michael had been my gentle, genial tutor all those years ago; and he had been more. Trinity, my college, had, as well as a president, a dean whose duty was to watch over the behaviour of the undergraduates. Michael was dean – although a less likely college police chief it would be hard to imagine. His spindly figure encased in baggy expensive tweed, his moustache and his preoccupation with the middle ages combined to remind me of the White Knight in *Through the Looking-Glass*. He may have been an effective dean; certainly he was merciful. One festive night an undergraduate friend of mine, awash with high spirits, took a pot-shot with a sporting rifle at a don in a neighbouring college. The don was standing up in his bathtub at the time and his naked silhouette against the frosted glass of the bathroom window apparently presented an irresistible target. The .22 pellet passed close to his head and lodged in the ceiling. In due course Michael appeared, looking stern and demanding some sort of explanation. It was only a joke, my friend said contritely; he had placed the bullet very precisely; he was an expert shot. Obviously the excuse was inadequate. My friend had perpetrated a misdemeanour serious enough to merit dismissal from the university. Nevertheless, Michael had perceived an excellence in his work, and he also knew that the case was not one of attempted homicide but of horseplay, however outrageous. The indignant don was somehow pacified; my friend's grovelling apologies, orchestrated by Michael, were magnanimously accepted; perhaps some relatively minor punishment was imposed. At any rate, my friend's academic career was saved, thanks to Michael.

Now we sat in the sun of Patmos. Michael was in charge, he said, of a Swan's tour party of three hundred, lecturing them on the Christian sites of the eastern Mediterranean. Two weeks in the sun; he did it every year; they were in Patmos for a few hours to see the monastery on the hill. They seemed in a holiday mood, but there was something else . . .

'Are your tourists giving you problems?'

'No, not at all. But I don't suppose you've heard the news?'

'I haven't seen a newspaper or heard a radio since I left Athens.'

'Yesterday the IRA murdered Mountbatten and several members of his family, including a young grandson and another boy. Blew them to pieces in Mountbatten's launch while they were on holiday in Sligo Bay. Pretty shattering, isn't it? As a herald, I'll have to go back to London for the funeral.'

Next morning I took one of the island's few taxis up the steep hill to the monastery. From Skala it had looked like a fortress, and it looked just as forbidding at the foot of the massive, castellated walls that soared up out of the narrow streets and white houses of the tiny town that encircled it. Below, I could see Skala like a fistful of knucklebones scattered on the bay, and the deep-blue peace of the Mediterranean − 'the cradle of overseas traffic and of the art of naval warfare,' Conrad called it − stretching away and out of sight. Small white launches moved slowly in the bay − not unlike, I supposed, the once-trim little vessel bits of which now floated on the surface of Sligo Bay.

The monks padded or shuffled about the ancient stones of St John over the still more ancient, hidden stones of Diana, the Huntress, and Goddess of the Moon.

A couple of tourists I met in a café warned me that leaving Patmos wasn't always easy. Sailing home to Piraeus, the *Alcheon* is sometimes overbooked, and passengers have been left behind. Sometimes the captain took a horrified look through his binoculars at the crowd of tourists waiting on the quay and quickly dodged away. So there was the possibility that I might be delayed still further.

But prospects looked brighter in the shipping office in Skala. The manager smiled confidently and said, 'Come back here at four o'clock tomorrow. The *Samos Express* will sail, definitely, at seventeen hundred hours.' Best of all, he allowed me to buy a ticket.

The tourist had also said, 'There is a nice British actor here called Clarence Standing.' I had never heard of a Clarence Standing, but I had seen a John Standing several times, most recently in London in *Plunder*, a revival of a Ben Travers farce of the thirties. As it happened, on my last evening, walking on the quay, I met a man wearing a T-shirt with *Plunder* written on it in big letters.

'I saw *Plunder*,' I said. 'You were excellent, Mr Standing. I hope you don't mind me saying that.'

'Not Mr Standing, please,' he said genially. 'The name's—'

'Clarence. You're the first Clarence I've ever met.'

'Clarence?'

I explained where the Clarence came from and, when he had thought it over, he came to the conclusion that he rather liked it. We had a drink, and the next day he brought his son down to the quay to see me off. We found a bar where we drank beer under coloured prints of skirted and scimitar-bearing Greeks in embroidered jackets slashing their victorious way through bloody barricades of Turkish bodies. Would old enemies never forget? The few Turks still standing were easily distinguishable from the Greeks by their turbans.

★   ★   ★

The *Samos Express* had arrived on time, a stubby little vessel despite its dashing name. Toward sailing time I hurried to the pension to collect my washing from the bathroom: underclothes and T-shirt. From my first-floor room I heard the *Samos Express* hooting twice; she seemed eager to be off. As I ran to the bathroom a priest forestalled me; bearded, with a black chimney-pot hat, muttering '*Kali mera*', he shot in ahead of me and bolted the door.

Two minutes, five minutes, passed. The door remained locked with the priest and my washing inside. My landlady climbed the stairs to say goodbye, saw my predicament and rattled the door handle in a commanding way. Inside we heard a shuffling, a small sound of breaking wind and, oddly, someone whistling several bars of the Warsaw Concerto. The *Samos Express* hooted again.

I had to go: to miss the *Samos Express* was unthinkable. Providence intervened. At the last possible moment, the priest emerged, straightening his hat with dignity. Like a fireman rescuing a baby from a burning house, I snatched my washing from the bathroom, seized my luggage and hurried breathlessly to where John Standing waited for me on the quay.

Tourists who had come across from Samos in the morning were back on board with their plastic bags of souvenirs and envelopes of picture postcards. When I had dumped my bags on the deck and looked around, I recognized some of the Germans from the daily queues in the shipping office, bowed like blond Atlases under their knapsacks.

'I envy you,' said Standing from the quay. The *Samos Express*'s crew had cast off, and the gap between stone pier and vibrating iron bulwark was already beginning to widen.

'This is the easy part, Clarence,' I said. 'This is child's play. Scheduled steamers. The hard part comes later.' I had to raise my voice as the distance between us grew. 'I think it's going to become nerve-racking somewhere this side of the Suez Canal, and get rapidly worse after that.'

'Look at the bright side,' called Standing.

But, of course, that was how it turned out.

Chapter Three

IT TOOK ME some time to realize that the little paper bags flying out of saloon windows of the *Samos Express* were full of vomit.

A good many tourists, mainly young and with raw and peeling Dutch, Nordic or Teutonic snub noses, boarded the ship at Patmos wearing T-shirts with slogans like 'Big Apple' written on them.

The *Samos Express* had two decks, and the upper one was also the roof of the saloon, where passengers sat in rows as if in a bus. A tiny bar had a sign over it: RECOMMENDED BY HOLLAND INTERNATIONAL. Whatever that meant, it sounded reassuring. I stood here for a bit and bought a paper cup of the bland Samos Koniak.

When I went out to the rail to look at the view, the bags began to fly. It was rough outside the protection of Patmos's headlands. We rolled and corkscrewed through a heavy choppiness, and spray formed a mist on the surface of the water. I thought the little bags must contain crusts

and cores left over from passengers' snack lunches. But no, ladies and gentlemen from Berne and Vienna were taking the plastic bags from the ship's toilet, vomiting into them and throwing them overboard. As I stood on the lower deck they whizzed past me like those little bags of water children sometimes enjoy dropping from windows on heads of passersby. Now and again a spray of unwrapped vomit fell from the top deck, splattering the rail.

I was joined at the rail by a six-foot Austrian lady who told me that she had crossed to Patmos from Samos that morning, and it had been rough then, too.

'This morning,' she said, 'I was so sick, and so scared by my face. It was all white. Now I'm awfully well, yes?'

A spatter of vomit fell on us, and I mopped at her coat with my handkerchief. She smiled bravely. 'No worry, no worry.'

On the upper deck a couple clasped each other and kissed standing up on the heaving deck among friends in sandals and sawn-off jeans. A violent roll sent them spinning across the deck, as if they were waltzing in a speeded-up film sequence, and they cannoned into a seated row of elderly Greeks dozing around the ship's rail who shouted at them angrily.

From the upper deck I zigzagged to the wing of the little bridge. Beyond the open wheelhouse door, the captain of the *Samos Express*, dressed in an old blue shirt, grey baggy trousers and gym shoes, stared ahead with a bored expression. A man whose stomach overlapped his shorts stood at the large wooden wheel. Two hunks of bread, a packet of cigarettes, matches and an ashtray on the ledge slid an inch or two back and forth with the rolling of the ship. Through a curtain behind the wheel I could just see part of the cabin, a child asleep on a bunk and a big woman with very white teeth: the captain's cabin, the captain's family.

The bulk of Samos eased like a whale through the spray: a big hump of hills, several times bigger than little Patmos; after Patmos, almost intimidating. Presently, I could see a fleet of yachts nuzzling a long stone quay.

The *Samos Express* would take me to the Turkish mainland next morning; then an hour and a half to the small port of Kusadasi. Meanwhile I was left to wish I were there already. I didn't care much for what I saw of Samos on the long horseshoe quay from which a fairly large town straggled back and up into foothills already swallowed by the evening shadows. Around the harbour, strings of coloured lights had come to life. European yachtsmen strolled in groups between their boats and the café tables that spilled across the busy quay. Glossy women sat with men with pipes and silk scarves. The men's grey hair was carefully swept back into curls at the nape of the neck, like the wash of a motorboat in a grey-rinse sea. Silk shirts by St Laurent or Cardin with blue anchor patterns seemed popular. There were a lot of deep tans about, and what used to be called 'expensive complexions'. Bulging blonde women tiptoed on stiletto heels trailing poodles; beautiful girls, with thighs that quivered with every step, trailed men; and there were a number of middle-aged women with bitter mouths and skin like orange tinfoil. I was glad I had been held up on Patmos, not Samos.

An old Greek insisted on carrying my heavy metal suitcase up a steep side street to a house where, he conveyed with signs, there would be a room for the night. He tottered alarmingly but, when I tried to take the suitcase from him, he protested loudly, '*Okhi! Okhi!*'

At last a woman appeared at the doorway. 'English?' she said from the rectangle of lamplight. 'Want a house?'

'Just one night.'

She showed me a room the size of a large cupboard; no window, no water, just a hard-looking bed and stifling heat.

'How much?'

'Six hundred drachma.' When I laughed, she said, 'Five hundred.' I said goodbye, tipped the old man, picked up my suitcase and walked down to the harbour. At the ramp to the *Samos Express*, I found two of the crew and said I would be travelling with them to Turkey tomorrow morning; could I stay on board?

'Okay. I'm the captain's son. It's okay.'

'I'd like to leave my bags here now.'

'Of course. No one steals in Greece.'

I stowed the bags under a seat in the saloon, and went ashore.

Several dozen yachts lay along the wharf, some pleasantly modest and workmanlike, some gleaming with chrome or aluminium and looking like kept women. A little way along I came to the king of them all; a red light glowed like the eye of a giant idol at the top of the mainmast, perhaps seventy feet high. It was a large sailing boat, a three-master, but it had engines, too; I could hear the purr of its generator. On board a muscular black member of the crew in impeccable whites lounged on guard, impassively watching the strollers who stopped to peer at this sailing palace. Who was it – Goldfinger or Dr No, holidaying in Samos this year?

From a café table, near some island boats – the Aegean caïques, single-masted wooden boats with wide noses curved like drawn bows – I could see a sign that said, 'Sail with Jiannis. Trips to have a nice time daily. Trips to the nice Island Samiopoula with a nice taverna and a sandy beach.' And over a fish steak and a half-bottle of retsina – 'Not too much sweet,' said the waiter – I thought of my perfect landlady in Patmos and the greedy one in Samos asking an outrageous price for her stuffy little room. Greedy, yes; but warmed by the retsina, I looked at the animated quay and thought, What of it?

A young Greek waiter was laughing with two Swedish girls at the next table, obviously making a rendezvous. I heard singing and the tinkle of a breaking glass coming from a back room. My waiter winked and put another half-bottle of the product of the Union des Coopératives Vinicoles de Samos on my table. As I drank it, I tried to imagine this quayside in winter, its café canopies furled, the tables stacked inside, windows and doors closed against wind and rain, and the chains of coloured lights switched off for another six months. Now, after all, it was the silly, sunny season when islands tried to forget the empty, lonely winter, when rain and winter gales have driven tourists and their money away and turned the islands' spirit to sludge. So why should anyone begrudge the fishermen, boatmen and landladies their modest killing? What harm was there in saving something for the winter? No harm at all, the retsina said.

Around midnight I went aboard the darkened and empty *Express*, felt my way into the saloon – a notice told me it was a '*place touristique*' – and stretched out on a banquette against the bulkhead. The fleas attacked three or four hours later, although I slept through their first blitzkrieg and only woke up when their occupation was fully established.

In the dark I could only turn, twist, curse and scratch and feel them running joyously all over my body. I had lived in the goat-filled tents of Bedouin tribesmen and the reed houses of Iraq's Marsh Arabs, but as biters these fleas were Olympic champions.

Where did they come from? From the cats of Samos? From the crew? Although the *place touristique* literally hopped with them, they only came out at night; luckily for the owners of the *Samos Express*, fleas are nocturnal creatures, because, if they had remained on the warpath the next day, the ship would have become a floating bedlam; passengers would have been leaping and twitching about the decks like victims of an advanced stage of St Vitus's dance.

From 4.30 a.m. I had to abandon the idea of sleep. My hands and ankles were covered with lumps that itched intensely; my waist seemed to be ringed by a nagging chain of fire. When daylight came I began a feverish search, but neither then nor later in the shower in a Turkish hotel did I glimpse an antenna of one of those seagoing fleas. They stayed with me just over a week.

At eight o'clock the *Samos Express* was ready to leave for Kusadasi. At the last moment a busload of Austrian tourists pulled up and came aboard, their bus driver handing over a plastic bag full of passports to the barman. We cast off. For a time crew ran back and forth to the accompaniment of a mechanical squawking from the engine room as a caïque's anchor rope was disentangled from the *Express*'s screws, and then we moved toward the Turkish coast.

The Turkish mainland is startlingly close to Samos. Soon we passed the red Turkish flag that flies from a small lighthouse on an islet to starboard, while the coast of Samos is still what looks like touching distance away to port. The Greeks have soldiers on Samos, which indicates an underlying tension here that is absent on Patmos.

Why shouldn't there be drama in this mere streak of water between Greek and Turk, whose enmity is so deeply rooted in so many massacres along these coasts, capes and islands that both races might be said to enjoy hostility as some elderly people are said to enjoy ill health? (The next day in Kusadasi, as throughout Turkey, the Turks would celebrate Victory Day – the military victory over the Greeks in 1921 and the violent expulsion of all Greeks from Anatolia by Kemal Ataturk – with goose-stepping military parades.)

There was drama, too, in the way Greece lay in sunshine, its rose rocks warmed in the sun while, ahead, the Turkish coastline could only be glimpsed dimly through thunderclouds that merged with a rising sea mist.

Someone on Patmos had praised a Hotel Imbat in Kusadasi, and I took him at his word. But by noon I was already leaving the Imbat. A haughty young man at the reception desk, who had taken a long time to appear, said, 'I can give you another room.'

But it had been a mistake to go there in the first place. I ought to have taken warning from the tourist-club insignia that bespattered the modern entrance hall. The room I had already been shown to was far too expensive to include a toilet that had no water, a telephone that didn't work even to the reception desk, and walls and doors that seemed to be a hundredth of an inch thick.

I pointed all this out to the cool, young receptionist, who said, 'That's only your opinion.'

'Naturally.'

Back in the town – the Imbat is quite a long way outside it – I found the Akman Hotel. It was near the sea, and also near where buses left several times a day for Smyrna, the port in which I counted on finding my next steamer – the one to take me the length of the south Turkish coast to Mersin. I registered at the Akman and walked to the shipping agent's office, but it was closed. The office was near the jetty where I had disembarked from Samos, and I was surprised to see the *Samos Express* still at her moorings. She had been due to sail some time earlier. I walked up to the jetty gate. The passengers for Samos, including those who had come across with me that morning on a day trip, were piled up there, sitting or lying disconsolately on the ground, or shifting from one aching foot to another. The *Samos Express* reared and plunged in wild and swelling water and, leaning his arms on the bridge and gazing sadly at his passengers, her captain rocked with her. The *Express* was delayed because of the sudden winds and high seas, but no passenger was allowed to go near it or even on to the jetty. The locked and guarded gate illuminated the contrast between a Greek harbour and a Turkish one, even the difference in the Greek and Turkish attitudes to life. In Greece anyone can wander down to the quayside; it is impossible to imagine anyone in seafaring Greece being arrested for wanting to look at the sea or at ships. Kusadasi is small and of no military importance, yet a cloud of police surrounded the gate, and big-chested loiterers in jeans and T-shirts, obviously plainclothes men, stroked their waterfall moustaches.

'Don't get locked up here,' a youngish man with a Canadian passport in his hand was saying to a despondent British girl who, I had overheard her saying, had run out of money. 'They take away your belt and shoelaces. They don't give you hygienic conditions. They're really rough on drugs here. Once you're in jail don't expect no hygienic conditions.'

By temperament, Turks are lockers-up and lockers-out. They have prison on the brain, and a belief that bars are all you need to make the world a safe place, if not a happy one. Few Turks seem to think the world is a happy place.

Mr Akman of the Akman Hotel doesn't believe in prisons, thank heavens. About happiness, he is sceptical too. He believes in fishing.

Mr Akman is tall, middle-aged and could be a distinguished professor of mathematics. He comes from Erzurum in the remote north-east of Turkey near the Soviet border, and until recently he was a consulting engineer, somehow connected with the building of the Hilton Hotel in Istanbul. He studied in Germany and he speaks good German, but his English, through lack of practice, is weak. He abandoned his job a few years ago to build and manage his own hotel in Kusadasi.

The first evening, when I came down to his simple bar, he asked me to have a vodka. Over it, I said how much I liked the hotel.

'Sank you,' he said with a gentle smile, as though he really was grateful. When I asked him if he enjoyed running his own place instead of building hotels for other people, he said, 'N-no, I want to retire.'

'What would you do then?'

'Fishing.' His smile broadened, and he cast an imaginary

59

fly across the room. 'Here,' he went on, 'too many problems. Staff come and go. Now we have room, breakfast, dinner. No lunch. Lunch too difficult. Maybe next year no dinner, only breakfast and room.'

'The year after that no breakfast?'

He laughed. '*Ja, ja.* Then no room. Then I go fishing in Erzurum.'

Mr Akman had a visitor from Ankara, an English-speaking friend, a doctor from the university, who said in a wise tone of voice, 'I know England. I like it. But you have so many problems with race there. I saw those notices in your restaurants: "No black men served here". Oh, yes, I saw them.' I wasn't going to let the doctor and politics get between me and Mr Akman by driving me to mention Armenia or the Turkish occupation of Cyprus.

The more I saw of Akman the more I liked him. He was shy, and had the lugubrious look of A. A. Milne's Eeyore – a look that I soon saw hid a heart of gold and a hefty degree of fatalism.

The first evening Mr Akman invited me to join his friend the doctor and himself for dinner: soup, kofte kebab, salad, then grapes. We shared a bottle of red wine: Dikmen, 'Turkey's best,' said Mr Akman, raising his glass. 'Chin-chin,' said the doctor, who, despite his feelings on English racism, was friendly. He was bursting with stories of the appalling political savagery at Ankara University that was disrupting any serious study there. 'The disease of Turkey,' he said.

After dinner every light went out in Kusadasi. 'They are always fusing,' the doctor muttered in the blackness. The hotel's television was cut off; its screen had been giving us ill-coordinated views of Turkish soldiers goose-stepping in the Victory Parade in Ankara and the sound of British military marches; I thought I recognized 'Garb of Old Gaul'. In the darkness beside me Akman's wan voice murmured, 'Problems . . . problems.' Waiters brought candles, and I saw Akman walking up and down in the shadowy bar, muttering to himself. He looked upset, and I postponed asking him about a phone call I needed to make to Smyrna; I would have to reserve a room there for a day or two before I sailed. But in a moment he came up to me, reached over the bar and filled my glass to the brim with brandy. 'From me,' he said.

Mr Akman's friendliness set the style for the whole hotel. It was a very ordinary place: not particularly well built, austere and certainly not beautiful or luxurious. I think Akman depended on groups of none-too-well-off Dutch and German families. Under a different owner it would have been a good hotel to avoid; adequate, dull and nondescript. But without playing a jovial extrovert 'mine host' role – quite the reverse – Akman somehow pervaded it with a life-enhancing property.

Sometimes his friend the doctor helped behind the bar. At other times the son of one of his Turkish lawyer friends from Kusadasi poured drinks or manned the reception desk. Having just left Istanbul University, this young man was waiting for the call to do his compulsory military service with the Turkish army – twenty rigorous months in uniform. He had shaggy hair and tugged at a stiff moustache with bristles an inch long, saying gloomily to me, 'In the army, all hair will go.' Turkish military barbers shave the skulls of draftees with a savage glee, he explained. In that case, several of Mr Akman's young waiters would be as bald as footballs within a year or two. Until that dreaded day they darted cheerfully about the hotel in well-coiffed hairdos, and spent a good deal of their time writing notes to pen pals in Europe, mainly to the German girls who came to Kusadasi for the summer holidays. Most Turkish boys, particularly those working in hotels, yearned for jobs in Germany. They said they wouldn't hesitate to marry *any* Germany girl – 'She could look like a sausage' – if it helped them to get work permits there. Many did marry for work permits, and were the envy of their friends, who had to stay behind in Turkey to go through their military service.

One of the Akman waiters, a wild-looking youth from Smyrna called Sukru, brought me a present of a cup of tea one morning as I sat writing in the empty dining room. When I thanked him, he said, 'It's nothing, *amga* [uncle].' Half an hour of writing then vanished while he took out his wallet and showed me, like a bridge champion slowly laying down a winning hand, a fistful of colour photographs of a number of German ladies of various sizes smiling in bikinis from an almost identical spot on the beach near Akman's Hotel – naturally, at different times, probably only days apart. 'Very beauty,' said Sukru, pushing the pictures back into his wallet.

Next evening, in the grip of some disorderly Anatolian zeal, Sukru rushed through the crowded dining room bearing a two-foot-high pile of plates, tripped, fell prone across a table and threw the plates among the diners like a Scottish athlete tossing the caber. There was the noise of an exploding china shop. Like Highland cattle disturbed by thunder, shaggy German men and women lumbered wide-eyed to their feet dabbing with napkins and crunching about in the debris of broken plates. Sukru lay across the table as if stunned. Then, still prone, he twisted his head anxiously toward Akman.

'Sukru, Sukru,' murmured Mr Akman, sadly shaking his head. Without anger, he lifted a large splinter of crockery from his lamb stew, smiled his resigned smile, and went on eating his meal.

I was grateful to Mr Akman because, while the police and the locked gates at Kusadasi harbour had reminded me of one side of Turkey, he showed me quite another.

I went back to the office of Turkish Maritime Lines near the harbour. The door was open, so I went in. A man came in from the back of the office, which was empty.

'Closed,' he said. 'After two thirty, closed.'

'But it's not two yet.'

'Well?'

'I have a ticket to sail on the *Samsun*, Izmir to Mersin, on 7 September.' It wasn't far from Kusadasi to Izmir, but I already knew it was not easy to find a boat and it didn't seem worthwhile wasting time looking for one. Also, the grand ruin of Ephesus lay beside the road to Izmir and I wanted very much to see it, so I would tackle that stage by road. I said, 'I want to confirm—'

'No tickets sold here.'

'I have the ticket and the reservation. I just want to con—'

'No tickets here. Izmir only.'

Another man, flushed with drink, came through the front door. 'No ticket here,' he said. So I left. I would go to Izmir (Smyrna, I preferred to call it, at least to myself) in a day or two. I had six days to play before the *Samsun* was due to sail, and it was cheaper to stay at Akman's than in a hotel in Smyrna.

Kusadasi (pronounced Kooshadasi, with the accent on the second syllable) has a population of farmers, fishermen and people intent on attracting tourists. It is popular because it is near Ephesus. It is not a big town; its population is about fifteen thousand, according to a guidebook. It clusters around the harbour and a seventeenth-century caravanserai with immense walls that once housed the Club Méditer-ranée and is now a luxury hotel.

Between the Caravanserai Hotel and the sea are many stalls and small restaurants, most of them selling fish; Kusa-dasi is famous for this. There is also a steak house, much grander than the other restaurants, where you are supposed to sit on a stool at a bar, push coins into a jukebox to keep the music pumping and roll your eyes around posters of pop stars on the walls. Blonde German girls sat there for hours on end, chewing gum, thighs spread, eyed by Turks of all ages, who watched the girls intently, as a boxer will study an opponent on film to decide whether to take it slow and tricky or go for a kayo in the first round.

Near an open-air waterfront bar, I saw a man with his trousers rolled up washing two large sheep in the sea. After a while a young Turk, with a handsome raddled face, who was drinking beer at the bar, said to me, 'Hello. You'll never guess where I come from. Uganda.'

'You're not black enough. I was going to say Congo.' We laughed and I asked him what he did.

'I was born here, but one day a few years ago a Belgian film critic came here and took me to Brussels to make a film. I made two films, actually. Not much good, I guess. I went to Paris, too. I had to come back because of work-permit troubles there. Also I had to do my military service here.'

'You haven't done it yet? You look—'

'I'm twenty-four. I could be in big trouble, so I leave on the Istanbul bus at eight o'clock tonight, register at the

barracks there tomorrow, begin my training the day after. For the first forty-five days nothing but physical exercise – you can imagine how tough the Turkish army is on recruits. All that long hair shaved.' He laughed again. 'Like a nut. But that's the least of it.'

'It'll pass,' I said to console him. 'Forty-five days of exercise, no drink, no women. You'll be the better for it.'

'I see military service as a mountain that has to be climbed. I confess I feel like a man facing a firing squad, and you are like the priest taking my confession. My name is Metin.' He held out his hand.

'I've had so many girls here,' he said. 'After all, I worked at the Club Méditerranée, then as a guide, then in Belgium. . . . I've done some strange things.' He grinned.

'Old women, too? Men? Sheep?'

His grin broadened. It was not unpleasant. 'You've met Ugandans like me before?'

'You'll need another beer if you're going to Scutari tomorrow to start a new life. Is it Scutari barracks you're going to?'

65

'Yes. Uskudar. Yes, thank you, one beer. You know, I could get a doctor's certificate and avoid that mountain.'

'Yes, a sharp attack of syphilis would probably get you off.'

He held up his hand and rubbed the tip of his first finger against the tip of his thumb. 'Money. That's easier, less painful.'

'Too late now. You've decided to be honest.'

'Too late, yes.'

We sipped the beer. The man led the dripping sheep out of the sea and rolled down his trouser bottoms. The sheep shook themselves and followed him slowly down the road, leaving parallel trails of water in the dust.

'I like Brussels better than Paris,' the young Turk said. 'I'll tell you why. It's the Parisians. Turks, as you know, are a bit quiet, reserved, but Parisians are much more so. I don't like that. Here's a true story. One day I was in a crowded Paris street and a girl in front of me tripped and fell hard on the pavement. Not a soul stopped to help her. I gave her a hand up. She was shaken. Her knees were badly cut and bleeding. I helped her to a café nearby. I put her on a chair, ordered her a cognac and asked the *patron* for a cloth or something to stop the bleeding. Do you know what? The *patron* – one of those bald, arrogant sons of bitches – said, "This is not an infirmary. Take her down the second street on the left, and after three hundred metres you'll find one. The cognac is twelve francs, and kindly don't put blood all over the floor." '

Metin frowned and shook his head in disbelief. 'Turks wouldn't do that. We can be selfish bastards, believe me, and tough. But not in that way. Never.'

I said, 'I'm going to have a fish lunch here. Join me?'

'Thanks. I ate earlier. I have to prepare for that bus. We might have a beer here at seven, yes?'

'I'll see you here,' I said. But for some reason I wasn't able to meet him. Three months later, in Colombo, just before I boarded an old Tamil sailing ship for southern India, a postcard with a Turkish postmark reached me. It was from Metin. He had begun his training at Scutari barracks, the towering early nineteenth-century barracks on the Bosporus that was once the hospital where Florence Nightingale tended the British casualties of the Crimean War. He sounded quite cheerful. He was not going to let the mountain defeat him, he said. He hoped we'd meet again.

The thought of Scutari and what Metin had said about the harshness of life in the Turkish army reminded me that a few years ago, as a correspondent for the *Observer*, I was given permission by the Turkish general commanding the Istanbul region to attend a military court he had convened in the Scutari barracks. Bombs had been thrown in Istanbul; there had been shooting, kidnappings, deaths, and martial law was in force. Hour after hour I sat in a white chamber with an arched ceiling and amazingly thick walls as the trial of the alleged terrorists went on. I had been told that once in the courtroom I would have to stay until the court adjourned for lunch. My wooden chair was uncomfortable; its seat felt like iron and its back was too upright. Quietly I crossed my left leg over my right. The proceedings, in Turkish, dragged gloomily on. Soon I saw that the presiding officers of the tribunal, medals flashing beyond a long table, were staring in my direction. The buzz of a voice giving evidence continued, but not only were the officers staring at me with hostility, they were also putting their bullet-shaped heads together and conferring about something – evidently something to do with me because their united and angry gaze never left my face. Then all talking ceased: a silence fell in court. Even the prisoners were staring at me.

It was disconcerting. I tried to think what I had done wrong. I had my permit to attend the court in my breast pocket; further, I was accompanied by a Turkish official. I checked my fly. I wasn't wearing a hat; I was wearing a tie. What could it be? The official with me seemed unaware of anything unusual. Finally one of the presiding officers beckoned a soldier to him and whispered into his ear. The soldier headed for us. At last the official at my side noticed something. He leaned forward, and the soldier lowered his brick-red face and crew cut and gabbled something into his ear before making an about-turn and marching stiffly away.

The official, a pleasant young civilian, looked embarrassed. He said to me in a low tone, 'The tribunal wishes to inform you that you are showing it contempt. You are not being respectful. It wishes to tell you that a military tribunal has powers to deal with disrespect to the armed forces of Turkey. It is giving you a warning.'

'What have I done, for God's sake?' I hissed back. 'I've been sitting here without stirring, not breathing a word. What do they mean?'

'You are sitting with your legs crossed. You must sit at attention in a military court. With both toes and heels together on the ground and your back straight. It shows proper respect.'

Luckily, I had to sit at attention for only two or three

more minutes before the court adjourned for lunch. 'Are you going back to the court this afternoon?' the official asked.

'No, we'll visit Florence Nightingale's sitting room instead. We won't have to stand at attention to show respect to her memory.' The official smiled. He hadn't wanted to go back among those officers either.

The corner room that the Lady with the Lamp had used as a study when the rambling barracks became a temporary hospital was almost directly above the chamber where the military court would resume its session that afternoon. It was the spotless, sparsely furnished room of a busy and practical woman. The famous lamp she had carried through the scandalously overcrowded wards that stank of bodies and excrement stood on a table. It was not the Aladdin's lamp I had expected, nor was it the kind of Victorian lamp they called a bull's-eye. It looked like an expanding Japanese paper lantern and resembled a small concertina standing on end.

Chapter Four

I BADE MR AKMAN farewell and caught a morning bus to Ephesus. There I toured the ruins before continuing to Smyrna by taxi. I found Ephesus full of ancient remains in fair condition, tourists – and cats.

Turkey is a cat country. In Ephesus you come across them everywhere: mother cats leading families down old Ephesian triumphal ways; gangs of cats in small temples to ancient pagan gods or big temples to Artemis; cats stalking the hillsides like miniature pards of Bacchus. (In Kusadasi I had seen groups of cats staring at the moon, wide-eyed, blinking lazily as if it warmed them.)

With Mustafa, a short, pear-shaped Turkish guide in dark glasses, I skirted the Gymnasium and made for the Upper Agora. Between the Upper Agora and the Odeon we became hopelessly entangled with tourists.

I had seen at least twenty large modern motor coaches parked near the ruins while the drivers drank tea in a string of coffee shops and snack bars. Near the Odeon we caught up with a group of Swedes and edged past them – Mustafa delivering his spiel as we did so – only to run up against a block of elderly Americans. To pass them would have meant a long detour halfway up a hillside and down again. In any case, I could see yet another group, possibly two, behind the Americans.

The situation was confused and the noise deafening. Our skins frizzled in the sun among soaring columns and burning slabs of historic stone. A Swedish-speaking lady guide was uttering loud uncouth sounds as if to invoke – or

70

provoke – a god, and the gentleman guide of the American group followed suit. The two harangues rose into the air and grappled in cacophony. A third voice was that of Mustafa, who seemed to see a ghostly ear trumpet in my hand and at the ready.

I sensed trouble. 'I can hear you better if you speak lower, Mustafa.' At intervals I murmured, 'Lower, lower.'

'Harry ap. Shake a leg. Gat a move un,' the voice of the Swedish party's lady guide rang angrily across the Nymphaeum. It was a duel; she was addressing the Americans' guide over our heads. In response, the Americans' guide closed disdainful eyelids over disdainful eyes. But his party began to move forward at what was a brisk amble after the snail's crawl of a moment before.

Irritable American voices began to be heard. 'Hey, aren't they kind of rushing us?' A bony lady whose face seemed to have melted into the folds around her neck, glared at Mustafa. 'Pipe down,' she snapped at him. But Mustafa was in full stride; nothing could stop him in mid-duty. 'The Temple of Diana, one of the Seven Vonders of the World,' he bellowed confidently into my invisible ear trumpet. 'Please looking at Temple of Westa, the Place of the Westal Wirgins.'

As if he had risen from the very stones, a dark, willowy figure appeared from behind us, moving briskly like some emissary of Diana herself. A jaunty creature among dejected foreigners, he tootled on a flute 'Rain Drops Keep Fallin' on My Head', and people made way for him. It was uncanny. They fell in behind him, and soon a single file of Americans and Swedes headed rapidly toward the Theatre, singing as though raised from the dead.

'Now they clear out,' said Mustafa with satisfaction as

he watched the crowd bobbing away like the children of Hamelin behind the Pied Piper. In the distance the fluting changed to 'The Sound of Music'.

'Yes, more better.' He was back on the job again. 'Now, please, you look,' he yelled. 'This is the largest brothel in the world. Was made to protect the girls of the East from the lusty seamans.'

'Sheep full op! Sheep full op!' In the wide deck area in front of his office the purser of the Turkish motor vessel *Samsun* was booming genially at a European couple who wanted to be shifted from second class to first class. I was in Smyrna, an hour before sailing time. 'Big problems. Sheep very full op.'

I had been referred to him by his assistant, who advised me to check my ticket with the 'poncer'. He was a cheerful man with a Cyrano de Bergerac nose who took my ticket in exchange for a radiant smile. That the ship was very full I could see from the crush on deck and the number of people still boarding. The two Europeans were out of luck.

For safety's sake, I had confirmed my second-class booking a few days before sailing. I had walked along the long seafront of Smyrna, past the Greek consulate, past the Ataturk Museum, past the big grey filing cabinet that houses 'NATO HQ Landsoutheast', to the pierside offices of Turkish Maritime Lines, and there a helpful lady had said, 'You have second class with a cabin for four persons. Second class is not good for you on *Samsun*. I want to change you to a better thing.'

'No, please. You are very kind. I'm quite happy—'

'Unfortunately, here we cannot make tickets or reservations,' she went on as if she hadn't heard me. 'We must telex or telephone Istanbul.' No ticket or reservations at Kusadasi *or* Smyrna? Turkish Maritime Lines have certainly centralized their system, I thought. 'However' – she smiled a smile of infinite sadness – 'today the electricity is out of order between Istanbul and Izmir, so telex is impossible. Telephones are also not working. But I will try later.'

'Please don't.' I would have three nights on *Samsun* before we reached Mersin, the port of south-eastern Turkey. I thought of the heat and socks of the *Alcheon*'s four-berther, but I saw no reason to move. I was more concerned about my course once I had reached Mersin; that was more important than cabins. At the moment my inten-tion was to reach a port – perhaps the Syrian port of Latakia or Beirut or Haifa – where, with luck, I might find a freighter to take me through the Suez Canal, the first great obstacle, nonstop. Perhaps Turkish Maritime Lines had something . . .

'No, we cannot help with that,' the lady said. 'To Haifa, no. To Latakia, no. Better for you to take the ferry from Mersin to Magusa – Famagusta, you call it – in Cyprus. Then cross to the Greek side in Cyprus. Maybe from Limassol you can find something Greek for the canal crossing. Maybe.'

I took a typed letter from her to the company's agent in Mersin, advising him to please issue me a ticket for the 'feri-bot' from Mersin to Magusa. Then I returned to the waterfront.

The Smyrna waterfront is spectacular. Modestly storeyed buildings face the wide expanse of a bay embraced by hazy wingtips of land. Behind the seafront the city begins to rise into clusters of tall buildings – banks mostly, hotels, apart-ment blocks. The statue of Kemal Ataturk gazes out to sea amid ranks of red Turkish flags fluttering in permanent celebration of the founder of modern Turkey, whose ghost haunts the souls of his countrymen as Lenin haunts millions of Russians and Eva Perón many Argentines.

The Ataturk Museum is the house the Grey Wolf moved into when the army drove Smyrna's Greek population into the sea and a great fire destroyed much of the city. The first thing you see in the museum's hallway is a huge frowning bust of the great man, and inscribed on its base '1881–1938'.

The museum has a moribund appearance. Ataturk's study contains a large, plain wooden desk, some high-backed, rather ecclesiastical-looking chairs, a wicker table and a smell of mothballs. You can see his double bed of varnished wood, dull carpets and dingy furniture, inlaid tables for *triktrak*, the Turkish backgammon. Glass cases display Ataturk's velvet overcoats lined with fox fur; dark metal statues of Seljuk or Saracen warriors pose under crudely ornate chandeliers of Paris, 1910.

The finest photograph of Ataturk in old age was not to be found here; I saw it in the shipping agent's office in Kusadasi. It showed him grey-faced and haggard, his expression not the official one of virile confidence but one of anxiety and pain. A little out of focus, it showed a human being, and one at the end of his tether. By then he must have begun his slow decline into terminal cirrhosis of the liver. The heavy-drinking Turks are not hypocrites; they have never held the manner of Ataturk's death against him.

Izmir, or Smyrna, is the third largest city and the leading port of Turkey, as any guidebook will tell you. The guidebook may not mention that its waterfront is notable for cafés and music. The music, from radios in the cafés and from television sets, is frequently interrupted by advertisements for banks or deodorants. Turkish music is the perfect Oriental music for Westerners. Much Arab music is too snaky, but the Turkish variety thumps along merrily with zithers, or slows to a gentle berceuse for lutes and two-foot flutes; it is, on the whole, simple and melodic and can be whistled. It issues from the cafés over the heads of the hubble-bubble smokers – the elderly men who sit in silent rows, sucking on their gurgling waterpipes like clarinet players negotiating a difficult passage in a score. From them it wafts across to the nut sellers, whose barrows at night are lit by pressure lamps, to the men toting samovars like silver pagodas, and to handcarts of plump red apples. It mingles with the smell of aromatic kebabs on portable charcoal grills, and, of course, fish of every kind, fresh in baskets or cooking on the grills.

At one end of the waterfront the sailing boats and fishing smacks draw up alongside the restaurants and food stalls, opposite the outdoor tables where waiters scurry with tumblers of buttermilk and pints of chilled raki or *yeni votka*, an old Turkish vodka that they drink with fresh lemon juice. Here the countrymen of Ataturk, who possess one of the world's finest cuisines, choose to eat and drink twenty feet from oily water slopping against the stone wharf, red flags with the Turkish crescent fluttering from mastheads, and seagulls fighting for scraps. At night they watch the ferryboats, full of lights, passing and repassing, looking like jewel boxes, on the dark surface of the bay.

The motor vessel *Samsun* is a big ship, six thousand tons or more, built in Genoa in 1950. A tall ship, too; it was a long drop from where I stood on the wing of her bridge to the quayside, from which Turkish stevedores were off-loading cartons of cigarettes.

At 1800 hours we were assisted out into the Bay of Izmir by a tug called *Kusadasi*. On the waterfront the only identifiable building was NATO's dull-grey filing cabinet.

I was glad that the helpful lady in the shipping office had been unable to change my second-class berth. Going below with the steward I found a cabin not much larger than the four-berther on the *Alcheon*, but a good deal cooler. It had one porthole, a washbasin with a mirror above it, a fan and four curtained wooden bunks. On each bunk the good-natured steward, all nose and eyebrows, laid a folded sheet, a small towel and a pillow; he showed me the four tall cupboards, opened one with a proud gesture and said, 'All the needful for your goodself.'

The cabin was still empty except for me, but someone had left a battered suitcase and a cardboard box on the deck near one of the lower bunks. I dumped my anorak on an upper bunk near the porthole like a prospector staking a claim in the Klondike. When I tried the reading-light switch over my bunk, nothing happened, but the steward promised to find a bulb.

After twenty minutes he reappeared, apologetic. 'Problems,' he explained sorrowfully. 'No bulbs in ship.'

'No bulbs at all?' It was difficult to believe.

'No bulbs. Company has no money, so no buy.'

A bed without a reading light is worse than fish without salt or lemon. I lowered my voice conspiratorially. 'How about taking one from another cabin? Maybe a bunk with only a baby in it?'

The steward looked at me with admiration, and wriggled his eyebrows furiously up and down like Groucho Marx.

'Very, very gutt,' he cried excitedly. In less than a minute he had returned triumphant and I had a reading light.

It soon appeared likely that I was to share my cabin with only one old Turk. The suitcase and cardboard box belonged to him, the steward said. Soon the old man himself sidled into the cabin on bowlegs, like an ancient jockey. He wore a felt hat, a suit of heavy, rough material, a waistcoat and a thin black tie. Later I found him praying, kneeling on a small mat he had unrolled in the middle of the cabin. For his prayers he had replaced the hat with a white cotton skullcap, and removed his shoes and his coat, but not his waistcoat.

I left him to finish his prayers in peace. When I came back he smiled warmly and toothlessly at me, and I smiled back; it was all we could do to communicate. His head looked like a ruddy wrinkled apple, set on broad rounded shoulders under a short white thatch of hair. He opened his cardboard box and, squatting on his bunk, began composedly to unpack it: apples, a loaf of bread, onions, a plastic container of what looked like string beans. He sat in his waistcoat cross-legged on one end of the bunk and spread his meal on the comic-strip pages of a 'girlie' magazine at the other end, his loaf of bread barely screening the naked midriff of a pin-up, although the rest of her was visible.

The cabin was cool and conveyed nothing of old socks. A broken thermos hung from the metal holder over the washbasin, and beside it were two glasses of different sizes, one of them cracked. At a pinch, the four passengers could stand up in the cabin side by side. The old *haji*, toothless in his bunk in blue striped pyjamas, didn't even snore.

In the showers facilities were not so ideal. The gents'

shower room was a plumber's nightmare, and the ladies' had odd grey foetus-like things sloshing about the floor in a lake of scummy water. When the old man had dressed, removed his dental plate from the washbasin and left the cabin, I made do with a thorough rub-down there.

I never saw the old man in the dining room. I had three table companions, all Turks, but he was not among them. One was a very old soldier with a fine strong-jawed face, snow-white hair and a silky white cavalry moustache; he wore a medal on his left lapel. When I sat down he raised his wineglass to me, and said, '*Sherefe!*' – 'Good health!' Opposite him a small man with glasses and a diffident manner introduced himself in bad English as a financial inspector working for the government. He even rummaged about in his coat and showed me his credentials – a frayed document signed by Ismet Inonu, a famous colleague of Ataturk from the early days.

A younger man, perhaps forty years old, sat opposite me; an architect, he said he was, from Istanbul. He looked more like an actor – easygoing, a bon vivant – and we shared a bottle of the Dikmen red, of which the old soldier accepted a glass.

'Excuse,' the government inspector said, 'I am sick, yes, from here' – he touched his head – 'all down. Drink offends me.' He only meant it didn't agree with him. At every meal he took a vial from his pocket and poured a little yellow liquid from it into a glass of water. I sneaked a look at the label and saw that it was for epilepsy.

'I speak English very bad,' he said. 'Can you speak French?'

'Yes. We can speak French if you prefer.'

'Oh, I prefer. Yes. I prefer very much.' But his French was worse than his English and we were soon bogged down in incomprehension. It didn't matter. The architect spoke fairly good English, although he said German, not English, was his second language; he translated when necessary.

'The old gentleman is an old lieutenant.' He translated, 'He wants you to know he fought the Greeks at Smyrna and also at Istanbul. He is seventy-nine years.'

'Did he meet Ataturk?' I asked.

'He says Ataturk gave him his medal. At Smyrna. He is very pleased to meet an Englishman.'

The architect could hardly wait to tell me about Turkey's catastrophic economic situation. It is a situation so dire that you can't blame Turks for their obsession with it.

'Do you know we have seventy-one per cent inflation? Seventy-one per cent!' He said it almost proudly. 'You ask why that is. Well, the government doesn't seem to be very good at economics. Do you know that Turkey has now three million unemployed?'

'So what's the answer?'

'Only one answer. Get out the leaders. New ones will come. Turkey was six hundred years under the sultans. Fifty years a republic, okay, but now Ataturk's work is gone.'

'Maybe you need a new Ataturk. A new sultan. A red sultan?'

He laughed. '*Ja*, a red sultan! Maybe!'

We ordered another Dikmen between us. The old soldier accepted another thimbleful and said, '*Sherefe!*' again. When the ship began to roll very slightly, the government inspector excused himself and slipped away.

The architect said, 'The CIA run this country.'

American capitalists – this was the opinion of Turks I had met in buses, hotels, coffee houses – wanted Turkey as a source of cheap labour and, to maintain this state of affairs, were deliberately holding back the country's industrialization.

The architect shook his head sadly. 'You could five year ago – no, two year – buy a *wunderbar* meal with *wein*, meat, all for fifty Turkish lira. Now, four hundred, five hundred.'

He sipped the Dikmen red. 'I sold a building on the Bosporus two years ago for five hundred thousand Turkish lira. How much now, you think?'

I made a wild guess. 'One million five hundred thousand.'

'Twe-e-nty million Turkish lira! *Ja!* Now you see how bad is situation?' Twenty million Turkish lira is about £200,000.

During the three-day trip to Mersin, the architect proved to be a useful informant. Most of the Turks on the *Samsun*, he said, were not on holiday; they used these coastal steamers as a means of transport to work. The government inspector, for example, was travelling to Antalya to investigate the ledgers of the local administration there. 'Maybe some shifty business.'

The architect's father had lived in a big house on the Bosporus and had given his wife all she wanted: clothes, jewels, anything at all. But there was a drawback: she was not permitted to leave the house – not ever. So she was denied the thrill of showing off her finery or jewels in public. The day he died was the happiest of her life. She threw an abandoned party for a few close friends to celebrate her freedom, and since then had married twice.

'Oh, old Istanbul!' the architect said, holding up his glass

80

to toast his birthplace. 'Before the traffic came, you could smell the girls, *smell* them in the street! Now gas you smell.' He pinched his nostrils together, frowning.

'The old days – twenty, thirty years before! Big-big villas on Bosporus in big-big parks, you know. Parks full of fish trees. Not fish trees? Ah pines. *Ja*, pines trees.'

He wanted to know if I had read the Turkish poet Nazim Hikmet. 'Famous poet.'

'No.'

He recited two lines and gave me a stumbling translation. Later I found them in a published English translation as follows: 'The life of a man is long, perhaps longer than necessary/Or perhaps is it shorter than necessary?' The poem, 'The Prison Clerk', goes on:

> Abdul Hamid drowned
> Medical students,
> Threw them into the water
>> At Seraglio Point.
> The currents swept the sacks away
> They were never found.
> Many,
> Many were hanged
>> In the days of the fight for freedom.
>
> In those days they hanged men
> At the head of the Bridge
>> Now at Sultan Ahmed Square.
>
> One last drink, you and I.
> 'Istanbul hath no equal anywhere,
> Her sparkling air, her limpid water give
> A new dimension to the sound.'

So sang
Master Nedim, the poet, so he sang.

At Antalya the old soldier and the government inspector
left *Samsun*, The inspector had his work to do; the old
soldier had a brother living nearby and would stay with
him for a few days. I took a photograph of them together,
and then another of the old man and his medal. They took
turns kissing me on both cheeks. The inspector said in
his hesitant English, 'I am–very–content–to–meet–you. *Très
content*,' and gave me his card. Shoulders back, the old
soldier said, 'Goodbye, Englishman,' and raised his hat.
Months later I received a Christmas card from Istanbul. In
a firm and careful hand the old soldier had written, 'As
you remember, we have met each other during the trip to
Mersin in the ship. You have taken the photographs of my
medal.' Touched, I sent him a card back.

Deprived of our table companions, the architect and I took
a taxi to a small beach covered with beautiful, small, egg-
shaped stones. The sea was greenish and felt like warm
consommé against the skin. Boys fished; fat Turkish ladies
stumbled over the stones, groaning happily like water buffaloes as they reached the water. Strange jagged hills shot up
a little way inland.

The architect eyed the fat women, who giggled and
groaned, trying to wriggle out of their bathing costumes
under their towels.

'I very much like womans,' he said. 'Sixteen years, sixty
years! Sixty years can be very good. London womans
sixty years old very, very good.'

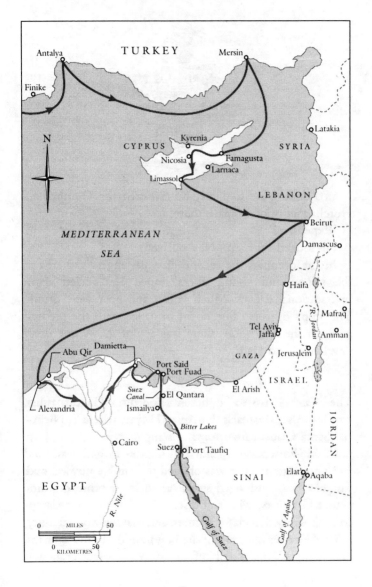

In London, he told me, he favoured the Cumberland Hotel. 'Plenty of womans there.'

'Expensive?'

He looked shocked. 'Never I pay!'

In the evenings the second-class passengers gathered in the saloon and young Turks leaped and reeled about in traditional dances. Much vodka and beer were drunk. The ship's officers came down to dance with the prettiest girls. In the afternoons there was a film show; one day I saw Laurel and Hardy.

The *Samsun* passed Ephesus, Bodrum (Halicarnassus), Cnidus. Also Marmaris, Finike and Myra, where St Nicholas (Santa Claus) came from.

E. M. Forster once landed in Cnidus in darkness, mud and pouring rain, and was obliged to stumble upward over vast blocks of dislodged stone 'amid the rapture of competent observers, who had discovered that the iron clamps were those used in classical times, and that we were straining our ankles over masonry of the best period'. In the darkness of a temple Forster fell off the stage into the orchestra,

which, luckily, was planted with Jerusalem artichokes set in glutinous mud.

Marmaris stretched along an unexpected bay, ringed with hills like a Scottish loch. I saw a rocky island streaked with rust, and four levels of mountain, in varying shades of purple and blue. Along this coast you can swim among submerged temples, theatres and libraries. There are valleys full of poplars, weeping willows and cypresses alive with larks and goldfinches. Among groves of olive trees whose bushy tops turn to silver as the sun dips into the Aegean, it is possible to believe that the great god Pan still lives. After all, who was the willowy flute-player of Ephesus?

It wasn't the fault of the radio officer of the *Samsun*, Haluk Bilgi, that he couldn't help much when I asked him how best to negotiate the Suez Canal.

We met one evening in the second-class saloon. Next midday I had a drink with him in a small cabin bare except for two pin-ups and a bottle of wine. 'I'm sorry, no gin. I drank it,' he said apologetically.

He considered my problem with frowning concentration. 'Now, to get through Suez to the Red Sea. Try take ship from Mersin to Haifa. Then from Haifa some ship to Elat – not difficult. Elat is in the Gulf of Aqaba, you know. Unfortunately it is still Israel.'

'Yes, from Elat it will be difficult to find a ship to Jedda or Dubai – in fact, to any Arab port.'

'Yah, maybe.' He thought for a while. 'Also avoid Djibouti. Ships I've been on down the Red Sea never want to take passengers from Djibouti. Political problem.'

That was that. I felt no further forward.

Haluk Bilgi was only thirty, he told me, but he had sailed nearly around the world. He showed me photographs of his wife and two children. He was happily married now, though he had once fallen briefly in love with a girl in Iloilo City in the Philippines.

'In Sula Sea, Philippines, there are many pirates who followed us in speedboats with heavy machine-guns. Sometimes they destroy the lighthouses, and then, when a ship is grounded, they kill the personnel on the ship. Many people killed there.

'In Singapore, prostitutes are coming to the boat to offer their body for two Singapore dollars, maybe same as one US dollar. They say, "Hello, how are you?" We say, "Very fine." After intercourse we pay two Singapore dollars. Man prostitutes, same like girl, are *five* Singapore dollars. Yah! Females cost less. Our astonishment was very much.' He roared with laughter, spreading out his hands in disbelief.

Bilgi said, 'I like Turkish ship. I have the company social-service help. Maybe my wife one year must be stay in hospital, I don't pay for nothing. In this company, if I have son and I die, he will be given education by government, to be pilot or engineer, go to university – everything.' He passed the bottle. He was a happy man.

Mersin. Modern jerry-building. Cranes. Neon lights. I had no time to drive out to see Tarsus, where St Paul was born, and where Antony first met Cleopatra. Instead, I walked to the shipping office pointed out to me by Bilgi, presented the letter given me by the helpful Turkish Maritime Lines lady in Smyrna, and was given a ticket for the night ferry to Famagusta or Magusa, as the Turks called it.

Afterwards I returned to the *Samsun* and said goodbye to the architect. 'We had nice talks,' he said.

With Bilgi, I took my luggage ashore. On a nearby wharf the night ferry, the *Yesilada*, had lowered her ramp to load cars and trucks. 'Green Island,' Bilgi translated. Sweating workmen were trying to push a truckload of tomatoes up the ramp. The truck was too old or too heavy, or the ramp too steep; it kept rolling back again on to the wharf.

'Fockin' vegetables,' muttered Bilgi with contempt.

I said goodbye to him and, when he'd gone, I stood alone watching the cursing men wrestling with the truck. With her ramp yawning open, the *Yesilada* looked like a hippopotamus refusing a pill.

Chapter Five

I CARRIED MY metal suitcase up the ramp after the re-calcitrant truck had at last been manhandled into the *Yesilada*'s hold, but saw no sign of a companionway leading up to a deck. A group of men in uniform stood there and must have seen that I was a passenger in need of direction but none of them made a move.

'Where do I go from here?' I called out to them, putting the suitcase down with a bump. They looked blank, and a full minute went by before a small man detached himself from the group. 'What want?' he said.

I showed him my ticket with the cabin number on it. He nodded, picked up my small bag and said, 'Come.' We found a stairway behind a battered Ford. One deck up was a corridor and a single-berth cabin. When I thanked my guide he said, 'Okay.'

I soon discovered that, if I lay on the bunk, the suitcase neatly filled the rest of the cabin. There was a porthole that didn't open. At 2.00 a.m. I woke up feeling like a character in the Edgar Allan Poe story who wakes up thinking he is in his coffin buried alive, although he is actually in a small cabin in a ship at sea.

The *Yesilada* was carrying a large number of poor Turkish Cypriot families returning from visits to relatives in Turkey, or poor mainland Turkish families being moved to Cyprus to be resettled in areas formerly Greek but taken over by the Turkish army when it invaded the island in 1974 and occupied its northern sector.

The division of an independent island nation, inhabited

mostly by Greeks, partly by Turks, is a modern tragedy awaiting a solution that may never come. Under President Makarios, the Greek Orthodox archbishop and politician, the two peoples of Cyprus had lived in peace – uneasily, it is true (the Greeks certainly had a tendency to bully the Turkish minority), but with no mutual problem that could not have been resolved by honest if dour negotiation. Yet *folie des grandeurs* drove political leaders in Athens and Ankara chose to use the Greek and Turkish Cypriots as proxies in a civil war.

The colonels who had controlled Greece since their coup in 1967 organized a second coup in Cyprus in 1974, which, for a time, put Makarios temporarily to flight and replaced him with a Greek Cypriot bent on achieving by force the extreme Greek nationalist dream: *enosis*, or the union of Cyprus with Greece, the unwilling Turkish minority included. This gave the Turkish generals in Ankara the excuse to fulfil *their* dream: the invasion and annexation of northern, mainly Turkish, Cyprus. The invasion was easily carried out: Cyprus is far nearer the Turkish mainland than it is to Greece, and the Turkish army is far stronger than the Greek army. Soon the Turkish soldiers gleefully bombed and bayoneted Cypriot Greeks out of the formerly mixed northern region, which they made exclusively Turkish. Turkish Cypriot peasants dragged themselves from farms they had worked for decades, if not centuries, among Greek neighbours in the southern zone, to the newly occupied Turkish zone. Turkish peasants who come over from the mainland – like those on the *Yesilada* – do so as part of their government's policy of increasing the proportion of Turks to Greeks on the island. The Greek colonels and their protégés in Cyprus have long since fallen from power;

the world's statesmen regularly urge the Turks to permit a reunited Cyprus; the Turks as regularly refuse to budge.

Every bench, chair and corner of deck space on the *Yesilada* was occupied by Turks and their roped suitcases, bundles and boxes of food. Many of them had put down mattresses so close together that it was almost impossible to move about between them. On the mattresses squatted or lay soldiers with shaven skulls and in shapeless, rough, threadbare uniforms, as well as elderly men in baggy peasant trousers and women in coloured petticoats. The area around the 'Snac' Bar smelled heavily of raki and tobacco.

'Would you like to sit here?' I knew I wasn't going to like the man who was offering me a place at his table the moment I accepted his invitation and sat down. There was a sharp-eyed cockiness about him, and his question was more like an order. But the *Yesilada*'s dining room was full, and there wasn't any choice.

Everybody else on the little 1500-ton ferry was in short sleeves. This man alone, despite the heat, wore a smart three-piece suit, a thick one, that caused his face to glisten with sweat. Doubtless he considered this gave him status, like the immense gold cufflinks the size of overcoat buttons, and the ring studded with what looked like diamonds on his left hand. He was fleshy, with a florid complexion and reddish sandy hair. His English, although not perfect, was very good, so I guessed he was a Cypriot Turk, not a mainlander.

'American? No, you are English,' he said. Again it sounded like an order. He might have been organizing a game: 'You are centre forward.' He told me he had spent nineteen years in London, and now lived in Cyprus. Since the Turkish invasion, he said, the Turkish part of the island had been transformed, and Turkish Cypriots were enjoying an unprecedented, almost unbelievable, prosperity. Tourists were flooding in. The Greeks on their south side of the Green Line, which, since the Turkish invasion, has separated the two communities on the island, were suffering, he said, with evident satisfaction. 'Are you a tourist coming to north Cyprus?'

I told him I would go from Famagusta to Nicosia, the island's divided capital. There I'd try to cross the barbed wire and the Turkish and Greek checkpoints on the Green Line in order to drive down to Limassol, the port on the south coast, a bigger, busier port than Famagusta. That was what the Turkish Maritime Lines woman in Smyrna had suggested. There might be a ship heading for the Suez Canal from there, she had thought; who knew?

My Turkish dinner companion did not like my plan to bypass northern Cyprus. His expression was sour and disapproving. 'The other side' – he meant the Greek Cypriot authorities – 'will never allow a crossing from north to south.'

'Surely, tourists can cross?'

'Not tourists, no one. Why don't you spend a nice holiday in the Turkish Cyprus? Go to the north. Fine place. Best beaches.' He sounded like a travel brochure.

Turkish Cypriot friends had told me that many of them, particularly the young, were disenchanted by the crude manners of the Turkish soldiers. They said that there was little hope of a really good job in the north of Cyprus, and that Turkey itself was bankrupt. 'Cypriots can get on with Cypriots even if they are Greeks,' these friends insisted. Older Turkish Cypriots recalled long friendships and former business relationships with Cypriot Greeks, and by now were even engaged in smuggling operations with Greeks across the Green Line.

I mentioned a little of this to my dinner partner when we had shared the best part of a bottle of red wine. He was indignant. Turkish Cyprus was thriving, he said; everyone knew that. I replied that my Turkish friends, simple, apolitical people, told me that young Turks longed to emigrate to Australia, England, anywhere, to escape the jobless claustrophobia of their demi-state.

My companion put down his glass with a thump and glared at me. 'If they say that, whoever they are, they have been brought up by the Greeks! They are traitors! The West helps only the Greeks.' It was a bitter statement across the fruit salad. By now I realized that my companion was one of those Cypriot Turks who have made a good thing out of the new dispensation. A businessman or a contractor, perhaps working for the Turkish army; a politician or a fat cat in local government. 'The West helps the Greeks because they are Christians and we are not!'

'That's not a very wise thing to say.'

It was a familiar cry. The Greeks echo it; the West favours the Turks, they say, because Turkey is more powerful and more useful to NATO. It's not an argument; it's the expression of a complex. I had heard, *ad nauseam*, similar expressions from Israelis about Arabs, Arabs about Israelis, Indians about Pakistanis, Pakistanis about Indians, and Iranians about everybody.

I said, 'The British don't give a damn who is Christian or who is not. You underestimate the West's indifference to religion.'

The Turk was drinking his coffee in agitated sips, his enormous cufflinks glinting in the neon strip of the dining room. 'The West is obsessed with all those centuries of Greek civilization. So what if they had some old play writers.' He wagged a thick forefinger. 'The Turkish army will never leave one inch of what they hold in Cyprus today.'

'A grim prospect for Cypriots.'

'Well, that's how it is,' he said, smiling with great satisfaction and calling for the bill. 'Have a nice time,' he said, 'but you cannot cross Nicosia, believe me.'

In the morning, watching the misty coastline of Cyprus growing larger, I began to think of my next step. From an assistant purser on the *Yesilada* I discovered that, after discharging cargo and passengers at Famagusta, the ferry would go on to a Syrian port, Latakia. This was certainly a possibility I had considered; being an Arab port, it would be easier to find a ship there bound for Jedda or the Gulf. But the assistant purser shook his head and showed me a Turkish newspaper of the day before, translating it for me. There had been serious riots in Latakia, and fighting between opponents of President Hafez al-Assad's ruling Alouite sect of Muslims and his supporters. Assad had sent troops and tanks to the city, and there had been heavy firing and loss of life. Latakia was not the place for a foreigner without a Syrian visa to wander about in looking for a ship to Eastern ports, so I ruled it out immediately. Later I was doubly glad I had. The port was a shambles, people said, with ships held up for two months or more, waiting for berths.

What about a ship from Famagusta to Haifa, and another from Haifa to Limassol? Limassol seemed a good place to head for, and the land route to it through the Green Line might be closed. I decided to consult the harbour master at Famagusta.

At the small walled port of Famagusta the police and immigration officials were quick and friendly. They scribbled chalk marks on the metal suitcase and stamped my passport without fuss. A police officer at once offered to lead me to the harbour master's office, indeed to the harbour master in person. In a small office on the quay I found a young, neat man who was amused by the idea of my ship-hopping to China. 'Slow boats to China,' he said, smiling. 'Would you prefer tea or coffee?'

'I don't think you can cross to Limassol through Nicosia,' he went on when tea arrived. 'Now we have very few ships to Haifa or anywhere else, except to Turkey or Latakia. There's not much commerce with Haifa.' Alexandria? 'None to Alexandria.' Suppose I reached Limassol? He didn't think I'd find much there, either, but, if I wanted to try, I could get there via Haifa, and a Turkish or Israeli ship sailed for Haifa from Famagusta once every two weeks or so.

'Nothing sooner?'

He looked at a list on his desk. 'We have a very small ship, a coaster, calling here tomorrow, sailing for Haifa after two days. It would be very cramped. I might get the captain to agree to take you.'

This sounded useful; only a brief delay. But I thought it worthwhile trying first to cross the Green Line to Limassol by land; if I could do so, there would be no ships going east from Limassol. On the other hand, what would I find to take me south from Haifa? This route presented the prospect of a chain of Arab ports hostile to shipping from Israel.

'The Israeli Zim Line would take you through the Suez Canal to Elat in the Gulf of Aqaba. You might find something at Elat to take you on.'

And I might not. The Zim line could not take me to any Arab port, so how would I get down from Elat to Jedda or to an Arab gulf port like Dubai or Bahrain? From Elat I might be forced to go *backwards* to Port Said, and Port Said, I had been told by someone, was only a transit port; you couldn't get on a ship there, you had to be *already* on a ship – to have boarded it in, say, Athens or Genoa. The harbour master confirmed this.

Limassol still seemed the best jumping-off point. I would try to cross to the southern part of the island through the Green Line checkpoints in Nicosia. If I failed, I'd ask the captain of the coaster to let me sail with him to Haifa from Famagusta in three days' time, and try to move on from there.

'Telephone me from Nicosia the day after tomorrow,'

the harbour master said. 'I'll tell you then if the coaster's captain will take you. I'll do my best.'

I found a taxi, a big white Mercedes, and told the driver, 'Saray Hotel, Nicosia, please.' We drove past the old stone walls of the fortress Othello is said to have lived in, but probably didn't, and out of Famagusta across the flat, dusty plain toward Nicosia, the divided capital of this divided, tragic and still friendly island. The early sun was cool on the peaceful surface of the plain.

To our right, northwards, the high mountain ridge I had seen so often ran like a dragon's back into distant cloud and haze. Also to our right, parallel with the straight road to Nicosia, lay the impassable Green Line, wholly visible only on a map, but viewable in detail in places where soldiers rested guns on the white barrels of roadblocks and signs warned that it was dangerous to approach. This was the cruel weal across the face of Cyprus left by the whip stroke of the Turkish invasion.

The guns and the barbed wire in this idyllic place brought back the memory of a winter in Cyprus just before the Turkish invasion in 1974. In the spring of that year, walking in the wilder hills above Kyrenia, I came across a strange phenomenon: a woman's string handbag suspended from the branch of an ancient carob tree. Soon I found a grove with other objects hung about: an elderly umbrella, a plastic shopping bag, a stone, a shoe. Far from the neat antiseptic villas of the British tourists on the shore below, far from Greek Orthodox and Muslim Cyprus, Cypriot peasants were still scrupulously striving to propitiate the spirits of this antique island as they had been for thousands of years.

In this new, divided Cyprus, in a new version of peace,

I did not have to be overly superstitious to feel that something had been killed here. Among those groves, shrivelled to charcoal by the Turkish shelling, the spirits of Cyprus, I thought, may be dead for ever.

I drove through the Turkish lines to the pretty port of Kyrenia in the occupied north. As far as the eye could see, Turkish shelling had blackened green hills like burned toast. Turkish troops goose-stepped past a newly erected bust of Ataturk, their eyes empty and moronic, dangerous as cobras. Their commanders had already flogged some of them for looting and rape.

When I drove up to a beautiful Greek village I'd known, I found it empty. It was a corpse: deserted, looted, silent. A gutted tank stood outside the church door, and two mules with no one to feed or water them tugged desperately at a vine.

'A dead place,' I said to a Turkish officer.

'Dead place, yes,' he said glumly.

Later, on the Greek side, I watched Turkish villagers moving north from houses they'd inhabited for decades. Their farm animals and tractors had been sold to their neighbours, Greek peasants, but they had loaded less precious possessions, such as Singer sewing machines and saucepans, on trucks provided by the United Nations. From years of habit, the old people had carefully padlocked their front doors with shaking hands, as if they had only gone out for a stroll and would be back for dinner. Their villages became so many earthbound *Marie Celestes*. Through curtains flapping against barred windows, I could see food on the tables and fires still smouldering in grates, but not a cat or a dog or a hen. Life had fled before the glow expired in these ancient hearths.

There were worse things down in the great central valley

nearer the capital, Nicosia. There the mass graves of massacred Greek Cypriot peasants were being uncovered. (There were similar graves on the Turkish side, too.) In Nicosia itself the young Greek soldiers cried for revenge and older people cried for grief. The keening could be heard around the city's school bulletin boards with their long lists of those still missing and the shorter ones of the newly traced dead.

Driving once more across the plain to the divided capital, I seemed to hear those cries now.

Although divided, Nicosia hadn't changed much in the year and a half since I'd been there. In spite of the pitiless killing and the madness of the destruction, I was still fond of it because of the Turks and Greeks I still knew there.

In old Turkish Nicosia you can look through open doorways at men cobbling, women sewing in cool, arched, stone-walled rooms, or at children playing in courtyards from which slender palm trees reach for the sky and bushier trees and shrubs spread shade. Here the older and poorer people live in space and greenness; the *nouveaux riches* pay through the nose for persuasive architects to slap together jerry-built houses and flats, hot boxes sitting in acres of brick rubble. Through old wooden doors one sees the precious things in unpretentious lives: sewing machines, photographs on dressers of smiling girls in wedding dresses and frowning young men in uniform, TV sets with bugle-shaped vases of plastic flowers set on them, coloured photographs of the mosque in Mecca, and chandeliers overhead like tinsel tiaras. There is no squalor.

But the absence of squalor is not enough. You can see

why young men want to leave for places where they think there's a bit of life – London, Hamburg, Sydney. A Turkish Cypriot friend once said to me, 'There are men here of thirty who are still virgins. Muslim tradition prevents them, on pain of death or a terrible beating at the hands of the girl's brothers or father, from touching a Turkish girl. They'd do anything to get their hands on a foreign girl, but, of course, it's not always possible. You have no idea of the intensity of the frustration here.'

Perhaps the mass graves are partly a symptom of the frustration. Repression and massacre, that legacy of a claustrophobic religious tradition.

The British vice-consulate on the Turkish side is a moderately grand building; before the partition it was the residence of the British high commissioner, and now also houses the British Council. A visa officer showed me to his room, and from there I telephoned the Greek Cypriot Information Department, a Mr Hadjiyannis. I explained why I wanted to cross over, and he said, of course, come across to the Greek side if I was proposing to travel to Limassol for the purpose of a book. Could I cross that morning, I asked. 'Yes. Come to my office,' he said.

As I put down the telephone a reddish-haired man with a moustache and freckles wandered in and said, 'Can I help in any way? Do you need transport?' He was obviously an Englishman.

'I want to cross the Green Line. The Greek information people say it's all right. If you could drop me at the Cleopatra Hotel?'

'I'll take you with pleasure. I'm the British Council rep, by the way, Richard Le Fanu.'

'I knew a Le Fanu some years ago in Aden, an admiral

of the fleet. Sheridan Le Fanu, the writer of horror stories, was his grandfather or great-grandfather. Yours too, probably.'

'Yes, old Sheridan's an ancestor.'

We drove to the Turkish checkpoint near the bullet-chipped walls of the old Ledra Palace Hotel, which before the fighting had been one of the famous hotels east of Athens, a home away from home for journalists, officials and diplomats in transit, and for foreign tourists who, year after year, visited Cyprus for its peace and quiet. Now it was a United Nations barracks occupied by Canadian soldiers. On its balconies their towels and bathing suits were hung out to dry.

At the checkpoint, while Le Fanu spoke to a Turkish policeman who knew him, a voice said, 'Mr Gavin, you are leaving us?' A fat, smiling Turk came up to me, and I recognized Inspector Ali, an old friend.

In the winter preceding the invasion, I had toured the north of the island with the idea of buying a small house there. One day I stopped to give a hitchhiker a lift; he turned out to be Inspector Ali. In return for the ride, Ali invited me to meet his family in their cluttered flat outside the old walls of Nicosia: a jolly wife, two roly-poly daughters, a teenage son offering me orangeade under the clothes line on their diminutive balcony. It had been easy to visit them regularly until the Green Line barriers went up, but on my last two trips to Cyprus I hadn't managed to cross the barriers to visit them. It was a pure fluke that I was seeing Ali now. And now there was no time to stop and reminisce about the good old pre-invasion days.

'Ali,' I said, grabbing his hand, 'I have to go. I'm travelling to China. I'll be back in a few months' time to tell you about it.'

'We've moved to Kyrenia now, all the family. We would like to welcome you when you come back. My salaams to China.'

I shook Ali's hand and Le Fanu drove me through the roadblock. A hundred yards on, the Greek police said they'd had a message from Mr Hadjiyannis's office to let me through. They wrote my name in a book and said, 'Okay. Bye-bye.' Le Fanu drove on toward the Cleopatra Hotel. I was through the Green Line; there was no reason now to return to Famagusta.

'You see, they're nice people in Cyprus.'

'Once again I'm grateful to a Le Fanu. Do you realize you have the hair of the Elphbergs?'

'Elphbergs?'

'The royal House of Elphberg in Anthony Hope's *The Prisoner of Zenda* was famous for its red hair. It was one reason why Rudolf Rassendyll managed the impersonation, remember?'

Richard Le Fanu laughed. 'My God, I'd forgotten that. Yes, the Le Fanus have that red hair.'

'I suppose Sheridan had it, even if his stories turned other people's hair white.'

'Stories like "Green Tea"!' That monkeylike thing crouching in the corner!'

'And Carmilla the vampire, do you remember her? All that panting and hugging. A Victorian lesbian nightmare.'

'Heavens, I must read it again,' Le Fanu said cheerfully, swinging right at the Chartered Bank.

I telephoned Alex and Mary Ephtyvoulou, and went to see them. The bunch of red carnations I bought for Mary from a mute street vendor outside the Cleopatra Hotel weren't dead, but they had no life and no smell, like plastic flowers, and Mary said, 'They've picked them in the cemetery!'

I have known Alex and Mary for fifteen years, perhaps more. Alex is a Greek Cypriot by birth and has represented the Associated Press in innumerable hair-raising forays into the battling countries of the Middle East. I first bumped into him in one of them – perhaps in Amman during the shambles of the Six-Day War of 1967, or in Damascus, or in Jerusalem. Our paths had crossed a good deal since.

There is no forgetting Alex once you've met him. He has shoulder-length hair that has nothing to do with – and long pre-dates – hippiedom, and a thick dark-brown beard that gives him a faint resemblance to Rasputin. This beard, surrounding a beautiful smile, can brighten one's day in the direst conditions. I have been cheered by it in the squalor of Beirut's sniper-dominated alleys and in the Street Called Straight as Israeli jets strafed the Syrian Ministry of Defence. But generally in my mind's eye I see Alex and Mary sitting by the sea in the sun during that peaceful winter in Kyrenia before the Turkish assault changed everything.

Mary has never reconciled herself to the Turkish occupation of the north of the island; I doubt if she ever will. Nor will Alex, but at least he has his work to think about. There are many like Mary who curse the roadblocks that keep Greek and Turkish Cypriots imprisoned in different parts of their country, and they all mourn their lost freedom. Mary is still a laughing, hospitable woman, but sometimes there is a melancholy in her that I don't remember from the easy times before 1974.

'I want to go to the UK,' Mary said over dinner on their

terrace behind its hedge of dusty oleanders. 'Now that we can't go to Kyrenia, I want to leave. There's nowhere to go for the weekend except Limassol, and I hate it there. Limassol, with its neon lights and Wimpy bars, is hardly Limassol any more.'

'All this emotion about Cyprus, Mary, and you from Samos.' Teasing her usually prises her out of her gloom.

The divided island has become like my carnations: not exactly dead, but without the spirit it once had.

In the Associated Press's ground-floor office behind his house, Alex and I looked through shipping advertisements in the *Cyprus Mail*. Apparently an agent in Limassol called S. Ch. Jeropoulos might have a vessel bound for Jedda sometime soon. Alex knew Jeropoulos and telephoned him. But meanwhile we saw another advertisement: 'The Red-Med Shipping Line: *m.v. Atlantis* loading Limassol 17/9/79; *m.v. Mini Lake* loading Limassol 30/9/79.' Both heading into the Red Sea, the ad said, but it didn't mention a specific port. Loading soon, it said, but it gave no sailing date.

Shipping advertisements are heady things. They are also a snare for the over-optimistic man who believes that, because it is written down in black and white in a timetable or an advertisement, a cargo ship will leave on the date mentioned to the destination specified. Sometimes it will; often it will not. It may sail a month late. The weather, port congestion – sixty-three days at Latakia – accidents, the availability of cargoes and the tactics of moneymaking, all are factors.

The next day I drove to Limassol. The town was full of holiday-makers, many of them from Britain or the two

British bases in the south of the island, there for the annual wine festival. I was lucky to find a simple room on the waterfront. From its French windows opening on to a small balcony I could see a small fleet of freighters lying in the bay.

The offices of S. Ch. Jeropoulos and Co. Ltd were conveniently close, only a few doors away. They had panelled walls, a high ceiling, and on one wall a picture of a clipper under full sail. A young man with a telephone to his ear waved me to a chair by his desk and excused himself. 'A container deal, sir. So sorry, but it's the weekend.' I looked at a shipping order on his desk for twelve casks of Keo wine for Singapore, Messrs Kuang Guan, Wine Traders (on SS *Mau Hing*). In a few minutes he put down the telephone and we discussed the possibilities. The ship to Jedda seemed elusive, but he found another vessel eastbound to the Red Sea and even further.

'There's a ship sailing from here to the Gulf, Bahrain, Dubai, Abu Dhabi on Tuesday. American. You might get on that.'

'Stopping anywhere?'

'Jedda, Saudi Arabia, I think.'

'That'd do.'

I thanked him and drove directly to the agent he had mentioned as being in charge of the ship. I found a short, bristling man, striding jerkily about a new office he had evidently just moved into; the furniture was modern, but there were hardly more than a couple of desks and three chairs.

'We have a ship, yes,' he said when I had explained my reason for being there. 'Limassol to Dubai.' My spirits rose. 'Stopping at Alexandria. I'd have to ask the captain's permission to take you, and the ship may not get here until Tuesday.'

'It's an American vessel, I understand.'

'American? No, Lebanese. Egyptian captain, but he's a very good man. When she arrives you could take a boat out to her. She'll be anchored in the bay.' It sounded just what I needed. After all my anxiety, had I conquered the Suez Canal so easily? I began to see myself on the deck of the Lebanese boat, her flag with the cedar tree stretching bravely in the Red Sea humidity, her sharp bows cutting through the waters, passing North Yemen, then Aden, abruptly turning up past Muscat and into the Gulf, which these days some call Persian and others Arabian.

I returned to my hotel, sat at a table on the street opposite the sea and opened an envelope of mail that the *Observer* had sent to me care of Alex Efty. In this delayed correspondence, I came across a cry for help so unexpected that I asked the waiter to bring me a Cyprus brandy before I read it to myself a second time. I downed the brandy and wondered what to do. How on earth could I, at a distance of a thousand miles, rescue a Pakistani from sexual atrophy?

The letter was from a Punjabi, the son of a friend I had known for several years in Pakistan. I had often visited the family in their home south of Rawalpindi. Walid, in his twenties, had worked in a hotel in Pakistan, but eighteen months ago he had decided – like hundreds of others – that he could do better for himself by emigrating and, by paying an employment agent in Lahore who specialized in sending Pakistanis to the Gulf area at exorbitant expense, he had found a job in a hotel in Dubai. He had really wanted to go to Europe – that's where the good life can be found, according to Pakistani friends who had gone there and written to him. Still, though Dubai was not England, it was on the way there. His father did not object to his trying to make good abroad. He was one more tiny ripplet in a sea of Asian humanity struggling westwards like fish to a lamp.

Walid had written to me from Dubai to say that it was a small, hot place; the hotel was grand, the pay adequate, but the social life very limited. He missed his girlfriend in Pakistan, a girl he had grown up with, and whom his parents wanted him to marry. His *cri de coeur* had the name and address of the grand hotel written on it, and it was dated more than a month before:

I am waiting for you to say welcome to Dubai. [I had told him I was on my way.] But I have an urgent request. If you do not mind can you bring me a 'Doll' which people use for sex I think that it is better than hands. I came to know that its price is about 25 pounds so I will pay for that. I think in Dubai it is good to pass the night some time because it is too difficult to get the girl here. I come to know that it is openly available in 'London'. So I will request to you to bring one 'Doll' for sex for me. That is rubber doll all the body is same like girl (please do not forget it) . . .

With best wishes to you,
Yours Walid

No doubt such dolls are openly available in London, but in Cyprus? What is more, I couldn't see myself stuffing a collapsible rubber doll into my metal suitcase in Nicosia and risk having it exposed to Muslim inspectors in the crowded customs at Dubai. Or at Alexandria, Beirut or

Jedda – particularly Jedda. (I had a clear vision of the scene: 'Open that one, please.' 'Oh, there's nothing in that one. Only personal effects in that one.' '*Awdha b'Illah!* Is this what you call a personal effect?') It might be good for sixty lashes in Jedda.

Poor Walid! He was suffering, but what could I do?

Next morning I heard from the bristling shipping agent in his new, meagrely furnished office that the Lebanese ship to Dubai was delayed – indefinitely, it seemed. 'Oh, one week. Or maybe early next month. Too early to be sure.'

I couldn't wait indefinitely. I continued to rummage through the shipping advertisements. And meanwhile to kill time I drove back to Nicosia to see Alex and Mary, who were thrilled by the idea of Walid's doll.

'Alex, you could get one here, I bet you could! You've probably got one hidden around the house, you monster!' Mary laughed so much that the children stopped watching television to come and see what it was all about.

'Not in Nicosia. No dolls!' Alex said. 'In London, of course. Strong rubber, inflatable, washable, lasts for years. But not here.'

'Oh, listen to him!'

'What do you mean, Daddy?' their daughter said scornfully from the doorway. 'Of course you can buy dolls in Nicosia.'

'Out you go now,' said Mary, hurrying her out of the room and making a face at Alex.

There would be no relief for Walid in Dubai.

* * *

I found the advertisement for *Al Anoud* in next morning's *Cyprus Mail*: '*F. B. Al Anoud*. Alexandria-Beirut-Limassol-Beirut-Alexandria. At Limassol every Tuesday as from 18th September.'

'That's it,' I said to Alex. 'A ferry carrying cargo and passengers, so it'll be more or less on time, I expect.' I telephoned the agents and booked a cabin from Limassol to Beirut to Alexandria. Better to push on, even if only to Alexandria; at least it was in the same country as the Suez Canal. I went round to a heavily guarded Egyptian embassy, where armed guards, expecting attacks from Palestinians, pushed my passport through a hole in the garden wall. In a quarter of an hour it was pushed back with a visa stamped on it.

I said goodbye to Alex and Mary and drove once more to Limassol. The *Anoud* was due in two days. In my hotel I wrote to Walid saying that I was still on my way, but didn't mention the doll.

Every night the public gardens near the waterfront of Limassol were full of coloured lights and avenues of stalls for its wine festival. Each stall had a covered counter with wine barrels on shelves behind it and Greek Cypriot volunteer barmen in traditional baggy trousers. The barrels were all labelled, but a red Afames 1962, which came only in bottles, was probably best of all. Crowds of local people and tourists surged about under the trees clutching long-necked flasks of red or white wine, which the barmen filled and refilled from the casks. The flasks of white wine looked like urine-specimen bottles. Nobody sprawled about on the grass or in the pathways, but most people were quite drunk. The wine was cheap and strong.

A snub-nosed British marine from one of the military

bases, his face flushed the colour of the red wine, swayed over to me. 'The wine takesh the lining clean out of your sh-shtomach,' he confided. 'Tha'sh wha' they shay.'

Greek mothers and fathers sat in the blue smoke of kebab stalls, watching the dancing among the trees. Big moths flew into the floodlights where crowds of younger Greeks howled with glee at clowns and a vaudeville act. 'Don't worry about young George,' I heard an English-woman say. 'We'll find him at t'gate soon enoof.' Police dived on pickpockets and hurried them away and, now and again, people stuck their heads into the shrubbery like ostriches and were sick.

A youngish Cypriot with a spotty face and a drooping moustache came up to me as I was leaving in my small rented car. I needed an early night before the next day's sailing on *Al Anoud*. He wanted a lift to the port area, not far from the hotel, and I told him to get in.

It was a mistake. When we reached the waterfront road with its bright overhead light I noticed something out of the corner of my eye. At first I thought the fellow had brought a wine flask from the gardens and was holding it between his thighs. When I realized my mistake, I said, 'I'd keep that for later. It might be useful for your girlfriend. A sort of wine-festival present.'

'Wine make too strong,' he explained. His eyes glim-mered off and on, like a mechanical doll's, as we passed under the intermittent lights. He sat there like an actor nursing a newly won Oscar. 'We go find a girl?' he said.

'Too late. Look, I'll drop you here on the waterfront.'

He sighed as I drew into the curb. I thought that when I stopped the car he might become truculent; instead, he got out, closed the door and said plaintively, 'No girl?'

'Not tonight.' I waved and drove away, leaving him under the light with the wine dying inside him. In the driving mirror I saw him wrestling with his clothing under the lights. Well, the festival had another night to run. I remembered as I turned into the hotel that Cyprus is the island of Aphrodite.

Next morning in the office of the agent for *Al Anoud* I was given a first-class voucher for the voyage to Alexandria. The agent explained that *Al Anoud*'s regular service between Egypt and Cyprus had been interrupted some time ago by political differences between President Sadat and the Greek president of Cyprus. Now it was resuming, he said, but the new tickets had not so far been received, and the Egyptians had agreed to accept vouchers instead.

'Also,' said the agent, 'please report to the ship at four o'clock this afternoon, not six o'clock as advertised. We hope *Al Anoud* will leave early.' That suited me. I was eager to return to sea as soon as possible.

I went back to the hotel, carried my bags down to the little reception desk with the helpful girl behind it and paid my bill. Cyprus is friendly. On the Greek side they overcharge tourists, no doubt, but, while Turkish attitudes are often surly or take-it-or-leave-it, Greek Cypriots usually smile and are usually helpful. A shopkeeper had photocopied some papers for me at no charge in his private office near the hotel. Truck drivers stopped and actually waved you across the street, and returned the thumb's-up sign you gave them to say thanks.

Over lunch I read the front-page story in the *Cyprus Mail*: 'Diplomat Quits over Antiques Scandal'. The

Austrian-born prince in charge of UN Aid for Refugees, appointed to look after two hundred thousand people who had lost all they possessed because of the Turkish invasion, had resigned, the paper said. 'Three lorryloads were removed from his house by police – thirty Byzantine Church ikons, much ancient pottery believed to have been looted [from the Greeks] by the Turkish Army. . . .' Trading in antiques, the newspaper said, is banned by the Cyprus government.

In the afternoon an old newspaper friend, Arthur Chesworth, formerly the *Daily Express*'s lively and hospitable correspondent in Beirut, now retired in a house in southern Cyprus, drove up to the hotel with his wife, Mickie. When I explained about the sailing of *Al Anoud*, they offered to drive me and my luggage to the dockside. I asked them if they'd been to the wine festival. Arthur has always felt at home in a taverna. 'We've stopped going to local weddings and wine festivals,' he said. 'So much cheap wine.' He pointed to his liver and sadly shook his head. We talked about the day's scandal. 'Does everyone come to Cyprus to loot and profit from this beautiful and unfortunate island?' Arthur asked rhetorically into a glass of beer. I could answer in a word: 'Yes.'

At the dockside we stopped by a customs shed in time to see men leaping with cries of alarm from *Al Anoud*'s ramp to the quay as a small and rusty tub swerving too fast into a berth alongside seemed about to ram her.

'You've got a weird and wonderful lot with you on that ship,' Arthur remarked, gazing at her. 'What about *that* load of scalliwags?' *Al Anoud*'s upper rails were lined, it was true, with a raggle-taggle crowd, several deep, of dark-skinned men in galabiehs, turbans, T-shirts and the odd fez. They did look a remarkably wild bunch.

I wondered where they had boarded and where they were going. 'Does Cyprus employ cheap foreign labour from Egypt?'

'Never seen any, have you, Ches?' Mickie said. She prophesied, 'You'll have fun with that lot.'

By now it was four thirty, but the customs and immigration shed showed no sign of life. It was as big as an abandoned warehouse, empty except for a few passengers, who, like me, had obeyed the agent's plea to arrive early, and one bored off-duty customs officer. 'Customs and immigration will open at six o'clock,' he said when I approached him.

'But we sail at six.'

'I doubt it,' he said, strolling away.

Chapter Six

'Ships? . . . Ships are all right. It's the men in them!'
Joseph Conrad, *The Nigger of the Narcissus*

THE EGYPTIAN FERRYBOAT *Al Anoud* of Alexandria
was a compact 2000-ton vessel, built a quarter of a
century ago in Denmark, which accounted for the cool,
irrelevant portrait of its Queen Margrethe in the captain's
cabin. Because of some Saudi involvement in the ownership
of *Al Anoud*, the Danish queen and Saudi Arabia's assassinated King Faisal were obliged to face each other across
the narrow cabin, while from a third wall President Anwar
Sadat of Egypt, in a blue Ruritanian-style uniform, all
sashes and gold with striped breeches and a large gold-
braided cap, stared with a curling lip down the length of
the cabin. His slight frown seemed to challenge anyone
present to smile at his extraordinary get-up (which, I'd
heard it said in Cairo, he had designed himself).

Al Anoud was small but not beautiful. To reach the
captain's cabin was like a journey through a Fellini film set,
or through a mob of extras from *Les Misérables*.

It is no exaggeration to say that the vessel swarmed with
the most wretched of Mr Sadat's subjects as bad meat
swarms with maggots. There were scores of them, and they
lined the stern rail five deep, wild of hair and scarred of
face, to watch developments on the shore. They milled
about, shouting inanely and obscenely, in the echoing steel
belly of the ship. Some of them had carried crates and bales
up the stern ramp, which were piled inefficiently around

the four or five cars and two tractors already in the hold and threatened to topple on to the cars. In stained pyjamas or torn and befouled trousers they squatted on the decks raucously talking and smoking among countless bundles and dilapidated suitcases. Spitting and scratching, they sprawled in every chair and even on tables in the communal saloon and the cafeteria. They lay in coughing, cursing groups on every inch of deck space. Some had laid down strips of cardboard torn from packing cases to serve as mattresses; some lay on single blankets, propping their heads on a grimy towel or on lumpy plastic bags with bottles protruding from them. Some were drunk and lay muttering in a clanking nest of beer cans. Others were either congenitally moronic or drugged. On the fetid lower decks they lay in accumulations of fruit peel, cigarette butts, gobbets of phlegm, twists of foul paper, streams and puddles of dark, unidentifiable liquid and a stench of urine and bodies. Once the ship reached the sea and began to roll, they lay in their own vomit as well.

To find my cabin required fifteen minutes of sweat and struggle up steel companionways against a flood of these aimless Egyptians. I needed to find the purser's office to show my ticket and be shown my bunk. But the corridors between me and the office were almost blocked by dim figures croaking 'Welcome' at me or lying inert and dejected. It was very hot. I could see air-conditioning outlets, but the system wasn't working and sweat poured down my body like rain. I wondered how a married couple with children and a baby would cope with this situation (the shipping company advertised itself as if it might welcome family parties). I wondered still more when I finally reached the purser's office.

The purser's office – a counter with 'Information' written above it – was locked and in darkness. It was six o'clock and, according to the agent and the captain, we should be about to sail.

After ten minutes a young officer in a crumpled off-white uniform and a bad temper arrived, unlocked the office door and shouted harshly to summon his assistants. Nothing happened, but more shouts from the office finally brought two ragged scullions, yawning, from dim bulkheads.

'Wait in there,' the information officer said abruptly to me. He pointed to a curtain, half opened to reveal a cabin large enough to contain a chair and a bunk whose sheets were grey and spotty. Thinking that to sit in there would undoubtedly give the information officer an opportunity to lock up his office and disappear once more, I said, 'Look, I'd like to be able to put this baggage in my cabin. Here is my ticket voucher.'

He took the voucher, glared at it angrily and said, 'Mister, you have no ticket. You must buy ticket.'

'I paid ninety-two dollars for this voucher. It's in place of a ticket. The agent has arranged all that with your company.'

'This not ticket. You have no ticket, mister. You must buy.'

'Look,' I said, 'I'm going to see the captain about this.' It was too hot to go on arguing here, as well as to talk in a busy aisle where people barged past us. 'Will you come?'

'Okay, I come. Captain also tell you go buy ticket.'

We struggled up more companionways to the bridge. I had convinced the sullen information officer that he could, without risk, lock my metal suitcase in his office until we returned. He made it clear with much sighing that he didn't like it, but he did it.

On the bridge I found the captain, a youngish version of Glenn Ford, amiable, competent-looking. He was actually smiling. It was a relief to see someone looking pleasant after half an hour on board *Al Anoud*.

He said, 'Hi! Everything fine?'

'Well,' I said, 'not entirely. This officer says this voucher I've paid for is no good, so I have no cabin. He says I must pay again for a ticket.'

The captain stopped smiling and turned to the information officer. 'Didn't you hear me tell you before?' he said quietly in Arabic. 'Vouchers are like tickets on this trip. This is okay. Give this gentleman the cabin he has paid for.'

From the look on the information officer's face, the captain might have told him that the pyramids had crumbled into rubble that very afternoon. 'Every voucher is acceptable?' His voice reflected disbelief and resentment.

'Every one,' said the captain sharply. He turned to me and asked, 'Which part of England are you from?' Vouchers and tickets were forgotten; we might have been continuing a discussion about holidays in Britain. 'I know England *very* well.' He smiled. 'I was two years on a Greek-owned ship between Liverpool and Antwerp. We must talk some more later.'

When we found it, my cabin was two-berthed, hot and airless. The sheets had been used at least once; they had dark stains and some yellow ones, and one russet hair and several black ones lay on their off-white folds. 'Wait,' said the captain's steward, who had carried my bag for me. He pushed it under a bunk, winked and went away. Soon he came back with newly washed but still-stained sheets, soap and a small towel. He himself, I noted, was dressed in white shirt and trousers as clean as a snowdrop. We pushed at the porthole for a minute or two, but failed to open it.

When I thanked him, he said, smiling, 'It is my duty.'

Al Anoud sailed from Limassol in the dark. She moved in a slow arc toward a narrow gap in the harbour wall, dropped the pilot there by a winking red beacon, and picked up speed abreast of the Limassol seafront.

Once we reached open water *Al Anoud*'s strange passengers began to form long, untidy lines between decks up to the steamy entrance to the ship's galley. There the kitchen staff, a brawny, sweating lot of overworked men, ladled rice, a pungent mess of steamed marrow and slabs of blackish meat on to metal trays. Sometimes a ragged figure would try to jump the immense queue and snatch a laden tray on the wing between a kitchen hand and the first in line. The staff cursed the interlopers and drove them off by bashing them on the head and shoulders with their soup ladles, and furious men in the queue kicked and punched them. The food was borne away to any available deck space and wolfed down among the cigarette stubs and the dirt. Soon the ship was full of men squatting like convicts, slurping food, belching, and wolfishly eyeing their neighbours' trays.

The cabin passengers' dining room was a long room with tables set one behind the other under a line of portholes, and led off the same steamy kitchen. By the time I found it, twenty or more Egyptian cabin passengers were already spooning up rice, the steamed marrow and pieces of dark meat. Between mouthfuls they fanned themselves with their hands. You could have absorbed the moisture in the air with a sponge.

Only one other diner sat at my table. He was an elderly

gentleman, unusually dressed for this time of year in a tie and white cotton shirt with long sleeves and long cufflinks, braces and a waistcoat of thick cloth over matching trousers. His jacket hung over the back of his chair. The older generation of Cypriot Greeks dressed like this. I could see that a conflict between the fibrous slabs and his dentures had to be resolved before any conversation would be possible between us, so I affected an interest in my tepid marrow. When he had cleared his teeth, he said, 'Good evening,' cautiously with a quick bow of the head.

'Not even serviettes in the dining room. Pah!' Two things soon became obvious: he was a Greek Cypriot by birth and a fine old man. Between scoops of rice and marrow, he told me he lived now in Wakefield, Yorkshire, where his son kept a coffee shop. He was going to Alexandria because he had lived and worked there as a young man, after his family moved there from Larnaca in southern Cyprus.

As we peeled and ate the apples that a steward with a bristly chin put before us after the rice course, Mr Pavlides told me, as if we'd been talking at this table for days, about his taxi business in 'Alex' in the thirties, and how later as a British subject from Cyprus he'd been called up and served six years in the Royal Army Service Corps, not as a driver but as a cook. Month after month in the desert with the Eighth Army, indefatigably spooning sand out of the soup, he had served boiled cabbage and potatoes, and finally risen to the rank of corporal. Sidi Barrani, Marsa Matruh, Alamein – he had seen them all. Cooking his greens and spuds 'under Rommel's nose', as he put it with a laugh, he refused higher promotion to stay 'with the lads'. When he said he'd never missed a day's duty in those six years, I believed him. He had a strong, square face, firm-

jawed and handsome, and a square head well covered with
neatly trimmed white hair; it was a face you believed in.
He could remember the names of his wartime officers as if
they were still close friends: Mr Reynolds, Captain Lyle,
and a Major Harry Piper from New Zealand who had
asked him to come and work as overseer on his sheep ranch
when the war was over (but it had seemed too far to go,
he said).

When Mr Pavlides took an envelope of photographs
from his pocket and began to pass them to me, I recognized
him at once, though they were pictures taken in the twenties and thirties. 'That's you!' I pointed to the dark-haired,
moustached figure in the twenties suit with high, stiff shirt-
collar, small knotted tie and wide-brimmed felt hat, posing
with other similarly dressed young friends, some of whom
wore spats. His big eyes, square head and face even under
the oiled black hair of fifty years ago was unmistakable.

He chuckled with pleasure, moving his dental plate up
and down with his tongue. 'How do you recognize me?
Eh? How?' But I think he'd known I would.

Pictures of old Alex: 'That's where we used to catch the
tram to work.' And: 'He's in Australia now. He's in America,
or was. This one is dead. Maybe that one is still in Alex; I
may see him.' Stocky, dark-eyed young Greeks in black and
white 'co-respondent' shoes, swelling with pride, elbows
and toes well turned out, beside a 1926 Fiat, his first taxi,
against the seafront at Alex. A little plumper, they posed
again beside a 1928 Chevrolet.

Last he showed me colour photographs of a red-tiled
Cypriot village near Larnaca, where his life had begun long
before the Alex days, and one of a Yorkshire suburban
garden under snow, where I suppose it will end.

Mr Pavlides visited his relatives in Cyprus every year, he

told me, and now, for the first time in twenty-five years, he was going back to Alex. Well, there'd be changes, no doubt of that, some good, some definitely bad. But he had to go back for one last look. So much of his life, most of his youth, had been spent in that soft Mediterranean city, and then the six unforgettable war years with not a day's duty shirked, which had led to security in sunless Yorkshire.

We had to push our way through the hot, overpopulated corridors to the upper deck. There, too, the mob seethed even more strangely in the eerie light of strings of red and blue painted bulbs, several of which were missing. Groups of men were bent over games of dominoes, slapping the pieces on the deck with the noise of pistol shots. Some played cards, throwing them down with shouts like war cries. A huge, swollen figure in cherry-coloured pyjamas swayed on its haunches, moaning quietly and rhythmically. Sleeping figures flung out arms and legs, their heads wrapped in filthy towels. Solitary men put their heads back and laughed inanely to themselves. It was like a scene from *Midnight Express*, the film set in a Turkish prison. My new Greek Cypriot friend edged gamely between men wrestling or exchanging screams of abuse, or men picking their feet or their noses. Egyptian music roared from several transistors. Empty cans of Dutch Oranjeboom pilsner de luxe clattered in the scuppers.

A light wind was lifting the sea and *Al Anoud* began to roll gently. Soon vomit lay on the deck like splashes of ratatouille.

I followed Mr Pavlides to the rail and we leaned over it with relief, breathing in the fresh air. 'Nice to look at the clean sea,' he said. He looked uneasily around before putting his moustache close to my ear to whisper, 'We must be careful not to catch louses!'

We must be careful not to be stabbed, I thought.

Most of the time there was nowhere to sit. The first-class saloon was locked until 9.00 p.m., partly, I found on inquiry, because the surly steward responsible for opening it seemed to be eating his dinner most of the evening and, partly, he said, because it would be invaded by the crowd and immediately transformed into an overfilled dormitory-cum-grogshop and toilet.

One of the cabin-class passengers was an American Seventh-Day Adventist – 'a very *strong* Adventist,' he explained earnestly – from Fresno, California. He was a biology teacher who had once taught in Beirut, and was now returning there for the sole purpose of selling his car before evacuating his family to Nicosia. Beirut now was a place of permanent and indiscriminate violence. It had undergone a horrific civil war with Christian and Muslim Lebanese showing the degree of unbridled ferocity toward one another that one would expect if the gates of two zoos were simultaneously opened and the wild animals released to battle in the streets. The shooting was not going to end there, and Beirut had become a good place to avoid. It was a sensible place in which to sell one's car and leave.

The Seventh-Day Adventist told me he was two decks down, actually *below* the level where the cars and tractors were parked. His tiny cabin had no portholes, no ventilation that worked, and he and an Egyptian lay on their respective bunks in pools of sweat, trying to breathe. I offered him the second bunk in my cabin, and he accepted immediately.

The second first-class passenger to materialize after dinner was a French-speaking Lebanese Christian, a businessman, obviously well-to-do, fingers ringed with heavy bands of what looked like gold, and heavy cufflinks on his sleeves. 'How terrible thees sheep,' he said. 'I'll never use it again.'

'Regard it as a unique adventure,' I advised him.

He began to talk of London, querulously and in French. 'I never want to put my foot there again. It's full of Arabs. It's no more London. Even my valuables were stolen from my hotel room in Kensington. Stolen by Arabs, that I'm sure.'

We moved into the first-class saloon as soon as the steward had unlocked it and beckoned us in. It had been unaired and uncooled all day and was stifling.

'Ah, my cabin is so hot,' the Lebanese panted in a mixture of English and French, thrown into linguistic confusion by the heat. 'No wind, and the *draps* are so *sales*.'

Later he abandoned his cabin completely. I saw him sleeping in a chair in the saloon, near a porthole that scooped in the sea breeze. Even so, his lolling head was glistening with sweat. Opposite him my old Greek friend sat upright, his eyes closed, dozing. Earlier he had told me that his cabin had no window, water or air. He was baffled by this, shaking his handsome old head and saying, 'How could I know the ship is like this? If the captain says he will give me one hundred pounds sterling, I am no more coming on this ship. Never!' I realized I was lucky to have running water and a porthole.

The Seventh-Day Adventist from Fresno and the Lebanese businessman disembarked at Beirut. *Al Anoud* went alongside stern first and lowered her stern ramp; then the shouting began. Customs officers marched up the ramp like big-bellied kings among their corrupt subjects, shouting for documents; Lebanese policemen shouted for something else; the ship's officers and the mob on *Al Anoud*'s decks shouted back. Shouting men ran up and down companionways carrying cartons of cigarettes, presumably contraband. In the vehicle hold they dragged crates to the ramp and dragged other bundles of cargo inboard, and men stood behind steel pillars counting banknotes into other men's palms.

The Lebanese businessman was slipping a handful of notes to a customs officer with one arm across his uniformed shoulder, and in no time, despite the seemingly impenetrable tangle of men and vehicles, he was soon driving his 1979 BMW 320 down the ramp with the customs officer clearing the way for him. At the top of the ramp the Lebanese looked straight at me through his window but gave no sign of recognition when I said goodbye. On the quay below, a taxi driver was kissing the hand of a policeman – obeisance, I suppose, to a 'godfather'.

Beyond the bedlam of the quay and docks that had a temporary, wartime look, high-rise buildings stood like shell-pocked abandoned lookouts. I was surprised we didn't hear rockets exploding or artillery; a day earlier or a few hours later we might have. Year after year I had watched Beirutis destroy themselves and their city, but it had always been much easier to feel sorry for, say, Phnom Penh. Beirut's pretensions to being the most civilized city of the region have always been skin-deep. It is truly a capital of unbridled intrigue, treachery, vulgarity and violence. It has always been a brutal city in a self-pleasuring, swaggering way – and in all sorts of hole-in-corner cowardly ways too. It has been a city of drugs, spies and gunmen, and, outside the novels of the late Ian Fleming, these ingredients add up to the antithesis of romance.

The Lebanese businessman on *Al Anoud* had talked about Arabs as if they were a different race, as though he were not an Arab. Yet Lebanon is a member of the Arab League, and he was not Armenian, Turkish or Kurdish. I wondered *what* he thought he was, but in an age of destitution and refugee camps, the Lebanese rich are generally irrelevant. They seem largely absorbed in increasing their fortunes in London, Paris or New York, in sunburning their bodies in beach clubs with names like the Elite, or being photographed for the glossy pages of Beirut's magazines. To them the refugee camps are unreal, but, of course, it is the camps that are the reality. Sprawling settlements as big as townships straddle the road to Beirut's international airport – one of your last memories of Lebanon is the sight of snotty-nosed urchins peering out through barbed wire, or out of nauseous lean-to shelters – and there are many more such camps disfiguring the body of this beautiful country like sores alive with human maggots. Mainly they house destitute refugees from the West Bank of the Jordan, fugitives from villages laid waste by war or set out of bounds to their own inhabitants by politicians drawing new lines on old maps. These Palestinian refugees share their misery with Lebanese fleeing the shelling and sniping of their own people, the gangsterism that flourishes in the name of religion and ideology. To the mindless brutality that fanatical followers of the Cross or the Crescent have practised on one another since the Crusades has now been added the brutality of nationalists, rightists and leftists.

On the ruined façade of a tall building across the waterfront one shoddy neon advertisement remained: SLEEP COMFORT. But true sleep and comfort have fled like refugees from the city that took itself for a ride in a homemade St Valentine's Day Massacre a hundred thousand times bigger than the original.

I remembered a horrifying crime of the sixties, an incident so relatively small that it failed to shock le tout Beirut. I told Mr Pavlides about it. 'At midday one ordinary working day, a young British diplomat was driving his wife along Beirut's seafront road, the Corniche. Behind him, a young Lebanese in a dashing car began hooting and swerving, making his tyres scream, changing gear with unnecessary revs – you know the sort of thing. Rich young Lebanese love to show off like that; it attracts attention and gives them exciting illusions of daring.'

Pavlides sniffed. 'Ha! Illusions! Cowboys!'

'Well, this cowboy finally swept into the fast lane beside the Englishman's car, drew a gun, aimed it through the window, shot the Englishman through the head and killed him.'

Mr Pavlides closed his teeth with a snap.

'Naturally there was a hubbub at the British embassy. It was discovered that it had nothing to do with politics. The Lebanese wasn't even after the Englishman's wife. There was no motive at all except impatience, petulance and the knowledge that the law wouldn't touch him because he was rich and well connected. When the Lebanese was arrested, it soon came out that he was closely related to a minister – a nephew or something. At the trial someone testified that he was 'sick' and, although he was found guilty, he was soon spirited out of prison and into a hospital. From which, of course, he soon disappeared. After a discreet absence he returned to Beirut and his normal life. It was as if nothing had happened. But something *had* happened: a young woman had seen her husband shot dead for no reason on the way home for lunch.'

Mr Pavlides tut-tutted loudly and shook his head. 'So much badness in the world,' he said. We turned from the dockside view and the line of mountains I had driven through so often over so many years since the fifties. I had come here then after five years of living among tribesmen in Iraq and in the Hejaz, and Beirut then had seemed like a gorgeous oasis in a desert. In the sixties and seventies as a journalist I had seen Lebanon engulfed in murder and religious madness. It was as if a monster had been revealed by the rolling over of a stone – a stone that could never be rolled back again.

It was pleasanter to turn away from that poisonous shore and look instead at the other ships in port: *René R* from France, *Dobrogea* from Constanta, *Kremnica* from the sealess city of Prague. Even if there'd been time, I wouldn't have wanted to go ashore in Beirut. I was glad when we sailed.

The captain asked, 'Do you know who all these deck passengers are?' He made circular motions with his hands to indicate the seething humanity belowdecks. We were in his cabin.

'Refugees from Beirut? Migrant workers?'

'No way. They travel on this ship all the time. It's their livelihood. They are the unemployed riffraff of Alexandria, from the gutter – and I mean the gutter. Egyptian importers scrape them up from a slum and pay them a little money – about twenty Egyptian pounds a month – to travel to Limassol and Beirut and then back again to Alexandria. You know what for?'

'I've no idea.'

'Look, there are two ways of importing goods into Egypt. One way, the usual way, is to import in bulk and pay regular import taxes, customs duties – quite high charges in Egypt today. The other way is to bring cargo in as accompanied baggage. There's nothing like the same duties for that.'

'Accompanied baggage?'

'The importer hires these people to divide his twenty tons of goods into small parcels, each man carrying a parcel or two. At Alex, they bring their parcels ashore as accompanied baggage. Understand?'

'And this is regular work?'

'Week after week. Another thing: these importers have

their bosses, *rais* is "boss" in Arabic. Six of them are on board at this minute. Sometimes the rais are themselves the importers – rich men themselves, and very tough, too. Each rais may hire forty or fifty unemployed riffraff to travel on *Al Anoud* to handle the cargo and divide it into parcels, which they will carry ashore at Alex.'

Mohamed Ali, the captain's steward in his snow-white shirt and trousers, came through the doorway and put cups of tea in front of us. When I thanked him, he said again, 'Pleasure and a duty, sir.'

'And let me tell you, they fight,' the captain said.

'It's the Alexandria Mafia,' I said.

The captain laughed. 'You're right.

I was hailed by one of the 'Mafiosi', an elderly former ship's engineer – ex-Egyptian navy, he said – sitting propped against a bulkhead outside the locked first-class saloon with a ragged group in jeans or galabiehs. He was taller than the rest, distinguished in a raffish sort of way, and he regarded his riffraff with barely suppressed disgust. He reminded me of Long John Silver contemptuously surveying his pirate shipmates on the *Hispaniola*. He was drinking a Dutch lager and his hand around the beer can was shaking. He had been pensioned off, he said; a monthly pension of 270 Egyptian pounds from the navy. 'This is my first trip on *Al Anoud*,' he added, 'and my last.'

'Why the last?'

'Too much *clifti*,' he growled, using the slang Anglo-Arab word the British army in Egypt once employed to mean 'stealing'. 'Too much fight. No good. I have my money from the government. Why work more at bad work?'

He picked up a piece of bread. 'This bread, I eat it. Enough.' He picked up another piece, curling at the edges. 'I eat this too? Why? One is enough. I eat only one. Why work more hard for two?' He was about to put down both pieces of bread but, on second thoughts, wrapped them in a torn newspaper and stowed them inside his shirt.

He confirmed what the captain had said. 'Yes, all bosses take men from street, all unemployed. Some bosses make money, start very poor, now very rich.'

I asked him what was imported into Egypt, and he shrugged: 'Machines, apples, anything.' A youth in a cheap white and red sweater, khaki flared pants and clogs clumped unsteadily up to us and flopped down on the deck. I pointed to him and asked, 'Look at him, is twenty pounds a month enough for him?'

The engineer laid a finger against his nose and narrowed cunning eyes. He only needed a parrot and a crutch to play old Long John. 'Oh, yes,' he said. 'Ho, yes! For him *very* good. He will stay on ship; he young man. But for me too much *clifti*, too much fight. After this I stop in my house.'

It was the young man with the clogs who, sitting in this identical place next morning, disarmed a man who seemed to want to stab Mr Pavlides.

The two of us had found part of a bench unoccupied on deck, an unusual stroke of luck. Several deck passengers were lolling about at our feet, dozing or smoking. Soon a dishevelled, twitching figure materialized in front of Mr Pavlides. Smiling murderously and flicking open the long blade of a knife, he began to flourish it very close to Mr Pavlides's waistcoated stomach. He waved it nearer and nearer, smirking and sniggering as he did so. Motionless, Mr Pavlides kept an admirable calm. His eyes grew rounder and his teeth clicked sharply, but 'Pooh, pooh!' was all he actually said. The stiletto weaving before him was long, thin and very sharp.

Luckily the young man with the clogs had seen all this. Looking on in some astonishment – his jaw had dropped open to reveal several missing teeth – he was even bestirring himself to rise to the rescue, if only at the speed of a drugged tortoise. I jerked my head towards the man with the knife and said quietly to the youth in Arabic, 'Take the knife. Quick. Take it.'

To my relief, the youth did so. He rose to his knees, which brought his head level with the hand that held the knife. Then he gently took the wrist and twisted it back and sideways so that the knife fell to the floor. Picking it up, he folded the blade back into the handle and dropped it into a trouser pocket, saying in soothing tones to the swaying figure above him, 'I'll keep it. Better. Afterwards . . .' Then he winked at me, pulled the owner of the knife down beside him and offered him a cigarette. It was a striking exhibition of calmness and tact. The man had stopped grinning and seemed suddenly exhausted. He said nothing and didn't look at Mr Pavlides again.

'I'm not a drinking man, but I'd like a drink,' said Mr Pavlides, wiping his forehead and walking with unusual stiffness to the rail.

We had a drink in the bar that night. I managed to find the steward to open it at nine o'clock, and we talked about the ship. 'Ship *ta'ban* – tired,' the steward said across the bar. 'Engine *ta'ban*. Can do only eight mile an hour.' I wondered why a washing machine stood on one side of the saloon door and an electric cooker on the other side, like pieces of pop sculpture. More contraband, perhaps. Mr Pavlides was saying that after tonight's dinner – rice and some sort of dubious stew – he was going to eat no meals except breakfast. I would have agreed with most of Mr Pavlides's opinions and tastes, but I couldn't give him my unqualified support on this because breakfast that morning had been ebony-hued tea and a kind of fried egg cake, quite hard and reinforced by a network of coarse black human hairs cooked into its fabric, as wire mesh is embedded in concrete to give it extra strength. I wasn't sure that I could get enough of it down to last a whole day.

On my way to my cabin I came across a knot of shouting people in the corridor and, in their midst, the sprawled, half-naked body of a man clearly in a bad way. He had blood around his head, neck, throat and chest, and his trousers seemed dark with blood too. The shouting group bore the body away, sagging like a waterlogged mattress, to the medical bunk (which was, I saw, the curtained cabin in which the information officer had ordered me to wait the afternoon I came aboard in Limassol). There the man, dirty, clothes awry, lay and bled. Eventually someone brought bandages for his head and apparatus for blood transfusion. Already he looked more dead than alive, a skinny desperado with a great slash around his skull.

The whole ship seemed to be in an uproar. A shouting crowd had gathered around another man who was bleeding from a stab wound or a clout with an iron bar. Several other people had blood on them. The captain and his chief officer were pushing here and there in the confusion, looking purposeful, bringing order. I saw Mr Pavlides, wide-eyed with interest, peering over the crowd, jiggling his dentures up and down with his tongue. He caught my eye and pushed towards me, shaking his head sorrowfully. 'If I don't see this I don't believe it,' he murmured.

I went to bed. A locked cabin seemed as good a place to be as anywhere on a night like this.

At breakfast next morning a hugely fat Egyptian woman – the only female rais on board, I learned later – leaped up and began to scream and struggle with a muscular waiter, who screamed and fought back, prudently grabbing a water carafe with one hand while seizing a fistful of bosom with the other. I was fleetingly reminded of the film *Godzilla Meets King Kong*. Mr Pavlides turned to me, his handsome face half horrified, half smiling. 'Now we'll have a fight, woman against man! Next, maybe woman against woman? You see!'

In a little while the chief officer came up to us on deck and reassured us. 'The man who threaten with knife is in calaboose, mister. Chains on foot and hands. Nobody see him again. No problem again.' Curtains for one pirate, at least.

After the stop at Beirut, Captain Musa had instructed the steward, Mohamed Ali, to set out two wicker chairs and a table on a small area of deck just behind the bridge-wing, the one part of the ship the deck passengers and the rais's men were not allowed to invade. With the saloon closed all day, these two chairs provided the only sitting place we had.

Captain Musa was a pleasant man, still young, who had seen service in many parts of the world since he graduated from Egypt's Naval Academy in 1962. Sitting with Mr

Pavlides and myself on the small rectangle of space he had lent us, he talked about the time when the lightning Israeli advance to the Suez Canal had trapped him in mid-canal for six months in a big tanker. 'It was dangerous. We were caught between the Israeli army on one side and our people on the other. The danger was from our side because in those days the Israelis had better weapons and could shoot over us, but our people sometimes fired short and hit the ship.' He leaned back in his swivel chair and laughed briefly at the ceiling, pitying the inadequacy of the Egyptian army of those days, shrugging at the way things were. It struck me that Captain Musa was very Egyptian, not a bitter man at all; alert, humorous, he would go through life dutifully supporting his family, observing with fascinated equanimity each manifestation of Allah's whim.

'After that, a crooked shipowner gave me a ship – a bucket, really – and I had my wife on board when we were both nearly drowned in it. You see, before I took over, the ship had been grounded on reefs in the Red Sea, and the owner had had it *pulled* off those blasted reefs, not lifted off. So, unknown to me, there was no bottom to speak of to the ship, and suddenly one day I found the old bucket was going down fast. I had to beach her near the Sudan-Eritrean border, just inside Eritrea. We got ashore, thank God, my wife and I and ten crew – all black men, as it happened. I thought that it might be safer in Sudan, because there was that rebellion against the Ethiopians in Eritrea and things were quite unpredictable. So I got some camels from a village and we bumped away to the Sudan. From there we contacted the Ethiopian officials at the border and they allowed us to reach Asmara. They arrested us there and accused us of running guns to the Eritrean rebels. They sent a helicopter with some officers in it to examine the ship I'd beached, but they found nothing, so we were released and sent back to Egypt safely.

'The Saudi owner wanted to hang me when he heard I was safe. He'd hoped the ship would sink – for the insurance – and he wanted me to drown with it. Well, he's in jail now.'

In his blue Ruritanian uniform, President Sadat looked severely down at us from the wall of the captain's cabin. 'It's much better with Sadat in control,' Captain Musa said, pointing to the portrait. 'The bad thing is the new breed of Egyptian businessmen who take advantage of freedom to make money by buying cheap, rotten ships, and creating bad working conditions.

'Take *Al Anoud*. I'm short of stewards, so the cabin-class saloon is closed all day. I have too many radio officers and six surplus hands whom the company – the Alexandria Shipping and Navigation Company – insists I take aboard, although they are useless and can't learn. That's how it is.

'As well as sail the ship, I must control two hundred and fifty of this riffraff from God knows where. The lowest riffraff in Egypt. I only have a handful of men to control them, but I control them. I have to go down and arrest them myself, as you saw; after all, I can't bring the engineers up on deck for riot control.'

I said, 'They look as if they might take over the ship.'

Captain Musa looked shocked. 'No way! No way! I make the rais responsible. If there's trouble, the rais see to it that the injured man's group is paid retribution money.'

Blood money. The Arabs' tribal way. And the Mafia's.

'I can get a rais banned from coming aboard, and he loses a fortune if I do. And they know me. They know I'll run a villain up the mast and leave him there for twelve hours or more. You can't play with these men, and I don't. If the men who were stabbed last night die, the police will be waiting at the dockside.'

When I told the captain about the creature who had threatened to stab poor Mr Pavlides, he laughed, as he probably had laughed when the chief engineer told him the bottom had fallen out of the engine room that day in the Red Sea off Eritrea. 'I tell you, we dealt with him – thoroughly. We know him. He used to give karate displays in the cafeteria. He's a fire swallower, too. *Was.* For him it's all over.'

I said I'd seen him pushing a beer-can top into the waistband of his pants under his vest to use as a knife.

'We've all kinds,' said Captain Musa. 'If you meet some of these men ashore, they'll demand your money. If you don't hand over, they'll—'

'Slash your throat?'

'First slashing themselves and yelling that *you've* attacked *them.* They'll claim self-defence and, though the police may not believe them, meantime you're dead.'

'In Alex, they kill sailors for money. Eh? You don't believe me?' A voice crept into my ear, the voice of the Greek barman from Kefallinia on the *Alcheon*, the man who liked screwdrivers.

'I hope you're not too angry,' Captain Musa said, holding out his hand.

'Not angry at all,' I told him. 'Just interested. But I'm glad I didn't bring a wife and three small children with me.'

In the afternoon, like a good omen, a small plump, brownish bird with white cheeks flew in from the sea and clung to a stay near *Al Anoud*'s bows. It was only hitching a short lift because soon the long Mediterranean coastline of Egypt appeared to port like a thick smudge. We were off Abu Qir (or Aboukir) and its bay, famous for Nelson's victory.

Captain Musa regretted that he had no advice on how to find a ship through the Suez Canal. I was beginning to feel like an inadequately trained Grand National horse approaching the green cliff of Becher's Brook. He did offer two suggestions, however. If you're stuck, he said, go to the operations office in Port Said or Suez. 'They know what vessels are expected, where and when they are going, all that. They regulate the convoys through the canal. There's no point in trying to see the harbourmaster in Alex. He's too busy. So many ships coming from every side, tours from Israel, important visitors. I know him well, and I can't get to see him for weeks.'

Before we parted, Captain Musa gave me his address in Alexandria. 'If you're here again, please phone. Or if you need something . . . We sail again in three days, back to Beirut and Limassol, the old round.'

It wasn't his fault, the anarchy of *Al Anoud*. I don't know where he is now. Perhaps he has gone to some better ship, or perhaps he is still with *Al Anoud*, holding the rais responsible, coping with the stabbings and slamming ragged cut-throats into irons. His employers might not like his frankness, so I have changed his name here. I don't want to get him into trouble; he's a good man.

By six thirty, we idled motionless among twenty-three other ships outside Alexandria harbour. The sea was a dingy grey, and the sun cast spokes of light between low, blackish clouds. It was quite cool.

By six forty-five *Al Anoud* began to move at a snail's pace, jettisoning rubbish, cartons, cans, crates, rags, bits of food and paper to the seagulls' delight. For a while the city was simply a long thicket of cranes, a silo, an oil flare, a cement factory and, beyond, the low outline of what is still a low-rise city. Soon the black and white light tower of Ras el Tin appeared and, inside it, Ras el Tin Palace, once King Farouk's, basking in the fitful sun like an elaborate sand castle. Near the palace lay Farouk's yacht, the *Mahrousa*, that sailed him into exile, distinguished by its desert-yellow funnel and sleek, pompous lines of forty years ago. A few submarines, a frigate.

We swung across the bows of a Greek freighter, the *Aliakman Light*, and began to trail a white Soviet cruise ship with red funnel and yellow hammer and sickle. The pilot came aboard, cautiously feeling his way along the ship's rail. On his launch, the paint peeling, its canvas awning stained by sea and salt and rust, the helmsman raised both palms to the *Al Anoud*'s bridge and shouted, '*Ma Salaama!*' then swung the wheel so that the launch veered away, '*Sura'a kamila b'il amam!*' from the wheelhouse: 'Full ahead' for Alex.

By 11.00 a.m. I am in the centre of a milling mob in the vehicle hold of *Al Anoud* just behind the ramp down which we are to disembark. We wait like marines in a landing craft about to storm a beach. But the ramp is stuck. '*Nezelu!*' the chief officer is yelling furiously. 'Down with it!' The heat is almost unbearable, and the hold is like the foul-aired belly of a sea monster. My metal suitcase seems about to tear my arm from its socket; it is hard to hold because of the sweat on my palms. The exasperated immigration officers who have done their duty aboard and want to return to Alexandrian docks begin to use elbows and feet to clear a path to the front. Around me, gap-toothed mouths reeking of beer scream, 'Your mother's c——!' and 'Up your arse!' Over the heads of the mob Russian tourists on the rail of the ship that has berthed ahead of us point down at the amazing spectacle of *Al Anoud* preparing to disembark her mad mob of passengers. Most people around me seem to be carrying a hundredweight of baggage on their heads. 'Pimp!' a furious man yells at someone with a crate who lurches into him on the metal deck, which is slippery with oil and spilled packets of smuggled cigarettes. The last individual action I witness is that of a man in a turban furtively folding the metal top of a cigarette tin into a makeshift knife and stowing it away in the waistband of his trousers.

At last the ramp drops on to the quay with the noise of a bomb in a metal vault, and the howling human flood bursts down it as if the ship were sinking, carrying me along like a stick in a stream. At the immigration check, a hundred yards further on, I find my clothes literally are dripping. I might have been standing under a shower. A small puddle forms around my feet and amuses the customs man.

Chapter Seven

GRATEFULLY I TOOK the pen from the fingers of the receptionist at the Cecil Hotel in Alexandria, signed my name in the register and dripped sweat on to the carpet. I was guided from the lobby to my room by a Nubian boy with a pearly grin and a fez, who operated a wondrously old-fashioned lift like an ornate, wrought-iron birdcage.

I was delighted to find that the Cecil, one of the most satisfactory of Egypt's older generation of hotels, was still as it had been two years before, just after the riots, and more or less unchanged since the day I'd first seen it in 1954. My room had a high ceiling, and the tall, wide windows opened on to a balcony over a narrow street running down to the sea. Across the street I saw washing strung out on lines and, through a gauze curtain opposite, a woman in a scarlet dress lying barefoot on a bed. On my second day, there was a wedding party in the street, with much drumming on tambourines and hand drums, and chanting, clapping and ululating by the women. Every balcony in the street produced two or three spectators who called to one another excitedly.

But now, after a bath, a change into dry clothes, and a drink, the thought returned: how was I going to get through the Suez Canal?

The Egyptian who was the general manager of the Cecil surprised me by his youth; I am not sure why I expected his age to match that of the hotel. ('Built in 1929. Architect: G. Lorca,' a plaque on an outside wall said.) I wanted to make sure that there were no plans to pull the Cecil down, as the old Semiramis in Cairo had been for no reason a year before. I explained that I had been conceived in the Semiramis, though not born there. 'On the third floor,' I told the general manager.

He smiled. 'Then you have a special interest in these things. The rich developers who bought it could have kept the façade of the old Semiramis and done what they liked inside. In fact, that was the agreement with the government, as I understand it. But one night after work had started, the façade fell down.' He raised a cynical eyebrow. 'Odd, wasn't it? So convenient for the rich developers. Here there's no such threat for the moment. The Cecil is a government hotel and is usually one hundred per cent full. They tried to give me new lifts, but I said, "No, give me new machinery for the lifts, and even new handles on the doors, but the wrought iron must stay." Do you see that big mirror in the lobby? I found that in pieces in the cellar. I had it cleaned and put back. It's a hundred years old.'

★ ★ ★

Alexandria may be shabby, but it is still beautiful, and as much Mediterranean as Arab. The lines of stately balconies swell out over tram-lined streets like the elaborately half-draped bosoms of nineteenth-century European matrons. Everywhere are names like Rue Verdi, Pension Acropole, San Stefano Beach, Antoniadis Garden.

I bought a booklet called *Alexandria Night and Day*, and sat in a café next to the Cecil to read it. Drinking tea, I looked across at the statue of Saad Zaghlul, a pre-Nasser-era nationalist, in morning coat and tarboosh, on a high plinth, striding none too steadily (all his weight is on his back foot) toward the eastern harbour. A small boy wove his way slowly between the café tables carrying an armful of woolly toy cats, crying. '*Awez biss-s-s-ss? Awez bis-s-s-ss?* Who wants a cat?'

Over tea I looked down a list of names under the heading 'Navigation Agencies'. I marked three of them, which should do for a start: Abu Simbel Shipping, Memphis Shipping Agency, Thebes Shipping Agency. Then I looked up the list of foreign diplomatic missions, with particular reference to the Sudan and Saudi Arabia. Both countries were represented in Alexandria. By now I had realized that, if a freighter was to be found that would take me through the Suez Canal, it would almost certainly stop somewhere in the Red Sea. Jedda was a probable port of call, Port Sudan another. Looking further down the map, there was Djibouti, for which I already had a visa. It would be unwise to risk a stop in Jedda without a visa of some kind, and the same might be true of Port Sudan. I had also calculated that, if worst came to worst, I might be forced to resort to a bus from Port Said to Suez, trains – if there were any – from Cairo down to Port Sudan, and there take a ship to Aden, Djibouti or the Gulf. This might prove difficult, but it would become impossible if I was held up at the Sudanese–Egyptian border for want of a visa.

First things first: the Sudanese consulate was nearest. On the seventh floor of a building on the seafront not far from the Cecil a policeman in dirty white sat outside an open door. I knocked and entered a newly painted apartment completely empty except for a kitchen sink and a desk or two glimpsed through a half-open door. The smell of paint was strong. A tall Sudanese in a dark suit came through the half-open door. I asked, 'Is the consul in?'

'He's in the Sudan. What is it about?' He had a gentle voice.

'A visa.'

'Visas not here. Only from Cairo embassy.'

'But I'm not going to Cairo.'

'Only from Cairo.'

'Why do you have a consulate here, then?'

'I don't know,' he said with a helpless shrug. 'Only consul know, and consul is in—'

'The Sudan.'

Downstairs, I found a taxi so festooned inside with pink and red plastic flowers, vivid green plastic leaves and toy plastic parakeets on swings that the driver peered through his windscreen like a hunter in the Brazilian rain forest. Perhaps he really needed the two toy compasses on the ledge above the dashboard to find his way. At any rate, he found it to the Saudi consulate and, when we got there, soft-talked a young policeman into allowing him to wait for me.

A mass of Egyptians were queuing at a small door for visas and work permits, or perhaps for *laissez passers* for the

Mecca pilgrimage. I walked around to the front door and up short, grand steps. Two armed Egyptian policemen hardly more than sixteen years old waved half-heartedly at me, and I waved back to show I wasn't a terrorist. Inside I found a big mock-baronial hall, beamed and panelled, which looked like a theatre set for *Charley's Aunt*. A secretary showed me into the consul general's office, where a portly, smiling Arab in an expensive suit said, 'Please have a seat,' in good English. I drew up a high-backed chair at his elaborate desk. 'Excuse me just for one moment,' he said and pressed a bell. A servant came in and the consul general said, 'Tea or coffee?' He made a few notes in a file with a gold pen, and another man came in, spoke deferentially to him, bowed and took the file away. The consul general wore a small silver-grey imperial on his chin and a silver watch strap on his wrist. On a wall hung a portrait of the late King Faisal, praying. It was painted from a perspective above and to the right of the kneeling monarch, and his face was partly obscured by a white silk headcloth, but Faisal's ascetic features were unmistakable.

'What can I do for you?' Not for the first time and certainly not for the last, I explained my intention of travelling to the Orient by sea. I wanted to sail through the canal, I said, and naturally I hoped my ship would stop at Jedda. It might be necessary to change ships there, and I might need a week – at the outside – to find something to carry me on to the Gulf. Could he arrange a transit visa for me with little delay? I hadn't much time.

With a smile, the consul general produced a form to be filled in triplicate. He needed photographs and my passport. His smile seemed to say that another hurdle was about to be safely overcome. But I misread it.

'I'll send your application by telex to Saudi Arabia,' he said, and my heart sank. 'I'll give you an answer in one week.'

'Couldn't you give me a transit visa? Does it have to go to Saudi Arabia?'

'Sorry, yes.'

'Could you make it less than a week? Perhaps get an urgent reply?'

'Two or three days, then.' He made a note with the gold pen, and looked up sharply. 'Where can I touch you?'

'I beg your pardon – oh, at the Cecil Hotel.'

'Very good. I hope tomorrow or the day after . . .'

I knew then that nothing would happen. I knew all too well Saudi Arabia's appalling bureaucracy. In my mind's eye I saw vividly the offices in Jedda or Riyadh full of indolent figures in white headcloths and ankle-length shirts, bare feet tucked up on the chairs beneath them, the tea glasses on desks stacked with papers, the nose-picking, the constant fumbling readjustment of genitals within the white cotton folds, the supercilious idleness of clerks with gold watches.

The consul general chatted on in a friendly manner. He had served in Geneva for five and a half years. I couldn't believe that Alexandria meant promotion for him but, in these days of kidnappings and attacks on consulates, Alex might be safer than Geneva. He sat benignly in front of a floor-to-ceiling bookcase containing bound copies of *L'Illustration* from 1913 onwards. I knew I was going to have to struggle for my visa.

My taxi driver was waiting, and I directed him to the Abu Simbel Shipping Agency fifteen minutes away. Its offices were massive despite the narrowness of the street. I walked up wide stone steps into a high-ceilinged building, and into a Dickensian confusion. With its interior divided into innumerable cubicles and offices by glass and wood partitions, the place looked like a bank. People ran back and forth; men in robes carried trays of tea; telephones rang and clerks shouted into them. I leaned over a desk and asked a man, 'Where's the boss?' He got up at once and obligingly led me through several small offices to a high open door. Through it I saw an even higher room, a large dark desk, a scattering of dark tables and heavy armchairs. As I entered a strong male voice shouted, 'Fatima! Fatima!' Two telephones were ringing on the desk, and a tall man with glasses, white sideburns and a trim white moustache instantly spoke into one of them, but he quickly banged it down to answer the other.

Finally he put down the telephone and said to me with great gusto and a sweeping gesture, 'English, French, Arabic, Armenian – what language do you want? Now, sir, please take a seat by me here and tell me what I can do for you.' He beamed, leaned over the desk, took my hand, shook it warmly, sat down again and handed me one of those visiting cards that look as though they are made from a wood shaving. His telephone rang again, and while he answered it I had time to read the card. It said:

I. I. Rashad, M.R.I.N.A. London
Master Mariner B.O.T. London
General Manager and Member of the Board
Abu Simbel Shipping Agency

'Now,' Captain Rashad said and offered me a cigar. Declining it, I told him my story. I told him about the *Alcheon*, *Samsun* and *Al Anoud*. He was interested, and it was soon obvious that, in so far as two almost constantly ringing telephones would allow him to do so, he was going to give my problem his serious consideration. He was friendly, he wanted to help and, although he was busy, he wanted to give me all the time he could; he seemed to have complete confidence in my story of sea travel to China for a book.

'My father', Captain Rashad boomed, 'was the first man to have four academic degrees from London, Mr Young. He was a landowner, a pasha. He was also a great friend of Dr De Valera of Ireland. He wrote a book, indeed, called *An Egyptian in Ireland*. Perhaps you've read it? Fatima!' A rattle of typing in a room nearby stopped abruptly and an attractive secretary came in, took up a bundle of files and withdrew, smiling. The walls were dotted with calendars from shipping companies. There was a good print of a British three-masted clipper, the *Swiftsure*, 1326 tons. A large sign opposite the desk said in Arabic, in gold and chocolate brown: SUBR (Patience).

Captain Rashad explained that, under Nasser, his company, like many others, had been nationalized. Although he was well-to-do and a pasha's son, 'They wanted people to administer these things. Now I'm a government official, you may say, but I make all the decisions. I'm my own boss. I speak *pure* French, pure English' – he did – 'Arabic, Italian and Turkish. I am a very good singer. I can sing just like Nat King Cole, Dick Haymes, Bing Crosby. You remember Nat King Cole's "Nature Boy"? I sang it in a New Orleans restaurant last year, where some American shipowners took me. When I was a seaman I used to go to the London Lyceum Theatre and sing there in French, English and Italian. I won many prizes there when I was a third mate. It was my hobby. I knew all the London pubs at that time. Now my dear London is very changed. Too many Arabs there now.' His big voice rumbled on happily; his eyes were round behind his spectacles. I liked Captain Rashad.

A decisive-looking man with a thick black moustache entered, picked up a Fabergé Brut deodorant spray from Rashad's desk, squirted his moustache, and left. Rashad didn't seem to notice. He was meditating.

'I have the impression, Mr Young,' he said after a moment, 'that it is advisable for me to give you a card to a very efficient man in Port Said – the most efficient man there. Because from Alex, I am sure, you will not find . . . Fatima!'

When his secretary came in, Rashad said something to her in an undertone, and then turned to me. 'You will have lunch with me at the Syrian Club. It will be a great pleasure for me. Does that suit? Now. . . .' He wrote for a while, then handed me a letter. 'Please read this.'

Written on a plain sheet of paper, the letter, in capital letters, said:

Dear Ahmed Bey,

Greetings. May I present Mr. G. Yong [sic] from The Observer. He wishes to join a V/O as a passenger, destination Jeddah. I should much appreciate your giving all help to facilitate joining a ship. Much obliged.

Cap. Rashad

Fluffing out his white sideburns, Captain Rashad said, 'Ahmed Bey Karawia is a most efficient man, as I said. You find him at the Aswan Shipping Company, Gumhuriyah Street in Port Said, right on the canal – anyone will show you. He is the commercial manager there.'

Rashad also gave me a letter to the manager of the

Aswan Shipping Company in Suez, and another to an Egyptian assistant harbourmaster at Jedda, which he signed, 'Your brother Ismail Rashad.' Then, over gin at the Syrian Club, a small, plush 1920s house, he shook his head. 'Oh, God, Jedda,' he said. 'In Alex the ships come into port, and first come first served. In Jedda the first one in is the one who pays the most.' An Italian captain entered, spotted Rashad and raised his arms. Rashad embraced him, asked him to join us and introduced him: 'This is Captain Roncallo, a good friend.'

We moved to the dining room and ate hot prawns. Rashad and Roncallo talked of the Red Sea; it was interesting because they hoped never to see it again and I was heading there.

'Oh God, Jedda!' said Captain Roncallo, putting on an abandon-hope expression and raising his eyes to the ceiling. 'Fifteen years ago, we had one hundred and eighty camels on the main deck. Other trips it was sheeps or cows. About six-a hundred. The heat. Terrible.'

Captain Rashad poured us some white wine. He said, 'In the 1960s Yemen War, I was shipping our troops to the Yemen, to Hodeida. One day I returned from Hodeida via Port Sudan, where I had to load a complete circus, including tigers, lions and elephants. And, before we reached Suez, one elephant – the biggest one, naturally – died, and at Suez we didn't know how to lift out of the hold this huge terrible thing! The stink!'

Rashad seemed determined to undermine my confidence in the Red Sea. 'Next month,' he warned, 'there's a wind, the haboub. It makes it impossible to see anything. Daytime becomes night-time. It's full of dust; you can't sail ahead. There are the reefs and islands, and the haze makes mirages and even hides the stars. There are no lighthouses in the Red Sea. And the heat! I remember in Massawa one time I asked for a steak. They took off the cover, and it was black immediately with one million flies. Impossible to live in the Red Sea.'

By now I knew that Alexandria was not the place to get my ship through the canal, but at least I had three useful names in Port Said, Suez and Jedda, and it turned out that without at least one of those letters I would almost certainly have been obliged to cross from the Mediterranean to the Red Sea by the humiliating land route.

But even at this moment I realized how lucky I was to know Rashad. As we said goodbye on the steps of the club, I took his hand in both of mine and gave it an extra-hard shake. 'Tell about it,' he said, laughing. 'Maybe you come back and I'll play you some records and you can hear me singing Nat King Cole's "Nature Boy".'

'Go to the Holiday Hotel in Port Said,' said Captain Roncallo. 'Say my name, or ask for Captain Mohsin.'

But for the moment I couldn't go anywhere. I had to wait for that Saudi visa.

It is easy to pass the time in Alexandria. There is plenty to see: a Graeco-Roman museum, the Amphitheatre, Cleopatra's Beach and Pompey's Column. There is also a racecourse. But, above all, there is the Alexandria built in imitation of the northern Mediterranean architecture of the last century or the early twentieth. It is full of façades from Marseilles and Athens, streets from Nice and Genoa.

Behind the rigid back of Saad Zaghlul's statue I wandered by chance into the Trianon Bar, a beautiful relic of pre-1914 that in any other city would be lovingly preserved and have become a famous place for rendezvous. A marble-topped long bar of carved solid wood, with a brass rail for the elbow and another for the feet, under decorated wooden pillars soaring up to a brownish lacquered ceiling with small inverted marble domes. The walls are high, and decorated with life-size paintings of ecstatic Turkish slave girls and bland eunuchs dancing in a swirl of baggy Oriental trousers, turned-up slippers, brandished tambourines, scarlet skirts and white legs: Eastern Isadora Duncans painted somewhat in the style of Arthur Rackham. They are signed 'G. Tolleri – Pittore – Vetrate d'Arte, Firenze', but, unfortunately, have no date.

Ancient waiters shuffled about the tiled floor. I ordered a *zebib*, the Egyptian equivalent of the Turkish raki, and ice.

An old gentleman at the bar saw me looking at the murals and said, 'You should have seen the old tiles they had on the floor. Beautiful.'

A second elderly man in a dark blazer with naval buttons, stiff white collar, well-tied wide-knotted tie, light trousers and highly polished shoes laid a short malacca cane on the marble bar.

'A nice cane,' I said.

'From Harrods, Brompton Road, SW1, 1926,' he said promptly, with a gratified smile. 'I was staying at the Hans Crescent Hotel.' His English was clear, and allowing for the faint tremors of age his voice, like his appearance, was perfectly poised.

'Only a horseman would have bought a cane that length.'

'You're right, sir.' He whisked it smartly under his left

armpit, straightened his old back, saluted briskly and laughed. 'I've several horses still. I even have fifty acres near Alexandria. I was a merchant marine engineer – that's why you see these buttons. I was a pilot, too. I flew in the Royal Egyptian Air Force – Farouk's air force in the 1948 war that Nasser was in. Now I can't wear those buttons because they've got crowns on them.'

'Surely no one would worry now.'

'You can't be sure. *This* chap's not bad.' He meant Sadat. 'And I suppose seventy-five per cent of the people would say the same. He wants peace – and who doesn't?'

A man in a galabieh drew up a little stool at my feet, gently lifted my foot on to a box and began to rub polish on my shoe.

I asked the man with the blazer what he was drinking.

'Rum. Egyptian rum. Jolly good stuff. Pure, you know. Does you no harm.' He motioned to the barman, who poured me a zebib and another rum and water for himself. When the shoe cleaner rose to go, he gave me a few coins before I could stop him, then offered me a Gauloise *filtre*, which I refused. 'When I'm not out planting potatoes on my little piece of land, I come here at midday to about a quarter to three. I never go out in the evening. My wife and I have a sixth-floor flat here, and at exactly six o'clock the electricity goes off. Well, at my age, six floors are too much to walk. My wife and I happen to be giving a party tonight. May I invite you?'

I thanked him and said I was going to see the British consul. I told him my plan to leave for Port Said, and mentioned Captain Rashad.

'Oh, Captain Ismail Rashad. He's of a *very* good family. I think he married a princess. He's a first-class fellow. I saw him the other day at the yacht club. Would you care to have lunch there one day with my wife and myself?'

I would have liked to, but I had to say I might be leaving in a day or two. 'But perhaps I'll see you here at noon tomorrow.'

'Oh, I'll be in the country. Pity. It *was* a pleasure to meet you. I love England, you know, although I haven't been there for many years.' When I asked for my bill, the old man made a sign with his cane and the barman said, 'All finished, sir. No pay. Fuad Bey pay.'

I walked out through the towering caramel pillars into a tumultuous street where a motorcycle policeman was buying a flute from a street vendor, playing a few trills to test it.

Next morning I looked into the Trianon Bar, but Fuad Bey was not there. Instead, I talked to a very fat Armenian who said, 'Fuad Bey is a real gentleman, a cousin of King Farouk. But Farouk never liked him because Fuad Bey is a man who never says anything except the truth. Others leaned, you know, on Farouk's arm, and smiled and flattered. But not Fuad Bey: he stood up, aloof. Under Nasser, he suffered too. Everything was seized. He hadn't ten piastres, but he never asked for anything. Now things are better. But what about the twenty years of poverty, the best years of our lives?'

Another man put on a mock-angry expression and said, 'Nasser, the English favourite,' and everybody laughed.

I asked why the beautiful décor of the Trianon Bar was not cleaned and restored, and who owned it.

'The owners don't care a thing about this place. It's beautiful, but they don't care. They never come here. They've no values. Egyptians are like that.'

'But the manager—'

'There's no manager. The waiters run the place. That's why it's dirty and falling down.'

'It could be one of the great bars and restaurants of the world. Is there any point in writing to the Minister of Tourism?'

Someone made a rude noise. 'Fuck the Minister of Tourism. No, Egyptians don't care about this kind of thing, sir.'

I looked at Signor Tolleri's dancing girls, the Isadora Duncans in slave trousers with their bangles and tambourines, the spangles on their costumes standing out in glistening relief. It seemed a terrible pity, but then I remembered the Egyptian saying, 'God has given earrings to those who have no ears.'

During all this conversation a large carton had perched on the bar between the Armenian and me. Just before I left, something made it fall and it burst open. Immediately the floor was alive with small flapping birds escaping in all directions. Laughing, the patrons dispersed on hands and knees, trying to catch them as they scuttled under tables and glass cases full of bottles. Feathers flew about. 'Quails,' said the Armenian, who was far too fat to scramble after them. 'Delicious, cooked on a skewer. Very expensive these days. And see how small they are.'

For form's sake, I waited for the call I knew would not come from the Saudi consulate general. Two or three days, he'd said. Next morning I waited until eleven o'clock. I bought a *Journal d'Egypte* to pass the time with my morning coffee at the Cecil, and on its front page the political world partly caught up with me: '*Quatre avions syriens et deux israéliens abattus au-dessus de Beirut*'. This sort of futile mayhem had been going on for years, and it seemed pleasantly far away from Alex. But, after combing the rest of the paper for an hour, there was still no message from the Saudis, so I called. The consul general's secretary assured me that there would be a reply the next day: 'We are sending another telex now.'

'Please, can you send it "urgent"?'

'Yes, of course.' She had a lovely voice on the telephone. Don't worry, it seemed to say; everything will be fine. But I knew better: we wouldn't get a squeak out of those supercilious bureaucrats − not in under three weeks or a month, and then the answer might easily be no. I'd give it one more day and then try to prise a visa out of the consul general himself. At any rate, I intended to try my luck from Port Said as soon as possible, trusting to Captain Rashad's friend.

For the moment I wanted to visit the house of Alexandria's celebrated Greek poet, Constantine Cavafy, the poet of the 'decadent' city, of strange gods and strange loves, of barbarians, Christians, Jews and Greeks; of ambitious Antony and Cleopatra and of dull, noble Ptolemies; of spoiled heroes and of the 'very handsome boy, assistant at a tailor's' whom he saw one day straightening his tie in a mirror, 'making the mirror proud'.

There was a Cavafy museum, I knew, in the Greek consulate. On earlier visits, lack of time had prevented me from seeing it: a meeting, for instance, between Henry Kissinger and Sadat at the Montazah Palace in 1975, and serious riots in 1977 in which official buildings went up in smoke, and the seaside villa of Sadat's vice-president was sacked by people protesting at the price of bread and oil. They claimed to have dragged out seven television sets – or was it seventeen? Too many, at any rate, for one man: that was the opinion of the impoverished mob.

The Greek consul was a lady with charm and a brisk manner. She talked of old Alex, before Nasser, when the Greek population was a hundred thousand (today, it was three thousand): the Alexandria of Lawrence Durrell's Justine, Pursewarden and Mountolive, and the even older Alexandria of E. M. Forster, and of Cavafy. 'But things haven't changed very much, you'd be surprised.' She laughed. 'The telephones: they steal the lines for the copper. They stole four hundred metres of cable between my house and my office – imagine that. Siemens, the famous German firm, went to Cairo to make a new system, and they had to give up! The lines were all rotten and everything was stolen. Now I can't even get through to your consul here, and never to Cairo or Port Said in less than two or three days.' Nevertheless she had succumbed to Alexandria's ramshackle charm: 'The winter's best. There's no dust in the air. You can smell the iodine in the sea.'

Cavafy's museum was in an upstairs room, shuttered against the heat. An Egyptian factotum led me in in darkness and opened the shutters. As I prowled about the sad, piously arranged room, he moved ahead of me with a cloth, dusting cases of manuscripts and relics of Cavafy's simple life in this great Mediterranean city. Sketches of Cavafy, busts, photographs, the dates of his life: 1863–1933. An open book: Κ.Π ΚΑΒΑΦΗ, ΠΟΙΗΜΑΤΑ. And one open at a poem: 'Α ΕΧΑΝΔΡΙΝΟ ΒΑΣΙΛΕΙΣ'. Strong handwriting on pages of letters. The furniture was predictable: dark wood, inlaid mother-of-pearl, folding chairs with

curving legs and red seats. Through the windows, palm trees and cooing pigeons:

> O how familiar it is, this room.

> Near the door just here was the sofa,
> And in front of it a Turkish carpet;
> Close by the shelf with two yellow vases.
> On the right; no, opposite, a wardrobe with a mirror.
> In the middle a table where he used to write;
> And the three big wicker chairs.
> At the side of the window was the bed
> Where we made love so many times . . .

> The afternoon sun fell on it half-way up.

> . . . One afternoon at four o'clock, we parted
> Only for a week . . . Alas,
> That week became perpetual.

In the hallway a secretary rose behind an ancient upright typewriter. 'The consul says will you please make use of her car. The driver can take you to the place of Mr Cavafy.

If you would send the car back in not too long time . . .'
It was generous of her. Cavafy's street, Shara Sharm el
Sheikh, is not smart or picturesque; on the contrary, it is
almost a slum. I walked up the narrow street through puddles and refuse. A sign outside his old building announced
that it was now Pension Amir. The entrance looked dark,
grimy and unwelcoming. Next door a garish sign advertised
HAPPY HOME, a small shop selling hair dryers, lemon
squeezers and cheap shaving brushes. An elderly doorman
appeared on Cavafy's steps and said, 'Give me baksheesh.
You want see Cavafy house?'

I looked up at the stone balcony of the apartment and
the few pieces of poor linen hanging on a sagging line. A
child, its face covered with snot, playing in the grime on
the bottom step fell off the step and screamed. I gave the
bouab some money and walked back down the lane through
the puddles to the car.

The driver took me to Pastroudis, which, like the Trianon, was one of Cavafy's favourite cafés. Pastroudis is in
better shape than the Trianon, and cosier; it has no caramel
pillars or spangled dancing girls cavorting on its walls. It is
more like a good Paris café of the turn of the century, with
wooden panelling and tiles, battered brass rails on a solid
wooden bar and wooden stools with wicker seats. Nubian
waiters in yellow galabiehs and turbans hover around small
tables with green cloths. A long terrace is shaded from the
sun by an awning and illuminated overhead by a row of
globe-shaped lamps, which give it a Parisian air – or rather,
the Parisian air of Pastroudis at the time of Cavafy. Several
old Greeks or Italians sipping Turkish coffee on the terrace
looked old enough to have known him.

The bar was enlivened by luxury: shelves of Russian

vodka, Black and White whisky, Evian and Vichy water. The Trianon is neglected, but someone is looking after Pastroudis; perhaps it's the shade of Cavafy. I sat down at a table and opened the volume of poems. By the time my coffee came I had come to this one:

> Yesterday, walking in a quarter
> Rather remote, I passed under the house
> I used to enter when I was very young.
> There on my body Love had taken hold
> With his marvellous strength.
>
> And yesterday
> When I passed along the old street
> Immediately beautified by the magic of love,
> The shops, the pavements and the stones,
> And walls, and balconies, and windows,
> Nothing left there was ugly. . . .

I thought of the Pension Amir and Happy Home, the grimy steps and the snotty child.

I ordered a sandwich, some olives and a beer, and watched the peaceful old men in wide-brimmed hats under the long green awning. Younger men began to come in from their offices. It was well after midday.

> Half past twelve. How the hours have passed.
> Half past twelve. How the years have passed.

These words are the last in a poem called 'Since Nine O'clock'.

★ ★ ★

The following morning, which I had decided must be my last in Alexandria, I turned my mind to the important matter of that Saudi visa. I telephoned the Saudi Arabian consulate general and was told by the secretary that nothing had been heard. 'Well, I must go,' I said. 'At this rate I may have to wait a month.'

'You might try for a visa at our consulate in Suez,' she said. 'We cannot give you one here.'

'Why should I get a visa in Suez easier than from your consulate general here?'

'Well, they can give visas in Suez.'

I knew a Saudi evasion when I heard one. It was obvious that she was suggesting Suez merely as a means of avoiding responsibility for giving me a visa in Alexandria. The cowardice of officials is usually obvious. I said, 'No. I'm coming round now. I have to leave for Port Said this afternoon. I expect the consul general to be kind enough to provide me with a transit visa, giving me just time enough to change from one ship to another. I can't believe he is not empowered to do that much.'

Once more I sat at the desk of the smiling man with the silver-grey imperial and the silver watch strap under the picture of King Faisal praying. 'I can give you only three days, Mr Young. A transit visa.'

'That is all I need. It would be better to have a week, but it's also better than having nothing.'

I waited in the mock-baronial hall until a clerk brought my passport with a three-day visa in it. It also had two pages obliterated by ineffectual attempts to stamp the visa into them – the visa officer's rehearsals, as it were, for the final successful one. Those damaged pages, it turned out, would oblige me to leave Jedda in a hurry. On the other hand, if I'd arrived with no visa, I might still be there.

I paid my bill at the Cecil while the Nubian boys brought my bags down in the wrought-iron birdcage. As I collected my change, a voice said, 'Oh, ho! Going?' Mr Pavlides was wearing his thick suit, waistcoat and a grey felt hat. 'How did you find Alex?' I asked him.

'Sometimes good, sometimes bad. As I thought.' He shrugged. 'I have good time. I found friends. Now I go back to Limassol in *Al Anoud*. Oh, yes! I paid my ticket for *Al Anoud*, so I go *Al Anoud*. I shall miss you, my friend.' He snapped his teeth with emotion.

'Give my best wishes to Captain Musa,' I said, 'and don't get stabbed.' We shook hands, and I followed the Nubian boys with my baggage into the street and found a taxi to Port Said.

Chapter Eight

NEAR THE PORT Said waterfront is a region of shops called, among other more Egyptian names, Boulangerie de Luxe, Queen Elizabeth, George Robey and Harry Lauder. Behind this area of merchants and touts, the city council's lighting gives a flush of glamour to the distinctly northern Mediterranean façades of streets and squares, and they become like faded opera sets whose central spirit derives from Nice or Barcelona, not old Damascus or Baghdad. In winter the people of Port Said never have to endure the icy wind that sweeps into southern Europe from the Mediterranean, and the city has not been badly damaged by the bombardments and invasions of the last quarter of a century.

As I turned left off Shara Gumhuriyah I saw a splash of bright light from an open door and a neon sign saying RITZ BAR. I crossed over to it, looking down the street to where it dissolved in a string of lights and a yawn of blackness. If I had continued past the lights only a hundred and fifty yards, I would have fallen into the Suez Canal.

The Ritz is a simple place with a long bar under slowly turning fans and tables for those who want a meal as well. One wall was taken up with a gilt-framed picture of a Regency drawing room with ten or twelve pretty girls in crinolines playing Blind Man's Buff with several young men in tailcoats. There were empty tables outside as well, under a wide arcade, and I took a cold Export beer out there.

An Egyptian on a bicycle pedalled up to the curb and said, 'You are Holiday Hotel, waiting for ship?'

'Yes,' I said, 'waiting.'

'You want anything?' He leaned closer over his handle-bars. 'Some joy?'

'Not now.'

'Okay, maybe later.' He pedalled away. I was surprised by the politeness of it all.

I had reached Port Said from Alexandria about an hour before, after 7.00 p.m. It is a long drive, but a rewarding one and, when I told the driver not to hurry, it was not because of the wrecked cars at the side of the road. The delta of the Nile is a wide expanse of glimmering greenness, water, villages and animals. Everywhere men and women walk behind ploughs, or sit in groups under eucalyptus trees or the weeping willows that bow over scores of canals and rivulets – all the myriad waterways that make up the miracle that has nourished old Egypt since before the building of the pyramids. You drive through white-pink fields of cotton dotted with the larger blobs of pink, white, red and blue that are the robes, turbans and dresses of villagers working in the sun. Behind mud-coloured village walls, pencil outlines of minarets rise from screens of palm trees. Men and boys wash naked in streams by the roadsides, the silt-thickened water modestly encircling them as if they stood waist-high in a mudpack. One sees railway lines, factory chimneys and pylons carrying high-tension wires that connect the industrial towns of the delta with Alexandria or Cairo, but the great rich greenness flows away to the skyline, never interrupted for long. It is a landscape with moving figures of countless men and animals and a restless profusion of egrets, kites and waders.

As evening fell, on the straight coast road between Damietta and Port Said, the taxi ran full tilt into a rock no smaller than the foundation stone of an average-sized bank, shattering the front axle. The stone was difficult to see at dusk against the asphalt road. My driver waved down a private car, and its owner drove us, crying, 'No problem, no problem. You do same for me,' to the Holiday Hotel, the hotel recommended to me by Captain Roncallo. The taxi driver, who had friends who owned a garage in Port Said, didn't seem worried about his front axle, and said goodbye in good spirits.

The hotel was quite modern. On a card in my room I read that television involved an additional charge but, when I turned it on, it showed nothing on seven of its eight channels and, on the eighth, a snowstorm from which came garbled American voices. After a shower I asked the receptionist if he would either remove the television charge from my bill or the set from my room.

He seemed astonished. 'But TV is compulsory,' he said.

'But there is no TV reception in Port Said.'

'You see here, sir, our card, it says – room service so-much, with breakfast compulsory so-much more. And then TV compulsory so-much more. And a fridge and radio and air-con, all so-much more. Tax extra, ten per cent.'

'Have you a room without TV, please?'

'Sir, all rooms have TV, fridge, and radio. No one ever said before what you say about not wanting.'

Another receptionist joined in. 'TV is like breakfast. Breakfast is compulsory. So is TV.'

'Yes, but breakfast is food – to eat, to live. TV actually doesn't exist here. Breakfast exists; you eat it!'

But there was no comprehension. It was written on the card ('What is written is written,' Muslims say), so I paid for the nonexistent television. I didn't begrudge it much.

Egypt is a very poor country of great charm and spiritual resource, and it deserves better times and a least minimal riches. The receptionists had charm too – like most Egyptians – and deserved a richer country. In any case, I hoped I wouldn't have to wait too long at the hotel. The following morning I would go to see Mr Karawia at the Aswan Shipping Company with my letter from Captain Rashad.

Like the other canal towns, Port Said is still convalescent. The Six-Day War of 1967 closed the canal, and until 1975 the port was paralysed, like a busy man felled by a stroke. It still had an empty look, despite the groups of tourists from the cruise ships that lay alongside the quay. These days the city is a free-trade zone, and you can buy luxury goods cheaper than at most other ports. This is why the tourists come ashore. Their ships – handsome white ships belonging to Cunard or Greek lines mostly – couldn't help me. They were either going north to Naples or to Casablanca or across the Atlantic, or going south in long smooth strides to Mombasa or Cape Town. In any case, their captains seldom, if ever, pick up stray travellers like me. They like groups. All the world, those Patmos landladies had reminded me, loves a group.

The tourists wandered the streets, occasionally bending

to peer at a window full of tape recorders or calculators. The women wore straw hats with small, coloured pompoms hanging from the wide brims. I could catch snatches of their chatter as they struggled after their guides in the north Mediterranean streets: 'We did the Valley of the Kings last year. Wasn't it adorable, Wilma?'

Port Said was also, I found, a surprisingly courteous city which had not been my recollection of it twenty years earlier. The Egyptian who had cycled up to me outside the Ritz Bar to offer joy had shown no irritation when I'd turned him down; I'd expected a stream of abuse. I was considering this phenomenon when a small boy put his head out of the door of the bar, hissed at me, grinned and stabbed his finger in the direction of a fat girl in a green shift and headscarf nearby who must have weighed about thirteen stone. When I shook my head politely, the girl smiled and said, 'Never mind,' with no hint of rancour for business lost, and waddled away.

Later I clambered up almost vertical stairs to the Star Cabaret, an establishment providing belly dancers in a large, dim, smoke-filled room with a spotlit dance floor and a small band where every face glistened with the heat. A lonely American engineer, a middle-aged Midwesterner, had asked me to accompany him there; we had met in the hotel lobby. 'Just have one beer,' he said. He had a small camera with a flash on it and wanted someone to take his picture as he danced with one of the girls. He introduced himself as Robert. He had spent two weeks in Port Said already, he said, and there were few foreigners he could talk to.

We sat a little way from the dance floor and drank beer. I looked at the spangled décor and the bead curtains while the American told me how he was laying a cable under the canal, joining Port Said to Port Fuad in some way.

A hostess in heavy white make-up like a mask and a green pleated miniskirt sidled up. 'Was friend nime?' she asked me.

'What's she say?' Robert said.

'She's asking what your name is.'

'Tell her Chris.'

'Chris,' she said, 'you buy whisky?'

'Nope.'

'Okay, buy chips?'

'Yeah, chips I buy. Also I buy beer.'

She drew up a chair beside him and sipped happily at the beer he'd ordered her. She held his hand and turned her white mask up to him, fluttering overthick eyelashes. I didn't remember ever having seen a cabaret hostess accept beer before. Usually they drink a dash of darkish liquid in a small glass that is 98 per cent Coca-Cola and costs a fortune.

Later, as requested, I took two photographs of Robert on the dance floor. For the first, he seized the white-masked girl in a violent Valentino tango hold; for the second, he posed behind her right hand, holding an imaginary castanet awkwardly above his left ear like a first-term flamenco student. After they sat down again, a danseuse went by waggling huge buttocks, and the American's eyes followed them like a bull's horns following a matador's cape. 'Hey,' he said, rising a little from his chair. I could see that, if he invited another girl for a beer, White Mask was going to start raving. 'That's Stanley,' I said quickly. 'He's taken on Tuesdays.'

Robert sat down again. 'You've been here before!' But he liked the joke and peace was restored.

Between dancing and drinking Robert confessed he was not greatly taken with Port Said; there wasn't much to do. But he confirmed my impression that the people were helpful and friendly, even the officials, which he hadn't expected. He'd heard a lot about xenophobic Arabs before he'd left the United States. 'I think the government is trying to encourage tourists. If a guy comes up to you offering, you know, girls or something like that, often, I've noticed, some other guy comes up and asks him for his identification card and what he's doing. Police. It's creepy in a way, but their aim, I think, is to look after people like us. To encourage foreigners and tourists, attract hard currency, that kind of thing. I like them.'

I left Robert holding White Mask's hand. 'See you at breakfast,' he called.

Near the hotel a voice at my elbow rasped, 'Jock Mac-grrr-egorrorr, sirr. You like to buy a camel, sirr?' I turned to find a smiling Egyptian with white-stubbled jowls and a mendicant manner. He was holding four or five fluffy toy camels under one arm, and with his other he held his hand to his forehead in a military salute.

'No camel, thank you.'

'You want to play girl, sirr? Egyptian girl, not Scottish, but verra nice girl.'

I gave Jock a twenty-five piastre note simply for the pleasure of hearing his name. He was a man in a long, if not necessarily distinguished, tradition. In the old days of King Farouk and the British, Port Said and Suez had several tourist touts calling themselves Harry Lauder, Wee Jamie Macdonald or Bonnie Prince Charlie. In Suez, one of them, known professionally as Will Fyfe, had achieved worldwide fame conducting lascivious tourists or tipsy British soldiers to witness bizarre spectacles involving large

Egyptian ladies and smallish donkeys. Nasser had cleaned all that up a long time ago and for ever.

I exchanged good-night salutes with Jock Macgregor outside the hotel. 'It's a bright moonlicht nicht,' he called roguishly over his shoulder. In my room, I turned on the bedside radio and an Israeli announcer in Tel Aviv introduced me to a piano piece by Ravel.

Ahmed Bey Karawia said, 'To get a ship to Djibouti from Port Said is difficult, very difficult.' He sat at his big desk staring thoughtfully out of the French windows of his office at the canal tugs and launches moving restlessly on the water.

The telephone rang and he said, 'Subhi Bey, yes . . . yes. . . . Good. Thank you.' He rang off. 'The port police say you can leave on a ship from here only if you are the owner's representative or if you have work on board.'

I had found Ahmed Karawia in a three-storey building on the edge of the canal, an attractive architectural throwback to the days of Lord Kitchener and General Gordon. The offices of the Aswan Shipping Company were built in 1894, twenty-five years after the opening of the canal. They were painted a faded green, and surrounded on each floor by wide covered balconies linked by wrought-iron balustrades. The offices within are tall and open on to the balconies, so that you can step through the windows and stroll about looking down on the river. One can imagine Victorians in solar topees and white linen suits lolling on those balconies in low chairs, sipping long cold drinks.

Mr Karawia was a plump, middle-aged Egyptian who spoke perfect English, and was the sort of Egyptian official who has long been in the same line of business, is well educated, has travelled, and who will do his best to be helpful. A man too who knows all the people worth knowing connected with the life of Port Said. It took me only a few minutes to explain what I was trying to do, to give an outline of the story so far, and of my conversation with Captain Rashad in Alexandria. Ahmed Bey grasped the situation at once, ordered tea, and began to be helpful.

'We must make sure you are not obliged to take a car or a bus to Suez from here. Now, we have a Greek ship arriving this afternoon, maybe not alongside but in the roads . . . We'll ask about a passage to Suez, eh? Just Suez, because other things are not going to be easy, and Suez is essential. And even if it's just a chair on the deck . . .'

The Greek-ship plan fell through; she was delayed. Undismayed, Ahmed Bey made other telephone calls and sent young clerks off in launches to talk to captains about their destinations and their timetables. From the balcony I looked at the jumble of vessels nuzzling the piers of the great Canal Authority Building. It stood a little to the left of the Aswan Shipping Company Building and on the lip of the water: blue and green cupolas, Oriental arches and windows, dominating the head of the canal. Its exotic grandeur matched other relics of British Raj architecture around the Middle East: the railway station at Mosul, for example, and the Basra Port Building in Iraq.

Mr Karawia talked about the ups and downs of life on the canal. First, there'd been the Anglo-French invasion of 1956. The people of Port Said had pulled down the statue of De Lesseps, the French engineer who designed the canal. The plinth could still be seen on the waterfront; the statue was tucked away in a warehouse.

'We are going to have a new memorial to the hundred and fifty thousand fellahin who died building the canal, and to commemorate the 1973 crossing of the canal by the Egyptian army.

'Port Said was relatively lucky. During the bombardments of 1967 and after, Port Taufiq at the southern end of the canal was really seriously damaged; Suez, eighty-eight per cent damaged; Ismailiya, thirty-five or forty per cent; lucky Port Said, perhaps seventeen per cent. Still, Suez has industry and agriculture; here we have only the canal to live off. Many of our people had to evacuate – not to Cairo, but to small delta towns. There was no work here for eight years, until Sadat announced the canal open again in June 1975. About one third of our company's experienced people went off to Iraq or Libya or Australia – at least one third.'

We looked across the roofs at the Mediterranean housefronts. 'Port Said was full of French, Maltese, Italians, Greeks and Cypriots at one time,' said Ahmed Bey. 'Now our population is half a million, with no foreigners, but business is almost as usual. Three convoys a day: one north to south, two the other way. We deal with six to seven hundred ships a month. Things are moving.'

Ahmed Bey failed to find a ship that day or the next. 'Well, tomorrow let's see,' he said, more cheerful than I. One trouble was that shipping people were wary of chance passengers, fearing saboteurs. 'Suppose someone bombed a ship in mid-canal?'

I returned in the evenings to the Ritz Bar and sat under the street arcade reading *Under Western Eyes*. In an upper room opposite, a man in an undershirt played snooker

under a naked neon light. Once I saw a pair of ghosts from the Egypt of the pashas shuffling out of the Ritz Bar: two old men carefully dressed in snuff-coloured suits with brown and white shoes. They wore bow ties and hats, and one of them held a cigarette in a long holder and carried a cane hooked over his arm. There was something rakish about them, but they were skeletally thin. They hailed a victoria, climbed stiffly into it and sat back, talking like courtiers with flourishes of the cigarette holder, cane and long bony fingers, as if they were off to the races or an opera. The driver adjusted the scarf wrapped around his head like a turban and flicked his whip; the two lean-thighed horses clip-clopped stiffly away through the shadows.

* * *

There was no suitable or willing ship even on the third day. I began to think seriously of the canal road to Suez. Ahmed Bey was apologetic, but still hopeful.

I walked down the cement breakwater to where the canal slops its tideless waters into the Mediterranean. 'A dismal but profitable ditch,' Joseph Conrad had called the canal. Under the blazing sun I inspected the plinth that for almost a hundred years had supported the statue of M. de Lesseps. 'He points to the Suez Canal', E. M. Forster wrote, 'with one hand and waves in the other a heavy bunch of large stone sausages. "*Me voici!*" he gesticulates . . . *Voilà* Egypt and Africa to the right, Syria and Asia to the left.' Now only a bare plinth remains.

That evening I had a dispiriting encounter with a British couple, both teachers, who had been trying for over a week to find a ship for India, plodding around the shipping offices without success. 'The days are over for ship-hopping, we've decided,' the wife said flatly, rubbing her feet. 'We're giving up. It's not possible.' My spirit faded as I listened to them. 'We've one more agent to try,' the husband said. We shook our heads and arranged to meet next day to compare our dismal notes and perhaps share a taxi to Suez.

That night the hotel room was hot and airless. I dreamed I had to catch a train in Cairo, but great heaving crowds blocked the streets and I couldn't make the taxi driver go faster. The train was going to Aswan and Port Sudan; I had failed to find a ship through the canal. This train went only once every two weeks, and it was obvious I was going to miss it. I woke up in a panic.

In the morning Ahmed Bey said, 'A French ship is expected in the roads today. Noon, probably. We'll ask her captain about you. She's going to Jedda. Don't move from your hotel room, please.'

At noon he telephoned me at the hotel. 'I have spoken to the captain myself. He was not willing at first. He is not stopping at Suez, and he must go to Aqaba, too. But I said we could get you off in a launch at Suez so that he wouldn't have to stop. Then he said he had no accommodation, but I told him you would need no more than a chair on deck – anything – so he agreed. We'll get clearance from the police and immigration. Can you come to the office at two thirty?'

In the Aswan Shipping office, Ahmed Bey handed me a letter: 'Give this to the captain.'

The letter said:

To the Commander, M/V *Patrick Vieljeux*, Port Said.

Dear Sir,

We have to advise you that arrangements will be made to our Suez office to arrange for Mr. G. Young's disembarkation at Suez. Please see that he will be ready on the gangway on his arrival there and oblige.

'Ali, my clerk, will take you,' Ahmed Bey said. 'Be ready at six o'clock at the hotel entrance. Give me your passport, and I will send it by messenger to our agent in Suez.'

It was difficult to express enough gratitude. 'Without you – you and Captain Rashad . . .'

'Well, it would have been much more difficult,' Ahmed Bey said with a smile.

Ali's launch swept up the canal northwards towards its mouth. The sun had long gone down, and the water glistened like wet oilskin under the bright lights of the harbour and the waiting ships. The French freighter loomed unbelievably high as we swung between her stern and the two giant hawsers that held her to her buoy. I saw her name above me, *Patrick Vieljeux*, and, under that, the word 'Dunkerque'.

We came alongside the gangway, and Ali, standing in the launch's bows, made her fast. I followed him up the stairs with my anorak and leather bag; the launchman followed me with my metal suitcase on his shoulder. A steward met us at the top and said, '*Bon soir.*' Up an outside companionway and into the superstructure of the ship. Inside another door, and then, after whining up a deck or two in a lift, we crossed a spacious landing with a wide staircase. On one bulkhead was a Picasso print, on another a Bernard Buffet reproduction of flowers in a vase. Over the stairwell hung a large photographic blow-up of a seventeenth-century engraving featuring a windmill, horsemen prancing, wagoners in white hats and a town on a river.

Ali halted before an open door labelled BUREAU DE CAPITAINE and knocked on the lintel. A tall, heavy, grey-haired man in white shirt, shorts and stockings came slowly into the opening. He stroked a close-clipped beard, looked momentarily puzzled, and said, '*Ah, vous êtes le monsieur qui . . .*' I introduced myself and thanked him for agreeing to take me. '*Non, non. Plaisir.* Come in, but give me one instant, please.' For a few minutes he and Ali talked business. The captain moved and spoke slowly and deliberately, as if he had just woken from sleep, which he might have while waiting for his ship to be allowed to move off with the southbound convoy. Later I found he always talked and moved like that, but his sleepy look was deceptive. Whatever his manner, the captain of the *Patrick Vieljeux* was wide-awake. There was also a stateliness about him that reminded me of a middle-aged actor in the Comédie Française; without difficulty one could imagine him in a seventeenth-century cloak, breeches with ribbons at the knee and a wide lace collar: tall, upright, magisterial.

'Two more crew lists?' he was saying to Ali with the mildly puzzled air of a schoolmaster who has just been informed by a prefect that today is Tuesday, not Wednesday, and that the subject is divinity, not applied chemistry. For a while he riffled through his papers, making a dive or two to fish others from a drawer. Finally he handed over a fistful of documents, and Ali disappeared.

The captain put on half-moon glasses to read Ahmed Bey's letter. 'No problem. Now, I have no passenger space, you know,' he said in an accent as pronounced as Charles Boyer's. '*Mais . . .*' Leading me down an air-conditioned corridor, he cautiously opened a door. I saw a cabin larger than my room at the Holiday Hotel: two bunks, a large wood-framed porthole and a massive wooden wardrobe. An electric iron sat on a sideboard and an ironing board lay on the floor. '*Alors,* this is all. . . .'

'I was expecting a simple chair on deck.'

'Oh, that's not good. This cabin is only for the pilots – if it is necessary.'

'You mean a pilot may come and sleep in the second bunk?'

The captain smiled. '*En principe,* the pilot should not be sleeping. He has to avoid hitting the side of the canal.'

Back in his cabin, I explained why it was that I particularly wanted to traverse the Suez Canal by ship, and he understood immediately. 'You will want to see the ship moving through the canal, is that it?'

'Exactly.'

'Of course. Come.'

We climbed a stairway to the bridge, one floor above the captain's cabin in the enormous superstructure. The bridge – the SALLE NAUTIQUE, a metal sign said – of the *Patrick Vieljeux* was staggeringly large, or so it seemed after *Al Anoud*. It was as big as a large living room; too big to encompass in the present half-light. The captain pulled open the door that kept the air-conditioned climate inside the wheelhouse, and we stepped out on to the starboard wing over the water, a long way below.

A ship was moving up the canal towards us. 'The convoy is passing from south to north,' said the captain, pointing to it. 'We will not wait too long now.'

'Is that the first ship in the convoy?'

'No, the *quatrième*. Four since eleven hours. One every ten minutes. It will take time. Let us see. . . . Three and a half hours all together.'

'How many ships in our convoy ahead of us, Captain?'

'*On ne sait pas.*'

The northbound ship moved past us, a huddle of light moving against the more numerous harbour lights of Port Said, which were so bright that they blotted out the stars in a perfect sky.

'You must get some sleep as we wait. You may not sleep much when we go through the canal. Come up here any time. See the steward if you want anything. Oh, may I give you this?' He handed me a card.

Jean-Noël Visbecq,
Capitaine au Long Cours Commandant
Société Navale Chargeur Delmas-Vieljeux

Avenue Matignone
Paris 8e

Then I drank a tot of whisky from my father's old flask, lay down in my clothes and went to sleep.

When I awoke it was 2.15 a.m. I found Captain Visbecq on the bridge, a cigarette hanging from his wide lower lip.

The pilot had appeared too, a thin, dark man with a black moustache, peering through the windscreen of the bridge with a thermos flask on a ledge in front of him, a large jar of Nescafé, a container of sugar and an electrically operated bullhorn.

'*Allons-y.*' The captain began switching off all the ship's deck lights, pushing small levers at a switchboard – snap . . . snap . . . snap – until only the navigation lights and a powerful searchlight remained. 'We are going to be a little late,' he said. 'There are four ships in front of us. Seven to ten minutes between each of us is the rule. Now we'll start getting into position.'

A red star on a white funnel – a straggler from the south-north convoy – passed, while those ahead of it began to disperse toward fifteen different destinations in the Mediterranean or across the Atlantic.

'Are there always delays?'

'And not much sleep.'

'Do you sleep at all during the crossing?'

'I may doze in the chair in the radio room, but something could happen. One ship ran into another two days ago, from behind, and, if there's fog, we must stop and pull to the side.'

The *Patrick Vieljeux*, Captain Visbecq told me, was a family name, and the vessel was one of thirty belonging to the family's company. She was six years old, 1600 tons, built near Marseilles, registered in Dunkirk. 'A good ship,' he said.

At night the beautiful old façade of Port Said looked even more theatrical. The palm trees like mop-haired sentinels, the neat box-topped trees, the arched, high-shuttered windows and the slim stems of pillars supporting verandas and balconies seemed to be waiting for scene shifters to clear them away. Like a one-eyed giant, a lighthouse glared around the harbour. From the *Patrick Vieljeux*'s dominating bridge I could see the distant necklace of lights along the road to Damietta and Alexandria on which my taxi had rammed the rock.

Near Ahmed Bey's darkened offices beside the blue and green cupolas of the Canal Authority Building, the ferries to Port Fuad were still loading passengers and cars at 3.00 a.m. Presently the shoreline began to close in as the waterway curved gently eastwards like a black scimitar. I could see the ship behind us adjusting its searchlight, stabbing white light at us across the water, and behind her the smaller lights of other vessels of our convoy moving after us, keeping their distances.

A little launch had guided us to the last of the harbour buoys; now it dropped back and curved away into the darkness. Ahead a pair of lights – red and green – the first of the many that point out the narrowness of the canal, like cats'-eyes on the verges of a main road. The mouth of the canal seemed incredibly narrow. A hundred metres? Less? The *Patrick Vieljeux* was a colossal steel camel about to be threaded through the eye of a needle.

My notebook reads:

Now the red light is behind us, and *Patrick Vieljeux* –
God bless Captain Ismail Rashad and Ahmed Bey for it!
– is inside the Suez Canal! My Becher's Brook, my first
dreaded obstacle, is slipping past in the darkness below
me in a double chain of red and green light. By tomorrow night, I am certain of it now, I shall be through the
Suez Canal.

A young officer brought me a mug of Nescafé from the
bridge. I raised it to him, and, grinning like an ape, said,
'*Salut!*'

Chapter Nine

THE WING OF the *Patrick Vieljeux*'s bridge, as high as a four-storey house, looked down on an avenue of red and green lights as straight as the Champs Elysées. A road ran along the canal on its west bank, but few cars moved on it at this time of the morning. We moved so silently, engines humming, so faintly that we could hear cocks crowing in the villages on the shore.

Once in the canal, Captain Visbecq drew a large white hand over his beard, yawned and said to the pilot, 'I am going to my cabin now. Call the mate if you need to.'

I stayed on the bridge watching our high bows stalking two white eyes, the stern light of the ship ahead. Delicate ripples fanned out from bow and stern to caress the canal's verge and then subside without fuss on the placid surface of the waterway. Oil is partly responsible for this serene passage through such narrow and confined waters; its slicks lie on the canal like the rainbow coils of a sea snake.

The night became colder, and a mist began to lay a low smokescreen. The beam of our headlight reflected back off the mist wall, and lights of the vessels following us became wavering spokes of white seen through gauze.

At 4.55 a.m. I went below to sleep. Once I woke up and realized that the ship had stopped. I woke again at 8.25, splashed water on my face and climbed to the bridge. The sun was already quite high, and the heat of its rays warned of a sticky day to come. It was bound to be hot; we were passing down a narrow funnel of warm water between sand and lagoons, patches of reed and swamp. Captain Visbecq was on the bridge and nodded good morning. A cigarette hung from his lip and on his head was a white tennis cap with a long jutting peak of green Perspex.

The first officer, a youngish, fair-haired man, asked me if I'd like breakfast, and an officer with a beard led me down a few decks to the officers' dining room, where a steward was laying out bread, jam, butter, jars of Nescafé and instant Eurotea (new to me) on a long table. Yesterday's menu propped against a kettle announced: '*Déjeuner – Salade de Tomates, Sole Meunière, Gigot, Pommes Boulangères, Dessert. Dîner – Potage, Pizza Napolitaine, Boudin au Four, Pommes (Fruits).*' Not bad at all.

'*En principe,*' the first officer said later, 'the canal takes fourteen hours, but it depends on the punctuality of the daily northbound convoy. If it is on time at the Bitter Lakes, we shall pass directly down to Suez. If it is late, we must wait for it in the Bitter Lakes.'

From my notebook of the Suez Canal passage, I recall Captain Visbecq instructing me that *pont* means deck (not bridge). *Château* means the superstructure housing the crews' and officers' living quarters. *Salle nautique,* he explained, was the enlarged wheelhouse, which contained not only the wheel and helmsman but radar, chart room and other automation.

At El Qantara the pilot said, 'The Egyptian army crossed the canal here in 1973.' I could see the barbed wire and thirty-foot-high bunkers, like crude sand castles not yet crumbled away, and even a few anti-aircraft guns poking their rusting snouts toward the sky.

According to his memoirs, President Sadat had sat in a bunker like these on the day of the attack, sipping tea and puffing his pipe, watching his soldiers race down to the canal and push their boats into the water, shouting, '*Allahu Akbar!*' In a few minutes they stood once more in Sinai.

I had a more distant memory of this place. In 1947, before Nasser, I had arrived in Egypt by troopship from Glasgow with an army draft. Our destination was Tiberias on the Sea of Galilee, and we passed through El Qantara because it was a railway junction from which a major line shot north across the Sinai desert to Gaza and Palestine. As a teenage officer, I had been particularly instructed by my superiors to make sure that our soldiers' rifles and equipment reached Palestine in the possession of their rightful owners. This stern instruction was not easily carried out, for half the population of Egypt seemed to be singlemindedly engaged, day and night, in desperate schemes to part the British army from its basic equipment. A rifle laid carelessly down for half a second instantly vanished. Railway stations were popular with the Egyptian snatch-and-run experts, who had become amazingly agile, daring and successful with constant practice. Large groups of bored and restless soldiers, sometimes waiting for hours for a train, became less vigilant, even falling asleep, as time passed. A junction like El Qantara was a thief's paradise.

Going north by train from El Qantara, we were packed for the long, slow desert journey into hot railway carriages with sealed windows, overflowing into the corridors and the guard's van. Doors remained open to admit at least a minimum of air. Egyptian scalliwags, a grinning lot in torn and dirty robes, perched dangerously on the metal platforms, even astride the swaying metal buffers between the carriages. With infinite patience they would edge gradually closer to the open doorways and the belts of webbing and their valuable attachments that the soldiers had taken off for greater comfort.

The flicker of a dark hand was all you might have seen. You heard only a soldier's startled yell. Two sets of equipment had vanished into the moving carpet of the desert: .303 ammunition in clips, bayonets, water bottles, mess tins, razors, toothbrushes, needles and thread, towels, undershirts and underpants, shorts, socks and perhaps a handful of pornographic pictures obtained from a persuasive Egyptian with a Scottish name near the gates of the transit camp in Suez. Two sets of equipment gone, and two guardsmen with hairless cheeks staring at each other in shock. 'Fuckin' 'ell, mun, he's nicked me bloody webbin' – the lot!' And to me, 'Me webbin', sir, it's gone. Some wog . . .'

Leaning on the bridge of the *Patrick Vieljeux* I could still hear the shock in the young Welsh voices and the rattle of the train. Now I stared down into the water of the canal, borne smoothly past the colossal sand bunkers (like the relics of some modern Ozymandias), the bombarded villages, the rusting snouts of guns, the scene of two great offensives and a hundred artillery duels. The distant image of that train journey from El Qantara and of myself, skinny, itchy with prickly heat and eighteen years old, found its sole reflection in my own mind.

'*Français!* French! *Ça va! Ça va!*' The canal spread itself at Ismailiya like a boa constrictor that had swallowed a sheep. On the bank a mosque, a church and a smart new-looking hospital appeared. Then a newly made beach on a spit of land, with a newly painted café, tables, yellow and red umbrellas. Families picnicked, young people swam, children ran about shouting.

'*Français! Ça va!*' the swimmers called from the water near the *Patrick Vieljeux*. The French officers, including the captain, eagerly crowded the starboard wing of the ship and waved at the girls. Excitement even emboldened one of them to snatch up the captain's binoculars and peer at the bikinis on the little beach.

'*Ouf!*' – the captain shrugged – '*Pas grand' chose!*' but he went on staring.

'Can't we stop and get wet a bit?' someone asked him. '*Non!*' Captain Visbecq snatched back his glasses in mock indignation, crying, 'Hey! My glasses, paid for out of my own pocket, *non?*' and he too peered down at the girls waving from shore.

We dropped our first pilot here, an unobtrusive man. Now a Nile-bred Napoleon – a short, abrupt man who wore, oddly, a pair of white gloves – replaced him.

Date palms, wheat fields; to the west, the oasis of Ismailiya. For a time the canal twisted and turned uncharacteristically. Through the tubular spars and derricks of the *Patrick Vieljeux* I saw wastes of the Sinai desert.

'*Droit senk. Zeero. Comme ça.*' The new pilot spoke French to the helmsman, but talked sharply to Captain Visbecq in English. 'Close the bridge door,' he ordered. 'Your air conditioning is working, no? Why waste it?' The captain raised his eyebrows mildly and stuck another cigarette in his lower lip without comment. A startled young officer closed the door.

In the Bitter Lakes we anchored while the northbound convoy already in its southern end – seventeen or eighteen freighters and two small American frigates – regrouped before proceeding up to Port Said. Two of the ships trailed black smoke across the great bowl of the lake, which is so wide that its rim is a mere smudge. I remembered poor

Captain Musa of *Al Anoud*, blocked on his tanker here for six months in 1967 while Israeli shells flew overhead and now and again the Egyptian shrapnel rained down on the ship.

At lunch Captain Visbecq said, 'Have you ever been to St Malo? I am from near there, a Breton, like most French seamen.'

We ate *morue* tongues, then pork and peas, and helped ourselves to French red wine, Spanish rosé, beer and Montjoie mineral water.

The officers carried on what must be a daily game: Bretons versus Corsicans and Basques (the chief engineer was a jovial Basque from Biarritz). '*Ouf!*' Captain Visbecq said with a laugh. 'Let Corsica be independent. Who'd miss it? They produce nothing and they cost a lot. At least the African countries produce coffee and cocoa. But Corsica . . .'

'They produce goats,' the Breton first officer said.

'Ha! Yes! Goats!'

At the end of the meal a message came from the pilot; the convoy was on the move again.

'Stand by, *tous!*' Captain Visbecq said, swallowing his instant coffee.

'Suez about five thirty,' the pilot predicted. 'Where you go after Suez, Captain?'

'Aqaba . . . Jedda . . . Djibouti . . . Aden . . . Mombasa.' He jerked his thumb northwards. 'Then back to Europe. Holiday: the garden, the fishing, the ski.'

In my mind's eye I saw the pilot vacationing on a crowded beach at Alex but, when I asked him he said he'd spent a very happy holiday in Italy last year.

★ ★ ★

During the afternoon Captain Visbecq invited me to his dayroom for a beer. When I mentioned that the *Patrick Vieljeux* seemed a very solid ship, the captain raised a warning finger. 'Yes, but *la mer . . . vous savez!*' In his thirty years in the company no ship had been lost, but suddenly this year two of the company's vessels had gone down. 'One sank off Vigo, Spain, in a tempest, with only six survivors, including the captain. It was his last voyage. His wife was drowned. The second was the *Emmanuel Delmas*, carrying logs. It collided with a small Italian tanker and went *boouff!* The explosion and fire killed all except four men in the engine room. They came up and found everything black – all their colleagues burned to death. You have heard of the German ship the *München*, from Bremen to North America? Disappeared last winter without a trace. In a big storm, a twenty-thousand- or thirty-thousand-ton ship disappears. No one knows why. We all forget that the sea doesn't change.'

Later on the bridge the pilot, agitated, suddenly shouted, 'That Liberian ship ahead of us keeps slowing down.' It was certainly closer than before.

'A mixed crew, that's the problem,' the chief officer said. 'Some Far East mixture.'

'The pilot on board her is radioing me that they have only one man who knows the front from the back. A Venezuelan,' said the pilot disgustedly.

'*Oh, c'est pareil!*' groaned the chief officer.

The canal curved to the east and immediately twisted back to the west.

'*Gauche senk!*' the pilot called.

'*Gauche, cinq!*' the helmsman repeated.

'*Zeero!*'

'*Zéro!*'

The *Patrick Vieljeux* moved slowly ahead toward Suez. With unexpected suddenness the air darkened and the yellow disc of the sun sank toward a horizon already dissolving into a mauve and flame-flecked haze.

After sunset, Suez. In the darkness the *Patrick Vieljeux* moved on, evidently not going to slow down for my sake. I prepared my baggage at the head of the gangway, which was now lowered almost to water level. A pilot boat frothed out from the west bank, where buildings sprang up in irregular silhouette against the evening sky. A second launch was down there too, and a young man in its bows waved a passport. I pointed to my own chest: 'Me?' 'Yes, you!' I could hear his voice. He climbed aboard, introduced himself as the shipping agent's representative, gave me my passport, and together we went to Captain Visbecq's cabin. There papers were exchanged and signed: the formalities of shipping. Then Visbecq stooped, opened a cupboard in his desk, reappeared red-faced with two large bottles of eau de Cologne and a carton of cigarettes and handed them to the agent's representative.

'Oh, Captain, please,' the young man importuned, showing no embarrassment. 'One more carton of cigarettes, please, for my friend at home who is so sick. He asked me specially . . .'

Captain Visbecq stooped again, groaning. More eau de Cologne and a second carton. 'That's enough! That's all!' He shut the cupboard door with a slam. 'No more!'

'Follow me,' the young man from the agency said to me, and headed for the lift, clutching his bottles and cartons. I said, 'I'll be along in two minutes.'

Captain Visbecq looked at me, smiling over his half-moon spectacles. '*Donnez-moi! Donnez-moi!* Eau de Cologne for the agent! Brandy, cigarettes for each pilot. You could understand it from bumboat men, but pilots! The only place as bad is Kuwait, and there it is also a kind of blackmail. It's forbidden by their religion, but the customs can be very annoying if you don't give them that brandy. You give one bottle – "Two," he says, "I have a friend." So many ships, so many bottles. Brandy from the French, Scotch from the British, vodka from the Russians. Good business, eh?' He held out his hand, '*Bonne chance, bon voyage,*' I said, 'Same to you. Many thanks.'

'See you maybe in Jedda. If not, you have my home telephone near St Malo.'

'Next year, I hope.'

I went down the ramp and into the agent's launch. My bags were already on board. The boatman cast off, and we swung away from the throbbing, moving hull of the ship toward a ramshackle huddle of wharves and tugs and warehouses. When I looked back at the fast-receding stern and soaring superstructure of the *Patrick Vieljeux*, our combined speeds had already drawn her so far away that my thumbs-up sign must have been invisible to the officers waving from the wing of the bridge.

I had spent only a night and a day on the *Patrick Vieljeux*, yet not for the last time on this long journey I was struck by a sudden sense of abandonment.

Chapter Ten

THE FRIENDLY NET of the Aswan Shipping Company was waiting to catch me in Suez – luckily, because I stepped ashore into pitch darkness, where black shapes shouted rudely with onion-scented breath for my passport. There had been a power failure in the dockside part of the city.

A long delay followed in the coal-mine atmosphere of an unlit customs shed, but at last a courteous, trim-looking Egyptian drove up, introduced himself as Mohamed al-Hattab, the manager of the company in Suez, and loaded me, my baggage and his assistant into his car. 'It's the security people,' he said, explaining the delay in the inky customs hall. 'They're looking for European terrorists. So many Arab countries are against us now that Sadat is trying to make peace with Israel, and they recruit Europeans to do their sabotage for them. They think Europeans won't be suspected, so our people must be very vigilant.'

Out of the area of the power cut, we dropped off the young assistant with his bottles of Captain Visbecq's eau de Cologne, and Mohamed al-Hattab drove me to the Bel Air Hotel in the centre of the city. I had stayed in this old hotel in 1968, when most of the buildings around it had been reduced to rubble by Israeli shellfire. I put my bags in a room at the top of marble stairs that had seen better days, and then we walked across the road to a second hotel called the Misr Palace, where it was evident from the welcome that the waiters and other clients gave him that Mr al-Hattab was a popular visitor. 'This is a good place for company,' he said. A table with a bottle of Red Label, a

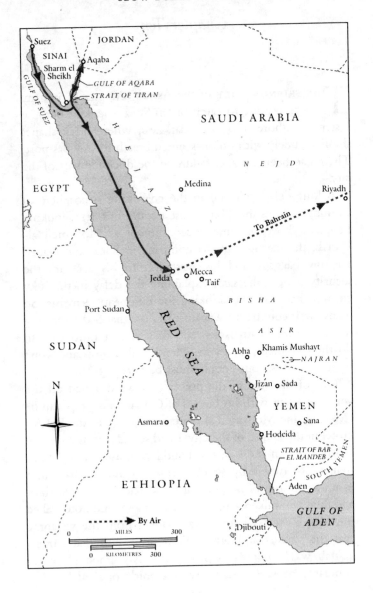

bowl of ice and a jug of water waited for him on a closed corner terrace.

From here we overlooked one of the city's principal traffic intersections, and probably its most lively one. It was a bedlam of cars, trucks and donkey carts, and, because it was a level crossing as well, with much hooting, clanking and blowing of steam the passenger and goods trains on the main line from Cairo passed almost through the lobby.

'First things first,' said Mohamed al-Hattab, briskly hospitable, and poured me a whisky two fingers deep. Then, with a broad smile: 'I've found a ship for you, sailing tomorrow afternoon for Aqaba and Jedda. A good captain, a friend of mine. Not a big ship, but not too small, taking pilgrims to Mecca and Egyptian workers to Jordan. No luxury, I must warn you. Called *Al Wid*.'

Luxury was not one of my worries, I assured him. I was delighted to be able to move on so soon. 'Ahmed Bey asked me to help,' he said. 'And so you are welcome.' Captain Rashad, Ahmed Bey Karawia, Mohamed al-Hattab: may Allah bless them.

Soon we were joined by a young captain from the Canal Company, and a few minutes later two large men with bullnecks rolled up and were introduced by Mohamed al-Hattab as marine contractors. They were enormously fat; their double chins quivered when they sat down.

When I told Mohamed al-Hattab I'd been here not long after the Six-Day War of 1967, he said, 'Suez really suffered then. It had a population of a hundred and thirty thousand. After the bombardments destroyed so much of it, only about three or four thousand people stayed. I was one of them, but I had nothing to do. The place was empty, so there was no work. Suez was dead.'

'You say Suez was dead,' I said, 'but I have a story for you. I came here on a brief visit from Cairo in 1968 with a friend, Nick Herbert of *The Times* of London. We had lunch in the Bel Air, the only place left standing. Just for fun we wrote a postcard to my foreign news editor in London and posted it in a postbox half buried in rubble. We thought it might be found a few years later when the war ended. But the card reached London before us, only ten days later. Some postman must have carried on through the shelling, like people in the London blitz. He deserved a medal.'

Now Suez was certainly alive again. Below us through the glass two elderly policemen in baggy white uniform with sergeant's chevrons on their sleeves cursed the traffic and blew piercing, angry whistles without effect.

Mohamed al-Hattab and the contractors talked about the laziness of Egyptian youth (we could see groups of young Egyptians in tight trousers or ankle-length robes hanging listlessly about in the street below). 'You can't fire the slackers,' one of the contractors complained. 'It's illegal. You can only dock their salary for a very few days.' The other contractor agreed. 'Only ten per cent of our people really work,' he said. They shook their heads and chins disapprovingly over the whisky.

The young captain from the Canal Company said, 'Sadat's ideas for peace are very good, but prices are the danger in Egypt. Food prices are too high for the millions of ordinary people. America and Europe should give Sadat money to keep food prices down in the local markets.'

'Subsidies.'

'Exactly. Ordinary Egyptians want to see their lives improving now. If they don't see that – phwee! – there'll be a big bang!'

Riots against the price of food in every major city of Egypt had shaken Sadat in 1977 – the year the demonstrators in Alex had pulled all those television sets out of the vice-president's villa. The mobs had cursed Sadat's mollycoddling of the 'new aristocracy': the rich businessmen, the owners of gaudy boutiques and the patrons of the smart nightclubs on the Giza road. 'Sadat Bey, Sadat Bey, you were born in a cabaret!' Egypt's sans-culottes had shouted through the streets.

Mohamed al-Hattab said good night, promising to reappear next day to introduce me to the master of the *Al Wid*.

Taking a turn before bed in the street that boasted the Greek consulate and the Ciné Chantecleer as well as the Hotel Bel Air, I thought of the *Patrick Vieljeux* pushing impatiently down through the Red Sea at that very moment. Outside the consulate, three grinning youths held up a magazine to show me the centrefold picture of a nude with an abundance of carroty pubic hair. 'Look, sirrr!' When I passed them again on my way back to the Bel Air, they were pushing the picture through the consul's letterbox.

Next morning I had coffee on the terrace of the Bel Air among elderly Egyptians and families in wicker chairs speaking Greek and Italian. A waiter in a tarboosh brought me a newspaper, and I read about a concert Frank Sinatra had given the night before outside Cairo. An article described the jewel-spangled gathering under the pyramids organized by a jet-set princess and a Paris fashion designer. I wondered how the ghosts of the pharaohs had taken to songs like 'My Way' and 'The Lady Is a Tramp'.

Below the peeling balustrade of the terrace, men in
galabiehs and sandals slip-slopped by and foolhardy raga-
muffins diced with death on the running boards of the
trains clanking down the street. A shoeshine boy in a stained
nightshirt importuned for custom by clicking a brush
against his wooden box of polish. Old men in high old-
fashioned collars and fraying ties waved horsehair fly-
swatters at a servant in a turban who was flicking a duster
at the brass wall-plate that said, BEL AIR HOTEL DIR.
PROP: J. JAHIER, and ignoring them.

That afternoon the Saudi vessel *Al Wid*, built in Sweden
in 1967 – the word 'Styrhus' was still there over the wheelhouse door – sailed for Aqaba and Jedda. At 3.50 p.m. the
tug *Omar* eased us out of Suez dock. All around us small
ships were ingesting long lines of poor Egyptians carrying
baskets, boxes and crates. They had queued passively, if
clamorously, since dawn, and the heat was their punishment.

Al Wid sailed leaving at least a hundred people on the
quay. In a last look through my glasses, I saw them tramping
dejectedly away, miserably humping Adidas and Alitalia
bags: ochre-skinned men like those who had come aboard,
with towels twisted around their heads like turbans, or in
woollen caps, and wearing shoes that didn't fit their wide,
thick-soled peasant feet.

We bore south-west, through an anchorage of vessels
that included a French warship. On the right-hand shore
appeared the Suez refinery and a line of new housing in
front of a dark escarpment.

I found a small cabin with two bunks in it, which the

steward said I had to myself. It was hot, but not unbearable with the air conditioning on and the porthole closed. On the stairs I had seen portraits of King Faisal and King Khalid of Saudi Arabia, and an illuminated ̣ or two from the Koran. Saudi Arabia is a dry state, but I had my Port Said Scotch in my bag. *Al Wid* was not another *Al Anoud*. The first-class dining room had middle-aged Egyptian waiters in white jackets, and there was a saloon where, my steward told me, videotaped television films would be shown at night. As it turned out, the films were Egyptian comedies with one exception: an American film about white mercenaries wiping out black men in Africa. The Egyptian audience sided unmistakably with the white mercenaries.

It was all certainly better than *Al Anoud*, even though a plaque informed me that the Swedes had licensed *Al Wid* for only four hundred and fifty passengers but she was carrying eight hundred to Aqaba and I don't know how many more to Jedda. I felt no anxiety; there wouldn't be much elbow room, but it was not far to Aqaba. I stifled the thought of what the effect of a collision at sea might have on a thousand Egyptians temperamentally alien to the concept of a boat drill. Oddly enough, I was more concerned by the discovery that the toilets were temperamental, although at least they were not permanently awash with urine and vomit as those of *Al Anoud* had been. On that ship the ultimate catastrophe would have been a loose bowel.

I am not particularly fussy about the absence of working toilets on small boats, for you can almost always find a convenient place to ease yourself over the side in reasonable safety and privacy. But on big ships you have nowhere to go. Their sides are too high for acrobatics and, in any case, the rail areas are too public. (Incidentally, if you fall from a big ship – or even from a relatively small big one – your chances of survival are virtually nil. Sea, wind and engines would overwhelm your cries, and you could wave until you were blue in the face but a ship's wake or a swell would hide you. Once overboard, ten to one you're a goner.)

Al Wid's toilet facilities would do, but it would be wise, I decided, to use them early, before rush hour.

Ships headed north, converging on the narrow funnel of the canal. To the west, land disappeared; to the east a grey-white line hardened into cliffs of treeless, fissured rock. There were no fishing craft to be seen on the blue waters off the coast of Sinai.

During the night, *Al Wid* wove craftily through the reefs and islands south of Suez, which appear as an angry black rash on the charts. Next day the immigrant workers sat up on the decks where they had spent the night lying huddled together for comfort on benches or bare planking. Now they looked around and pointed to the coast, the terrible peninsula where in three wars – 1948, 1967, 1973 – fathers, brothers and cousins had died in their thousands of thirst, sunstroke, bullet wounds, burns, or even of sheer bewilderment and fear. El Arish, the Mitla Pass, Sharm el Sheikh are names on every Nile boy's mental map of Egypt. Those places lay behind the shore we were now passing, and not a soul aboard could have been unaware of the fact. They peered over the rail in that unusual silence as the first rays lit the terrible shore of Sinai. Dreaming of a certainty of peace? Grieving for dead generations? Or forgetful of the past, not looking back at all, simply invoking the blessing of the One God on the new life that *Al Wid* was bringing nearer by the second?

The mood seemed to pass. Soon they pulled themselves back to the normal, vociferous world, and resumed their animated chatter – which, for peasant voices born and bred to carry long distances across villages and fields, meant something more like raucous shouting. Excited hands rummaged in the Adidas and Alitalia overnight bags and found country-made rusk-like sweet cakes (like English shortbread), fruit and flat bread, bits of processed cheese and stringy carrots bought a day or two before at a friendly stall in the delta. These rations might have to sustain them until Baghdad. They even had bottles of water. After the food they brought out photographs of relatives stiffly posed by village photographers, passed them around and then carefully reburied them, a shade more creased, under the spare shirt, towel and bathing wear in their overnight bags.

Then they explored the ship; they'd never been aboard one before. Woollen-capped swarthy heads rose cautiously over the tops of companionways: was this a forbidden area? The ship was alive with laughter. Cabin doors opened and shut, and officers sharply ordered giggling passengers away from the sacrosanct engine room or the bridge. I, the only non-Egyptian aboard, was greeted with shouts of 'Good morning, misterr!' When they had inspected the ship with as much thoroughness as they would devote to a new water buffalo or a wife, they milled off to drink tea in the ship's cafeteria and raucously debate their prospects in the unknown and immediate future that for eight hundred of them would begin at Aqaba.

Iraq was their destination from Aqaba, the port of Jordan. Aqaba, whose capture from the Turks by the Arab irregular armies of Faisal, Abdullah and T. E. Lawrence in the First World War had created the springboard for the offensive that eventually carried the Arab revolt in triumph to Damascus. Aqaba, where King Hussein went to water-ski, would be their springboard to an expatriate life in Mesopotamia. I knew their route; I had followed it several times myself. From the seaside town of Aqaba by truck or bus up the dramatic escarpment road, through the splendour of Wadi Rumm – where Lawrence and Faisal were bombed by Turkish biplanes – along the snaking track of the old Turkish-built Hejaz railway to Amman, the track that Lawrence spent so much time and effort blowing up. From Amman, Hussein's capital, to Mafraq (which means crossroads), the hub town from which the roads to Damascus and to Baghdad radiate. Then the long, dreary desert crossing by bus to Iraq: the descent into the steamy lushness of the basin of the great twin rivers, the Tigris and Euphrates, which keep Iraq alive, just as the Nile has sustained Egypt. Past Nineveh, perhaps, and Ctesiphon, the capital of the old Persian kings, past Babylon perhaps as far south as Ur of the Chaldees. The Nile to the Euphrates and Tigris: they wouldn't know it, but *Al Wid*'s hopeful passengers were leaving one of the world's nurseries of civilization for another as great.

It was an interesting experiment in human transplantation. Iraq, rich in oil and land and poor in population, and Egypt, nearly destitute and barely able to support a population that seemed hell-bent on doubling itself in a few decades, had come to an agreement. I had seen fellahin from the Nile clumping about the riverine towns of Iraq, easily distinguishable from the native peasants by their browner skins, round-necked galabiehs and speech (the

accents and idioms of Egyptian Arabic are as strange to the
Arabs of Iraq as the English spoken in Kansas is to the people
of Yorkshire). But not only fellahin were transplanted.
Young Egyptians with some minimal experience in hotels
in Cairo are to be found in the hotels and restaurants of
Baghdad, Basra and Mosul. It is good to see them there,
because however adept or inept they may be in their work
they are always cheerful; Egyptians are inveterate jokers.
Iraqis, on the other hand, like the English, feel that waiters'
work is mysteriously demeaning to the soul, and work off
their humiliation on the diners.

As *Al Wid* steamed up toward Aqaba, there was no singing
or drumming from the mass of Egyptians on her decks.
Most noticeably, there were no transistors; these men were
too poor or frugal for such dubious luxuries. After all, no
pop group can ward off the Evil Eye.

Unlike Suez, the heat was dry here. The cliffs of both
sides of the Gulf of Aqaba closed in; Arabia on the right,
lifeless and bare; Sinai, still occupied by the Israelis on the
left, with an occasional car or jeep speeding down a road
parallel with the water.

'Sinai, Egypt's land!' a ship's officer announced, pointing
to the coast. I handed my binoculars to a group of bejeaned
Egyptians who said, 'Thank you, misterrr,' and passed them
round, each one gaping at the strange mountain-girt bay
and the ships we could now see anchored in it off the little
port of Aqaba and, a little way to the west, the Israeli port
of Elat. They goggled at the strange sight of an Arab and
Israeli town side by side. 'Is that Aqaba? Is that Elat? Is that
Palestine? Is that Israel?'

In Arabic I asked them where they were heading. One said, 'To Baghdad.' Another: 'To Basra,' adding, 'I'm a mechanic.' Someone asked, 'Is Dohuk cold?' (Dohuk is in northern Iraq.) 'How far is Dohuk from Baghdad?' 'How far is Baghdad from Amman?' 'Is Baghdad like Cairo?'

An innocent abroad, more pushy than the rest, in a red and white sweater zipped up the front, said his name was Gamal – 'But call me Jim.' Like most of them he was going to Baghdad. 'I have friends there. Look.' He handed me a card from the Ibn Khaldoun Hotel with an Egyptian friend's name on it. I had been to Baghdad recently to complete a book about the Marsh Arabs of southern Iraq, and knew one or two Egyptians there. I gave him another Egyptian name – that of Samir, the head barman at the Dar es Salaam Hotel, a kind man who would no doubt help him over his first baffling, homesick days in a strange city. He tucked the name gratefully away in his wallet.

'Are you nervous?'

'Not a bit,' he answered boldly. 'People say there are thieves in Baghdad, but thieves are only people like me, aren't they?' Sententiously he added, 'I am afraid only of God.'

I pointed out that he was taking this adventurous step into a country whose government was at loggerheads with his own. This meant nothing to him. He said, 'You see, misterrr, I've eight brothers and five sisters in Cairo, so someone has to travel to find money and send it back to them. I am the eldest, so who else should go but me? I give myself ten years' hard work abroad, suffering maybe, until I'm thirty. Then I'll marry and take a settled job in Egypt. By then I should have saved enough for a house and a car. Am I right, misterrr?'

I said, 'You are happy to go, it's a duty to your family and you are not afraid. So you are right.'

'Thank you, misterrr.' I looked at Gamal's – Jim's – flushed and beaming face, the thick red hands with broken nails, and for some reason I thought of Sinatra in his tuxedo under the pyramids, facing that scintillating audience and singing to the Sphinx in the desert night.

Chapter Eleven

'*HUT AL HABIL, Hutuh!* Make fast!' Deckhands threw lines ashore from bows and stern and shouted down to make sure they were secured. *Al Wid* had come alongside a wharf not far from a huge column of smoke; a bush fire seemed to be nibbling at the outskirts of Aqaba. But we came safely to rest bow-to-stern behind a Saudi ferryboat, the *Yarra*, which plied regularly between Suez, Jedda, Port Sudan and Aqaba.

There was a long wait before the gangway went down, and then a torrent of fellahin and other Egyptian passengers began to tumble on to the quay in an avalanche of baggage and unwinding turbans. Scenes of anarchy and despair filled the ship. Like juveniles abandoned by their parents at a pop concert, desperate Egyptians wandered through the decks of *Al Wid* calling for friends or searching for passports or lost belongings. At the head of the gangway a howling confusion prompted the whirlwind appearance of Jordanian policemen, one of whom in drawing back his fist to drive a way through the crowd caught me a hefty clout on the shoulder with his elbow. 'Sorry, mister,' he said and, on the rebound, swung at an innocent fellah who was too astounded to resist a tremendous clap on the chops.

The Jordanian security men were faced with the problem of identifying every individual in a shouting crowd that flowed and seethed like water in a stormy bay. The loud-speaker system began an interminable appeal to missing Egyptians to report to immigration control, and here a problem of names revealed itself.

'Will the following report at once to the passport depart-
ment in the cafeteria,' official voices, sharply irritable or
limply indifferent, grated or drawled repeatedly over the
crackling Tannoy. 'Mohamed Ahmed Mohamed,
Mohamed Mohamed Ahmed, Ahmed Mohamed Ahmed,
Ibrahim Mohamed Ibrahim, Ibrahim Mohamed Ahmed,
Mohamed Ahmed Ibrahim, Ahmed Mohamed Ibrahim,
Ali Ahmed Ibrahim, Mohamed Mustafa Ali, Mohamed Ali
Mustafa, Mustafa Ali Mohamed . . .'

Like an atavistic incantation, the calling out of names
went on and on in barely perceptible permutations. 'Musa
Ali Musa, Musa Musa Ali . . .' Yes, one could see the problem, and it delayed us in Aqaba for some hours. There
were known troublemakers aboard, it seemed. One or two
had smuggled drugs; others had caused political trouble
during earlier visits to Hussein's kingdom. Several would-
be immigrants were now rudely refused entry into Jordan.
I heard an angry immigration officer shouting into a dark
and tearful Nilotic face, 'We've had enough of you in
Jordan. Go away! Fly to Iraq from Egypt if you can, but
don't ever enter Jordan again!'

To add to the general irritability, long before we sailed
again the air conditioning was shut off and there seemed
to be no cold water. In appalling heat, and with nothing
better to do, some of the passengers going on to Jedda sat
about indignantly comparing the uneven value of their
tickets.

One man wailed bitterly, 'I paid eighty-four Egyptian
pounds for a cabin berth and no food. My friend paid
only sixty-five for the same thing.' His listeners rocked and
groaned in impotent indignation. Another fumed to the
accompaniment of angry cries that he had paid fifty-six

pounds for a place on board – no question of a cabin and not a bite of food – 'yet the travel agent in Cairo told me that food was included'. Cries of 'Pimp! Dog!' rained on the agent's absent head. On top of this, people said that tea cost six or seven times the price in Egypt, and this was true. In such ways are the poor of the Middle East eternally cheated out of the little money they have.

With my binoculars I searched the bay in vain for the sight of King Hussein on water-skis; instead, their pitted lenses found the familiar rearing *château* of the *Patrick Vieljeux* lying offshore in a huddle of several other large foreign vessels. A lighter lay alongside, and her derricks swung back and forth, so at least she was working. I imagined Captain Visbecq in his air-cooled cabin impatiently smoking a Gauloise under his green visor, and in my mind's eye I saw a *gigot* in the galley next to a simmering pot-au-feu. The *Patrick Vieljeux* would certainly make much better speed than *Al Wid*; she would reach Jedda before us if she sailed within the next twelve hours.

I had been thinking hard about my future hops from Jedda. My aim was to reach Djibouti, and from there to bypass Aden on my way up the side of the Arabian peninsula and around the corner to Dubai. (I doubted whether the Adenis, now friends of the Russians, would welcome a solitary ship-hopping writer from Britain – or rather, they might welcome him with an immediate jailing.) Going from Jedda to Djibouti might be accomplished direct with any luck, or, if necessary, by a swift passage across the Red Sea to Port Sudan in a ferry like the *Yara*. I would have to pray for a ship from there down the west coast. But I was doubtful about Port Sudan. I had no visa for Sudan and, thanks to the spineless consul at Port Said, I had a Saudi visa for a mere three days. Only an idiot would have the slightest confidence that the Saudis, truculent and bureaucratically hidebound, would extend it; unable to count on this extension, I would have to act as if it wouldn't be granted. That is to say, I would have to find a ship to take me southwards out of Jedda with a minimum of delay. There would be precious little time to tour the shipping agencies. I began to think about Captain Visbecq and the *Patrick Vieljeux*: a captain I knew and who knew me, and the more I thought about him, the more I felt that he might help me out of a Saudi Arabian impasse. Still, the first thing to do was to consult Captain Mohamed el Zenati of *Al Wid*.

Al Wid sailed from Aqaba that evening, and by the time I was awake at eight o'clock the next morning we were passing the Strait of Tiran at the entrance to the Gulf of Aqaba. The ridged dragon's back of rock outside my porthole was Tiran Island, according to the map.

From a useful and friendly publication called *Ports of the World* (Benn Publications, London) lent me by Captain Rashad in Alexandria, I had noted the following random characteristics of the port of Jedda: 'Two anchorages: inner and outer. The Outer between the second and third line of reefs off Jeddah ... The practice of throwing refuse into the harbour discouraged – no tides to take it away ... Vessels strongly advised not to enter or leave port during hours of darkness due to difficult passage through reefs.' Then came some words of great importance: 'Holidays. Fridays, Ramadan and Eid el Hajj, both eight-day holidays. No work on these days.' This news came as no surprise, but it impelled me in sudden alarm to see what day of the week *Al Wid* would strand me in the port of Jedda. The answer was Wednesday afternoon. This meant that I would have no more than half a day in which to find a ship – a half-day because in every Arab country, the Thursday before the full Friday holiday is a half-day, just as Saturday is in Christian countries, and often rather less than a half-day, given every man's eagerness to start the weekend.

Moving on, I read: 'No navigation aids mark the approaches to port, and therefore there is no night navigation. A light-house and lighted marker are scheduled. . . . The Saudi Arabian flag (in good condition) must be flown from 0600 hrs. to sunset.'

Poring over his charts with Captain Mohamed el Zenati later in the day, I could see the name Jedda tucked away behind a snowstorm of reefs up a narrow channel. 'Very few lights in the Red Sea,' sighed the captain, shaking his head. 'Many ships have gone aground here, especially Greek ships. Greek captains go aground here very much.' Presumably, as E. M. Forster had noted, with their charts locked up in a drawer.

At noon Captain el Zenati, a brisk, cheerful man of about forty, invited me to his cabin. He told me that while waiting for the emigrants to disembark at Aqaba he had gone next door to see his friend the captain of the *Yara*, and bought a bottle of whisky. He proceeded to open it, and poured two hefty ones, adding cold water from a small refrigerator.

Though still a youngish man, Captain el Zenati had served eighteen years in submarines of the Egyptian navy, ending up as a captain. 'I loved subs,' he said. 'Even though ours were old Soviet vessels, they were exceptionally stable.

I must admit that some of the technical aids were certainly not of the latest.' He laughed. 'Still, they were as good or better than French or American subs of the same age.'

He had served through the wars of 1967 and 1973 against Israel, and surprised me by saying that the Egyptian navy had never lost a submarine. 'The Israelis lost three,' he added. He himself had torpedoed a ship in the Red Sea during the war of 1973. 'Do you know, what I enjoyed about subs was the necessity for extreme precision. One mistake – pouf! – and you're gone. Cheers!'

Captain el Zenati seemed typical of his class and age in Egypt. He had actually enjoyed eighteen years in submarines, so perhaps he was braver than most. But, like many Egyptians, he was a man of much laughter and kindness; he was also very serious and a passionate talker. He had strong convictions: why not, he said, after what Egypt had been through? For instance, he was convinced that after 1973 Egypt could not have fought another war. He blamed Nasser for the defeat of 1967 and for the 'pointless debacle' of the Yemen War, where Egyptian troops – those boys from the delta – were required to fight a bewildering mountain war for which they were never trained, against Yemeni tribesmen who knew every peak and gully. Nasser was responsible for the pauperization of Egypt.

'Are you happy, then?' I was eager to know whether he thought Sadat's plans for peace stood any reasonable chance. If not, was the alternative 'phwee! . . . a big bang', as the skittish officer in Suez had said as the trains hooted past our terrace table?

'Directed democracy,' the captain said. 'That's what I think is necessary. Strong government based on Islam. A modern state on Islamic lines – but not extremist or intolerant, like Khomeini. Modern, but more aware of Arab culture, so that Arabs will be proud people.' Yes, perhaps Egyptians could do with a little more pride, but I was sure that the Saudi bourgeoisie were too proud already.

We walked out on to the wing of the bridge and watched the Red Sea water flow by. It was windless and sticky. 'You know, Egypt and the Arabs need another really big leader. God knows where he'll come from, but we need him – now. Sadat is right to look for peace' – every Egyptian I had met since I stepped on *Al Anoud* at Limassol had said this – 'but there will be no end to the conflict if Arabs and Israelis don't agree to share a state together.' At this point a shadow fell on the conversation, for neither of us could imagine that this desirable state of affairs would be effected during our lifetimes.

In a lighter tone, Captain el Zenati said, 'About your best plan at Jedda, I'm not sure what ships go to Port Sudan or when. Our agent there is a good Saudi; I'll ask him. Maybe you should try to return to the French ship. At least you know the captain and you want to see Djibouti.' Remembering something, he shook his head and added, 'I knew a ship that foundered near Djibouti. She was over-loaded above and below decks with camels, sheep, buffaloes, cows and I don't know what. There was a heavy swell and she began to list and then kept on going. The crew got off in time; they were close to shore. But you ought to have heard the pandemonium in the holds – the animals, all packed in down there in the dark, feeling the ship going, smelling the water, smelling death . . . And the sea was full of sharks. What a field day for the sharks!'

'Can sharks get into the hold of a ship?'

'When a shark smells meat he'll get in anywhere.' For a

moment I thought of that roaring, struggling mass in the black steel belly of the doomed ship, and took a second large whisky without being asked.

'Not a nice idea,' agreed Captain Mohamed el Zenati. He changed the subject. 'Let's see if the French ship is near us when we dock at Jedda. I'll do what I can.'

The Jedda skyline astonished me. I had seen it, though not from the sea, in 1964 on a return visit at the time of the Yemen War. Travelling down to the Yemeni border at Jizan, I had walked across into northern Yemen with the Imam's tribal supporters, and then returned to a semi-modern Jedda with an ugly new hotel where Western businessmen sat about drinking non-alcoholic beer.

Such a sign of Western encroachment was matched by saddening experiences I had endured with the Imam's forces. The *Observer*, for which I was then a foreign correspondent, had required me (quite properly) to take a look at both sides in the war, and by the time I joined the Imam's men I had already spent ten days in Sana, the capital of Yemen and the base of operations for the Egyptian expeditionary force engaged in making sure the Imam never returned to the throne from which a republican coup d'état had ousted him. Because of my excursion into their enemies' camp, the Yemeni royalists regarded me with suspicion; they thought I might be an Egyptian spy. I found myself obliged to eat, walk and sleep apart from the Yemeni tribesmen whose way of life interested me more than the actual war itself; I suppose the Imam's officers, knowing that I spoke some Arabic, feared I might coax from them some military secret of vital importance to the Egyptian high command. But that wasn't all. Unfortunately, the Imam's cause had already attracted hordes of Western mercenaries and journalists, whose empty corned-beef cans, Coca-Cola bottles and toilet paper (tribal Arabs use water or sand) disfigured a mountainous landscape of hitherto unsullied beauty where heretofore no more than a handful of European explorers had ever set foot. My dispiriting experience in the mountains culminated in a dreary week in that new hotel in Jedda, waiting to be summoned to an interview with Prince Faisal, the crown prince of Saudi Arabia – the man whose portrait, though he is now dead, had dominated the office of the Saudi consul general in Alexandria.

In the old days Jedda had been a small but important port of the kingdom of the Hejaz, an entity that ceased to exist when in the twenties the Bedouin armies of Ibn Saud swept out of the eastern province of Nejd, deposed the ruler of the Hejaz and gathered the region into a united kingdom of Arabia under the Saud family. Jedda retained its importance as the largest Arabian port on the Red Sea and as the sea gateway to Mecca.

My best memory of the city was the first time I had seen it. In 1954 I arrived in Jedda to join the British-run part of an international organization called Desert Locust Control, which tried to destroy those devastating insects by poisoning the swarms as they laid their eggs in the Arabian wilderness. I had already spent two years with the Marsh Arabs of southern Iraq, and the Englishman who had taken me to meet them – Wilfred Thesiger, the last of the great Arabian explorers – had urged me to see the wild and beautiful west of Arabia before it was too late. I had arrived in Jedda from London in an old propeller-driven aircraft to embark on two of the best years of my life, two years freely roaming the highlands and lowlands of Arabia from Mecca to the Yemen, alone with the Bedouins of the desert and the long-haired men of the well-watered valleys of the Asir.

Western Arabia was still unspoiled then, and Jedda was an antique Hejazi port with a mere handful of modern buildings. Now, from the deck of *Al Wid*, I saw something unrecognizable: a skyscraper city high-rising round a vanishing curve of sealine; a bristling of cranes and masts; glass and steel gleaming in the sun. Was this Chile, Spain, Japan?

The Saudi pilot was a huge, discontented-looking man in a white *thobe*, the Arabian ankle-length shirt. He seemed overweight for the job. A wave leaped up as he sprang awkwardly from his launch and soaked the thobe from the thighs down, so that when he waddled up to the bridge his massive buttocks shifted back and forth under the white cotton like captive balloons. Over the ship's radio came a gabble of voices – voices of captains, mainly deferential Greeks or feebly imploring Scandinavians, begging to be allowed to move into port to escape from the sun-broiled roads where their ships lay, a score or more of them, among the hulks of rusty freighters that had gone aground on the port's famous reefs. Jedda filled the minds of seamen with a peculiar dread of delay – days, weeks, even months, of baffling, almost insupportable delay. Who could stand out among the reefs, burned by those terrible temperatures and soaked by the humidity, with no relief, no alcohol (Saudi officials insisted on coming aboard and searching for it), no shore leave, no women? Delay, at least, we were spared. Our pilot brought us straight in to the wharf. Of course the blessed difference was that *Al Wid* was a Saudi ship.

Another pleasant surprise, the last one for some time: as we approached the quay, Captain el Zenati pointed – 'Your

French ship is very near us. Look. Three berths away.' It was true. The high *château* and pale-blue funnel were visible over what looked like a large customs shed. Somewhere over there was a captain called Jean-Noël Visbecq, a Breton first officer and a Basque chief engineer.

At first things seemed to go very well. With Captain el Zenati's introduction, I met the chief immigration officer, who permitted me to enter Saudi Arabia without fuss. I lugged my bags ashore and, thanks to the same officer's intervention, was permitted by a suspicious and unsmiling man in a thobe to leave them in a corner of the shed while I walked over to the *Patrick Vieljeux* five minutes away – long enough to stick the shirt to my back in that heat. There I climbed the gangway and pressed through the crowd of dark-skinned Orientals wearing hard hats and jeans ('Malays?' I asked, glad to see those familiar cheerful, high cheekbones; 'Filipinos,' they winked back over flashing teeth.)

Captain Visbecq took the surprise with a smile and a shrug. '*Ouf!* If you can bear the pilot's cabin again.' Within an hour or two I had retrieved my baggage, said a warm goodbye to Captain Mohamed el Zenati (who sailed as soon as he had off-loaded his pilgrims and on-loaded a new mob of passengers for Suez), and returned to the *Patrick Vieljeux*. 'Hodeida, then Djibouti, then Aden. That's our programme!' said Captain Visbecq. '*Eh bien*, have a beer!'

But it was not to be that easy. Already, the captain told me with gestures of frustration, his Jedda agents had shown themselves to be slack, even uncooperative. Just at this moment, the agency's representative came on board. An unprepossessing and slouching youth, he was a surprising human being to find in a position of such relative authority. He wore sloppy Western dress and looked more like a tout for an Alexandria disco than a shipping agency's clerk. He was tailor-made for a job at the Star Cabaret in Port Said; his manners would have been appropriate there. He had already delayed the cash the captain had ordered in advance so that his men could go ashore and shop for souvenirs. It seemed probable that part of the cargo to be loaded would also be overdue, which meant that either the sailing of the ship would be delayed or the cargo left behind. None of this was of any visible concern to the agent's representative as he lolled on Captain Visbecq's banquette, legs crossed, a young man of malignant expression, waving a disdainful hand in the air as he talked.

When the kindly Captain Visbecq turned to this youth and observed that he was willing to take me as passenger to Djibouti, my anxiety rose. 'We have nothing to do with this man,' the clerk said with a dismissive gesture in my direction. 'I take no responsibility for him.'

'But I am willing to take him. I know him,' Captain Visbecq nobly persevered.

'It cannot be done. We will take no responsibility.'

Captain Visbecq said heavily, '*Merde!*'

'The captain gives his permission for me to travel to Djibouti,' I said to the agent's representative. 'All I need is an exit stamp from the immigration office. You could arrange that. How about it? If you don't feel like doing it, suppose I talk to your boss?'

'What boss?' His expression was one of quiet triumph. 'I am the boss.'

'Your boss. The managing director of the agency.'

'In Paris.'

'Your operations manager, then.'

'In Beirut. I am the boss, I tell you, and I will not be responsible for you.' He got up, said, 'I'll be here early morning,' and left. '*Merde!*' Captain Visbecq repeated. 'Sheet!'

I had not, at this point, met many shipping agents, although of course Captain Rashad and Ahmed Bey clearly had been admirable representatives of a fine profession. Agents are scattered around the ports of the world to assist distant shipowners in the matter of the procuring of cargoes and their loading and off-loading, and the provision of necessities for the running of their vessels and the well-being of their officers and crews. As far as I knew, ships' owners or masters were responsible for any decision concerning the acceptance of passengers aboard. But Jedda is not like other ports. In Jedda, attitudes to foreigners – any foreigners, not only sea travellers – depend largely on the whims and personal relationships of individual Saudi officials. It was outrageous that Captain Visbecq should have to kowtow to this young man, but he was certainly prudent to do so in a port like this. Here such a young clerk had it in his power so to engineer delays in the loading and sailing of the *Vieljeux* – by 'forgetting', for example, to order trucks or stevedores or by 'mislaying' essential papers – that her owners would be faced with hideous expense and a horribly disrupted schedule. The young man's motive would be sheer malice; we were not acting illegally, but Jedda is different. Even my inexperienced brain told me to stop embarrassing kind Captain Visbecq. If in the morning the agent's representative hadn't softened his attitude to my presence on board, I would leave the ship immediately.

At Captain Visbecq's invitation, I occupied the pilot's

cabin and took a shower. After a few hours in this heat I looked as if I'd had a ducking in the harbour, and my clothes were full of salt. I changed them and returned to the office. '*À table!*' I heard Captain Visbecq's commanding voice like that of a genial cavalry general ordering a welcome advance.

At dinner the captain and the chief engineer from Biarritz made a pantomime of closing the dining-room curtains before we helped ourselves to the Spanish rosé or the French red. (The official puritanism of the Saudis involves depriving even passing sailors of so much as a glass of wine or beer, while behind their high marble walls the Saudi élite make merry with their cellars of smuggled Scotch.)

'Let not the Saudis see us wicked persons drinking the wine and the beer.'

'And eating pig meat!' It was true; the steward had served us with a nicely cooked leg of pork.

'*Oh là là là!*' Captain Visbecq moaned richly, rolling his tragedian's eyes around the room. 'Pork, too! *Mon Dieu*, steward, what were you thinking of?'

Early next morning, the agent's representative appeared looking, if anything, more malignant than before. I had hoped that by now his stubbornness might have mellowed. In a brief conference with me, Captain Visbecq had proposed typing a letter stating clearly that he was prepared to have me aboard. The kindly Breton could hardly do more, and I was grateful. Sitting with great solemnity at his own typewriter in the dayroom, he tapped out slowly and carefully: 'I undersigned, Captain of m/s/ "PATRICK VIELJEUX" declare accepté as passenger from Jeddah to Djibouti Mr: GAVIN DAVID YOUNG – Ship expected sailing from Jeddah on the 3rd of October.' He signed it. 'You have a visa for Djibouti, yes?' I told him I had.

'Now,' he said in gentle but confident and businesslike tones when the agent's representative appeared, 'about this problem—'

He was rudely cut short. 'There is no problem,' said the Saudi with a moody insolence. His eyes fixed malevolently on a patch of carpet, he added, 'I will not talk about it to you. Or to this man,' and he flicked a thumb in my direction.

There was nothing for it but to leave the *Patrick Vieljeux* before she sailed. Who knew what mischief a man like this might not get up to, what charges he might trump up to inflame the Saudi authorities? I imagined all sorts of evils befalling poor Captain Visbecq: the ship delayed, himself arrested, fines, God knows what, but, not least, bitter recriminations from the owners in Paris.

Once more I lugged the suitcase – its metal body seemed solid lead – down to the deck at the head of the gangway. The first officer was there, and I asked him if I could safely leave my baggage there while I said goodbye to Captain Visbecq.

'*Ouf! Oui! Il n'y a rien à craindre de ces philippins, hein?* They steal nothing.' I knew that he was right, and glad that he knew it too; I like Filipinos. I quickly said goodbye to the captain in his cabin, and thanked him for his efforts on my behalf. '*Eh bien, je regrette . . .*' he said with a sad smile.

Much later I found the key of the pilot's cabin in my pocket.

★ ★ ★

A friendly Filipino volunteered to drive me in a small pick-up to the dock gates some way from the *Patrick Vieljeux*. He told me he was the overseer of this particular gang of workers. Jedda docks are largely populated by Filipino stevedores: cheap, imported labour, part of a foreign work-force of thousands, mostly Filipinos, Koreans and Pakistanis. I had seen the old hull of a French ship, the *Pasteur*, where the Filipinos were barracked like battery hens, moored just off the wharf as *Al Wid* sailed in. The *Pasteur* was big, about 32000 tons, built in 1938, a fine trim ship then. She had ferried troops in the Second World War, then been turned over to North German Lloyd as the *Bremen* on the North Atlantic run from Bremerhaven. Subsequently she was bought by a Greek company, renamed *Regina Magna*, and finally sold to the Filipinos as a 'hotel ship': a floating dormitory, bunks slapped everywhere, for five thousand Filipino workers.

The Filipino drove me past dozens of his countrymen manhandling cargo or resting, on ships or on the docks, skins dark as treacle, coloured scarves around their heads, like pirates in oily jeans, naked to the waist. He seemed to find it a relief to talk to an outsider. A stocky, dark-skinned man with scarred arms, he opened his mouth wide and threw his head back when he talked, revealing several gold teeth. He drove through the containers, crates and ware-houses in erratic bursts of speed, wrenching the wheel from side to side in some kind of eccentric counterpoint to his animated chatter.

'We're about three thousand men in our company,' he shouted above the engine, 'and we get about five hundred dollars US a month – that is for supervisors like me, the others less. Not so much because here is hard. No drink

here. We live in that old ship for two years. Tough, eh? Yeah, tough. Two years no girl! But we save some money. Philippines is a very poor country. Only we are not happy that the Koreans here get one thousand dollars US a month. When we say to our boss, "Why we only get five hundred dollars?" he says, "Take it or leave it. You want work or you no want work? If not, we bring other Filipinos and you go back home." So what can we say?'

Like Cubans, Filipinos are easygoing, irrepressible people, and their country is an uproarious mélange of spontaneous song, easy sex and flamboyant spirits highly spiced with a strong dash of day-to-day mayhem, mostly by shooting. But two years cooped up in the *Pasteur*! It was not pleasant to imagine it, whatever the pay.

The overseer dropped me at the dock gates and I went through the police control and found a taxi. Captain el Zenati had told me of a small but adequate hotel in central

Jedda, so I took the last available room there. Jedda hotels are always full of affluent pilgrims or businessmen. People come to Saudi Arabia to find God or gold; there is nothing else there.

My urgent need was for a ship out of Jedda next day or the day after – or else to get an extension to my visa. But the next day was Friday, and nobody worked on Friday. If I wanted an extension I would have to acquire it today before noon. I stayed in the hotel just long enough to wash, and then went to call on one of the biggest shipping agencies.

The shipping manager in a big airy office high over the port was as unlike the young agent's representative who had insulted Captain Visbecq on board the *Patrick Vieljeux* as a man could possibly be. He was courteous and understanding, and he wanted to help; unfortunately, there were, I soon saw, considerable problems. A major one was the attitude of the Saudis.

'Their attitude to what?'

'To everything. Your difficulty here will be documentation, Mr Young. It is our difficulty too. Indeed it is!' The shipping manager was a Pakistani by birth. From the precision of his English he might have come from Oxford instead of a college in Karachi or Lahore. 'I have to tell you – warn you – the documentation is fantastic. We are bombarded by circulars from the government. Often they contradict themselves. Sometimes they are impossible to comply with unless we want to put ourselves out of business.'

Behind him through a wide, tinted window I could see the anchorage of Jedda, the ships lying helplessly inert on that steaming water, the abandoned wrecks listing on the reefs.

'Then there is the fiddling. The government is trying to stop all the fiddles that go on here. Deals involving sale of cargoes on the high sea, that kind of thing, mostly involving Lebanese in cahoots with Saudis.'

'So I'm a bit of a documentary nuisance.'

'Frankly, most shipping people won't want to bother with someone like you, a single individual who doesn't fit in the normal routine pattern of sea travellers.'

He ran a finger down the shipping lists: ships in port, ships due, ships sailing, where they were going and when. Nothing fitted my timetable or itinerary. Either the ships he handled were the wrong type – container ships, perhaps, with no accommodation of any kind that wasn't occupied – or the dates and destinations didn't fit. Later, perhaps; he would let me know as soon as something promising turned up. 'Don't despair.' He gave me his telephone number and urged me to return on Saturday. My heart sank. Without a visa I could not be here on Saturday.

I sped around to another agent, whose name the Pakistani had given me. He, too, wanted to be helpful. I had seen a Hansa Line vessel in the port; the black Maltese cross on her funnel took me back to the fifties, when I had worked in a dingy shipping office in Basra and supervised the loading of grain into the ships lying in the river. There had been many Hansa Line ships there, and I can still recall the taste of the schnapps and Beck's beer in the un-air-conditioned cabins of sweating, jovial German mates. But now the agent told me that to hitch a ride on a Hansa vessel would mean telexing Hamburg or Bremen for permission from the owners. This he would do, he said, but the answer would take time, or might never come; the owners were the sort who would probably ignore a request involving a single, unknown man. As for the Saudis, now if only I had been a *group* of *pilgrims*! 'Come back next week to see if Hansa has answered.' I wished I could turn myself into a group just long enough to leave Jedda by sea.

Now it was a question of extending my stay. It was also time, I felt, to let the British consul know that a lonely Briton was on the loose with a near-moribund visa in his pocket. I hoped that someone in the consulate would know a way of getting a week's extension of the wretched little three-day permit so begrudgingly handed to me by the bearded Saudi consul general in Alex. A week would be enough. Hanging about Jedda indefinitely was out of the question. I couldn't afford the time if I was going to reach Canton in under a year, and God forbid that it should take anything like *that* long. My heart sank still lower. I began to feel like Napoleon when his aides told him that the first few blocks of Moscow were in flames. A retreat was in the offing.

At the British consulate – a longish drive by taxi from the centre of Jedda – I discovered two Englishmen behind a locked door. They admitted me cautiously. One was tall and slim, the area around his mouth and chin disfigured by a few days' growth of beard. There was a kind of suave alertness about him, combined with an impatient irritability. The second man was, I surmised, a kind of Dr Watson to the other's Sherlock Holmes; he wore a moustache, jacket and tie and smiled genially, if warily, over a pipe.

The tall, unshaven one intimated with all the delicacy

of a circus barker that I was really intruding pretty madden-ingly into an area of intense and secret activity. I gathered that someone of importance, whose identity could not be revealed (the Duke of Edinburgh?), had soon to be met at Jedda airport. Time, his attitude brayed at me, was precious and, in any case, belonged to Her Britannic Majesty. (As I remember, it turned out that the visitor was some minimally important Foreign Office inspector.) Nevertheless, when I had rattled through my story – which sounded embarrass-ingly trivial, I had to admit – Dr Watson took enough pity on me to telephone a shipping agency he thought was friendly and obtain a promise from someone there to call me back shortly. (It was not the good doctor's fault that no return call ever came.) He also gave me the names and office telephone numbers of one or two British shipping men. But it soon developed that they had sneaked away from Jedda some months previously without, apparently, informing the British consulate. At this rate, I thought, I will soon be not only shipless but on the run from the Saudi Immigration Department as well.

'I think I'd better get this visa extended, don't you?' I said.

'Try the passport office,' Holmes suggested hopefully. 'It's by the old airport. They may help you there, or they may not; it depends how they feel. If you don't speak Arabic I don't suppose they're likely to.'

'Could you speak a word on my behalf then? Or give me the name of somebody there? It's Thursday and almost noon. I would be very grateful.' I didn't feel like telling them I spoke Arabic. In any case, I didn't think that Arabic by itself would be the key to a week's extension (nor was it). But I did know that it was halfway through a Thursday morning, and that the passport office would close at noon. Any delay there could be fatal. 'A little note, perhaps . . .'

Holmes waved a careless hand. 'If we did that for everyone who came here, we'd be doing nothing else.' He and Watson exchanged the weary smiles of the permanently overworked. In addition, Holmes had the exasperated air of one who feels that the world underestimates him. 'Of course,' I said humbly. 'But perhaps a short note – in Arabic, of course.'

'Well, perhaps a note. Then you'll be on your own.'

They gave me a note asking for a week's extension, and then Holmes had to be on the move again.

But the genial Watson called for tea and seemed disposed to talk. What he said made me sympathize with him; he obviously had a wretched job in a wretched place. The Saudis were, almost to a man, deliberately rude and unhelpful, he said. 'They actually put obstacles in your way for the hell of it. Yet if *they* want something from *you*, they expect you to go miles out of your way on their behalf.' There was only a hint of indignation in his diplomat's voice.

'Take an example. Suppose some Saudi prince decides to go to London. It's twelve o'clock at night and I'm in bed. The phone rings – and this has *happened*, believe me – and it's the prince's secretary saying, "The prince and seven other people want to fly to London on a special plane tonight. Give them all visas. Now, please!" Of course I say, "Sorry, the consulate's closed. But I'll get there by seven o'clock tomorrow morning, though we don't officially open until later, and will have your visas ready in five minutes, I promise." ' Watson paused to drink, then set his teacup down. 'Slam!' he cried suddenly. 'Down goes the receiver! And a few minutes later, after I've fallen asleep again our ambassador is on the line, spluttering, "Look, Prince So-and-So just phoned me in person demanding visas immediately. He's absolutely livid. For God's sake, give them to him. Get up and give them to him now!" '

'You mean to say that our ambassador gives in to this bullying in the middle of the night?'

Watson nodded his head ruefully and began scraping his pipe with what looked like a paperclip. 'It wouldn't stop there,' he said in mournful tones. 'That's the problem. That prince wouldn't hesitate to speak to some other royal bigwig – some even bigger prince – who in his turn wouldn't hesitate to throw a deliberate spanner into some important commercial transaction of value to Britain.' He shrugged. 'Of course, it's blackmail.'

'So to connive in one's own humiliation is good diplomacy, is it?'

'As we all know, they have all the money,' Dr Watson said with a sad smile. 'And, as we all know, we need it, don't we?'

Chapter Twelve

THE PERMIT OFFICE near the old airport was besieged by scores of Saudis, jostling and shouting. The last minutes before the weekend began were running out. At any moment the doors might slam shut until Saturday morning, a day and a half later.

It wasn't easy to find the office of the colonel who dealt with cases like mine. (Ask ten urban-dwelling Saudis directions, and you'll probably get at least six different answers and four arrogant shrugs – and, if you can't speak Arabic, you'll get no answers at all.) In the end I found him at a desk in a medium-sized office, surrounded by a frantically heaving crowd in thobes and headcloths. Two telephones at his elbow rang constantly. From three sides of his desk, petitioners were brandishing pieces of paper – applications for permits of one sort or another – like flags at a nationalist rally.

With few words, the colonel impassively waved away petitioners as if they were flies hovering over his food, or glanced carelessly at the pieces of paper and added a few scribbled words on them with a gold pen, signing and dating the scribble.

He wore a uniform and his head was bare, showing blond hair, unusual in Saudis, but he may have been Palestinian or Syrian. Shoved and shoving, I made my way to his desk and laid my passport and the consulate's note on it, keeping my hand on them to make sure they were not snatched away in the turmoil. With a momentarily deafening shout, the voice of a muezzin rose above the babble and the telephones, calling everybody to prayer. I hoped a good number of the people around me would rush out to their devotions, but nobody moved from the colonel's desk and the scrimmaging went on as before; when it came to getting a permit, prayers evidently could wait. '*La ilah ill' Allah . . .*' The muezzin's nasal tones filled the room with a metallic roar of static. The prayer call was too highly amplified for the loudspeakers, and, to judge from the volume, the minaret it emanated from might have been in the permit office itself. Everything audible, including the colonel's throw-away voice, thereafter had to be heard against that ear-splitting background.

When at last the colonel glanced up at me, unsmiling, and took my passport and the note from the consulate, his telephone immediately rang. 'Could you give me a week more?' I asked him in Arabic, but he was talking into the receiver and pretended not to hear. He had already written something brisk on the consulate's note and, when he rang off, the nib of his gold pen was tapping on the visa from Alexandria in my passport.

'This says "Transit only",' he said in an accusing voice. 'And there are these . . .' He turned back two pages and rapped with his pen the two unsightly smudges the ham-fisted clerk in Alexandria had made in stamping the visa in my passport. To the colonel they seemed to have been put there as deliberate warnings – a sort of code – to any Saudi official in Jedda not to trust me with an extension, and perhaps, I suddenly thought in burgeoning paranoia, that's what they were.

'You can stay four days,' said the colonel, not looking at me. His calculated indifference was positively aggressive. 'Saturday. Then you must go.' He had given me no more than one extra day. Already he was reaching out impatiently for an application flapped at him by a shaking old man with a grey beard. Arabic and the note from the consulate had availed me nothing.

There was now no question about it: Moscow was truly alight and burning merrily; a retreat was inevitable. I would have to leave Jedda before midnight on Saturday, the day after tomorrow, and it would not be possible to wait for sailings or telex messages from Hamburg or anywhere else. I would have to forget Djibouti and fly direct to the Gulf. Fly!

'Go and see Mr Fuad downstairs,' the colonel said curtly in my direction. No one seemed to know or care where Mr Fuad's office was. When I found it, a clerk drinking tea said, 'Fuad is praying. Later.' I sat on a hard chair and waited with four or five silent Saudis in white cotton robes, all of whom wore gold watches and rings and had gold rims on their spectacles. Mr Fuad turned out to be a grim Mr Punch in a soiled thobe and a cheap red and white headcloth. He added his signature to my passport in green ink, and snapped '*Sanduq*' – meaning cash desk. There was no sign of such an object in his tiny office, and a clerk who pulled himself slowly to his feet beckoned me to follow him, and led me to another building across a courtyard. There I paid ten riyals (£1.50) to a cashier, and was led across a courtyard by the clerk. Halfway across, a handsome Saudi, whose face was as black as any face I've ever seen, called to the clerk in whose footsteps I was following, 'Brought your slave with you?'

'What?' The clerk was puzzled.

The black Saudi jerked his head toward me. 'You've brought your slave with you.' The clerk glanced back at me and they both hooted with laughter. I laughed too. It wasn't a bad joke. Most blacks in Saudi Arabia and other Arab countries are descendants of slaves brought over from Africa. And slaves walk at the heels of their masters just as I had been following the clerk.

Slavery in Saudi Arabia was a strange system. Despite an official ban on the practice, there were slaves there until quite recently. The term can be misleading. In Arabia slaves often became affectionate servants rather than the pitifully ill-treated human beings we read about in *Uncle Tom's Cabin*. Furthermore, eventually a faithful slave was almost invariably rewarded with his freedom.

The impudent remark by the black Saudi suddenly reminded me vividly, as if he stood before me, of the slave boy Saad. I paid about £30 for Saad one day in 1955 in the scruffy backwoods town of Bisha, on the long dust and lava track that led from the city of Taif to the remote – and to foreigners almost unknown – town of Najran on the Yemen border. I had driven into Bisha with my small band of Locust Control helpers – four mountain dwellers from the Medina region, a man from the east, and a young Yemeni from the fortified town of Ib – to buy stores in the market. The next day I was sitting reading in the doorway of my tent when Mubarek, the elderly and reliable overseer of my group, returned from the town to say that he had been approached by a black boy of about sixteen – a slave, he said, whose parents had been sold to the other end of the kingdom, and who wanted to get away from Bisha. Saad had shyly told Mubarek this in a coffee house; the man he worked for was willing to let him go, he said, for a reasonable sum.

'But do we need anybody else? Another mouth to feed?'

Mubarek said, 'He would be very useful washing pots and pans and helping with the cooking. If he's too much trouble, we can let him go in Najran.'

So Saad joined us, and was as useful as Mubarek had prophesied he would be. He was also cheerful, and the others seemed to get on with him. He liked music, and sometimes in camp in some wild spot between the mountains and the desert, I would see him alone, cross-legged in the shade of the thorny umbrella of an acacia tree, his head thrown back to reveal a crimson tongue, singing in high falsetto and flicking on a saucepan lid the African rhythms he heard in his head.

We had a football in camp and sometimes the Saudis awkwardly tucked up their long skirts and kicked it about barefoot. Saad was good at it; he was short and bowlegged but nimble. His hair was tightly curled, and his teeth gleamed in his black face like a set of dentures in a coal scuttle.

Sometimes I found him feeding biscuits to the harmless fluffy tree rats that now and again infested the camp. If a locust swarm descended nearby, Saad gathered handfuls of them into a sack, then threaded them together like beads on a necklace, and grilled them on the embers of the open fire as if they were chestnuts. They had a dull taste – like singed cardboard, I imagined – but were said to be nutritious.

There were worrying times. Saad's pleasantly ugly face was so expressive that sometimes I could see some high emotion playing across its black glossiness like electric waves through a steel plate. His speech was punctuated with explosive exclamations – 'Ah!' and a squeaky 'Eeh!' More than once I found him sitting alone behind the tents, silently staring at a small patch of ground as if he'd lost something precious there and was searching for it. Then I would call Mubarek and the others to get out the football or take my .22 rifle and clamber about the rocks looking for partridges or quail, and soon Saad would be laughing his high-pitched black boy's laugh again. To the others Saad wasn't a slave but a younger brother. That is what Saudis were like outside Jedda.

'Are you happy, Saad?' I asked him when he'd been with us about six months. 'More than ever before,' he answered.

He stayed with us for a year, and then, when I left Saudi Arabia, went on his way, a slave no longer.

Now, in 1979, twenty-four years later, in the taxi going back to the hotel, I wondered where Saad was now – fortyish, plump, married, perhaps a shop owner, a taxi driver, a bowlegged mechanic in the eastern oil fields?

As it happened, the driver of my taxi was also black and no longer young. When I asked him where he came from he said, 'Oh, Abha,' casually, as if he was certain I had never heard of it.

Abha! The capital of the Asir province on the northern Yemen border, a mountainous but watery region intermittently green with orchards and grain fields between jagged ridges full of wild cats and colonies of fierce baboons that threatened men and tore large dogs to pieces. It was a region of some of the loveliest villages I had ever seen, with miniature skyscrapers that were really mud towers with small shuttered windows. After sunset they glowed like dolls' houses.

Hardly any outsiders had been to Abha then; I can only think of St John Philby and Wilfred Thesiger. It had a solid fort of stone built by the Turks and used, when I pitched our camp there, by the all-powerful Saudi governor, an imposing, stern but kindly man, bearded, robed and encircled by retainers, some of them black, wearing pistols and swords. I made Abha our base for six months. The people of Asir were short and dark, and their long hair, held by a fillet around their foreheads into which they pushed sprigs of fragrant herbs, hung down to their naked shoulders and chests. They wore short cotton skirts bound at the waist by a thick belt, which usually held a sharply curved dagger in an intricately embossed sheath of some silvery metal, perhaps silver itself. In the market they crowded around me – they had never seen a human being six foot three before or one with fair hair – and shyly and experimentally fingered my shirt or felt the hair of my arms. They were like Lilliputians examining Gulliver, and ran away giggling if I turned suddenly and spoke to them. In time they grew bolder, and eventually one of the bravest broke the ice by asking me to come to his five-storey Alice-in-Wonderland house for dinner.

My small group enjoyed Abha. It was cool up there after the desert; the food was good; and the girls, who were beautiful, went about unveiled and often bare-breasted. One of our young men from Medina fell in love with an Abha beauty and, because she evidently didn't think much of him, he fell into a decline. He actually turned his face to the wall and refused to talk or eat. As birds do, he was pining away; the others said such a reaction was quite common. But after a few days of this I bounced him out of his mood with a prodigious and explosive dose of Epsom salts, which gave him little time to brood over love. I could not imagine that the Desert Locust people at headquarters in Jedda would really accept a report from me that one of their employees had died of unrequited love.

Now I told the taxi driver that I knew Abha well, and

immediately he became excited. His family was still there, he said. 'It's changed, of course, since you were there, but the weather is still good, and the cool breezes, the gardens, the fruits.'

'The grapes and the pomegranates.'

'We had so much running water.'

'And the green grass at Khamis Mushayt and the long-haired people.'

The governor's name was Ibn Madhi, a man with a power of life and death over the people of the region, and a brother who was governor of Najran. I told the taxi driver that as I entered Najran for the first time a procession came towards us, leaving the town, kicking up a great cloud of dust in the valley; it was that governor being led off in chains. He'd been arrested by order of King Saud for some misdemeanour and summoned to Riyadh to explain himself. It had been a dramatic scene, like something from another time: the tall moustached men in Arab dress, the sun flashing on their guns and swords, some on horseback, the fallen governor – a Nejdi from the northern deserts – in their midst manacled but still imposing in disgrace.

'You were certainly there!' The driver had slowed down in the Jedda traffic, and was talking and listening with his head turned more to me than to the road. A green Rolls-Royce swerved past us, and a princely figure in the back seat glared at us through the smoked-glass window. 'Drive a longer way round, then we can talk,' I suggested to the driver, and he laughed and agreed.

Talking to him, I remembered more about that long valley of date gardens, wells and mud mansions. Ten years later the valley became something of a tourist trap, its peace ruined by the soldiers, European mercenaries and journalists who crowded in to participate in or cover the Yemen War from the Saudi side. Abha and Khamis Mushayt were smothered by urbanization and new military installations. 'There are too many new buildings,' my taxi driver mourned, turning out of the centre of Jedda for the Mecca highway.

In the Asir there had been an Arcadia worth mourning: it was not a place of beauty where people died of malnutrition; it was a granary, an orchard, a waterfall, a seventh heaven – that is, if a heaven will admit witches and magic. A number of witches were said to live around Abha in those days in isolated villages amid a landscape that had a strange Grimms'-fairy-tale look about it. There were huge rocks with holes in them like Henry Moore sculptures. Obelisk-shaped rocks shot up from flat, stony plains, and hills rounded like domes were strangely grouped in pairs. The Arabs, who like giving things names, called such landmarks the Sultan's Penis or The Bosoms.

The witches of Asir specialized in love potions or curses. In southern Arabia the spirits or genies we read of emerging from magic lamps in the *Arabian Nights* were more like the little people of Ireland, and lived under bushes, rocks or small hills where they guarded treasure. My Arabs hated to pitch a tent without first consulting a local Bedouin. After all, they said, if you urinated on a subterranean household of ill-natured djinns, you were asking for smallpox or a heart attack. Djinns could strike back. The Arabs believed in these things as people in America and Europe believe in haunted houses, and could become irritable if their beliefs, or half-beliefs, were mocked. Riding beside me in a jeep towards the great mountains behind Najran, the Yemeni from Ib, Abdullah, pointed and said, 'See those mountains?

There are dangerous people living at the very top of them who kill everyone they get their hands on. They are called the Beni Chilab, and they have long hairy tails.'

'Who told you that!' I asked, conscious too late of the disbelief in my voice.

'My cousin told me,' he said sharply. 'He's been there.'

'Well, did he say whether they wore their tails inside or outside their skirts? If they were inside, how did anyone see them?'

Abdullah turned a darker shade of butterscotch and began furiously stuffing handfuls of qat leaf, the Yemeni equivalent of pep pills, into his cheeks. I had seldom seen him so angry. 'You don't believe a simple thing like that,' he exploded, 'yet you tell me – we all heard it – a ridiculous story of an air pilot, married and with children, who goes into hospital in London and comes out of it a woman.' He jammed another wad of the bitter leaf into his mouth. 'You tell me, furthermore, of a country somewhere in the north where the people have six months of day and six months of night. All that I am expected to believe, and yet men with tails is all lies . . .'

Abdullah's diatribe went on for some time, until qat swelled his cheeks like a hamster's and began to redden his eyeballs. I didn't blame him. Why shouldn't there be human tails – or at least why shouldn't Abdullah reasonably expect me to believe that there might be? Luckily, the qat made him giggly, and his anger faded away.

Now, in 1979, I said to the taxi driver, 'Let's go to Abha tomorrow. You drive me, and we'll visit your family there.'

He saw I was joking – Abha was a very long way off – and his shoulders shook with amusement. He said, 'Which way? Down the coast road and up the mountain highway to Abha? It's all asphalt now.'

'Never! We'll go the old way, past Mecca, through Taif, eating noodles at a Bokhari restaurant on the way, down to Bisha across the lava fields. The old, long way: three days and nights.'

'I'll come,' he shouted. 'Let's get away from this hot, damp city and up to the breezes and the pomegranates. Welcome to my Abha house!'

But by now the asphalt highways are everywhere; Bisha is a modern town; the orchards of the south are ringed and dwarfed — even replaced — by missile sites and air-force bases. I wondered about the Darb el Fil, the Elephant Road, that used to wind through the mountains north towards Mecca from the Yemen. This was the undulating way of great stone slabs, the width of a bus, that the Ethiopian kings of Yemen had built so that their battle elephants could advance on Mecca. (God had smitten the poor beasts with hailstones.) Probably the Elephant Road, which I had often explored in those days, had also been paved over for heavy motor traffic.

When we reached my hotel at last, I got out to pay the black driver, who was by now beside himself with the excitement of reminiscence. 'Let's go, let's go!' he cried, displaying the gaps in his teeth. I told him of my three-day visa, and we looked at each other sadly.

'When you see Abha next, give it my regards,' I said. He smacked his pink palm into mine, clasping it, and threw his other arm around my neck and kissed me on both cheeks. A party of stubble-chinned men who looked like Iranians stared at us in astonishment from the entrance of the hotel. Then, ignoring the money I held out to him, he hopped in his taxi and drove away with a wave and a grin. A small pendant sign in his rear window saying ALLAH swung back and forth as he went down the street.

At least one Saudi had survived the oil boom with his humanity intact.

The avalanche of memories the taxi driver had shaken loose from the past – and his own sweet simplicity – had made my stay in Jedda worthwhile.

In my hotel at lunch I shared a table with a Lebanese businessman whose hair resembled corrugated tin, and who wore a cream silk shirt with green cufflinks as big as saucers. He informed me genially, 'I am in big business here. No good coming here unless you have big business.' He waved a fork. 'Mine is worth four million sterling pounds.'

'Bravo,' I said. I saw that he had sheaves of typewritten paper by his plate and, by his chair, the inevitable leather briefcase with a combination lock.

'Yes,' he said, 'with small business you lose.' He looked round the dining room at other Arabs poring over papers as they ate kebab and chips. 'No one ever comes to Jedda except for good big business. You know what my trip is? Three days here, three days in Riyadh, three days in Kuwait, three days in Baghdad.' He seemed satisfied. 'All very big business.'

'Better you than me,' I said.

'Kuwait is more expensive even than here.' He pronounced this as if it was a recommendation. 'Have you seen Sana, capital of Yemen? It's dirtier than Jedda.'

'I like Sana.'

'Just a living museum.'

'At least it's living,' I said. 'People here have heads full of gold watches, and as a museum it's zero.'

He laughed. When he asked, I told him I was a writer.

'A writer! In Jedda?' he exclaimed. 'No business?' It was as if I'd said I was a unicorn trainer. 'You must be the most unusual man in Jedda.'

Whenever I saw the Lebanese again, he was running busily about the lobby, in and out of taxis, dashing to the telephone, always in a hurry. He had given himself only three days in Jedda and didn't have time to say hello again. He was four million pounds of big business on the move.

I went to the Saudi Airlines office near the hotel. A sign on the door said, CLOSED FOR PRAYERS. After an hour I returned, survived a stiff dose of rudeness from two Saudi clerks, and finally bought a ticket to Bahrain from a jolly Pakistani from Lahore. Then I wandered around the centre of the city. Old buildings in piles of rubble alternated with modern structures of no distinction; Jedda looked like a poodle in a diamond collar suffering from the mange.

And gold poisoning. New, high, arched emporia filled the city centre; rambling covered markets that seemed to go on acre after acre; mazes you could get lost in, an Ali Baba's Cave. Over the high plate-glass shopfronts – window after window – the words sparkled in gold lettering: JEWELS, WATCHES. Gold and gems sparkled out at the gaping shoppers from every side: necklaces, brooches, bracelets, watch faces studded with diamonds and sapphires. I squinted at the price tags: the equivalent of £700, £1650, £5000 and more. The robed figures of Saudi men and women elbowed their way into these treasure-houses, while once more the voice of a muezzin rose deafeningly over us: *La ilah ill' Allah!*

I realized with joy that people like my taxi driver existed

– exceptions to the evident rule that wealth and its arrogance had deprived too many Saudis of all grace, generosity and tolerance. Did God feel at home among the Cadillacs so matter-of-factly ranged in window after window like those in a Los Angeles used-car lot? What did He think of the whisky and the pornographic films behind high villa walls? The soul of Arabia lay entombed in the bazaar, behind the plate-glass and burglarproof grilles, with the gold rings and diamond necklaces.

The next morning, the last day I was permitted by my 'extended' visa to remain in Saudi Arabia, I remarked to the manager, a Palestinian, as I paid my hotel bill, 'Well, I hope the flights leave on time from Jedda. I have a connection from Bahrain to Dubai.' He gave me my last jab of fear. 'All go on time,' he grinned, 'except Saudia. With Saudia, some prince comes along with eleven persons and everyone is turned off the flight,' then added, patting my shoulder, 'Don't worry, I'll try to keep a room for you here if you're turned off the plane.' With longing I thought of the sea.

My taxi driver to the airport was a sturdy fellow, like Mubarek in the old days. He came from Medina, he said, as he pushed through the jams of Cadillacs with a fine nervous dexterity. When I pointed to a group of Pakistani labourers and said, 'Once all the work was done by the Yemenis, and by black Takrunis from Nigeria,' he answered, 'The Koreans are the strongest workers now.'

'Pakistanis?'

'Lazy, lazy.'

In the chill of the air conditioning in the airport waiting

room, Filipinos in orange overalls swept the floor with brushes and emptied the ashtrays. They looked neither happy nor miserable. 'If you don't like it, go home!' their boss had told them. The departure board read, 'Abha, Flight SV 833 09.10', and I remembered Saad saying he was happy – 'more than ever before'. Then my own flight to Bahrain was called. No prince wanted to hijack it that day, and it left on time.

Near Bahrain, after miles of wilderness occasionally interrupted by sheer buttresses of sand, the Saudia Boeing banked and dropped toward the sea through a sandstorm. It was as if a giant were throwing handfuls of red pepper at the plane's windows.

I caught my connection to Dubai from Bahrain and, as the Gulf Air aircraft crossed the shallow waters off Qatar, looked down on the dhows and fishing craft moving slowly on the surface of water so shallow and still – and therefore so invisible – that they seemed to be suspended in air, not water. It was so clear that I could see strange delicate seabed shapes like dragonflies' wings, and what looked like gold-flecked folds of silk undulating there as if trapped under glass.

Chapter Thirteen

I SAT ON my bunk and opened *Lady Sustant's Recruit* at random. Where the pages fell open, I read:

Peggy sat up to ease off her black lace briefs . . .

Hands wormed into the waistband of her tights, stretched the thin material outwards and eased down. She wriggled her bottom on the rich leather . . . 'Well, do you fancy me?'

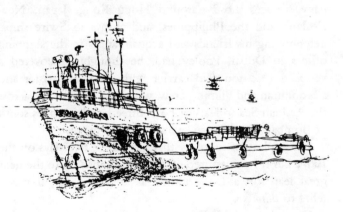

It wasn't the only reading on the *Pacific Basset*, a 360–ton tug with, as I saw from a brochure provided by the owners, Swire Pacific Offshore, two Yanmar G250E engines totalling 2600 b.p.h. at 820 revs. per minute, and a speed of twelve knots. In Captain Peter Barton's cabin I had spotted Stendhal's *The Red and the Black*, Jacques Prévert's *Paroles*, Priestley's *Bright Day*, an Agatha Christie, Francis

Chichester's *Lonely Sea and the Sky*. Barton had studied French in Paris and wanted to live there, which perhaps accounted for the air of catholicity aboard the *Pacific Basset*. It was not really Lady Sustant's ambience, perhaps.

I was spending a couple of days at sea in the Gulf to watch John Swire's *Pacific Basset* tow an oil rig from one position to another somewhere off Abu Dhabi.

Arriving from Jedda, I had telephoned Swire's offices in Dubai and been invited around by Swire's manager, Chris Pooley, an energetic veteran of eighteen years' merchant navy service, mostly around Hong Kong, Japan, New Zealand and the Philippines, and always in Swire ships. Telephoning his friends and acquaintances in the shipping offices in Dubai, Pooley had, he thought, discovered a vessel, a 1200-ton acid carrier with a British master and a Honduran and Filipino crew, which would take me across the Arabian Sea to Karwar port, three hundred miles south of Bombay. That, I said, would suit me nicely.

It was pleasant to know that after these two days on the *Pacific Basset* I was assured of a smooth transit on to the next great leap forward. Or rather, as it turned out, it was a relief to *think* so.

'Are you seasick?' Captain Barton asked.

'Not up to now.'

'Nor was I until I began to work offshore. The *Basset* is very solid and very stable, so it takes a hell of a lot of pressure to push her over. But once she's over it takes an age before she gets back.'

'Doesn't she have stabilizers?'

'Anything sticking out – rudder, propellers, stabilizers –

are a liability on a tug. Anything that sticks up is a liability, too,' he added, patting the top of his head. Peter Barton was six foot five, and was continually banging his head on something, he said. 'I trust men who are tall,' he said. He was thirty-five years old, long-nosed, long-jawed, highly articulate.

The *Pacific Basset* was a handsome tug with a spick-and-span firehouse-red hull, white bridge, and the squat, nimble tough-guy look of a middleweight boxer. She looked capable of bashing her way through the short, steep waves you find in shallow water, and of riding the bigger, more gradual but heavier waves of the oceans.

Seen from her roomy fore-to-aft bridge, the rigs of the biggest Abu Dhabi offshore field sat on the hazy horizon like grey spaceships. A long tapering flare rose from a tall sticklike pipe in the water. Helicopters hovered and swooped down to alight on platforms of rigs like tentative bees. Closer to the rigs, in the midst of them, it was like being in a Meccano world of robots and miniature Eiffel Towers. In certain conditions of light and mist, their widespread legs seemed to turn them into striding mechanical men. In my notebook I wrote:

We approach the rig named Penrod stern first, edging alongside one of the three towering legs and spreading floor of the drilling platform. The voice of Penrod comes over Barton's radio speaking in a French accent. 'Please 'urry urp an we'll gate on wiz eet.'

'Jesus Christ, first you say "Starboard", and then you say "Port" . . .' A clash of French and British temperament seems in the offing. Men in hard hats shout down at us from the rig.

'Stand by with the boathook,' Barton calls to his Filipino first mate. The mate throws a line up to the rig; a big noose of wire is hauled up after it, and draped over the bollard. We edge away, tightening the wire.

The body of the rig starts to settle silently on to the water, moved by machinery slowly, foot by foot, down the three thick Meccano legs. The platform is really a kind of barge as well as a mass of rails, steel ladders, radar antennae, pipes, things that resemble generators and a small helicopter pad. Finally the subsided rig is more like a small grey aircraft carrier with three metal-strutted towers sticking up from it.

A Filipino puts his head into the bridge and says, 'Chow?'

'What is it today?'

'Fly lice.'

'Fried rice is good. Okay, bring it up.'

But, mysteriously, what appears is omelettes, raw tomatoes and a dish of tinned peaches. 'Fly lice, eh?' Barton moans. 'Bloody 'ell.'

We begin to tow the rig. The wire between us tightens as we turn and drops sizzling into the sea as if it were red-hot. Tight, it becomes a quivering white snake with water trailing like threads of cotton between the rig and a winch just behind the bridge. 'Towing under full power,' says Barton. The disparity in size is laughable: Goliath dragged along by a pygmy for twelve miles.

For Barton it's the Centre Court at Wimbledon. The wheel and telegraph are on one side of the bridge, the radio at the other. He leaps from one to the other like a tennis champion playing himself from both sides of the net at once. Even stooped, he is unable to avoid an occasional crack of his head on some protuberance in the ceiling. It is an impressive performance.

'Imagine this for three months on end. It's pure escapism.' Escapism from what? Barton wanted to be a seaman from the age of thirteen. After nautical school, he took his master's certificate at twenty-five ('Par for the course'). Not a bad life. Travel – yes, some element of romance. In practical terms, you get four months' leave a year (six weeks every three months), although it's a sixteen-hour day for those three months. 'We've worked eleven hours today already. No one bothers at sea. If you have work, you finish it.'

After dark the rig lights up with neon strips. We are dazzled by the strong light blazing down on us. In the limelight we cast off, pirouette to starboard, then throw up another line: more manoeuvres of balletic precision. The rig is positioned very exactly, according to delicate instruments. At last, at 8.00 p.m., the unseen French voice says, 'Fine. Fine positioning. Jacking down now.' We wait. The mechanical legs probe down through the water under the white light; they find the seabed.

'Very fine. No more tonight.'

In the morning: 'Bass–et. Well, we 'ave everything in order 'ere. You ken 'ead beck to Dubai. Good treep.'

Barton says, '*Bonjour* and thanks.'

'All ze best.'

'Happy landings.' All quite friendly now.

I asked Simeon Furio Junior, the first mate, if he minds when a captain shouts at him. 'Oh, no, no,' he says. 'He's busy and all alone up there mostly. It's the job.' Simeon Furio has had some tough jobs: for instance, towed barges of ammunition up the Saigon river under fire, sandbags around the bridge, rockets and bullets crisscrossing the deck, crewmen wounded. He got a 50 per cent bonus for that, plus extra for any direct hits on the vessel by rockets. Hot work, if you can get it. This was before he joined Swire's, of course.

Towing a barge *without* being fired at, Barton says, is hazardous enough. Erratic movements in bad weather? 'No, the towline is very long. What can happen is that, while manoeuvring, your tug engine can fail, and the barge keeps going and overwhelms the tug. Still, that doesn't happen often.'

He stands up and bangs his head on a small Japanese shrine on a bulkhead. It has two little doors like a cuckoo clock. I open the doors and find inside, like an effigy of the Buddha, a small head-and-shoulders photograph of John Swire, the supreme boss of Swire Pacific Offshore and the whole Swire group. 'It brings us luck,' says Peter Barton, rubbing his head.

From my hotel room I overlooked the creek that is Dubai's watery heart and gives this brand-new, unreal city its cohesion, much as a magnetic rod attracts and holds iron filings. Commerce is the reason for Dubai: trans-shipping, and gold.

The creek is about a hundred and fifty yards wide, lined on its eastern bank now by medium-sized skyscrapers, with a second bank of taller ones behind them. Towards its mouth are two pale, graceful minarets: along its eastern bank, a clutter of dhows, some from Aden, most from Iran, and a quay heaped with bales, crates and coils of rope and the sea chests of sailors, whose newly washed sarongs and long cotton drawers hang out to dry over spars on the dhows' awninged decks.

The sailors of the dhows are a mixed lot. Some with white skullcaps and beards are almost certainly Iranians. Some wear baggy Baluchi trousers; others, long Arab night-shirts or red and green checked Adeni sarongs (called *futas* here) and white cloths around their heads. Some wear the loose, knee-length Pakistani shirt. Beyond the western side of the creek, a fringe of lower buildings, palms and aerials wavers indistinctly in haze and rising dust. Beyond them nothing: an empty undulating stretch of sand and stone, interrupted less and less frequently by strands of telephone wire and perhaps an asphalt road that wanders off into the Empty Quarter, the ocean of great sands.

Twenty-five years ago Dubai was little more than a mosque, a modest palace, a shipping office and a clump of palms. No census has been taken in Dubai for some time, but estimates circulate of an immigrant population that outnumbers the Arabs of Dubai by ten to one. The vast majority of the expatriates are Indian or Pakistani – perhaps seventy-five thousand of them. Then come the Iranians, it is presumed, followed by Arabs from outside the Gulf, then

Filipinos and, finally, Koreans. None of them plan to settle, but all have come, sometimes at the cost of great effort and anxiety, to save money. Having done so, they will return home again – or, if they can, keep travelling west, to the eldorado of Europe.

Soon after reaching Dubai, I called Walid, my son-of-the-soil Pakistani friend, and he appeared, hot and flushed, at the hotel and, for a while, jumped around like a puppy at feeding time. I ordered tea for us both. He was plumper – he wasn't starving in Dubai; people working in hotels never starve – but otherwise unchanged by the heat and limitations of this isolated desert port. His job bored him, and I had no doubt that with his honesty, energy and good nature he deserved a better one.

Walid now earned more than he ever could in Lahore or Rawalpindi, and perhaps he could eventually leap the gap between Dubai and London or Paris, the cities he longed to see. He hoped to make, if not a fortune, a good nest-egg here; perhaps he would be 'spotted' by some hotel talent scout, if such people existed, as unknowns were once snatched out of Hollywood drugstores and raised to stardom.

He had paid a lightning visit to Pakistan the month before my arrival. 'I had a very good time,' he said. 'My girlfriend was very happy to see me. I was enjoying her very much.' He shook a finger at me and smiled. 'I do not mean that I played with her body. Oh, no. In Pakistan we never do that before marriage. We went to the Muri Hills to see the snow falling.' He fell silent and his smile faded. His thoughts, I could see as he sat in this place of sandstorms and humidity, were on the green trees, the familiar language and the unfamiliar snow he'd held in his hand north of the Punjab.

I was sure Walid had been waiting impatiently for my arrival with the sex doll he'd asked for in his letter. I said awkwardly, 'Walid, look, about the sex doll. Don't be too upset, but I haven't brought it. Your letter reached me in Cyprus; too late – and my Greek friends told me such things are not on sale there.'

'Oh, my letter was late, was it?' He looked crestfallen but, considering the head of steam that must have been building up inside him since his letter, he didn't seem too depressed. 'Never mind, it is not worrying.'

'You realize I'd look very stupid if the Dubai customs officers found a sex doll in my suitcase and inflated it in the baggage hall in front of two hundred people. Suppose it had broken free and floated slowly over the rooftops of Dubai?'

Walid sat back and giggled, and I pointed a finger at him in mock severity. 'Walid, I'd have blamed you. You'd only have been deported back to Pakistan, but I'd have gone to jail for months in a deafening scandal.'

His giggling turned into open-mouthed glee.

'A *really* deafening scandal, Walid. Is the sex situation really so desperate?'

'Deafeningly desperate.' He laughed, slopping tea. 'Some Korean chap told me about these dolls. Did you know that you can even wash them?' He repeated bleakly, 'Desperate I am saying. You know, I've been back to Pakistan only once in two years, and there's no sex for people like me here. The prosses have all gone.'

'Prosses?'

'Prostitutes – girls and women, mostly from India. The Dubai government sent them off home, so now there are only the air hostesses.' His eyes had a dreamy look. 'Very love-lee. Their boom-booms are very lovelee.'

'Boom-booms?'

He made pyramid shapes with both sets of fingers and clamped them to his chest. 'Very lovel-ee and shape-lee.'

'Well?'

Walid shook his head mournfully. 'They go only with the hotel's front-office managers and assistant managers, who have more money. Of course, there are also the Filip-ino girls working in hotels here.'

'*They* sound promising.'

'They all make jigajig with Arabs for money. We are not being able to pay them on our salaries. Some male Filipinos also make jigajig.'

No wonder he wanted a doll.

'I'll tell you something very privately. Twice in two years – only twice – a Filipino kid called Dave in Food and Bev was obliging me—'

'Food and Bev?'

'The food and beverage department of the hotel. And once a Filipino in the night telephone staff – on a friendly basis.'

'Well, he can't have been exactly hostile.'

'I mean not for money. Only twice in all that time. Not much, is it? I prefer fucking girls to boys, as you know, but some Filipinos, nice kids, are being more free in their conduct. They are going to parties with Arabs on their days off. Dave from Food and Bev has a big mountain of hi-fi stuff from his Arab friends.'

'Watch out, Walid,' I teased. 'When I visit your house

in Pakistan, I'll point to the stack of hi-fi equipment you've got there and denounce you to General Zia. He'll chop off your hands – at the very least your hands.'

'You'll not be finding the smallest transistor radio there,' Walid protested. He began to laugh again. 'I'll tell you another thing. Jackie from the night switchboard had to go to hospital last month with six stitches in his what-you-call – his anus. Five Arabs damaged him like that.'

'Five?'

'He couldn't sit for a week.'

Walid's laughter rocked him back and forth in his chair. 'Luckily he was not taking phone calls at the time. Perhaps only incoming and trunk calls, you might say!' I saluted the joke by raising my teacup. 'Don't look so shocked,' Walid spluttered. 'Jackie is fine again now.'

'And you, Walid?'

'Well, there's always HP.'

'What's HP?'

'Hand practice, as we call it here. Masturbation. Not very often. I'm saving up for marriage in three years' time.'

'Unless you can get your hands on that doll.'

Whether or not he was conscious of it from minute to minute, Walid's every waking moment was part of a war to keep his head above the stagnant surface of a dead-end life, to avoid drowning in a Sargasso Sea of faceless, penurious humanity. This struggle to keep alive the hope of enjoying a mere shadow of the affluent life European workers are blessed with – and find inadequate – was not something he could ever resign from. If only the peoples of America and Europe, and those of Africa, Asia and Latin

America could change places for a week – for a single day! But would it do any good?

'Any more British airline pilots come your way?' I asked, referring to a surprising story he'd told me in Rawalpindi.

'No more. And to show you I'm not interested like that any more,' he continued sententiously, 'I'll tell you this story. The other night I was standing in the hotel with my Pakistani boss on duty at 1.00 a.m. and an old businessman – a German, I think – came up and gave us each fifty dirhams [about six pounds sterling] and just said to me, "Come up to my room in fifteen minutes." '

'Did you go?'

'Certainly I did not go. But imagine it. My boss said, "But we've taken the gentleman's money. You really ought to go." '

'An honest boss you've got there.'

'I didn't go, and the businessman checked out the next morning.'

'Minus a hundred dirhams chargeable to expenses.'

'I didn't feel badly about taking his money because he had been in the hotel before and never left any tips.'

'Serve him right, then.'

Walid and all the other immigrant workers in the Gulf needed any tips they could get. His father, who for thirty-six years had been a senior supervisor in a machine shop – 'in charge of it, you might say,' he had told me – had recently retired. According to Walid, his provident fund and other monies would bring him about two thousand pounds a year in all. Later, for some reason I couldn't grasp, there would be another twenty pounds a month. 'And he will go on working,' said Walid. 'Maybe he will open a poultry farm, or a tractor business. We have fields, but we can't depend on them.'

The talk of the tractor business sounded ambitiously unreal to me. I had seen the family home; the 'fields' were indeed undependable – 'unworkable' seemed more accurate. Still, to help out, Walid was sending home a hundred pounds a month out of the one hundred and fifty he earned at the hotel.

'I earn a little from part-time jobs, too – say, forty pounds a month. But I have to spend much money when my sisters get married.' Weddings are a great burden for Asian families. 'And on gifts for the family every time I go home.' Yet he earns double what he earned in Pakistan.

Before going off to his hotel shift, Walid had a question to ask about Eldorado. 'In London, it's easy to fuck? I hear girls do it in parks and streets and discos – everywhere.'

'Well,' I said, 'practically everywhere, but usually in bed.'

Walid looked intent. 'How many times? Once a day? Two or three times?'

'Walid,' I said, 'first get there, then make your own arrangements. And meanwhile lay off the HP.' I heard his gurgle of laughter going down the corridor. If he ever reached London, I reflected, he would certainly find it easier to get into bed than into work.

By the time I reached Singapore there was a letter waiting for me from Walid. A beautiful English girl was staying at the hotel, he said; they had made friends, and might even be in love; he was trying to persuade her to stay another month. He hoped I was fine and that my sea trip was going well. Well, he's happy now, I thought, but he added a PS: 'Dave in Food and Bev says you can buy sex dolls in Manila. Don't forget!'

★ ★ ★

Chris Pooley reported a delay. The acid-carrying tanker that might have taken me on to Karwar was sinking at its moorings, or so it seemed; at any rate, it was certainly not sailing to India in the foreseeable future. Indefatigably, Pooley continued to telephone his contacts, including the British firm, Gray Mackenzie, the commanding position of whose offices at the very lip of the entrance to the creek proclaimed its seniority in Gulf shipping circles.

I went to the office at the mouth of the creek and saw Jay Walton, Gray Mackenzie's shipping manager. He said they might find a place for me in a week or so aboard a small vessel called *Bacat 2*; he would telex Bombay for Indian permission to put me aboard as a supernumerary. Then he took me to lunch with one of the company's experienced captains, David Maudsley, master of a small tanker, the *Arrisha*. With a crew of twelve Iranians and two Bangladeshis, he regularly passed through the Strait of Hormuz just north of Dubai on his way to Muscat, carrying oil and jet fuel.

Maudsley was a quiet, dry-voiced man, the sort of man you wouldn't mind sailing with in a highly flammable tanker. Not the sort to irritate a militant Muslim or anyone else. 'I don't mind Iranians,' he said. 'These Iranians are not Khomeiniites. Even if they were, you can't let prayer interfere with sailing a ship – anyone can see that – however fanatical they are.'

It was the time of great Western fears that oil supplies might be cut off by a blocking of the Strait of Hormuz, but Maudsley didn't think it would happen. 'You could block the inner passage; it's five miles wide. But I doubt if you could bottle up the outer passage, which is twenty to thirty miles wide.'

Maudsley said bluntly that, though British seamen probably weren't any less good at sea than others, and perhaps just as good, they certainly could be a liability ashore, delaying the ship. This was the downfall of British seamen. 'My last deep-sea job,' he said, 'we had British and Portuguese seamen. Terrible trouble we had with the Brits – knifings, fights, arrests. It's always been unusual to have *no* trouble with British seamen. You have to have someone standing at the top of the gangway when they come back on board, taking bottles off them. We'd have to go around all the brothels to rout them out, and they'd be hiding under the beds and I don't know what else. Of course, the Scawegians [Scandinavians] can be the wildest cowboys, but the Brits always seem to find the lowest dives possible. The British seaman has always had a reputation ashore.'

Maudsley also told me that his day cabin had an artificial fireplace. It reminded him of his home in the cold north of England.

Apart from the *Bacat 2*, the American Tycoon Lines seemed to offer hope. (I have changed the name somewhat; the line's agent seemed a muddler to me, but it's possible I misjudged him.) The line's container fleet had spacious passenger accommodation and a reputation for comfort. It was hard, however, to get passage on them and, because they were cargo vessels first and passenger handlers second, they were subject to delays in loading and unloading. A strike in Bombay, for instance, had delayed the line's *Samuel Goldwyn* in Dubai, and she didn't know where to go next; at least this was what her agent seemed to convey. But the situation remained confused even when news of the end of the strike in Bombay came through. Apparently the *Samuel Goldwyn* was destined for Cochin in southern India and was carrying her full complement of passengers – or else they'd been put ashore and repaid their full fares; the truth was elusive. In any case, another idea had come into my head.

After a week in Dubai I was sitting alone at the bar of the International Seamen's Club, sipping a beer and wondering which film to kill time with. The list was not long: *Scream and Die*, *Sexy Merilla*, *Madhirikkunnha Raathri* (a Tamil comedy with music), and a love drama in Pushtu.

I decided against all of them and in favour of another beer, even at the expense of watching the Keralan barman plucking his eyebrows over a bowl of chips and hearing him croon, '. . . Only trouble is, Gee whizz, I'm dreaming my life away.'

Soon a friendly Englishman hoisted himself on the next barstool. He was, he said, Captain Bill Nelson; he had worked in Dubai for some years, and supervised shipping in the creek and the dhow harbour at Hamriyyah, a little way up the coast. 'Surely, you shouldn't bother with ordinary freighters and such,' he said. 'It's the dhows and native motor launches crossing to Karachi and Bombay that would interest you more.'

Of course. Next day I accompanied Bill Nelson on his daily tour of native shipping. He drove his yellow Mazda while his clerk jotted down the tally of vessels in harbour: tugs, dredgers, every ship from Dubai to Hamriyyah.

Hamriyyah is a small harbour full each day with motorized dhows loading and bound for Iran, Aden or India, and with Pakistani 'launches', which could be transformed into sailing vessels simply by raising canvas.

Coolies ran up planks with bales and crates, timber from

Malaysia and milled American rice. Water buffaloes were winched up from fetid holds and dumped, eyeballs rolling, on the quay.

'This is the place to find something, mark my words,' said Nelson. 'Meet my man here, Majid.'

And so I met my saviour. Even so, I still had several days to wait – Majid couldn't work miracles – and I had *Bacat 2* as a fallback.

I sat in Chris Pooley's office and thumbed my way through the 'Casualties' page of *Lloyd's List* of shipping. The alarming entries made one realize how much of an illusion the bland surface of the shipping world really is:

London. Vessel *Sheng Hsing*, 125 tons gross, built 1973. Last message received 1700, Sept. 29. No further information since then. Left Keelung with 11 crew. At present north-east monsoon blowing with strong winds and heavy seas in this area . . .

Overdue Vessel, *m.v. Myrina*: US Coast Guard, New York, advised the *Myrina* overdue on a voyage from New York to Naples . . . All ships to maintain lookout . . . US Forces, Azores, briefed . . . Three aircraft . . . Assumption is that the *Myrina* had broken up and sunk . . .

Port Louis, Mauritius. The sole survivor of the *Induna* has reached Mauritius, from where he will fly to South Africa for the inquest into the fate of the vessel . . .

Supply vessel *Keith Rhea* sank in the Gulf of Mexico due to striking an oil rig during heavy weather.

A fire had badly damaged the historic yacht of Kemal Ataturk. The *Savarona*, which was anchored off the Princess

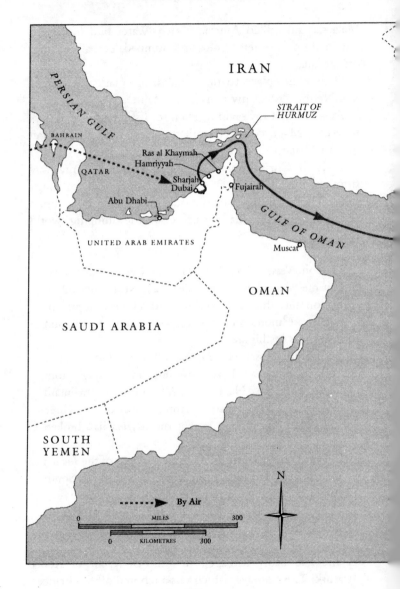

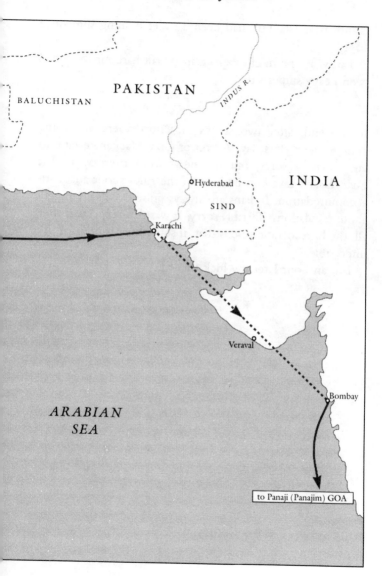

Islands near Istanbul, had been a cadet training ship since 1951.

Lastly, as one might expect, in Beirut harbour there had been heavy sniper fire.

In the end, after two weeks in Dubai, there was some definite news. First Jay Walton of Gray Mackenzie rang to say, 'Terribly sorry, but the news from Bombay is that *Bacat 2* can't take you because of the rules about adequate accommodation. Indians are always quite needlessly niggly about regulations. Terribly sorry.' It wasn't unexpected: after all, the bureaucratic rule is that, if something is unusual, it's impossible.

But an hour later my luck turned.

Part Two

DUBAI TO SINGAPORE

Chapter Fourteen

THAT MORNING IN Hamriyyah Majid said, 'A dhow, the *Khalid*, will sail for Karachi today at one o'clock from Sharjah. A passenger dhow. The agent is Chishty Trading; you find the office on the creek there.'

I found the dhow, the *Khalid*, heavily laden with crates, a truck, two or three small cars and about thirty passengers perched on the cargo like egrets on a water buffalo's back. She was a hefty vessel with a big, steep, square stern. 'We sail at three thirty or four thirty,' a moustached *nakhoda* (captain) said.

In the agent's office all was agreed. All I had to do, it seemed, was to return to Dubai to pick up my bags and my passport, a matter of an hour. But when I returned to the Sharjah wharf I found an empty space where the *Khalid* had been. 'She sailed,' some men on the dockside said.

The exasperation of that moment comes back to me in full force even now. The Muslim Id, or holiday, was about to paralyse the region. Every office would be closed tight as an oyster for five days – longer in Dubai, where there was a local closure as well (the ruler's uncle had died). No customs man would operate, no passports would be stamped, no dhows would sail. The *Khalid* was likely the last boat for a week.

In the Chishty Trading Office, up the same narrow staircase, the fat, unsmiling agent, who passed me a card telling me his name was Siddiq, said he had no hope of any sailing before 7 or 9 November. More than a week – eleven days. It was now 27 October. All the sailors, he said, wanted to enjoy the holiday ashore, not waste it at sea.

With its wall calendars and inevitable colour photograph of the mosque at Mecca, the small office was hot and seemed a hopeless place. The agent looked at me without apparent emotion. 'No more passenger vessels,' he said firmly. I was rising from my chair, prepared for the miserable drive back to Dubai when, to my surprise, he said, 'Have some tea.' We drank it looking at each other in silence. I should be drinking tea on the *Khalid*'s deck on my way to the Strait of Hormuz, I thought. I took a sip and frowned at the teasing cargo price list over the agent's desk: 'From Sharjah to Lahore and Karachi – Motor Car dirhams 1000; Motor Cycle dirhams 125; Fridge 60; Gas Cooker 40; Sewing Machine 20.' Passenger?

I took another sip, and it came to me. It might have come earlier if I hadn't been so stunned by the heat and the *Khalid* fiasco. The *Khalid* was the last passenger boat for ten days. What about—

'What about a cargo dhow?' An outside chance, admittedly. If passenger-boat crews liked to spend their big holiday of the year ashore, so presumably would cargo-dhow crews.

Mr Siddiq's eyelids seemed too heavy to keep ajar as he murmured, 'They cannot take a single passenger without a big payment. That payment is three thousand rupees for the Karachi Port Authority. Cargo dhows have no special licence to take passengers.'

I brooded: 3000 rupees was about £150. A lot of money, but Karachi was a long way off.

'Perhaps I can get a letter from the Pakistani consul general in Dubai to Karachi – a permit to travel on a cargo dhow.'

The agent blinked. 'You know the consul?' His interest, I saw, had quickened fractionally. After a pause he said in a louder tone, 'If you can get a letter from him, I could possibly get you on a cargo launch tomorrow or the next day.'

'Sure?'

'Sure.' He even gave a flicker of a smile.

I wasted no time in asking where this vessel had suddenly materialized from; I was already on my feet. 'Don't worry.'

Mr Siddiq said, 'Go to the consulate at nine and I'll join you there.'

Colonel Shufaat Hasan Khan, consul general of Pakistan in Dubai (may his shadow never grow less), sat upright in his office chair looking very military with his parade-ground alertness and black moustache, let alone the English accents of a gentleman from Sandhurst.

I had told him my story and made my request, and we now awaited Mr Siddiq. There was no sign of him. The colonel had sent an aide to search for him in other offices in the consulate, but Mr Siddiq was elusive. I told myself bitterly that I might have expected him not to turn up, and my unease returned. The colonel, however, wasted no time. In a few minutes he had a visa stamped into my passport – although, strictly speaking, I didn't need one – 'For safety's sake in Karachi,' he said. He even dictated a telex message to the Karachi port authorities to expect a European to arrive on the launch *Al Raza* (I had ascertained the name from Mr Siddiq) some time within the next seven days, and asked them not to arrest me.

'If there are any hitches, let me know. Call me.' He added, 'I'm lunching with a very big Dubai trader, but never mind that. Call me at home if you need to.'

'You're a very kind man, Colonel.'

'Not at all, not at all.'

Then I telephoned Mr Siddiq. He seemed to have forgotten any idea of coming to the consulate, but was surprised and impressed by the colonel's prompt assistance. 'Be here at four thirty,' he said. 'Sailing at six o'clock.'

At four thirty I handed up my bags from the wharf to a dusky seaman, who lugged them to the wheelhouse high up over *Al Raza*'s stern. 'Don't sail without me,' I said. 'No worry,' he called back. I saw a blue-painted bridge balustraded off from a main deck cluttered with bales, crates, refrigerators and four or five minicars.

In his office Mr Siddiq raised gratified eyebrows over the consul's note and visa. I handed him the money, and he grunted his thanks and gave me a receipt: 'Received Dollars 300/- From Mr. Diavan David Young.' 'Food', he said, 'is provided. Rice, chapatis, tea. No bedding because this cargo boat not for passengers. Crew all Baluchis.'

In the little bazaar of Sharjah I bought a torch, a towel and some soap. I knew there'd be something to sleep on. Like their houses, Asians' boats are always provided with spare mattresses and blankets or, if not mattresses, woven mats. I wondered if this was the moment to dig the money belt out of my metal suitcase and use it for the first time, but somehow I knew I needn't bother. Traveller's cheques were locked behind the combination of the metal suitcase. In the zip-bag, the cameras, binoculars, the bottle of Gordon's gin and the much smaller one of angostura bitters, all that would be Wanted on Voyage, would be easily accessible. I didn't believe Asian sailors would steal on a small boat like this.

There was a delay and it was dark before we sailed. I heaved myself on board. Through the shadows cast by one bright mast light and the illuminations from the wheelhouse, I scrambled across bales and crates and swung myself up over the balustrade on to the bridge. The nakhoda was on the strip of deck by the wheelhouse, and warmly shook my hand: a short, fairly young man in a knee-length grey Pakistani shirt and white cotton pyjama trousers. He led me into the wheelhouse as big as a chicken coop and said, 'You sleep' – miming sleep, he put his palms together on his right cheek and bent his head to that side, closing his eyes – 'here!'

Someone, I saw, had roped a tiny table and chair to the corner of the bridge overlooking the sea and the main deck forward. 'For you,' the nakhoda said, making energetic writing motions with his right hand. On a raised bunk running the width of the wheelhouse just behind the helmsman, blankets and a pillow in a plastic cover lay in a heap on a thin mattress. I protested to the nakhoda; obviously, he had given me his own bunk. 'No, no, for you,' he said with finality, and I knew that protesting was futile. You can't argue with a Baluchi demonstrating hospitality; they are among the most stubborn peoples of the world. In my distant days as a shipping clerk in Basra, which at the north end of the Gulf seemed quite close now, Baluchis had been much prized as watchmen, as much for their stolid honesty and unshakable devotion to whoever employed them as for their physical toughness.

We sailed much later, at about ten thirty; new cargo was constantly appearing. At last the nakhoda called over the

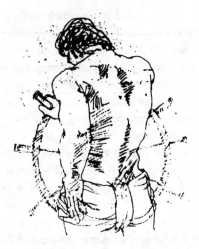

balustrade: '*Hather?*' From the semi-darkness among the cars and bales, voices replied, '*Hather*. Ready.' He turned to me. 'Okay?' '*Yalla, meshena!* Let's go!' I saw the crew casting off fore and aft, and the engines spluttered into life. A massive man in a turban paused to blow his nose in his fingers over the side, and then squeezed into the wheelhouse to take the helm. In the light thrown up from the binnacle I saw a thick nose and a heavy moustache.

Al Raza began to edge away from the quay. Soon we were in the middle of the creek, turning towards the sea, then moving smoothly down the creek, and slowly and gently rolling as we entered the relatively open waters of the Gulf. I sat at the table the nakhoda had taken the trouble to have lashed to the front corner of the bridge, and felt the excitement now; this was a small ramshackle launch and I would be closer to the sea, literally and figuratively, than on any earlier ship; even on the *Pacific Basset*, its heavy steel and technological equipment got in the way.

From the bridge, I could see that *Al Raza* was not a thing of beauty. About sixty feet long, she was certainly not the classic dhow with high, carved medieval stern, thick slanting masts and billowing sails, running down to Zanzibar. Locally she was called a launch, pronounced 'larnch'; she was decidedly stubby, and her single mast was more like a twig than a tree and carried no sails. Yes, *Al Raza* lacked glamour. She was a working launch of 100 tons and looked it. A thin tin tube amidships was her funnel, and she had a crew of eight, including the nakhoda, all of them Baluchis except for the 'driver', who was Indian-born, and one elderly Iranian. Her home port was Karachi; her maximum speed was ten knots with luck, but more likely four or five.

A light swell cradled us. A large half-moon dominated half the sky overhead, and Orion lay above us on his side, his belt perpendicular to the sea. Over the jagged mountains of Ajman and Ras al Khaymah, lightning flashes lit up a kidney-shaped cloud like a neon sign. Sharjah soon receded into a thin necklace of meaningless light.

Most of *Al Raza's* deck was in darkness. The wheelhouse was only faintly lit by the glow-worm light of the single small bulb in the binnacle. There was a strong light in the prow; another, less strong, astern of the wheelhouse roof, and a red navigation light on the corner of the wheelhouse roof over my head, matched by the starboard green on the other side. Occasional sparks flew out of the narrow funnel, arched languidly over the side and died before reaching the water.

Soon the nakhoda went to his mattress on the other side of the bridge deck, and the crew slipped below. I lay down on the bunk behind the muscular back of the helmsman, who paid no attention to me, put my torch on the mattress beside me, took a large swig of Gordon's, kicked off my shoes, lay back in great contentment and fell asleep instantly.

I was woken by silence: *Al Raza* had stopped. Everything was dark, but the luminous hands of my watch said 4.30 a.m. I got up quickly and, peering over the balustrade of the bridge, saw at once that the whole midsection of *Al Raza* was enveloped in a dense white haze. Smoke? I muttered to myself, 'God Almighty!' Fire at sea in a wooden boat? Torch beams flickered. The nakhoda and the rest of the crew were already scurrying about the overloaded deck, opening hatches, heaving aside heavy crates. The helmsman had deserted the wheelhouse, the engine was silent and every light had gone out. We rocked quietly in darkness except for gruff Baluchi cries from the deck, under silent stars. Looking around, I saw a few remote clusters of lights on the shore and a few nearer, unmoving, and denser clusters further out at sea: oil rigs. The smaller light of a fishing boat bobbed quite close ahead. Would we soon be taken aboard her to bear gloomy witness to the hulk of *Al Raza* burning to charcoal off the coast of Ajman? I saw myself back in the agent's office in Sharjah, hearing him murmuring glumly, 'Now you'll have to wait ten days, until after the Id' – that is, if he himself had not already closed down and disappeared for the holiday.

It was not smoke; after a while I realized that, if it had been, the crew in the engine hatch would have keeled over, asphyxiated. It was steam, and slowly it grew less thick. After an hour it was barely noticeable, and the nakhoda seemed satisfied, so we moved on; we had drifted with our nose toward Dubai, and now the engine weakly pulsed into life and we swung round again to head toward the Strait of Hormuz, the narrow gullet leading from the ocean into the belly of the Gulf. *Al Raza* remained in darkness; we had no lights at all; the helmsman steered with a torch. 'Dynamo *kharban*,' he explained from the shadows, meaning, 'The dynamo's kaput.' He shrugged: never mind.

From my bunk I saw the helmsman's wide back, bulky in a gown with a sash around the waist. The wind had risen, and blew fresh and strong over the wooden windowsills of the wheelhouse. Once more I laid my feet on my suitcase and my head on the plastic pillow cover. I wondered sleepily what our fate would have been if the steam had indeed been smoke (the bridge boasted two rusty fire extinguishers, as effective as spitting into the flames if a fire took hold), then willed myself asleep again.

As usual, the situation looked better when a sunny morning broke. A crewman with grey hair and a long comedian's face brought me a plate with two fried eggs and a chapati on it, and a mug of hot milky tea.

We were moving into the Strait of Hormuz, a mountainous profile of the land to starboard. To port, a long white tanker bulldozed its way into the Gulf, and soon I spotted the *Arrisha* creeping towards us near the shore, heading back from Muscat. I thought of the mock fireplace in the captain's dayroom and tried to see Captain Maudsley through my glasses, but the little tanker with 'GM' on her funnel was too far away. As she faded, steam billowed up again from *Al Raza*'s engine-room hatches and we stopped and rolled again for fifteen minutes, while our dark-skinned driver, with a towel round his head, hammered metal and manipulated screwdrivers and spanners.

A good breeze cooled us as *Al Raza* passed the two little

wedge-shaped Quoin Islands, and a number of large vessels moved westwards into the shallow waters of the Gulf. Anyone who wanted to block this opening by sinking a tanker here certainly had a problem. The strait is far wider than it looks on the chart.

To starboard the islands and coast of Oman fell sheer into deep water. The sun revealed deep fissures and caves in some; smoother ones were grey and wrinkled like the hide of an ancient elephant. In the lee of one such island, a small sailing dhow was anchored in the shade, as if in ambush. Our helmsman spun the wheel, we veered towards it and soon came alongside. Without delay a man and a boy in shorts hoisted up a basket of fish, long and pike-like or fat and brown; in exchange, someone from *Al Raza* handed down a can of what looked like engine oil. Everyone waved and grinned and we moved on down the strait. It was obviously a harmless and routine bit of barter. A glance into the 'galley' – a primus stove and a primitive open metal oven set on the strip of deck in the stern near where the 'thunderbox' hung over the side – revealed rice, strips of dried fish, eggs, a few vegetables and tea. The fish flapping on the deck looked like emergency rations.

Just as well, for we might, I thought, be considerably longer than four days at sea. Every two or three hours steam poured up out of the engine hatch, where a 380 h.p. Japanese motor seemed to be in the throes of irreversible senility. Whenever the steam erupted, the lanky driver switched off the engine and renewed his hammering while *Al Raza* rocked and dipped. I opened a book.

The nakhoda grinned at me: '*Shweya, shweya, insh' Allah,*' conveying, 'It will be all right.' As well as their native Baluchi, the crew spoke Urdu – all Pakistani citizens do –

and certain phrases of Hindi, Arabic and Persian. This meant we were going to have to communicate in broken Arabic; mine was basic, and rather better than theirs, but we would manage. My memory now is that we chatted away as if we had at least two languages in common. Somehow we communicated quite adequately and became friends.

Presently I understood that, after the dynamo, the starter motor was also kaput: perhaps you couldn't have one without the other. A bulky Baluchi with black muttonchop whiskers and baggy trousers explained this with signs and bits of Arabic, and there was a certain embarrassed air around the wheelhouse. '*Allah karim* – Karachi!' the helmsman proclaimed, sticking out his chest reassuringly, and I agreed, wanly hopeful that God would see us safe and sound in Karachi.

What followed, in the engineering sphere, was beyond me. The crew set on our cargo of cars like bulldogs baiting bears; they ripped wires loose and ran them into *Al Raza*'s engine, and the car engines were revved, then revved again. Evidently the driver had forgotten that we might need some engine spares – dynamos, for example. We slid on through oil slicks that smoothed the sea into a flat, glittering sheet of purple, yellow, green and blue like brocade. Dead sea snakes, ivory-coloured bellies uppermost, floated on the surface. The coast of Oman to the west slowly disappeared; in the evening it was replaced to the east by smudges of Iran.

In one of *Al Raza*'s motionless interludes I tried out the thunderbox. It was suspended over the sea but felt reassuringly solid when I clambered over the stern rail and down into a thick wood box. It was open to the sky and had walls some three feet high. The hole was a wide pear shape, with two raised footrests on either side. In the sea below, swarms of small jellyfish floated near the surface. Muslim sailors never use toilet paper. A tin can on a long cord stood by the footrests to be swung down into the sea and had to be hauled up carefully, or else all the water would slop out before it reached the thunderbox. The only tricky aspect of the arrangement was the possibility of your foot slipping as you climbed out of it in rough weather. What you had to do was to keep a firm grasp on the wooden stern rail.

The weather held. I thought of *Al Raza* caught powerless in a storm. That night, dark continents of angry clouds formed in the sky, but there were plenty of stars between each continent. In the sea off the Iranian coast an unexpected and mysterious fragrance drifted across the water, not unlike the scented breezes off the lush tropical islands of Borneo and Celebes. Yet the Iranian coast is a bleak desert region. Gleaming blobs of phosphorescence streamed past *Al Raza*'s low rail like reflected stars winking in spun sugar. I noticed that the nakhoda kept an eye on the Iranian shore because we had no charts or radio, much less radar. Now and then he borrowed my glasses as the helmsman changed course at the heavy wooden wheel behind the brass compass housing.

The compass's little light had returned, but for some reason other lights were less reliable. Our navigation lights came on and went off mysteriously so that the crated air-conditioning units, washing machines and sacks of cotton piece goods heaped on the deck were either looming up in a half-green, half-red glow or receding into blackness.

During the day I began to take Polaroid pictures of the

crew. They posed together and singly, always demanding just one more. Even the nakhoda joined in. We had been getting on well in a shy, tentative fashion, but the Polaroid broke the ice once and for all. I began to know them as individuals.

The nakhoda was a quiet, stocky man who had been on this run several times. He was shy, but seemed glad to have me on board. He was baffled by *Al Raza*'s half-cocked engine, and depended as much as everyone else on the driver, Hasan, the thin Pakistani of Indian birth who spent most of his time streaked with oil in the boiling depths of the machinery for which he had been denied adequate spares – or which he had neglected to buy through an excess of Islamic fatalism.

Hasan's two assistants, Shapur and Osman the Iranian, were respectively young and wild-eyed, and elderly and impassive. Shapur was given to loud, impulsive, cheerful cries in my direction, while Osman did no more between Sharjah and Karachi than gravely incline his head and say, '*Zen*,' the Iraqi for 'good'.

Sumar was the big, bulging, huffing-puffing bear of a man with the muttonchop whiskers – big, happy whiskers he fluffed out proudly, booming, 'Ha, haaaaa! Arabs say these are Israeli whiskers! I am Israeli!' He invariably wore the baggy Baluchi trousers and knee-length shirt. To counter any new setback with the engine, he would point his forefinger to the heavens, roll his big eyes up until they almost disappeared into his thick Groucho Marx eyebrows, and slowly intone in sonorous Arabic, 'God will see we reach Karachi. Oooh, yes.' After which he would roar with laughter and pump my hand energetically.

That left three: Lal Mohamed, Mir Mohamed and

Khalat. Khalat was the youngest, about twenty, a dusky sprite who brought me a plate of rice from Mir Mohamed's 'galley' now and again and, when I said I wouldn't eat before they did, replied, 'Baluchi peoples eat finish' – which demonstrated the level of his English and meant, 'That's all right. We've eaten already.'

Lal Mohamed was twice Khalat's size, a thick slab of muscle who looked as though he might have been carved out of a single piece of mahogany. He was built like those Olympic Games wrestlers traditionally bred in such surprising numbers in Turkey, Iran and Baluchistan, and I believe he could have been one if he had chosen to be. He looked as if he could break a man's neck with a flick of his fingers, though not like someone who would ever want to. I guessed he was in his mid-twenties.

Finally, Mir Mohamed, the cook. Every barrack room and ship in the world has a clown like Mir Mohamed – sly, canny, harmlessly dishonest ('fly' is the army word), the disreputable butt of everyone's practical jokes. He could fry an egg, cook rice, make curry, gut fish, and no one asked him to do more.

With the exception of Khalat, Mir Mohamed and Lal Mohamed, the crew were practising Muslims, or, at least, praying ones. But there were no religious fanatics aboard *Al Raza*. 'Ha!' Sumar yelled at Khalat and Mir Mohamed for my benefit. 'You infidels don't know the meaning of "*Allahu akbar*"!' But he was only laughing at close friends.

In any case, Islam didn't stop some of them, including the nakhoda, from chewing the mildly intoxicating leaf drug they call *mushok* in Baluchi – all except Khalat and Hasan, the driver. When I asked Khalat what effect mushok had on him, he laughed and made circles near his temple with a forefinger to denote tipsiness. Mir Mohamed, the clown cook, and big Lal preferred gin.

Another day went by. In Dubai the holiday period of the Id had begun, and we were suddenly alone on the Arabian Sea; all the dhows that regularly plied this route remained tied up in port, their crews ashore celebrating. Now we had a new crisis; the clouds of steam issuing periodically from the engine suddenly turned to black and oily smoke, which rose out of the engine hatch like an evil genie from a bottle. The sight of it was frightening, the smell of it appalling.

The nakhoda rallied his men with urgent cries and they began to wrench feverishly at the crates in the bows, revealing a small, buckled, coffin-shaped bathtub of flimsy metal; this was our lifeboat, the only one. I climbed down to lend a hand, but the scrimmage was so hectic – it was particularly dangerous to approach the bull-like Lal Mohamed's flying elbows and knees – that I retired to my wheelhouse perch. The nakhoda shouted to Shapur at the helm and *Al Raza* swung off course, aiming for the bleak cliffs of Iran. The smoke was pouring out so heavily that any onlooker would surely have thought we were on fire. I worried about the driver. I could see his frantic silhouette in the stinking black fog, coughing and swearing, and was afraid he would be suffocated by the fumes.

Al Raza limped shorewards, trailing a black scarf of pollution like a mourner at a funeral. A school of dolphins came alongside, lazily leaping and diving. Perhaps, I thought, they are curious to know what will happen to us. Perhaps they will wait and carry us ashore when *Al Raza* finally goes down; after all, the Romans told stories of drowning seamen rescued by dolphins.

The driver emerged from the smoke with a coil of rope, and Sumar tied a lump of lead to it and swung it over the side, testing the depth. It was too deep, and we puttered on for half an hour before the anchor went down. *Al Raza*'s engine expired with a sigh, and she lay smoking and motionless on the abandoned sea.

Hasan wasted no time. He plunged back into the engine room, hammering and shouting. Under his orders, Shapur and Khalat threw open the hoods of the cars on deck and began detaching collars, pipes, a radiator, wires and batteries. The nakhoda came up to me, looking hot but unflustered. He said, 'We stop here maybe two hours. Then go . . .' He pointed vaguely towards Iran, or did he mean Pakistan? I wondered if we were going to end up engineless, foodless and waterless on some remote beach in the wild west of Ayatollah Khomeini's Iran.

As I took a discreet nip of gin behind the wheelhouse, the hoarse voice of Mir Mohamed murmured at my elbow, 'A little for me?' I poured him a couple of fingers, and he gave me a sly grin and a wink before going back to chop fish in his 'galley'. After a while I heard him singing a lugubrious Baluchi lament.

The dolphins had disappeared; I hoped they were lingering somewhere within earshot. To pass the time I opened *Decision at Delphi* and immediately found Helen MacInnes's Greek Special Branch man musing on Westerners: 'Totally incomprehensible . . . living as they did in a child's world of indulgence and pleasure, out of touch with reality. Did they really believe that life owed them happiness?' It was not a belief that touched people east of Delphi – certainly not these Baluchis straining and sweating, their chests and backs naked, their cotton trousers sticking to them like cellophane.

The Iranian coast reared up in shapes like organ pipes and castle turrets. Sometimes there were grotesque protuberances in the skyline that could have been fortified Sassanian towns or Babylonian terraces, and shafts like the first New York skyscrapers. But my binoculars told me that these shapes were illusions in weathered sandstone, and that there was nothing on this coast but drought and death.

Chapter Fifteen

AFTER THREE HOURS Lal Mohamed, the bull-like wrestler, and young Khalat heaved up *Al Raza*'s anchor, and with a splutter or two the old launch cleared its throat and chugged on again. God knows what repairs had been carried out while we were at anchor, but they had been extensive: pipes and other bits and pieces cannibalized from the cars on deck had been sawn in half (one hacksaw snapped in Shapur's hand), or hammered into shapes to fit the Japanese engine. The lean driver, Hasan, sat on the engine hatch with his helpers and drooped with fatigue. Poor man, he had little chance to rest on this voyage.

As soon as *Al Raza* moved on, oily smoke belched out of the inadequate funnel, thicker, if possible, than before. 'Damn,' I said to myself, and heard Mir Mohamed tut-tutting behind me. This time the smoke was so heavy with oil that the breeze could hardly lift it clear of the vessel before its black coils slumped down on the waves like an undulating black sausage.

We continued to move forward through that perfect sea, but I knew it couldn't last. I wasn't sure what was causing the smoke – the last thing I am is an engineer – but surely, if it was a question of overheating, wouldn't there be a fire sooner or later? Sooner, to judge by the solid density of the smoke.

I clambered over the balustrade and across the bales and crates to where the driver and the nakhoda sat in dismal palaver near the engine housing, the black opaqueness of the smoke coil overhead throwing them into deep shadow.

I, an ignorant passenger, didn't want to risk irritating them by interfering, so I said cautiously, 'Why not try going slower? Half-speed. Reduce heat.'

They both looked at me passively, not irritated, and then the driver slowly swung his legs over the edge of the hatch and dropped down into the choking heat and fumes of the engine. The rhythmic thumping moderated and *Al Raza* slackened speed. At the same time, the sun burst down on us and the long, deep shadow overhead began to fade; the colour and density of the smoke was returning to normal. Spluttering, the driver reappeared, wiping his sweat- and oil-streaked face with a dirty rag, and the three of us sat on a soft bale of cotton clothing labelled 'Abu Dhabi to Kabul'. (I never discovered why Abu Dhabi should be exporting clothes to Afghanistan via Karachi.) The nakhoda called out, 'Khalatu! Bring tea,' then turned to me and said, 'Like this to Karachi three days. If the engine works. The engine', he added in a dreary voice, 'is tired.'

'You're telling me,' I said in English, and added in Arabic, 'That I see.' I could also see that even this self-composed and experienced seaman was uneasy.

Then the nakhoda unveiled a plan. 'Tomorrow night we should get our first sight of the Pakistan coast, the coast of Baluchistan. We'll stop at a small port there. Get a new, good launch, and tow this one to Karachi. 'Or,' he went on, tapping my arm, 'from that small port we will fly. To Karachi. Pakistan Airways.'

'Who will fly?'

He pointed to himself and then to me. '*We* fly, and send a launch from Karachi to tow this one.'

Fly? The idea astonished me. Could we even make that small port? We had no chart on board, so I couldn't see

where it was in relation to us, to Karachi or anywhere else.

The nakhoda was smiling and pointed to the heavens; God will help us, he was telling me. Tea arrived with Khalat, who handed us each a mug, took one himself, squatted down with us and murmured sententiously (I knew from Sumar's remarks that he considered himself a nonbeliever), '*Insh' Allah*.' If God wills. He began to crack his knuckles with an abstracted air.

I had no desire to fly from Baluchistan to Karachi; I wanted to stay with *Al Raza* – at least until she actually began to sink. I can see us now: Hasan streaked with oil and silently cursing his moribund engine, the nakhoda lost in dreams of finding a small port with an airstrip, Khalat and I drearily sipping tea. Lounging in the sun on a sack of men's shirts and women's bloomers destined for Kabul, we made a dismal little group.

That night we had no electricity, or next to none. I awoke in the dead of night to see the navigation lights of two small boats to port: fishing boats from Iran, which meant that some scattered life existed on that awesomely barren coast. I slept again, and woke up two hours later to find the same lights in the same position on our port bow. Then I saw that our helmsman, the old Iranian, Osman, was bent so low over the pathetically dim compass light that he must be either losing his sight or nodding off to sleep. Every now and then he straightened up with a jerk and frantically began spinning the wheel like a demented croupier, first one way and then the other – far over to port and immediately afterwards all the way over to starboard. Through the wheelhouse windows Orion arched wildly through the sky into sight, then suddenly out of it as we tacked back and forth. Our wake had become a series of S-bends. I could hear the voice of Peter Barton of the *Pacific Basset* demanding, 'What's he bloody doing, then? Writing his fucking signature?'

I didn't feel I could put the question to Osman, and was relieved when Khalat came up from the dark bunk area below the wheelhouse. He peered at the compass and said something to the old man. The veering lessened and I lay down again on the red and yellow mattress. Khalat wrapped a white cloth around his head and went outside to sit with his back against the front of the wheelhouse, his knees drawn up under his knee-length gown, his feet on the balustrade. It was cold, but he was going to stay on the bridge. The two men talked in low voices through the open wheelhouse window while *Al Raza* sputtered on through the night slowly, feebly and without lights.

I pulled my blanket up to my chin and the low ebb of 2.30 a.m. took over my imagination, filling it with pictures of *Al Raza* in flames or helpless, her engine finally an inert mass of scrap, overwhelmed by gigantic waves. I thought morbidly of the 'Casualties' pages of the *Lloyd's List* I'd pored through in Chris Pooley's office in Dubai. I remembered the bulletins telling of the disappearance of the Greek motor vessel *Myrina* somewhere between New York and Naples: 'Assumption is that the *Myrina* had broken up or sunk . . . The US Coast Guard reports the search was negative, and therefore they are suspending further active search . . .'

The next day I took out my copy of *The Mirror of the Sea* and read what Conrad had to say about missing ships:

> The unholy fascination of dread dwells in the thought of the last moments of a ship reported as 'missing'. Nothing of her ever comes to light – no grating, no lifebuoy, no piece of boat or branded oar – to give a hint of the place and date of her sudden end. The *Shipping Gazette* does not even call her 'lost with all hands'. She remains simply 'missing'; she has disappeared enigmatically into a mystery of fate as big as the world . . .

I thought of our wooden hull and wooden wheelhouse, and of our dented tin bathtub of a lifeboat buried under a small mountain of heavy cases in the bows. The only other lifesaving possibility lay in a huddle of dirty, moth-eaten life jackets on the wheelhouse roof; what good they would be in shark- or barracuda-filled seas I wasn't sure. Some of the cargo might float – the crates, perhaps – but if the *Al Raza* was burning like a torch it was unlikely that the fire and inevitable (I supposed) explosions would spare anything as flammable as a wooden crate. We would disappear enigmatically . . .

'The word "missing" brings all hope to an end and settles the loss of the underwriters,' said Conrad with finality, and I put him back into my bag.

The next morning the smoke was back, pouring like black treacle from the funnel and in shimmering waves from the hatches. Once more the driver dropped down into the engine hatch, and the nakhoda and others busily siphoned petrol into jerry cans from all the cars but one. This they poured into the remaining car, whose engine had to be kept running. At least one battery was needed to illuminate the compass and one masthead light.

To port lay the savage Baluchi coast and a white line of surf. To distract everyone from gloom, I took still more Polaroid pictures, which never fail to steal attention. Mir Mohamed loped up winking and smirking, rolling his eyes towards the hidden gin bottle. Khalat, who wanted to be snapped at the wheel, hopped on to the helmsman's stool, squatting on it cross-legged, his thobe drawn up over hairy ankles and calves. 'You have jig-jig pictures?' he asked eagerly. Miming obscenely, he jabbed a forefinger into an orifice formed by his forefinger and thumb. No, I apologized, I had no pornographic pictures in my bags. 'General Zia ul-Haq says' – I drew my finger across my throat – 'forbidden! Death!' Khalat, his eyes fixed dutifully on the compass, sighed unhappily. 'Bhutto dead, Pakistan jig-jig dead,' he said. Whatever his virtues and failings, Zulfikar Ali Bhutto, the former president of Pakistan executed by General Zia, had certainly had nothing against jig-jig.

Portly and jolly, Sumar joined Khalat and myself on the bridge and posed for his picture, turbaned, arms folded, like a pirate chief. I learned from them that Khalat earned a salary of about fifty pounds a month and Sumar, who was older, a little more. The captain, Ghani Adam, and Hasan, the driver, got the equivalent of a hundred and twenty-five pounds, they said. *Al Raza*'s owner in Karachi paid for their food, and they also took a share of the value of the cargo.

Combing and perfuming with a green oil his whiskers that seemed to grow bushier each day, Sumar told me he had been a fisherman once, but for the last four years he had sailed as a seaman on dhows to Bombay, Dubai, Abu Dhabi, and all the way up the Gulf to the big ports of Kuwait and Basra.

'Are dhows often lost at sea in these waters?'

'Oooooooh, often,' said Sumar, waving his arms happily to indicate fatal storms. 'Big winds – phweee! Big waves – oooooow! They go over. Many, many. Oooh, yah.'

Just after noon, with *Al Raza* still belching smoke that again seemed too heavy to clear the gunwales before flopping wearily on to the water, we saw a distant smudge on the horizon behind us. The nakhoda looked through my glasses and said, 'Larnch.' It was a launch, all right, and at the rate we were limping it would easily overtake us before long. Immediately the crew broke into song. Above the chanting, the nakhoda shouted orders, and Lal Mohamed, the wrestler, and Shapur, the wild one, dragged a large piece of cloth from a locker under the wheelhouse. It was a huge red flag with a white border, big enough to cover a restaurant table for ten diners.

'It means we need help,' the nakhoda explained for my benefit, and soon they had hoisted it up the twig-like mainmast, lashed to a bamboo sheet that other crewmen excavated from under a crate of washing machines. The wind had dropped, so the flag hung limply, but later it would attract attention. I looked back and saw the plume of smoke on the horizon standing straight up like the tail of an angry cat.

'When that launch comes up with us,' said Sumar, bouncily optimistic, 'they must pull us. Nakhoda will say we have Engleezi on board, so they must give us a tow to Karachi because our engine is so tired. You show your English passport. Very important, oooooooh, yes. *Allah kareem!*' He pointed like a contemptuous tourist guide towards the coast. 'Look at that coast. Half Iran, half Pakistan.' So at last we were crossing the frontier. 'Before sometimes I go to fish in there.' Sumar frowned indignantly. 'But Irani militia there shoot at me – *tuk! tuk!*' He mimed a man firing a rifle. 'I go away quickly – Khomeini peoples no good.' He added scornfully, 'Old man with beard.'

The sight of the smoke from the launch behind us revived everyone, and things began to happen in a rush. First, Lal Mohamed found a fishing line and threw it over the stern (I had wondered why we hadn't had a line out long before; most seamen throw them out at the first opportunity). Almost immediately the line snapped taut. Mir Mohamed the cook, who was peeling onions close by, yelled in excitement, and Lal Mohamed bent his great muscular back to grab the line and pull it hand over hand. The old Persian, Osman, had been squatting in the thunderbox, blatantly farting and peering round like an elderly hen in a nesting box, but now Shapur, with one of his wilder cries, chased him out of it with a boathook and took his place, poised to help Lal Mohamed land the fish. It was a big one, and it struggled desperately all the way to *Al Raza*'s stern. But Lal Mohamed and Shapur between them wrestled it on board, and there it leaped, snapped and slashed with its tail until Lal Mohamed stunned it with a lump of heavy wood.

The second and much more important event was the transformation of *Al Raza* into a sailing dhow. Leaving the dead fish to the attentions of Mir Mohamed the cook, the driver and the rest of the crew began to rig two ragged sails in a prolonged burst of activity (this Baluchi crew was not lazy) with two long bamboo poles and ancient sails – both much patched, one large, the other about the size of the 'need-help' flag. Within an hour, two pieces of patched cloth, stretched diagonally before the mast, and the red flag with a white border were billowing in a fresh breeze, and the engine had been idled down still further so that the black fumes once more all but dispersed. The catch was that our speed had dropped to a rocking crawl. This was maddening, but we were not nearly so likely to burst into flames and, provided the wind kept up, would not drive helplessly and indefinitely, a passive prey for any passing storm.

In a new mood of relief, the Baluchis decided to celebrate the Id holiday by turning on their radios, and soon the vessel echoed to strange clickings, the rhythmic rustling of metal discs, the whirring and thrumming of Eastern string instruments. 'Baluchi music, yah, Baluchi,' Khalat shouted, determined that I should appreciate it. Across the empty ocean – the dhow behind us was still far off – gongs and drums from a studio in Quetta provided a background of clashes and thumps for the high whine of Baluchi girl singers. Mir Mohamed produced a meal of rice and fish, and the Baluchis lay back belching loudly in contentment. Once, on my behalf, the nakhoda switched the radio dial to the BBC Overseas Service, and I heard an excited English voice gabbling, '. . . setting yet another record of five minutes fifty-eight point oh five seconds, which is one point oh four seconds better than . . .' 'No, thank you,' I said hurriedly. He switched it off and moved closer, saying in scrambled Arabic, 'We will not call at any port here. No launches go out from here in the Id holiday time. Maybe we get a tow from the launch behind us.'

'Good.' I wanted him to know that I was relieved we weren't going to abandon *Al Raza* in some godforsaken fishing port on this coast and – of all humiliating things – fly.

'Sail good,' he said, seeing my mood and smiling. 'Flying no good.' We shook hands warmly on that.

Yet we didn't get a tow from the launch behind us, after all. At 10.00 p.m. she caught up with us with surprising suddenness. Her navigation lights appeared out of the darkness as she came alongside. An eighty-footer, she cut her speed to match ours, and we dipped through a mild swell parallel to each other. Khalat had leaped up to shine the torch on the red flag and the larger of our two sails to catch the attention of the other nakhoda and show him we wanted help. And now the two captains were shouting hoarsely at one another across the dark, watery trench between the two vessels.

It was no good. The captain who had overtaken us yelled back that he, too, had engine trouble, that he was overloaded – 'carrying two hundred and fifty tons,' he shouted, spreading his hands apologetically – and that any further strain on his engine would be disastrous. His own weak engine accounted for his delay in catching up with us. Our nakhoda, Hasan the driver, Lal Mohamed and Khalat sat back on the engine housing in dejection and watched the launch throb away and move ahead of us. In the morning there was no sign of the launch, and *Al Raza* plodded on with the sea to herself again.

A day and a night went by. Winds rose and fell. Once the engine clanked to a stop, with sparks flying from the funnel. Again Sumar responded with a reassuring volley of '*Allah karim*' and hopeful stabbings of his finger upwards to regions where, he clearly wished to convey, God the Merciful had our welfare in mind.

'No trouble with the weather,' Ghani Adam, the nakhoda, said. 'If a storm comes and the waves are really big, we throw this' – he pointed to the crates and bales on deck – 'into the sea.'

On the morning of the fifth day the wind picked up again and swung behind us so that the crew could rearrange the two sails and swing their sheets out over the sea on either side of the mast in a butterfly pattern.

'Five miles an hour, perhaps six,' Hasan said, with the satisfaction of a sailor who sees sail again, overcoming, for the moment, the exasperation of an engineer with a faulty engine.

A large island lay ahead, an impressive lump of rock flat-topped like a giant aircraft carrier two hundred feet up. Later *Al Raza* threaded her snail's way through other islands, and with rising excitement the Baluchis began to recognize home territory.

'Snakes and wild goats there,' Sumar cried, pointing to a couple of miniature table mountains in the sea. 'Many fish. Oooh, yah!'

It was very hot, and suddenly the water was very shallow. 'The big steamers on their way to Karachi follow a route much further out,' Ghani Adam said.

Here the sea was a browny-green, but abruptly, as if we had crossed over the lip of a high shelf in the seabed, its colour and texture turned to a sombre commingling of rust and earth, and the rays of the sun could penetrate no more than six inches below the surface, illuminating clusters of small, pale jellyfish.

By 2.30 p.m. the dilapidated sails were bulging again, and the failing engine was tuned down to almost no revolutions at all. The smoke panting up from the tin funnel now had the grey, exhausted look of a man who, having survived a near-fatal illness, has been told by his doctor that any over-exertion could bring a disastrous relapse. The wind behind us and the heaven-sent benevolence of the weather were our salvation. A lot of praying had been done on *Al Raza*; five times a day the believers in the crew had washed themselves and spread their mats in corners of the deck.

Lal Mohamed was at the wheel staring at the compass so fixedly that he might have discovered the future in its depths. Indefatigable, like a great faithful watchdog – a mastiff with a waterfall moustache – he turned the wheel with strong, decisive movements. 'Lalu! Lalu!' Khalat shouted, teasing him, but Lal smiled without looking up and gently pushed him away with a big dark paw, like Baloo the Bear brushing away young Mowgli.

The crew bathed in the sun, clambering in turn into the thunderbox, soaping their bodies and then pouring water over themselves from the tin can. Shapur pulled in another fish, a tuna like the first one, but this time with a bright yellow belly and steel-blue back.

That evening was my last on *Al Raza*. Near sunset the long, quick-eyed face of Mir Mohamed appeared over the steps to the little bridge like a distorted grey moon, and he crept up to me with the exaggerated tiptoe steps of a villain in a Victorian melodrama from the area of the thunderbox, revolving a finger near his temple, closing his eyes and frowning piteously to show me how much he was suffering. It wasn't aspirin he was after, I knew, so I cured his affliction with two fat fingers of gin. He thanked me with a grin and a lot of nodding, and went down the steps with his palm cupped round the mug like a man protecting a candle in a draught.

Later I lay on the wheelhouse bunk, watching the moonlight shine through the windows and listening to the Baluchi voices around me. It was odd how, to the half-wakeful brain, Baluchi sounded like English, and once or twice I started up, thinking that someone had said something to me. But it was only Khalat pretending to fight with Shapur, or Sumar telling some rambling tale to the nakhoda, punctuating it with sharp but muted exclamations. By now the hard bunk and its knobbly red and yellow flower-patterned mattress had come to feel as comfortable as any bed I had ever slept in. The pale-blue wheelhouse itself seemed snug and solid, although one big wave could have brushed it overboard like an eggbox. At times *Al Raza* seemed indestructible, at others horribly vulnerable. But then an illusion of strength masking an incurable inadequacy in the face of overwhelming seas will always be the reality of ship construction. A dhow is a freighter is a supertanker.

There was no place for enmities or secrets aboard *Al Raza*. She had no cabins, and no one could steal a little privacy behind closed doors, for there were no doors. The eight men slept, in shifts as their watches dictated, on small wooden bunks in four partitions two feet high and opening on to each other. Every word, every action was public property except in the thunderbox, and even that was not soundproof. But there is no privacy on any Asian native craft between Suez and the Sulu Sea. Asia is no place for privacy.

At last the cry came: 'Karachi!' It was Khalat's voice. I saw another wedge-shaped island, and behind it a long headland. Ghani Adam strolled up in undershirt and pyjama trousers and said, 'Karachi seven hours more.' Hasan had begun replacing the batteries he had removed to keep our lights glowing at least weakly. 'Lucky we had those cars aboard,' said the nakhoda. 'We needed the petrol to keep the batteries charged. Now it's almost finished. What else could we do?'

I said, 'Always be sure to load two or three cars before a voyage.'

Passing a black and white striped lighthouse, a brown-walled village, and the looming chimneys of the Marupur Power Station, we approached Karachi, and the Baluchis began to prepare for their arrival. Personal preening came first. Mir Mohamed sidled up to ask for a razor blade. Lal Mohamed took a minute pair of tweezers and a small round mirror from his ditty box – a small metal trunk decorated with Swiss lake scenes in vivid green and blue – and, with infinite patience, plucked straggling hairs from his moustache. Sumar shaved, trimmed, washed, brushed, combed and, finally, rubbed strongly scented oil into his whiskers. 'Ooooh . . . aaaah,' he sighed contentedly, examining their silky gleam in Lal Mohamed's mirror. Khalat washed and put on a new *kemis*, the knee-length Baluchi shirt, and wide black and white checked trousers. Hasan, the driver, free of oil for the first time for days, was also a changed man. The crew of *Al Raza* approached their home port dressed to kill.

We approached slowly on the engine, sails stowed away. While Shapur took down the red distress flag – we had no wish now to be rescued by a well-meaning Pakistani navy ship – the others, with the excitement of children on Christmas morning, examined the presents they had bought in the bazaars of Dubai for themselves or their families. One or two had radios or record players. There were tins of Vinolia Cream, tubes of 'Twain' Budlet lipstick, something called Prophecy Cologne spray mist 'by Prince Matchabelli', and a good deal of Brut spray lotion, much of which wild Shapur squirted over us with indiscriminate *joie de vivre*. There were brightly coloured tins of biscuits, too: Britannia Creams, manufactured in Taratola Road, Calcutta. And there were clothes, most of which – with the exception of the diminutive woollen bootees and jumpers Sumar had bought for his baby – the crew were tugging on like men wrestling with serpents. The idea, they explained, was to wear the clothes so as not to trouble the Karachi customs with unnecessary work. Lal Mohamed had managed to force his massive frame into six T-shirts, and was pulling on loose blue trousers over two pairs of football shorts. Sumar lifted his shirt to show me three undershirts, one of them stencilled with the words 'Take It from Here', and two sports shirts. He seemed to be having some difficulty in breathing. Suddenly everyone had put on six inches around the chest, waist and thighs. Shapur was so absurdly swollen with extra clothing that the nakhoda ordered him to take some of it off: 'Because of you, everyone will be stripped naked in the customs,' he said severely, whereupon Shapur sheepishly clambered out of enough garments to see two average-sized men through a severe Baluchi winter.

Peter Barton of the *Pacific Basset* had said, 'Funny how the adrenalin or whatever it is begins to move when you return to port, however short a time you've been away or how long you're going to stay there.' The adrenalin moved in the Baluchis now.

Ghani Adam, the nakhoda, whom I had come to like and respect, came and sat with me, and Khalat brought us tea. He wore a carefully pressed Baluchi shirt and *shelwa*, the pleated baggy trousers people wear from the point west of Karachi where the province of Sind ends and mountainous Baluchistan begins.

'Can you find me work in London?' he asked.

'It's difficult,' I said, surprised by his sudden question. 'Don't you earn enough here?'

'Three thousand rupees a month [about £185]. Good work,' he admitted, 'a living.'

'But tiring,' sighed Sumar, looming as big as a galleon with his undershirts, moustache and baggy trousers. He wore a cloth like a turban on his head. 'And no women in Dubai. Before, there were women – Pakistani women, Baluchi women, all sorts; a pound a time; maybe less.' He shook his turbaned head and looked mournful. 'Now they've all been sent home.'

Ghani Adam asked, 'Why do you travel with us on *Al Raza* when you can fly?'

I would have liked to quote Graham Greene about 'the universal desire to see a little bit further, before the surrender to old age and the blank certitude of death.' Or Kipling: 'For to admire an' for to see,/ For to be'old this world so wide.' But my Arabic was not good enough, so I said, 'To see the world. To meet people other than my own.'

We were turning through the outer anchorage. A large number of ships waited there: tankers, rusty freighters in need of paint, Greek, Panamanian, Cypriot, Liberian. As evidence of what storms could do, two large ships lay beached, and another sat on the bottom of the harbour, only her masts showing above the oily surface. I could see a crowd of bathers on the beach. The Id holiday was evidently not yet over; it had started late in Karachi.

'To meet you,' I added, and the nakhoda put out his hand to shake mine.

'Good,' he said, smiling.

We puttered past a great stone mole, a fort and a very English-looking garrison church. In the harbour ships lined the wharves on both sides of a curved waterway: dredgers, many smart or bedraggled cargo vessels, two blue-grey American frigates, a Soviet tanker. From the complicated superstructure of one of the frigates a group of sailors waved to us. Launches packed with holidaying Pakistani families shuttled back and forth and up and down the harbour; they, too, waved and pointed me out to each other – the tall foreigner with a sunburned face in red and white checked shirt and white trousers standing among the tur-baned Baluchis on *Al Raza*'s stern. Of course, I looked incongruous.

Past a Pakistani coaster and the *Tamy* from Singapore, we turned into the dhow harbour, Ghas Bandar. Instantly *Al Raza* was a galleon sailing into an armada of other galleons: dhows big and small; dhows wide and heavy with polished dark wood, or low in the water with spars grey with age and salt; huge vessels with soaring carved sterns from the era of Drake's *Golden Hind*, and with what looked like acres of deck space around the wheelhouse, and with not one but two massive, thick-sided thunderboxes aft.

There was the aspect of a great medieval army about the dhow harbour. The heraldic standards of the French knights at Agincourt could have been only slightly less vivid than the pennants and ensigns of this tightly packed fleet of wooden ships. In the fair offshore breeze the colours of Bahrain, the United Arab Emirates, Qatar, Pakistan, Iran and Kuwait – reds, purples, greens, whites and browns – stirred and flapped over scores of vessels tied up eight or nine deep alongside the wharves of Ghas Bandar. They lay lazily rubbing sides, cushioned by fenders of old truck tyres. Their cargoes, sacks of rice or grain, crates of furniture (descriptions of their contents stencilled on their sides), bicycles, scooters, bales and boxes of God-knew-what stood on their decks undisturbed. Their crews on holiday had gone ashore, or squatted in skullcaps and sarongs, chatting and gesticulating, playing cards on the planked decks; some slept on thin woven mats or drank tea or smoked in silence.

As *Al Raza* drew near, men sprang up shouting, 'Come in here! Come alongside us!' and *Al Raza*'s crew shouted back. I heard Sumar's 'Ooooh . . . aaah,' as he and Lal Mohamed threw lines to friends on other vessels who hauled us in, making fast the lines, releasing them, hauling, making fast again, until *Al Raza* was in perfect alignment and at rest, her engine silent and smokeless at last. The crew of the vessel we lay alongside crowded aboard and told us they had arrived three days earlier. They greeted

Mir Mohamed with ribald cheers and slapped the backs of the rest of the crew. Their vessel was *Khalid*, the passenger launch that had left Sharjah without me. Now I was glad I had missed the *Khalid*, although I remembered well my anguish at the time. Since then I had become deeply attached to the jolly crew of *Al Raza*, that inelegant polluter of the breezes of the Arabian Sea.

Chapter Sixteen

THE STRETCH OF coast from Karachi to south-west India turned out to be a region of dismal, stop-and-go uncertainty. Dock strikes, diverted ships and the timidity of ships' agents all combined against me. In the background lurked the repulsive Indian bureaucracy – the niggling regulations that, brandished in the trembling hands of myriad minor officials, achieve the menace of loaded clubs. Regulations: the gelatine that prevents the jello of the Indian state from dissolving into slush. Perhaps that's the best that can be said for them.

Aeroplane, ship and aeroplane again: such mixed transport conveyed me to Sri Lanka. As it turned out, my luck changed there, and thereafter I had no further need of buses or jets until I reached my destination, Canton. But in Karachi all I knew was that I would have to fly again. The cat-versus-dog political obsessions that haunt governments in Delhi and Islamabad made it impossible to continue to Bombay by sea from Karachi's dhow harbour at Ghas Bandar.

A 10.30 p.m. flight to Bombay. My notebook begins once more to register the agonies of flying: the delay – two and a half hours – at Karachi airport, the crumpled and irritable crowds. The banks were closed or not working, the cashiers sat behind their counters chatting in a haze of cigarette smoke, surrounded by cups of tea, indifferent to the pleading of passengers who wanted to change their useless rupees and whose plane was leaving. 'Regulations say we cannot work between nine and nine fifteen,' a cashier told them, hardly looking up from his crossword puzzle.

Miserable, I wondered when next I would be leaning on a ship's rail. I missed Sumar's whiskered huffing and puffing, Khalat's good nature and Mir Mohamed wheedling for a nip of gin. Before saying goodbye to them, we had all driven along the coast from Karachi to a beauty spot, a strange formation of rocks dramatically battered by the surf, and spent an afternoon walking there, jumping from ledge to rock ledge dodging the spray, and finally drinking tea at a small shop where students had scribbled their names (or obscenities) on the walls in big green Arabic letters.

Khalat, Lal Mohamed and Sumar were excited to be ashore in the brown wilderness of their hard country. They talked proudly of the size of Baluchistan, which stretched from the tawny cliffs we had seen to the mountains of Afghanistan. Still, they said, they were glad to be sailors; travel meant freedom from the cruel and absurd restraints imposed by unpredictable rulers on those who lived ashore. Travel meant freedom from regulations: 'In Pakistan everything you want to do is *memnu'h* [forbidden],' Khalat mourned. 'Everything is *haram*.' Lal Mohamed and Sumar shook their moustached heads in agreement. 'Generals, colonels, mullahs . . . *memnu'h*.'

On the Indian Airlines flight to non-Muslim Bombay, young Pakistanis celebrated their freedom from generals and mullahs by ordering Scotch and half-bottles of Rémy Martin. In India they might find an obliging girl for the first time in their lives. From the toilet came a muffled sound of retching.

★ ★ ★

At Bombay airport customs, my skinny porter, a puckish man with a mischievous mouth, said, 'India three hundred and fifty declared. Australia fourteen for two.'

This friendly shaft of cricket talk in the gloomy barn of Santa Cruz airport did me good. So did a newspaper story in the *Times of India* next morning:

> Mr Harisinh Chavda, Minister of Roads and Buildings, will personally enquire into the flush tank collapse in the government resthouse at Idar . . . in which the former Prime Minister, Mr Morarji Desai, had a narrow escape . . . It could be a deliberate attempt on the life of Mr Desai . . . As soon as Mr Desai pulled the chain, the flush tank collapsed and crashed on the ground and missed him by inches.

Out of my window in the Taj Hotel I stared out across the Indian Ocean in the direction of the Arabian Sea and the Gulf. Or thought I did. Actually, the Gateway to India, the stone imperial arch high as a three-storey house under which the King-Emperor George V and Queen Mary had stepped for the coronation durbar in 1911, faces India, so George and Mary were walking away from the mainland when they arrived in Bombay. The city's obese and still-growing bulk covers and overflows a narrow peninsula, which protrudes like a fin from the coastline; the Gateway stands on the inside edge of the fin.

In the offices of the Great Eastern Shipping Company, one of the most important private shipping organizations in a country of largely nationalized shipping, I found good news and bad. From Mr B. N. Adappa, Great Eastern's operations manager, I learned that the Mogul Line ran a regular daily service to Goa.

'You sail at ten o'clock in the morning and arrive at Panaji – that is, Goa – at seven or eight o'clock next morning. The passenger steamer service down the Konkan coast is very fine.'

So at least there was a sure way ahead to Goa by sea.

'Does it continue on down to Calicut or Cochin?'

Once, it had done so, said Mr Adappa, but recently this service had been suspended as an economy measure. Just my luck, I thought.

'The Mogul Line is a very old and respected line, but now it is a government undertaking, like the Shipping Corporation of India, which you must be knowing.'

I asked Mr Adappa's advice on how I might bridge the gap between Goa and Colombo. Below Goa, Calicut and Cochin were the two ports I had hopefully underlined on my map, both of them on the Malabar Coast and both in the state of Kerala.

Mr Adappa shook his head. These days, he said, very few ships plied that coast. I might find some 'country boats' – the Indian term for small private vessels like dhows or launches – but these days the traffic came from Calcutta, and very little of it went the other way. This state of affairs seemed illogical: surely what went westwards had to return eastwards in order to come westwards again? I had a vision of all that shipping from Calcutta piling up in Bombay harbour. But Mr Adappa explained that, westwards or eastwards, sea traffic around India's shores had been considerably reduced. 'People prefer road and rail transport. It's like England. There used to be many coasters, but the fuel costs and the labour problems . . . Oh, my God, the labour problems.'

I was going to hear a good deal more about India's labour problems. Indians talk about dock strikes as Englishmen talk about the weather, and there are probably about as many workless days in the country as there are rainy ones in Great Britain. In Calcutta they talk not only of strikes but of silt as well: the Hooghly river is being choked to death by it, just as a man's veins and arteries are fatally blocked by cholesterol. Mr Adappa told me, 'Calcutta is no longer India's number one port. Now it's first Bombay, then Goa, *then* Calcutta.'

Mr Adappa arranged for me to visit the Bombay docks. To enter them was to take a backward step in time, into an old engraving. In the maze of Victorian brick godowns, among the derricks that bent their heads together over ships like guardsmen's swords arched over the bride and groom at a military wedding, among the clerical black of rotund and venerable steam cranes, bulbous bollards and heavy, cogged swing-bridge mechanisms with their nineteenth-century look of complete dependability, there was, as Conrad wrote of the London docks, an ugliness so picturesque as to become a delight to the eye. Dark-skinned workers, made darker by oil and grime, swung in cradles, chipping paint from the sides of freighters, or squatted in groups in the shadow of containers. Victoria, Princess and Indira (once named Alexandra) are the three docks of Bombay. Unexpected trees grow among them. Fine old buildings of old British trading houses, still in use, cluster like dignified old gentlemen in retirement between the dock gates and the grand Victorian pile of the Bombay Yacht Club and the Gateway to India.

The Royal Bombay Yacht Club is such a splendid building in such a striking situation – next to the Taj and behind the great Gateway – that I walked in and asked if I could have a look at this fascinating example of Victoriana. A friendly Indian secretary welcomed me, and added, 'You should talk to Captain Philip Bragg. He knows all about it.'

Where would I have to go to meet him? Not far; Captain Bragg was in one of the tall public rooms, reading a delayed London *Times* over a cup of tea. The breezy friendliness of the Royal Navy flowed out of him; so did the spirit of Indian hospitality. 'If you're here for a few days, you'll find the club useful. Prices are . . . well, helpful.' I hoped to leave Bombay very soon, but I was grateful for the offer.

Founded in 1846, the yacht club had moved into these spacious quarters in 1948 from a venerable building on the Wellington Reclamation nearby. The present clubhouse was built as residential chambers in 1897, and stands, like much of Bombay, on reclaimed land. It is the grandest yacht club in India, said Captain Bragg. It's grand in the way that a grand old man is grand; not plush, far from it. Surely Kipling came here; his father's college stands just behind it. Its touches of the modern are tentative; like a newly joined midshipman, they know their place. Notices inform you that the King and Queen visited the club in December 1911, that Admiral of the Fleet Viscount Jellicoe of Scapa came here in 1919, and that, in November 1921, 'His Royal Highness the Prince of Wales had Tea on the Lawn.' Did he also have a siesta in the club chairs, the old wicker-backed kind with extendable arms for propping up one's legs in the heat? Some have holes in the arms in which you can slot your burra peg. Captain Bragg lives in the club in a large apartment high up in a turret, like a ship's lookout. A brass spyglass, two tables of ships' wheels and his naval sword on a wall befit the retreat of an old British seadog.

We were borne aloft in a lift decorated with Corinthian columns. Doors are of teak – one from the deck of HMS *Achilles* – with real portholes and their brass wing nuts still in place.

'Sit ye down,' said the captain. 'What's your poison? Pink gin? Jolly good.'

The captain's windows looked not only down on but *through* the Gateway to India. Sun shone on sailing praus out to sea; an island wavered vaguely in a haze; green parrots swooped from tree to tree in the club's garden.

Captain Bragg retired here in 1945. When I asked him if he planned a final retreat to England, he said, 'You must be joking.' There are bearers to sweep out his rooms, to shake out the floppy cushions in his old armchairs, and to dust his old HMV phonograph, his few pictures, his books.

I told Captain Bragg of my journey, my progress and my fears of future difficulties, particularly in Indian waters. He, too, suspected that the west coast of India would produce snags, but he promised to give me a letter to an Indian shipping friend in Goa. He still had an office in a Bombay shipping company, and the letter might help.

Over the pink gin, the captain told me of the decline in yachting; apparently the sun is setting on this innocent and character-forming pastime. 'India has its troubles, as you know. Poverty galore. We all realize that to display wealth is unwise and undesirable, and sailing has become wildly expensive. If you want to import a sail, much less a yacht, you must pay a hundred per cent duties, plus one hundred and twenty per cent extra charges. It's a pity. There's marvellous sailing here.'

He got up, selected an old acetate-coated record and blew on it before laying it with extreme care on the turntable of an old phonograph. The suave, precise rhythms of Victor Sylvester's orchestra sounded, and the captain, beaming, wandered to the window of the turret, and stared out to sea through his spyglass, his foot tapping to 'Cochabamba Samba'.

I scouted other shipping possibilities. There was, I found, an American President Lines container–passenger ship due to leave for Colombo in a day or two, but after Dubai I didn't care to depend on the vagaries of her schedule. In any case, I wanted to see the west coast of India. Mogul Lines seemed the best bet, so I went to their office in Bank Street and arranged a cabin-class booking to Panaji, Goa. Once the ticket was in my pocket, a weight fell from my mind.

That settled, I made a serious attempt to arrange for a permit for the Andamans. In vain. Travel agents I consulted were ignorant of official procedures for procuring such a document. I resorted to the telephone. Someone in the British high commission said I must arrange it through the Indian Tourist Board; the procedures involved the Ministry of External Affairs, he said. The Andamans were a sensitive area, it seemed; permission to go there was seldom, if ever, granted. The senior Indian tourist official in Bombay seemed reluctant to discuss the Andamans at all.

His high, impatient babu's voice complained that it was an unusual request – a futile one, too, he implied. My application for a permit would have to go to his office, he said, then be sent to Delhi, then returned to Bombay after 'due consideration' by more than one government department. In six months I could return to Bombay to collect it – if indeed it was approved by Delhi.

What were the chances of approval?

'Fifty-fifty, at best,' the impatient voice said.

'Is there nothing you can do to speed things up?'

'Nothing.' Did I detect a hint of triumph?

'Suppose—' But he had rung off. And that was that.

Captain Bragg and I had our last drink together in the yacht club: Hayward's beer, brewed in Maharashtra, then pink gin. A crested menu propped against a tankard offered dhal soup, pork vindaloo and rice. Pennants and ships' crests painted on little shields, presented by visiting officers grateful for the club's hospitality, hung behind a barman who swirled angostura bitters around the inside of the glasses, coating them pink before pouring in the gin, the drink of the Royal Navy and of east of Suez. The dining-room tables had brass tops, and the gents' toilet had brass handles on the slatted cubicle doors. Indian and non-Indian members drank or lunched together. The club has long been more Indian than Royal or British, and in that sense it is not an imperial relic at all.

The kind captain drove me to the ferry wharf to catch the Goa steamer. A long street took us through jams of battered trucks and hordes of half-naked coolies, chimney-sweep black, pushing carts and humping bales.

'See all those big houses? They once belonged to the foremen of the dock navvies.'

'Indian or British?'

'My God, British. Even at that level, people were British in the old days. You notice I don't say "good old days".'

At New Ferry Wharf, the Mogul Line steamer lay waiting, and Captain Bragg handed me the letter he had promised me. 'May do some good.'

I thanked him and said goodbye. In the waiting room, passengers gathered slowly. I counted thirty, including two hippies, one of whom, a young man, wore a spangled dress and orange lipstick.

A sign in the afterdeck of the *Konkan Shakti* said, AIRING SPACE FOR LOWER-CLASS PASSENGERS. A tea seller strolled among the deck passengers, announcing himself by clicking little cups against little saucers. Hippies lay about the deck on bedrolls. One of them was a tall, completely bald, middle-aged man in sleeveless undershirt, a belt with a large metal buckle and filthy trousers. I had seen him come aboard, pushing through the ruck of the gangplank, followed by a porter carrying his big rope-meshed bed. Now smoking a cheroot on his wooden bed, bulging obscenely in his tight pants, and totally hairless, there was something villainous about him. 'We must be careful not to catch louses...'; I could almost hear the calm voice of Mr Pavlides and the disapproving snap of his dentures.

Luckily, my cabin was nothing like *Al Anoud*'s. It had two fans, white sheets and pillows, two portholes, bed lights and neon strips in the ceiling, and contained, besides myself, a small man shaped like a cannonball and of mild appearance named Mr Chowdury.

The *Konkan Shakti* glided past Victoria Dock, a small island or two and praus with tattered sails. It was eleven o'clock in the morning of a hot day. A Bombay-registered ship, the *Rajendra*, dribbled smoke near the forest of cranes made by Jessop of Calcutta fifteen or twenty years before. Soon we passed the Taj and the Gateway to India. I peered at the arch, focusing my binoculars behind it on the Gothic turrets and red tiles of the Bombay Yacht Club so reminiscent of Torquay or Bournemouth. I wondered if Captain Bragg was in his window, his spyglass to his eye, tapping a foot to Victor Sylvester.

Captain M. I. Kadir put two fingers in his mouth and released a piercing whistle. In response a large young officer appeared and the captain gave him a burble of orders. Turning to me, he said, 'Myself, my chief officer and second officer, we are all from Daman in Goa. My chief engineer comes from Punjab and the third officer from Kerala. Mixed bag.'

Soon after sailing, the captain had invited me to the bridge. I think someone in the Mogul Lines office had told him I was a writer. He had been all over the world, he said, but had spent thirteen years on this run between Goa and Bombay. It was not a profitable route any more; fuel prices were the problem. The *Konkan Shakti* was a good ship, though, Yugoslav-built, fourteen years old, 2000 tons.

Yes, Goa was now a very busy port, but there was a weather problem for small vessels. For example, June, July and August were months of heavy swell and strong winds because of the south-west monsoon. 'In these months we are not running the ship.'

'Have any ships been lost in these monsoons?'

'Five or six years back, yes. At Malwan. Ships going aground on reefs. Ships lost, not people. In 1977 a cyclone made us put back to Bombay and disembark all the passengers. Now if we have a bad weather report we don't sail.'

Mr Chowdury shifted uneasily in his sleep. His black stomach heaved restlessly as his white vest rode higher and higher and his cotton bloomers sank lower and lower. I feared total exposure before morning. A fart overrode the whirr of the fan.

At a very early hour we anchored off a small port. Coolies came aboard and loaded and off-loaded cargo with a thunderous banging of barges against the ship's side. Mr Chowdury heaved himself up. 'Is that a door banging?' he demanded. 'Are we sinking?' I didn't feel like conversation and feigned sleep.

At daybreak, while we drank the early morning tea our steward had brought us, Mr Chowdury said, 'So hot, so very hot at night. Did you hear that amazing noise?'

'What sort of noise?'

'I am referring to a really rude, ill-mannered noise. Almost intolerable, you might say. A gun fired at the porthole, possibly, although that would have been illegal, of course, and would have merited summary arrest.'

'No, I doubt—'

'No, no, not a gun, obviously. But the effect was the same. You didn't hear that bloody man whistling and shouting at 1.00 a.m.? Dementedly shouting, you might say. I thought we were being attacked by hooligans after our blood. And you, sir, quietly sleeping. If I may say so, like a baby, like an innocent baby.'

He swung his short legs to the ground. 'How tall are you, sir?' he asked. 'Six foot three? My son is also very tall, six foot, yet his mother is like me.'

Mr Chowdury said he was from Patna in the north-eastern state of Bihar; he would stay two days in Goa and then fly back. 'A change is as good as a feast, I always say.'

'That's very true.'

'Ah, then,' he said seriously, 'we are agreeing on a very important thing.'

Bingo in the second-class dining room. The second officer calls out the numbers to a packed and sweating audience bent over slips of squared and numbered paper. 'Grandmother's age – eight zero . . . Republic day – twenty-six . . . Punjab Day – number five . . . A round dozen – number twelve . . . Hockey sticks – seventy seven.'

Sikhs played cards on the perfectly scrubbed deck; Indian families made little picnics. Hippies peeled oranges, slept or studied pornographic pictures in sex magazines. Four miles away the green coastline moved by.

On time, Captain Kadir brought the ship into Goa in a blue morning mist, passing through a fleet of trawlers with light roofs. 'We're going right inside,' he said, like a surgeon announcing his next probe. An old fort, a white church,

land becoming reddish and lumpy, a line of broken water under a cliff.

'Slow ahead . . . Dead slow ahead.' The engines die to a purr. Trees and beach come down to the water. 'Here the water is very shallow, only thirteen feet, and our draught is twelve foot six.'

A fine Portuguese jail on a bluff. A lighthouse with a prau in front of it like a postcard. Palms sprouting like unkempt hair, behind them ridges and trees: Mowgli country. A small town on the water's edge. A wharf.

* * *

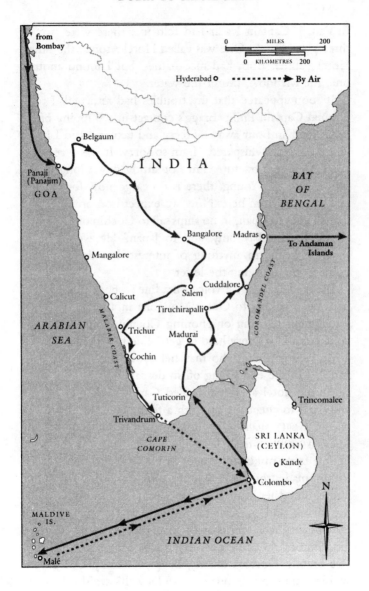

In Panaji, Captain Kadir had told me, there were two or three good hotels. One was called Hotel Aroma; the other, Hotel Fatima. Both had nice names, but I found another one, the Mandovi, nearer the water.

It soon appeared that my troubles had returned. I telephoned Captain Philip Bragg's contact in a shipping office more than an hour away by ferry and taxi and said I had a letter. A voice whispered, 'I am so sorry.' It was a very sad voice. 'I have a fracture. I'm not sitting down long in the office. But, Mr Young, there is no cargo now for Cochin or Colombo from here. Now we expect iron ore only, and that all goes to Japan, so no ships sail to Cochin or Colombo at all. To Bombay only, and to Japan.' He would be in touch if he heard anything of interest, but there was no point in my bringing the letter.

Blocked again, by a voice on a line so poor that I might have been talking to Outer Mongolia in a blizzard. When I suggested telexing or phoning Cochin, Captain Bragg's contact said, 'It's very hard to get a line to Cochin. There's a Mr George there who may help you. But the line is so bad . . .' In the end I rang off in despair.

At the hotel a barman called Carlos took pity on me and tried to cheer me up with a fenny cocktail; it was, he said, a Goan speciality: a double caju fenny, Rose's Lime Juice, a dash of fresh lime juice, ice. Fenny is the local liquor, fairly mild, and comes in two varieties: one, called Patrão, made from cashew nuts (caju); the other, Diva Goa, lighter and drier, from coconuts. It makes a smooth, uplifting drink and at seventeen pence is far cheaper than the Indian-made spirits with magnificent names: Carew's gin, Forbes' London gin, Hayward's white rum, Honey Bee brandy, Doctor's brandy, Bagpipe whisky, Old Tavern whisky, and – my favourite – McDowell's whisky.

Over the fenny I considered what to do. Even the news from Cochin was bad. In the bar a man who had just come from there by road told me that the port was closed by a strike of stevedores. Nothing would be going in or out, he said, for days.

Nevertheless, I wanted to push on, although, from what I could see of Goa, it was very beautiful indeed, one of the loveliest places I had ever seen. It reminded me of Cabinda in the old days, the tropical Portuguese enclave north of Angola on the south-west coast of Africa. After the second fenny I decided to stay a day or two and see the churches and a hippie or two – Goa is famous as a hippie hangout and is the burial place of St Francis Xavier – and then press on somehow.

In the street outside the hotel I ran into a man I had seen on the ship from Bombay. He was youngish, blond, very tall and slim, with a pale moustache. He was dressed like a Mississippi gambler in a film, in a white three-piece suit and shoes, very elegant. I had watched him at the rail of the ship and, for some reason, had found him sinister, like a villain in literature – Conrad's Mr Jones in *Victory*, perhaps.

I couldn't have been more wrong. Although we hadn't spoken more than a few words on the ship, he recognized me in the street, and there was no avoiding shaking hands and reintroducing myself. I needn't have worried because as soon as he spoke his charm was apparent, and I couldn't think why I'd thought him sinister. He was Richard Wesse, a German, and he and his wife lived in an old and most unusual house, he said, at Naicavaddo-Calangute, some way out of Panaji. He would be delighted if I could come and see it.

It was indeed an extraordinary house, about an hour

away. Thick, silent coconut groves behind one of the biggest hippie beaches screened it from the world. Villa Nunes it was called, and the owl-light of the trees gave it a mysterious haunting look. The date 1904 was carved on a small, over-grown bridge on the grassy, stony path that wandered up to it from a village, and the name 'John Nunes' faced you like a curse from the mildewed stones of tall pillars through which you passed into a walled garden and up to a front porch that had the aura of an Eastern temple about it. There, coloured glass over the porch dappled us in green-blue and blood-red, and a ten-foot double door opened into tall rooms with arched, ecclesiastical windows – the top third of them glowing with the same red and blue glass – and furnished with fine dark wicker chairs, dark wood tables and potted plants. On the walls a print of *The Meeting of Dante and Beatrice* faced grandly framed and mounted photographic portraits of some of the departed Nunes family: the grandfather stern-faced in evening dress with three medals; his wife, firm, big-bosomed, unkillable (but dead now, of course); his grandchildren in mortarboards displaying their newly awarded diplomas. They were lugubrious; it was like inspecting the photographs, blotched and dimmed by the weather, you find on tombs in Catholic cemeteries.

As he moved through the gate ahead of me, momentarily a harlequin as he passed under the porch's coloured glass, Richard Wesse's lean white-clad figure seemed wholly appropriate; he reminded me of a photograph of R. L. Stevenson on Samoa.

He waved a hand around the shaded and taciturn rooms. 'The old lady, the surviving Nunes, is widowed and lives in Bombay in a dismal slum on the railway line. I saw her there once, sitting over the railway line with a few sticks of furniture and one plastic table shaped like a kidney. Imagine, after this, she prefers it there.'

This was how minor Portuguese officials once lived, raising a family, retiring, dying in this obscure and modest grandeur. Outside, black crows flopped about in the palms, and mangoes and hibiscus grew on both sides of the crumbling gate. Except for the squawks of the mynah birds, the heavy silence was unbroken. I supposed John Nunes must be buried near here, not far from St Francis Xavier.

Wesse's young wife joined us, a cheerful Berliner whose laughter broke the sombre spell the place imposed. A bird-like black gardener's boy – he might have flapped down from a tree – trotted behind her, carrying a watering can. He put his head on one side and said, 'Your country is not like this, sir. Better than this.'

'This is a beautiful country.'

'No, sir, not good.' He shook his head. 'Not good.' Was nobody contented with his country? He poured water on a scrubby plant, then perked up. 'This is a garden. I am watering flowers here, sir.' Well, at least he liked flowers.

Some way down the green bumpy path that ran past the stone gateposts, a little white cross stood near a tiny shrine. Palm branches had been stuck in the earth beside it, and on a palsied stone I saw blobs of candle wax.

The countryside around Naicavaddo-Calangute was a region of white ornate churches, dotted like pious blocks of sugar icing among the iridescent greenness.

'Every day the churches are full,' said Richard Wesse. The services were still held in Portuguese, and there was organ music. Elaborate tombs, hull down in the long grass, to people with names like Da Santos and Pinto encircled the churches. Inside there were blue ceilings, blue walls, statues, tumbling scrollwork in gold, and fans on long stalks suspended over light-wood pews. The churches looked as though a lot of money was still being spent on them; they exuded a stifling richness. Yet the bedraggled world of the hippies was only a fifteen-minute walk away.

Richard had been a hippie. As we strolled down to Andrew's Bar, a shack near the beach selling beer and fenny, he told me about it.

'Well, hippie is an attitude of mind. It started in sixty-seven – the political thing, anti-Vietnam. All my friends were hippie, so I was too. I tried to run away from home. I liked long hair and to be dirty. It was just – well, something else. Then I didn't see any point in it any more. For one thing, I like my parents.'

We drank caju fenny at a creaking wooden table in the open air under palms from which coconuts thudded down. A Frenchman with a thirty-year-old drinker's face called Paul, and Jo, a plumber from Newcastle, joined us. When Paul went into the bar to buy more fenny, Richard Wesse told me that Paul had once been a successful *Vogue* model, but had dropped everything to settle here. 'He's at Andrew's Bar all day. Well, not all day because they close from three to six.'

A plump girl roared up on a powerful motorbike with a long-haired Indian on the pillion with his arms around her. 'Yoo-hoo,' she shouted, snatching two hockey sticks from the Indian and disappearing into the bar, 'Yoo-hoo. Yoo-hoooooo.'

'Spaced out,' Richard Wesse explained. 'She's Lilli, from Berlin.' In the bar someone began to sing 'Surabaya Johnny'. A pale man naked to the waist, displaying prominent ribs and skinny arms, slouched by, watching his own feet pushing uncertainly forward on the uneven ground. '*He's* a real junkie. Neglects to eat. Ninety per cent of the youth are here because of the drugs. Why here? There's no harassment and it's cheap. Not that they're all real junkies. You can take drugs without being an addict. Some are addicts; some just like drugs.'

Jo the plumber said, 'You're English. Let me tell you, this is a really lovely place, this is.' He hesitated a moment, and then said, 'Funny thing happened. Like to hear about it?'

'Please.' He didn't look like a junkie. He was sipping beer.

'I bumped into a friend here, someone I'd known since childhood in Newcastle. I hadn't seen him for bloody ages.

There was a bloke playing a guitar on the beach here. I said, 'There's a good guitarist,' and I looked at him, like, and all of a sudden I saw it was old Nipper. I don't know how I knew him, I just did. Truthfully, he'd completely changed. He's only twenty-three, but as God's my witness he could be any age. It shocked the life out of me – really shocked me rigid. He used to be a big, solid bloke, Nipper. Now in Goa I saw this skeleton, small, all wizened. You could see all his chestbones sticking out, like that bloke who's just gone past, his chest sort of caving in.'

Jo waited while Richard Wesse went in to the bar to order more beer and fenny. A coconut fell near a family of black-backed pigs rolling in a mud patch.

When Richard returned, Jo resumed, 'Well, he peered at me, Nipper did. "Is that you, Jo?" he asked, as if he couldn't take me in, so to speak. "You want a beer?" he said. He seemed scared and confused, and wanted to get us away from the others . . . Christ, he was that nervous. Still, after a bit we started talking of the old days. We saw where he lived, sharing with lots of junkies. Some of them obviously looked after themselves nice and seemed healthy, but not old Nipper.'

Jo shook his head, seeing Nipper again. 'His teeth had gone completely rotten, and his hair was all going. I tried to laugh. "Well, then," I said, "what's it like to be with the Health and Happiness Group, eh?" I didn't have to ask if he was happy or wanted to go home. He'd been asked that too often, I knew, and it was too late for that now. He asked me for ten rupees – that's just over fifty pence – for food, although I doubted if he'd eat with it. He can't have been eating at all.'

Jo took a mouthful of beer. He looked as if he wanted

to cry. 'If you could only have seen him aged twelve, and now . . . I only recognized him by instinct – nothing but instinct.'

Paul went for more drinks, and Lilli, invisible in the bar, carolled again. 'Yoo-hoo.'

Nipper had been here three years without a break,' said Jo.

'How did he get into drugs?' I asked.

'He'd been a junkie in Newcastle years ago. I knew that. He went to prison there, see, for raiding a chemist's. After that, he'd taken off for Bombay. He got through all his money there – two grams a day of smack cost a lot – and sold everything he had, clothes, everything. He'd become like a lost soul, he said; he even sold his body. Then he came to Goa, and here he was, talking to me. Well, sort of talking; it wasn't real somehow. I felt I was with someone in a trance. Serious questions seemed to bounce off him, like.'

'How does he live now?'

'I don't think he has any money. Sometimes he plays in that band at parties.' He wagged his head again. 'I'd have given him a hundred rupees when he asked for the ten, but I thought it might seem patronizing, so I said, "Of course, Nipper boy, here's ten." '

When I asked Jo whether he'd stay on here, he said, 'I'm off tomorrow back to UK. I love it here and I'll be back on a visit, but I've a job. Plumbing, that's what I do. Good money, so, when I get another holiday, I'll be back. I may see Nipper again; I don't know. But what the bloody hell will I tell his family in Newcastle, eh?'

Paul was back with another glass of fenny; it might have been his fifth or his fifteenth. 'Some junkies live by selling bad drugs,' he said. 'There are some really bad people here.'

Richard Wesse said, 'But others – me, for example – live by selling local materials to Europe. Some of the materials here are very beautiful and very cheap. You could stay here for ever doing legitimate work like that, no problem.'

Paul said, 'Richard says you're trying to get to Sri Lanka by sea. Try a port on the south coast of India, at the very tip. A small port called Tuticorin. They have country boats; you've heard of them?'

'Paul's travelled all over southern India,' Richard said. 'He has good advice. Try Tuticorin.'

Chapter Seventeen

I WALKED BACK to the Villa Nunes with Richard Wesse, to the twilight house, with its stained glass, fine tiled floors and gaunt but stately windows, that had nothing to do with the bar on the beach. Two little girls in school tunics wandering under the trees sold me a one-rupee ticket for the Christmas draw at their church of St Alex. The ticket told me that the parish priest, Fr. José Francisco Vaz, promised the winner: '1 hen, 1 Bottle of Brandy, 2 beers, 1 tin of cheese, 1 tin of Mackerels, 1 Pk. of Toffees.' I wondered if their parents warned the girls away from the beach where, among the Richard Wesses, Jos and Pauls, other far less human strangers lived and carried on. I had seen young men with taut, pallid skins, thin grim mouths and hair pulled back into buns so that they looked like discontented governesses, and young women from whose faces all youth seemed to have leaked away. There was a little bit of heaven and something of hell here, and the century was immaterial.

Richard and his wife took me to Old Goa to see the tomb of St Francis Xavier, another slice of unreality in this gloriously unreal region of India. The Basilica of Bom Jesus, a sign said, was built between 1594 and 1605. St Francis, who lived from 1506 to 1552, lay before us in a silver casket. A glass section of the casket revealed a small grey wizened face staring blindly up at the golden barley-sugar pillars. A tiny, pretty Indian nun gazed at the saint, her head on one side. VOX INIMICA FUGAR, I read over the ornate silver of the casket. Above the altar, a weird apparition leaped from the ceiling: a grotesque golden statue, more than life-size, moustached, obese, aproned, skirted and shirted under a great bulging golden turban, rosy arms raised in benison, or to conduct an invisible orchestra, among the barley sugar. It gave me a foretaste of the astonishing churches I toured later in southern India.

'Stay a few days,' Richard suggested. 'They're making a film in Goa. Roger Moore, Gregory Peck, David Niven.' But Charlie Chaplin and Greta Garbo themselves couldn't have held me. I was beginning to experience intimations of mild panic. Even though Cochin might not turn up a ship for me, I had to get on.

We said goodbye. 'Remember Tuticorin,' Richard Wesse said. I wrote the name down in my notebook, and turned away from the charming creepy house that John Nunes built.

Next morning I took a seat in the bus to Bangalore. This was what Richard had advised, and I trusted him. I had made inquiries at the hotel and had been warned that Bangalore is in the centre of southern India, as far from the sea as it is possible to be. Why not go down the coast? But Richard had told me that coastal connections by rail, bus or taxi were hopeless. It might seem daft, he said, but the safest way was by bus to Bangalore and then by bus or hitchhiking from there down to the coast again at Cochin.

It may have been the safest way, but it was not the most comfortable. Bangalore was sixteen hours away; sixteen hours in the seat of a crowded bus, mostly at night. I boarded Super de Luxe bus number MYF 9571 in Panaji. It cost very little, but then it was not de luxe. It was un-air-conditioned, the seats were so close that it was impossible to stretch one's legs, and the roof was so low that I couldn't stand upright without banging my head.

The bus was full, and the journey was one I prefer to forget. Indeed, depressed less by the discomfort and the lack of light to read by than by the mere necessity that had driven me to take this inland route when by now I had contracted a feeling that the sea was my home, I made very few notes of the next twenty-four hours. I remember the corkscrew motions of the bus as it wound its way up from the coast into hill and a plateau, past animal reservations, villages and widely spaced towns. Sitting hunched up with my knees scraping the back of the seat in front, I soon felt the prick of the first insect bite. But rain intervened – heavy, relentless downpours in which no mosquito could fly.

In the dead of night the bus pulled up in the muddy main street of a small town. Street lights shone feebly on puddles of water. Hunched men with clothes over their heads crept up to look at us. Passengers bought fruit, cakes and tea from stalls. When we drove on, I found a large Sikh next to me, his eyes badly bloodshot. He peeled off his socks and then, to my surprise, his turban. Later he had a nightmare and leaped up with an ear-splitting howl, waking up everyone and causing the driver to brake to a jarring halt.

Two students said their college was on strike. 'So we're taking a tour. Good time to see this part of India.'

'Have a really long strike and see it all.'

It was not their strike, they explained; only one thousand

out of two thousand students had gone out. It concerned the vice chancellor of their college, who, the strikers alleged, had three jobs outside the university, 'so he has no time to think of the students'.

At Bangalore the rain fell as steadily as ever. At the West End Hotel, I found a forceful lady called Mrs Das at a travel agent's office. I was tired and ached all over from the constant motion of the bus. My knees felt as if they would never take me upstairs again.

'I want a train or plane to Cochin, please,' I said.

'You'd better walk,' said Mrs Das. Strange talk from a travel agent. 'There's no train for a week because of a coal shortage just now. As for planes, there's no seat for eight days. Fully booked.'

It seemed incredible. 'What if my mother was dying?' I asked.

'You can get an emergency ticket if you can produce a doctor's certificate.'

Buses went half around the world before reaching Cochin from Bangalore, so I braced myself and ordered a taxi. It would cost the equivalent of eighty pounds, but I wasn't going to waste time in Bangalore. I stayed in that fine city just long enough to buy Conan Doyle's *The Sign of Four* in Higginbotham's bookshop, have a meal and a bath, and to allow time for Mrs Das to flush Andrew, her taxi driver, out of a tea shop.

Now it seems absurd to me that I had set so much store on getting to Cochin. Once more I bumped for several hours across the Indian landscape. At dawn next day Andrew and I began to descend through Kerala's coconut forests and paddy fields, now and then giving way to elephants. The nearer we came to the sea the more excited I became, but it was excitement for nothing.

Andrew deposited me at the Sealord Hotel on the waterfront, then drove away, bent on taking the opportunity to visit relations. I slept, awoke refreshed but stiff, and asked at the reception desk for directions to the port and shipping agents' offices. In blazing heat and appalling humidity, I staggered, pouring with sweat, into the office of the Cochin Shipping Company. (It was this office that Captain Bragg's contact in Goa had said it was pointless to telephone.) A man with brows like hairy caterpillars replied to my explanation of my presence, and of my urgent desire to proceed by sea to Colombo, with the unsmiling remark, 'You can fly from Trivandrum in half an hour.'

'I'm travelling by sea.'

'Oh, of course.'

There was a strike, he explained, and it would be a long one. It showed no sign of ending; on the contrary, it was expanding to other sections of the labour force. He himself could suggest nothing. He looked at the current list of shipping. A Yugoslav freighter might leave tomorrow, but Yugoslavs never took casual passengers. No hope there.

A tour in the almost unendurable heat of other shipping offices confirmed this dire news. No ships from Cochin. One man gave me the name of a shipping friend in Colombo. I returned to the Sealord, flung myself down on my bed and let my mind spin like a runaway dynamo.

I had learned one or two other things from the gentleman with the caterpillar eyebrows. I now knew that Cochin was the only deepwater port in south-west India, and that it exported tea, timber, spices and cashew nuts. I had learned that coastal trade had dwindled year by year; traders now preferred road transport. Possibly I could find a country boat from Tuticorin – I had read this name from my notebook; otherwise he would not, I'm sure, have mentioned the place – but it was a long way, only reachable by bad road. On second thoughts, Caterpillar Eyebrows said he wasn't even sure that the country boats would take me. He'd only mentioned the place because I'd asked him . . . I could telephone a Mr Miranda there, a merchant and a shipper; perhaps he would help.

I sprang off the bed and badgered the Sealord's telephone switchboard to connect me to Miranda's office in Tuticorin. It took an hour to get through, and then someone seemed to be frying bacon and eggs on the line. But at last, with a good deal of shouting and repetition, I heard a voice, which told me that Mr Miranda had gone to Madras. I rang off and made a decision to cut adrift from south-west India, to take a train to Trivandrum and fly from there to Colombo. I would give up this stage of my struggle. Indian port strikes had temporarily defeated me, and looked like driving me crazy. Very well, I would leave them to their victory. I would abandon the Malabar coast, perhaps the most beautiful in all India, to breathe new air and make a fresh start. Colombo – I was on my way!

Chapter Eighteen

THE OFFICES OF P. B. Umbichy Ltd, Shipping Agents, Contractors, Colombo, took some finding. They were hidden away near the docks in a two-storey row of ramshackle offices and shops off a narrow street in which, on the rainy Saturday I went there, processions of bullock carts, rickshaws and ancient, diminutive taxis crept through potholes and mud. A strong smell of dried fish pervaded the area.

Umbichy was the name I had been given by a shipping man in Cochin. Having just arrived in Colombo, my immediate concern was the means to leave it for my next major destination, Madras, so I tried Umbichy.

'Upstairs.' One of two skeletal men crouching in a narrow doorway pointed up a dim staircase. Squeezing up to the third floor, I found a small office and two clerks at a desk. We exchanged greetings.

'Oh, yes, we know Mr Muthukaruppan of Lakshmi Lines, Cochin,' one of them said when I handed him the card I had brought. 'What can we do for you, sir?'

I explained my presence in Colombo and said, 'According to Mr Muthukaruppan' – it was not an easy name to pronounce – 'the steamer *Raj Lakshmi* is due to sail from Bombay for Colombo soon. Her destination from Colombo, he told me, might be southern India, Madras.'

'That certainly seems likely. Not Madras, though. Tuticorin might be her destination.' Again that name. It was beginning to mesmerize me.

'She'd take me?'

'If the captain agrees.'

'Of course, I'd really prefer to take a country boat to Tuticorin.'

He shook his head. 'Country boats will not take passengers, certainly not in this weather. We are in the time of the north-east monsoon, and it is very rough. Country boats would not take you.'

'It would be at my risk.'

'Ha, ha. Yes.' He was amused. 'But personally, I doubt . . .'

'To Trincomalee?'

'The east coast is battered by the monsoon gales. Nothing will sail to Trinco until February.'

The gentleman promised to call me at my hotel when the *Raj Lakshmi* arrived, but as I splashed from puddle to puddle in the decaying street I was only marginally encouraged. By now I knew I couldn't put my trust in freighters. The country boats could hardly be less reliable, and they offered a greater adventure. Perhaps I could find a sailing vessel to Madras, Calcutta or Rangoon.

My itinerary now became a process of elimination. There were four ways ahead, apparently. A steamer to Tuticorin? Unlikely; perhaps the *Raj Lakshmi* later. A sailing ship to eastern India or Burma? Or to southern India? Hmm. A steamer to Madras or Calcutta? Possible.

Using an introduction that Angus Wilson, the novelist and biographer of Rudyard Kipling, had given me in London, I met Mrs De Mel, a Colombo hostess and travel agent. Like others, her agency loved airlines and spurned ships, but she put me in touch with the father of the Sri Lankan navy. In vain: Admiral Rajan Kadirgamar politely dismissed the idea of sailing boats to the Bay of Bengal.

'There used to be marvellous brigs – sailing brigs, three-masted, square-rigged, full-fledged sailing ships to Rangoon and Chittagong.' Dismally I noted the words 'used to be'. 'All gone. These chaps used to take salt to the Andamans and bring back rice. All gone.'

The second weakly soaring bird of hope folded its wings and plunged lifeless to earth. Two to go.

Meanwhile I looked around Colombo. Someone – a shipping man in Dubai, I think – had told me the city was 'a dump'. If he was right, I like dumps. Colombo retains the look of an early twentieth-century city. It has a splendid seafront, grand trees and open spaces, and a great many charming or dignified buildings. The heart of Colombo, around the port, is ennobled by handsome rows of awnings and perfectly proportioned pillars outside the Senate, by the red and white arches and decorative cornucopias of Cargill's emporium, by the vice-regal grandeur of the Chartered Bank guarded by stone ceremonial elephants, and by the towering halls of the post office. In the side streets behind the Taprobane Hotel one might expect to see ladies driving with their grooms in horse-drawn gharries and English tea planters in topees on horseback trotting past the Pagoda Tea Rooms ('Bare-bodied people not permitted inside'), the offices of Canon, Cumberbatch and Co. Ltd, Agents, and the square clock tower topped by its lighthouse dome and weather vane, sniffing the pungent air of the Toddy Shop and giving the men with mottled noses who staggered from it a wide berth. Now saris and sarongs have replaced the topees and divided skirts.

The Taprobane Hotel was a perfect lodging for anyone concerned with the port or the sea. From the moment the dark wood-panelled and mirrored lift rose to the Harbour Bar on the fourth and top floor, the Taprobane seemed to me one of the most interesting hotels between Suez and Singapore.

Taprobane was the Greek and Roman name for Ceylon; the Muslims called it Serendip. Once the hotel had been known as the Grand Oriental Hotel. Mrs De Mel showed me some old advertisements for the GOH, as people called it: 'The first modern hotel known in the East . . . Lift, Electric Light and Electric Fans in the Bed Rooms and Public Rooms . . . The Hotel Porter meets all Steamers and takes delivery of Passengers' Luggage. Hire of Carriages or Rickshaws from the Door Porter.'

My room was immense, a relic of those days, with high ceilings and a bathroom as big as most hotel bedrooms. It looked down on Colombo's old harbour, horseshoe-shaped, an artificially made haven full of vessels of all kinds, with godowns (or warehouses) all around and a lighthouse where a plaque said, 'This great work Projected by Governor Sir

Hercules Robinson KCMG . . . was completed April 1885.'

From the Harbour Bar and Restaurant above my room, wide windows looked down on the same scene. The restaurant specialized in curry 'tiffin' (the Anglo-Indian for 'luncheon'), and the bar was a delightfully old-fashioned place, something like the snug, unpretentious wardroom of an old sailing ship. From it, the harbour very much resembled a photograph Mrs De Mel showed me that had been taken ninety years before. Here and in the rest room of the Mission to Seamen Hostel (or Flying Angel Club) I had a few odd encounters.

There was the English ship's engineer, for instance, who had been put ashore by his captain with instructions to the company's agent to get him aboard a flight to London without delay. But delays there had been. At first the engineer had refused to go; then, when the unfortunate agent managed with great difficulty to drive him to the airport, the airline captain refused to take him, on the ground that such a dishevelled and liquor-soaked apparition would terrify his other passengers.

I found myself sharing a table with the engineer in the Harbour Bar. His arm was heavily bandaged. He commented that the bar was 'nicely put together; must be some carpenters around'. A drink or two later he asked, 'What's "a whopper" mean?'

'A whopper? Well—'

'I've fallen a whopper. That's what I've done. What's tha' mean?'

His bandages hid a wound, a big bad one, I could tell. 'Is it painful?'

'Not yet. Delayed shock must follow a thing like that, mustn't it?'

'Caused by a human or an inanimate object?'

He liked the long word. A grimace altered his features into a brief smile. 'Inanimate . . . inanimate . . . very, very inanimate. A glass door.'

His face twitched as he took a long gulp of beer. He had very pale blue eyes, completely expressionless. Some people would have called them killer's eyes.

A youngish man with yellow hair lurched over and sat down with us. He, too, I saw, had been drinking for a long time. He held out an uncertain hand, which I shook; the engineer ignored it, or perhaps he didn't see it.

'*Monro Stahr*. Tycoon Lines. Know what I'm talkin' about?' the newcomer asked. (I have changed the names here.) He had an American accent, Midwestern. I'd seen his ship, a big container vessel, in the harbour, and I ordered him a whisky (a dram was the official measure in Colombo). 'God is love' was tattooed on his right forearm.

'An instant in time,' the engineer said, as if the American didn't exist. 'Who said that?'

'God knows,' I said and the word God seemed to press a switch somewhere in the American.

'God,' he said in a loud, dramatic voice. 'God is beginning to fade on the *Monro Stahr*, I'm tellin' you. God has gone below.'

The engineer ignored him. 'The moment of birth, that's what an instant of time is,' he said. 'A sad moment. Or it could be the moment of death, I suppose. Another sad moment. Or the time in between. Sadder still. What's the important thing about dying?' His cheeks sagged, and he seemed to be looking for the answer under this chair. Or preparing to vomit.

'How to avoid dying full of tubes in a hospital bed,' I suggested.

This cheered him. 'Yes. How right. To avoid tubes.' He looked at me and demanded, 'What carries oil to an engine?'

'Tubes?'

'Tubes, yes.' He raised his eyes and his glass. 'Glorious tubes.' He toasted them gaily.

The American said, 'Let me also inform you that God is now back on that ship. I have brought him back – in full strength. It just don't matter no more what the devil tries.' He pointed at me. 'I'm tellin' you. Even if the devil opens all the valves and tubes on the ship, it ain't goin' to matter one shit. That son-of-a-bitch ship will keep goin'. Because why?'

The engineer looked at him but was silent.

'Because those fuckin' valves and tubes would not be *really* opened, no sir. God's will ain't goin' to be stalled – know what I'm sayin'? Those open tubes would be a god-damn illusion, nothin' more.'

'Are you leaving tonight?' I asked, turning to the engin-eer. I'd heard that the agent might make a second attempt to extricate him tonight.

'I am always bein' thrown out of bars for preachin',' the American said, draining his beer. 'It always happens, so I know the pattern. They tell me to shut up, but I go on preachin'. I'm one hell of a preacher. I stood up for God when I was five. I was reborn aged five. I was being devoured by mosquitoes; the bites I could see, but not the mosquitoes. Can you imagine that? That's how I knew I was reborn. An' now I jest go on preachin' the fuckin' Word of God in bar after bar.

'Some guys' – he leaned forward and lowered his voice – 'some guys look as if they're goin' to zap me. Their fists start comin' at me, then they stop in mid-air. God has stopped those fists. Then the bartenders say, "We won't serve you," so I move on, and it starts all over again in another bar.'

'Are you going to start preaching in here?' I asked.

'No. This ain't the right bar. God tells me – know what I mean? Just talkin' to you may be all He needs tonight. He knows. He'll tell me what to do. Like, I might maybe visit the White House and tell the president to move over. If God tells me to.'

The engineer's blue gaze had settled on the American's nose. I waited to see if God would catch his fist in mid-air.

'So far God ain't told me to do that. So far I've jest brought God back to the ship. Other day, the captain called me up and said, "Boy, they tell me you've brought God back aboard again. I'd bin wondering where the hell He'd got to." He said, "I sure as hell see the fuckin' Will of God movin' in you, boy." That's what he said. Yes, sir. The captain's seen the light. Now that he sees God movin' in me, he says he ain't never goin' to let me out of his goddamn sight.'

He got up and moved unsteadily to the bar. The engineer didn't bother to watch him go. 'Are you flying to London tonight?' I asked again.

'I shall endeavour to,' he said mournfully. 'Nice word, endeavour.' His face twitched, and he demanded in low, furious tones, 'Endeavour to what? Eh?'

'Endeavour, if you'll excuse me, to get us both another drink.'

Nothing would stop the engineer from drinking himself into oblivion. Perhaps the agent would come to collect him soon.

336

In the Harbour Bar of the Taprobane a jumpy figure on a stool knocked his glass of arrak to the floor. He had a young, grey face, which, although not exactly sour or malevolent, was uninviting. He might have been on drugs. He was about to step down shakily from his stool on to the splinters of the glass when I pointed them out to him. He sneaked off, muttering, 'Zank you,' sounding French.

The next day he was back in the bar, and we sat on adjoining stools and began to talk. He was excessively nervous, and there was an aggressive furtiveness about him. His lips shook, and he sipped his arrak convulsively, swallowing with a gasp. Behind us two Englishmen talked in businessmen's tones. 'Ah, that's a good drop of beer after a walk,' one said. 'Yers. Yers, indeed. Hits the spot. I say it hits the spot. Realler does,' said the other.

The Frenchman talked jerkily of Paris. I told him that I sometimes lived there. 'There'll be trouble there this winter. An uprising.'

'Do you mean of those hooligans who call themselves autonomes?'

'*I* am an autonome,' he cried, suddenly sitting up straight, 'and I am *not* a hooligan. We are very, very serious. We are very, very numerous.' His voice rose, and his hand fumbled toward his glass. 'The struggle is growing. It is only just beginning ... Perhaps a holocaust.' His eyes seemed to grow larger in a face so pallid that it might have been raised in a cellar like a mushroom. The little mouth turned down, half baleful, half pleading, seeming to say, Please believe me – and also, Watch out.

Autonomes had made their appearance in the streets of Paris in recent years. They are anarchists, mainly middle-class, extremely violent wreckers with no definite left-wing ideology but dedicated to the destruction of property, even by bombs. Parisians had seen them rushing about in commandos – peeling off from peaceful and legal demonstrations of, say, trade unionists, to engage the police in pitched battles and to wreck cars and shop windows. Their attitude, it seemed from their spasmodic statements to the press, was: destroy everything – then let's see.

From behind us, English boardroom voices came to me in snatches. 'Werll thern, what's the problem?' . . . 'So I said, "Now look here, just you look here . . ." ' 'Go werst, young man, go werst, eh? Huh, huh, huh.' One of them was laughing.

At the bar the big eyes looked at me intensely. 'What do we want, we autonomes? We want work for all. Minimum wages. No more support for Idi Amin and for fascist colonels in South America. Idi Amin' – his face contorted in disgust – 'was a sort of black Englishman. Uganda was a new British colony, with Amin at the head.'

'But he was hated and ridiculed in England.'

'I know all about it. You're wrong.' He spoke fiercely. 'Britain wants to control the riches of South Africa – the gold and the copper. They want to use it to make the black peoples poorer. Everyone knows that. It's well known.'

'Where do you find this unquestionable truth?'

'From the newspapers. Luckily, all important problems in the world are quite simple. Black and white. It's all so clear when you come from the ranks of the deprived.' He was beginning to shout.

The imperturbable voices behind me never faltered: '. . . In a bit of a merss, I'll be bound . . .' 'Well, he ran off to – where was it? – somewhere beginning with "s". Bromley; that's it . . .' 'Bromley doesn't begin with "ers" '.

Something wrong there. Same again?' 'Why not? Hits the spot . . .' 'God blerss.'

I said, 'All right, calm down. You'd better eat something.'

Over lunch, the autonome – his name was Jean-Marie – quietened down. He was a dropout, he said, and lived with his parents, who ran a restaurant near the Rond Point on the Champs Elysées.

'You're hardly one of the deprived, then.'

He let that pass. 'A poll taken by *Student* magazine in Paris recently showed that fifteen per cent of the students are with us. There'll certainly be a big upheaval. Oh, certainly we can't take power in France, but by violence we can push the system into an extreme fascist reaction. We can force people to make the choice: the fascist system or us.'

'Do your parents worry about you?'

'They worry about me not have a job.'

'What do you do for money?'

'I steal. I love going into those big stores and taking things under the nose of the guards. Then I give a lot of it away, just hand it to people in the street, for fun.'

'If you're deprived, why are you here? How can you afford it?' He was wearing an expensive watch.

Jean-Marie shrugged without answering. 'I liked Mexico. The people have dignity there. Poor, but dignified. Here they've no dignity.'

'Hospitable and friendly, though.'

'I don't want that. I can't stand sentiment, although I like dogs. In Ceylon a dog bit me.'

'A hard one, are you?'

'I'm a cyclopath.'

'A what?'

'A cyclopath.' He made an up-and-down movement

with his flat palm. Mad for bicycles? Smiling a Mona Lisa smile, he held out his arm. 'Look.' I saw a thin grey arm, nothing more. Impatiently he jabbed with a finger at a faint line or two across the wrist. 'I wanted to kill myself.' It was a proud declaration. (Ah, a *psychopath*.)

'Recently?'

'In July. That was the third time.'

'Slash your wrists each time?'

'First two times I tried gas.'

'The restaurant's oven?'

'The gas ring in my room.'

'And?'

'My sister noticed I was in that kind of state, so she was keeping her eye on me. She turned off the gas twice, and bandaged me up in the bath the third time.'

'In the bath?'

'That's where I did it.'

'Please don't try again now.'

'No, no, I don't feel like that any more. Not now that the uprising is coming. I'll be ready for it. In February or March.'

'To the berst of my knowledge,' a familiar English voice floated across our chopped paw-paw, 'it wasn't a shotgun wedding so much as a popgun wedding.'

'Werll, God blerss my soul. Oh, wine. Thanks much-ler.'

February or March is a year ago, more or less, so Jean-Marie is still waiting for his upheaval. I hope his poor sister hasn't had to save his life yet again.

Admiral Kadirgamar had advised me to visit the harbour master. It was good advice that worked like magic to dispel my problems.

The Port Authority building lay below my window at the Taprobane. In a spacious Victorian office, all dark wood and polished brass, Captain George Henricus murmured, 'Take a pew. Cup of tea?'

A slender man, he wore a white shirt and shorts, high white stockings and black slippers. A telescope hung on a wall; wide windows looked down on the harbour. On his door was a sign, MASTER ATTENDANT.

There are only two Master Attendants in the world; one is in Colombo, the other in Singapore. All other ports have harbour masters. It is not clear why. In 'The End of the Tether', Joseph Conrad writes of the Master Attendant in Singapore:

> A Master Attendant is a superior sort of harbour master . . . a Government official, a magistrate for the waters of his port, and possessed of vast but ill-defined disciplinary authority over seamen of all classes. This particular Master-Attendant was reported to consider it miserably inadequate on the ground that it did not include the power of life and death.

It was impossible, I soon discovered, to imagine the gentle Captain Henricus, descended from a Dutch Baptist 'burgher' (the term for Dutch or Portuguese colonists of Sri Lanka), pining for such powers. (In an old book about Ceylon I read that 'the Portuguese came with sword and cross; the Dutch with ledger and law-book; the British with roads and railways'. The dates it gave for their respective periods of supremacy were 1500–1650; 1650–1800; 1800–1950: a hundred and fifty years each.)

A servant with a wall-eye poured tea from a large brown teapot, then wound a brass-fronted wall clock with a heavy key. A board listed the names of all Master Attendants since 1815; mostly they were captains in the Royal Navy. A chalk scrawl reminded Captain Henricus that the liner *QE2* would arrive on 7 March 1981. 'We like to know in advance,' he said, smiling.

The captain's duties were contained in a copy of the *Legislative Enactments of Ceylon*, 1956 edition, which lay on his table. He could, for instance, 'penalise captains who threw overboard stones or ballast or rubbish, or any other thing whatever likely to form a bank or shoal or to be detrimental to navigation'. (Fine: two hundred rupees.) He could claim as government property all anchors recovered and not claimed within twelve months. He could enforce prohibition of diving for money. (Penalty: one month in prison.)

Further, the master attendant raised wrecks impeding navigation and gave assistance to ships in distress. He also licensed bumboats and their tindals. Tindals were the men in charge of the bumboats, and bumboat is the term for private boats, perhaps carrying laundrymen or ships' chandlers with stores alongside vessels, or jolly boats or gigs carrying passengers about the harbour.

Oil pollution? 'That will be part of my duties soon,' said Captain Henricus. 'But even now I don't hesitate to say to captains, "Look, you know what you've just done – now clear up the mess you've caused." I don't hesitate.'

Captain Henricus confirmed that it was useless at this time of year to look for sea transport to Trincomalee or Madras. 'Why don't you take a look around the harbour?' he suggested. 'There are a couple of Tamil sailing ships in from Tuticorin.' That name again . . .

He gave me a pass, and I set out to wander around the

walled harbour, visiting the old breakwater and its light-house, pausing by the ancient steam tug with a long funnel that still whirred and panted about the harbour. In their very names, old landmarks advertised their age and the international maritime history of Colombo: the Leyden Bastion, the Delft Warehouse and the Baghdad Gate (an old and still-existing trade with Iraq accounts not only for this name but also for the Muslim population of Colombo).

There were two schooners at berth, as Captain Henricus had said, and I stared at them and stared again at these magnificent ships. I couldn't believe my eyes. Great heavy-timbered three-masters, with soaring thick black masts like sooty columns in a burned-out temple, and mainsails that arced up, Arab style, from the deck on sickle-shaped spars. They looked as I imagined those ships the great Captain James Cook first went to sea in, the Whitby colliers. These had broad decks covered with coils of ropes, tarpaulins and sails, and a swarm of very black men with muscular limbs who gathered around me pointing and laughing when they spotted the camera around my neck.

A man in shirt and trousers, an agent's representative, I suppose, asked if he could help me, and then said, 'Yes, these ships will be sailing to Tuticorin as soon as they've loaded a cargo of seeds. A few days more, depending on the weather.' Did they take passengers? What about me? The men laughed, and the agent's man said he doubted if it would be comfortable for a passenger like me. They had no engines, only sails. 'Very primitive.'

'I don't mind that.'

'Well, you could talk to our office about it. Ceylon Shipping Lines, Apothecary Buildings.'

I thanked him and made for Apothecary Buildings, my heart pounding. Soon I was talking to the general manager of the Ceylon Shipping Lines, a young, courteous man, who was surprised and amused by my request.

'You're not afraid of taking one of those sailing ships, Mr Young? There's a risk . . .'

'Can you arrange it?'

'Well, actually, it is not we who, strictly speaking . . . I'll just use the telephone if you'll excuse me . . . to the man who . . .'

He dialled, and soon a voice sounded faintly on the other end. 'I have a Mr Young here,' the general manager said, and explained the circumstances. Laughter followed at both ends of the line. In a moment he rang off.

'Mr Missier says the last European passenger he allowed on one of those ships turned out to be wanted by Interpol. Are you wanted by Interpol, Mr Young? In any case, Mr Missier is waiting for you.'

Mr Missier's office was even harder to find than Mr Umbichy's had been; it was deeper into the tumultuous maze of muddy streets around the old port. I had to squeeze between roaring trucks, under the snuffling noses of oxen in shafts, and against the sweat-streaked skins of coolies in sarongs knotted at the hips who heaved at long iron-framed barrows and still found the breath to shout, 'Helloo, sir.' I ended up at the corner of a narrow cobbled lane carpeted with squashed coconut tops, mango skins and ox dung. Here and there a dead rat lay in the gutter.

Mr Missier's office was in a small rectangular loft at the top of steep wooden steps. You approached it from the street through a long shadowy room at the entrance of which clerks with the Hindu spot on their foreheads tabulated the weighing of sacks of small onions, potatoes, green and red chillies, dried prawns and peanuts. Sacks of these commodities were stacked against the walls. In an aroma of onions an old woman squatted in a corner chewing betel and squirts of betel juice marked the floor.

As my head slowly rose above the level of the office floor where Mr Missier made his living, I registered two pairs of legs, two waists and finally two pairs of hands stretched out to help me up the last three steps. An elderly voice said, 'Hullo, sir. Well, well . . .'

Mr Missier was sitting at a desk, looking at me over his spectacles. An elderly man with a long, thin face and nose, he stretched forward a bony hand. 'Please be seated.'

The clerks and the teaboy who had helped me up now offered a rickety wooden chair, and placed before me on the desk a small glass, a bottle of fizzy, sweet barley water, a packet of cigarettes and a box of matches.

A telephone on a high, old-fashioned cradle rang and Mr Missier answered it.

'Yes, yes,' he said into it, waving at me to drink the barley water. 'If . . . if . . . for the sake of argument . . . the documents, there's some hitch. Can the goods be shipped back . . . I mean with no fuss and that sort of thing?' His face set into a sterner expression, although it was not a face that could be very stern. 'No, no, impossible . . . Exchange-control regulations . . . That would never do . . . Quite, quite.' As he rang off his face cleared again. A kind face. I liked Mr Missier even before he arranged everything for me.

He pushed a card across the table, and I pushed mine back. His read:

R. Missier and Co.
Sole Agents for Ceylon Shipping Lines Ltd,
Sailing Vessels, Shipping Clearing and
Forwarding and Customs House Agents

A sketch of a sailing ship like the ones I'd seen in the harbour was printed in blue under the lettering.

The basic contents of Mr Missier's headquarters were whitewashed walls, a single overhead fan, two wall calendars, a tiny safe, a filing cabinet, three tables and six people, one of them a teaboy. There were other objects, of course: his desk, covered in black leatherette with a ziggurat of torn files; an umbrella hanging from the top of the plastic curtain over the bottom half of a window with rusty bars. The window opened outwards, and a large crow perched on the frame, cawing loudly. One of the clerks poked at it every now and then with the umbrella, and it flew off, returning a moment later to continue its cawing.

A wax Virgin and Child in a glass case, lit with one small bulb on the wall behind Mr Missier's head, attracted my attention. He said, 'Formerly, Mr Young, our family was Hindu. We were converted by Francis Xavier when he came to Tuticorin. We're all Catholics in this shipping business – one hundred per cent. My father-in-law owned sailing vessels in Tuticorin, but he became very old and so gave it up. We came here many years ago now, in 1926.'

The crow let rip with a string of caws that were like the harsh noise of a man wrenching the fender off a bus. Mr Missier's soft voice disappeared under the sound for a while, although his lips continued to move.

'That's my future son-in-law,' he said audibly at last, pointing to the young man who was trying to jab the crow off the window frame with the umbrella. 'It's a family business, here and in Tuticorin. I was born, bred and married in Tuticorin.'

'Those sailing ships I saw in the harbour—' My pulse accelerated. 'Would they take me?'

'That depends, Mr Young. Let me tell you about them. At Tuticorin there are no mechanized boats at all, but these sailing ships, built there, sail up to Cochin – sometimes even to Bombay in the right monsoon. From here to Tuticorin it is too rough when the south-west monsoon blows. They've lost several vessels on this crossing.'

The trade with southern India, he said, was in buffalo hides, graphite, grams, dried fish, betel leaves, gypsum, salt (Tuticorin is famous for salt), safety matches, cement – everything.

'Another thing. The last man we put aboard a ship of ours' – Mr Missier smiled and shook his head in mock disapproval – 'was a German fellow, and it turned out Interpol was searching for him. Very embarrassing, as you can appreciate.'

An obvious question seemed to hang silently in the air, so I explained why I wanted to sail to Tuticorin.

He listened carefully – the whole office listened – and

then sat back and smiled an angelic smile. 'I love England, Mr Young. We used to do such a *lot* of good business with England. Lace business. Nottingham. I had so many friends in England, very big merchants and very good friends to me.'

He opened a drawer and handed me a photograph, taken in a studio in Colombo, of a comfortably built Englishman posed with a younger, black-haired Missier. 'Very rich men. Millionaires, I suppose. The war changed everything. Before it, commerce was free; you could do what you wanted, and all you needed was energy, keenness, hard work. But after the war, so many controls made it nearly impossible to trade. Now . . .'

His face looked sad and pinched, contemplating the dead past. Then he said, 'You'll be very uncomfortable on those ships,' and smiled. 'You'd better take some biscuits with you. And a pineapple.' He hadn't said, 'Why don't you go by air to Madras?' I knew then that he would arrange everything.

'I'll speak to the captain. You will have to see the immigration people here. Captain Henricus, you've met him? Oh, well, that's all that matters. Get a letter and perhaps a visa for India. I shall write to the customs in Tuticorin; I have a nephew there. The ship will take on cargo in a day or two. Please come and see me tomorrow.'

While I finished my barley water Missier's future son-in-law slapped at the wire mesh over the window with a rolled Sinhalese newspaper. The crow sprang away, flew a lazy circle, alighted again on the same spot and the cawing resumed, like a man ripping the roof off the same bus. The sequence repeated itself like a Morris dance: slap, spring, circle, slap . . .

I pushed back through the lane of sweaty black bodies. The heat was intense, but the sweat of anxiety and urgency had left me. I stopped at the Nawa Rasa 'Cool Spot' stall and sucked a pineapple, strolled past the row of clothing stalls near the Sri Bodhiraja Temple opposite the Baghdad Gate, sidestepped the crowds around the Sir Cyril De Zoysa Building, which houses the Young Men's Buddhist Association, and skirted the offices of the *Sunday Times of Ceylon* and the *Ceylon Daily Mirror*. Beyond a grogshop and a crumbling hostelry I turned right and found the Taprobane.

The stately Edwardian lift took me to the third floor. From my window overlooking the harbour I focused with my binoculars on the black spars of the two Tuticorin sailing ships. Their sails were partly expanded, limply drying in the sun after a downpour, so that they looked like the wings of an exhausted moth.

The Tuticorin adventure was not to take place right away, however. Mr Missier was outraged by the churlish attitude of the captain of the sailing ship he had planned to put me on. Having agreed to take me, the captain had started to argue over what I should pay. It was never clear to me exactly what was said, but whatever it was shocked Mr Missier's sense of honour. Later he said, 'Such shouting. I told him, "Don't be so hard. Hardness in life does no one any good." And he is a Catholic! I told him he should be proud to have you on his ship, not go shouting like a wild man. It was not Catholic behaviour – that is what I told him.'

The upshot was that I had to wait for the next ship to arrive from Tuticorin, which would not be for a week or ten days. I composed myself, and luckily, two possibilities arose to keep me busy.

Mrs De Mel had introduced me to Admiral Kadirgamar. At a party at the house of this all-knowing lady I now met the admiral's brother, Sam, one of Sri Lanka's best lawyers, and also a former acquaintance from Singapore, Tom Abraham. At this moment, he was the Indian high commissioner in Colombo, which could hardly have been a better stroke of luck.

When I had moaned to him about the delay, Sam Kadirgamar immediately advised me to fill the time before Tuticorin with a visit to the Maldive Islands – 'a necklace of tiny jewel-like atolls,' he said, four hundred miles west of Sri Lanka. Small vessels went there at regular intervals, and some of them took passengers, he thought. It was an appealing notion.

Tom Abraham did even more. In the middle of yet one more recitation of my plans and progress so far, he stopped me when I mentioned the unhelpful Tourist Board man in Bombay.

'Wait. The Andamans. You couldn't get a permit for the Andamans, is that right? And you want to go there?'

'Very much, but I'm afraid Indian government regulations—'

'I have no time for red tape.' He thought for a minute, then told me that if I could occupy myself for a week or so, he would see what he could do about a permit for the Andamans.

'Tom, with every respect, I doubt—'

'You want to bet?'

I didn't want to bet, so I took a supportive drink instead, and time showed that it was by far the wiser thing to do. I left Mrs De Mel's feeling so blithe that I fairly skipped through the doors of the Taprobane.

My rough ride to the Maldives sticks in my mind as the 'Tale of Two Bird Men'. I shall never really know how close I was to being drowned. On the other hand, I now know how to open a coconut with a spanner.

There was a good bird man and a bad one. The bad one sat in an office in Chatham Street, cold, white-haired and hunched over like a vindictive sea eagle. He represented the owners of the small Maldivian launch, a mere twenty-five tons, that would accommodate me for three days and three nights across that quite wide stretch of water. He took obvious delight in keeping customers seated on hard chairs while, with excruciating deliberation, he busied himself with other matters without so much as a glance, much less a 'good morning'. There was no offer of tea here, nor even a minimum of Sri Lankan warmth. The only good thing about Sea Eagle was that he finally arranged my passage, and this was all that really mattered.

The voyage to Malé, the capital of the Maldives, began badly with a dispute between the captain of the launch and Sea Eagle that delayed our departure by several hours.

It was a filthy night when I reported to the harbour for sailing. Rain was bouncing off the docks, but it would have been difficult in any weather to spot the launch, the smallest of all the vessels I sailed in during my odyssey: twenty-five tons, forty feet long, powered by a Thorneycroft 125-h.p. engine making six knots – with luck. I found her at last, crouched like a frightened pygmy between two metal giants, a Sri Lankan freighter and a ship from Canton. The comparatively huge hawsers of these two towering neighbours somehow added a puny absurdity to the launch's littleness, so that she looked more like a dinghy. I stood in the rain and thought, Is this what we're going to cross more than four hundred miles of water in? Three days or more in *this*?

Naturally Sea Eagle did nothing to raise my spirits. His dispute with the captain postponed our time of departure to 11.45 p.m., trapping us all in solid sheets of rain. Despite, or because of, the rain, it was muggy almost beyond endurance on the cramped deck of the launch, and a nauseous smell rose from the stygian, stagnant water trapped in our corner of the harbour, the area farthest from the outlet to the sea.

The angry Sea Eagle kept urging the crew to cram an immense cargo of furniture from trucks into the tiny holds of the launch: large, heavy panels of compressed wood, chairs and dozens of lavatory seats. 'The owner's representative has accepted this cargo,' he snapped when the captain protested, and refused to allow any of the shipment to wait for a later vessel. Truck after truck drew up, the crew forced more chairs and tables into the last nooks and crannies of the hold, and we settled lower and lower into the water. I waited, getting wet, noticing Sea Eagle's avian ability to turn his head rather more than ninety degrees, and fighting a desire to go ashore and forget the whole adventure.

The launch had two bunks, no mattresses and no awnings. Space in the tiny hutchlike cabin area, apparently constructed out of a handful of nails and a hundredweight of driftwood, was further diminished by the metal trunks of the crew, a spare outboard motor, and the exhaust pipe of the engine that thrust up through the middle of the cabin to the upper air. This exhaust was a serious cont-inual danger to the unwary because in rough weather it was exceedingly well placed to serve as a natural hand-hold, and yet was almost red-hot. As a result, by the time we reached Malé, I lacked skin on three fingers of my right hand.

When Sam Kadirgamar, QC, had urged me to take a look at the Maldives, I knew nothing about them, and the next day I had accepted his invitation to consult a book or two in his library. From these, I discovered that the Maldives were an archipelago four hundred miles south-west of Ceylon, a chain of two thousand coral islands stretching six hundred and fifty miles, some only a few yards long. Maldivians were Muslims, the books said, and their ancient rulers had titled themselves Sultans of the Thirteen Atolls and Twelve Thousand Islands. The islands produced fish, breadfruit, coconuts, pumpkins, paw-paws, limes, and the inhabitants spoke their own language, although words from other tongues had been fused into the original, like new coral into a reef: Sinhalese, Arabic, Urdu, Persian, English, Malay, Sanskrit and Portuguese.

'The Maldivians are a civilised and peaceful race,' a monograph informed me, and dark brown of hue. Patroniz-ingly it added, 'The women are somewhat fairer than the men – some of them distinctly pretty.'

The *West Coast of India Pilot* informed me that in 1960 HMS *Scarborough* reported that the coral islands on the atolls could be detected by radar at a range of just over twenty miles, but that the intricate channels between them required

local knowledge. Between Sri Lanka and the Maldives were great sub-oceanic trenches, some perhaps thirteen thousand feet deep. 'There is no bottom at the depth of 200 fathoms,' the *Pilot* said.

We moved out of the harbour at last, past the friendly light at the end of the breakwater, and felt the light lift and fall of the open sea. Lightning flashes silhouetted mountainous cloud formations.

I moved back to the stern of the launch – it wasn't far to scramble over the roof of the cabin with its protruding funnel – and found the captain, a thin young man with big teeth, and a helmsman, an even younger Maldivian, standing in a small raised, roofed area, an even tinier hutch than the cabin and engine housing. The launch had no wheel; the helmsman steered standing up by straddling a long thick, rounded wooden spar attached to the rudder, pushing it or restraining its movements with the muscles of his thighs. It looked agonizing. The spar was heavy, and in a high sea I imagined that it would slam back and forth almost uncontrollably.

The helmsman was having no trouble now. He stood in a red undershirt and bathing trunks, peering at the compass on the ledge formed by the roof of the engine housing in front of him, the helm spar protruding between his upper thighs like a giant phallus, each vibration of the rudder travelling up the spar and shaking his leg muscles like jelly. He looked at me, grinned and wrapped a tiny, inadequate towel around his hips. If this was modesty, it was misjudged; the great spar thrusting through the towel only increased the effect.

My notes read:

A light rolling. I take one of the two ledges – or bunks, if that is what they really are. It has a wafer-thin woven mat on it. I roll my anorak into a pillow and spread my towel like a blanket. The engine pounds away; its chimney throws up a bright jet of smoke and sparks. A breeze stirs the fug of the cabin but cannot dispel it.

Through the night, I see the crew (I don't sleep much) changing their watches. Six men plus the captain. They scramble agilely about in the cramped space, changing from towels to sarongs and back again. Sometimes they bathe on deck outside the cabin door, pouring sea water over their wiry hair, drying themselves with small coloured towels, rubbing scented ointment into their chests, cheeks, armpits and under their sarongs. The sweet smell of the ointment tempers the prevailing odour of fuel oil, hot metal, sweat and vegetables.

A young Australian was on the launch. He was taciturn – shy, I think. He was travelling – slowly, he said – to Europe. 'What is Time?' he asked, and was silent.

There were also two Maldivian passengers who travelled on the cabin roof. During the night, they offered me a cut or two from what looked like a hard plug of dark, rich

tobacco, but which was in fact a dark, rich plug of compressed fish. It looked like the dried meat of South Africa
called biltong. The Maldivians extracted it from the folds
of their sarongs and hacked pieces off it with a penknife. It
tasted mildly fishy and was very hard on the teeth.

I wondered what fish it came from. 'Maldive fish,' they
answered.

'Mullet?'

'Mullet,' they agreed. But they were repeating what I
said.

The launch's crew spoke very few words of English, and
that included the Starling Cook, although when I think of
him I recall that somehow we communicated quite effec-
tively. I call him the Starling Cook because of his looks.
He was more or less the colour of a starling, very dark in
blue shorts and shirt. He was short and fat-bodied, and his
skinny bowlegs protruded out of his shorts like a black
wishbone. He had long bare feet and very little neck; his
shoulders were hunched, his arms long, and his nose was a
beak that curved thinly between large expressive eyes. I
suppose he was in his forties or fifties. Some seamen, I have
noticed, quietly observe the pitch and toss of a deck and
time their moves across it like a computer, perhaps quite
unaware of their calculation. The Starling Cook was not
like that; he scuttled crablike over the deck, hardly laying
a hand on any support.

The first morning, the wind rose and the broken water
swayed and rocked us quite a bit – a foretaste of things to
come. The launch was so small that anything affected its
stability. I could hear the fresh water sloshing in the two
tanks of the foredeck. The sea looked very big.

The Starling Cook's domain was near the bows. Here

he presided over a wooden-box structure that shielded a small metal stick-burning stove about a foot high. From it the wind blew clouds of sparks that showered across the rusty barrels of diesel fuel, crates, piles of rope, pineapples and tyre fenders, as well as a tangle of bamboo chairs that were part of Sea Eagle's cargo. We might, I thought, all go up (or down) in a spectacular Viking's funeral. Here the Starling Cook cut and served pineapple chunks at night, and for breakfast made tea and *nan* – flat, oily bread – with a very sweet form of custard. Breakfast was at first light. At 9.00 a.m. the first day, and on succeeding mornings, the Starling Cook appeared at my elbow. I felt a very gentle plucking at my sleeve, and a sound it is difficult to describe – a mew is perhaps the best word. The Starling Cook was offering me *pan*, the tiny sandwich of betel leaf, areca nut and lime that all Asia east of the Gulf chews the way Westerners chew gum. It has a tart, clean taste, not bitter or fiery as I had expected, and the juice trickles from the corners of the mouth like blood. I remembered seeing middle-aged Vietnamese women, their teeth blackened from years of chewing, sitting with red juice glistening on their lips as if they had just eaten their babies.

I watched the Starling Cook for hours as he moved about his restricted kingdom. I saw, for example, how he opened a coconut with a spanner, holding it in one hand, the spanner in the other, and tapping it with many small, firm strokes around its middle until it fell apart in two neat halves. He scraped each half against the upturned sharp metal prong of what looked like a shoehorn, which he clamped between his knees; then he wrapped the gratings in a porous cloth, and dunked them into a wide pan of water and rice. He scooped up seawater to cook the rice in, and always cleaned his pots and pans in seawater too. On vessels like this, no one dreams of using fresh water for anything but drinking. His implements were few but sufficient; a huge soot-black kettle and two deep cooking pans were the basic containers. There was also a wide, open tray on to which he poured uncooked rice before he and a wild-haired assistant of dishevelled aspect picked out the bad grains. Just inside the cabin door were arranged his little sacks of cabbages, beans, leaves, chillies (green and red), cardamom, small cumin seeds, coriander, black peppers, cinnamon and garlic.

What did the Starling Cook make us for dinner that first day? My notebook says: rice, dried fish, diced and curried potatoes, onions and raw chillies. He ladled it out of pans into chipped metal plates, and we staggered away with our portions like squirrels catching acorns, and sat on diesel barrels or coils of rope to eat in silence with our fingers. We got no tea with meals, only tepid fresh water from the tank.

The weather was unfriendly. The sea was black and ominous like the sky, and soon seemed to grow bigger. Although it retained its oily smoothness, I felt as if under the surface something very big and unpleasant were waiting to burst up and horrify us. It was a menace not unlike that at the opening stages of my recurring nightmare.

In this dream I am sitting alone on a flat, empty beach, or perhaps in mid-ocean in a rowing boat. The sun is shining; the sea sparkles; I am happy and at peace. But soon small shadows begin to smudge the sunlight. Little by little, terrifyingly, the sky and the sea darken, and at last the sun is extinguished by immense black clouds; what has been a perfect day becomes at last a sort of night. A roaring noise, a slow diffused thunder makes itself heard, filling the seascape like a swelling drum roll, a prelude . . .

I am prepared for what I see next, which is why I grip the sides of the boat. What I see looks like an immense island of wet slate slowly rising from the water; it stretches almost a hundred and eighty degrees before my eyes. But it is not an island. It is a whale – the biggest whale anyone has ever imagined.

Soon the whale is fully surfaced, and the roaring grows even louder – another prelude. I know that the whale is not going to lie there. It is going to do its trick, and its trick is to imitate a salmon; it is going to leap.

It leaps. Can you imagine a leviathan as big as the *Queen Elizabeth* leaping several hundred feet in the air? I sit alone in that sea, clinging to the sides of the rowing boat. What else can I do but hold on desperately, knowing what will follow when the whale falls back into the water? A tidal wave from horizon to horizon . . .

But I always wake up before the tidal wave.

When the Starling Cook had finished swilling out his pots and pans with seawater, the waves started to grow larger, and a big and mounting swell from the starboard began to push the launch over to an angle of thirty degrees. The sky was quite bright, not at all like the sky in my nightmare, and a full moon was rising behind us, coming up over Sri Lanka, which by now was well out of sight. The moonlight turned the agitated water into heaving sheets of wet mackintosh. I thought of the immense depths below us. 'No bottom at the depth of 200 fathoms.'

The Starling Cook was watching me; he was obviously

fascinated by the presence of this European passenger on board. When he caught my eye he grinned and danced a few steps on his piece of deck, pointing excitedly at the moon. He made a hoop with his long arms, miming a full moon, and then jabbed a finger at the waves. The moon's to blame for all this, he was saying. His expressive eyes looked anxious.

I paid a hazardous visit to the captain in the stern, who gave me all his white teeth in an ugly grin and said, 'Storm. Moon make big sea. Big sea storm.' I staggered back to the bows and lay down tensely on my towel in the hard little bunk. The Australian was already in his, and finding it difficult to stay there. A discarded volume of Kurt Vonnegut lay on the deck, and a forty-degree list threw me violently after it. Scrambling back bruised into the bunk, I tried to wedge myself by pushing one foot against the ceiling and the other against the bulkhead, grasping with one hand the window frame over my head. The strain on my legs and arms soon became too great. Hauling myself out on deck, I saw that clouds now covered the stars and that the moon was only an area of bright haze in the sky. The wind took one's breath away.

My notes become sea-stained here:

We are nearly on our beam ends once every minute and a half. The planks shuffle back and forth on the deck as the waves strike us, and the grinding and creaking parts of the old launch drown the noise of the engine, pistons, prop shaft, wind and sea. The chimney seems to be red-hot, and acts like a stove in the already overheated, confined space of the cabin. Boxes slide and fall; metal trunks shift. A heavy case – it must weigh a lot because it was the last thing to be loaded, and the whole crew had to struggle to manhandle it aboard – has begun to crash into and buckle the only lifeboat, which in any case is a poor light metal thing buried under a small mountain of pineapples, bamboo furniture and ceramic lavatory bowls.

One of the fresh-water tanks is leaking. The crew ladles the water from it to the other tank, which requires much rushing up and slithering down sodden decks in semi-darkness, with sarongs hitched up, slipping down or falling open. (Sarongs, it seems, are fair-weather garments.)

The sight of Hassan Ali in the wheelhouse window alarms me. He is clutching for dear life two- vertical beams on either side of the compass. His face is fixed in an expression of agony or terror, teeth gritted, eyes staring. He looks terrified to dementia: a man facing a watery death? But I remember what I cannot see. His lower half is straining to control that heavy rudder handle, which must be vibrating and jerking about like a bucking bronco, battering his thighs. Hassan is grimacing with effort, not fear.

The seas are very big; they are breaking over us. The moon has gone behind two banks of cloud: one grim, thick and unmoving, the other low and scudding. From my 'porthole' I can see the black and grey strips of cloud streaming past back and forth according to the roll and dip of the launch. The corkscrew motion is exhausting. Two of the Maldivian passengers have already been very sick; they huddle together, green and horrified. I have offered them my ledge and seasickness pills, but they have refused both.

Now the Starling Cook joins the drama. Facing me, he is smiling and gibbering unintelligibly. Suddenly his eyes switch from my face to something over my shoulder – something, to judge by the horror on his face, too appalling to imagine. His eyes stretch open to an amazing size, and he opens his wide mouth and screams, '*Eeeeeeeeeee—aaaaaa—aaayyyyyyyyyy.*'

The sound was shattering, rising like the mixed sound of a whistling kettle and an air-raid siren above the racket of creaks and thuds of shifting cargo, wind, and crashing of the sea against the old wooden hull. Even if the whale of my dreams had surfaced behind us, I would have had to follow his pointing finger, turn and look. There was no whale; instead, I saw a low black cliff, visible because it was darker than the grey-black of the clouds. Higher than our stubby mast, it was about eighty yards away and advancing.

Thanks to the Starling Cook's scream, I had time to wedge myself into the cabin doorway, bracing myself with feet and elbows. The Starling Cook himself leaped with astounding agility for the mast and clung to it, wrapping his arms and wishbone legs around it like a koala bear on a eucalyptus trunk. The impact of the wave was awesome. The launch heeled over – ninety degrees? God knows. Solid slabs of black water toppled over the gunwales, and everything on deck or in the cabin seemed to go adrift. Water filled my clothes, eyes and ears. Water cascaded from the legs of the Starling Cook's shorts. He squawked like a wet hen and gestured at me, pointing once more at the moon with one hand and at the waves with the other.

The Australian, I saw, was out of his bunk again, and as

the launch righted herself – she surprised me by managing to do so – he crawled his way past me in the doorway, shouting, 'Someone's got to tell that captain to steer a different course. He'll have the bloody thing capsizing.'

'Leave him alone!' I yelled into his ear. 'Must know this route by now. Must know the weather. It's his beat.' I knew enough about seagoing to be well aware that passengers should never try to advise a captain on how to sail his ship, whoever he is, whatever the size of the vessel, or however frightening the storm. I can imagine some captains taking such backseat driving very ill indeed – even, perhaps in an emergency, taking a pistol from a pocket: 'I must ask you to leave the bridge at once.' Like Captain Ahab, or Captain Bligh.

I didn't catch more of the Australian's reply than '. . . do something . . .' as he scrabbled his way astern. Later I looked back to see if he'd been thrown overboard, but he was only crouched near the ramshackle wheelhouse, where by now another unfortunate was straining and grimacing astride the rudder bar in Hassan's place. Next day the Australian told me he had politely suggested that the captain might alter course by a degree or two in order to take the seas nearer to head-on. The captain had smiled toothily – had he even understood? – and had altered nothing.

Again and again, the clifflike waves came at us and every few minutes the eyes of the Starling Cook forewarned me of impending disaster. Sometimes he tugged at my shirt before releasing his awful cry – '*Eeeeeeeeeee—aaaaaa—aaaaayyyyyy*' – and again we would cling: I in my doorway, he like a monkey to the mast. There was nothing else to do but hope – although once or twice I did ask myself what I was doing there at all.

During the night I saw the lights of three or four big

ships going north or south. They were small comfort; we could have capsized quite near them and they would have been none the wiser, for we had neither radio nor rockets.

In the early morning I fell uneasily asleep. The first thing I saw when I woke up was a big Maldivian sailor perched on the rail brushing his teeth under a triangular sail. The crew had hoisted canvas during the early hours when the sea's fury abated. The wind was now north-east, and the sail filled satisfactorily.

The Starling Cook was up and about, too, shaping lumps of dough into white cricket balls, and then rolling them out flat on a hot plate on the stove. His woolly-headed assistant had already mixed jam and butter to make a very sweet custard, and we dipped the bread into it and drank dark, sweet tea.

The horror was over. The seascape had changed into a gentle blueness. The wind was benevolent, and in its way our mild roll was soothing. Soon it became very hot. The crew raised a tarpaulin over the roof of the cabin and I went and lay there.

Later the crew wanted their pictures taken in Polaroid. I discovered their names while I took them: Ali Qasim, Hassan Ali, Musa, Ibrahim, Captain Azia Ali – all Muslim names. I wrote them down in Arabic script to amuse them; peering over my shoulder, they murmured 'Muslim' to me, but when I said, 'No Muslim. Christian,' they showed no disappointment. They were pleased enough by the Arabic writing and murmured approvingly, 'Arab, Arab.' Their reaction to the Polaroid was immediately to throw off undershirts and shirts and to pose, stripped to their bathing trunks or sarongs, flexing their biceps and holding in their bellies like Asian Charles Atlases. In fact they were only fairly muscular, verging on the plump.

As the Baluchis had done on *Al Raza*, the crew made a great play with combs and mirrors. Hassan Ali caressed his long hair with a metal-bristled brush, looking with great attention at his reflection and going back over a certain swoop of hair, turning his head this way and that like a vain girl at her dressing table. After meals they relaxed in tumbles of tangled limbs on the cabin roof, always shifting arms around shoulders, legs over legs, lighting cigarettes, laughing, jumping up to dip a mug into the fresh-water tank or to spit over the rail.

Like an ageing film star bored with all that, the Starling Cook was uninterested in the Polaroid, and quietly continued to grind a stick of cinnamon to powder with a stone rolling-pin. His assistant made tea and carried it to the Maldivian passengers, who by now had recovered from their sickness. He even played a trick on them – I don't know what – which is how he became known as the Black

Devil. His face was very black and knobbly, and usually he was grinning. His trick made the passengers shout and laugh, and because of it I said, '*Shaitan!*' ('devil' in Arabic), which I suppose is the same in Maldivian because from that moment they began to call him Shaitan, one of them adding 'Black'. 'Black Devil!' they shouted, and he shouted back in glee, 'Blaack Divil.'

The Black Devil was really anything but devilish. He had a good nature. I found him up in the bows blowing his nose in his fingers and watching the result slowly unstring itself to fall into the sea. He was turning back to knead the dough when I called to him and motioned to him to wash his hands, and at once he trotted away and washed them meticulously. Then he smiled warmly and nodded at me. A bond seemed to have been established; from then on, he gave me the first mug of tea. I was the first to feel his invariable invitation to take the mug, the finger tapping my forearm three times, like a gentle tapping at a door.

An odd incident occurred on our last day at sea. Hassan Ali, the crewman I had seen first at the helm, came to me weeping and distraught. The passengers gathered around, and with signs and bits of Arabic I learned that the captain had confiscated from Hassan Ali all the Polaroid pictures I had taken of him. 'Master take, master take,' was all he could splutter out. I didn't want to tangle with the captain and I would never know his reasons, so I snapped Hassan Ali again out of the captain's sight. He whipped the picture into the top of his trunks and smiled once more.

★　★　★

On the last day it also turned out that one of the crew, Musa, spoke quite good English. He came up to me, my notes remind me, and said, 'Please, I have a pain in my penis. Have you a medicine?' What was the trouble? I asked. Inflammation? Discharge? When had he last had a woman? In Colombo? I imagined that almost any disease of the penis was freely procurable in a seamen's bordello in Colombo.

One month ago, Musa answered. He'd need an injection from a doctor there, I said. Would the injection be enough? he asked. I told him it would be.

'Have you hashish?'

'No, Musa.'

'Have you hero-een?'

'No, Musa. Why? You want?'

'No, no. Five weeks in island jail. But you drink beer?'

'Yes, I drink beer. Muslims also drink beer.'

'Sometimes. Khomeini no drink, you know why?'

'I don't know,' I said, feeling that our conversation was sidling up to the delicate subject of fundamentalist Islam and had gone far enough. I didn't want to discuss militant Islam.

If the captain's grin was awful, his navigation was excellent. On the third evening the outlines of Malé lay dead ahead of us.

The Starling Cook was beside himself with relief and the thought of home. First he cooked a magnificent curry full of chilli and pungent exotic leaves – a dish I would like to try again. I gestured at him, 'Good, very good,' and he wriggled about the deck in a happy dance step, arms raised, stamping his black feet, swaying sinuously on bowlegs, laughing. Everyone laughed back, even the Australian.

Dolphins leaped alongside the launch, a reassuring sight. The ocean was flat, the horizon clean and so well defined that it seemed we might drop over the edge if we could only reach it. The clouds were milk-white; had I really seen those ragged strips of grey scudding past my 'porthole' at the height of the storm?

The Starling Cook began to sing in a high undulating whine, '*Feni, feni, sarna . . . feni, feni, sarna . . .*' a chant he repeated over and over. The crew joined him, and the Maldivian passengers jumped down from the cabin roof on to the foredeck and began to clap in time with the Starling Cook's singing, arms in the air like Scottish reelers, and stamping around in a circle. '*Feni, feni, sarna . . . feni, feni, sarna . . .*'

'What's that mean?' I asked Ibrahim.

'It mean, "Good heavens, look, look, it's love. Look, it's love!" '

How could I have asked myself with such anguish in the storm, 'What am I doing here?' I was delighted to be exactly where I was at this moment.

Chapter Nineteen

A FTER THE STORM, the calm in which we glided into
Malé harbour made our arrival seem unreal. We
might have been moving over a rink of black ice.

In a fever of excitement, the Starling Cook seemed to
be brewing more and more tea; the Black Devil tapped my
arm with a fresh mug of it every few minutes. Presently
we anchored within the reefs and the captain welcomed
aboard the Malé customs and immigration men, who, on
inspecting my luggage, ignored my cameras but snatched
my two Penguin books out of the hands of Musa. Earlier,
Musa had fallen in love with the John Singer Sargent portraits on the covers of Edith Wharton's *The Age of Innocence*
and Henry James's *The Awkward Age*, and had spent an hour
or two gazing awestruck at them by the light of the mainmast light, softly tracing their outlines with his forefinger.

My books were returned, but the Australian was less
fortunate. He had been rash; the customs men soon
removed from his knapsack several small bottles of pills.
Worse, he had elected to travel with some highly suspicious
objects – sticky Indian sweets in silver paper, for example,
and what looked like sesame seeds in a matchbox. They
were harmless, the Australian protested, but the customs
men weren't at all convinced, and threatened to saw into
small pieces the tubular struts of his collapsible tent. It was
a long time before they allowed him to join me in a boat
heading shorewards with some of the crew, looking back
without affection at the old launch with its wobbly exhaust
pipe. With the the truculent presence of Sea Eagle and the
delays and the downpour, the trip had started in gloom.

The storm had been a bonus in its alarming way, but now it was almost impossible to identify it with this inert and ugly little craft. Also, though I had been glad to sail with Maldivians, somehow the crew lacked the spirit of other seamen I had met. Was it shyness, wariness or xenophobia? Shyness, I think. The Maldives have always been isolated, and the islanders have little knowledge of outsiders. Today fifteen or sixteen islands of the archipelago have been turned into tourist resorts. But everything has to be imported, from the first nail to the next meal, so the resorts are horrifically expensive and have little to do with the people of the Maldives, except for those who work there. Everything has to be paid for in American dollars or pounds sterling; Maldivian money is not accepted. I tried to imagine large fenced-off beauty spots in the United States or Great Britain within which, say, only Saudi Arabian riyals could buy a meal or a bed for the night.

I stayed one night in Malé, a diminutive, attractive town entirely surrounded by the turquoise water indicating shallow sea and coral reefs. Going to buy my air ticket back to Colombo the next day, I felt a plucking at my arm, and looking down, saw the Starling Cook grinning and wagging his head at me. I took his hand and shook it and pressed ten dollars into his palm. He stuffed the note into the pocket of his old blue shorts, and danced a little bowlegged jig in the middle of the road, singing as he did so, '*Feni, feni, sarna . . . feni, feni, sarna.*'

★ ★ ★

In Colombo again, I hurried to the office of Mr Missier.

'You must take biscuits or something like that,' Mr Missier said. 'You may not like the food at all.'

'Is it rice?'

'Rice and curry, yes.'

'I like them. And tea, I suppose.'

'Coffee,' said Mr Missier. 'In south India they grow good coffee. Ooh, *very* good coffee they grow in south India.'

I felt like hugging Mr Missier. He had kept his word and arranged matters exactly as he had promised. A schooner would take me; bound for Tuticorin, she lay in the harbour almost ready to sail.

'Do we sail at night?' I was recalling the miserable, rain-soaked sailing to Malé.

'Of course, sailing depends on the weather. Remember, the vessel has no engine, only sails. Morning is usually preferred.'

'I can be there very early.'

'The captain is a good man. He is Tamil like all the crew. Here is his letter accepting you on board.'

I read:

I, A. Cellathural, the Master of TTN 15, the *Herman Mary,* have no objection to have Mr G. Young to take along with me on outward voyage from Colombo to Tuticorin,

Thanking you, Yours faithfully. . . .

Mr Missier had also written letters to immigration and customs, and even to the Sri Lankan navy. 'The *Herman Mary's* owner is a very strict Catholic gentleman,' he assured me.

I made my way down the dark staircase, and through

the knot of tallymen weighing sacks of onions, vowing to see Mr Missier again.

A message at the Taprobane from Tom Abraham, the high commissioner of India, asked me to drop in to his office as soon as possible. I found him looking downcast deliberately – I knew this in a minute – as a joke. 'I'm afraid I have to tell you . . .' he began heavily, 'that . . . your request for permission to visit the Andamans has been' – he paused, and then quickly stood up and put out his hand – 'granted. You can pick it up in Madras. It allows you to stay one week. Lucky you didn't bet me.'

Another man had kept his word. Sam Kadirgamar, QC, Mr Missier, Tom Abraham and Captain Henricus had done all they could. Perhaps my luck had turned.

I joined the *Herman Mary* at 4.30 a.m. At that silent hour I seemed to be leaving a dead hotel, and to be walking through a doomed city, 'a city taken by storm, where none are left but the slain!'

A watery moon still hung in the sky. A few white figures scurried past in the street, and in the Leyden Bastion a voice said, 'Hey, *baba*, railway stay-shun that way.' At the Baghdad Gate, the guards waved me through with a 'good morning'. On the docks, barges sloshed and squeaked against each other and the quay. Two men were shovelling coal into the glowing furnaces of two ancient steam cranes. The lights of big ships in the harbour glowed, but a tug was the only vessel that moved. The harbour still slept.

The *Herman Mary* showed no sign of life. On her wide

deck the shapes of the sleeping bodies of her crew were lumped under the sail they were using as a communal counterpane. An occasional cough or snore escaped from the heavy canvas. I put down my bag, sat on a bollard and waited.

At five thirty a Sri Lankan navy jeep drove up and a man in white shirt and shorts politely checked my passport. His arrival acted as a wake-up call. 'All hands,' cried a voice, and the crew began to emerge from under the sail, yawning and stretching. Two small boys hastened to hang a wreath of white jasmine-like flowers around the base of the bowsprit, and then planted smoking sticks of incense at the foot of the mainmast. Having performed their first religious duty of the day, they dropped down a hatch near the stern, and soon the light of a stove flickered and wisps of smoke rose from below, followed by the smell of coffee.

Meanwhile some of the crew cleared the deck as others hoisted into position over the stern a huge steering boom – a rounded piece of wood, like the steering spar on the Maldivian launch but bigger, perhaps ten feet long, and painted red, white and green. I counted eleven men on deck, all in loud checked sarongs. One of them, a smiling young man, came up to me, saying, 'Good morning, sir. I am Chandra, brother of the captain. Are you Catholic, sir?' When I said, 'Protestant,' he answered cheerfully, 'All same, sir. Excuse us now while we go to pray,' and under the black masts of *Herman Mary*, against a backdrop of grey-white warehouse walls, the Tamils stood to pray in the bows of their ship.

These prayers were brief compared with the later services at sea. In two minutes the sailors had crossed themselves, and then began to swarm about the ship. The mainsail was hauled up, ropes were cast off, and Mr Missier's supervisor waved from his bicycle on the quay. 'Sit here, sir,' said Chandra, patting a ledge near the helmsman. Suddenly transformed into something like a giant moth poised for flight, the *Herman Mary* silently and slowly edged away from the wharf.

It takes some time, I found, to get used to a sailing ship's slow, silent ways, particularly to her utter dependence on a breeze, after weeks of noisy but self-reliant motor vessels. At first, the *Herman Mary*'s progress, though silent, was almost nonexistent. We hung about. The sun came up, but no breeze followed suit, and we continued to be becalmed. An hour and a half after casting off we were still in Colombo harbour. It was a little embarrassing. Ropes had to be flung to barges and other vessels ahead of us, and our crew took turns jumping across to them and pulling the dead weight of the *Herman Mary* along like mahouts trying to shift a recalcitrant elephant. At one point a young crewman stripped off his sarong, dived into the harbour with a rope around his waist and carried it with a vigorous breaststroke to a dredger, whose crew helped him aboard. Before diving, he was careful to kiss the talisman he wore on a chain around his neck, and he held it firmly between his teeth as he swam.

For the first time in my life, I heard sailors whistling for a wind. The Tamils wandered about the deck, lips pursed, uttering plaintive birdlike sounds, which eventually seemed to work. At last, as we reached the old white lighthouse at the harbour entrance, something swept a wisp of my hair across my eyes. A breeze.

Immediately the captain – I could see the fraternal resemblance to Chandra – shouted an order, and in a flurry of sarongs and black limbs the crew ran up other sails, which devoured the masts like white flames and filled out. We moved.

At a fair speed the *Herman Mary*, alive at last, dipped through the troughs of sea, alive in the creaking of her spars and the hiss of water under her bows. I hadn't felt a greater elation since leaving Piraeus. One of the boy cooks brought me a mug of grainy coffee and, as we tacked down the Sri Lankan coast, my strongest desire was to canonize Mr Missier as soon as it could possibly be arranged.

The crew soon rigged other sails on heavy booms which they pushed out on either side of the *Herman Mary* between her mainmast and bowsprit. A sail was run up below the foresail, then a topsail on the mainmast; by now we had five sails over our heads. Steering west we moved briskly into the Indian Ocean.

Now that I could have a good look at her in daylight, I saw that the *Herman Mary* was a formidable vessel. Even the caulking between her deck planks was as wide as my forearm. Decking, crossbeams and stanchions were knotted, gnarled, and bolted together with enormous pieces of metal, so that they looked as if they had grown together like parts of a single tree. The planking of her sides was four inches thick, and a lifeboat containing two spare sails had the solid look of a dugout.

Through Chandra, the captain's brother, and a grey-haired seaman called Darson who spoke some English, I learned that the ship could take no less than thirteen pieces of canvas, and that the mighty mainmast had cost one hundred thousand Indian rupees (fifty-five thousand pounds), and the mizzen half that. The *Herman Mary* had been built in Tuticorin, and there were plenty more like her, some a good deal bigger, they said.

At noon we began to steer north-north-west, going nicely. The two young cooks scrambled up through their hatch from the smoky darkness of their 'tween-decks galley, and laid out on the deck half a dozen bowls: rice, curried vegetables, pieces of crisp dried fish, fried eggs, small sweet bananas, and drinking water in a large kettle. After a short grace from the captain, we squatted in a circle and ate with our fingers.

After the meal I took some Polaroid pictures. The first to pose was the young man who had leaped overboard to carry the rope to the dredger. His name, he said, was Hentry Rodrigo. He was slim, wiry and short, like all the crew except Chandra, the tallest man on the *Herman Mary*, who was what in the West we would call of medium height.

At siesta time the sun ran behind monstrous clouds and rain like Niagara Falls hit us. Soon the *Herman Mary* glistened from deck to masthead. The crew simply let the water cascade over their half-naked bodies; they could always discard wet sarongs and slip into dry ones later. Perhaps I would have been wise to take off my shirt and trousers, too; instead I ducked below, down the forward hatch, and discovered a more mysterious world.

A short but dangerously steep wooden ladder led to a

small, amputated 'tween-deck area halfway down the hull of the vessel; it was really more of a cramped semicircular ledge shaped like the *Herman Mary*'s blunt bows. Its open, near edge fell precipitately into the belly of the single hold, a stygian cavern that ran the length of the vessel, uninterrupted by bulkheads and nearly full with a cargo of black lentils in sacks. Any swift movement here was tricky, for the ledge had no rail. In the near-total darkness it would have been easy to slip backwards off the edge; the fall would certainly result in a broken back or neck on the floor of the hold. An additional problem was that, because torrential rain was falling through the hatch on to the cargo, the hatch cover had to be pulled across the opening with a tarpaulin over it. What little light there might have been from the sky was thus cut off, and the only illumination came either from my torch – or from the shrine.

The shrine took me by surprise; how could I have expected such a thing in such a place? All I saw at first was a faint, flickering light in the far corner of the ledge where the massive black timbers of the ship converged under the bowsprit. This dim corner reminded me of old bookplates of the cockpit of the *Victory*, and of Nelson dying by the light of a lantern. It was even darker here, and it took a minute before I saw the wreaths of faded white flowers and the joss-sticks, and smelled the incense. Three candles burned on the little altar and, while water slapped and gurgled four inches away, the wax faces of the Virgin, Jesus and St Anthony seemed to come alive in the faltering glow of their pale flames. Speculatively, two cockroaches looked down on them from a beam.

It was hot and humid in the hold with the hatch closed. The crew's sarongs and shirts swung back and forth on lines attached to the bulwarks and in the rank-smelling cavern below me sacks of cargo lay like white shrouded bodies stacked thirteen deep.

One or other of the cooks – they couldn't have been more than twelve or thirteen years old – bobbed up from time to time to keep an eye on the altar candles; I suppose the Tamils believed something fearful would happen if they went out. The boys had made a tunnel through the sacks, and were small enough to squeeze from one end of the ship to the other without bothering to go on deck. Once they somehow fumbled mugs and a full kettle of tea through the tunnel for the shivering crewmen coming off duty.

These included Hentry, who tumbled down the companionway, his hair plastered to his skull and the rain running down his chest as if he had been swimming again. He and his mates immediately threw off their sopping sarongs and rubbed themselves dry with frayed towels. Then they sat in dry clothes, looking at me, grinning and wagging their heads in the Indian way to signify (a wagging head can have a number of meanings, according to context) that all, though wettish, was well. Two of them pointed to their chests and pronounced their names, Nobel and Ignatius. They wore cheap miniature crucifixes on neck chains, and seemed to draw comfort from fingering them constantly.

The hold was dry but airless, and claustrophobia and the stale, muggy heat finally got to me. The wind was fierce and the sea broke over the deck, but it was worth getting soaked to watch the crew in action, never still, adapting the sails to every rise, fall or shift in the wind, shouting and chasing one another up and down the back of this wallowing 215-ton, man-made whale of wood and iron. I could hear the booming of the sails – the origin,

Conrad said, of the sailors' saying, 'It blows great guns.'

By afternoon, when the rain had stopped, the crew had hoisted eight sails. The vast diagonal sweep of the mainsail, now at full stretch, was awesome; I had never before seen a working sail anything like as big. High above me, Nobel and Hentry were poised on its spar like flies on a curtain rail.

I told the captain, Darson and Chandra of my fears of capsizing on the Maldivian launch, and they didn't laugh. Chandra said, 'Two of our ships were lost a year before last year.'

Apparently a cyclone had caught them between Colombo and Tuticorin, more or less where we were now. Sixty-foot waves had overwhelmed them, Chandra said, and they'd gone down with all hands. I could imagine the irresistible cataract crashing on to the deck of the *Herman Mary*, carrying all before it: hundreds of tons of ocean descending on the ship, winkling the boy cooks out of their galley like escargots from their shells, hurling overboard Chandra, the captain and myself, snapping the mainmast, pouring down the hatch and swamping the great cave of the hold, engulfing the whole ship. If such a wave came when I was below, I thought, perhaps the last sight my eyes would register would be the final flicker of the candles on the little shrine.

This image reminded me of the Maldivian launch again. The little vessel had seemed so helpless in that comparatively unexceptional sea. It had been only twenty-five tons; now 220 tons didn't seem much, however indestructible the *Herman Mary*'s beams, planks and spars might at first appear.

I wondered how big the early sailing ships had been, those of the navigators who first risked ocean crossings and typhoons. Later, I found a book that told me that Magellan's *Trinidad* was only 110 tons, and Columbus's *Santa María*, *Pinta* and *Niña* nearer sixty tons. Much later, Cook's *Resolution* was 462 tons, while the English Admiral Anson's *Centurion*, which went round the world, was a comparative giant of 1005 tons, with a 521-man crew.

According to my notebook:

I join Chandra and Darson beneath the mainmast. It's like standing beneath a redwood tree painted black. Chandra is singing, but all I hear is the creak of this mighty mast and, when I put my hand against it, I can feel it shifting and shivering like a muscle under great stress. The spar holding the mainsail is as thick as a fat man's body and feels like iron. It jabs skywards like an iron bar, surely fifty feet from the end nearest the deck to its distant point that seems to scrape the heavens – the height of a four-storey house. The mainmast is shorter but much thicker; it has to be to support the great weight of a lopsided rectangular sail that wrenches about as if struggling to get away. The sail opens and contracts under the different pressures of the north-east wind like the hood of a very vigorous cobra.

Just now a staysail sheet parted far overhead and fell like a black mamba at our feet: everyone nearby sprang up. Ignatius and Hentry were aloft in a trice to make good the sheet, both taking time to cross themselves first. They climbed the halyards by grasping them between their big and second toes; descending, they dropped down swiftly, hand over hand, their legs hanging free.

Ten sails up! They are hauled up with much effort and loud chanting, and everyone, including the captain and old Darson, turns to the haul. What are they chanting? It's difficult to grasp from Chandra's phonetic version of the words. One chant goes something like: '*Mada-ve un udave maravain – uru na lung,*' which means, according to Chandra and Darson, 'Blessed Mary, don't forget to give me a helping hand.' A reasonable prayer.

These Tamils are far more open, friendly and less shy than the Maldivians – the Starling Cook excepted, of course. Physically they are not so different. Although their skins are very black, their backs and shoulders are lightly covered with a very faint down of brownish hair. On their chests, arms and legs, however, the hair is as black as pitch.

I asked Hentry and Nobel how much they earned per voyage. Four hundred Indian rupees, they said – that is, fifty American dollars or twenty pounds sterling, with all food provided. 'Hentry is a very hard worker and knows everything about sailing,' Chandra whispered. 'His father is also sailor.'

How many years have Hentry and Nobel been at sea?

'Three or four. To start they were the same size as cook-boys.'

Twice a day, at sunset and sunrise, the entire crew, led by the captain, repaired to the stern of the *Herman Mary* for prayers. 'We will pray now,' the young captain said to me, shyly trying out his English for the first time. I noticed his betel-red mouth and the Virgin Mary locket on his chest. Pray they did: not just a mumbled prayer or two, but twenty minutes of litany and hymns. They sat cross-legged in two rows, the captain a little in front, near the compass with its oil lamp in a green box and a large alarm clock, a white rosary in his hand and a prayer book open on a towel neatly folded on the deck before him. Only the helmsman, wrestling with the huge steering boom behind the captain, remained standing, so I sat and tried to be inconspicuous.

The captain read fast, low and clear, in Tamil, of course, so that only later did I learn what it was. 'Remember, O most gracious Virgin Mary, that never was it known that anyone who fled to thine aid was left unaided . . .' The crew spoke their responses loudly, and later sang a hymn with enthusiasm. More prayers followed. 'I fly unto thee, thou Virgin of Virgins, my mother . . .' Then another hymn, followed by more prayers and responses.

As the *Herman Mary* moved on, brandishing her spars against a perfect sunset of orange and gold, the male voices rose and fell to the background of her humming and groaning. This moment remains one of the most vivid images I carry with me from the seven months of my journey. The great mast loomed as black and menacing as Beelzebub above the bowed figures. 'O, Mother of the Word Incarnate . . . hear and answer me.'

At prayers' end, the squatting sailors crossed themselves but remained seated for a time, as if in meditation. When at last they stood up, each one salaamed the captain, briefly bowing his head and pressing together the flats of his extended palms, level with his mouth. The captain salaamed back, then, to my surprise, walked up and salaamed me. Touched, I joined my palms together and bowed back in the same way.

The second day we were becalmed for long, sun-baked hours. The men lay about on deck, seeking the shade of the lifeless sails. Chandra, Hentry, Nobel and an old man called Ganananam peeled a bowlful of small Indian onions while Darson pumped out the bilges with a small mechanical pump.

Now and again the captain played with a radio. Thin, high Indian singing floated about us. Once we heard a burst of pop music from Colombo; a voice said, 'I think – don't you? – there's no more truly magnificent way to end this evening's session of "Grandstand" than with this beautiful song by Neil Diamond . . .'

The sea sparkled, and we watched a school of dolphins playing with the *Herman Mary*. 'Do you want to wash your body?' Darson asked, indicating a kettle of hot water, but I decided to wait until Tuticorin.

With our fishing lines we caught two tuna and a long thinnish creature, which the boys threw into the midday curry and served with rice, onions and beetroot, but which turned out to be all bones.

The wind rose again during the night, and by the early morning we were near the tip of India. Hentry borrowed my binoculars and shinned up the mainmast to scout for lights, and after a short while he came down to announce with a satisfied nod of his head, 'India.' Sitting down, he pulled up his sarong and, after some contortions, drew from the recesses of his bathing trunks a handful of sticky green and pink acid drops, one of which he offered me.

Under a sky suddenly full of shooting stars, we approached Tuticorin from the east in a wide flanking movement, in sight of the harbour lights for five or six hours before we reached it.

My notebook registers some first impressions:

A long, low line of trees and houses. Fishing boats bobbing around us everywhere; we almost run one or two down, and the captain shouts at the fishermen angrily. A lighthouse ashore, blue and white striped like a barber's pole.

Our magnificent sails come down. Three boys take in the forward staysails; the various booms are swung inboard and made fast up the centre of the *Herman Mary*'s deck; the movable boards that served as gunwales are stacked. The captain has put on his shore-going sarong – mauve, black, yellow and red in big patterns. I tell him I'd like to sail to Bombay with him. 'Bombay, okay,' he says cheerfully. 'Why not Karachi?'

End-of-term permeates the air again. Darson says, 'Tomorrow we all want come see you at your hotel.'

'You must all come,' I say.

Invitations follow: to the captain's house, to Hentry's, to Nobel's, to see Chandra's baby . . . All very nice, but

I am not sure yet what the reaction of the Tuticorin immigration people will be to my arrival in their port – a port not, I suspect, geared for passengers, certainly not for Europeans on sailing ships, particularly since the German wanted by Interpol passed through. I am glad Tom Abraham gave me a visa, even though technically I don't need one.

Beaches ahead backed by palms, a patchwork of red roofs, more sails, Arab style, very white. Many church spires.

The last meal – tuna, cabbage, eggs, rice – is served by the little cooks; I can't complain about the quantity or quality of food on the *Herman Mary*.

The crew begin to spruce up; the little round mirrors carried by all Asian sailors appear. Nobel has thoroughly greased his hair and combed it into great black, glossy whorls, like black whipped cream. All of them rub their teeth with pink tooth powder they carry in small cellophane bags.

Now the great sails are down, the bamboo booms – their 'bark' an inch thick – stowed, the huge mainsail lowered by means of a hand-turned iron winch. Suddenly the *Herman Mary* has a bare, plucked-chicken look; it is a hulk with two masts, a moth without wings.

Boys catch our lines ashore. The *Herman Mary* bumps heavily, bow first, into a ruck of sailing ships, and we come to rest in a forest of masts and a solid mass of black hulls.

Chapter Twenty

IT HAD BEEN a wise thought of Tom Abraham's to put an Indian visa on my passport. With equal foresight he had told his attaché to write, in green ink beside the visa, the following words: 'Permitted to enter India at Tuticorin by sailing boat *Herman Mary.*' Even with the visa and those added words, the customs official at Tuticorin was baffled; without them, I tremble to think what might have happened – perhaps an enforced deportation to Colombo. Mr Missier would have been mortified.

Hentry and Nobel helped me ashore with my bags, and I gave the metal suitcase's combination lock a whirl to make sure that the spray from *Herman Mary's* deck hadn't rusted the tumblers solid. Two hours passed in a hot, bleak shed before a plump man in plain clothes who introduced himself as a customs officer said, 'Come with me,' and showed me to a car. We drove out of the gates of the little port to a two-storeyed building with a barred door and windows, opening into a pitted street full of creaking ox-carts.

A fan turned with maddening sloth in a small room behind a curtain where a large man in khaki sat behind a desk. 'My superior is at lunch,' he said. 'Please be seated.'

'Can you please clear me through customs? This is my visa, and this green ink—'

'I am a customs officer, but arriving like this at Tuticorin is most unusual.' He looked at me like a disapproving schoolmaster. 'Most unusual. I must consult my superior.'

'Unusual?'

'Definitely.'

'Is your superior in this building? Perhaps we could—'

'He's at lunch. He'll be back at four o'clock or five.' It was then two fifteen. 'Have you anything to declare?'

'Just these cameras. I use them for my work.'

'That's customs, then,' said the plump man, and drove me back to the bleak, hot shed to register the numbers of the cameras in a crumbling ledger. Seeing me glance at my watch, he noted this in the ledger as well.

'That's interesting,' I said. 'No one worries about watches at Bombay or Calcutta airports.'

'Here we do worry. We've worried about watches for years.'

He couldn't find a number on the watch, so he wrote down, 'Omega watch.'

We waited in the shed for half an hour longer, but no officer came from lunch or from anywhere else. I wondered whether we could drive to the officer's home; he might be having a siesta. But at his house his wife said he had gone to a wedding thirty kilometres away. The plump man drove me back to the office of the man in khaki, who this time offered tea with milk and suggested that I go to a hotel, wash and wait. 'If there's anything wrong,' he said, smiling at last, 'I am here.'

It was lucky he allowed me to go because the officer didn't return from the wedding until 10.30 p.m. A sullen man, he called at the hotel, and took me to his office in the port. There he sat at his desk, turning my passport over and over in his hands, reading and rereading the words 'Permitted to enter India at Tuticorin' as if he couldn't believe his eyes, and scrutinizing the official stamp as though I might have forged it.

'Fill out these forms,' he said at last and, when I had

done so, he stamped me in to India. Suddenly I was another step nearer Canton.

The office of Mr E. P. Rayer, the owner of the *Herman Mary*, contained obvious clues to the main preoccupations of the little port of Tuticorin: shipping and the Church. On one wall was a large, lavishly coloured calendar from Dr Johnson Fernando, Fish Exporter, showing the Virgin Mary with the Infant Jesus, both crowned, on a stylized stormy sea with a three-masted schooner in obvious trouble in the background. The legend under it said, 'Our Lady of Good Health, Vailankanni.' On another wall was a board with the names of Indian ports on it – Bombay, Calicut, Mangalore, Veraval – showing the present disposition of Mr Rayer's fleet.

It was a small fleet for Tuticorin – even smaller since 1977, Mr Rayer said, when two of his vessels went down with all hands. 'Overloaded,' he said. 'Twenty-five per cent above the beam. A heavy sea and they went over.' Now he had only three thonis (*thoni* is the Tuticorin word for sailing ship): *Herman Mary*, the smallest at 215 tons, *Mary Isabel*, 350 tons, and *Arockya Mary*, 370 tons. The last two were both in Calicut loading timber and plants for shipment to Veraval in north-west India. There was, Mr Rayer said, a 500–tonner under construction in Tuticorin at this very minute.

The Tuticorin fleet of seagoing thonis now numbered about forty-seven, and their crews were all local men. From Tuticorin they carried salt and fertilizers to the west coast, returning with ballast. From April to August they took imported wheat, fertilizers and rice up the east coast to Madras and Calcutta.

Mr Rayer was a jovial man shaped like a barrel and wearing thick glasses. He was proud to have been at sea for thirteen years before buying ships of his own. He took me to his modest old house, where his wife brought out home-made cakes and we looked at family portraits and a blown-up photograph of a three-masted thoni under full sail that he had snapped himself.

'There are fewer thonis now,' he said, 'because the cost of building and maintenance has gone up, although of course the cost of fuel is even worse. Another problem is the constant strikes in the big ports.'

I complimented Mr Rayer on his captain and crew, and asked how much money I could give them as a parting present.

He became quite agitated. 'I don't want you giving money to the crew. I don't like that.'

'Then can I give it to you to pass on to them?'

'Mr Young, I will never take money from you. I don't want your money, I want your love.'

'At least let me pay for the food I ate.'

'Love is better than money. It is a pleasure to have you on my ship.'

The great man of Tuticorin, Mr Missier had told me, was the chevalier Machado. 'You certainly must see him,' he had insisted. 'He is a most important man. A fine person.' 'Chevalier' was an impressive title; I'd never come across a papal knight before.

I found the chevalier in his office on the dusty street nearest the port; from his door I could see the masts of the thonis sticking up like black asparagus. A notice announced the name of the building as 'Captain Machado's Building', and polished plates and painted boards informed all con-cerned that the chevalier was the highly approved agent for

the Maersk Line, the Hansa Line, and the Mogul Line, as well as the representative of Harrisons & Crosfield.

The chevalier's offices were arched, cavernous and venerable, with high beamed ceilings. His personal sanctum was decorated with photographs of Gandhi and Nehru, a Catholic mission calendar and a head of Jesus. Neatly dressed in spotless white trousers and patent-leather shoes, the chevalier was a pleasant, dignified man of about fifty-eight, with black eyebrows and hair, who rose to greet me with a warm smile. Evidently he was the patriarch of the shipping community – not only of the shipowners, but of the families of the captains and crews as well. Tuticorin's population consisted of Hindus and Muslims as well as Catholics, he said, but the non-Catholics were shopkeepers or workers, while those involved with the sea were, to a man, members of the Church.

The chevalier himself was obviously wealthy. Someone, perhaps Mr Missier, had told me that his money had been made in salt. Tuticorin is surrounded by flat land as white as snow. 'We drill down, take out the salt and let the seawater evaporate. The salt here is marvellously pure,' the chevalier said. 'In fact, one third of India's salt comes from Tuticorin.'

He went on: 'You may be interested to know that Tuticorin has been a port for only one hundred years. The Portuguese and Dutch had another one not far away, near Cape Comorin, the very last point of India, but it had a very low draught.'

The Catholic community was his overriding concern, the chevalier said. 'We were once all fishermen – *paravan* is the caste name for that – and we were all – our ancestors, I mean – baptized by St Francis Xavier. We've had our own bishop here since 1923.'

He invited me to his house, Fátima Lodge, a rather grand yellow and white building in a quiet street of pleasant, ageing villas.

'You'll see our church, I hope, Our Lady of Snows. It's very fine. We hold four or five services there every Sunday, and all of them are overflowing.'

The chevalier showed me a photograph of himself in his uniform, brass-buttoned, wide-striped trousers, with cockaded hat and ceremonial sword. I said I'd certainly see his church and perhaps attend a service.

'I'd like you to see the clinics I paid for, too.'

When I said goodbye, the chevalier's last words were, 'God bless you. Happy Christmas.' Christmas? I had forgotten time. Christmas, I realized, was only a week or so away.

The Church of Our Lady of Snows was like a gorgeous slab of marzipan; lavishly decorated with statues of the Virgin, Christ and the saints, lit by neon, with slabs of white marble here and there, it was high-vaulted, with a planked ceiling of delicate sky-blue. Chirping sparrows flew in and out of the doors at the back, and the sides were left permanently open to catch the cooling breeze.

More extraordinary than the church itself was its congregation. As the chevalier had said, the attendants at early-morning mass on Sunday, the next day, overflowed into the courtyard outside. It is difficult to describe the rainbow spectacle presented by the women. They looked like so many Madonnas in their saris, which covered them from head to foot except for the oval of their faces, unveiled to reveal clear skins and big long-lashed eyes. There were saris of every conceivable shade and mixture of colours: mauves, yellows, white with the palest blue, deep reds and purples gleaming with gold and silver thread. They trooped in as a heavy bell pealed overhead and a bellows-operated organ began to play quietly. The chevalier had done Our Lady of Snows proud: an electrically operated curtain around the altar of a statue of the Virgin sighed open on runners, and the statue shone out at the congregation, bejewelled, gold against white.

SANCTA MARIA ORA PRO NOBIS. Under an arch with this painted injunction to the Madonna, a man in rags pressed himself against a wall near me, his hand grasping the pierced and bleeding feet of a statue of Jesus. From his attitude and stillness it seemed as if he himself was suspended from the nail.

I couldn't see the chevalier in church because near the altar the crowd was very thick. I slipped out before the service ended, while the priest, a brisk young Tamil, assisted by two small boys, moved through the congregation dispensing wafers among the believers in their unbelievable saris, walking in black through a shimmering field of gold, silver and many-splendoured colours.

Later I met the captain, Chandra, Wilson (the captain's small son), Hentry, Nobel, Ignatius and Darson in the sunlight outside the church. They had all attended the service and were spruced up in their Sunday best. The captain wore a gleaming white shirt over his white ankle-length sarong. In fact, he gleamed all over, and his eyes shone as if he had used make-up. For some reason, Tamil eyes often seem larger and brighter than other people's. Like all Asian seamen, Tamils seem to be compulsive washers; I had seen Hentry, Nobel and Ignatius painstakingly scrubbing and preening themselves on the *Herman Mary*'s deck and, on the second evening ashore in Tuticorin, Hentry had come to the Ashok Bhavan, the tiny, shabby but friendly hotel in the heart of the bazaar where I was staying, and had spent at least ten minutes rubbing my Johnson's Baby Powder into his shoulders, neck and face. When we stepped over the sleeping bodies in the corridor outside the room to see a Tamil comedy at the local flea-pit, he still had a clown's smudge of powder on one cheek.

Now we were going to visit the crew's houses one by one, starting with Hentry's. His was very small; in Europe it would, I suppose, be called a slum, and possibly be condemned. Despite this, it was remarkably clean. There were two small, low rooms – I had to duck to get through the door – for which Hentry paid forty-five rupees a month (less than three pounds). The ceilings were beamed, the floor cemented, the walls of flaking whitewash. Photographs of Hentry's sisters in communion dresses hung on the wall, and a couple of coils of ship's rope lay in a corner.

I am not sure how many of the assembled men and boys in the house were Hentry's brothers, cousins, nephews or friends. His father, a smaller, stout version of Hentry, showed me the certificate issued by the port office announcing to whomever it might concern that he was permitted work 'in the registered Harbour crafts plying at Tuticorin, a Minor Port in the State of Madras'. He was a *sokaní*, the father said – that is, a licensed helmsman of a sailing ship, with the basic pay of four hundred and fifty rupees a voyage. Romans, Hentry's youngest brother, had already made several voyages, although he was only sixteen. On the baptism card he showed me, his caste was given as paravan.

All the houses were much the same size and rent, all overflowing with giggling children, staring women with babies, and hospitable men showing their work permits and certificates, while cats, dogs and chickens ran underfoot. I copied down their addresses, they took mine, and all of them, from the captain down, whispered into my ear their dream of work in London.

On the third evening I took a train to Madras, about three hundred and twenty miles away, and the whole crew came to the station to see me off: the captain, Mr Rayer, Hentry's father, Hentry, Hentry's brother Romans, Nobel, Ignatius, Chandra, Darson, the chevalier's son-in-law Winston Corera, and even the immigration officer, who was suddenly no longer sullen but smiling.

At the last minute, Hentry rushed on to the platform with a box of mixed Tamil cakes and sweets tied up with string. Darson, too, had a present, a garland of white, orange and red flowers; he put it round my neck and pressed a small lemon into my hand – a Tamil sign of respect, Chandra told me in a quiet aside. 'Don't forget my address,' said Darson.

Just before the train moved away, Hentry ran into my compartment to check my luggage – 'One bag, two bag, okay' – his head wagging back and forth, tears running down his cheeks. At the last minute, as I shook hands with them all through the window, he grabbed my hand and kissed it.

As the train pulled out I waved until I thought they'd had enough, then moved back into the compartment and laid the garland on my seat. But I couldn't resist a final look back. I waved again and instantly, far away on the receding platform a thicket of arms shot up, so I waved again until the sign saying TUTICORIN at the end of the long platform nearly took off my hand at the wrist. I felt a sudden spasm of loss, a feeling as palpable as nausea and so strong that I sat down quickly, sensing the curious gaze of the only other person in the compartment, a clerkish-looking man.

In a minute I recovered a little, and got up and hung the garland on the wall. It swung there, slowly shedding its small orange petals, already wilting, but filling the compartment with its lovely sweet smell.

Chapter Twenty-One

'WHY SHOULD PYTHAGORAS strangle me?' Harry Miller asked, lovingly stroking the thick scaly folds of the snake under his bearded chin. 'He doesn't want to eat me – why should he?'

'Well, anger. Fear?'

'Anger and fear would be expressed by a bite. The python has over a hundred teeth and, if he becomes angry with you and wants you to leave him alone, he'll bite you, like a dog or a cat. If you pick up a monkey that doesn't want to be handled, he'll bite you, and Pythagoras would do the same. But, having bitten you and hurt you, he'd let you go again. He certainly wouldn't constrict you, would you, Pythagoras?'

It was nice to be reassured. Pythagoras was clearly too strong for one European (me) and one small Tamil (Sampath, Harry Miller's assistant) to control if suddenly he became fighting mad.

Harry eased the ten-foot python off his shoulders, dropped the sleepy creature back into its box and lowered its glass side. Pythagoras fell back inert; he could have been stuffed. We could see his beady eyes looking back at us, and a blunt nose to the glass.

'Suppose he got into a rage for some reason? That glass doesn't look very strong.'

'It's thick enough. He wouldn't even try to break it.'

'Kipling's Kaa in *The Jungle Book* used to hit things with his nose, and he was a python.'

'Kipling was a brilliant novelist, but he was a lousy

naturalist. A snake's nose is very delicate. It can be damaged by striking a hard object, and ulcers form. The last thing they want to do is hit walls or anything else.'

I had to admit that Pythagoras looked too lazy to punch his way out of a paper bag.

Harry Miller knows a lot about fish, animals, birds and snakes – particularly the last. Pythagoras lives with him in his bungalow near the Madras Club, and Miller and Sampath often take him out of his glass-lined box and let him have a wriggle.

Two essential pieces of good news awaited me when I reached the Connemara Hotel in Madras from Tuticorin just before Christmas. The first was that the Indian government's permit to travel to the Andamans had arrived; the other was that a Shipping Corporation of India steamer would leave for Port Blair, the administrative capital of the Andamans, in a few days. I went to the agents, booked my passage and collected my ticket, which said: 'Madras to Port Blair – 559 rupees, *m.v. Nancowry.*' I tucked it away in my metal suitcase and turned the combination lock on it as if it were a bar of gold.

The permit, from the Ministry of Home Affairs in Delhi, had been sent on by Tom Abraham in Colombo, and stated that I was allowed to 'enter and reside at Port Blair for a period of one week' and that I would 'arrive at Port Blair by ship from Madras and leave Port Blair for Calcutta by air'. I immediately made three photocopies and put the original beside the sea-ticket. Then once more the waiting game began.

It was lucky that Harry Miller took pity on me. When

he was not manhandling pythons, or collecting rat snakes, writing, photographing, or spotting cyclones and eclipses of the sun or moon, he was to be seen at the Madras Club. It was still an imposing Raj building. Colonnades overlooked a sweep of fine lawns, a couple of large, handsome trees and a river. Servants in white carried bottles of beer out to the terrace for Indian and European members and their wives, and turned on the old overhead fans. Gin *pyaj* (gin, a pearl onion and bitters) was much fancied.

'The club has the finest mulligatawny soup in India,' Harry Miller said, introducing me to it. 'The name comes from pure Tamil, *millagu tunnir*, meaning simply pepper water.' I looked up 'mulligatawny' in Hobson Jobson, the famous dictionary of Anglo-Indian slang, and, of course, Harry was quite right. The dictionary cited a song composed in 1784 by 'a gentleman of the Navy, one of Hyder Ali's prisoners':

> In vain our hard fate we repine,
> In vain on our fortune we rail;
> On Mullaghee-tawny we dine,
> Or Congee, in Bangalore Jail.

A note added that congee meant rice water.

On the wall of my hotel room, an old eighteenth-century print showed catamarans drawn up on the beach at Madras (they still are), and the dictionary also gave an Indian derivation for that word. 'Catamaran', it said, came from *kattu*, meaning binding, and *maram*, wood. Hence, a catamaran was a raft formed of three or four logs of wood lashed together.

At last there was time for reading, and in the club I found

the *Observer*, which told me about the Russian invasion of Afghanistan. It also carried an interview with the English poet Philip Larkin, who was quoted as saying, 'Thrift, hard work, reverence . . . those are the virtues, in case you wondered.' I liked the 'in case you wondered'. They were virtues I associated with the crew of the *Herman Mary*, and the last line of a Larkin poem quoted in the piece, 'What will survive of us is love,' seemed to fit the sailors of Tuticorin too.

My arrival in Madras and the imminence – I thought – of my departure for the Andamans drove me to *The Sign of Four*, the Sherlock Holmes novel I'd bought in a rainstorm in Higginbotham's bookshop in Bangalore. Lunch with Harry Miller reminded me of the first chapter, Holmes's dissertation on the science of deduction. Harry's cigar case was in front of him, and I asked him what he was smoking.

'Phipson's Club Number Three,' he said. 'Made in Worur, a tiny village near Trinuchinapalli – the place we know as Trichinopoly.'

'Listen to this, then.' I read from the book an extract from Sherlock Holmes's monograph *Upon the Distinction Between the Ashes of the Various Tobaccos*, in which he listed a hundred and forty forms of cigar, cigarette and pipe tobaccos: 'To the trained eye there is as much difference between the black ash of a Trichinopoly and the white fluff of bird's eye as there is between a cabbage and a potato.' (Harry's ash didn't seem particularly dark, though.) 'If you can say definitely that some murder had been done by a man who was smoking an Indian *lunkah*, it obviously

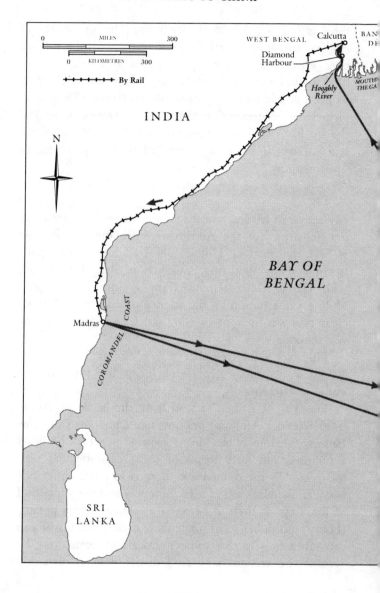

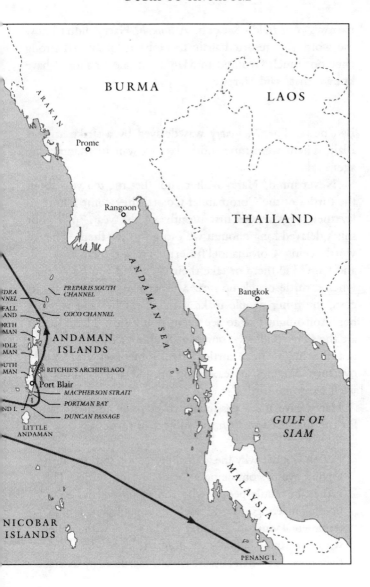

narrows your field of search.' A *lunkah*? Harry didn't know the word, so I resorted again to Hobson Jobson: 'A strong cheeroot much favoured in Madras,' it said. 'I should have known that,' said Harry.

Bad news. The *Nancowry* was delayed by a strike at Port Blair. There were nine more days to wait in Madras, the agent said.

'Never mind,' Harry Miller said. 'Let me tell you about the turtles of the Coromandel Coast. They come ashore to lay their eggs in the first months of the year, so if your ship's delayed long enough we can go to see them. They're worth seeing. Coromandel fishermen regard them as sacred, and won't kill them or take their eggs. Did you know that, when a turtle crawls up near a fisherman's house to lay its eggs, the fisher people make garlands for her and worship her? You might like to see them doing this. These turtles are the Olive Ridleys – quite small, about a metre in length, not the huge "boat turtles" that sometimes accidentally overturn dinghies at sea. Hang around a few weeks and we'll see some turtles.'

Harry gave me a passionate *cri de coeur* he had written for the *Indian Express* on the subject of turtles:

I often wonder why the animal protection societies turn a blind eye to continuing atrocities against turtles. The earnest but futile people who run these societies enjoy holding meetings, passing resolutions, publishing foolish, sentimental journals, and they can be severe with coolies who beat their bullocks or even the rich who starve their dogs; yet when pigs are ritually sacrificed by having a crowbar thrust through anus to mouth, or are beaten slowly to death so that their bleeding will not spoil the meat, when the eyes of living animals are torn out for 'eye medicine', or when turtles from the cool seas are roasted upside down for hours in the hot sun before being ripped up alive, they remain strangely silent.

Strong words, and why not?

Harry Miller has lived in India since the war. He is an excellent naturalist, a useful writer, knows a good deal about such subjects as stars, eclipses and cyclones, and practically all there is to know about southern India. He is a humourist, a professional photographer, and writes a regular column called 'Speaking of Animals' for the Madras edition of the *Indian Express*. It was there that I met him. I had been in Madras a few days waiting for a ship to the Andaman Islands, and Harry's hospitality had taken charge of me. Thereafter I spent my days sightseeing and listening to Harry Miller's stories – sometimes both at the same time.

For instance, while driving to St Mary's Church, where Robert Clive was married and Arthur Wellesley, the future Duke of Wellington, worshipped, Harry said, 'Do you know the story of the old lady who had two pet monkeys, male and female? The male died and then the female pined and died too. The old lady called a taxidermist. "Please stuff these two dear things," she said, "and please be sure to take good care of their little bodies. They were so fond of each other." "Certainly, lady," said the taxidermist. "Would you like them mounted?" "Oh, no," said the old lady, "just holding hands." '

Harry restrained himself in silence under the marble

effigies of dragoons and fusiliers in the old church the East India Company had built by the sea. Plaques commemorated early nineteenth-century British generals and brigadiers struck down young – aged only thirty, perhaps – by cholera, wounds or simple *coups de soleil*. 'Affection weeps! Heaven rejoices!' the inscriptions on the marble scrolls read.

My departure for Port Blair was delayed yet again; there were another three or four days to wait.

'Never mind,' said Harry. 'We'll go to the snake farm.' There he walked about an enclosure full of cobras like a gardener in a bed of tulips, the snakes rearing upright around him, hoods open, forked tongues flicking. I could only stand with a crowd of Tamil tourists and watch him ignoring my pleas to come out.

'Look,' he said as we drove back to Madras, 'India has two hundred species of snake, and of those only five are dangerously venomous to man. Of the five, the king cobra is so rarely encountered that you might as well make it four.'

'Vipers, kraits?'

'Vipers are venomous, yes. You've heard of the big, fat Russell's viper – that's the Sherlock Holmes chap in "The Speckled Band". The krait is India's most venomous land snake. But I say again, snakes are not aggressive to human beings at all. They've no reason to be; they don't want to eat you. You saw me walking among those cobras just now, and nothing happened. All snakes want is to be left alone. They hiss or strike to say, I'm dangerous. Of course, if you hit them or tread on them, what can you expect?'

★　★　★

In default of a departing ship, kindly officials drove me around the harbour breakwaters of the port of Madras expounding on its growth and traffic. It is an entirely artificial port. The coastline here is flat, swept clean of sheltering wrinkles and comforting indentations by the terrible currents and swells of the Bay of Bengal. In the hall of the Port Trust, charts show the steady addition of break-waters by which the port has now expanded to handle a thousand ships, including containers, a year, overtaking Calcutta in importance on the east coast.

'Calcutta has many political problems,' a Port Trust direc-tor, a Tamil himself, said. 'Here we have too large a labour force, but less troubles, partly because Tamils are quieter characters.'

Unlike the Hentrys of India or the Walids of Pakistan, officials at the managerial level in India have no desire to emigrate west – I assume because they are doing nicely where they are. Another factor is that, if they have been acquainted with Britain in the recent past, they find differ-ences there now that horrify them. The director, an extremely polite man, was moved by his overpowering disappointment to say, 'People in the West – the UK, especially – are so lazy. I don't like going there. Four years ago I was in a posh London hotel, just arrived, very early in the morning. I rang room service for coffee. The waiter said, "What do you want with coffee at four in the morning? The kitchen opens at seven." I said, "Just some hot water. I've got instant coffee here." "I can't serve you," he said. In the morning the girl who brought my toast and tea was lazy and exhausted. I don't know if she'd slept or not; she just dropped it in front of me. When you see things like that in London your heart just fails. Maybe Mrs Thatcher will change them – but no, it's too late.' He looked at me mournfully and shook his head.

I discovered from this director that a Shipping Corporation of India vessel still plied regularly between Madras, Penang and Singapore, mostly carrying Tamil and other Indian settlers in Malaysia back and forth. The settlers usually had heavy baggage that would cost too much by air, which was why the sea service survived.

This news stirred me out of a deep depression; I was growing more worried by the delays. I foresaw others – perhaps from Port Blair, almost certainly from Calcutta with its strikes, cyclones and red tape. I felt no confidence in a possible passage to Rangoon, so I booked a berth to Singapore from Madras. It was two weeks hence but, with South-east Asia yet to cross, I preferred safety to more disappointments. I felt better for having that ticket in my metal suitcase. When Harry Miller took me down to the Madras Club for dinner, I was less depressed and marginally less obsessed with my failure to get to sea again.

Harry was his usual cheering self. 'For God's sake, have another pink gin, and I'll tell you about the octopuses around Madras. We trawl them up often. Have you ever felt the suckers of an octopus on the back of your hand? Each of those hundreds of small but powerful suckers attach themselves to you like glue, with a delicate tickling sensation, as though you were being plucked at by a multitude of tiny wet hands. Stay on here another month and we'll catch some octopuses and see the turtles, too.'

But the next day the agents telephoned me to say the *Nancowry* would sail for Port Blair the day after. Would I be aboard by 5.00 p.m.?

Harry drove me to the docks and said goodbye. A wharf inspector took me aboard – sent, he said, by the Port Trust director – and wove through the wharfside crates, dodging pools of rusty water and scurrying coolies, incongruously chattering about religion. 'I want to work for God, sir. I'm Anglican Church of South India. Follow me, sir, and watch that puddle. And what church are you?'

The last barrier on my way back to sea, a sleepy man in an office on the dock, blinked at my ticket which he had to stamp. 'Where are you from?'

'London.'

'Why are you going to Port Blair? Why are you not flying?'

'Could you please just put your stamp on this ticket?'

'Oh, yes, stamp. Of course, a stamp.'

Four hours later, the *Nancowry* moved across the harbour basin from the west quay and through the narrow jaws of the breakwater.

Two hours later still, I was talking in his cabin to Captain Balasubramanian of Madras, a man who, like three successive Shipping Corporation of India masters, would become and remain my friend. His first words after pouring whisky for us were, 'Look here, sir, I have something of importance to propose. You are unlikely ever to be able to pronounce my name, leave alone remember it, so why not call me Bala. Everybody calls me Bala. Does that strike you as a sensible thing, sir?' And so Bala he became: jolly, no-nonsense, generous, friendly Bala. A portly figure in smart whites, greying but not above fifty, with a quickness of speech that matched the rattle of a Gatling gun. An old hand with bubbling humour that seemed a match for any misfortune.

I learned all about the *Nancowry* from Bala over that first tumbler of whisky. Built in 1949, an ex-British India Company ship, 10,300 tons, with capacity for 950 passengers. He liked her: 'She's a sweet thing,' he maintained. What if she was old? Her oil-fuelled steam turbines were virtually inaudible; she moved along in stately style without so much as a tremble. 'Look at the whisky in your glass, sir. Is it trembling? Is it so much as shifting slightly? No, sir.' Thirty years old, moving like a dream at eleven knots, the *Nancowry* left my whisky unshaken and unstirred.

I shared a cabin with a doctor travelling to take up his new posting at Port Blair. Bala had said that most passengers were government officials, workers or their dependants, and doctors and teachers, all from the mainland and assigned to the islands. The Andamans were still jungly and sparsely populated. Like Australia, their population consisted of aborigines, who mainly lived hidden in thick forests; newly arrived mainlanders; and settlers descended from the con-victs of the great penal settlement established during the Indian Mutiny.

The doctor, a tubby man, who had studied medicine in

Madras, opened my *Vintage Wodehouse* paperback. 'Ah, my favourite author. English is such a beautiful language.'

We drank whisky together and he invited in three young men who put their heads around the door – two of them his pupils and one, called Francis, a teacher at the government college in Port Blair.

'Mud in your eye,' the doctor said.

'Fluff in your latchkey,' I replied, and then had to explain that I was only repeating a favourite toast of Bertie Wooster.

The doctor was eager to know from Francis if people on the Andamans felt isolated. Sometimes, said Francis, but luckily the islands were beautiful, if you liked wild nature. The isolation was partly the result of the difficulty of transport. You had to trust to the steamer service to and from Calcutta and Madras; otherwise there was only the twice-weekly air service to Calcutta, and nothing to Madras. Francis said to me, 'You must see the old prison. It is now a museum, a national monument.'

After breakfast – cornflakes, eggs, bacon, Madrasi cakes with curry sauce – next morning in the spacious dining room, I inspected the library-music room. Indian Muzak drifted around bookcases filled with titles like *To Glory We Steer* or *Ill Met By Moonlight*. I gave up a long time to reading the *Bay of Bengal Pilot* (1978, tenth edition) lent me by Captain Bala:

> The Andaman Islands consist of a group of about 200 islands and rocks. The aborigines live in the forests by hunting and fishing; they are of a small Negrito type, and their civilisation is about that of the stone age. The

forest-dwellers comprise the Jarawas and Sentinelese, of whom little is known, as these tribes are hostile and avoid contact with civilisation . . .

Andaman Indians consist of ex-convicts who were released under declaration of amnesty in 1947, together with penal administrative staffs and merchants who settled in the island after the penal settlement was abolished.

Port Blair, the capital, the *Pilot* said, exports timber, coco-nuts and copra, and imports textiles and plants, notably pineapples. In 1949 the population of the whole archipelago was eighteen thousand.

The Andamans have some wonderful Robert Louis Stevenson names: Jolly Boy Island, the Labyrinth Islands, Turtle Reef, Elfin Patch, Bacon Bay, Egg Island, Curlew Island, Diligent Strait, Fusilier Channel, Grub Island. According to the *Pilot*, Viper Island contained several build-ings formerly part of the penal settlement. ('The gallows, too,' Francis said.) I wanted to visit Mount Harriet, 1193 feet high, which stood over Perseverance Point; at its foot, in 1872, a viceroy of India, Lord Mayo, was stabbed to death by Sher Ali, a convict.

Port Blair was named after Lieutenant Archibald Blair, of the old British-run Indian navy, who arrived there in 1788 with two ships, *Viper* and *Elizabeth*, to survey for harbours. He wrote an ecstatic report on the anchorage, the 'perfect harbour . . . large enough to contain about fifty sailes of the Line'. Blair planted fruit and vegetables there, and built a wooden wharf. Some artificers, soldiers and two Chinese gardeners were settled there, and the first two hundred convicts followed in 1792.

'I think Arthur Conan Doyle was really off his rocker,'

the nice-looking Indian lady who was my neighbour in the dining room said sternly. 'As far as the Andamans are concerned, at least.'

'How so?'

'Well, he described a wild pygmy from there, armed with a blow-torch—'

'Blowpipe, surely.'

'Blowpipe. And poisoned darts. Well, no pygmies live in the Andamans, although there are some tribals who are quite short, it's true. He really meant the Philippines or somewhere further east, where there *are* pygmies, and he should have said so.'

Though I didn't care to argue, I wasn't sure that Doyle ever described poor Tonga in *The Sign of Four* as a 'pygmy'. 'Unhallowed dwarf', yes; 'a little black man with a great misshapen head', certainly. My neighbour was the daughter of a settler, a marine engineer now dead, and was returning home after nine years. Of course, she was right about there being no pygmies in the Andamans, but Doyle's story was rooted in the treasure of Agra and the opportunity the anarchy of the Mutiny had provided for unscrupulous men to steal it. He could hardly have shifted things to the Philippines (where there are no pygmies either). So it is the word 'Andamans' that sombrely evokes that 'fairly fine' night at Pondicherry Lodge in Upper Norwood in London when Holmes and Watson discovered the body of Bartholomew Sholto, formerly a major commanding native troops at Port Blair, seated all in a heap, with a ghastly and inscrutable smile upon his face, and his limbs twisted in fantastic fashion. And twenty years of building breakwaters in the penal settlement of Port Blair will remain the sentence passed on Jonathan Small, the one-legged convict, who owed a temporary freedom and the satisfaction of revenge to his friend, Tonga, 'the little hell-hound' and his poisoned darts from the distant Bay of Bengal.

A sudden change of course. Francis, the teacher, ran down to the cabin saying, 'Come quickly. They've spotted a drifting boat.'

The *Nancowry* was bearing down on a tiny bobbing shape, and Bala was on the bridge peering at it through binoculars. As we approached it he ordered a long blast of the steam siren to rouse anyone dozing or comatose on a boat that was too far out to sea to be a shipping vessel. Was it a castaway family of Vietnamese boat people?

But the siren's mournful call went unheard; no one emerged from the ramshackle chicken coop in the stern of what turned out to be a two-decked bamboo raft. Perhaps it was only a Thai or Burmese river ferry washed out to sea by a flash flood. We circled it and hooted again, looking for traces of blood or a sun-shrivelled body, while inquisitive passengers packed the rail. But there was no life or death, only a small mystery four hundred miles into the Bay of Bengal.

On the way up to see Bala on the second evening, I was startled by a flick of something quite large at the head of a companionway ahead of me.

'Captain Bala,' I said to tease him. 'Do you have any bandicoots on board?'

'Oho, sir,' Bala said, laughing, 'that would be impossible. A bandicoot is not a seafaring animal. Bandicoots will come out in the early hours of the morning and dig up your yams, tapioca, sweet potatoes – that's their delight. Dogs can deal with them. But you will not find a bandicoot at sea – never, sir.

'Now, rats, that's different. I've seen them sitting up. Big bastards, they are; I don't like them at all. They gnash their teeth and I respectfully salute them. I remember, once off Madras, rats crept up to the crew's feet while they slept and began to nibble. It was the socks, you see, sir. These seamen hadn't washed their socks, so the rats came out to enjoy them. And they gnawed all the sock toes and then all the soft skin of the actual toes, the bottoms of the toes and their edges, so that they were red and raw, though not actually bleeding.

'When the seamen woke up, they began shouting, "What's this?" I painted their raw toes with tincture of iodine – you don't know what will come from a rat's bite. And then – *aha!* – I held a spirit lamp under each toe to cauterize it. You should have heard 'em howl, sir. Ooooh, my God, how they howled and cursed and swore, and said dreadful things about my father and mother. But I had to do it. A rat bite, a nibble even, is very dangerous indeed. But the bandicoot, sir, is a land animal.'

One night we heard wild cheering, which seemed to be coming from the foredeck. 'What's that?' Captain Bala said over his curry to the chief officer. 'A mutiny? My goodness, it had better not be.' He laughed. 'I haven't got so much as an air pistol aboard.' It was passengers applauding an announcement from Port Blair radio that Mrs Gandhi's candidates in the general election were sweeping southern

India. It reminded me of similar cheering in northern India two years before when Mrs Gandhi had suffered a landslide defeat.

The cheering continued until a Tamil film was shown. An enthusiastic audience, including soldiers in sarongs printed with hand-sized flowers, packed into a small space on deck, standing or perched on chairs. The sailors of the *Nancowry* watched the film from the wrong side of the screen; the image came through quite clearly.

At dinner I asked Bala, 'Would you encourage your son to go into your profession?'

'No, I would not, sir,' he said immediately. 'It's a lonely life, sir, a lonely life. I'd steer my son towards electronics – that area. It has a good future.' After a moment he added, 'Not that I grumble. I'll work until I'm forced to stop.'

Fifty-four per cent of Indian masters' earnings go in tax, so Bala can't be a wealthy man even after all those years at sea. At one time he was on the Shipping Corporation of India's northern run to Odessa, and he has a Russian wife. They had to wait four years before the Soviet authorities would allow her to leave the country and set up house with Bala in Madras.

A passenger – an immigrant worker – fell ill two days from the Andamans. Called in by Bala, the doctor bustled between my cabin and the sick bay. No one seemed quite sure if the man would live or die. He was said to be in a coma; his jaw was paralysed; perhaps he had tetanus. Soon it seemed he might die before we reached shore. That would mean a burial at sea, or locking up his corpse in the fridge. On the other hand, expert hospital care might still save him (although, in the event, it didn't). So Bala decided to divert the *Nancowry*, which had been scheduled to make a short midnight stop off Car Nicobar, the northernmost of the Nicobar Islands. Instead, we veered northeastwards, taking a short cut.

At 6.15 a.m. a whitish sun lit the back of Rutland Island, the southernmost of the Andamans.

Port Blair soon appeared as a rash of old mansions and pleasant bungalows spread over low hills, a new wharf, and a small tin-roofed factory with a smoking chimney, all just inside the mouth of a deep bay. On our right, Perseverance Point was marked by a small light, and over it rose a green pyramid of trees: Mount Harriet. Islands dotted the bay; I could see a topknot of trees on tiny Viper Island at the far end against a forest background. Overlooking the town of Port Blair and its tiny port, the great prison displayed a long flank of wall with blank windows, like the side of a liner.

Chapter Twenty-Two

A CURLEW CALLED from the dark forested mass of an island. Sea eagles, white and chestnut, lazed about the treetops. An elephant carried a log down to the water, like a dog with his master's walking stick, and laid it carefully in the shallows, where half-naked men were pushing the timber together to make rafts. I felt I was in a soundproofed room or, at least, a timeproofed world. You could choose your century out here.

I had been two days in the Andamans. Bala had finished his chores on the *Nancowry* and was free until she sailed back to Madras the next day. He had taken me to meet an amazing man, his old shipmate Captain Dennis Beale, who had opened a magic door to the Andamans.

In 1966, Beale had decided, in early middle age, to leave the Shipping Corporation, settle in Port Blair and, as people used to say, 'follow his bent'. This meant setting up a small boatbuilding business, fishing from one of his tiny launches among the islands, studying the flora and fauna and towing the logs of the timber company to the sawmill at Port Blair. A simple, idyllic and useful existence.

Beale had invited me 'to potter about' in the western islands. He loved them and thought I would too. Here, on Rutland Island, men were cutting the timber that his boats would tow.

'Elephants here are imported from Assam. They're less temperamental than the ones from Burma,' said Beale. Smiling, he added, 'I should know.'

He looked like a Burmese, although he was only half

Burmese. His rich English father had owned a rubber estate in the Moulmein area of Burma before the Second World War. Forced to flee to India with his family when the Japanese came, Beale's father returned to Moulmein after the war. But somehow life there was never the same again, and he died in 1950. Young Dennis Beale, who had walked out of Burma with the family across the Naga Hills clutching a revolver, decided against following his father into the rubber business, and had joined the Shipping Corporation of India instead.

Dennis Beale's unpretentious house on the outskirts of Port Blair was made of wood and, like many houses in the Andamans, its creaking rooms stood on stilts. Hi-fi equipment filled his front room. Planks of wood were stored under his house, and in the garden, by a row of slim, upright areca palms, his Indian employees hammered a half-finished launch into life. His little car stood in a lane outside. Plates of fried tuna or barracuda stood on one table, a bottle of whisky on another. In a backroom was his record collection: Gracie Fields, Chevalier, Tauber. We had more than one night of song before I left.

'This is Gavin Young, a writer who's visiting. I told him you were just the man,' Bala had said.

I shook hands with a stocky, round-faced man of about fifty, who immediately astonished me by turning and yelling, 'Hey, Gavin!'

In a second, two boys came running in, sixteen and fourteen perhaps. 'My sons. Gavin's the small one, Nicholas the big one,' said Beale. 'Surprised?' He laughed. 'Just wait, you'll be surprised again.' When we reached his hidden bay, I discovered that Beale's favourite launch was also called *Gavin*. 'This meeting must be predestined,' he said.

Perhaps it was. The Andamans had turned out to be exactly what I had hoped. My visa gave me a week here, and the steamer to Calcutta left Port Blair in precisely a week's time. On this occasion the timing could hardly have been worked out better. I was staying in a pleasant guest-house, the Megapode's Nest (the megapode is a big-footed bird about the size of a coot, found only in the Andamans), and my room looked down over the bay and the slopes of Mount Harriet. A few small inter-island ferries crossed and re-crossed the bay. Not many bigger ships came here, apart from the *Nancowry* and her counterpart on the Calcutta run. Rust-red godowns lined the horseshoe of Phoenix Bay beneath me, and a low line of buildings marked a street or two leading up from the bay to the district of Port Blair called Aberdeen where administrative buildings sheltered behind a fringe of trees.

Port Blair is pocket-sized, about the size of a small

country town in Britain or America. It has no newspaper or bookshop, although there is a newsletter, the *Daily Telegrams [sic]*, which, on the day I bought it, carried a front-page article headed 'Tribal Welfare: Greater Attention to Be Paid'. The government college had, I was told, a good library. Bars are banned by law, though drinking is not; a wine store is open three days a week.

The Indian government, more than most, takes a sensible attitude to forests. The Andaman trees – perhaps the oldest trees I've ever seen – were still close-packed, even after the selective trimming we were witnessing. Bala, Beale's two sons and I stood in the airless, sticky heat of their shade and watched the elephants stacking immense timbers. Using trunks, forefeet and tusks, they advanced and retreated, bowed and rose again, in a kind of minuet. Their mahouts, perched on their heads, were their dance masters, ordering their movements by kicking them behind the ears with bare feet. The timber company also used buffalo, twin-yoked, grunting up and down the red paths dragging logs with chains.

The forests of the Andamans are not undergoing the indiscriminate ripping out of trees without reforestation that decimates forests in Borneo, Celebes, Brazil and elsewhere. The government seems to have seen the danger in time.

'Here's a story,' said Beale. 'A female elephant resented the drunken ill-treatment she was getting from her driver, so she "rampaged" his house, as they call it here, and killed him. Although people said she seemed to have a demon, she only killed him; no one else was injured in any way, although the houses in his village were very close together.'

Bala said, 'There's a story going round Tamil Nadu. Some bloody fool gave an elephant a coconut full of bleaching fluid to drink. He lived a long way off, but she had recognized him and she waited. When he came back to the same place five years later, she killed him. Tossed him – wheeee – high in the air.'

Around the islands the water was deep and dark. Through the Labyrinth Islands, we passed Alexandra, Jolly Boy and Pluto to Macpherson Strait, where the water was shallower and gave out a green-blue luminosity as though the light were coming up from the seabed.

Bamboo stalks poked upright in the water, marking channels between rocks and pinpointing ridges of murderous coral that glowed below the surface only when the sun was out. 'Daylight navigating,' commented Bala. 'Very difficult at night round here.'

Dennis Beale's three Bihari Indians steered the *Gavin* up from Rutland, and we trailed two lines over the stern. Near a pair of coralbound islets called the Twins, Beale's sons yelled, 'A fish!' Another yell: another fish on the other line. Then a shark came after them, its torpedo body a stream of silver only inches behind their tails. The Biharis hauled in the two tuna just in time; as the second was half out of the water, the shark threw itself up in a last vain snap of jaws. It might have left us nothing but two heads.

Off the white beach of Snob Island we caught rockfish and the beaked parrot fish, exquisitely coloured – yellow flanks speckled with turquoise, pink fins with turquoise fringes.

On Redskin Island we swam in water like glass. Bala wallowed and dived into a big, dark cave, roaring like a sea monster to scare Beale's sons. 'Oh, my God, I thought I saw a sea monster in there,' he cried, laughing. There was a canoe on the shore and a hut with sugar-cane leaves for a roof and sugarcane or bamboo walls. A very dark man in a white sarong who walked to the water's edge said he'd come here from southern India three years before. He lived on this island alone, spending his time fishing and noosing the spotted deer that infested the undergrowth.

When the light began to fail, Beale stood near the *Gavin's* Bihari helmsman as we slipped homewards through unlit rocks. Against the darkening background of the sky the cliffs of huge trees made silhouettes of battlements, pinnacles and spires. '*Thora obaju*,' Beale's voice murmured. 'A little that way. *Tik hai*. Okay, fine.'

An eagle beat its way home. Ahead, where Dennis Beale moored his boats, were the lights of small fires and spirals of smoke. Charcoal burners carried sacks ashore from a heavy wooden barge. Fishermen flicked their skiffs about a creek, rowing while standing upright, wagging oars that they also used as rudders. '*Ruko*,' said Beale to the helmsman. '*Bandhao*. Stop. Tie up.'

We waded barelegged to dry land. I could see through the open doorways of a few shaggy houses men and women sitting around fires that illuminated their faces orange-red. The silence of the sea, the surrounding islands and the trees settled around us as comfortingly as an old overcoat. I didn't even mind the mosquitoes that attended us as we drank a sundowner of Honey Bee brandy on the beach before the corkscrew drive back to Dennis Beale's house on stilts and an evening with the records of Sinatra and Vera Lynn.

I spent most of my seven days with Dennis Beale, and several evenings under those areca palms. He told me of the fauna of the islands – of the robber crabs, for instance: big creatures, shaped like a giant fist, with seven or eight legs. They were also called coconut crabs because they would scrabble up the slender, silvery trunks, pluck a coconut down, husk it fibre by fibre and, when their huge claws had broken open the shell, drink the water and eat the kernel.

I should return one day, Beale said, to see all the creatures unique to the Andaman region: the regal python, the Nicobar quail, the Andaman red-breasted parakeet and the saltwater crocodiles.

I had seen a 'Dugong Creek' marked on a map, and asked about it. Dugongs are rare sea creatures with heavy bodies, not unlike seals, with big blunt, whiskered heads. Olden-day sailors often mistook them for mermaids – heaven knows why.

'The sea cow?' said Beale. 'Rare now. The aborigines kill them sometimes, I think.'

The headline I had seen in the *Daily Telegrams* about government concern for the welfare of the tribes obviously reflected the truth; everyone seemed agreed on that. The matter was literally one of survival or extinction, and the government had a difficult task. The tribes of the Andaman Islands need all the protection they can get. Two of the four tribes, the Jarawas and the Sentinelese (they inhabit Sentinel Island), are 'outside the scope of friendly contact', according to a government report of 1979. Few survive: they number only two hundred and fifty, and fifty people,

respectively. As for the two 'friendly' tribes, the Great And-
amanese and the Onges, only twenty-four of the former
and ninety-four of the latter remain. No wonder the
government is engaged in protecting them from outsiders.
Diseases introduced by foreigners, including the convicts,
almost decimated them. The more friendly they were, the
more they caught syphilis, measles, mumps and influenza.

The curator of the excellent museum in Port Blair
showed me tribal spears and arrows whose iron heads were
presumed to have been made from vessels shipwrecked here
in the nineteenth century or earlier. But there were no
blowpipes or poisoned darts. In that detail, then, as the
emphatic lady on the *Nancowry* had insisted, Conan Doyle
was 'off his rocker'.

The museum showed a documentary film of a few years
ago in which the camera crew's boat was seen approaching
the beach of Sentinel Island and facing a hostile reception
committee of aborigines gathered on the shore. Short, slim,
muscular men, practically or completely naked, raced down
to the surf – and waist-high into it – obviously beside
themselves with fear or fury, shaking their fists at the boatful
of Indian intruders. Others waved spears. Still others fired
bows and arrows from the shore or from the water, and
one arrow struck a cameraman in the boat on the thigh. It
was impossible to land.

In a fascinating book on the Andamans by an Indian
writer, Iqbal Singh, I found an account by Lieutenant Blair
in 1788 of the first meeting with these tribes:

I met two canoes, and gave the people which were in
them, some bottles with which they were highly pleased,
or seemed to be so, but to my astonishment one of them

suddenly jumped out of his canoe, ran within twenty yards of the boat and shot all his arrows at us, which luckily did not hurt, though most struck the boat.

This, of course, mirrored what I saw in the Indian documentary film shot in the 1970s.

The Sentinelese, anthropologists say, are probably the world's only surviving paleolithic people. But these prototypes of Tonga are not pygmies. The average height of the men is four foot ten and a half inches; of the women, four foot six. Their origins are obscure. As they are Negritos, not Negroes, they may have the same ancestors as the people of the Malacca peninsula in Malaysia, or of the Philippines.

In 1874 two tribal boys nicknamed Kiddy Boy and Topsy were taken by kind Englishmen to Calcutta. (Topsy was a name applied as often to boys as to girls; other common names were Snowball, Friday and Crusoe.) They did not transplant well. Topsy died of 'inflammation of the lungs', and Kiddy Boy was soon carried off by consumption.

Captain Beale and Francis, the young teacher at the government college, took me sightseeing after Bala had sailed back to Madras in the *Nancowry*, giving us two hoots on his siren at Perseverance Point.

Beale obligingly posed for me on the trapdoor of the double gallows of the Cellular Jail, the museum and monument that once housed thousands of prisoners – a tall, austere system of single-windowed cells fanning out from a central tower like the spokes of a wheel. It was completed in 1910, and only part of it is used now. A large room on the ground floor is given over to photographs of the Indian martyrs of the struggle for independence in the first half of the twentieth century.

There were pictures of convicts in 'punishment dress' – a sacking shirt; of men convicted of ancient murders: the Cornwallis Street shooting, the Barisal police inspector's murder case, and other cases involving dacoity, gang robbery or murder. An official notice of 1908 admonished: 'Transportation entails hard labour under strict discipline *with only such food as is necessary for health* . . .'

There were statistics: Three months after the establishment of the penal settlement in 1858 the total number of convicts received was 773, of whom the following had already died:

In hospital 61
Escaped and not captured (probably died of starvation
   or killed by savages) 140
Suicide 1
Hanged for attempting escape 87

By 1874 there were 7567 prisoners at Port Blair, of whom 5575 were murderers. And the figures bounded upwards. In time, a number of prisoners through good behaviour became 'ticket-of-leave'; among other labours these men cleared the lower slopes of Mount Harriet. This – or rather the fact that their desire was to be clean-shaven – accounted for the murder of the viceroy, Lord Mayo, on 8 February 1872.

As it happened, Lord Mayo was interested in building a sanatorium for the convicts suffering from tuberculosis and, just before leaving the islands at the end of an official visit, he walked up Mount Harriet. 'How beautiful,' he said at the top. This would be the ideal place for the consumptives to recover.

It was dusk when he and his entourage reached the little jetty – I walked on it – to embark on his steam launch, and the viceroy stepped quickly in front of the rest to descend the stairs to embark.

Now people in the rear heard a noise as of 'the rush of some animal' and saw 'a man fastened like a tiger on the back of the Viceroy'. British officers and native guards seized the assailant on the spot while the Viceroy, who had staggered over the pierside, was dimly seen rising up in the knee-deep water. He was hoisted up and seated on a rude native cart, but the blood streamed out of a wound in his back. 'After a moment he fell heavily backwards. "Lift up my head," he said faintly. And said no more.'

His murderer, Sher Ali, went to the gallows on Viper Island. A massive Pathan convicted for a murder at Peshawar, he was the barber for the ticket-of-leave men on Mount Harriet. 'God gave me an order,' he said when questioned. On the gallows he shouted, 'Brothers, I have killed your enemy and you are my witness that I am a Muslim.' He died reciting the Koran.

'In the midst of life' – you can barely see the inscription in the murky light that filters down through the trees of Ross Island on to the graves in the British cemetery opposite the Cellular Jail. 'To the Memory of Lawrence, the Infant Son of . . . 1863.' The stones are half obliterated by moss, rot and age. 'Sergeant William Henry Irwin, "B" Company, 2nd. Bn. 10th Foot . . .' 'Gone before, but in our love never forgotten.' Roots like writhing snakes have forced up the stones. Creepers smother them or have smashed them into fragments. Inquisitive spotted deer sniff at them and the splendour of blue kingfishers and peacocks seems inappropriate under the disembodied tower of a ghostly church through which a tree has grown, withered and died.

Beale and his children accompanied me to Viper Island, the oldest part of the prison colony: before the Cellular Jail was built here, the convicts had either tents or shacks thatched with atap or nipa palm leaves.

The little island looked deserted and was very silent when we landed at an old stone jetty projecting from a crude sea wall and walked up a slope glowing green as emerald in an early sun. A few men appeared carrying *darbs*, the tender coconut of the Andamans, and Beale hailed them. 'The water of the tender coconut', he told me, 'is the purest in the world. You could mix it with medicines, like distilled water, and inject it into a patient.'

'Can we have a coconut, Daddee?' asked Gavin. 'I'm so thirstee.'

We sat on an old wall and the men hacked off the tops of several coconuts.

'Any ghosts here?' I asked them.

'No, sahib, we've never seen any on this island.'

The gallows had been erected at the top of a small knoll above the jetty. A ruined building, red-brick, cupolaed, more like a temple, now stood there among coconut trees. The old guardhouse was beneath it: six arches in a colonnade, then a brick-vaulted chamber. Springy grass covered the condemned cells.

We wandered over gradually rising green knolls, skirting half-buried causeways, half-hidden brick stairways, the surviving half of a red-brick sentry box. In a hollow the coconut cultivators have built atap huts, just as the first convicts, who had planted the first of the coconut plantations, had done.

'There's a cemetery at the highest point of the island,' Nicholas Beale said. 'Shall we find it, uncle?'

'Of course,' I said.

We came to a frangipani tree, spreading more white blossoms and smelling more sweetly than any I can remember and, beyond it, a crumbling flight of brick stairs.

'That's it. The cemetery's up there, uncle.'

We started to climb the stairs, but soon they turned an awkward corner and disappeared into a wilderness of scraggy bushes, creepers and spiteful thorn-fringed trees. Two long thorns lodged deep in my shoulder, but we pushed on, drenched in sweat, wrenching and tearing our way upwards to the hidden graves.

We never reached them. They weren't far ahead; in fact, there were old stones underfoot already, but the undergrowth was too dense to be stormed. The light under the trees had become dim, and my will to press on was flagging; the thorns in my shoulders were beginning to feel like Tonga's poisoned darts. Cut off from Nicholas Beale by a bamboo thicket, in my imagination I could hear Sher Ali's triumphant roar from the gallows down the hill: 'Brothers, I have killed your enemy.'

I was relieved to find Dennis Beale sitting under the frangipani. He and the innocent sun banished ghosts from the green slopes of little Viper Island. 'I wish I'd been born twenty years earlier,' he said, looking around with a planter's eye. 'I might have bought some land just here.'

The day I left Port Blair it was not a happy moment saying goodbye to the Beales and to Francis. I was appalled by the thought of what I might have missed if I hadn't run into Tom Abraham in Colombo. But my visa had expired and another ship, the m.v. *Harsha Vardhana*, was at Haddoo Wharf preparing to leave for Calcutta. I had packed and paid my bill at the Megapode's Nest guest-house. There was nothing for it but to go aboard and prepare to follow Bala out of the narrow gap between Perseverance Point and the dying graves of Ross Island.

Chapter Twenty-Three

BIFF! BOP! I opened my cabin door and stared. At 11.00 p.m. an elderly Bengali in cotton pyjamas was staggering about as though possessed, wildly thumping a whimpering youth of eighteen who was trying to protect himself from a hail of punches and slaps.

'Yow . . . yow . . . yow,' the enraged Bengali howled with every blow of his skinny arms as they reeled about the empty corridor ricocheting from wall to wall. Were they drunk? Should I help?

They moved slowly but violently down the corridor away from me, punching and staggering, until at the far end a woman in a sari appeared at a cabin door and leaped into the mêlée. 'No! No!' she cried. Momentarily she was the blurred centre of a flurry of resounding slaps, then the three of them fell through the door in a tangle and out of sight. Another 'Yow' or two and a muffled thud could be heard, then silence.

At breakfast in the dining room next morning, I looked around and saw the battling trio of the night before. The elderly Bengali was happily dribbling his porridge. His son, unbruised – I passed close enough to check – simpered beside him, pulling long rinds of bacon from his mouth like a conjuror drawing strings of coloured handkerchiefs from his sleeve. The lady in the sari sat opposite them both, smoking a cigarette and regarding them fondly. Did I detect a dark smudge on her left cheekbone just below the eye?

★ ★ ★

The voyage from Port Blair to Calcutta took two quietly enjoyable days in spite of the quirks of the passengers. Surprisingly, we were on time despite the fascinating revelation that the little people who inhabit the banks of the Hooghly river, the threshold of the great port, have stopped all navigation on it by big ships at night, not out of any anarchistic desire to sabotage the port, but out of a collector's love of the brass light fittings on the buoys that mark the safe channel in the waterway.

The *Harsha Vardhana*, a well-run, modern ship, vibrated more than the old *Nancowry* but moved twice as fast. In her dining room – a large one – I found myself wondering whether Indian government servants had been starved in the Andamans. They ate like famished refugees, wolfing down potatoes, fat bacon and porridge, grabbing two thick wedges of toast at a time, slapping a quarter of an inch of butter between them and shouting to the waiters as they did so, 'Bring toast. More butter. More potatoes.' Cries for second or even third helpings rent the air, crumbs showering from callers' mouths. I even had the awkward experience of finding the arm of my fat young neighbour between my mouth and the fork with which I was about to convey a mouthful to it: he was collaring the last piece of bread, being too impatient to ask me to pass it. Breakfast on the *Harsha Vardhana* became an athletic competition: to the fleetest the butter, to the strongest the toast.

Captain John's laughing explanation for this phenomenon was that Indian passengers were very much aware of their rights. If they or their government had paid a supplement for food, they would certainly eat as much as they could for the money.

It was not only the table manners that suffered from such insistence on passengers' rights. 'Government servants just don't worry enough about the fittings. We've gone to trouble to make everything nice, and because people's fares are paid by the government, they don't care. They pull out the fittings.' Once upon a time the cabins had telephones, Captain John said, 'but the children were always calling up the bridge and the engine room, so I had them taken out'.

The *Harsha Vardhana* was a modern ship, named after the Indian emperor who ruled between 606 and 647 AD. A generous man of liberal spirit, he had worshipped both Buddha and Shiva. The ship had been built in 1974 for the East Africa run in the days when that continent had as large Asian population. But East Africa had ceased to be profitable. 'Too many Idi Amins,' Captain John said. 'The Indians have left for the UK or India. Aeroplanes can cope with the rest, so here we are.'

A booklet in my cabin gave more details of the *Harsha Vardhana*'s parent company, the Shipping Corporation of India, with which I had now sailed twice – three times if one included the Mogul Line vessel to Goa. The pamphlet said that the SCI had a hundred and thirteen ships of over 2.77 million deadweight tonnage, with a new one being added practically every week. 'The SCI has but one way to look – forward!' The *Harsha Vardhana* herself was 132 feet long and could make seventeen knots.

Captain K. V. John came from Cochin; a good-looking Keralan, he must have been one of the youngest captains in the company's passenger fleet. He had a deadpan way of talking, and a deadpan humour, too. I told him of my delays in his home town. 'Strikes!' he said, rolling his eyes in mock agony. 'Poor Calcutta. Labour unrest is proving to be the death of that great port. Once we were about to sail, and I heard there'd be a strike of the lock operators. The passengers, hundreds of them, arrived at the ship. No sailing. We had to send them away – furious, of course. They went to the chief minister, the labour minister, the union boss. No one would do a thing. Finally we sailed, eleven days late. Who suffered? Not the company. Not me. Not the strikers who were paid by the state government. The passengers suffered. The public.'

And the port. Foreign ships were avoiding Calcutta.

There was even a surprising, though minor, labour dispute on the *Harsha Vardhana*. A film was to be shown to the passengers, but the crew wanted to see it too. Furthermore, their spokesman said, they wanted to be seated, just like the passengers. 'There's no chance of that,' said Captain John, quite reasonably, 'if the passengers come to the film. If there's room, members of the crew can stand; if not, I'll have it shown again tomorrow.'

The first officer reported that this had been received with angry mutterings. But the captain said, 'I can't offer any more. This is a passenger ship. If the crew want to see the film, they can see it tomorrow.'

Later the first officer, an experienced and genial Keralan named Joseph, a good man to negotiate with strikers, returned to say, 'Some booing. But they finally cooled it.'

Captain John said, 'This is not the worst I've had. But you have to be strict. I feel I have no choice in these decisions. I have a duty. There are standards, don't you think?'

★ ★ ★

At the Bingo session a young officer called out, 'One fat lady – number eight. You and me – thirty-three. Watch your son – twenty-one.'

A clerk from Baroda, who had been to the Andamans visiting his girlfriend, the daughter of a government employee, confided, 'This is my first time at sea, uncle. I am a lonely person. I want to go to Abu Dhabi, or anywhere outside India. Can I get work there?' Yet another little fish trying to swim westwards . . .

The first entry in the ship's complaint book was signed by a Mr Lal, who wrote, 'I am glad to certify that the service given me by the staff is really good. I feel just homelike comfort and this is due only from their sweet association.' Mr Lal had taken the words out of my mouth.

But there were grumbles, too. An Indian navy lieutenant had written, 'The standards of "HV" have come crashing down. All the facilities which were taken for granted when you travelled as a De Luxe class passenger have vanished into thin (salt) air.' A Professor Patel said: 'I received a piece of glass in my rice plate.' A Mr Kukherjee fumed that he had found 'certain indecent and unruly passengers in drunken condition'.

But the most elaborate complaint came from an irritated Bengali: 'I request Master of the ship to step in Cabin just for experience . . . Stewards attend cabins at their own whims and favours. Passengers boarding ship should be instructed about correct methods to use heads, and socio-economic differences keep some in dark . . . I am in habit of taking tea about six or seven times in a day, but saloon refused to entertain my request . . . There is a common

bath and lavatory for several Second Class passengers and in morning there is a terrible rush and it is difficult to attend to natural call. Also, as it is known, we are Indians and prefer to use water and never paper napkin . . .'

I'd had a long-standing ambition to travel up the Hooghly river, and now, on the bridge of the *Harsha Vardhana* with Captain John and Chief Officer Joseph, I was to do so. The following are jottings from my notebook:

> The great grey-green, greasy mouth of the Ganges. Sun white and bright in the mist. It reminds me of the mouth of the Nile. Mud swirls around us, contributed to by the dredging that is going on at intervals up the channel. The chief officer, Joseph, was with Calcutta Port recently and laid the buoys we see here. He also helped build the artificial spurs of brick and cement into the bank in order to push the water into mid-channel to deepen it. Labour unrest is one port killer; silting is another.
>
> The water is so thick that another ship in the channel,

the *Robert E. Lee* of New York, makes a sort of milky porridge of her wake. The banks close in, and flat, dusty-green countryside spreads out around us; here and there a red roof, cattle, a sailing vessel with men straining on two long oars. We pick up a pilot. Fifty-five miles below Calcutta the river is amazingly narrow.

10.30 a.m. The famous Balari Bar lies across our bows like a submerged whale, its brown length clearly visible. We reduce speed and slip across with only two or three feet clearance.

Diamond Harbour. Palms, houses and a brick factory. Fishing boats scattered about the river like that aquatic insect the water boatman. The pilot focuses his binoculars on the *Indian Trust* and waves to her bridge, then swings *HV* diagonally across the river. We zigzag at great speed, overtaking one or two foreign ships.

I read bits of Appendix C of the Storm Warning Service booklet, sold by the director of marine, Calcutta. Under 'Special signals used on the river of the Ganges Delta', it says:

It has been found desirable to arrange a simpler system for the inland waters of the Ganges Delta, as the signals there are used mainly by men of little education. Experience has shown that all that is required in this case is to indicate three degrees of danger.

Signal I. A storm may affect you shortly.

Signal II. A storm will soon strike you.

Signal III. A violent storm will soon strike you.

Appendix B reads: '. . . Great Danger Signal indicates

the approach of a storm of great intensity. Masters and pilots are cautioned not to . . . proceed down from Diamond Harbour, and they should make their vessels as snug and secure as possible . . .'

The river is like Henley during the regatta. Fleets of small boats. An old man and a boy in a dinghy nearly capsize in our wash, but right themselves and wave up to the bridge, laughing.

'There's Calcutta,' Captain John proclaimed. What do I see? Through smog, the whitish gleam of a few skyscrapers. On a bend, chimneys, derricks, plumes of oily black smoke. Flatness, alleviated here and there by archaeological sites in the making: the ruins of ancient jute mills, holed and pocked like buildings bombarded during the Mutiny. Near one ruin, an amazing and sickening concourse of vultures – a hundred or more. There are dark, unspeakable things on the bank: bodies, but whose? The vultures wrangle and tear and gobble. Some, bloated, waddle away too heavy with carrion to fly. How is it that they are so beautiful on the wing?

'Half ahead.'

'Half ahead, sir.'

I notice – it's difficult not to from the click-clacking on the deck – that the ship's apprentices – young Indians training to be officers – are wearing, of all things, high heels. High heels! They teeter awkwardly and dangerously about as if they were fashion models showing off the latest in naval styles. 'Aye, aye, sir.' Click-clack, click-clack.

We have to make dock in the slack water before the ebb, so we almost careen up the last bends. Soon the white dome of the Victoria Memorial. We swing around to the lock mouth – the docks here are tucked away among the buildings, only approachable through locks – scattering a midge cloud of barges and tugs with a basso-profundo blast which echoes through the part of the city that has now closed dingily about us. A city of Victorian godowns with Gradgrind faces, interspersed with occasional unexpected palms.

The lock. A tarnished tug the colour of an old, soiled tennis ball, the *Stalwart*, a good tug-worthy name (tugs usually have such names as *Titan* or *Giant*), creeps up behind us, at the ready. On our foredeck the passengers are ready to rush ashore. Bundles everywhere, bright clothes, soldiers in khaki again after holidaying in their sarongs. Wooden chests with brass corners, hockey sticks and umbrellas, thermoses.

'Dead slow ahead.'

'Stop. Make fast.'

A twenty-minute wait in the lock as the water level rises to match that of the dock. We give out four long blasts of the siren, then four short ones. Beyond the lock gate ahead sprouts a forest of derricks, and masts of the ships jammed end to end alongside the quays. The port of Calcutta may not be the glory it once was, but it isn't empty. A small tug waits for us, fussing about like a matador loosening up his muscles before the bull is released. Gates open. The tug is no longer a matador but a mother duck; back and forth from one side of us to the other, nudging, guiding. We pass through a swing bridge over which a road normally passes. On each side of it cars, rickshaws, motor scooters and pedestrians pile up, waiting for us to pass.

On either side, the *John* (Panama) and the *Lok Palak* (Bombay), her crew gathered on the stern rail to wave to friends arriving from the Andamans. They point at me, a strange foreigner to be coming from Port Blair. I feel elated to have been there. I wish I could go right back with the *HV.*

'Mid-shee-ips.' The pilot almost makes an aria of his orders.

Four short blasts on the siren. 'Hard a p-o-o-o-rt.'

We bump against the wharf behind *Vishna Vihram* (Bombay). Now I can see all Calcutta: skyscrapers, Victorian domes, chimneys, a park. A fusillade of triumphant whistles from the pilot: Calcutta, we are here. The passengers bunch themselves expectantly like an invading horde, longing to storm ashore and sack the city of their dreams.

Not the city of *my* dreams, however.

It was my bad luck to arrive in Calcutta on the eve of a public holiday. Offices would close tomorrow, the pilot said, and remain closed for several days. Long enough to make me try to flee the city.

With the help of Captain John's friends ashore, I tried to find a ship leaving within two or three days for Rangoon or Chittagong. They were pessimistic at first, and at last politely but frankly apologetic. 'It's just very difficult. If you had a week or two to wait . . .'

A week or two could stretch into three or four. But I didn't want to spend more than two or three days. I was impatient to get on.

At four o'clock that afternoon I rang the Everett Steamship Company and their travel service: no answer. I called the SCI; nothing doing, they said, from Calcutta to Rangoon or Chittagong. Of course, their regular steamship service would take me to Madras, Penang and Singapore. I told them I already had a reservation on that. Thank God I did, I thought now, sitting on my hotel bed with the telephone book open on my knee. After more abortive calls, it was obvious that the holiday shutters had come down in all offices in Calcutta.

I decided to give the impasse two days of thought and exploration, but two events crushed hope in my breast. First, the city of Calcutta was in a state of revolutionary ferment all the next day – which is to say that the various left-wing and communist parties of West Bengal took to the streets in those mammoth demonstrations involving the hundreds of thousands that only India can produce. They overwhelmed the centre of the city; the streets were impassable, with armies of chanting men and women carrying red flags. They overflowed on to the grassy park called the Padang, stopped all traffic to and from the port, and almost blocked the door of my hotel. The holiday and this human deluge put the seal of despair on any thought that shipping agents would take the time or trouble to help an unaccountable Englishman travelling for pleasure down the Hooghly in a ship. There would be no more ships from Calcutta – ever.

This may seem like hysterical pessimism now but, whatever it was, it received a palpable boost from a newspaper article that fell open before my eyes as I lay on my bed waiting for a telephone call that never came. The *Amrita Bazar* carried a story headed 'Foreign Shipping Lines Bypassing Indian Ports':

Mr. V. P. Punj, Chairman of the Engineering Export Promotion Council [meeting with the representatives of the two national shipping lines, SCI and the Scindia Navigation Company] said that Indian ports had never been free from problems like labour unrest, low productivity, inadequate and outmoded handling equipment. These problems had assumed such alarming proportions that the entire economy of the country was in jeopardy.

For instance, he said, *the Calcutta Port was virtually closed since mid-September 1978 because of strikes and other forms of agitation by the port and dock workers.* Once one group of workers called off their strike another group bobbed up and started agitation . . .

The words I have italicized above danced before my eyes like liver spots on the morning after. I thought of all those ships inert behind their untended lock gates: no swing gates opening, no tugs moving. I thought of that sluggishly swirling water like milky porridge. I thought of silt.

Going down to the lobby, I took another look at the Ganges-like, mud-coloured flood of human beings seething past the door, and then made a beeline for the hotel telephone operator. 'How long would it take to make a call to Madras?'

'Can you wait an hour?'

'Not possibly.'

'Well, you can make a lightning call, but it's expensive – two hundred rupees for three minutes.'

'I'll wait an hour.'

I waited half an hour. The shipping agent's office in Madras was open. 'I want to confirm my passage on the sailing to Singapore,' I said.

This accomplished, I begged the concierge to send a boy

through the human flood, if necessary with a lifeline round his waist, to the railway ticket office to buy me a sleeper ticket on the Coromandel Express for the following night's train to Madras. I had two days in which to catch the steamer from Madras to Singapore; to miss it would mean a delay of two weeks.

The next day I had lunch with an old acquaintance, Lindsay Emmerson, the English editor of the *Statesman*, a great Indian paper. We had pink gin and beer and curry in Amber's, one of India's – the world's – finest restaurants. I hadn't seen Lindsay for several years. He had grown older, of course – he must have been in his late sixties – and reminded me as always of an old but comfortable armchair bursting its seams. He had spent all his life in India; his father had been a pilot on the Hooghly.

He said, 'You once wrote that, when you came to my flat, you could hear the jackals howling from the cemetery.'

'What a memory.'

'No longer do they howl in my hearing. I've a new flat, very grand, very . . . well, Victorian, very . . . Balmoral.'

Lindsay told me a political joke about the time in 1975 when Indira Gandhi, the prime minister, had declared a state of emergency and herded the leaders of her parliamentary opposition into jail. 'This is true, on my honour. Someone I know went to a big bookshop in Delhi during the emergency and asked for a copy of the Constitution of India. And the bookseller said, "I'm sorry, sir, but we don't stock periodicals." '

I asked Lindsay about something that had puzzled me in the Andamans. 'The Japanese behaved so oddly there,' I said. 'They captured the Andamans from the British, and then, instead of befriending the population, they brutalized it. They even treated their Indian collaborators badly. Can you explain that?'

Lindsay had been a prisoner of war of the Japanese in Singapore. 'Well, they are peculiar,' he answered. 'They're a bit like the Dead End kids with tommy guns. Sometimes you could fool them, though, or make a successful appeal to their better nature. For instance, you had to salute Jap guards if you had a hat on, and kowtow if you were hatless. You could be very roughly handled if you didn't. But I saw one of my chums, a Scotsman, smoking a cigarette – another thing you were never supposed to do because it affronted the emperor – as he strolled past a sentry. The sentry, of course, shouted, "Come here," and, when my friend went over, the sentry put his little face close to his and barked, "Why are you smoking that cigarette? Why?"

' "Because I can't bear a pipe," replied my friend. And to my amazement – to this day I can't think why he did it – the sentry appeared to consider this and then after a pause said, "Yes, well, get along. Go." '

We talked of the poets Lindsay liked – Betjeman, Kipling – and in his Cambridge-accented voice he recited Kipling's 'Cities and Thrones and Powers'.

Our lunch lasted a long time, and then I had to prepare for the journey to Madras. Lindsay, in tweed jacket, food-stained, nondescript tie and voluminous trousers, climbed into his shaky little car, his hand waved, his creased old face smiled. A few months later, in England, I saw in a news-paper that he was dead.

Almost all I remember of the Coromandel Express is its speed and shining-chrome newness. There was a farting baby, and a sweet brother and sister who laughed over their holiday studies, and a guard's van just behind my sleeper full of bowlegged Assamese soldiers with ruddy round faces and slanting eyes.

Harry Miller said, 'You're lucky I'm still here.'

'Why? Travel plans?'

'No, a krait got into my snake bag!'

It turned out that a gardener had caught a krait not knowing what it was, and put it into a bag Harry normally used for storing rat snakes before taking them to the snake park. Rat snakes are perfectly harmless. 'I give the local boys a rupee or two whenever they bring me one. But a few days ago I noticed a bag with a snake in it in Pythagoras's crate, so I picked it up and squeezed it all around to discover how big it was. It was, I thought, a medium-sized rat snake but then Sampath asked, "What shall I do with the krait?" I looked in the sack and, sure enough, there was a healthy half-grown krait. As I explained to you, the krait is India's most venomous land snake. So you see, snakes don't want to attack you if they don't have to. I'd squeezed it all over, and even then it didn't bite me. Isn't that a tribute to the snake's docility?'

Before I left to find out about my sailing time to Singapore, Harry invited me to watch him feeding a long whitebellied snake that hadn't been in his house the last time. Feeding consisted of pushing three mice into the snake's crate. It seemed to inspect the mice like a housewife selecting a ripe grapefruit in a supermarket; then it seized one and began to squeeze it.

'A rat snake crushing a mouse?'

'Let's say,' said Harry, 'a *cat* snake preventing a mouse from breathing. A cat snake is common but harmless.'

'Cruelty to mice.'

Harry laughed. 'No mice would be cruelty to cat snakes.' From his crate window, Pythagoras looked on with an eye like the head of a hatpin. When I collected my ticket from the agents, they said the ship, *Chidambaram*, would sail on time next day.

That evening I telephoned my friend Dennis Bloodworth, the *Observer*'s man in Singapore and the author of bestselling books on South-east Asia and China. I had written to him from Colombo, asking him if he could get in touch with the operations manager of the Straits Steamship Company and find me a passage east from Singapore. Straits Steamship is one of the oldest shipping houses in the East. I knew it had passenger ships plying from Singapore to Borneo, in particular a famous old ship called the *Rajah Brooke*. My letter to Dennis had also suggested inquiring about a ship heading up to Borneo or Bangkok – either place would do.

On the telephone Dennis was apologetic. 'Bad news, I'm afraid. The *Rajah Brooke* is being scrapped this month, so she's out of it. They have no other passenger carriers left, except to Australia. Bangkok seems very difficult from here, but I'll keep trying.'

I thanked him and told him of my date of arrival in Singapore. 'The ship's name is *Chidambaram*.'

'Shit damn bum *what*?' the great Orientalist shouted across the Bay of Bengal. 'Kindly spell that.'

Chapter Twenty-Four

THE VOYAGE OF the *Chidambaram* to Penang and Singapore was an uneventful glide over submissive blue waters. She had formerly belonged to Messageries Maritimes, and had plied between Dunkerque, Le Havre and the Canaries. Since her maiden crossing of the Bay of Bengal and the Malacca Strait in 1973, she had carried hundreds of holidaying Malay and Indian students, workers and businessmen back and forth with stabilized aplomb.

There had been a rampage when Madrasi students ran wild, assaulting passengers, throwing chairs overboard, even stripping a girl or two – so terrifying them, the purser told me, that they wanted to jump overboard. But the leaders of the rampage had been handcuffed in their cabins and later fired from their university, and on subsequent voyages peace had become the rule. 'I know students who are barely literate,' the purser said contemptuously.

The captain sent me a message that I was welcome on the bridge any time I wanted to see the charts. Of the same school as Bala and Dennis Beale, he knew and loved the Andamans, especially for the fishing. He told me all this the first afternoon, and showed me the bridge, wide and deep like that of the *Patrick Vieljeux*.

'No brass fittings,' I noticed.

'Brass is a thing of the past.'

'Bala's got a lot of it on *Nancowry*.'

'Oh, yes, there.'

Captain Sujit Choudhuri lived up to the standards of no-nonsense friendliness I had come to expect from Indian masters like Dennis Beale, Bala and John. In fact, now that I think about it, I found this quality in all the masters I met between Cyprus and Singapore. It is as if ships' captains live at some isolated level of self-assurance, philosophically removed by a life sandwiched between sea and sky from the landlubberly pettiness of the rest of us. The wide world must contain petty ships' captains, but I have yet to meet one. Perhaps the reason is contained in Joseph Conrad's remark that, 'of all the living creatures upon land and sea, it is ships alone that cannot be taken in by barren pretences, that will not put up with bad art from their masters'.

I spent a considerable time reading on this leg of the journey. I had a cabin to myself and, although the ship was quite full, its saloons were usually empty and the Muzak was muted. The French decorator employed by Messageries Maritimes had done something bizarre to a main wall of the largest saloon, transforming it into a massive tableau of a frozen city of unreal turrets, weed-filled streets and ghostly ships at leprous wharves. This romantic nightmare he had underscored with a quotation from Baudelaire:

> *Cette ville est au bord de l'eau*
> *On dit qu'elle est bâtie en marbre . . .*
> *Voilà un paysage selon ton goût;*
> *Un paysage fait avec la lumière et le minéral,*
> *Et le liquide pour les réfléchir . . .*

It was an unexpected picture to come across in the Bay of Bengal. It struck me even more oddly in the evening when the reading room and saloon became alternately a cinema and a miniature casino where, surprisingly, two British girls presided over games of blackjack. The brittle lights of the fifties décor twinkled happily, a group of mountainous Parsee ladies and gentlemen whooped with high spirits and laughter, and the comforting clink of glasses came from the bar. A pop song that throbbed from speakers over a small dance floor had an unusual title: 'Save All Your Business for Me'. Above all this the crumbling turrets and spectral quays of that inappropriate mural seized the attention and chilled the heart.

A middle-aged Australian couple travelling back to Adelaide had been touring Afghanistan in a minibus for some months. 'You could stand up in it,' she said, 'although it had no fitted things. I mean, I had to use a plastic pot, but I managed. We've taken it all over the world.' Near Hunza or Gilgit in Pakistan's extreme north, they had been attacked by tribesmen and badly beaten up, but they told the story as a joke.

'Bob loves anything mechanical,' she told me. 'He's got a beaut bike he can't wait to get home to. He rode it from Sri Lanka to London in 1952.'

Later I was talking to Bob when she came up laughing and said, 'I've just been in the loo. Do you know, a man tried his best to join me while I was squatting in there. When I came out, I found he'd peed in the washbasin.'

'Who was it, then?'

'One of those Kurds.'

There were indeed three Kurds aboard the *Chidambaram*. Later I tried to talk to them in mangled English, French and Arabic. They were a thick-set, blue-chinned trio. 'You are from Germany?' they asked.

'No, England.'

'We are Kurds,' they said gruffly.

When I asked them who they preferred, the Shah or Ayatollah Khomeini, they answered, 'Both are bad. The Shah is looking too far forward, Khomeini too far back – he wants to see 700 AD in 1980.'

They were Kurdish nationalists, they said, and were confident that one day their country would be united and independent. 'There are problems but in fifteen, twenty years . . .' Were they, I wondered, on an arms-buying mission?

They bought bottles of Teacher's whisky from the bar and drank fiercely, toasting 'Kurdistan or death'. I never discovered which one had peed in the washbasin in the ladies' lavatory, or what they were doing crossing from Madras to Singapore on the *Chidambaram*.

Sheltering behind the funnel, I read copies of Harry Miller's 'Speaking of Animals' columns in the *Indian Express*. In one on whales, he quoted Hilaire Belloc:

> The whale that wanders round the Pole,
> Is not a table fish.

You cannot bake or boil him whole,
Nor serve him on a dish.

In another column, Harry considered the large forms of squid, a creature which, even more than snakes, fills me with revulsion. He wrote:

Attacks on boats appear to have been made by giant squid, but even the largest come nowhere near the size of the monsters depicted in some old prints. However, such stories have given rise to many legends, such as the persistent Scandinavian belief in the Kraken, a colossal sea monster measuring two kilometres in diameter with mast-like arms capable of dragging the largest ships down into the sea.

The combination of whale and giant squid jogged my memory about an old sailor's story that had impressed me some years before, and I looked it up again in a book by Sir Francis Chichester called *Along the Clipper Way*:

A reliable eyewitness of what happened said later that near Sumatra in the Indian Ocean, something he thought might be a volcano lifted its head above the sea. It was a large sperm whale locked in deadly combat with a cuttle-fish, or squid, whose tentacles seemed to enclose the whole of his body. The eyewitness, Bullen by name, estimated the mollusc's eyes to be at least a foot in diameter. The silent struggle ended when the whale clamped his jaws on the body of the squid and 'in a businesslike, methodical way' sawed through it.

I quickly scanned the sea. After all, we were in the waters north of Sumatra where Bullen had witnessed this spectacle, and it seemed uncomfortably close to my nightmare. But the sunlit waves winked innocently back at me.

I went ashore only briefly in Georgetown on Penang Island, but the beauty of South-east Asia struck my eyes with the full force of an old love suddenly revived. I suppose to the superficial eye the landscape on Penang is almost the same as that in Tamil Nadu, the Tamil state in southern India more than a thousand miles away, but it is not. There is as subtle a difference in the size and shape of the simple buildings, in the appearance and arrangement of trees, and in the rig of native craft in a bay as there is in the colour and physiognomy of men.

I passed through Georgetown's customs office, showing my passport to big Sikhs in boastful turbans, and wandered down the Pesara King Edward, stopping to take in the orientally domed ochre and cream clock tower presented to Penang by Cheoh Chen Eok 'in commemoration of Queen Victoria's Diamond Jubilee'. I admired the olive and white pillared and porticoed colonial buildings; there is nothing over-bearing about them. A parade of Malay Muslims chanted '*Allahu Akbar*' on the Padang, and I ate a plateful of flower crabs at the Anchor Bar of the handsome old Eastern and Oriental Hotel, a small version of Raffles in Singapore, and one of the great hotels of the East. A young European tourist came in from the garden wearing a dressing gown and a white plastic beak to save his nose from the sun, and I wondered what Khalat or Hentry or Dennis Beale would say about that.

The next day we reached the Strait of Malacca. *The Malacca Strait and East Coast of Sumatra Pilot* said:

> The Malacca Strait is the main seaway used by vessels from Europe and India bound to Malaysian ports and the China Sea. It provides the shortest routes for tankers trading between the Persian Gulf and Japan.

The strait not only is narrow and busy, but contains critical areas like one called One-Fathom Bank, a menace of shoals and sand waves. Furthermore, the *Pilot* warns, 'Navigational aids . . . in Indonesian waters are reported to be unreliable.' Thus, 'since passage through the strait entails a run of more than 250 miles, long periods of considerable vigilance are necessary in order to maintain safe standards of navigation'. Nothing could be more blunt than this warning.

Captain Choudhuri talked about collisions in the strait. 'There are quite a few unreported – if it's just two ships grazing or bumping and no one hurt. In the latest the smaller ship went down. Luckily, no one was lost.'

Like the Strait of Hormuz or the Suez Canal, the Malacca Strait is a funnel of the sea world where the appalling vision of colliding supertankers is a distinct possibility. There are smaller hazards, too. The water was dotted with tiny Sumatran or Malaysian motor trawlers, seemingly contemptuous of our approach, which chugged across our bows and sometimes made us change course.

'The trouble with them,' said Captain Choudhuri, fixing his glasses on them severely, 'is that the crew are often asleep, tired from their hours at sea, so they don't look.'

The sea traffic had relatively the same density of a weekend city street. A Panamanian freighter passed so close to us that without glasses I could see a man leaning on the rail in a red bathing suit, a man in a hammock dangling a leg, and another, squatting on the deck, slicing a watermelon.

Opposite Malacca, the coast of Sumatra pushed east and narrowed the channel still more. A white octagonal tower on piles signalled One-Fathom Bank. The coast is described by the *Pilot* as 'mostly muddy, low-lying and uniformly covered with mangroves'. But on my side of the wing of the *Chidambaram*'s bridge there was nothing to be seen save for a slight smudge.

The radio began to bark and whine; magnified human voices chatted irritably, and babel invaded the bridge.

'Listen,' said Captain Choudhuri. 'One ship's captain is complaining that another ship has hit him and gone on regardless. A hit-and-run. And they're all speaking different languages, so no one is understanding the others. A real mix-up.'

As a vision from the sea, Singapore is still exciting. Stamford Raffles's creation remains a great Eastern port. The sweep of its anchorages, the graceful green frontage of the Padang, the white dignity of St Andrew's Cathedral and the pillared public buildings behind, even the cluster of very new skyscrapers – all have grandeur. The city has supermarkets, too, but it is still the East. I seem to see a signpost here – a fantasy, of course – reading, 'From here on is the East – behind you, the Rest of the World.' The long elephant's trunk of Malaysia and the spray of islands at its tip form a screen between the wider world and the concentrated Orient.

The western approach to the Empire Dock is the inner one curving around to creep inside these islands. A strong

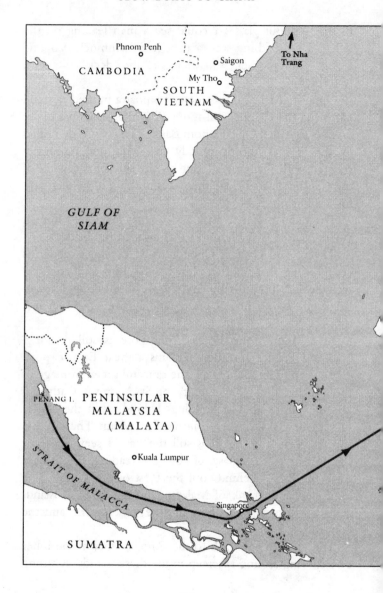

454

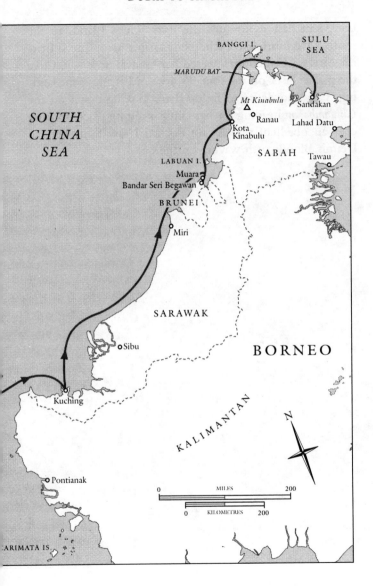

455

tide went past us towards the hazy Rhios Islands to the south. Overhead, like a schoolboy's paper aeroplane, a British Airways Concorde lowered her conical nose – just like the plastic beak on the tourist's nose in Penang – for landing. I had no desire to be up there looking down on the *Chidambaram* heading for her familiar resting place, moving over an obedient sea. As we docked I saw from her rail Dennis Bloodworth waving on the quay.

Part Three

SINGAPORE TO CANTON

Chapter Twenty-Five

I N BETWEEN WRITING his columns for the *Observer* and
a book on Mao Tse-tung, Dennis Bloodworth had
worked nobly on my behalf. As the *Chidambaram* crossed
the Bay of Bengal he had kept in touch with the Straits
Steamship Company, and at first he had heard nothing from
their offices in the Ocean Building to comfort me. On the
contrary, Tony Blatch, the man in charge, had a case of
euthanasia to report: the old and much revered *Rajah Brooke*
was even then under the shipbreakers' hammer in Keppel
Dock.

The Straits Steamship Company's passenger fleet was
not, Dennis warned me, what it had been in the high old
days of Somerset Maugham. The recent decisions of the
company's management reflected a depressing trend, and
portended, it seemed to me, the total demise of passenger
vessels throughout the East.

In the Ocean Building on Collyer Quay, it was possible
from a high window to survey an impressive fleet – scores
of ships of all sizes and flags lying in the eastern and western
anchorages – but few would have accepted a passenger
aboard.

The general manager of Straits Shipping, Mr Khong
Chai Seng, explained the two simple, obvious reasons for
the shrinkage in passenger ships: the high costs of fuel and
maintenance. Fuel, we all know about. As to maintenance,
a passenger or cargo–passenger vessel is subject to more
stringent regulations by Lloyd's – for example, an annual
dry-docking.

'The *Rajah Brooke*', Mr Khong said, 'was not built as a passenger ship. She was built as a cargo ship that would carry passengers – a subtle difference. In the good old days she carried thirty passengers regularly to and from the Borneo states of Sarawak and Brunei.'

Fuel costs, maintenance and airlines are the three major and victoriously advancing enemies of passenger sea travel. In the days of Maugham, how could ships have failed to do well? How else could far-flung planters and government servants travel on business or cart themselves and their wives and children back for leave in Singapore? How else could they have made sure of connections with the grander P&O or British India Company ships to Great Britain?

'*Rajah Brooke* had to be replaced because of sheer old age,' said Mr Khong sadly. 'We had to decide whether to replace her on the Brunei run with a passenger–cargo vessel or a purely cargo vessel. We had to bear in mind that Air Brunei is advertising ten flights a week to Brunei. So . . .'

So the new *Rajah Brooke* is a pure cargo vessel – the middle-aged *Nahoon*, newly named. The passenger *Rajah* is dead; long live the cargo *Rajah*.

For me, however, arriving in Singapore in the twilight of passenger sea travel, not all was yet lost. 'There is hope,' Dennis said comfortingly. Tony Blatch had told him about the little *Perak*, once a cargo–passenger ship but now purely devoted to cargo, which sailed to Kuching in Sarawak about every nine days. She had one or two panelled Maugham-style cabins still, although they were never used. Perhaps he could arrange for me to travel on her to Sarawak as a supernumerary. She would be leaving in a few days.

This was one possibility. The *Perak* was sailing in a direction I preferred to the only alternative: a voyage north to Bangkok, with the hope of a ship from there to Hong Kong. I decided to investigate this alternative, although it would short-circuit the detour I had looked forward to – the slow swing up along the coast of Borneo and across the Sulu Sea (that traditional and still-flourishing haunt of pirates) to the Philippines.

I tried a Malaysian line, but the rebuff was immediate. 'A passenger', the agent said, aghast, 'would be most unusual. Quite impossible.' It was a response of the Jedda and Dubai variety, and I felt again the chill of exasperation. But, of course, it was quite useless to work oneself up in nervous frustration over the lack of obliging shipowners and the commercial interests that now have turned their contemptuous backs on the innocent serenity of sea travel. 'Ah!' Conrad exclaimed in 'A Smile of Fortune', 'These commercial interests spoiling the finest life under the sun.'

With as much equanimity as I could muster, I crouched over the shipping pages of the *Straits Times* spread out on a table in the tropical splendour of the terrace of Raffles Hotel. Japanese cameras clicked, gin slings tinkled, golden orioles, mynah birds and tailor birds all failed to break my concentration on the essential business of finding an onward ship. Only an importunate black starling, which reminded me of a certain cook in high seas off the Maldives, disturbed me. '*Feni, feni, sarna,*' I murmured foolishly at it over the newspaper, and wondered how many waiters at Raffles knew how to open a coconut with a spanner.

The shipping pages had little to offer in the direction of Bangkok. A company called the Singapore Union Line was the only possibility that caught my eye. 'Regular Singapore–Bangkok Service,' a notice said; the *Mulia* was loading for Bangkok, and the Heong Leong Building housed the company's offices. But on the fortieth floor of that giant structure a Mr H. C. Lau flatly refused to discuss the matter – or, indeed, anything at all. 'Mr Lau is so busy,' his pretty secretary apologized. I could see the disobliging Mr Lau through the glass door of his office; he didn't seem to be busy. His refusal was a pity and, without the *Perak* at my back, it might have meant a setback on the Jedda scale. For his churlishness, I now bracket Mr Lau in my mind with the agent's representative in Jedda who made me leave Captain Visbecq and deprived me of a look at Djibouti. His shipping manager, a young Chinese, murmured dubious excuses: 'An Asian crew would never agree to a super-numerary. Passengers, even one like you, would delay the ship.' (In all, I travelled by sea between Piraeus and Canton on twenty-three vessels, and only three had non-Asian crews. Crews don't mind who travels with them; they are a tolerant lot, and never once was there a delay because of me.)

These two men were exceptions in a long series of voyages, and were more than offset by such glowingly bonhomous people as Captain Rashad in Alexandria and dear Mr Missier in Colombo.

So Kuching in Sarawak was the next stop. And now, Tony Blatch said, the *Perak* – exceptionally – would be going on to Brunei. I was in luck. I consulted my Bartholomew's map of South-east Asia and followed the coast of Borneo with the tip of my pen: Kuching to Brunei to Kota Kina-balu, the capital of the Malaysian state of Sabah, formerly known as North Borneo, where another Straits Steamship Company vessel, the *Straits Hope*, was due to arrive soon;

she would take me around the serrated north-west corner of Borneo to . . . where? Sandakan, nestling discreetly in a bay in a coastline so indented that it might have been gnawed by bandicoots, seemed the best-positioned place to make the leap across the difficult Sulu Sea. Then I had to find a way to Zamboanga City in Mindanao, the southernmost island of the Philippines.

Tony Blatch, ever helpful, telexed the agents Harrisons & Crosfield in Sandakan. Their answer was less helpful: 'For Blatch presently no sea passage available to Mindanao from Sandakan suggest take scheduled flight from Sandakan to Zamboanga.' At least the reply was not a prohibition to travel.

First things first, I thought. Get to Sandakan, then look for fresh possibilities. My eyes roamed more closely over the map. Assuming I could cross the Sulu Sea to Zamboanga, I would need ships north to Cebu City and Manila, and from there a vessel to Hong Kong. Swire's. For the last hop, Manila–Hong Kong, Swire's came to my aid.

I called on John Olsen, Swire's representative in Singapore, at his office in the by now familiar Ocean Building, and learned that two Swire ships were scheduled to leave Manila for Hong Kong at about the time – a month from now – that I, with luck, would be arriving there. The ships were the *Hupeh* and the *Poyang*, and they would stop at Taiwan before reaching Hong Kong, he warned, but to me that was a welcome bonus. As for the Philippines themselves – well, all island nations had plenty of inter-island transport; I'd find something.

But that small hurdle disappeared when by a stroke of luck I met in the house of a Singaporean friend, an Englishman named Kerry St Johnston, whose first words to me were, 'I hear you may want a ship to or from Cebu City in the Philippines. Have you any objection to meeting a Filipino millionaire shipowner with a fleet of inter-island ships?'

At that moment there were few people I would have preferred to meet if he could allay my fears of further defeats in the last long lap of my journey. 'My God, no!'

'Then you must meet the Chiongbian family,' said Kerry St Johnston. 'They own the William Lines based in Cebu City. Want me to telex them to say you'll be bobbing up?'

So Kerry St Johnston and the Chiongbian family joined the golden rollcall of those who helped. Into my notebook went the name William Lines, and an address and telex number in Cebu City. The William Lines had a branch office in Zamboanga, and it turned out that, if that branch hadn't existed, I might have been obliged to swim back across the Sulu Sea to Borneo.

With the decision taken to forgo Bangkok, I could relax with Dennis and his family for a day or two until the *Perak* completed her loading in Empire Dock.

In a way, it was a homecoming. I had worked as a reporter for the *Observer* based in Singapore. During my ten years in Vietnam, Cambodia, Thailand and Indonesia, I had returned to the city regularly as to a rest house after the physical and emotional hurly-burly of wars and disasters.

Dennis and Judy, his Chinese wife, now listened patiently to my stories of the Starling Cook, Dennis Beale, Bala and Hentry, Chandra and Darson; of Sumar the Baluchi and Captain Musa the Egyptian. Captain Sujit Choudhuri of the *Chidambaram* met the Bloodworths and they became friends.

With them, in honour of Maugham, I drank the Raffles's 'million-dollar cocktail' for the first time. Invented, it is said, by the wife of the defence counsel in the murder case Maugham adapted for his story 'The Letter', this cocktail – which some people would call a killer in its own right – is made by mixing gin, sweet and dry vermouth, egg white, pineapple juice and bitters. Of Raffles and the million-dollar cocktail, I began to feel, as S. J. Perelman once said about the old Semiramis Hotel in Cairo, that, if I stayed there drinking pink gins long enough, all the world and little black specks would pass before my eyes.

I lightened my baggage by leaving notebooks and exposed film at the Bloodworths'. I had been worried about the possibility that sea-water, the daily humidity or an accident might deprive me of several months' work by ruining film or notes.

I also thought of having my Pentax cleaned; I had a lurking fear of a rusted shutter in the steam-bath atmosphere of these seas; an expensive watch, in theory waterproof, had rusted on my wrist during an earlier visit. But there was no time for that, nor for the overhaul of my Leitz binoculars, bought in Aden so many years before.

I have spoken of the strange blotches on the lenses of the Leitz. They had increasingly worried me. Not only did they impair the vision; worse, they were reminders of something better forgotten, and they had seemed to grow like the loathsome stain in a story by Edgar Allan Poe. This troubling flight of fancy wasn't affectation on my part, though clearly it was a superstitious absurdity. Yet this awareness in no way cleared from my mind the intolerable half-belief that the disfiguring blobs and blotches were physical traces of an afternoon fifteen years before when a shell fragment burst open the stomach of a Vietnamese soldier and he died across my knees.

In 1965, before the American forces landed en masse in Vietnam, the Vietnamese army seemed to be heading for total destruction; it was losing a battalion or two every week, most of them in engagements very close to Saigon. One day I travelled from Saigon to the riverside township of My To, south of the capital, in a bus crowded with Vietnamese civilians and soldiers; bundles of shopping and chickens cluttered the floor under the seats.

We crossed bridges fortified with sandbags and barbed wire, and sometimes soldiers stopped the driver and peered in at the passengers. Two laughing Vietnamese behind me leaned over my shoulder: 'Aren't you frightened of VC? Maybe Vietcong come on bus.'

A day later, with my Leitz binoculars strapped around my neck, I was walking in a single file of Vietnamese soldiers along the narrow banks that divided the paddy fields of the Mekong delta. The column was part of a larger force scraped together to clear the Vietcong out of an area of several square miles of trees, paddies, water buffaloes and hamlets. Sometimes we heard a propeller-driven aircraft overhead, and the deep voice of artillery.

On the wider tracks it was possible to break the single file, and I walked beside the young Vietnamese soldier who had been in front of me. He looked like a child playing soldier; his helmet was absurdly big, his American carbine too long and heavy. His dull-green battle dress revealed the amazing slightness of his body. Small dark crescents of sweat stained his armpits and the small of his back. He pointed at my suede boots and said admiringly, 'Shoes you number one.'

'I give them to you.'

'Oh, no. You very big. Small, me.' After a pause he looked up at me again. 'Home America?'

'England.'

'Home me Nha Trang. You see Nha Trang?'

I hadn't, up to then; I got to know it later, a small and beautiful city on the South China Sea. It has fine beaches, and in those days a French restaurant served fresh lobsters.

'So much fishing in Nha Trang,' the soldier said, smiling.

I hadn't met many Vietnamese at that time, and I looked at him with interest. Where the fine line of his Oriental cheekbones swept down to the rosebud mouth there was no hint of hair. He couldn't have been much over nineteen.

It began to rain, and the dark stain on my new friend's back quickly widened as water dripped from his helmet. He turned his carbine upside down on his shoulder so that the rain wouldn't run down the barrel, then he put a hand on my sleeve and smiled up at me.

'You number one friend. Come Nha Trang, okay?'

'I come Nha Trang.'

A sergeant waved impatiently and laid a finger on his lips. In silence now, except for the drumming of the rain and an occasional clink of metal or a cough, we approached a tree line. When the shell burst, my impression was that a small volcano had sprung out of the ground, not that something had fallen from the sky. I felt a tremendous shudder through the soles of my boots, and then the blast threw me to the ground.

I lay there waiting for other shells, but it was not an ambush or even a sustained harassment. Another shell roared much further away, and then heavy silence fell. My heart thumped and my hands shook. Then I heard a human

sound quite close, half-sob, half-gasp. A helmet lay on the ground like an abandoned seashell, and near it was my friend from Nha Trang, clasping his stomach with one hand, pushing feebly at the ground with the other, trying to get up. I went over and stopped him.

I put my left hand around his shoulders and made him lean back across my knees, but I didn't know what to do next. His eyes were closed, and the rain poured through his hair and down his face and neck. There was a terrible smell. I opened his sodden shirt and saw below his breast-bone a dark, shining mess – ripped clothing stained black with rain, blood, bile and whatever else comes out of bellies torn open by metal splinters.

His eyelids flickered open and he frowned. 'Hurt, me,' he said faintly.

He was dying. He fumbled for my right hand – in a futile way, I had been trying to wipe the rain from his face – and pressed it to the warm, liquid mess. I didn't feel the least disgust. I had an idea that between us we might hold him together.

'Hurt, me,' he whispered again. At the inner corner of

the delicate half-moon fold of his eyelid a drop of water had lodged. Rain? A tear?

Soon people came and carefully carried him away, limp, with his head lolling back as if a hinge in his neck had snapped.

I was left with my hands and clothes stinking of an abattoir. The strap of the binoculars around my neck had snapped, so that the glasses were slippery with blood and bile. Something seemed to have got into the lenses, for later, however much I wiped them, blobs and blotches remained that had not been there before.

From then on, because of those blobs, I felt a revulsion for my excellent glasses, and when I was on leave in Singapore I bought another pair and put the tainted ones away. But years later in Paris someone stole the new binoculars, so for this adventure I had been obliged to fall back on the old ones.

Now, staring through the blotches at the anchorages of Singapore, I remembered with anguish my friend from Nha Trang.

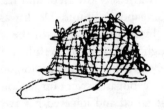

Chapter Twenty-Six

'**m**.v. *Perak*. Wharf 20–21. Gate 2. Empire Dock. Sails 15.00 hours. Board 14.00 hrs.' I noted all this as I talked on the phone to Captain MacGregor, the Straits Steamship Company's operations manager. The *Perak* would sail the next day.

'I warn you, she's not the *QE Two*,' he said.

'I'd be extremely disappointed if she were.'

'I hope you like curry.'

'I do.'

'Good. You're the only passenger, of course.'

'Two days to Kuching?'

'That's the theory, but the *Nahoon* had a very stormy crossing the other day and took three days. North-east monsoon. The weather's still unpredictable.'

Next day Dennis drove me to Empire Dock, and after a short search we discovered the *Perak*. I say 'discovered' because the *Perak* was easily dwarfed, and the godown on Wharf 20–21 of Singapore's Empire Dock was a long, high building. Hidden by it, the *Perak* lay in the water looking almost small enough to float in one's bath. I liked the look of her immediately. She had almost no foredeck at all; her bridge and officers' cabin area swept up abruptly just behind twin winches that raised and lowered her two anchors, so that from the dock she looked as if her face had been flattened by a tremendous blow on the nose. Amidships, two elderly Chinese in straw hats and dirty shorts, shaded from the fierce afternoon sun by paper parasols, pushed and pulled the winch levers that lowered the last few slings of cargo into the *Perak*'s holds. There was a smell of fruit on the cluttered deck and a sound of ducks quacking. A steward, a spare, pleasant-faced Chinese with grey hair, led us up a companionway to the officers' dining room and the three former first-class passenger cabins that led off it. 'This is for you, sir.'

Somerset Maugham would have been satisfied: a bunk, a dressing table and a mirror, a wardrobe, two armchairs covered in white leatherette and a stool. The two portholes were square wood-framed windows with curtains; a thermos of ice water hung in a wall bracket, and on the ceiling a large fan rotated inside a cage designed to protect abnormally tall passengers like myself from a scalping. I took my copy of Maugham's *Short Stories* out of my bag and laid it on the dressing table, where it looked at home.

As soon as we stepped into the cabin, Dennis said with surprise, 'This was my cabin twenty years ago. Sailed in it to Palembang in Sumatra with Keyes Beach of the *Chicago Daily News* and Pepper Martin of *US News and World Report*, to cover the rebellion in central Sumatra against Sukarno's government in Jakarta. Remember? Revolt in Paradise, someone called it. We landed at Palembang after thirty hours in *Perak*. Her captain was called Brown, a nice, rather eccentric character who caused a stir in Singapore by bringing back a Sumatran panther as a pet. It got loose on the deck. Yes, this was the ship.'

Now the elderly steward was offering us a drink. But Dennis had to go ashore. 'Good luck and *bon voyage*,' he said. 'By the way, those Sulu pirates still make their victims walk the plank.' A minute later he called from the quay, 'See you – maybe.'

The tug *Teman* moved the *Perak* cautiously into the

narrow dogleg of the dock, edging her past the *King Dragon* of Penang and the *King River* of Labuan. Heads turned to point to the *Perak*'s old-fashioned silhouette, to her prizefighter's nose. Along other wharves the angular shapes of container ships formed rigid cubist patterns, the sky-scrapers of Singapore behind them. To our right, a noisy craft dashed through the water spewing smoke, and faces peered intently from a long row of portholes. Compared with the *Perak*, it was almost a Martian spacecraft.

The steward's voice again. 'Tea, sir?' He laid a tray on a small table. 'My name is Wong,' he said. 'Sir, *Perak* now cargo ship. Good cook at home sick. This cook maybe make European food, maybe not.'

'Mr Wong, I'll eat Chinese or Malay food.'

'Chinese cook no good, food very greasy,' cautioned Mr Wong. 'Captain and chief officer eat Malay, hot food, more better.'

'I'll eat Malay.'

'No problem,' he said, relieved. 'I tell Cook.'

The *Perak* moved sedately through the anchorage cluttered with ships. There must have been forty or fifty of them at anchor before the grand buildings of Singapore's Padang, the porticoed Supreme Court and the white needle of St Andrew's Cathedral spire, the only part of the great port now that Maugham, Conrad or his Captain Tom Lingard might have recognized. Tankers belonging to BP and Esso; one disturbingly long, green Japanese one; a Soviet tanker, the *General Kravtsov*; a Maersk Line ship in a coat of unfortunate green and blue; a Singapore navy gunboat; one of the Singapore shipowner Mr Y. C. Chan's modest vessels in from Jakarta or Surabaya. As she has regularly for many years, under a pale cloudy sun, the *Perak* picked her self-confident way eastwards on the 436 miles to Borneo at 8.5 knots.

'Dinner six o'clock,' Wong informed me. 'Now I bring you duty-free drink.'

'Good. I'll have a gin.'

At dinner, I met Captain Abdul Rahman Hadi, the master of the *Perak*, a short, jolly cannonball of a man in his forties with a shy smile that exposed gold teeth. The dining room was panelled, and the windows could be raised or lowered by wide leather straps with round brass eyeholes of the kind once found in British railway carriages. Malay and Chinese officers ate separately at two tables. The *Perak* even had two galleys and cooks. The pork that is loved so much by Chinese could not be prepared in the same galley as the Malay food; pork is *haram* (forbidden) to Muslim Malays. Two galleys in a small ship like the *Perak*? 'British system,' said the captain. 'No problem.'

Captain Abdul Rahman was a Malay Singaporean, born in Malacca. He had joined the Straits Steamship Company as a cabin boy in 1952, and his first command had been a 2500-ton rice carrier between Bangkok, Penang, Christmas Island, Singapore and west Sumatra. He was waited on by Mr Wong and a second elderly Chinese, a massive old man in bulky blue shorts and sandals with a shock of white hair standing straight up on his big head as if thousands of volts were permanently running through him. They had been with the company for ever, the chief officer said. The *Perak*'s swaying deck failed to disconcert their old bowlegs.

I asked the captain if he had many problems with the behaviour of the crews. He looked surprised. 'No problem. All our men old employees of Straits Steamship Company. If young men come and make trouble, I kick them out!'

'In India that might be difficult. The unions might delay the ship and organize a walkout.'

'If a man is not working, how can ship work, make money? Man not work, kick him out.'

The chief officer added, 'Young men don't like Sarawak and Borneo so much. Nothing to do.'

'They like Jakarta, Bangkok, Manila, more girls.' The captain laughed.

'Young men like to enjoy.' The chief officer was himself about thirty. From his cabin, one deck down, Western pop music could be heard when he was off duty. The captain's dayroom and sleeping cabin were one deck up, behind the wheelhouse and little chart room. No pop music there. He watched the sunsets from a wicker easy chair on the deck outside his dayroom.

Although the *Perak* gave the impression of being tiny, she weighed 1400 tons – huge compared with the *Herman Mary* or the Maldivian launch. On this trip she had on board 580 tons of cargo, much of it for Chinese New Year celebrations in Kuching. We were due to reach the Sarawak river on the eve of the Year of the Monkey, and the decks were stacked with crates of Chinese apples, mandarin oranges, Korean peaches, sacks of cabbages and vats, gaudily labelled, of salted vegetables from Thailand. In addition, she carried a general cargo of canned goods, clothing, and frozen chicken and meat. As Kuching produces very little meat of its own, the *Perak*'s arrival was a popular event.

In the stern I found two Chinese busily plucking ducks; white feathers overflowed an enamel bowl, webbed feet pointed pathetically into the air. Malays with sweat cloths around their brows and long hair were chipping rust off the deck like decay from an old smoker's teeth.

474

At breakfast – paw-paw, porridge, egg, bacon or sausages (for non-Malays), toast, marmalade and Nescafé – the chief officer said that a Malay had fallen sick with a fever during the night, and that he'd taken his temperature and found it to be 110 degrees. 'A hundred and ten degrees?' I said. 'He must be dead.' I thought of Groucho Marx feeling a patient's pulse: 'Either he's dead or my watch has stopped.' But the man was up and about the next afternoon, so either I or the thermometer was wrong.

'Look, Vietnamese ship,' the captain said. On an island hardly bigger than a Hyde Park bandstand a small ship lay stranded. The vessel had brought a fortunate group of Vietnamese boat people here. They had beached it and been taken off by the Indonesian navy.

By the afternoon, with misty rain falling, Captain Abdul Rahman seemed to think that we might have rough weather that night. 'Better get sleep now. Maybe at night no sleep.' My siesta, I noticed, was sanctioned by a relic of the *Perak*'s passenger-carrying days. On my cabin wall an 'Information for Passengers' notice said:

> There is normally a quiet period at sea when passengers, and also officers off duty, may be resting. If parents would be kind enough to aid in maintaining this atmosphere, it would be very much appreciated.

By 7.00 p.m. we were halfway to Kuching. The captain expected to arrive in the mouth of the Sarawak river at sunset the next evening. If the holiday had started, customs and immigration officers would be at home celebrating, and we might have to anchor in the river overnight.

The night was a rough one, as the captain had predicted. The *Perak* lurched and bucked, the wind howled and thunderous waves slapped her sides. It was uncomfortable, but I don't suppose the Starling Cook would have been worried, and neither was I. I wondered if he had ever sailed on a ship as big as the *Perak*.

In the morning the voyage was almost over. We were still rolling, but on the skyline there was now a pale smudge in the morning haze, the mountainous outline of Borneo. Or of Kalimantan (Indonesian Borneo), to be precise, for the part known as Sarawak of this immense island lay beyond the still-invisible spur of Tanjung Datu.

The captain said to Mr Wong, 'Tomorrow Chinese New Year. Year of Monkey, yes?' The steward answered, 'Tomorrow Monkey Year. Year of Golden Monkey.' For my information, he added, 'Very mischeevious monkey.' I thought, a mischievous monkey might cause delays.

'Can you expect a quick turnabout once we are in a berth?'

'Can,' said Captain Abdul Rahman. 'Ten hours' work. Very quick.' The *Perak*, he said, would pick up rubber, paper and rattans for Singapore and proceed to Brunei. But how much work would be done during the four days of the New Year celebrations? From Kuching it was thirty-six hours to Brunei. This would give me 21, 22 and 23 February to catch the *Straits Hope*, which was not due in Labuan from Singapore until the 24th. It was the sort of timetable Tony Blatch and Captain MacGregor had envisaged in Singapore, but I was not the optimist I had been at Piraeus.

By noon we were abreast of the great forested fist of Tanjung Datu and began our last rolling progress across the last bay before the entrance to the Sarawak river. Between banks of mangrove and tree trunks entwined with creepers, the river twisted its way like a shining green caterpillar towards Kuching, the former capital of the White Rajahs. Soon, to starboard, an awesome dark shape reared up, dwarfing the landscape ahead: Santubong Mountain, a vast, shaggy sentinel at the entrance to the river. Behind it the waves of the mountains and forests of Borneo lay blueblack in rain and swirls of thick, low, grey cloud. The *Perak* slipped into the narrow mouth of the river just as the burning disc of the sun reached the western horizon.

The Chinese members of the crew began their New Year celebrations. Mr Wong came up to the bridge as First Officer Omar Oman was ordering the old Malay quartermaster at the wheel 'half ahead', easing the *Perak* over the bar at the entrance of the narrow waterway. '*Tengah-tengah* – amidships.' The *jermudi*, his wrinkled, highcheekboned face shining like polished mahogany, echoed impassively in the fading light of the wheelhouse, '*Tengahtengah*.' Mr Wong said to me, smiling, 'Chinese crew would like invite you join them in their special holiday dinner. Please follow me to stern.'

The Chinese were already seating themselves at a round table they had positioned near the stern rail. Under the ship's lights in the thickening darkness, bowls of soup, pork, vegetables, fish balls, chilli and other dishes were already scattered across the table. The duck's feet rose above the surface of the soup. Junior crewmen were pouring Tiger beer into glasses and three bottles of Johnnie Walker Red Label stood among the dishes. Mr Boon Koh Peng, the elderly steward with the shock of white hair and bowlegs, poured three fingers of whisky all around, dropping ice into mine from a jug. A clatter of dishes and chopsticks soon drowned out the rumble of *Perak*'s propeller shaft under our vibrating stools; glasses were raised and emptied, and excited holidaying Chinese faces began to turn a deep pink, the inevitable and undisguisable effect that liquor has on pale Oriental skin. '*Kong hee fat choy!*' they cried rosily across the table at each other and at me. 'Happy New Year!' And Mr Boon genially raised his glass and leaned over to say, 'Monkey coming. That what this means.'

It was a good moment. Only a tongue of dark-red cloud lay across a flaming orange sky, so that the *Perak* crept across the inner bar through black water that glittered with golden splinters of light. '*Kong hee fat choy!*' As the Chinese sat carousing in their circle of light in the stern the tangled trees on the riverbank merged into mysterious conglomerations of shadow, and behind them to the east the mountains merged quietly into the night.

'*Kong hee fat choy!* Must finis' Johnnie Walker!' After the feast, the handshaking, the draining of beer, whisky and small saucers of tea, the Chinese dispersed to put on smart clothes and to gather the New Year presents they were taking to friends and relatives in Kuching. Most of them had been on this run for years and were going to a second home.

I found the captain on the bridge in long khaki shorts and an undershirt. 'Good dinner?' He gave me a smile and the flash of a gold tooth. He had news. Kuching immigration had agreed that the Chinese members of the crew and I should be allowed to go ashore tonight, that all the berths were full, and that the *Perak* should anchor in the river a few miles downstream at a place appropriately called Pending until a ship's departure left a free berth. However, there would be no work for a day or two at least, so the *Perak* might spend four days here. A launch was on its way to pick us up.

It soon arrived, and on it was the Straits Steamship Company's agent, Mr Paul Ho. Well scrubbed and neatly dressed in clean tropical shirts and pressed trousers, clutching their bundles of presents, the Chinese filed down the gangway and, smiling to right and left, took their seats in the motor launch that growled alongside. I waved to the captain (I would be in touch with him through Mr Ho), a Malay boy cast off, and we spluttered away into the darkness of the narrow, meandering, silent river. Now and again the lights of a small village interrupted the blackness of the riverbanks, and a pressure lamp or open fire revealed the wooden wall of a little house on stilts or people in sarongs standing in a doorway. We passed through a knot of small ships, clusters of white lights in the blackness, anchored in mid-river in Pending, then landed among the barges and moored rivercraft and warehouses of Kuching. The Chinese hurried off under the street lights as Mr Ho drove me across the neat, leafy town to the Aurora Hotel. I thanked him for interrupting his New Year's Eve at home. 'Relax,' he said, 'I'll be in touch. I guarantee *Perak* will not sail without you.'

Half an hour later, from the cramped balcony of my room in the Aurora, I watched young Malays and Chinese hurrying arm in arm about the Padang under the ancient, thick-trunked trees that screened the hotel from the golden domes of the mosque. Occasionally the peace was broken by youths in crash helmets who sped past on scooters to New Year parties. The sound of firecrackers, no louder than thorns crackling in a fire, came distantly from buildings across the Padang. Kuching is a gentle, unassertive little place, a friendly garden town not yet ruined by high-rise pretentiousness. Its name means cat, after Sarawak's cat's-eyes trees. Across the river, on a grassy eminence, the White Rajah's palace, the fortlike Istana, seems to fix the time firmly in the nineteenth century.

I lay on my bed, feeling it sway as if I were still aboard the *Perak*. On the ceiling a painted arrow showed any of the faithful who might sleep and pray in this room the direction to holy Mecca.

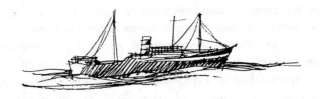

Chapter Twenty-Seven

NEXT MORNING I thought for a moment that a revolution had started. Chinese firecrackers rattled around the town like rifle fire, and truckloads of singing Chinese boys roared past my hotel window banging drums and clashing cymbals. New Year's Day – the first day of the Year of the mischeevious Golden Monkey.

The crackers were particularly impressive, considering a government ban I read about in the the *Sarawak Tribune* that had been pushed under my hotel door. The following 'items of fireworks' had been banned, the paper said: Coloured Pearls, Silvery Chrysanthemum, Ground Bloom Flowers, Sparkling Wheel, Flashing Wheel, Dancing Fresh Flowers, Spider's Web, Peacock Fountain, Silvery Glittering Flower, Fire Splinter, King Cat Sparklers, Small Bee, Red Ground Chicken, Friendship Fireworks, Moon Flitting Phoenix and coloured Electric Sparks. It seemed a pity to have missed all that.

I drank green tea and telephoned Bushey Webb. 'I can hardly hear you,' he shouted. 'The illegal firecrackers. Deafening. Must have been smuggled in somehow!'

I was downstairs when he strode in through the glass-fronted door in a short-sleeved flowered shirt, shorts and sandals. 'You see me in my who–gives–a–bugger kit,' he announced, beaming like a large and overwhiskered ginger cat. 'Let's go home.'

Alan Webb has lived in Sarawak for nearly thirty years, and is one of very few – perhaps four – foreign residents to have been granted Malaysian citizenship since that country

became independent of the British in 1957. He is a solid man of medium height with a reddish round face. A massive pair of bushy sideburns come together at his upper lip and give him his nickname. He is a Buddhist, a convivial drinker, and describes himself with a hearty laugh as a gourmet. I had met him two years earlier with my seafaring friend Brian McGarry, towards the end of a six-month search I had made in McGarry's old ketch, the *Fiona*, for the Eastern world of Joseph Conrad – scouting the places Conrad had visited as the master of ships in the 1880s and later written about in novels like *Victory* and *Lord Jim*. When we had reached Kuching in the *Fiona*, Brian found he needed to repair a life raft. The firm Webb owns was able to provide all that was required, and a good deal of unexpected hospitality as well.

He is a hospitable man in the unstinting tradition of all the local people – Dayaks, Malays, Chinese or British.

Little jungly Sarawak – the domain carved out in the early nineteenth century by James Brooke, the first of the White Rajahs – is a place of outstanding interracial harmony, despite, or perhaps because of, the furious nineteenth-century sea and river battles between, on the one hand, Brooke, his British and Malay followers and allies, and odd ships of the Royal Navy, and, on the other, the rebellious chiefs, intruding pirates and marauding sea rovers from wild north Borneo and the ill-famed Sulu Sea. The peace the victorious Rajah Brooke imposed and maintained has survived the threats of communist terror, banditry and three hectic years of Indonesian armed confrontation in the 1960s, when British troops came to help the Malaysian armed forces resist an Indonesian invasion. Malaysia had just achieved independence from Britain and President Sukarno of Indonesia was contesting by force the inclusion of the western Borneo states of Sarawak and Sabah within Malaysia. That was when I came to Kuching for the first time. The little port had become a bustling military cantonment, and the nights were raucous with the Hogarthian revelry of young British soldiers down from the thousand-mile-long border with Indonesian Kalimantan – down from the mountains, from the heads of half-lost rivers, from the tents and longhouses of Dayak headhunters, from patrolling jungles inhabited by snakes, wild boars and orang-utans. Actually, their revelry was more Rowlandsonian than Hogarthian; the troops were rowdy and drunken, but not in the ugly, vicious way of a Hogarth print, and the people of Kuching seemed to understand.

Now the fighting was long over and the foreign troops gone. Sarawak, a state of independent Malaysia, was as peaceful as it had been in the twenties and thirties in the days of British administrators, bank managers, young company assistants, police officers, museum curators, the days of British clubs, memsahibs and scandals – the world you can read about in the short stories of Somerset Maugham.

Bushey Webb lived in a pleasant Maugham-like, wood-frame bungalow on the edge of the town. It was set back in a cleared rectangle among trees where bright-coloured birds flitted among frangipani, bougainvillaea and clumps of tall pale-green bamboo. I clumped up wooden steps across a creaking wooden veranda and entered a large L-shaped room whose front part had a home-made curving bar at one end and bookcases at the other. An overhead fan stirred the sticky air, and harmless *chichak* lizards flicked about the walls. Motionless, their black pinhead eyes looked sharply about them for insects, and they breathed quickly in the heat, their sides labouring.

'Oi Fah,' Bushey called from the bar. 'People are dying of bloody thirst in here, you know.' When his young smiling Chinese wife appeared carrying a dish, Bushey said, 'What's this, then? Spare ribs? Jolly good show.' He poured Tiger beer into mugs for all of us. '*Kong hee fat choy!*' he toasted across the foam. 'Happy New Year,' said Oi Fah.

I said, 'Oi Fah, I read somewhere – in Somerset Maugham, I think – that, to the Chinese, Europeans have the smell of corpses. Is that true?'

'Not of corpses,' she said promptly. 'Of cheese.' She and Bushey laughed. 'And yet you married me,' he said.

An Italian-made electric organ stood in the other part of the room and a pile of old copies of the *Observer* and the *Sunday Times* lay on a bamboo table. The books in the shelves were about Borneo or cooking, and there were novels by John Masters and memoirs of the India of the Raj by Philip Mason. Firecrackers sounded distantly. A golden oriole, a bright-yellow bird the size of a thrush, perched on a rail of the veranda. It could easily have been 1934. 'Did you clap your hands and shout "Boy!" to bring your servants running in the old days?'

'Never, I promise. Anyway, now we only have an amah who helps Oi Fah in the kitchen, and a Malay who cuts the grass.'

I knew from Maugham that life for the British residents in Malaya in the good old days had not been all hectic sex in exciting mansions with bowing servants and slippered ease. 'I don't know if you've been much to planters' houses,' a Maugham character says. 'They're a bit dreary. A lot of gimcrack furniture and silver ornaments and tiger skins. And the food's uneatable.' The Webbs' food was far from uneatable. After the Tiger beer and pink gins ('*Gin merah*, they're called in these parts, red gin'), we sat down to curry. Bushey pushed a dish of sliced red chillies in my direction. 'That's the real stuff, that is. Make you hold on to the rail later on. Just the thing.'

'Bushey!' Oi Fah reproved him, patting his arm.

'About Maugham,' Webb said, 'there was a certain amount of resentment in Malaysia towards him, you know – abuse of hospitality, that sort of thing.'

I said, 'Maugham answered that in a preface. He admits that his stories are about the exceptions. British government servants, traders, planters, ordinary people living in Malaya were as happy or unhappy with their wives as most people elsewhere. I think he calls them "good, decent, normal people". But there must have been some peculiar people about, surely? And dramatic incidents. After all, stories like "The Letter" were based on fact, weren't they?'

'Yes, oh yes,' said Bushey. 'Certainly, there were eccentrics out here. Take old Fred Salt, an ex-sergeant major from the Gunners, who always wore one gold earring in his ear, while his dog, a bitch, went around with the other gold earring in *her* ear. He now lives in Darwin with his Dayak wife.

'Nowadays the British community here is very small. There's me, there's a bank manager who is also the honorary consul, and there's a Guinness representative, Frank Burke-Gafney, a very young-looking Old Hand. But he's usually travelling because Guinness is popular in Borneo and Indonesia. A potent aphrodisiac, people think, and cheaper than snake wine or rhino horn.'

Bushey took more rice and scattered red-hot chillies over it. 'In the days of the Rajah, I lived up-country at Sibu. The Island Club there would have thirty to forty members. Just a wooden bungalow with an atap roof, a tennis court and a bowling alley. With old English bowls, mark you, made by Gamages out of the hardest wood there is. There was the resident, the district officer, the police superintendent, the land-survey wallah, an agricultural officer, the public works engineer, a judge, a doctor and business people like me. Timber in my case.'

'Any Chinese or Malay members?'

'You could bring them in as guests, but Malays don't usually drink and the Chinese preferred their own clubs – we played bridge, not mah-jongg or fan-tan. There were no planters here; there's no rubber in Sarawak. The planters were all in the Malay Peninsula – in the Federated Malay States, the FMS, as we used to say. Raffles's Long Bar was full of them.'

I had often seen in my mind's eye the newly arrived young planters, fresh off the P&O steamer from home, catching their breath at Raffles, so to speak, before taking the train to the rubber estate up-country, where they would work for an initial stretch of seven years before their first home leave. Thereafter, leave came every five years. 'They call the young planter a creeper,' wrote Maugham, 'and you can tell him in the streets of Singapore by his double felt hat and his khaki coat turned up at the wrists. Callow youths who saunter about staring and are inveigled into buying worthless truck from Birmingham which they send home as eastern curios, sit in the lounges of cheap hotels drinking innumerable *stengahs*, and after an evening at the pictures get into rickshaws and finish the night in the Chinese quarter.'

Maugham had eyed the creepers from the window of a room very like the one I occupied in Raffles. Now he would see only tourists – mainly American, Australian and Japanese – loaded with electronic gadgets from Hong Kong or Japan. Singapore no longer has cheap hotels to lounge in, and to drink 'innumerable' stengahs would be to squander a small fortune. But it is still possible to spend an evening at the pictures and then get into a cycle-rickshaw to finish the night in the Chinese quarter – but only just possible, because the government is rapidly demolishing such parts of old Singapore.

If Maugham returned he would find another change. No doubt the English accents that assailed his ears in the card rooms of all those clubs he frequented were monotonously upper class, although perhaps the limited social shake-up after the First World War might have intruded an occasional sound of something more regional. I recalled the expressions of dismay he overheard in the bar of an up-country club when the news appeared in the *Straits Times* that one of its pillars, a Mr Harold 'Knobby' Clarke, had died on the ship taking him home on leave:

'I say, have you heard? Poor Knobby Clarke's dead.'

'No? I say, how awful!'

'Rotten luck, isn't it?'

'Rotten.'

'Damned good sort.'

'One of the best.'

'It gave me quite a turn when I saw it in the paper just by chance.'

'I don't wonder.'

Nowadays in, say, the Singapore Cricket Club, which has long been multi-racial, the British members are more likely to address each other as 'Squire', 'Vicar' or even 'mate' than as 'old man' or 'old boy'. Mr Warburton, the tetchy and snobbish Resident in Maugham's story 'The Out-station', would not be amused. He was the official who had been brought close to apoplexy by the action of his callow and insubordinate assistant, Cooper, when he returned from an up-country tour to find that the young man had torn open and read his most recent batch of newspapers from London:

'I wonder you didn't open my letters as well.'

'Oh, that's not quite the same thing. After all, I couldn't imagine you'd mind my looking at your news-papers. There's nothing private about them.'

'I think it extremely impertinent of you. They're all mixed up.'

Mr Warburton's newsagent, Maugham tells us, had instructions to write on the outside of the wrapper the date of each paper he dispatched. Mr Warburton then numbered them, and his head boy's orders were to place one on the table every morning in the veranda with the early cup of tea. This gave Mr Warburton the illusion of living at home. Every Monday morning he read the Monday *Times* of six weeks back, and so on through the week. On Sunday he read the *Observer*. Returning to the scene of his lifework, Mr Warburton's irascible ghost might be interested to find that, while in those days it took him a week in a coaster from Singapore and forty-eight hours lying on the bottom of a native boat to reach his outstation, it would now take him a couple of hours by air and a few more by motor launch. But he might be amused to find that the techniques of newspaper distribution have failed to keep pace with aerodynamic progress. On my last visit the most recent

Observer hanging on the newspaper racks in the Singapore Cricket Club was exactly six weeks old, the same time its predecessors sixty years ago used to take to travel by water from London to the back of beyond.

'It wasn't all beer and skittles being a planter in Malaya, you know,' Bushey said. 'In Maugham's time, there probably wasn't any ice to cool your drinks, though later some planters had swimming pools. It could be bloody boring. The *tuan* – the white master – got up at five in the morning for the rollcall of his workers. Then he inspected the estate, a long, tiring walk. Breakfast at nine, then some office work, and he'd be finished by twelve. You have to tap rubber early in the morning; while it's cool, it runs, but in the heat it congeals like latex.'

In a setting very like that of the old days we were discussing, I could imagine the planter in his khaki shorts and flannel shirt (a bit thick for the climate), heavy boots and stockings, doing the rounds between the rubber trees in their prim rows, assigning the day's work to the mostly Tamil workers – 'coolies' they called them – some to tap, some to weed, some to dig ditches. Then, at noon, relaxation in a sarong and a loose shirt with warm beer and a pipe. Tea at the club, dinner in the bungalow at eight, bed about nine thirty.

I thought of the wives in their cool, fresh, simple frocks, with not nearly enough to do, working at their pillow lace to keep busy. Maugham had noted it all. 'Pretty dull for the memsahibs,' Bushey admitted. 'But worse for their opposite numbers, the Dutch wives, over in Sumatra. A general manager of an estate there might order a young married assistant to take his plain old wife to the club film, and himself invite the assistant's young wife up to his bungalow for you-know-what. The assistant wouldn't refuse; it guaranteed his job with the company.'

We stood up and walked to the doorway looking down to the trees. Mynah birds whistled and cursed one another, stalking stiff-legged on the lawn, and a pair of golden orioles flew past the veranda.

I said, 'Maugham's story "The Letter" revolves around the disgracing of an unmarried Englishman because he kept a Chinese mistress.'

'It has never been a disgrace here in Sarawak,' Bushey said. 'A mistress might not go to the club, but her English boyfriend, her tuan, certainly could – no stigma there. In fact, the Rajahs encouraged their young whites to have local birds to keep them happy on the long five-year tour. Sarawak came to feel like home, so they stayed on. Good policy.

'Talking like this brings back so many stories. I'll tell you one or two if you like. They're not libellous, and they may interest you.'

Oi Fah said, 'Bushey adores telling stories. You'd be doing him a favour by listening.'

Bushey said, 'In 1953 there was a young English chap named George out here, working in timber like I was. He must have lived in Kuching for about a year before being sent to Miri in east Sarawak, and he formed a liaison with a Malay girl there who moved in with him. She used to play him up a bit by going off now and again with someone else, but he'd have her back again. He would never be harsh to the opposite sex. I know it sounds odd to say it, but – well, he was a natural gentleman.

'Anyway, his company rented him a wooden bungalow two miles out of Miri, and she went with him. It was a

pleasant area on the edge of the town opposite a cantonment where the Borneo Company Europeans lived.
Now, being a Malay, the girlfriend was very fond of golden
ornaments, and had purchased on credit a lot of ornaments
from an old Malay woman who used to go around the
houses selling them. Finally she owed this woman a hundred
dollars.

'At last the old woman demanded that she pay up what
she owed. According to the evidence in court later, the girl
said, "All right. My tuan has given me the money, so come
round tomorrow when he's at the office and I'll pay you
what I owe. I may even buy more, so bring your entire
stock with you."

'Well, in the late afternoon of that day, George's office
boy went off to the house to cut the grass, and he noticed
that all the windows of the house were closed, and that the
place looked desolate. But all of a sudden a window swung
open and the girlfriend leaned out and said, "Look, you
don't have to cut the grass today. Go away. Come back
tomorrow." The Malay noticed that there was blood on her
arms, so he dashed back to the office and reported this to
George, who immediately drove home.

'Unfortunately – or perhaps fortunately – he had a puncture, and didn't arrive at the house until well after six
o'clock. By that time, whatever had transpired in the bungalow had been sorted out. The windows were open again,
and his girlfriend seemed calm. With her in the house there
was also her brother and her brother's boyfriend – among
the young Malays, homosexuality is not rare.

'Anyway, George asked what all the trouble was, and
what was all this about blood on her arms. She claimed
that she'd had a miscarriage that afternoon, although

George noticed there were also bloodstains on the wall of the lounge. He said, "All right, you'd better go and see a doctor," but she said, "I'm all right now. I'd like to go to the pictures." So he had his bath and then took her off to the Palace cinema.

'Well, in the back of this house was a large kitchen, or *dapor*, with a Chinese type of stove made of concrete, rather like a table with two holes in it through which the heat of the charcoal is forced up. Underneath this sort of table very large pieces of charcoal were stored. When the old Malay woman had come to the house, she had been attacked by the girlfriend, her brother, and her brother's boyfriend. Apparently they had strangled her with the cable from the electric iron. They hid the body under the charcoal in the *dapor* when George returned. While George was out at the cinema, these two characters got the old woman's body out of the back window after dark and carried it down to the jungle at the back of the house with the intention of burying her in a grave they had dug in the morning before she visited the house. This was probably fatal to their case, since the digging of the grave showed premeditation. At the same time it was also their undoing because Miri is subject to floods, with the river rising and falling fifteen feet every six hours or so. The grave was now a pond full of water, and quite useless for their purpose. So they stuck the body in a hedge, covered it over with jungle, came back and went to bed.

'In the Malay *kampong* [village] where the old lady lived there was a hue and cry. Next day, more hue and cry, the police also joining the hunt, and eventually, of course, their inquiries led to George's house. The arrest of his girlfriend and brother and boyfriend followed. George was questioned closely, a search of the area produced the body, and the game was up.'

Bushey broke off. 'You can't listen to this without a glass in your hand. Brandy? Beer?' Even under the fan, the afternoon temperature felt like 120 degrees, and the lizards on the walls were panting even harder. 'Beer,' I said. He poured two mugs, and went on.

'Now, in Sibu at that particular time – bear in mind that Sarawak was still a colony – the head of the police was a very able European called Roy Henry, who later on became commissioner of police, and today is the number one of the police in Hong Kong. Roy was the investigating officer because it was a very serious crime, particularly since a European seemed to be at least partly involved. Anyway, in the course of the questioning, the girlfriend changed her evidence and said that the blood on the wall was not human blood but animal blood from a chicken she had slaughtered. Roy decided that in order to check her evidence she should have a medical examination, so he sent her up to the hospital. The examination showed that she had not had a miscarriage.

'Eventually the trial was held, and the three of them were accused of murder. It lasted about ten days. There were amusing incidents during the trial. The boyfriend turned out to have a rather low intellect and, when questioned as to where he was on that night when George and his girl-friend were at the cinema, he claimed that he had not slept in the house that night, but was sleeping with a European. "What was her name?" His answer was that it was a he, a young European of the Borneo Company across the road. This evidence was not produced in court.

'The girlfriend's appearance in court was that of a nun

or saint. She had no make-up on, wore a drab, grey, full-length dress, and had her hair done up in plaits. Questions were asked about this: "Would it be fair to say that normally you would not dress up as you are today?"

'She replied, "Normally I would not dress like this, but it is in respect for the court I'm dressed like this today."

' "Do you normally wear European-type clothes?"

' "Yes."

' "Would it be true to say that normally you would wear lipstick?"

' "Yes."

' "And nail varnish?"

' "Yes."

' "In fact, would it be truthful to say that you look after your appearance very well?"

'But the Malay translator made a mistake, and asked, "Would it be fair to state that you look after Europeans very well?"

'And, before the translation could be corrected, she answered, "I look after Europeans very well!"

'This produced a great deal of laughter from the court, including the judge himself, who, being an old Rajah hand, could also speak fluent Malay.

'Anyway, judgement was given, the brother and sister were both found guilty, and the judge felt that he could not recommend mercy for either of them, mainly because the grave had been dug. The boyfriend was found not guilty – largely because he was of such low intelligence.

'Late in the afternoon of the last day of the trial, the two accused in handcuffs were led outside the court, where a tremendous crowd of relatives of the old woman was gathered, and were taken away in a Black Maria to the prison. They would be taken down to Kuching the following day on the steamer anchored at the wharf about a hundred yards away. Roy Henry, whose office was immediately above the court, instructed the boyfriend to be brought to his office immediately after the case ended. Roy explained to the boy in Malay that, but for the grace of God, he, too, would have been sentenced to be hanged. The law being the law, he was free, but for the boyfriend's own safety, Roy said, he was going to keep him in the jail that night. "See all those Malays outside? If I let you loose tonight they'll kill you. For your own protection I'm going to take you into custody, and tomorrow you'll go down to Kuching. If I ever see you in my division again, I'll make sure that you're arrested." To which the boy said, "Tuan, before I go I would like to ask one favour." And Roy said, "Yes, what is it?" "Tuan, could you lend me five dollars?"

'Two or three months later the appeal for clemency failed, and it was the last night before they were to be hanged. George was down in Kuching, and went to the jail to say farewell. He always maintained that, had she been found not guilty, he would have taken her back to his house, despite all that had happened. I think it was pretty plucky for George to say that. That's the end of the story. She was the only woman ever hanged in Sarawak.'

The yellow bird had returned to the veranda rail, this time bringing a mate. They were beautiful creatures perched there, beaks open, breathing with difficulty in the heat. They flew off when the Webbs' cat sidled around a shaded corner.

'What about George?' I asked. 'Did people steer clear of him once it came out about his Malay girlfriend?'

Bushey looked shocked. 'Good God, no. He stayed on to be a very successful and popular member of the community. As I told you, he was a natural gentleman.' He put a big red arm around Oi Fah. 'Sometimes, though, there are difficulties the other way, but I think your family have finally accepted that I'm a reasonable barbarian husband, haven't they?'

She laughed fondly. 'It's lucky you're a Buddhist, or they might not have.'

Later, when I reached Hong Kong, I met Roy Henry, the policeman who had investigated the case. He remembered it well, particularly the girlfriend. 'She was a very haughty woman. Very brave, her head high – unlike her brother, who had to be carried to the gallows. It was widely believed by Malays that she could cast spells and work magic with incantations and herbs. Even my Malay officers believed it. I think she thought that because she was with a tuan she might get off. But she was very brave.'

In the evening coolness, Bushey walked with me to Kuching's museum, famous in the region. It contained a reconstruction of a Dayak long-house, Dayak weapons and tools and artifacts, cases of local fish, birds, animals and old Chinese porcelain. We looked at the ancient embossed cannons, the paintings of James Brooke and his dashing sailing ship, the *Royalist*, the scourge of marauding sea rovers from Sulu. We stared into the angry glass eyes of stuffed orang-utans, red and shaggy, half the size of a man, their huge arms draped over reconstructed branches, and gazed in awe at the long, red, glowing nose of the proboscis monkey, another large creature. The Malays call it *orang blanda* (Dutchman), showing what they thought about their overlords in the East Indies.

We paused before a case of birds of paradise, perhaps the

most wonderful of tropical creatures, and, a few paces further on, looked at the grotesque hornbills with their unwieldy-looking bills and the long tail feathers that the superstitious Dayaks like to wear as headdresses. Then we saw that the custodians were closing the museum.

As we walked slowly down the hill to the Aurora, Bushey said, 'I ended the war in Burma, you know. Place called Prome. Now at Prome there was as queer a coot as you'll ever find. The local province engineer said to me one day, "Would you like to meet a real prewar British type?" This odd chap had been in the Burmese police, right up on the Burmese–Chinese border. He'd been left alone by the Japs because even then I suppose they thought he was too old to do any harm.

'We drove up in a jeep to his pleasant timber bungalow, thatched roof, raised off the ground. The old boy had very little hair, and must have been eighty. He wore a *lungi*, the Burmese sarong, and a collarless Burmese shirt with no buttons but with studs joined by a golden chain – the usual formal dress of Burmese males. He gave us pink gins – no choice, take it or leave it. His friends were there, some Burmese, some Brits who had come back to restart their timber concessions, and we sat on teak cane-bottom chairs with extendable arms and slots in them for the glasses.

'Old Montague lay back, feet up on his chair, talking about tiger shooting in the Arakan area. Tigers had snatched one or two chaps from the Eighty-second West African Division when they passed through. After a drink or two, he called out, and an aged Burmese woman shuffled out from behind a curtain – his wife, it turned out – carrying a spittoon. She lowered his legs, put the spittoon under his lungi, and we realized he was peeing.'

We turned from the Padang into the bar of the Aurora and sat down at a small table behind a trio of large Sikhs, who sat talking volubly over a thicket of empty bottles. Bushey resumed: 'Well, he kept on chatting, and after a bit he said something to her, and she bent down and dived under the *lungi*, then bore the spittoon away covered with a piece of cloth. Talk went on as before, no one had taken a bit of notice, and the old man put his feet back up.'

I wonder whether Eric Blair of the Burma Police, later to change his name to George Orwell and write *1984* and *Animal Farm*, knew old Montague?

Next day Bushey Webb got out his old car and made his annual round of New Year courtesy visits to Chinese friends. Through the leafy avenues of Kuching he drove like a Panzer officer afraid of slowing up a blitzkrieg, waving gaily at people on the pavements who waved back, Malays and Ibans – the local people – as well as Chinese. Once we passed three young Malays who pranced and giggled in women's dresses. Bushey said, 'Malays don't mind that sort at all. They accept transvestism as quite normal. Look, one of them, the one in the beautiful red dress, has the whole works – tits, brassière, the lot. Wonderfully tolerant about that, the Malays. Good for them, I say.' Good for Bushey, too, I thought.

As we slowed at a corner, two Malays called out cheerfully, '*Orang putih!*' – 'white man' – and we exchanged waves. 'Funny how they call us white,' said Bushey. 'We're anything but, really. Pink, purple – pink and purple – off-white. Red – the Chinese are right to call us red barbarians.'

Chapter Twenty-Eight

B Y THE TIME Mr Ho announced our departure I had been in Sarawak four days and the crackers had stopped exploding. The Chinese lion-dancing – boys hidden under a great grinning animal long enough to accommodate several dancers – had come to an end. The holiday was over, the Year of the Monkey was launched and even Bushey's stories had almost run out. When he drove me to the little riverside port where the *Perak* lay, I found I was glad to see her again. 'Send me a postcard from Zamboanga,' he said. 'Something with a pirate on it.'

The *Perak* swung out at high tide. The crew of a little ship behind us, the *Getah Kinabalu* of Singapore, waved and called, according to the custom of Asia, and out in the stream we moved steadily away. '*Barrrp!*' The *Perak* belched like the battered tuba in a street musicians' band. '*Barrrp!*' Sampans and a few motor fishing vessels scattered before us. '*Baarrrrp!*'

A timber yard disfigured the east bank: logs and planks, a tall, thin metal chimney. Rusting tugs. A decrepit riverboat or two on slipways. Then we turned a bend, Kuching disappeared and mangrove and nipa palm closed in. Occasional figures in plate-shaped hats slid by in canoes heading for lonely waterside houses on piles. Angry clouds towered in the sky, growing nearer and darker by the minute. At the mouth of the river, where we crossed the inner and outer bars, a Chinese temple stood in the woods above the ramshackle pier of Muara Tebas village, and to seaward sheets of rain advanced. Hundreds of smooth round coconut shells blackened by long immersion floated in the water like heads severed by Borneo headhunters, and nipa-palm fronds floated like skeletal ribs. We began to roll slowly but decisively.

In the dining saloon, the *Perak*'s little cannonball captain ran up and down the steeply sloping deck, intuitively judging each roll. 'Must take exercise or be sick-sick,' he said, flashing a golden molar. The rolling created a fleeting intimation of space travel, but I had no feelings of sick-sick.

The storm continued through the night. At breakfast next morning the little captain, scooping up the egg yolks in his cup with a spoon, said, 'Not sick-sick? Weather threw ship up, down. Very confused. Brunei maybe five o'clock tomorrow evening.' I wondered where the *Straits Hope* was after our four-day stopover in Kuching.

The second officer said, 'I've never been to Brunei.' I had been there once with the *Fiona*. I told him, 'There's a town – a large village, really – built entirely on stilts over water.'

'Brunei produce fish?'

'Oil, natural gas – worth about a billion pounds. Apart from oil, fish and timber, I suppose. I read somewhere that the people of Brunei are the fourth richest per capita in the world.'

In a year or two Brunei would become an independent sultanate; for now, it was under British protection. In 1841 a sultan of Brunei had rewarded the English adventurer James Brooke with the territory of Sarawak in return for his aid in putting down rebellious chiefs and fighting off, in his sailing ship, the *Royalist* – and sometimes in alliance with the ships of Captain George Keppel of the Royal Navy – the swarms of Sulu marauders.

As the *Perak* rolled through the South China Sea towards Muara, the port of Brunei, Mr Boon, the white-thatched steward, scuttled on his bowlegs across my cabin like an albino crab, backwards, forwards, sideways, wielding a dustpan and brush. Looking for exercise, I staggered along the deck towards the stern.

Two Chinese with bandannas around their heads were hammering rust off the rail. 'Where you go after Brunei?' one of them asked me. Manila, then Hong Kong, I told him. The other man said, 'Hong Kong more better. Have subway now. And China better than bee-fore.' As an after-thought, he added, 'China soya-bean countly. Countly for soya bean.' I suggested a photograph, but they smiled, immediately shy, saying no, they were in working clothes. They had a fishing line over the stern.

'Any fish?'

'No fish this place. Oil ligs, dlilling. Fish lun away.'

Oil rigs were all around us like bits of abandoned Meccano.

In the chart room, Captain Abdul Rahman was striding his dividers across the chart. We were, I saw over his shoulder, passing south of Ampa Bank, where there was a light. We had skirted Iron Duke Shoals and Victoria Patches; these seas, explored, surveyed and charted over two or three centuries by British buccaneers and naval navigators, have Malay or English names. The words 'Densely wooded' cover the land on the chart, and they certainly describe the shoreline.

'Poosy cat, poosy cat!' Mr Boon was staggering along amidships with a dish of food pursued by the ship's cat, a small grey and white animal with a lump on the end of its shortened tail, which looked as if it had been caught in a

mangle. A small bell tinkled under its chin. 'Poosy, poosy-cat,' Mr Boon called seductively again, setting down the dish. 'Ship has cat, no rat on ship,' said the captain. 'Nobody see rat on this ship.' I made a mental note to present Captain Bala of the *Nancowry* with a cat to deal with his bandicoots the next time I passed through Madras.

Captain Abdul Rahman was the antithesis of the ebullient Bala; quiet, though friendly, wearing trousers rather too short for him and very narrow at the bottoms, which gave him the look of Mr Micawber. Suddenly he turned into Winnie the Pooh as he stood on tiptoe holding the hood of the radar screen and peering down hopefully as if scanning the bottom of a honeypot. 'Muara, Muara, Muara, Muara,' he called into the radio, and '*Perak, Perak, Perak.*' A prolonged gabble answered him; to judge by his smile, it did not displease him. We were very close to Muara and would anchor offshore for the night in sixty feet of water.

The morning was grey but calm; the bad weather had blown itself out. The harbour master gave permission to enter the port, a little bay at the end of a narrow opening in a tongue of land, and marked by an avenue of green and red lights. A big, serious Malay pilot came aboard and guided the *Perak* to a mooring next to a Japanese freighter, whose crew waved when I stared at them through my mottled binoculars. The crew of the dredger had done the same at the entrance to the bay: the waters of South-east Asia are full of waving, smiling people.

Alongside the quay were three Singaporean freighters in line behind a shoddy Panamanian, six slick police launches and a tiny tanker, rather like a toy, with an elegant awning encircling a dainty bridge more appropriate to a steam yacht. There were a few acres of modern warehouses, and then the undergrowth resumed. Along the water's edge were the wooden stilted houses of South-east Asia. As usual, they were small and simple, but at each door lay at least one boat with an expensive Japanese or American outboard engine.

I bought a bottle of vodka from Mr Wong's pantry, then tipped Mr Boon, thanking him for having been so attentive. 'Oh, no,' he said, shaking his big head with its white hair standing up like a cockatoo's crest. 'Thank *you*. Come soon.'

An assistant from Harrisons & Crosfield, the agents, arrived on board with the immigration men. I said goodbye to Captain Abdul Rahman, Chief Officer Oman and the rest, including Mr Wong and my Chinese hosts at the New Year's Eve feast in the mouth of the Sarawak river. 'Happy travels,' they said. As the launch pulled away towards the jetty, I looked back affectionately at the little *Perak*'s perky bridge, snub nose and decks smelling of fruit.

I was lucky to be looked after in Brunei by two helpful Englishmen. One, Guy Nickal, general manager of Harrisons & Crosfield, was on the quay at Muara and drove me into Brunei. The other was someone I'd bumped into in Brunei two years before, when I called here in the *Fiona*: Derek Hewett, manager of the Chartered Bank, who gave me a room for my two days' stay. The Harrisons & Crosfield office looks out over one of the most extraordinary water scenes in the world. The lake-like expanse of smooth water runs back to green slopes and looming wooded hills, or up broad creeks out of sight into the impenetrable tangle of mangrove roots and mud. The sprawling village of wooden bungalows on stilts is linked by raised wooden catwalks, and between that quarter and the modern town on dry land, where sit Harrisons & Crosfield, the Chartered Bank, shops, hotels, government buildings and the dominant golden onion domes of the grand mosque, there is a frenzied, unceasing roaring and splashing of scores of outboard-powered boats – the taxis of Brunei – crossing and recrossing, bearing families, housewives, children to and from the dwellings suspended above the water.

The news from Harrisons & Crosfield's shipping manager was that the *Straits Hope* was expected to arrive in a day or two at Kota Kinabalu, the port and capital of the Malaysian state of Sabah, or North Borneo. Thereafter she would probably call at Sandakan, Lahad Datu and Tawau – in other words, make the full semicircular trip around the wild coastline from Brunei to Indonesian east Borneo. These ports were tiny places – most people would regard them as 'off the map' – and my task was to find out which of them was the best jumping-off point for a sea crossing of the pirate-haunted Sulu Sea to the Philippines.

I consulted my map. As Tony Blatch had said in

Singapore, Zamboanga on the western tip of Mindanao would be the most convenient port on the Philippines side of that sinister and dangerous expanse of water. Most convenient, yes, and the name appealed to me, too, but the problem was that every island between Sabah and Zamboanga – and there were a great many – was a potential, perhaps actual, haunt of one of three groups of ruffians with a formidable reputation for kidnapping, torture and murder: pirates, smugglers, or the Muslim desperadoes of the rebel Moro National Liberation Front who had been giving the Filipino armed forces a bloody time of it for years in their bitter struggle against the regime of their enemy up in Manila, President Ferdinand Marcos. The area was one of great political and military tension. I couldn't be sure that any steel-hulled ships crossed from Borneo to Mindanao, and it looked as if another Becher's Brook was just ahead of me. Was I going to have to make another miserable compromise and fly from Brunei to Hong Kong in order to get a ship to Manila? And then return from Manila to Hong Kong by sea to complete the itinerary I had planned? But this would mean missing the great tract of sea and island between Borneo and Luzon, and that would be intolerable. Once more, anxiety began to nag like an aching wisdom tooth, and it grew more insistent the closer I got to Sandakan.

Chapter Twenty-Nine

I DON'T KNOW a place where the mood of the landscape can change so swiftly from happy to sombre as Borneo, except perhaps the Andamans. Now, in spite of its beauty, it was gloom-laden.

Derek Hewett's house looked down from a fringe of frangipani and flame-of-the-woods trees on a snaking strip of water. In the morning the mist hung thickly about the forest trees on the other side, obscuring the water, mud, mangroves, a small jetty and a smaller launch. The sun, lurking behind its smoke veil, had no brightness or heat. *Le soleil noir de la mélancolie.* A bird nearby made a maddeningly regular sound like a man chopping wood. I read through the odd scraps of information I had collected about the Sulu Sea, weighing my chances. What I read was depressing, but it didn't make me afraid; that came later.

My notes read:

November 1979: Hijacking of local ferry *Saleha Baru* with forty-four passengers and crew on board as it plied its way from Semporna to nearby Lahad Datu. (This is from the *Straits Times* report. The *Straits Hope* is going to Lahad Datu.) I may have to take a boat from there to cross the Sulu Sea. Launch captured by a gang of pirates who took it and the passengers to an isolated island in the nearby Philippines. There they were robbed of valuables while the pirates set about repainting and disguising the captured launch. It was two weeks before the remaining passengers returned to Semporna; in the meantime two had died, one from gunshot wounds, one from drowning. Seven of the hijackers were killed when Filipino troops went to the rescue.

December 1979: The Japanese fishing vessel *Daisan Hokko Maru* attacked by gunmen off Sarangani Island. Thought to be Moro National Liberation Front separatists fighting for greater Muslim autonomy in the predominantly Christian Philippines.

Same month: 'Pirates shot dead a young mother in the Sulu Sea while she was sailing with her Norwegian husband and three-year-old son from the Philippines to Borneo.' (The *Borneo Bulletin* reporting.) 'Mr. Peer Tangvald told Brunei police that his wife fell overboard after being shot by the pirates, who boarded the fifty-foot schooner on the high seas and took away all valuables. Mr. Tangvald said he had not believed that it could be possible in this day and age.' It is not only possible but has become so frequent as to verge on the humdrum from what I've heard.

In the last year, there had been more than sixty people killed and nearly five hundred wounded in political violence in the southern Philippine islands, all part of the eight-year-old Moro war. Bombs seemed to be exploding everywhere, including Zamboanga. I read that the Filipino commander in the Southern Military District, Rear Admiral Romulo Espadron, was inclined to think that anyone killing or hijacking in his area was a Moro, although that might be professional bias. More seriously, there were political strains with the Malaysian state of Sabah in northern Borneo. Everyone seemed to agree that about ninety thousand southern Filipino Muslim refugees had taken refuge there from the fighting on the island. The admiral's charge that the Moros were getting arms and fast boats from Sabah was, of course, hotly denied by the Sabah chief minister, Mr Harris Selah, who said that the pirates were probably Filipino soldiers; at least they had cropped hair like soldiers and called their senior colleagues 'sir'. To which the admiral retorted, 'What about the fact that these pirates and terrorists are using fast Volvo-Penta speedboats made in Sabah?' So the political cannonade went on, back and forth. In an anarchic situation, truth is elusive, but the case of an ore tanker called *Berge Istra* hardly seemed to fit Admiral Espadron's ideas about the exclusivity of Moro terror. The tanker had vanished south of Mindanao five years before, and nothing more had been heard of it except for faint SOS signals. Who would have done away with a tanker?

Piracy was nothing new to this strange region, to which an aura of the eighteenth century still clings. Scenically, it cannot have changed much since Dampier, the English buccaneer, and Captain James Cook, the Yorkshire navigator, boldly sailed this way into the virtually unknown Strait of Macassar and the Java Sea. No cement jerry-building has sullied these palm-covered islands, looking so deceptively meek in sky-blue seas full of dolphins and turtles; the greatest change in this beautiful and perilous backyard of Asia is that the pirates have equipped their outriggers and praus with high-speed engines and heavy machine-guns. Piracy was an honoured way of life in these obscure parts for several hundred years before the Moro Liberation Front added its idealistic brand of terror to the prevailing tradition.

I didn't brood much on the risks that waited for me around the corner; I was depressed enough by the gloom that suddenly and mysteriously struck me that misty morning in Derek Hewett's pleasant living room. My immediate concern was to find a ship to take me to a place where it might at least be possible to cross that long stretch of treacherous water to Zamboanga. The pirates might crop up in due time, but first things first.

To reach Kota Kinabalu, Guy Nickal of Harrisons & Crosfield had suggested, take the ferry, a powerful and reliable motor launch, to Labuan Island two and a half hours offshore, where Harrisons & Crosfield had a branch office. Labuan was becoming a busy, free-trade port; it belonged to Malaysia and was part of the state of Sabah. From there Kota Kinabalu was a long stone's throw by air. I decided impatiently that my pride could accommodate a plane-hop over an inconvenient ditch. The *Straits Hope* might even be at Labuan, but more likely it was at Kota Kinabalu; Harrisons & Crosfield's Captain David Corrie in Labuan would know the exact situation, and could be in touch with his office in Kota Kinabalu, and with Blatch or MacGregor of the Straits Steamship Company in Singapore.

I left Brunei on the ferry, the *Seri Sungai Express*, to Labuan. Derek Hewett's driver delivered me at the landing stage on Jalan McArthur, or McArthur Street. A Murut, one of the tribesmen of the Sarawak–Borneo border, he drove with dogged caution at a good speed so that we arrived early and watched the motor taxis ploughing up spray between the landing stage and the village on stilts across the hundred yards of water. American Johnson engines were outnumbered by the Yamaha and Suzuki 25s but the drivers could have been in Florida or California. A slant-eyed daredevil who hurled his boat into a ninety-degree swerve to stop just in time, deposited two fat and startled Chinese women at the jetty near the Brunei ferry, and saluted me by raising his hand to the peak of a military baseball-style cap bearing the words 'Don't Ask Me' on one side and 'Deputy Dawg' on the other. The Brunei ferry launch was modern, sleek and white, and had a notice on it saying, 'Powered by Caterpillar'. On time, it roared throatily down the winding forest-bound waterway to the bay at Muara and out into the sea towards Labuan, then surged into full speed. The crossing was short, pleasant and uneventful. At the wharf at Labuan an old Chinese porter loaded my bags into a handcart and wheeled it to Harrisons & Crosfield's office just outside the harbour gate.

In his office, young Captain Corrie was helpful. The *Straits Hope*, he said, was in Kota Kinabalu waiting for a replacement captain, Bob Barker; her previous master, Captain Rankin, was going on leave tomorrow. I breathed a sigh of relief. David Corrie booked me on a flight to Kota Kinabalu, then took me on a drive around the tiny island of Labuan. The Japanese forces in this theatre of military operations during the Second World War had surrendered on Labuan; a memorial marked the spot. It was a green and pleasant island, thriving on a barter trade with the Philippines. Corrie pointed out one sign of our times in the waters of Brunei Bay off the harbour: a huddle of tankers laid up because of the cutback in OPEC's oil production and the world's oil consumption. Shell, BP and Chevron tankers stagnated here, some well into their second year of idleness. The largest of them was the *British Resource*, 133,000 tons, and there was no one on her but a single watchman. Like elephants, but not nearly so precious, the huge vessels looked as if they had sought out this quiet corner to die in.

Corrie talked about the Sulu pirates. 'A Japanese freighter anchored near Semora Island a little while ago was approached by a launch full of wild-looking Filipinos – you know, bandannas around their heads and all that. They shouted to the captain that they wanted to come aboard to sell fruit. Well, the captain was no fool; he'd heard all about the pirates around here, and so refused to let them come up. At which they opened up with their automatic guns, punching a number of holes in the hull and around the bridge. Luckily, no one was hurt, but it shows they've started attacking full-sized ships now.'

I asked if merchant ships in these waters carried weapons for self-defence.

'Some do now. The Filipino government has made it illegal for their barter traders to do business in Sandakan and Tawau because they think the Moro insurgents will kill or kidnap the crews and use their boats. The Filipino authorities don't want their nationals coming and going unchecked between the Sulu Islands and Zamboanga to just anywhere in Sabah. Therefore they can trade now only in Labuan and, for their protection from pirates on the way here, they are allowed to carry arms up to Banggi Island, where they deposit them with the Malaysian authorities. On the way home from Labuan they recover their arms from Banggi before running across the Sulu Sea past the risky spots around Sandakan and the islands of Tawitawi and Jolo.'

That afternoon Corrie drove me to the little airstrip. As the Fokker Friendship crossed to North Borneo, I wondered glumly how I was going to continue if the

Philippines government had banned barter-trade boats between Sandakan and Zamboanga, and if merchant vessels avoided the area. Disguised as an old fisherman in a canoe? I decided to think about this tomorrow.

I had visited Kota Kinabalu during the Indonesian conflict in the sixties, when it was still called Jesselton. Since then it had acquired a Malay name and grown. Like many ports hereabouts, it had been needlessly bombed by the Allies in the war, razing its two-storey houses and dignified arcaded shops. Now it is all concrete and trying its best to be high-rise and up-to-date. It has none of the charm of Kuching, which was spared such senseless bombing attacks. But beyond it is the glorious savagery of Borneo's landscape. The mountains of Sabah rise up like a series of tidal waves, with Mount Kinabalu dominating the skyline at fourteen thousand feet, the highest peak in South-east Asia. The indigenous tribal people, the Dusuns, consider it sacred; until recently, at least, many believed that the spirits of their dead gather now and then on its top two thousand feet.

Dennis Bloodworth had told me that, according to local custom, you should be careful to sacrifice a number of cockerels before climbing Kinabalu. 'A British governor of North Borneo,' he said, 'thoughtlessly climbed the mountain without sacrificing a single rooster. He came down, was taken ill and died. The Dusuns said, Serve him right. One night, as his successor waited for guests to arrive for a reception at the residency, he was horrified to see an unearthly figure in dress uniform floating down the staircase. He shakily grabbed an aide, and was told, "Oh, that's the last governor." '

The anxiety that had accompanied me to Labuan

persisted in Kota Kinabalu. I took it with me to the seafront offices of Harrisons & Crosfield, where, Captain Corrie had informed me, Mr John Fung was shipping manager. When the clerk told me he was on board the *Straits Hope*, which had arrived the day before, I walked down the street to a travel agent, pessimistically intent on taking out a sort of insurance policy.

In the travel office two pert young Chinese girls struggled Laocoon-like with ringing telephones amid posters showing Malaysian Airlines System jumbos, Thai jets ('smooth as silk') and beefeaters in 'Visit Britain' advertisements. When one of the girls had freed herself from the telephones for a minute, she answered my inquiry about a flight to Zamboanga from Sandakan or Tawau (Corrie had said he thought there was one) without a second's pause: 'No flight. Only from Labuan.'

'I'm fairly sure there is one from Tawau. If you could just ask . . .'

She telephoned a friend, enjoyed a long, laughing conversation, then turned back to me. 'Sandakan or Tawau to Zamboanga on Thursday and Sunday. But the flight only goes if they have enough passengers – like a taxi service, you know.'

I asked her to make a reservation from Tawau, the timber port at the head of the Macassar Strait, and took the ticket with a minimally enhanced sense of security, but without joy. To have to fly over the Sulu Sea . . . I read the Sabah Air ticket: 'Tawau–Sandakan–Zamboanga'. A slip of paper clipped to the boarding pass said, 'Smallpox vaccination required.' I pushed it into my hip pocket and tried to forget it.

Mr Fung was back in his office with Captain Barker,

newly arrived from Singapore, and the man he was replacing, Captain Rankin. I knew Rankin's dark, sleek head from a voyage I had made two years before from Brunei with him in the *Rajah Brooke*. Sitting at Mr Fung's desk, he was reading Captain Barker's hand. 'You'll live to seventy-five,' he said. And Barker exclaimed, 'Oh, not that long, surely!'

'You own three houses and forty acres of land.'

Barker raised eyebrows like small wire brushes and winked at me. 'I'm not sure that's accurate. I've never counted my acres.'

Captain Barker was in his fifties, tall and rangy, with long, thin white legs beneath blue shorts and greying hair going thin on the crown. He had a face as red and cheery as Rankin's was pleasantly solemn. Between them, John Fung sat listening; he was a tall, thin elderly Chinese with a lined face, gold-rimmed spectacles and a serious legal air, like a benign solicitor out of a novel by Dickens, an oriental Mr Wemmick.

The *Straits Hope*, I gathered, was due to sail the next day at ten o'clock. '*Straits Hope* won't call at Tawau this trip,' Mr Fung announced. 'Read this and sign it, please, Mr Young.' He handed me a typed piece of paper as if he were requesting my signature on a new will.

I read: 'I, Gavin Young, hereby declare that I will not claim on your company nor the Master of the *Straits Hope* for responsibility for any accident which may happen to me during presence on board between Kota Kinabalu and Sandakan. For Harrisons & Crosfield (Sabah), John S. Fung.' I signed it without delay. 'There we are, then,' said Captain Barker.

★   ★   ★

The *Straits Hope* was a bigger ship than the little *Perak*, but still no giant of the seas. She had strange bows that curved up sharply and narrowed into a sort of towering peak, so that when I stood there my head was almost level with the line of sight from the bridge. 'Bloody nuisance,' Captain Barker complained cheerfully. 'Sometimes I can't see a damned thing ahead.'

Barker was no exception to the rule I had discovered: that ships' officers are an easygoing, friendly – though often bitchy – lot with an interest in talking as a safety valve for the restrictive nature of their monkish existence. Relationships on ships are generally easy and casual, and antipathies are kept well in hand, even ashore. I suppose they have to be, for what alternative is there but bodily harm and murder?

Barker had a nice line in mock anxiety. He liked to sprinkle chilli sauce, so to speak, on the blander periods of shipboard existence. 'I hope we can muddle through between here and Sandakan,' he said glumly as we rocked out into the South China Sea, heading north-east. Why shouldn't we? I wondered.

I had discovered an unused bar and game room on the deck below my quarters in the owner's cabin, a large though not luxurious room with a bunk, chest of drawers, and shower attached.

Barker came into the game room, a relic of passenger days, a couple of hours after we'd sailed, and found me sitting at a low table with a writing pad in front of me. I had already inspected the posters of Swiss lakes, a wall chart identifying several varieties of ferns and a collage of nude girls cut from magazines. Over the three-ply bar stood a TV set, and near it a dartboard.

SINGAPORE TO CANTON

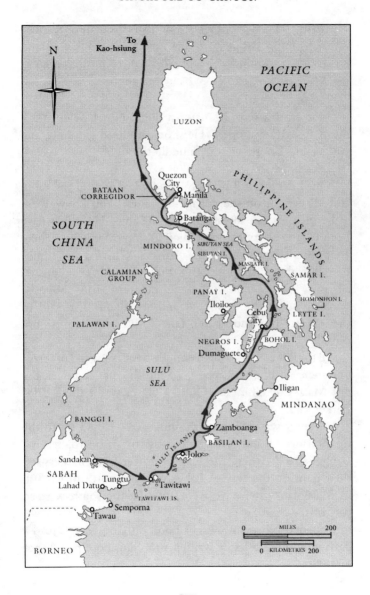

'Writing letters?' asked Barker, and immediately went on, 'My God, I find the third mate's never been up this coast before, and none of the officers have been around to the Macassar Strait.'

'None of them?'

'Not on this ship. It's new to them. Nor have I, so it'll mean an extra eye open.' He shook his head gloomily, and said again, 'I hope we can muddle through.'

'Let's hope so.'

'Oh, I daresay it'll be okay.' He looked around the cabin and his eyes lit on the collage of nudes. 'You know, these girlie pictures can spread all over the ship.' He might have been talking about some pernicious tropical fungus. 'There are pussies all over the crew's quarters. What do you think? It's all right, I suppose. But there shouldn't be pussies all over the *outside* of their quarters, too. Suppose female visitors come aboard and see them? I've said to the crew, "No, no. Fair's fair. Inside the cabins, not outside!" '

All told, the *Straits Hope*'s complement consisted of forty-one men: an English captain, a Scottish chief engineer, the rest Malays or Chinese. 'Quite a big crew for these days,' Barker said.

Darkness was falling by the time we steamed up to the tip of Borneo and swung due east to starboard, leaving Banggi Island (where the Filipino barter-trade masters left their guns on the way to Labuan) to the north of us. Still in Malaysian waters, we were entering the south-western part of the Sulu Sea.

I opened Norman Sherry's book on Conrad and read a passage quoting a letter written to a Singapore newspaper in 1879:

Sir:

I notice a paragraph in your issue of Wednesday last commenting upon the action of H.M.S. *Kestrel* in burning a native piratical village on the North East Coast of Borneo . . . Well, Sir, I was attacked in the *Subahani* six months ago by pirates at the mouth of the Beelungan River. I was apprehensive of an attack, knowing the coast, and put on deck rattans 8 ft. high and my guns were double shotted, when about 200 piratical sampans attacked me and I fired upon them . . . A horde of pirates infests the coasts, and I, for one, am delighted that H.M.S. Gunboat *Kestrel* has taught them a lesson.

Yours truly,

John Kelly,

late master of the schooner *Subahani*

Journals kept by travellers and seafarers in the nineteenth century spoke of the broken coastline just south of Tawau as a pirate haunt and slave market. Conrad wrote that the pirates were 'very fine men, brave, fierce, never giving quarter to Europeans'. The Sulu Islands' capital of Suq had been a fine slave market too, and so had Palawan Island, the long rib of land pointing like a dagger to Mindoro as it lay north-east across the sea above Banggi Island – where the *Straits Hope* now moved in the dark with Captain Barker on her bridge.

Of course, I had read of Joseph Conrad's Sulu pirate, 'the one-eyed statesman', 'the one-eyed crocodile, factotum, harbour master, prime minister to the Rajah of Sambir' – the crafty Babalatchi of *Almayer's Folly* and *An Outcast of the Islands*:

★ ★ ★

He was a vagabond of the seas, a true Orang Laut (man of the sea), living by rapine and plunder of coasts and ships in his prosperous days; earning his living by honest and irksome toil when the days of adversity were upon him . . . He was brave and bloodthirsty without any affection, and he hated the white men who interfered with the manly pursuits of throat-cutting, kidnapping, slave-dealing, and fire-raising, that were the only possible occupations for a true man of the sea. He found favour in the eyes of his chief, the fearless Omar el Badavi, the leader of the Brunei rovers, whom he followed with unquestioning loyalty through long years of successful depredation . . .

Babalatchi, the one-eyed boaster, in conversation with an English seaman, regretted the days of glory:

'Ah, *Tuan!* . . . the old days were best. Even I have boarded at night silent ships with white sails. That was before an English Rajah ruled in Kuching. Then we fought amongst ourselves and were happy. Now when we fight with you we can only die . . .'

It has been convincingly pointed out by Mr Sherry that Babalatchi, the crafty, one-eyed *shahbandar* – harbour master – of Sambir, was partly modelled on a real Sumatran, Jadee by name, who first became a slave of the Sulu rovers and later fought with them. The author of an eighteenth-century book of travels, *My Journal in Malayan Waters*, met Jadee, who by then had given up piracy after an unfortunate encounter with a British man-of-war. One can see that he must have led a grand life. Opium, curry and rice, and wives galore:

'We were all very rich then – ah! such numbers of beautiful wives, and such feasting! – but, above all, we had a great many holy men in our force! . . . such brass guns, such long pendants, such creeses [krisses, or Malay daggers]! Allah-il-Allah! [*La ilah ill' Allah*, is what he meant] . . . fighting cocks, smoking opium and eating white rice.'

There were sultans of Sulu in those days (Sulu City is called Jolo now). For fear of retribution, they were not always willing to embark on wild adventures in alliance with the sea rovers who came and went through their scattered island possessions, but the rovers visited the court or took refuge there when the contest with *orang putih* (the white man) grew too hot for them.

The headlands and forests of North Borneo remain as mysterious and reticent as ever. As I did now, the turbaned rovers had stared at them as they sailed bravely south through these glittering seas to pillage the coast and river settlements of Brunei and Sarawak. These are the shores of the Land Below the Wind, as Malay sailors still call the wilderness of Borneo because it lies ten degrees below the typhoon belt from Japan to Luzon.

The Land Below the Wind! The moon was not full, but it was very bright and the stars were enormous. As we passed through Marudu Bay I saw a beacon ahead; I counted a flash every ten seconds. Islands began to loom up amazingly fast; we were on top of them in no time, as if we were going to ram them.

Captain Barker came up to the bridge in his curiously cheerful 'disaster-ahead' mood and said, 'Sometimes when we get close to an island like this, I wonder if the radar is working.' He sent an officer of the watch below, and murmured to me with a comedian's grimace, 'I don't want idiots up here in this time and place. One idiot's enough.' He pointed to himself. 'Ha!'

Later he said, 'Once upon a time my radar *did* break down, so I stopped and anchored. Bless me, another ship came up behind us and rammed a little island – just there.' He pointed at a group of shadows on the sea. 'Twelve knots. But no puncture or leak, apparently. I asked him if he needed any help from me, but he seemed not to.' He embraced the sea around us with a circling finger. 'Crews don't like to anchor here.' He drew a finger across his throat. 'Pirates.'

Do captains use talk of possible disaster as a verbal talisman against the real thing? Perhaps Barker did, although most of what he said was sheer irrepressible clowning. On sea hazards: 'Luck. You need it all the time. If your ship comes alongside fast in current and you get the anchor down in time – luck! If you don't get it down, crash, into the wharf – *bad* luck. No one's fault necessarily.'

At breakfast next day, present besides Barker and myself were Mr Low, the Chinese radio officer, and the chief engineer, a Scotsman called Ian Guthrie, with a rutted face and bristle of grey beard of the 'torpedo' variety I associate with schoolboys' pre-Second World War sea stories by 'Taffrail', 'Bartimeus' or Percy F. Westerman.

'Nae,' said Guthrie, tackling his herring's roe as a surgeon digs for an appendix. 'No one's fault, necessarily, at a'.'

'Sparks here puts everything down to magic, don't you, Mr Low?'

The radio officer smiled bashfully. 'Tell Mr Young about your mysterious fishing allergy,' Barker said.

'Well,' said Low, 'I'd been a month on a Straits Steamship Company ship and fishing all the time. At one o'clock in the morning our agent came up to me when we were alongside the wharf at Port Dickson, up west Malaysia way, and said, "Why is it that every time you fish here a Malay woman cries in that *kampong* over there?"

'Soon I found strange white patches on my skin, dead white, spreading from my calf to my buttocks. I put ointment on it, and after three days it went away. Next day I threw a line over the side, and this time my hands and arms turned dead white. So I stopped fishing there and then in a panic.'

'Any pain?'

'Only itching. Six months later I tried fishing again, and the same white patches appeared. The third time, a year later, in the Malawali Channel off North Borneo, we were anchored and I'd really forgotten how scared I had been. The same thing happened.'

'You could be allergic to your bait.'

'No, the bait was only cuttlefish. It was something spiritual.'

'Look, try again now. Throw a line over and let's see.'

'No! Never! The fourth time, there'll be no cure.' He shivered. He was perfectly serious.

I was telling Bob Barker about the man who died on board the *Nancowry* on the way to the Andamans, and about Captain Bala's dread of having to bury the corpse at sea or stick it into the freezer to prevent it from putrefying before we reached Port Blair.

The captain had strong views about it. 'Put the body in the fridge? No way would I do that. My word, if the cold-storage people who install these things heard that you'd put a body in the freezer!' He slapped his forehead with his palm, bowled over by the thought.

The morning we berthed at Sandakan I groped my way in the semi-dark up to the bridge. I had rolled out of the owner's bunk at cockcrow in order to see our approach to Sandakan; 'It's like a miniature Hong Kong,' Captain Rankin had said, 'cliffs and islands and a bay. Imposing.' It *was* imposing. By the time the sun was well up we were passing under soaring rock faces that looked as if they'd been carved with a cleaver, and past forests still half hidden in cloud, their tops rising out of early mist like brush-strokes in a Chinese painting.

' "Oh, the monkeys have no tails in Zambo-ang-a," ' sang Barker. 'By God, you'd better not sing *that* old American song when you reach Zamboanga; they'd kill you for sure.'

'What are the rest of the words?'

'I can't remember. It's an old song from the time the American forces were there.'

'Terrible, being out of bed so early,' Barker said cheerfully a moment later, stamping up and down. 'That's the trouble with this life at sea. You get half the amount of sleep most people get and at fifty-five you feel it. If I started life again and had the wife I have now, I wouldn't do it. I would not, sir.'

'What would you do?'

'Well, I'll tell you – my wife would be better off as a housemaid and me as a gardener. Honestly. At least I'd see her all the time.' Barker genuinely missed his wife after all these years of marriage. I'm not surprised. I met her later over a curry tiffin at Raffles in Singapore, an amusing, intelligent Filipino lady.

A personal aura of drama attended Barker on the bridge rather as it does a major actor. He cocked an ear to his ship-to-shore radio like Macbeth hearing the Porter's knock, and when he said irritably, 'The harbour people say they've got no agent's instructions for us. What the hell's going on, I'd like to know. I don't see any bloody tugs, do you?' he might have been Napoleon at Austerlitz demanding to know where Marshal Murat's cavalry was.

'Dead slow ahead. Stop engines.' At the wharf, Barker gripped the forward edge of the wing of the bridge and pushed it convulsively, urging the *Straits Hope* around, moaning to the chief officer, 'She's not coming around, is she? Tell the tug to give her a push.' He gave his final order – 'Finished with engines' – in tones of unforgiving gloom, as if his ship had deliberately let him down, and he was finished not only with the engines and the *Straits Hope*, but ships in general and almost with life itself. But in a moment his usual high spirits returned, and he turned to me proudly. 'We made it,' he said, spreading out his arms. And now he was Amundsen at the South Pole.

Chapter Thirty

As soon as the *Straits Hope* berthed a little way down the coast in the middle of the morning, I told Bob Barker I'd be back and took a taxi to the centre of town. I wanted to be sure that Sandakan was a better jumping-off point to Zamboanga than Tawau further around the coast. If Tawau was better I would have to sail on with the *Straits Hope*. I didn't fancy any more delays.

In Harrisons & Crosfield, one of the firm's senior men, Rodney Jago, who had worked for seventeen years in North Borneo, said doubtfully, 'You really want to cross to Zamboanga by sea?'

'I certainly do.'

'Well, I think Sandakan is a better place to start from than Tawau. Things called kumpits cross fairly regularly, I believe. They're launches – Filipinos in the barter trade run them back and forth. But you'll find out more about it if you come with me today to a Rotary lunch. Are you free?'

I hadn't expected a Rotary Club in Borneo. Nevertheless, at lunchtime I found myself sitting at a long table in a hotel restaurant. I had shaken hands with several Rotarians – an easygoing company of young Chinese businessmen and British trading-company representatives – and had time to read only one of the several jokes on the bulletin of the Rotary Club lying by my plate. 'A mistake', it said, 'is something a virgin and a parachute jumper can only make once.'

A Chinese meal came and went, and once the bowls and chopsticks had been removed an American Peace Corps worker lectured us on the problems of malaria control in the sprawling wilderness of North Borneo; he warned us that the local mosquitoes could impregnate us with lethal cerebral malaria unless we took a new drug whose name I forget. When we stood up to leave, Jago said to a Chinese Rotarian, 'Mr Young wants to cross to Zamboanga by boat. How would you advise him to do it?'

'By air is by far the best way. Of course, the planes don't leave if there aren't enough passengers, but by boat is very risky. I definitely don't advise it.'

'But Sandakan is the place for a boat crossing, is it? Not Tawau?'

'Sandakan is the best place if you *have* to go by sea. Kumpits cross now and then. They're dodging the pirates, you know, but they go. If you insist, go and see a government shipping-control official, Inspector Ahmat, at the kumpit wharf, which is in the centre of town. He should know the kumpit schedules, such as they are.'

'He's near our office,' said Jago, and drove me back. But I thought I'd call on the police before I tried the kumpit wharf. They might not take kindly to a strange Englishman snooping around a wharf full of Filipino kumpits looking for a crossing on a sea so busy with piracy and intrigue. Arrest and deportation back to Singapore would be a disaster.

Sandakan's police headquarters were housed in low, modest buildings near the water. The superintendent, a stout and friendly Malay wearing a casual shirt outside his trousers, offered me a chair and sent for his colleague, the local representative of the Malaysian Special Branch. After I told them my story, the police chief said, 'What have you heard about the situation here?'

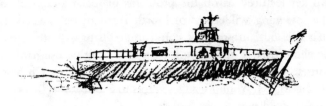

I told him what I'd read about the hijacking of ferries, the boarding of trading vessels, the pillaging of cargoes, the murder of crews, the machine-gunning of merchant ships, and of the battles between the Moro separatist rebels and the Filipino government troops. When I had finished he said that I had more or less got the picture. It was not a good situation, he added.

'What I would like to know before starting out', I said, 'is whether you hear of many cases of offhand unprovoked murder? I mean, boats boarded, throats cut indiscriminately, bodies thrown over the side?'

'Let's say that the Sulu pirates are not as bad as the Thai pirates in the Gulf of Siam. They don't rape *all* the women they capture, and don't kill *all* the men. I can't say I'm sure of the percentage.'

'We're not sure at all,' the Special Branch man admitted. He was small and slightly paler than the superintendent, a Dusun – a man from the indigenous people of North Borneo – with sharp, alert eyes. 'You see, we patrol our waters around here very well, but they don't go very far out to sea – twelve miles at most – before they become Filipino waters. Beyond that we don't know what goes on. We may *hear* this and that, but we can't be certain.'

'You have no direct communications with the Filipino authorities?'

'None at all. So, you see, I'd be worried about your safety out there beyond our control.' I began to wonder if he was making up his mind to prevent me from leaving.

The Malay police superintendent said, 'If you're stopped out there by the Filipino navy bobbing about in a kumpit, they'll ask you why you're travelling in a kumpit; it's illegal, they'll say, for foreigners to travel to the Philippines like this. They'll tell you that if you want to go to the Philippines legally, you should go by boat to Manila, or *fly* from here to Zamboanga. The immigration people in Zamboanga don't let foreigners come ashore from boats – especially from kumpits. You could be a foreign mercenary helping the Moros. You'll have trouble at that end, I expect.' He smiled. 'Still, if you are stopped on the way, it had better be by the Filipino navy and not by pirates or Moros. The navy doesn't kill offhand, eh? It's a civilized world, the navy, isn't it?'

'I have a passport and a visa.'

'The navy wouldn't treat a foreigner *too* badly.' He paused, then added, 'Of course, if the navy took the kumpit for a Moro rebel boat – ah ha! – I don't know what would happen then. They might shoot first and ask about you later.'

'I'd rather you didn't do this,' said the Special Branch officer. Again I felt that a direct order to take a plane was only a breath away.

'I have an idea,' I said quickly. 'Surely the men who know the risks of the crossing best are the kumpit captains, who make the trip quite often. Could I talk with one or two of them who have arrived recently? Would you help me to do that?'

To my relief, the superintendent said, 'Oh, yes, we could

do that.' He rose from his desk, opened a drawer, took out an automatic and put it in his hip pocket. Then we drove to the wharf.

A large shed on the water's edge served as an office for immigration, customs and police officers, and as a waiting room for the crews and passengers of the kumpits arriving or leaving for the Philippines. Five or six large ones lay alongside each other on a seafront reinforced by a wall of solid wooden piles. A kumpit, I saw, was nothing more than a large launch with a roof over much of its deck which provided shade for those beneath it and a sightseeing platform with a low wooden rail for anyone who sat on top of it. A wheelhouse and a small cabin like a chicken coop protruded above the level of the roof, the cabin containing the captain's bunk and three spare ones for a charterer or senior members of the crew. The bunks were narrow and lined with wafer-thin mats. A thin metal funnel protruded from the roof over the deck. The kumpits were made of heavy wood from stem to stern and were about a hundred feet long.

A number of men lounged nearby, and I asked one of them if the kumpits came from Zamboanga.

'Yes, tuan.' He spoke with the Hispano-American accent that distinguishes a Filipino from a Malay.

'Are you from there yourself?'

'I'm living this side now, tuan.'

A young police officer who had joined us and been introduced to me as the shipping-control official, Inspector Ahmat, said, 'He's living here, but he's from Mindanao Island in the Philippines.' Zamboanga is the westernmost town of Mindanao.

I asked the man how many days a kumpit took to cross

the Sulu Sea between Zamboanga and Sandakan. I had an idea it would take eight or ten hours, although I can't think now how I'd invented such an absurd timetable.

'About three days, tuan,' the man said. Three days! It was a long time to be dodging pirates and the Filipino navy. Later, when I looked at my map again, I saw that this was a reasonable length of time, and that I'd misjudged the distance.

At the superintendent's bidding, Inspector Ahmat led us into his office and then went out to the kumpit wharf. Soon he returned with a stocky, dark-skinned kumpit captain with a wide nose and eyes far apart in a long high-cheekboned face. The man shook my hand. He looked strong, but he took my hand in a tentative, lifeless way, not limply, but as if he hadn't done much hand-shaking and wasn't sure how it should be done.

I said to Ahmat, 'Can you speak to him in Malay and then translate?' He laughed; the man couldn't speak Malay, he said. His native language was Tagalog, but he could speak a little English.

To the kumpit captain I said slowly and distinctly, 'How many trips have you made between Sandakan and Zamboanga?'

'Maybe, ah . . .' – he looked up at the ceiling trying to count the times – 'maybe, nine, ten trips.'

'How many times you stopped by pirates?'

'Two times.'

'Only two?'

'Only two.'

'They kill anyone, shoot anyone?'

'No killing. But they have guns. Take money. Take every wallet, everything take.'

'You think pirates attack us?'

He smiled. 'Cannot tell. Sometimes attack, but not always. Sometimes not attack.'

'Two attacks out of ten trips,' I said to the superintendent. 'Not a bad percentage. Makes it a fair risk.' He shrugged, as much as to say, That's your opinion.

To the captain I said, 'Will you take me?'

'What about emi-gra-tion?' he asked.

Ahmat said with a glance at the superintendent, 'No problem here.'

'When do you sail?'

The captain said, 'Saturday.' It was Thursday. The *Straits Hope* sailed on Friday at noon, and the little weekly plane came to Sandakan and returned to Zamboanga on Saturday. I hoped he really would take me on Saturday. If he was delayed or refused me, I might be stuck once more for at least a week, this time in the relative wilds of North Borneo, and would risk missing the connection with Swire's steamer, the *Hupeh*, in two weeks' time in Manila.

'Will you take me?' I repeated with greater urgency.

'I want to consult my companions, please.'

'Of course.'

'We meet here tomorrow 9.00 a.m., okay?'

'Fine, okay.'

'See you,' he said, flashing a gold tooth.

I had checked into the Nak Hotel, the nearest to the kumpit wharf. There, that evening, I sat with the Special Branch officer and pondered the situation. I had returned to the *Straits Hope* and informed Barker of the opportunity with the kumpit, at which he'd muttered dourly that he couldn't say he envied me.

I needed a drink. 'Only Black Label, no Led Label,' the Nak's barman said. I ordered a double.

'On lok?'

'Yes, on the rocks, please.'

John, the Special Branch officer, took a glass of milk. Chinese pop music floated over us from loudspeakers over the bar. 'I think the kumpit captain is going to say no to me,' I said.

'Better for you if he does. Well, I won't go so far as to say that. But we can do nothing for you after you pass that frontier on the sea.'

'I'll survive. If not, I won't blame you. I promise I won't sue you for responsibility if I'm thrown to the sharks.'

John laughed and ordered me another whisky.

To my surprise, when we met next morning at nine o'clock in Inspector Ahmat's office, the kumpit captain said he would take me. He didn't want any money, he added, but could I eat their fish and rice? Of course, I said; again I held out my hand to him, and this time he took it more firmly. A tall, broad Filipino who looked a bit like Anthony Quinn had accompanied the captain, and he, too, shook hands and said, 'Welcome.'

Inspector Ahmat said, 'The captain told me that he can't take you all the way to Zamboanga. You see, what he is doing is illegal – the barter trade, I mean. In any case, his real destination is Cebu City, not Zamboanga, so he wants to drop you off at an island before Zamboanga. A friend of his will take you on from there, he said.'

'I don't much like the sound of that.'

'Exactly. I told him that he must take you right to Zamboanga.'

I turned to the captain. 'Do you agree, Captain?'

He smiled and shrugged. 'Okay. I agree to Zamboanga.'

It was arranged that I should present myself at the wharf

the next morning at ten o'clock with my baggage; the kumpit would sail soon after.

The day was left to me. I took a taxi to the *Straits Hope* and told Barker regretfully that I would be leaving him. I had enjoyed my short voyage and his stories and mock gloom as we threaded our way through the islands at night.

At the head of the gangway we said goodbye. 'Take care,' Barker said. 'See you in Singapore,' I told him.

'You've got a nerve, haven't you?'

'Well, you have to admit that creeping across this sea by plane would be cheating, and it would take much more nerve to explain that away when I get home.'

' "Oh, the monkeys have no tails in Zamboanga, ta tatatatatatatatata *ta* . . ." ' Singing like a music-hall comedian Barker winked and waved as I lugged my cases down the gangway. From the quayside, I took a snapshot of him looking down at me from high up on the wing of the bridge.

'Have you permit to photograph this ship?' A policeman was coming towards me.

'Of course,' I said, and quickly got into the taxi.

A young Englishman I had met with Jago in Harrisons & Crosfield who had something to do with timber and forests had asked me to lunch. As we drove down the main street before turning off to his house in the hills above the port, I noticed the high percentage of Chinese names over the shopfronts and restaurants, although the Chinese are a minority here.

'It's a pity Sandakan was bombed during the war. Not many old houses survive,' my host said.

'It was the same story from Brunei to Macassar. Senseless bombing.'

The Allies, as much as the Japanese, were responsible for the destruction. But thinking of the Second World War reminded me of the puzzle I had discussed with Lindsay Emmerson in Calcutta. The Japanese army came ashore in North Borneo and Sarawak, defeated the British and Australians, and took many prisoners. As elsewhere when they captured British or Dutch or French possessions, the Japanese commanders announced themselves to the local populations – Chinese, Malays, Dusuns, Dayaks, Ibans and the rest – as liberators, brothers come to free fellow Asians from the European imperial yoke. But, having made that point, they began to behave towards the local population they claimed to have 'liberated' with a good deal more savagery than the former European masters had ever meted out. They had the hearts and minds of millions of Asians in their grasp, and then proceeded to treat them like enemies, jailing, torturing, humiliating and beheading them. It was an amazing psychological error, induced by the Japanese 'master-race' attitudes of the time.

Like the rest of North Borneo and Sarawak, Sandakan had experienced the harshness of Japanese occupation, and many of the indigenous Dusuns and Kadusans formed an active underground resistance. It was in this obscure port in 1945 that the Japanese command, seeing that the war was going against them, decided to eliminate the eighteen hundred Australian and six hundred British prisoners of war still alive in Sandakan. They organized a death march through a hundred and fifty miles of malarial swamp and thick jungle to Ranau, a small town at the base of Mount Kinabalu. The prisoners were given a ration of two and a half ounces of rice a day; they supplemented this lethally inadequate diet with snakes, rats – anything they could find. If they collapsed from exhaustion the Japanese soldiers shot them where they lay. Dennis Bloodworth told me that one of the six survivors later recalled that Kinabalu towered over them higher and higher, like a 'gigantic tombstone', as they staggered towards it – and for most of them this was exactly what it was.

Those who reached Ranau heard there of the Asia-wide Japanese collapse and surrender. There weren't many of them. The six Australian survivors – the six hundred British were all dead – weighed, on average, less than sixty-five pounds when loyal Dusuns began to nurse them back to health. Now, thirty-five years later, driving to lunch with this amiable timber expert, it was difficult to imagine such horrors. What was the point?

My host led me into an open verandaed house with polished wood floors. We kicked off our shoes at the door, and from the terrace looked down on a breathtaking view of Sandakan Bay through the spreading foliage of large trees. A European meal was served by his amah, a smiling Muslim girl from Macassar, who moved silently on bare feet. Over the chicken, he told me that his immediate boss had worked in North Borneo for seventeen years, and that his general manager was entering his thirty-fourth year.

'Almost a working lifetime.'

'It is, when you consider that these days people who work in the tropics retire in their mid-fifties.'

Sandakan has a very small British community. I wondered if, à la Maugham, there was much infidelity and 'going off the rails'. 'No,' said my host with a smile, 'these days wives don't seem to do that sort of thing out here.'

Since he was young, personable, available, and so a natural prey for predatory wives with too much time on their hands, he must have known what he was talking about. Perhaps TV diverted their minds into less active channels.

And the Sabah people?

'Well, I'm beginning to think there are hidden depths to them. I had thought that without exception they were the nicest people in the world, but not long ago I went to a bar here – a bit sleazy, I admit – and, without warning, someone smashed a chair over my head. Lucky the chair was made of wood.'

'What did you do?'

'I was too stunned to do anything, but my friend, a big chap with a black beard, stood up and they all scattered. It shows that some sort of antagonism is simmering near the surface, doesn't it?'

'Possibly. But in a dark bar there might be no significance whatever. Just drunkenness.'

'I hope that's what it was, because I like the people of Sabah.'

Knowing he was a timber man, I asked him how the government looked after North Borneo's magnificent forests. In Indonesian Borneo and in Celebes, a cruel and common sight is an expanse of bald mountainside, the result of the ripping out of forest and undergrowth by mechanical grabs imported by greedy foreign timber companies. Once destroyed, rain forests can never be restored.

'It's not as bad as that here,' my host said, 'although there's too little replanting, and generally it's pine trees for quick money.' He added, 'I love being in a forest. I like wandering further and further in, you know, so that I almost get a feeling that I'm lost. I love the sense of wave after wave of huge trees stretching up around me, of the canopies of foliage overhead blotting out the sky.' He laughed. 'Once I was carried away like that, feeling I was quite lost in the wilds, when suddenly I was astounded to hear a police siren, loud voices and shots. Fifty yards on I found timber workers in a camp gathered round *Charlie's Angels* on their telly. That's modern Sabah for you!'

He told me of a government centre for orang-utans near Sandakan, a praiseworthy effort to save those shaggy, sad-faced creatures from extinction.

'They have eight orang-utans there. There's one lovely great male, tame and friendly, except that, oddly enough, he can't stand European women. Attacks them. God knows why.'

Before I left, my host recommended that I have a word with a local old hand, Dr Nigel Lever, who knew about the Sulu Sea area and Zamboanga.

In the evening I had a drink in the Sandakan Recreation Club, where I found Ian Guthrie, the chief engineer of the *Straits Hope*, in the bar in an undershirt and old shorts with the bottoms rolled up. He and Captain Barker were sailing next morning, he said. I felt as if a bridge were burning behind me.

Later, in the Nak Hotel café, Dr Lever, a friendly man and unexpectedly young, gave me the name of a satisfactory hotel in Zamboanga, which he described as a pleasant town, if dull. He had crossed the Sulu Sea only by air, but had two things to say about my journey. The first thing was that patients of his – local seafarers, Dusun, Malay and Filipino – had been made to walk the plank in the Sulu Sea. Walk the plank? 'Usually it's the boats the pirates are after, not you.' It was nice to hear that one could be made to walk the plank and still survive to tell the tale.

Dr Lever's second point was, 'Don't on any account let the kumpit captain drop you at any island en route.'

Alone at the table, I reflected that my situation was a little nerve-racking. Zamboanga was a longish way; I didn't know the kumpit's captain or the crew from Adam; and I had no firm facts about the Sulu Sea. On the Baluchi boat to Karachi and on the Maldivian launch to Malé, the risks mainly involved the weather or fire. Here the weather hadn't entered my thoughts. The monsoon rains were ending. There had been rain today, but nothing like earlier downpours that had washed gaping holes in the asphalted roads. Besides, bad weather might keep the pirates and the Moros in port.

Anyway, I thought, the choice has been made for me. After all, I have chosen travel by sea from Europe to Canton; the Sulu Sea is on the way; I must cross it by boat, not by air; and that is that. The priority is clear, the requirement obvious, and it only remains to get on with it. In which case, instead of worrying about it over cold coffee or nervously prodding the plastic tablecloth with the prong of a bent fork, it's best to go to bed. I went upstairs, stared from the window for a few minutes at the darkened kumpit wharf, read a few soothing paragraphs of Edith Wharton's *The Age of Innocence*, and slept.

In the morning, John of Special Branch came round early with a police friend, and we had coffee and omelettes together. Slicing the toast in two, the friend said, 'These pirates of Sulu are very merciless.'

John glanced at me. 'But they haven't killed any foreigners yet.' This wasn't quite true, recently they had shot the wife of that Norwegian yachtsman and two other European sailors near Jolo Island. Still . . .

'Thank you, John,' I said.

Chapter Thirty-One

A DARK-SKINNED, half-naked man with the shoulders of a wrestler was squatting on the water's edge at the kumpit wharf when I arrived. His slanting eyes stared as though he had been waiting for me. Great activity encircled him. A dozen kumpits had nosed in to pick up cargoes and passengers for Tawitawi or islands further down the Sulu chain. Their shouting crews were humping cargo ashore, passengers squatted chattering among their bundles, merchants and captains of kumpits darted about, impatiently flourishing export permits for boats' manifests or shore passes for themselves and their crews.

I found Inspector Ahmat in his office and gave him my passport, which he stamped at once, muttering, 'If you must go.' Presently the captain of my kumpit appeared displaying his gold tooth. 'We go soon. Please put bag on board.' Ahmat said, 'No stopping at islands.' 'Okay, okay,' the captain answered, and led the way to the head of the narrow tilted plank spanning a ten-foot gap between the bank and the deck of a yellow kumpit loaded and low in the water. 'Carlos take bag,' said the captain, and the dark-skinned wrestler rose from his squatting position and flicked my heavy suitcase on to his shoulder as if it were an empty cardboard box.

I shook hands with Inspector Ahmat and teetered after Carlos down the bucking plank to the heavy bows of the *Allimpaya*. The boat was stacked almost to the gunwales with thick bundles of branches, each of them perhaps an inch wide and of a dark reddish colour. I wondered what

the cargo could be. Carlos led me down under the roof and pushed my suitcase and the smaller bag beneath and behind these bundles so that they were well hidden – a sensible idea, as it turned out – and then was gone with an effortless leap from the deck to the top of a small water tank, from there to the roof and back to the wharf, like Tarzan springing from one jungle branch to the next.

The captain, I was glad to see, was not one for hanging about. From the roof-deck he watched Carlos and other men casting off, and soon the *Allimpaya* nudged out between the other kumpits into the bay, her engine put-putting parallel to the straggling town and the misted high ridges of forest. Before long, her nose pointed to the slabs of cliff and an island like a small Gibraltar crowned with trees and a lighthouse at the bay's entrance. Small steamers lay at anchor, and launches and outriggers powered by outboard engines sped between them. At the wharf where Bob Barker had berthed *Straits Hope* two days before was a sad, empty space.

★ ★ ★

I had slung my binoculars around my neck and kept the Polaroid in my hand. There were several packs of film in the pocket of my anorak, which I hung over one of the two wooden chairs on deck. It was shortly to become an object of almost murderous dispute.

As we came abreast of the miniature Gibraltar, families were visible picnicking on a small beach, and one or two children waved. When we had left them behind, a lumbering motion of the kumpit signalled our emergence from the bay into less protected waters. We were in the Sulu Sea.

'Why do you enter the Philippines through the back door?' a dull tenor voice singsonged at my elbow, and I turned to see a tall man of about thirty-five with unusually pale features, more Chinese than Malay or Filipino. 'I am Haji Daoud,' he said. 'I live in Zamboanga. Are you from America?'

'No, from England.'

'Why are you going to the Philippines?'

'I am writing a book.'

'But why you go to Philippines illegally through the back door?'

'It's not illegal, is it? If you come to England you can enter any port you choose if you have a visa.'

'But Zamboanga is not a port like that. There are many troubles there. Have you heard of the Moros?'

I asked Mr Daoud what he thought about the Moro rebellion and how the Moros were faring against President Marcos's forces.

'I think the war is dying,' he answered. 'The fighting is very hard for the Moros. They are in jungles, and their families suffer. Who will pay if they are sick? Who will look after their children and wives?'

He'd mentioned 'many troubles' in Zamboanga. What else did he mean?

'Zamboanga is a violent city. Many grenades explode in crowds, in the market, in the movie houses.' He shook his head sadly. 'I'll give you advice. The bad time for grenades is between six and seven o'clock every evening, when the streets are full, so go out in the city only at eight or nine at night. In any case, you will have trouble with the immigration people in Zamboanga.'

I promised to remember his warnings, but I wasn't going to worry about Zamboanga now; it still seemed a long way off.

'Do you know what "Haji" means?' he asked, and when I said I knew it meant that he was a Muslim and had made the pilgrimage to Mecca, a glimmer of satisfaction appeared on his calm Chinese face. 'I was a Catholic as a boy and was taught by the fathers; that's why I speak English well. Later I read about Islam and was converted. My conversion stopped my heavy drinking. I drank very much at one time. I am a Muslim now, so I no longer drink.'

I said I supposed he was Chinese by birth. 'Half Chinese and half Eurasian,' he said. 'But Filipino by nationhood, of course.' He added that he traded between Zamboanga, Jolo and Tawitawi, shipping Coca-Cola in his own kumpit to Tawitawi and bringing back copra. He had visited Sandakan to search for spare parts for his kumpit.

In the wheelhouse the captain was drinking a mug of coffee with an elderly Filipino helmsman. They stared out like human prisoners in a hen house with glass windows. Carlos–Tarzan had changed from brief, ragged shorts into a sarong, and he and two other Filipinos had sidled up to listen to our conversation. Carlos interrupted in a high voice that contrasted with his deep chest. 'What time ees eet, surr?'

'Ten thirty,' I said, showing him my watch.

He peered at it. 'Lucking thirty minutes beefore eleven?'

'Yes, lacking thirty minutes to eleven.'

'I am Carlos,' he said and produced an identity card, which said 'Licensed for barter trade only. Issued in Zamboanga City,' over a smudged photograph.

One of his companions thrust out an open palm for me to shake. 'I'm crazee man,' he announced cheerfully as I took it. He was about twenty, rather skinny, and certainly looked zany, a comedian with a swarthy face and a wild long black moustache. He had a very wide mouth, and his lips drew far back to display acres of teeth and gums in a smile that made you grin in return. The blue and yellow sweatband around his head, the red towel around his neck like a kerchief and a yellow shirt gave him something of the look of a very humane and jolly pirate. 'I'm Jan,' he cried. 'Eef you forget my name just theenk of the crazee one!'

'I don't think I'll forget you, Crazy One,' I told him, and he gambolled about the deck with delight, returning to pull up a shorter, plumper, shyer man of about his age.

'Thees my friend Jalah,' he said. 'Veree good friend, same school in Jolo. Haji Botu's Inst-it-uto of Arr-ts in Jolo. Jalah wants to see you telescope.'

I handed Jalah the binoculars, and he scanned the deck through the wide end with a baffled expression until I turned them round for him and pushed them up so that he could see the fading line of trees on the horizon behind us.

While Jalah gazed at Sabah, Jan introduced another member of the crew. 'Thees ees Armando,' he said, holding a small grubby sparrowlike youngster by the shoulder. 'He

ees second engineer. See, he ees black. His name ees Small-But-Terrible. Please call him that.'

'Hello, Small-But-Terrible, how are you?' I said, and he and Jan fell into each other's arms, howling with laughter. 'Armando ees kung-fu champion,' said Jan when he had sufficiently recovered. To demonstrate the truth of this, Small-But-Terrible threw himself into a succession of acrobatic contortions, striking the air with the sides of his hands and kicking out like Bruce Lee, the kung-fu film star. I could see that travelling with Filipinos would be an enlivening experience. I liked them already.

The Haji had watched these shenanigans with a tolerant smile. Now he said, 'There is food.' I followed the others to the stern section of the roof, where lunch was waiting in the form of a bowl of cheap, almost powdery rice, a plate of strips of dried fish and a saucer of raw red chillies. We ate with our fingers, standing under the blazing sun and washing down the dry food with water from chipped enamel mugs. Like the Bedouins of Arabia – who would have expected a better meal than this – the Filipinos crammed the rice into their mouths in big handfuls, and the meal was all over in five minutes. The captain asked, 'Food okay?' and I said, 'Food is fine.' I would lose weight on the *Allimpaya*, but I hadn't the least objection to that.

The others washed their mouths as most Asians do after a meal, swilling water around their tongues, using their fingers as toothbrushes to rub their teeth, and spitting over the side. Then they delicately picked remnants of dried fish from their teeth with matchsticks or splinters of wood torn from the handrail.

I took my mug below and sneaked a mouthful of gin from the bottle in my bag, but for all my stealth I didn't escape Jan's curiosity. As I swallowed the gin, his big front teeth, partly veiled by his ragged moustache, appeared at my elbow as they were to do constantly, at all hours, during the whole voyage. Jalah, his less ebullient friend, was just behind him.

'Do you drink wine?' Jan asked.

'Sometimes.'

'What ees the name of your wine?'

'It's called gin.'

'It's called jeen-jeen,' Jan informed Jalah.

'No, just gin.'

'Give me leetle beet.'

'Jan, it's *haram*, forbidden to Muslims.'

'Just a leetle,' Jan begged, putting on a pleading expression. I gave him a sip and he made a face, then laughed at Jalah. 'He knows *haram*. You hear heem? He says *haram*!'

I was not, I discovered, the only non-Muslim on the *Allimpaya*. The chief engineer, an elderly man called Jesus with a puffy drinker's face (though I may do him an injustice; perhaps he never touched a drop), was a Catholic, as were José the cook, Armando (Small-But-Terrible) and Ernesto, a beefy deckhand capable of as many Tarzan-like leaps about the boat as Carlos. As for the old helmsman, who later developed a passion for wearing my anorak during his night watches, I never learned his name or religion. Apart from the nine men who formed the boat's complement, Haji Daoud and I were passengers pure and simple. The tall, saturnine man I had seen in Inspector Ahmat's office with the captain, and who resembled Anthony Quinn, was also aboard. He had chartered the *Allimpaya* and was accompanying his cargo to Cebu City, a port far beyond Zamboanga on the route to Manila. Anthony Quinn, the Haji, the captain, Jan and I were to share the wooden structure that opened off the wheelhouse and contained five small, narrow bunks.

Jesus slept in some obscure corner near his engine, and I think his assistant, Small-But-Terrible, did too, burrowing beneath the cargo like some small rodent. The rest of the crew slept haphazardly below, on or near the cargo of red, flaky bundles, which took up most of the space under the roof-deck. These, the Haji informed me, were a valuable cargo of tanbark, the bark of the mangrove. The dry cylinders were reduced to powder in Cebu City, he said, and mostly exported to Japan to give colour to floor wax or shoe polish. In the Philippines tanbark gives a mellow whisky colour and mild tang to the local coconut toddy called *tuba*. I wondered whether any other more dubious cargo was hidden underneath the bundles.

By mid-afternoon we were still in sight of Sabah on the starboard bow as we edged down towards the Sulu Islands. I presumed that for safety's sake the captain wanted to keep Malaysian territory in sight as long as possible.

'Tawitawi Island is ahead on the right side,' said the Haji. 'They export copra, seaweed, fishes and tanbark there. They cultivate seaweed too because, without it, the island economy would suffer. You see, the coconut trees do not produce much. It is a damp place with many wild hogs.' I remembered that Tawitawi was the headquarters of Conrad's fictional one-eyed Babalatchi of the enterprising and merciless Balanini pirates. Further to the right, round a now-invisible headland, lay the town of Tungku, the home of the pirates defeated in 1879 by HMS *Kestrel*.

The weather was perfect, the sun hot, the sea blue, but by evening there was bad news. It was obvious that the *Allimpaya*'s engine was failing. Sometimes it puffed and panted like a dying asthmatic; sometimes it faded completely. First, *Al Raza* in the Arabian Sea, now the *Allimpaya*, I thought with exasperation, each at the worst possible time and place. Sumar, the Baluchi, pranced back into my memory, puffing out his whiskers and cheerfully booming '*Allah karim!*' I could have done with his cheerfulness here.

Our speed was soon down to only three knots an hour from a possible seven or eight. Speaking as a kumpit owner himself, the Haji said he believed the trouble was a slipping clutch. 'If I were the captain,' he said, 'I would steer to an island – there are many just out of sight – and anchor there for the necessary repairs. Also, I would not take this course; nearer the islands is quicker.'

But when I laid a pencil across my map, it showed that the shortest distance between Sandakan and Zamboanga was along the course we were following at present. Besides, I asked the Haji, weren't there pirates on those islands? And, although he had just recommended this alternative, he now exclaimed, 'They are full of pirates! I have been attacked by pirates there myself. Luckily, we beat them off with grenades. Two pump boats – outriggers, you know – came at us very fast. The pirates fired rifles – automatic rifles, *tut, tut, tut, tut.*' He imitated automatic fire. 'Oh, I was very scared, but we put out all our lights and went full steam ahead.'

'How fast?'

'Seven miles an hour, not much. Then I threw a grenade. That makes a big noise, you know, and it worried them. You have seen pump boat? It has problem coming alongside another boat. The outrig makes it very difficult to come close alongside quickly. While they try it, you drop grenades on them. Very dangerous for them.'

'Do we have grenades?'

'I don't think. No.'

'What if they'd boarded you?'

'Cut throats of us all. They cut throats to save bullets. Maybe they sink kumpit, too, maybe not. Maybe only take cargo – they like barter goods. Last month two barter pump boats were shot *to-tal-ly*, everybody dead. What do you say? – "Dead man tells no tale," eh?'

The Haji joined the captain for evening prayers. Kneeling far apart from each other on the roof-deck, they bowed towards Mecca. Carlos and Jan were wandering about as usual, and I didn't see anyone else praying.

When the Haji returned, he told an even worse story. 'One year ago, my two brothers were massacred in their kumpit. They smuggled five hundred cases of Champion cigarettes, and they were killed for them. In my idea the Filipino navy killed them because soon navy men were selling the cigarettes in Jolo market. Very bad. Who else could have killed them? Smugglers may rob other smugglers, but they never kill each other. *Pirates* may rob smugglers and *sometimes* kill them. The navy kills smugglers and pretends it was fault of pirates. That is not good.'

It certainly was not. To the list of human hazards of which I was already aware – pirates, smugglers, the Moro rebels – were now added what I had regarded as a deterrent force, not a threat: the Filipino navy.

But it wasn't the Filipino navy that stopped us; the Moros got to us first. Early next morning a pump boat came alongside, a narrow, nippy outrigger with a Japanese outboard motor in the stern, and seven wild and agile men scrambled aboard the *Allimpaya*. Even now I am not sure where they sprang from.

Anthony Quinn peered out of the cabin window and Haji Daoud muttered, 'Savage people, savage people.' I couldn't see Carlos or Small-But-Terrible, and I supposed they were on the deck below, trembling amid the tanbark. The captain was politely assuring the Moros that we were helpless, harmless people with nothing more than a failing kumpit and eighty tons of uninteresting cargo.

I sat on the roof-deck rail in the sun and watched them. Three or four of them had twisted coloured cloths around their heads from which long hair dangled to their shoulders, and some had straggling hair on their lips or chins. They wore a variety of coloured shirts, and several had old military khaki jackets with buttons missing and inked doodles of hearts, hands holding daggers that dripped blood, or topless women. Some wore tight khaki trousers, stained and much worn, and scuffed basketball shoes or jungle boots with thick soles. The older ones were flat-faced men

with short grey hair and empty, dangerous eyes. Old or young, all were dark-skinned from the island sun and had high cheekbones, wide noses and slightly slanting eyelids. They spread out over the kumpit, and the older men immediately went into conclave with the captain, who never for an instant permitted a wide smile to leave his face. I could see his hands spread and his shoulders moving up and down as he talked earnestly with them, his head bent attentively to what they were saying. Then they disappeared below the level of the roof into the belly of the boat.

It wasn't long before three of the younger Moros snooping about clambered on to the roof. They stopped dead when they saw me sitting on the rail; the last thing they'd expected to see was a white man. Then they slowly came forwards, edging up to me without speaking – so surprised, I suppose, that they didn't know what to say. I waited until they were very near, and then said, 'Hello. How are you?' I put out my hand, and the nearest Moro took it cautiously as if making an experiment and said, 'You who? American?'

'No, English. You from Tawitawi?'

'From Jolo. You from England? Where you go?' He

spoke with great hesitation; obviously, his English was limited. There were bulges of what I took to be guns in their hip pockets, and two of them had long, big-handled knives in their belts.

'I go Zamboanga.'

'Zamboanga? You . . . ah . . . selling?'

'No, not selling, not merchant. Writer, writing book.' I mimed someone scribbling.

'Ah, book?'

Another Moro asked. 'Magazine also?'

'Sometimes.'

'Yes. All kinds.'

At last the first Moro grinned. 'Very famous, yah?'

'No. Not famous. Very poor man.'

He sat on the rail so close to me that our shoulders touched, and they all stared at me as if I were an exotic and possibly dangerous species of animal in a zoo.

'Very poor, yah!' He laughed. 'So go in kumpit, no go aeroplane.'

'That's right. A poor writer travelling in a kumpit. And you are – Moros?'

'Yah, Moro.' He watched for my reaction.

I continued to smile. 'Moro people very brave.'

He asked, 'England people say that? In England people know about Moros?'

'In England not many people know. But in Singapore they know about Moros. Moros are famous.'

'You go Manila before?'

'Yes.'

'Why you go Manila?'

'I go everywhere. A writer must go everywhere.'

'Sure. True.' He thought for a moment, looking at the

deck as if he saw something unpleasant there. 'Goddam Marcos government no good. Goddam President Marcos.'

One of his companions echoed. 'Goddam fuckin' Marcos government,' and spat over the side.

The man next to me had spotted two Malaysian fifty-dollar notes in the breast pocket of my shirt; I had forgotten they were there. Now he tapped the pocket with his finger and asked, 'Malaysia dollar? Show me?'

I took out the two notes, each worth ten pounds sterling, and he took one and examined it. 'You give me?' he asked politely.

'Yes, I give you that. This one' – I flourished the second fifty-dollar bill – 'I keep this one. I need it for Zamboanga. Otherwise no money.'

'Oh, yes,' he nodded understandingly, one traveller to another. 'You travel with leetle money. Maybe someone steal. You find your money from bank in Zamboanga Ceety, yah?'

'Yes. Carry very little money. Maybe pirates come on the kumpit. Any pirates here in Sulu Sea?'

The other two said something that sounded like '*Mundo?*' and he answered, 'Yeah, *mundo*,' and they said something else.

Turning to me, he translated, 'My friends say, yah, pirates here. *Mundo* means pirates in our language, Tausuq language. But Moro not pirate. Moro fighting goddam Marcos. You scared?'

'Scared?' I said. 'Why scared? You and me are friends.'

'Ha! you *good* man.' With a wild grin he threw an arm around my neck, jerked me down to his shoulder level and kissed me loudly on the cheek. 'Good man. Friend,' he informed the others with his arm around my shoulder.

'Friend,' he confirmed to me. 'My name Musa. Your name?'

'Friend,' I agreed and told him my name with considerable relief. Had I defused at least these three? I studied my new friend. All three of them were in their twenties. He had a longish, pleasant face with an easy, lopsided grin and there was a two-inch scar over his left eye. His eyes were strange: glowing green, the colour of the base of a green bottle. It was a nervous face, constantly and subtly changing its expression as the nerves chased around under the skin. Like the others, his hair was long and pinioned by a rough headcloth.

All three wore ragged khaki jackets. On the T-shirt under his jacket one of them had drawn a crude sketch of a Moro in camouflaged uniform with a sub-machine-gun over his shoulders, a panga – a long jungle machete – in his belt, and his girlfriend, a large, busty girl in a short dress, at his side. 'That is Ibrahim,' said my new friend. He pointed to the third man, who wore the same costume as the other two but whose hair fell longer than theirs, well below his shoulders. 'That is Ali.' Ali had a bad-tempered expression, thick liver-coloured lips, and mean eyes in a pudgy face. He was tall and tough, and I didn't care for the look of him; I hoped my friend, as I now thought of Musa, would want to control him. I suspected that a Moro's mind could change rapidly from friendly to suspicious to hostile. It was not easy to foresee what might alarm or enrage them.

Suddenly a sharp call from below roused the three from their contemplation of me, and they ducked under the roof-deck and disappeared. Soon Jan and the Haji joined me, Jan jumpy but giggling, the Haji apparently calm in the recollection of Allah.

'You make friend with Moro, yah?' cried Jan. 'You make friend with very Muslim man – yah, yah – with Ayatollah!' Thereafter Musa, the friendly Moro with the bottle-green eyes, was known to Jan as the Ayatollah.

The Haji said, 'Moros take arms from Brazil revolutionaries. FN rifles and pistols. Their chief is living in Libya with his wife. They want independence for Sulu, Mindanao and Palawan Island, all Muslim areas. But, of course, all that is too small for independence. It has nothing. I am a Muslim also, but I think independence is nonsense and Moros are too savage.' The Moros made no show of guns; in retrospect, I realize they had no need to – and no desire to be caught flourishing weapons by a patrol launch of the Philippine or Malaysian navy.

An Oriental palaver had begun below that lasted most of the day. The Haji left me now and again to sit in on it and listen to the negotiations that pursued their desultory way through the heat of noon. Anthony Quinn, whose cargo was at stake, joined the captain in the talks. Jesus, the engineer, had stopped the engine, and in stifling heat we lay motionless except for a gentle rolling. Now and then a Moro or a member of the crew clambered on to the bows and urinated over the side while the spasmodic murmur of voices, and sometimes laughter, continued. Small-But-Terrible and Carlos bobbed up occasionally with anxious expressions to wave or wink at me. I sat on the roof and tried to read. It was not easy. I couldn't stop wondering what all the talk below was about, and whether we were going to be made to jump overboard and swim to the nearest island. I was relieved, therefore, when at last the Haji clambered up to report on the talks so far. 'The Moros say the captain must take them eight or ten hours away to some island near Tawitawi, so they can return secretly from there to Jolo Island, their base. They say there are many navy boats around Tawitawi. Too dangerous for them, but this kumpit can go there freely.'

I didn't like the idea of sailing in a kumpit loaded with armed Moro rebels into a region of remote islands infested with still more Moros and gunships of the Filipino navy. 'What is the captain saying? Will he take them?'

'Captain says he cannot take them because he has only enough fuel and food for three days to Zamboanga, not enough for two extra days at sea and seven more men to feed. He must convince them this is true or maybe they kill him next time he come this way, so he tries to convince them peacefully.'

As time wore on, an absurd rhyme entered my head and refused to budge:

> It's a long way to Zamboanga,
> It's a long way to go,
> It's a long way to Zamboanga
> And the nearest land I know.
> Goodbye, Tawitawi,
> Farewell, pirates' lair.
> It's a long, long way to Zamboanga,
> And my heart's right there.

I varied the time by trying to invent lines to follow. 'Oh, the monkeys have no tails in Zamboanga,' but I couldn't concentrate for long.

Big, muscular Carlos and his friend Ernesto brought up bowls of the powdery rice, dried fish and red chillies, and Moros, passengers and crew gathered round and concentrated on eating. The Moros had caught a fish on the way; one of them fetched it from the pump boat floating alongside and they shared it with us. Captain Amin asked me, 'You okay? Not too hot?' I replied that everything was okay. The older Moros looked greyly at me without saying anything. I suspected that they probably didn't speak any English; I had noticed them asking Musa about me.

After the meal and the usual mouth-washing and spitting, the captain, Anthony Quinn and Haji Daoud led the older Moros below once more to continue their palaver. I dragged a crude bench into the shadow of the wheelhouse, but had no sooner sat down when the ill-tempered young Moro called Ali loomed up. His brows bent into an intimidating frown and his lips like strips of raw liver pouted furiously. Abruptly he pointed to my wrist. 'Geeve me watch,' he said fiercely, 'geeve me jacket also.'

Chapter Thirty-Two

IBRAHIM, THE MORO with the sketch of the rebel and the girl on his camouflage jacket, stood at Ali's shoulder. As Ali's face scowled, his was blank. My friend Musa, the one Jan had called the Ayatollah, had vanished.

'Geeve me watch,' Ali ordered again. 'Geeve me jacket.'

'Give me, give me, give me – what's all this "give me"?' I said, smiling.

'Geeve me watch.' He was gruff and impatient.

'You give me your shirt.'

'I want watch,' he said angrily through the curtain of his hair.

'No, I want *your* shirt – oh, *and* your boots.'

'You no understand. I want watch and jacket, too.' He was scowling, but was also beginning to look baffled.

'No, Ali,' I said slowly, emphasizing my words but still smiling. 'I' – I pointed to myself – 'want' – I pointed to him – '*your* shirt and *your* boots.'

He looked really bewildered by now, perhaps as much by my smile – I was holding it as steadily and nonchalantly as I could – as by my unexpected and apparently unworried parrying of his threatening finger. Always smile: I had learned that lesson years ago in the Congo, where the penalty for dropping your grin, even for an instant, in the face of nervous soldiers or tribesmen, was slow death with both legs hacked off above the knee with pangas.

Ali turned to mutter something to Ibrahim, receiving nothing more in return than a shrug and a glazed look. To my relief, I saw Musa, the Ayatollah, approaching. His green eyes opened wider when he took in the situation, and wider still when Ali said something angry to him, pointing at me. Smiling, the tic fluttering his eyelid, Musa said quietly, 'How about your jacket?'

'How about it, Musa?'

'Ali says your jacket ees very good. In the for-est veree good.'

'I need my jacket, Musa. The kumpit is very cold at night. Maybe there will be rain in Hong Kong.'

Musa nodded. 'Hong Kong rain . . .' He turned the notion over in his mind. But Ali was not going to be put off. He took a step towards me and bellowed, 'How abo-o-o-out your jacket? How abo-o-o-out your watch?'

'How about your boots?' I asked politely.

'Ho-o-ow abo-o-out—?' His breath was on my face and I saw his hand working round to his hip pocket. 'Ho-o-ow abo-o-out your jacket? . . . Ho-o-o-ow abo-o-o-out—?'

'Ho-o-ow abo-o-out . . .?' I chanted back, and felt my heart thump when, his fury at its peak, Ali opened his thick lips for a still more terrifying 'How about . . .' – the last, I felt sure, before he drew a gun. Then Musa acted with a diplomat's aplomb that was quite unexpected. Twitching like a copper-coloured St Vitus, he threw an arm over Ibrahim's shoulders and pushed and wrenched at him, forcing him to sway back and forth. Ali was ignored as the two Moro desperadoes began to rock to the rhythm of my ludicrous chant, 'How about . . . How about . . . How about.' High spirits possessed them, and an upsurge of love for the universe overflowed even to me. A moment later, Musa had flung his other arm across my shoulders – symbolically, I felt – demonstrating an Anglo–Moro treaty of friendship from which only the churlish Ali was now

excluded. 'How about ... How about ...' we yelled
between Musa's and Ibrahim's gurgles of mirth like three
juvenile drunks. But, of the three of us, only I was acutely
aware of what in effect it was that we were chanting: an
uproarious incantation against murder at sea – my murder.
So, although nerves made it an effort to draw enough
breath to keep the chorus going, I made the effort.

The incantation worked. His mouth open, Ali gazed
appalled at this unprecedented spectacle, frowning, puzzled,
shaking his head like a bull that has entered the ring to find
not one matador but three, and all of them engaged in a
mad fandango. For a long minute he considered the situation, biting fiercely at the skin around his fingernails,
glaring at our vaudeville act; then, as the Ayatollah put out
a hand to bring him into the group, he capitulated. In a
moment, from having been a potential killer of a man
with a desirable watch and a delectable anorak, he became
someone who could have been mistaken, if not for my
bosom friend, at least for a fond acquaintance. Such is
the erratic character of the descendants of old Babalatchi's
people, the corsairs of Sulu, the lawless scourges of every
sea from Cagayan de Oro to the Carimatas.

Musa's arm embraced my neck from one side, Ibrahim's

pungent armpit cupped my shoulder on the other. We jiggled and chanted, 'How about . . . How about . . .' until the afternoon sun became too much for all of us and we flopped, still laughing, into the shade. Ibrahim and Ali, his frown evaporated in the scalding light, sprawled on the deck, their arms and legs spread out and overlapping, and I collapsed on the bench. Musa slid down beside me and, without letting go his armhold on my neck, swivelled his khaki legs so that they lay heavily across my lap. Then he released my neck and lay back, resting his head against the arm of the bench. In the sudden animal abandon of their limbs the three Moros suggested leopards in human form, hunters in the shade of a forest.

In his relaxed position, Musa said, 'You see many wars and fighting?'

'About fifteen wars in twenty years.' I was including coups d'état and revolutions, but only two or three – a small cheat.

'Why you not come see the Moros on Jolo Island?'

'I'm too old for that now.'

'Too old at thirty-eight, thirty-nine?'

I didn't correct that estimate. 'Also I'd be scared,' I said.

'You scared?' Suddenly he swung his feet to the deck, swelled out his chest and put on a warriorlike scowl. 'You no scared. We no scared. We all brave men. How can you be scared after fifteen wars?'

'I think everyone is scared when bullets go ppz-ing, ppz-ing.' I punched the air around his head with my finger. 'Aren't you?'

Musa's nerves chased across his face and the tic twitched the lid of his green left eye. Indignation leaked away from him like air from an old tyre. 'Yeah,' he said, lying back

again. 'Okay. When bullets come I scared. We all scared.'
He paused, and then his crumpled smile reappeared. 'But
I have thees. Look.' He reached into his shirt and drew out
a plastic cord that hung around his neck with a small piece
of bone threaded to it: a talisman.

'Also we have' – he jabbed his finger skywards – 'Allah.
You know Allah?'

'I know about Allah, yes, of course.'

Ibrahim and Ali had been whispering and giggling.
Now Ibrahim said something, and Musa began to laugh.
'He says you so beeg, so maybe have beeg steek?'

I was certainly taller than them. 'Stick?'

'Yah, you know, steek?'

He pointed to Ibrahim, who sprawled languidly massaging his groin. 'Ibrahim nearly lose his steeck by bullet.
Now all time he hold eet for safe-tee.' He began to wriggle
out of his jacket. Across his shoulder, near the neck, a
shining sheet of skin stretched over a deep hole three inches
long. 'See,' he said, 'hole from bullet.'

Ali also had something to show. Lying back, he pushed
his pants down over his hips to reveal a wide, fresh-looking
scar beneath his navel where a bullet seemed to have passed
clean through his abdomen. So all three had been wounded.
'Goddam Marcos,' Musa muttered. 'Sonofbeetch.'

When the Moros came aboard I'd had time to push my
Polaroid camera in through the wheelhouse window. (My
Pentaxes were locked in the metal suitcase under the
tanbark.) Now I brought it out and, as I had suspected they
would, Musa, Ibrahim and even Ali leaped up in delight.
Their pleasure increased when I explained that this camera
could deliver pictures on the spot. They were beside them-

selves clamouring for attention. They demanded pictures singly, in pairs and as a trio; standing and sitting; always frowning or at least set-faced, never smiling: a smile would not befit a posing warrior. I must have pressed the camera's button twenty times and had the pictures snatched from my hand and flapped wildly in the air to aid their development. I had to keep instructing them – 'Not so roughly, Musa! Keep your fingers off the colour!' – but most of the pictures came out well. Like the Bedouins of Arabia, they often preferred to hold the photographs upside down: it seemed to give them a better view.

Informed of the Polaroid, the other Moros suspended their negotiating with the captain and hurried to join us on the roof. I took their pictures, too, and they passed them about from hand to hand, pointing and laughing at each other's likenesses. Even the older, wary Moros with cropped grey hair and lustreless eyes begged me for more, holding up a forefinger to show that they wanted individual shots.

First Musa had saved me from the ruffian Ali; now the Polaroid made me the friend of all the Moros. They patted and hugged me, wheedling and begging for more pictures. In his latest paroxysm of affection, Musa grabbed my neck again and bumped his bony forehead against mine repeatedly and painfully. When finally one of the grey-haired Moro chiefs clamped my hand in his knobbly one and said, 'You good man,' I felt that an immediate danger had receded – at least, any personal danger. The more general one that remained lay in the question of whether the Moros would force the captain of our crippled kumpit to carry us into the lairs of a daunting variety of armed and homicidal men.

The captain's delicate but unshakeable insistence on our

shortage of fuel and food played a role, no doubt, but I think it was the state of the *Allimpaya's* dilapidated engine that finally saved our skins. The oil-spattered old 'driver', Jesus, cranked the engine into wheezing life once or twice to show the Moros that mechanically we really were not up to any diversion whatever. No gauntlets could be run in the *Allimpaya*, it was clear. 'The captain told them again and again that we might break down properly at any time,' Haji Daoud recounted to me later. 'Properly' was the word and Jesus certainly rose to it. Few people anywhere can have been invited to bear witness to such mechanical decrepitude. Like the old trouper she was, the *Allimpaya* gave a heart-rending and utterly convincing demonstration of a crippled kumpit taking her last staggering steps before terminal collapse. I hope that Jesus, as stage manager, received some sort of reward at journey's end, but I doubt it. We moved through the sea like a dying turtle, making no more than two knots. This decided the grey-haired Moro leaders. Still smiling, but not as broadly now, they began to wind up their discussion by turning to more general things: the state of trade, the prices of contraband and allied subjects. There was no more talk of diverting the kumpit, Haji Daoud said.

Meanwhile, over their heads, while Ibrahim and Ali lolled on the deck, Musa had been chatting with me. By now he was quite at ease, leaning his head on my shoulder and massaging my knee in a platonic, dreamy way, as someone might pass the time with petit point. He asked about the world I had seen. Was England a town in America? Was Sarawak part of England? (His Balanini pirate forebears would have known the answer to this. The Sulu fleets of twenty to a hundred ships raided the coast all the way down to Sarawak every year when the north-east monsoon wind, the Pirate Wind, began to blow.) Were there Americans ruling in Singapore? How many Americans lived in Morocco?

I began to think that it could really be true that Libyan agents had been helping the Moros. Colonel Qadhaffi would have liked to fortify them on nourishing tales of a despotic American rajahdom over Singapore and Morocco. But, when I asked Musa what he thought about Libya, he said he had only vaguely heard of such a place, and Musa of the twitching face was not a man able to disguise a lie. I don't think he had any idea where Singapore was, much less Morocco. I incline to believe that the Moros asked about Americans simply because, like all Filipinos, they are more or less entangled in that deep attachment for the United States that is sometimes called the 'little brown brother complex'.

Even these young Moros' conception of Islam had a typically Filipino rock beat. 'Goddam communists not like Islam,' Musa said at one point. When Crazy Jan, giggling, rashly thrust under my eyes a magazine open at a two-page spread of the most lurid pornography, I feared a volcanic outbreak of Islamic ire that another twenty Polaroid exposures might not succeed in appeasing. I needn't have worried; Musa slowly flipped a few glossy pages of by now well-fingered photographs depicting what might at first glance have been close-ups of sea urchins or attacking man-eating spiders. Some he tilted sideways or even upside down for a better view; then he passed them down to Ali and Ibrahim, saying with a laugh, 'Veree loveful. In Jolo, no have.'

'In Jolo, *haram*.'

'Yeah,' he sighed. '*Haram*, no have.' He fell to massaging my other knee with a clownish, melancholy expression.

Ali and Ibrahim reacted to the dirty pictures in much the same unexcited way. Lazily tumbled together cheek by cheek, they peered at breasts and vaginas, indicating the more brightly coloured parts to each other with a finger, like two tourists idly tracing the outline of a foreign country they had no immediate hope of visiting. Only Jan showed any emotion; he bore away his magazine with the haughty umbrage of an artist whose latest work has received less than its due. I felt no sympathy for him; a Muslim himself, he had been absurdly thoughtless. It seemed to me very lucky that the pictures had not aroused the Moros' anger. Jan might have been walking the plank by now. I would have been sorry to see the splash, but he would have brought it on himself.

An hour later the Moros sailed away. Musa gave me his full name and an address on Jolo Island. 'We een forests very of-ten,' he said, 'but please send letter.' Ali, Ibrahim and the other Moros shook hands and moved to the side of the kumpit. With them went my fifty Malaysian dollars and my binoculars, the haunted ones with the spotted lenses; Jan had produced them from somewhere and Musa immediately wanted to handle them, and having peered through them at length, decided he couldn't live without them. 'They be veree good een for-ests,' he said.

'All right.' I didn't want to risk another squabble, certainly not with my protector. Better that they leave us as quickly and quietly as possible. Volatile as they were, they would be dangerous until they vanished over the horizon.

Anyway, I wasn't sorry to see the last of those disturbing stains.

'You veree friend,' Musa said. He shook hands, pressed a cheek against mine, gave me his side-slipping smile and a twitch of the left eyelid under the scar, and followed the others over the side into the pump boat. The outboard motor started with a readiness that the *Allimpaya*'s engineers, Jesus and Small-But-Terrible, must have envied, and the outrigger, with the Moros bunched up between its narrow gunwales, skittered away like a water boatman on the calm surface of the sea. Soon its wash and the two lines of flecked water under the outrigs unreeled behind it as if it were laying a trail from the kumpit to the horizon ahead. The elderly Moros sat low in the boat and hardly glanced back. Jan had mounted to the *Allimpaya*'s roof-deck and was waving and shouting, 'Ayatollah, yah, Ayatollah, so long,' and pointing at me. Musa's strange bottle-green eyes turned towards me in the stern. He and Ali, the troublemaker, raised two hands over their heads while Ibrahim shouted, 'Steeck-steeck.' When I waved, most of them made some gesture of farewell.

Then we turned back to the world of the kumpit. Metallic bangs rose from the direction of the engine. The captain said, 'Now we go to Zamboanga. First we stay here short time, make good the engine. Not long.' It was late afternoon. Soon Carlos the wrestler came bounding up with a mug of coffee as if he had delivered us single-handed from the Moros. 'Double Dragon coffee,' he said, showing his very white teeth. 'Veree shtrong.' He had stripped to ragged shorts and had knotted a white towel around his head.

When the Moros were on board, the crew had made

themselves conspicuously scarce while the captain, Haji Daoud, Anthony Quinn and, from time to time, Jesus, the engineer, had been locked in earnest discussion on which all our fates depended. I had hardly seen anything of the others except at the midday meal. Jan and Jalah had taken refuge in the shade of the wheelhouse, making one or two sorties, such as the tactless flaunting of the porno magazine. Heaven knows where Carlos, Ernesto and Small-But-Terrible had been hiding. They had all been very scared, I realized; and I didn't blame them. Small-But-Terrible could hardly be expected to take on a complete boarding party of Moros, however expert his kung-fu. As for Carlos, I saw that, for all his muscles, narrow hips and agility, he was endowed with the sweet, timid and pacific nature of Ferdinand the Bull. He would never raise a finger against a living soul if he could avoid it, although, if he ever did, he would surely break someone's neck by accident. 'Moros gone away,' he said, watching me drink the coffee. 'They no keel you.'

'Yes, all gone.'

Gone out of his mind as well as his sight, apparently, because he then continued as if our earlier conversation hadn't been interrupted, 'Look at theesh.' He drew from the waist of his bathing suit a piece of paper and handed it to me. It was a letter written in English on part of a lined page from an exercise book that had been much handled and folded. It read: 'Dearest Carlos, this is to remember me when you are in far places,' and was signed 'Loyola'.

'You have a Christian girlfriend and you are Muslim?'

'Oh, yah,' Carlos agreed indifferently. 'Never mind.'

Yet another example, I thought, of the tolerance of seagoing men. 'Very pretty?'

'Veree prettee. Her nose eesh too shmall.'

'*Very* small, not *too* small.'

'Yeah. Too *shmall.*' Now that danger had vanished over the horizon, he wandered happily about the roof-deck singing, softly in his surprising falsetto, 'You urr always un mah ma-a-a-ah-nd.'

The repairs continued until at last Jesus mastered the slipping clutch. We had bobbed and swayed gently on a fair swell but in sticky heat; now the *Allimpaya* set off again at a much better speed, creating its own breeze.

'Weather will not be bad,' the Haji assured me. 'Sulu Sea well enclosed by Palawan Island, Mindoro, Mindanao and Sulu Islands. Palawan is a very long island. People have bows and arrows there, though they are friendly. They'd be most astonished to see you.' As usual, the flame-flecked sunset brought a cool breeze, and I joined the Haji under the roof where he had spread a bedroll. I lay down on a folding canvas bed I found there that belonged to big, moustached Ernesto, who did not need it; he was at that moment asleep and lightly snoring in the arms of Carlos on a similar bed a few feet away. They were naked except for sarongs. Through half-closed eyes, Carlos was gazing abstractly at the ceiling, smoking a cigarette. ' "Oh, kees me aga-ee-ee-n before you go-o-o," ' he crooned, not to Ernesto, I judged, but to Loyola, whose too-small nose, from his lovesick expression, he evidently beheld affectionately in his mind's eye.

The Haji said, 'See, Carlos is singing. Filipinos are very jolly. Only the Moros are angry and dangerous. People are very fed up with Moros. They came to Jolo, which was peaceful; the army came too, and many were killed. Moros are not popular, but of course Marcos, too, is not popular in this region.'

He lit a Champion cigarette and switched his thoughts to religion. 'Do you know what attracted me to Islam? The prayers. They are so beautiful, and they mean you must wash five times a day. It is good to wash five times a day, and also to be reminded of God five times a day. If you pray five times a day you have less time to do something bad.'

'Or something good, for that matter.'

The Haji ignored that. 'It is good to talk to God five times a day. Also, if you go to the mosque, you must take off your shoes. In Catholic church, no, so the church is full of dirty things you bring in on your feet. The smell is horrible. It can put you off your prayers. Don't you find that? Another thing: in Islam women pray separately from men and wear long dresses, which is very healthy.'

' "Kees me, oh kees me aga-yeen . . ." ' Carlos crooned sweetly to Loyola, despite the arm that slumbering Ernesto had thrown across his chest.

'Why healthy?'

'Because you are away from temptation. If you see the legs of women with short dresses, your mind is distracted from God. That, of course, is bad.' He thought a moment. 'Now I know through Islam the purpose of life.'

'Tell me.'

'To live for the praising of God.'

But the Haji was not a fanatic; he confessed he felt temptation too much. 'Japanese and Chinese girls are best, very beautiful. Lucky in Philippines we have all kinds of girls. I have wife *and* girls. But in Jolo everybody very jealous. If your finger touches a girl's hand, trouble – a bullet!' Formerly a heavy drinker himself, he had no objection to my gin, although his attention was inevitably drawn to my occasional clandestine swigs by the delighted cries of Jan and Jalah, who pranced around proclaiming, 'Gaveen is drinking wine. Give me leetle jeen–jeen.' The Haji ignored this, and was pleased to be able to practise his English, which evidently had once been relatively good. 'Shakespeare's language,' he announced, 'is not very good. Not good, I mean, according to the best rules of English. Some of his writing is very slum English.'

Shakespeare used slum English, I suggested, when he wanted to convey the language of slum characters. But the Haji was not one for discussion so much as for the release of his long pent-up beliefs. '*Romeo and Juliet* is the best of Shakespeare's plays,' he announced to the waves. 'It has the best rules of English language. "Tomorrow and tomorrow and tomorrow . . ." At school we read Chaucer, Poe, Longfellow. "To His Coy Mistress." Sometimes Wordsworth.' Just then the face of Small–But–Terrible appeared disconcertingly upside down at the corner of the roof. He shouted something down to us, and the Haji stood up. 'Time for food again.'

That night I couldn't fall asleep, and spent hours on deck or in the wheelhouse. Jalah slept on the wheelhouse floor on a thin mattress of towels, with a knapsack as pillow. The first night after the Moros had gone, Carlos took the wheel but, because he kept falling asleep, Jalah and Jan made Double Dragon coffee – very weak because there wasn't much of it, they said.

It had been very rough, they told me, coming to San-dakan from Zamboanga six weeks before. No one could hold the wheel at all easily except Carlos, though apparently even he had suffered. 'Terrible rains and winds,' said Jan. 'Crew all sick. Carlos very hurt in his body. He drink coffee for three days to keep awake. If not, maybe we hit stones. Sometimes kumpits hit big stones in the sea. *Big* stones. So!'

'Are there rocks here?'

'Rocks, yah.' But I think he meant small islands.

To pass the time, Jalah, who spent much of the day on his bedroll and emerged at night like some nocturnal forest creature, said, 'You know Magellan?'

'Yes, he discovered the Philippines.'

'Yeah, right. He discover us, that's why Philippines so famous. You want to hear famous song about Magellan?'

'Yes, please.'

He began to sing a kind of wobbly calypso:

'In March 12, 1521, Philippine was discovered
   by Magellan,
They were sailing day and night across the
   beeg ocean
Until they saw small Limasawa Island.
When Magellan landed in Cebu at noon,
Rajah Humabon welcome on the shore. . . .'

'This is not real words,' interrupted Jan. 'Onlee like the words, yah?'

'Rajah Humabon makes them veree happee,
All people will baptize under the church of Christ,
And that's the beginning of our Catholic life.

'But Lapu-Lapu is veree bad
To drive Magellan to go back home.
When the battle began at noon,
Bow and arrow versus cannon,
Lapu-Lapu is veree bad, he drive Magellan
To go back home.'

Here Jalah broke off and, with a loud laugh, began to chant:

'O, Mother Mother
I am seek,
Call the doctor veree queeck.
Doctor, doctor, eef I die,
Tell my mother do not cry.'

'That's song for keeds,' said Jan. 'But Lapu-Lapu was King of Mactan who keel Magellan. Maybe we go to see Cebu Ceety and the island of Rajah Lapu-Lapu.'

'I hope to see that,' I said.

A night or two later I was alone in the wheelhouse with the old helmsman whose name I never learned. His eyelids refused to droop shut like those of Carlos; he stared dutifully, with a wild surmise, at the compass (the only navigational aid we had), or else dead ahead, shading his eyes against the dim compass light – looking, I supposed, for islands, fishing boats or pirates' pump boats. The *Allimpaya*'s long nose dipped and rose. The moon was full and beautiful. By 1.00 a.m. it was cold, and I draped my towel over my shoulders like a shawl; the old helmsman had my anorak. The snores of the captain and Anthony Quinn came to us

573

from the cabin that opened out of the wheelhouse. Small-But-Terrible bobbed up from time to time with glasses of watery coffee – loathsome stuff, which forced me to plead with him: 'Small-But-Terrible, more coffee, please, in goddam water.'

'Fineesh co-ffee.' He would grin back and dive below.

The old helmsman said, 'Mon-kee boy. That boy is small mon-kee.'

Just as I was thinking seriously of sleep, the Haji appeared from the cabin, apparently refreshed by several hours of rest. 'Who is the Queen of England?' he asked me. 'Has she power? What is her name?'

'She is called Elizabeth.'

'The first Elizabeth or the second? And the Prince Charles? Which Charles will he be?'

When I told him, he paused and thought for a moment. 'I saw a very good movie in Zamboanga. *The Prince and the Pauper*. A very good movie. Mark Twain.'

Suddenly there was Small-But-Terrible, tiptoeing out of the wheelhouse with the rest of the Double Dragon coffee, about as furtively as a wicked uncle in an old melodrama. Coffee fineesh, indeed. He had the gall to wink at me.

My eyes began to close. It was too late for an appraisal of the British royal family or Victorian melodrama.

Chapter Thirty-Three

ON THE FOURTH day Jan informed me that the coffee was 'fineesh'. 'Ask Small-But-Terrible why,' I said. Yes, he knew about Small-But-Terrible pinching it, but this wasn't the problem; the kerosene had run out and we had no way of heating anything. Who could drink cold coffee?

'Four days from Sandakan and no more kerosene?'

'Ah, sheep dancing like thees, kerosene go like thees.' He made a spilling gesture. 'I fall down, kerosene go.'

I said to myself, 'The engine is weak, the kerosene is all spilled and there's little food. How careless can such born sailors be?'

I was irritated and baffled. The *Allimpaya* had been six or eight weeks in Sandakan – long enough, surely, to buy spare parts for the engine and enough kerosene for emergencies like Jan spilling it, long enough to procure a better variety of food than mouldy rice and strips of dried fish. Malay sailors would have concocted a fiery stew with tomatoes, chillies and onions; Chinese sailors would have cooked noodles and made soup. The Tamil boy cooks on the *Herman Mary* had whipped up a curry in high seas, and the Starling Cook had done the same in even higher seas on the launch to Malé. The only explanation that made sense to me was that the *Allimpaya*'s owners were a very stingy lot who paid their crews a minimal food allowance for the sake of a trifling increase in profit. Still, no one was complaining, and Carlos's beefy physique showed every sign of being well nourished. But suppose we were shipwrecked for a week on one of Jan's 'big stones'?

There was a bigger blow to come. A few hours later the captain came to me and, leading me to the bench on the roof-deck, drew me down beside him. He looked embarrassed.

'I not can go to Zamboanga. Not can go because police take me. This kumpit not legal to go Sandakan to Zamboanga, understand, surr? Veree sorree. If go, I lose kumpit – maybe confiscate. Big problem for me, big loss to owner of kumpit.'

'All right. What do you want to do?'

'More better we stop at small island. Then I put you on small pump boat which take you to Zamboanga.'

This was just what Inspector Ahmat, Dr Lever and others in Sandakan had advised me against. Anything could happen to you on a godforsaken island, they had warned me.

The Haji now arrived to explain things. He said, 'Not you only will get down at the small island. I also and the charterer will come.' This was reassuring; I didn't believe the Haji would be a party to my murder.

'I also will come,' the captain said with a comforting flash of his gold tooth.

'We'll take the pump boat to Zamboanga,' the Haji said,

'leave you there, finish our business and return to kumpit. The captain also. Then we and the kumpit sail on to Cebu City.' Safer still.

'When do we arrive at the small island?' I asked.

'Noon time today.' So we'd be in Zamboanga that evening? 'If we have good luck.' We would have taken five and a half days from Borneo to Mindanao, but we still had to reach the island and find a boat to ferry us to Zamboanga. There the immigration officers awaited me, but they were the smallest worry of all; they might imprison illegal immigrants, but surely they didn't kill them, did they? The Haji said he doubted it.

Through the same dazzling azure screen of sea and sky, the *Allimpaya* pushed on. Standing on the roof with Carlos an hour later, I saw, one after the other, a chain of small islands – first a tiny blur, then an outline of palms, finally a white beach encircling an islet like a collar.

When we were close to the islands and were about to slip between two of them Carlos pointed ahead and snatched at my arm so roughly that I shouted, 'Hey!' His mouth hung open, his slanting eyes had widened with fear, and he quavered, '*Pirate*'.

From the cover of one of the islands a pump boat had appeared and was sliding at right angles across our course. It was still three hundred yards away and low in the water, but I could see the heads and shoulders of three or four men in her, sometimes obscured by the water as the boat rose and fell and her speed tossed up spray.

'*Tut-tut-tut-tut-tut*.' Carlos mimed a man firing a machine-gun, then stabbed a finger across his chest to indicate bullets perforating his lungs. 'Go down,' he advised.

If Carlos, a local seaman, was scared, I had every right

to be, too, but I preferred to seek refuge in the wheelhouse. There I found the captain reading a magazine while Ernesto steered. 'Captain,' I said, resisting a strong inclination to lie on the floor (my imagination envisioned the sweep of machine-gun bullets splintering the wooden walls of the wheelhouse), 'Captain, see that boat? Carlos says they're pirates.' I looked as calm as I could.

We had no binoculars now; I pictured mine hanging around the neck of green-eyed Musa as he played deadly hide-and-seek with the Filipino marines on some jungly island. We stared at our fate. The captain, Ernesto, Jalah (who had roused himself from his bedroll at the word 'pirate') and I fixed our eyes on that splinter of wood moving low and fast in the sea and now immediately ahead. The more we stared, the more sinister the three or four bent figures in the boat became. I thought I could see the barrels of guns resting on their huddled shoulders. The power of suggestion is immense. Three minutes went by. Then, 'No pirate,' said the captain, smiling and returning to his magazine.

Feeling limp, I went out on to the roof-deck to find Carlos. He was hiding in the shade of the wheelhouse and looked up at me with such a penitent expression, like a pet dog conscious that it has done something wrong, that I couldn't help laughing. 'No pirate,' he said dimly. 'Only look like pirate.' We watched the pump boat, which had stopped and turned sideways as the *Allimpaya* passed it. Four islanders were unfolding fishing nets into the water. When they waved, I waved back, filled with a relief topped only by the recent departure of the Moros.

★　★　★

The island group we were aiming for was beautiful. Robert Louis Stevenson might have written *Treasure Island* about the sugar-white sands and soaring palms we soon saw on every side. Among these pocket islands, the captain said, we would rendezvous with the pump boat that would take us to Zamboanga. The *Allimpaya* crept slowly between islands like turquoise sea jewels, fragments of paradise floating in water as clear as pale-green glass that shimmered as if sprinkled with a million silver mirrors. Small houses on stilts came into view between the palms, and men in sarongs mended nets on the sea's edge. Outriggers with one or two paddlers hurried across the water or lay in rows on the beach.

'Jish eesh So-and-So Island,' said Carlos (I hesitate to give the place its true name and betray its inhabitants). He wrote its name on his palm with my pen. 'See? Four hour from Zamboanga.' He held up four fingers.

'Will you come to Zamboanga, Carlos?'

'Noa. I shtay this kumpit. Maybe shee you Sheebu Sheetee.'

Soon we nosed in to an island shore where a large conglomeration of houses with atap roofs straggled out through the trees to a brilliant white beach. Here our appearance caused a sensation. Men and children poured out of the trees or houses down to the water's edge to meet us; behind them in the village, women smiled from windows or verandas and held up their babies. Five or six pump boats came swiftly alongside, and the captain scrambled into one to go ashore.

'Come to see island?' he called up to me.

'Of course.'

Wading ashore barefoot through warm shallows, I might

have been Magellan landing at Cebu or James Brooke at Kuching. I may have been the first white man the population had seen. About two hundred Sulu islanders had already gathered on the beach, and others were running up. They surrounded me laughing and shouting, and led me to the village. 'What are they shouting?' 'They say "White man, white man," ' the captain said. 'Very simple people, but good. They are speaking Tausuq, language of Sulu.'

A tumult of infants and teenagers ran giggling behind me, and young men, jostling each other, took my elbow to guide me towards a group of houses to which several outriggers had been drawn up. Quickening his pace, the captain disappeared behind the houses with three islanders who clearly knew him and weren't in the least surprised to see him, and I was left with the mob. Most of the men were naked to the waist and wore brightly coloured headbands and sarongs tucked up like shorts; others wore T-shirts, and a few had American-style caps. They flowed around me like a bronze flood, parting ranks almost under my feet as I walked slowly up the beach. Chattering excitedly, they raised their hands parallel above their heads to indicate how tall they found me; I knew what it was like to be Gulliver in Lilliput, to be a giant in paradise.

Even in paradise the heat was infernal; the midday sun was barely tolerable, beating down like a hammer. I pointed to the sun and shook my head saying, 'Too hot,' and the crowd immediately swept me into the shade of the trees and houses. Here it was cooler, but in that confined space the noise echoed and the crowding increased, as did the twitching of inquisitive fingers at my shirt and trousers. Luckily, a sort of discipline was soon imposed by an unex-

pectedly dramatic intervention. A middle-aged villager in a red baseball cap and an undershirt strode like a pagan high priest into the uproar and raised his arms over his head for attention. A relative silence fell, interspersed with giggles and murmurs, when he put back his head, opened his mouth as though about to eat a bunch of grapes and roared like a sea monster, 'Go-o-o-*ddam*, go a-wa-ay, go-o-o-*ddamit*.'

If he had fired a musket over our heads, the effect might have been the same. The chatter, when it began again, was much reduced. Clearly, the man in the baseball cap was respected both as king and clown; the frown he had worn soon faded, and he began genially ordering boys hither and thither. One ran happily away to return minutes later with cold drinking water in a calabash; others shinned blithely up the nearest coconut palms, sixty to eighty feet high, cutting down several large coconuts. Slithering down the smooth palm trunks, they lopped the tops off the coconuts with pangas the way one beheads a boiled egg, exposing a pint or so of cool, semi-sweet water. Presented with five or six coconuts, I took one and passed the others around to the crowd.

We didn't stay long on Treasure Island. Still surrounded by islanders, I threaded my way below the windows and terraces of houses packed with cackling women and saucy smooth-skinned girls with big eyes, whose Muslim smiles, despite the all-seeing eye of Allah, were about as bashful as a wink from Doll Tearsheet. On the beach beyond I found the captain inspecting our outrigger sitting in the shallows. He soon completed his negotiations; the outrigger was quickly launched into the clear shallows, and its driver cranked the outboard engine, which started without a cough and took us out to the *Allimpaya*. Even then the mob followed us, swimming or in boats. The sea around the kumpit seethed with the damp skins and white teeth of dog-paddling islanders who surrounded us like a chorus of sea dryads. Carlos and Ernesto, minimally assisted by Small-But-Terrible, who badgered me too late for a final Polaroid, handed into the pump boat my luggage, followed by a large, heavy case belonging to Anthony Quinn and a wooden box of the Haji's tied with string.

Even Jan had decided to come. He stepped shakily into the narrow waist of the wobbling boat, followed by the two others and the captain. I waited to be last, wanting to say goodbye to those nocturnal creatures I'd hardly seen: Jesus, the engineer; José, the cook who had boiled the appalling rice; and Ernesto of the small beard and big moustache. Jalah gave me his address and a hug; Carlos offered a bone-grinding handshake and a quick, brotherly butt on the cheekbone with his head. Small-But-Terrible couldn't resist a last demonstration of kung-fu, letting loose a kick that misfired and smacked Carlos on the back of the thigh. The last close sight I had of him was the soles of his feet as he rolled about the deck, pushed there impatiently by Carlos as easily as a fighting bull repels an undersized matador.

The kumpit fell away rapidly behind us. The crew stood waving on the roof-deck – Small-But-Terrible seemed to be climbing on Carlos's back – and the chorus of islanders waved and called from the water or the beach, their sarongs as bright as a border of flowers.

I had little chance to wave back. As soon as the driver opened the throttle, the pump boat began to buck and dip, and large sheets of water descended on us. We sat very cramped, our knees drawn up, our buttocks balanced on the sharp edges of the baggage. Soon, when the boat roared out of the sheltered water of the islands, we became wet from our hair to our toenails.

Chapter Thirty-Four

Don't you go, don't you go to far Zamboanga,
Where you may forget your darling far away,
Don't you go, don't you go for if you leave me,
How can I without you stay.

O weep not, my dear Paloma,
O weep not for I'll return.
O weep not, my little darling,
I shall remember and I shall yearn.

With feathers of loyal dove, dear,
With red ink of my warm blood,
I'll write you my burning love, dear,
My own Paloma so true and good.

Song of the Filipino Scouts

IN THE PUMP boat we were plagued once more by
engine trouble. Three times our headlong progress
through the spray of a confused sea was halted by that
familiar choking splutter from the outboard in the stern.
Three times our driver, stripping down the engine to
hammer in its bowels, disclosed a murky tangle of rusty
metal clearly far from its first youth. And three times, after
half an hour of rocking from one outrig-bar to the other
while waves broke over gunwales no more than a foot
above the surface, the engine unexpectedly returned to life
and we battered our way onwards towards Mindanao.

At each breakdown, Mindanao was still a long way out

of sight. The captain had calculated the pump boat would take at least four hours to reach Zamboanga. With the stops, I thought, it would take longer: an uncomfortable thought, since we were all soaked to our underwear. To keep to our course, the pump boat had to drive across the grain of the main swell, so that the outrigger scuttled like a crab diagonally up and down waves as high as bungalows, tilting steeply and taking aboard slabs of green water.

It was not so bad for the driver in the stern or for Captain Amin, who had cannily taken a seat beside him, huddling in a mackintosh and peering out from a cap with a green eyeshade. Nor was it hard on Crazy Jan, who crouched just behind me in an outsized yellow oilskin, from time to time yelling into my ear, 'Ooah, thee sea ees sonofbeetch,' or 'Ya-a-ah! I want to pee-pee.' The Haji beside me shouted, 'Fasten seat belts,' as the pump boat careered like a roller coaster into a deep trough; once, to reassure me, he said, 'Don't worry. We will be in a Zamboanga nightclub by six o'clock.' I wondered what the Haji would find to do that was not *haram* in a Zamboanga nightclub.

I was mainly concerned that my anorak, rescued from the *Allimpaya's* old helmsman, was adequately protecting the films, cameras and notebooks in my metal suitcase. This water treatment might be exactly what was needed to rust the tiny tumblers of the combination locking system, leaving me with a portable but extremely heavy and unopenable safe. Water coursed down my neck, roared in my eardrums and filled my shoes, but the charterer, Anthony Quinn, was getting the real battering. Whenever the boat nosedived into the heart of a wave, a wall of water seethed over him as if he were a bollard on a breakwater. He must have been very cold, as well as half drowned, for he was covered by nothing but his dripping jeans, a T-shirt, a towel twisted around his head like a turban and another around his neck. He showed amazing fortitude. Every now and then he unwound the towels, wrung them out, and then replaced them, hardly less sopping wet, around his head and neck to await the next ducking. For three hours he emerged from successive waves shaking his head and laughing.

Small craft crossed our path; sometimes outriggers, their crews only intermittently visible in the rise and fall of the waves; sometimes vessels with square striped sails of pale- or cypress-green, sky-blue, white, yellow and an autumnal brownish gold – colours an artist might have chosen – transfigured by the strong rays of the afternoon sun.

At last the high whale-back outline of Mindanao emerged through the spray. 'One hour and half more,' Jan shouted in my ear. When the pump boat bucked and plunged into the strait that separates Mindanao from Basilan Island, now a long ridge of land on our right, the waves diminished. In another half-hour we could see woolly forest shapes and the small white cubes of the city of Zamboanga.

A large sea snake wriggled past us, twisting its loathsome coils of yellow and chocolate-brown stripes under my elbow; it must have been six feet long. 'Keep arms eenside boat,' called Jan. But, when three shining fins sliced through the water like headsmen's axes, he couldn't contain his glee. – 'Ja-a-a-a-aw!' he screamed to me, pointing, 'Ja-a-a-a-aws!' and leaped up, so that the captain had to grab the tail of his yellow oilskin cape and pull him down again.

'I want to urinate,' the Haji said with prim urgency, looking around as if selecting a spot to aim at. I shook my head, shouting, 'No, no,' and he thought better of it; he would certainly have toppled overboard. Accustomed to acrobatic motions at sea, Jan had earlier tried to overcome the barriers of the oilskin, a zipper and tight underwear in an attempt to pee in a wildly rocking boat, but in vain, and had had to give up. The Haji retained a pained expression until we landed on Mindanao.

On Mindanao, not at Zamboanga. I was surprised to see the high outlines of Zamboanga City far off to our left as the pump boat approached a shaggy shoreline disfigured by a couple of low buildings and a few nondescript houses. I craned my neck to the huddle of oilskin in the stern and asked the captain, 'Zamboanga, no?' A tooth flashed, and the Haji answered for him, explaining that the captain didn't dare be seen in Zamboanga harbour. He was not meant to be anywhere near Zamboanga. The police would ask him where he'd come from, what I was doing with him, and all manner of awkward questions, the true answers to which would land the lot of us in jail accused of espionage, smuggling, insurrection, or all three. 'So we land,' the Haji said, 'some miles from Zamboanga, and find transport to take us into the city by road.'

'We will find a jeepney,' said the captain from the depths of his yellow mackintosh. Ah, a jeepney: a nice idea. A jeepney is an exclusively Filipino phenomenon: a long-bodied jeep arranged inside like a bus, gaily and garishly painted and chromed all over its outside in the style of a fairground merry-go-round, with silver models of horses adorning its hood and loudspeakers booming heavy rock music at the passengers. When I boarded that jeepney, I would know without any doubt that my arrival was a reality. I could be nowhere else but in the Philippines.

★ ★ ★

Our landing lacked style. Once out of the boat, which quickly turned away to sea and disappeared, I found myself floundering on the edge of a shoreline of mud under some ramshackle wooden houses on stilts. The others were wading ankle-deep to a track behind the houses, splashing through water black and thick with mud, oil and unnameable substances. We were in a tiny horseshoe-shaped bay with two warehouses, a couple of rusty chimneys and piles of wooden planks nearby – some sort of timber yard.

Jan met me ashore, puffing, his jeans caked with black slime to the knee, carrying my small bag, teeth and gums agape with joy, and the captain, the Haji and Anthony Quinn followed. We all looked like walking corpses washed up by the tide, but to the people watching us from the houses we were all old friends. Many of them exchanged greetings with the captain.

Near the road we stopped. 'I leave you now,' said the captain. 'Go straight to hotel. Immigration closed already. Open tomorrow 8.00 a.m. No worry.' He shook hands and left us. The rest of our bedraggled group of four, our shirts and trousers sticking to our bodies like cellophane, stood by the roadside and waited. Not for long. Within three minutes I heard the sound of a discotheque in full swing rapidly approaching. The thundering beat, the falsetto voices and howl of over-amplified guitars seemed to envelop us from the surrounding banana groves like a stereo system turned carnivore. Around a bend, heading towards Zamboanga, a jeepney appeared like a moving carnival, gleaming with silver horses, festooned with young Filipinos, shuddering with the beat of the rock.

The driver braked hard, raising dust. 'Hey, man, you bin for a swim?' he yelled. His assistants leaped down, grabbed my bags and shoved them under the legs of a full load of Filipinos, sitting seven a side, who dragged us aboard, shouting loud words of welcome, showing no resentment as our sodden bodies squeezed them uncomfortably.

'Hiya, Joe, you goin' to Zamboanga Zeety?' asked the young man next to me. He nursed four mangoes in a basket. Jan leaned over: 'I'll pay to Lantaka Hotel, okay?' he told me. 'I go down before you. See you tomorrow at hotel.'

'You from America?' the young Filipino asked.

'England,' I said.

'Oh, that's very fine. My name ees Jerry Abdallah, schoolteacher.' He held out his hand.

I was wet and feeling cold, and the coating of road dust stuck to me like a clown's make-up. An angry Immigration Department awaited me, and, for all I knew, a Zamboanga jail. I didn't give a tinker's damn. Nothing on earth mattered. I wanted to hug these cheerful Filipinos who, without turning a hair, welcomed a shivering, dust-caked scarecrow of a foreigner from the sea. I had crossed the Sulu Sea under the Pirate Wind without having walked the plank. My throat was uncut, my notes were intact, and I could have kissed them all.

We bumped and rattled, half deafened by bass guitars, past handsome wooden bungalows in gardens vivid with tropical flowers, between avenues of slender coconut palms beside a sea that looked as pretty as a picture postcard. I stared at the horizon, imagining those invisible islands and the grey-faced Moro elders; hearing Ali growl, 'Geeve me watch, geeve me jacket also'; remembering Musa the Ayatollah, his knees across my lap, his bottle-green eyes, his tick and lopsided grin. I saw again the low, cunning shape of the mysterious pump boat sliding out of the islands across the *Allimpaya*'s bows, and felt the twist in my stomach when Carlos whispered, '*Pirate.*'

The jeepney rocked and swayed past more banana trees interspersed with roadside establishments called Dennie's Place or Ernie's. The Philippines! I felt cold, tired and exultant.

The Haji and Anthony Quinn got off in a suburb, nodding to me briefly. I saw they were nervous and now found me an embarrassment. Not so Jan; he knew friendship and had never heard of embarrassment. Before he hopped away he called to me loudly, so that every passenger could see and hear, 'Tomorrow I come, yah?' and darted off with a flash of teeth. Even that wasn't the end of him; in the middle of the street, his legs black with slime from knee to foot, and despite carts bearing down on him from both directions, he stopped and waved.

Before we reached the centre of Zamboanga, the jeepney developed a puncture. While three young Filipinos were changing the tyre, shouting, laughing and pushing each other, Jerry Abdallah, the teacher, introduced me to three girls who were fellow passengers. 'These are teachers also,' he said, and they smiled and bowed. 'You are quite safe. I will take you to your hotel. Please take one of these mangoes.' He passed the bag. 'They are for my wife.' I accepted his offer to guide me to my hotel.

I could hardly wait to get there. My face was burning, my eyes smarted whenever they caught sunlight, and my back ached from the hours of pounding in the boat and the half-hour in the jeepney. When we stopped again some way from the hotel, Jerry Abdallah said, 'You are too tired. I'll get a taxi. Wait here.'

The Lantaka Hotel is on the seafront, and the balcony of my room gave me a beautiful view of the strait that separates Zamboanga from Balisan Island, and Mindanao from the Sulu Sea. I looked again at the sea I had crossed; already it was becoming hard to believe I had done so.

BIENVENIDOS, said the notice on the back of the door. I felt thirsty; my system was still full of ocean salt. 'Time for a beer, Jerry?'

'Okay. It is still early. My wife is not yet worried.'

'Two San Miguel beers, please,' I said over the phone to room service.

'Family size or regular size, surrr?' crooned a sweet female voice. 'Family size.'

The beer was a reward for Jerry Abdallah's kindness and a celebration present for myself. When he had gone, I pulled back the bedcovers, threw off my damp clothes, bounced once on the unfamiliar springy softness, and fell into the deepest sleep I'd had since I'd left the Nak Hotel in Sandakan.

'I can hardly believe you have come by kumpit from Sabah. It is very risky, very unwise. I would say never do that again. Many bad things can happen.'

'I won't,' I promised.

'You came from Balisan Island?'

'I'm sorry. You won't mind if I don't tell you the names of the places we passed through, or the name of the kumpit or her captain. I don't want to make mysteries, but you know . . .'

'Of course, I understand. You are right. People could make much trouble if they knew. No sweat.'

It was the morning after my arrival and I was in the

local office of the William Lines not far from the hotel. Anticipating immigration trouble, I had decided to enlist the aid of Victor Chiongbian, the president of William Lines, whose number in Cebu City Kerry St Johnston had given me in Singapore. Thanks to Kerry's letter, Chiongbian would be aware of my impending arrival in Zamboanga, and I might need his help if the immigration authorities decided to play it rough.

Across a desk on the first floor I had introduced myself to the William Lines representative in Zamboanga City, Frank Manching. He was a young man, friendly and willing to help. He had called in one of his experts on local shipping, and I told them my story. The shipping expert, older than Manching and a local man, looked as if he knew every island and pirate from Mindanao to Labuan. 'You are quite right,' he said again. 'Names only make much trouble. Let's not talk of names.'

Manching said, 'Mr Victor Chiongbian wrote me to expect you by plane from Sandakan. It is surprising you come by sea.'

'Do you think I should report to immigration now?'

'Definitely. I will come too. It will take five minutes.'

But it took considerably longer. In a dark, narrow, ground-floor office with wood-panelled walls and a concrete floor, an elderly immigration officer flicked through my passport, lifted a stamp and said, 'You come by the plane from Sandakan?' When I told him by ship, he put down the stamp and frowned, then consulted a broad, white-haired man in gold-rimmed spectacles at a bigger desk, who said sternly, 'Mr Young, you are here illegally. Why?'

I explained my purpose in being there, but failed to

move him. 'I admire your enterprise,' he said, 'but you are here in violation of this country's laws. You cannot land here.'

'I'm sorry. I was not aware that to enter the Philippines through Zamboanga was illegal. It is a port. If you come to Great Britain you are not obliged to enter through the port of London. There are other ports – Liverpool, Cardiff, Southampton . . .'

'You came in a kumpit. Did you stop at any islands?'

'Only one.'

'Was it Tawitawi?'

'No. It was very small. I don't know the name.'

'What was the name of the kumpit? The captain?'

'The kumpit had a difficult Filipino name. The captain I simply called "Captain".'

'And where is this kumpit now?'

'On its way to Cebu City, I guess.'

'Hm!' He looked at me heavily. 'Mr Young, you are in violation. No foreigner may enter this country by sea through Zamboanga.'

'Where, then?'

'I should turn you back. I should say, "Go back the way you came." I cannot let you in.'

'But I must get to Cebu City. I can't go back to Sandakan now.'

'If you try to go to Cebu, I must arrest you and put you in jail.'

After crossing the Sulu Sea, I wasn't worried about a Zamboanga jail, but I did want to get on. He examined the visa I had thought it wise to get in Singapore. 'You are going to Cebu and Manila, yes? Mr Manching's company knows you? Well, I'll do this: I am sending now a cable to my head office in Manila, the office of Commissioner Reyes, who is in overall charge of immigration and deportation' – I noted the last word – 'announcing your illegal entry. He will say yes or no. If yes, I will stamp your passport and you will be free. If no, I will put you in jail. It's a fifty–fifty chance.'

'When will he get your cable?'

'This afternoon. Maybe tomorrow morning if he is busy.'

I turned to Manching. 'Could I phone the British consul in Manila?'

Back in the William Lines office, I called the British consulate in Manila, praying that I wouldn't have to explain things to one of those British officials who regard such problems as mine a waste of time and energy, a barely tolerable interruption to the task of solving the *Times* crossword puzzle.

I was in luck. Mr Ferguson, whose voice soon came thinly down the line, took my story in his stride, sounded relieved when I assured him that I had not been wandering about Tawitawi and Sulu to cover for a newspaper the Moro rebellion against the Marcos government to which he was accredited, and promised to get in touch with Commissioner Reyes and ask him not to deport me. He added, 'The commissioner is sometimes extremely difficult to find. A busy man, you see.' All those deportations, I presumed.

Reading the copy of the cable that had gone to Commissioner Reyes, I didn't care for its wording:

Young reported today his arrival this port from Sandakan via Tawi-Tawi aboard Philippine motor-boat thence boarded another Philippine motor-boat for Zamboanga stop subject claiming to be a writer ... entry through back-door contrary to existing regulations ... request immediate instructions ... Francisco F. Banez, Alien Control Officer, Zamboanga City

The wording made it seem as if I had landed at Tawitawi; if I had, I could have been in touch with the Moros.

Meanwhile, Frank Manching took me to an excellent seafood restaurant opposite the Coca-Cola bottling plant for lunch. It had bamboo walls, mother-of-pearl chandeliers and bamboo furniture, and our waitress might have won the Miss Zamboanga beauty contest the week before.

'Take her with you on the next ship,' Manching said when she brought our lobsters.

'I am always sea-seek,' she said, smiling.

Across the road, Coca-Cola bottles exploded in the heat singly and in bursts like sub-machine-gun fire.

That evening in a café off Pershing Plaza I bought the daily *Zamboanga Times*, and found in it the sort of violent events the Haji had warned me about. Eight people had been killed and seventeen wounded in three separate incidents in Zamboanga del Norte and Basilan districts by the Moro National Liberation Front in west Mindanao. Six labourers of the Basilan Timber Company had been killed and eight wounded when their logging truck was ambushed by men with machine-guns and grenades. A report from Iligan City said that groups of medical specialists had begun operating on the critically wounded victims of grenade explosions in the cities of Iligan and Ozamis.

On another page an advertisement said: 'The Search is

on! Join the search for the 1980 Miss Gay Universe. Coronation will be on Sunday, March 9th. Interested parties are requested to please contact Juan Cruz of Juan's House of Unisex.' The contest was sponsored by Philippine Airlines, the Zamboanga Coca-Cola Plant, Beautifont by Avon and Zamboanga Barter Traders.

I wondered whether to see a movie. 'Strictly for adults: *The Love Butcher* turns a quiet neighbourhood into a slaughterhouse.' Alternatively, I could see a 'very special presentation' of *The Thundering Mantis*, a kung-fu film from Hong Kong starring one Ricky Wong. Instead, I promenaded with students and soldiers in Pershing Plaza, the tiny green island at the heart of Zamboanga, and at last, feeling hungry, came across Jimmie's Happytime Eatery near Manching's office.

A uniformed guard stood at the door with a pistol in a holster in his belt and a twelve-bore pump gun on his hip. The place looked closed, but a pleasant-faced young woman said, 'Come in. Half an hour more.' Only when I was seated at a small plastic-topped table did I notice that she was scared. I ordered Chinese noodle soup and a San Miguel beer and looked around. The room was nearly empty, but on my right three thick-necked, heavy-shouldered men sat at a table covered with empty beer bottles, their faces coarse-skinned and mottled from the beer before them and all the liquor they'd consumed over the years. They were muttering, their heads close together over the bottles. One man had wrapped his hand around a glass, and you could hardly see the glass for the hand. They wore long, loose shirts over their trousers, and their clothes looked lumpy, as though they were carrying books in their pockets.

Before my order came, a man at a table on my other side pushed back his chair and darted quickly out of the door, holding a hand to his face. When they saw him go, the other three got up too and lumbered after him – not in a rush but not dawdling, either. As soon as they had gone, the woman with the pleasant face called to the guard, who entered quickly, closed the door and bolted it top and bottom.

The woman put down the noodle soup and the beer and looked relieved. 'Muslims,' she said. 'Very bad.' The three had come in earlier; later two other men had taken the other table. The three had looked hard at the new arrivals, and when one of the two went to the toilet the three had followed him. There had been a sound of shouting, and the man's companion had gone to the toilet too. More shouting and a 'bad noise'. Then the three had reappeared and gone back to their table and beer. The other two had staggered out bleeding. One of them, evidently the worst hurt – perhaps stabbed, she thought – had zigzagged out into the street. His companion had stayed only long enough to pay for their beers, and I had seen him leave. He might now be calling the cops, she said, or perhaps calling his friends to come to Jimmie's Happytime Eatery and 'redecorate the joint' – and maybe Jimmie, too.

'You can take your time,' the woman said. 'I am Jimmie's wife. You saw the guns in their shirts?'

'Why didn't you call the police?'

'I don't want shooting in here. It would make too much damage and maybe kill somebody.'

Could Moro bosses wander about Zamboanga, bulging with illegal weapons like Sicilian Mafiosi? The Eatery's guard was a young man. His peaked cap and blue uniform, emblazoned with 'scrambled egg' and decorative badges, gave him a half-and-half look, part bellboy, part American colonel. 'You no shoot them?' I asked.

'Aawww . . .' he said, swaying shyly from foot to foot. 'They three tough men, have guns.'

'I don't blame you.'

'Will you come back? In daytime better,' said Jimmie's wife.

'Tomorrow, I hope.'

Next morning Commissioner Reyes's answer reached Mr Banez, the alien control officer: I could stay. I went with Frank Manching to Banez's office on the other side of the Flavorite Refreshment and Coffee Shop and confirmed what I had sensed before, that despite the threats of jail and deportation Mr Banez was a kindly man. He was delighted by the reply from Manila and, in a few minutes, stamped my passport and pronounced me free to proceed with a long, pumping handshake and wishes for good luck.

Frank Manching said, 'Good. Now, when I've found

you a ship, I will phone Victor Chiongbian in Cebu City and tell him your arrival time. How's that?'

Back at the hotel's reception desk, a hand slapped my arm and I swung round to find Jan, arms open as if he were about to deliver a song. 'Eet's your crazee friend,' he cried. He had come with a cousin, a crop-headed soldier. I took them to the terrace and offered them drinks, but they refused politely. Jan told me he and the captain would take a pump boat back to the kumpit next morning and set out immediately from there for Cebu City.

I said, 'Well, take this for the boat fare,' and pressed a hundred pesos on him – about ten pounds, a lot of money in the Philippines. He refused, shouting, 'No, no,' in genuine distress, but I made it a matter of my unhappiness and he reluctantly tucked it away.

When I told Jan about my troubles with the Immigration Department and how they were resolved, he looked upset. 'Haji come see you?' he asked. Well, I said, on the kumpit the Haji had suggested I stay with him and that we would go to a nightclub, but once in Zamboanga he had vanished with hardly more than a nod. Again Jan became agitated.

'No good, Haji. Yah, no good, no good.'

'Never mind. Here is better. Crazy Jan, you came here. Much better than Haji's house, more free.'

'Yeah. More better.' He got up. 'Maybe we meet in Cebu Ceety. I contact William Lines offeece. You find me in kumpit harbour.'

'Remember me to Carlos, Small-But-Terrible, Ernesto, Jalah and Captain Amin.'

'Yah, yah. Also you remember Jan? You not forget Jan, the crazee one? You write, send book, yah?'

'Of course.'

'We all life friends now.'

'Yes, Jan.'

Even this wasn't the end of Jan. A few minutes later when I walked to the William Lines office, I saw a jeep stalled in the street, and a man pushing it to restart it. His shirt had ridden up over his jeans and an automatic stuck out of his hip pocket. It was Jan's soldier cousin. Jan's voice rose in anguish from the driving seat. 'Yah. Engine number three broken. First kumpit, then pump boat, now thees! Ooah!' I put my shoulder to the back of the jeep and in a few yards the engine fired and it leaped forwards. Jan leaned out and waved, and was still gesturing as he careered around a corner into Pershing Plaza, brushing the skirts of three schoolgirls who screamed indignantly. Then he was gone.

Chapter Thirty-Five

MY DEPARTURE FROM Zamboanga for Cebu City bore no resemblance to my arrival; the half-drowned rat had had time to dry out. I was to have the luxury and the loneliness of a cabin once more.

When I talked to Victor Chiongbian on Frank Manching's telephone, his friendly voice assured me that he expected me on the motor vessel *Jhuvel* in two days' time. He had received Kerry St Johnston's telex message from Singapore explaining matters, and his father – the tycoon owner-founder of William Lines – was also looking forward to meeting me. 'What is your short name?' asked Victor. When I said, 'Gavin,' he said, 'Well, call me Victor, please.'

Now that Manching had booked me to Cebu, where I would be pressed to the bosom of the Chiongbian family and the biggest shipping line in the Philippines, I could toss aside all worries about the next two stages of my progress to China. As far as Manila, at least, I faced no problems. It was the first time I had enjoyed the luxury of being certain of the next two stages of my journey since my night departure from Turkey six months before. *Two whole stages.*

Frank Manching took me to the harbour. There one realizes what a seafaring people Filipinos are; the bustle of the port was greater than anything I'd seen since Singapore. Zamboanga is not a big city, but its port serves all the south-west of the Philippines. It is also beautiful and, despite my impatience, I was not overjoyed to leave this city of exotic flowers and trees and the heart-melting combination of blue sea and low white buildings. The terrace of the Lantaka Hotel was lapped by the sun-drenched strait that linked the Sulu to the Celebes Sea. I sympathized with Mr Banks, the elderly American tourist I had met there who told me he had been in Zamboanga for six weeks and couldn't bring himself to leave.

I liked Mr Banks. He said he had tried to take the ferry to Basilan Island but the police had stopped him at the jetty. 'It has to do with pirates,' he said. 'Whatever you do, don't try to go out to those islands. Several foreigners have disappeared there in recent months. Still, I suppose you only flew down from Manila for a day or two and will go straight back there.' He blurted out the last sentence with an expression of sour condescension.

'No, I came here by launch from Sandakan past Tawitawi and Jolo,' I said.

Mr Banks didn't believe me. He knew I had to be lying or mocking him, and turned away insulted, abruptly ending our little game of one-upmanship. I wondered what he and Jan would have made of each other.

Zamboanga. Reading my notebook, I again visualize and pine for that obscure and sunbathed frontier of a religious war:

Outside the harbour gates the tricycle drivers shout for custom like circus barkers; the atmosphere is more of a circus than a port. The tricycles are gaily painted, some with garden or mountain scenes, and each one has a name – Milbert, Clifford, My Lucky Baby or Jesus Christ. On the gates, there is written on a big wheel, like something from a fun fair, 'Ciudad de Zamboanga. Bienvenidos.'

The wharves are not long but there are several of them, and all are crowded with trucks and ships and kumpits. Bare-chested men load crates of Coca-Cola, 'special brandy' and sacks of corn grits into two- or three-deck kumpits bigger than the *Allimpaya*. They have names like *Sweet Vilma*, *Luizmundi* and *Emily*. Spectators stand around waving goodbye to passengers, exuberantly blocking the quays with motor scooters and jeeps – laughing, chattering, whistling, singing. 'See that white steamer, the *Almalyn*?' asked Manching. 'She used to make Singapore. Not now. Only to Labuan these days.'

Several large steamers, one called the *Don Eusebio*, alongside a warehouse with COMPANIA MARITIMA painted on it in tall letters. 'A competitor of William Lines,' said Manching.

My passage is to be on the George and Peter Line's m.v. *Jhuvel*. We board her, and inspect my cabin, No. 2, which has four empty bunks and no washbasin. But it's better than the coffinlike bunk of a small kumpit. On the back of the cabin door an advertisement says: 'Be one of the faces at the festivities. Join the Loveboat Cruise to Kalibo, Ati-Atihan '80, aboard *Geopeter*, George and Peter Line Inc.'

With Manching I visit the wheelhouse and find again that I have to stoop. 'This ship must have been bought from the Japanese,' I say, and the captain shouts delightedly, 'Aah! It ees, it ees!' The captain's name is

603

Captain Maximo L. Clamohoy, Jr. He tells me that the *Jhuvel* is 691 tons, does approximately 11.5 knots and was built in Japan in 1954. She will stop once between Zamboanga and Cebu City, at Dumaguete on Negros Island fourteen and a half hours away.

The chief officer, Edilberto ('Eddie') Manuel, is a plump smiling man in a flowered shirt and blue tracksuit trousers with a six-inch stripe of red and white. Apprentices move about the wheelhouse polishing brass work on the binnacle and telegraph. They jive gently as they move to the silent disco music all Filipinos carry in their heads morning, noon and night.

Eddie was with the *Geopeter* for six years. He explains that the festival at Ati-Atihan is 'the sort where people are dancing and playing and dirtying their faces'.

'Painting their faces, you mean?'

'Painting, yeah.'

Eddie warns me about life in Cebu. 'Many peoples smile,' he says, 'invite you, take you see this and that thing, but they are really, umm . . .'

'Waiting to take the shirt from your back? Hustlers?'

'Hustlers, yeah. Watch your wallet.'

The ship's decks are covered by folding beds or bedrolls with hardly any space between, so men and women of all ages are stretched out side by side. They are workers on the move between islands, students or holidaymakers. It is not cold at night, so many make do with nothing but a sheet or a coloured blanket to lie on and an overnight bag or bundle to serve as a pillow. Young men and young women lie together, their brown skins almost touching, but this doesn't seem to create any problems; no one takes advantage of anyone else.

Such a mess of humanity on the deck of a shipful of Arabs – imagine *Al Anoud* – would soon create a shambles of spit, dirty paper, bits of food, babies' pee. Here people eat and drink from flasks or beercans, smoke, peel fruit – and then clear it all up. There is no squalor or smell. Once again I notice the extraordinary cleanness and almost finicky neatness of people in South-east Asia. Their clothes and bodies are always clean; they never stop scrubbing themselves. They don't seem to sweat much, and even the men's bodies are virtually hairless, which I suppose helps. They think Europeans smell of death. To me, Asians smell faintly of straw-green tea, a pleasant smell. In the eastern Mediterranean or the Red Sea a ship's toilets are soon clogged and stinking, the floors awash with urine and vomit. How do they get so much of their shit on the seats and walls? On m.v. *Jhuvel*, at 11.00 p.m. off Zamboanga del Norte, with hundreds of passengers aboard, the toilets are immaculate.

0600 hours the next morning. Coffee in my bare cabin. I join the chief officer for a view of the islands from the bridge. Soon I am called by the long-haired steward, Oscar Yap, for breakfast: a square, thin omelette with green leaves in it, a big grey fish and plain grey rice. No coffee or tea; I drink warm water. Grey fish is unappetizing, grey rice dries the mouth, and at 7.00 a.m. I can't say that Royal Banana ketchup helps much.

Music from the film *Close Encounters of the Third Kind* follows me about the ship from ubiquitous loudspeakers; it even sneaks ahead of me into the wheelhouse and chart room. From this vantage, the east flank of Negros Island unrolls like a shoreline of the Mediterranean. There is nothing tropical-looking about its higher slopes at all; they are high and dry, with only the outlines of trees on the uppermost ridges; their feet stand in a ruff of coconut trees from which a plume of smoke or two rises, signalling the odd house. It's quite unlike the flowered greenness of Zamboanga.

Nearer our first stop, Dumaguete, the coconut plantations thicken along the shore and reach up the mountainside. Men are fishing from outriggers, and an old Spanish-looking church and bell tower nestle in the trees. Two small boys on deck politely ask if I am getting off the ship at Dumaguete and, when I say I am going on to Cebu, they say they live there and volunteer their names: Bulbul Mendoza and Leil Belumba. We are leaving the world of Musa the Ayatollah, Ibrahim ('big steek') and Ali-Get-Your-Gun. Filipino names are usually Spanish in the Christian regions – not in the southern Muslim islands of the Sulu, of course. On the bridge the work certificates of several of the ship's engineer officers are framed on a bulkhead: Rezaldo J. Cagang, Romeo A. Badillon, Pedro A. Jaume, Jaime A. Labstida.

Also on the bridge are a couple of beautiful girls who certainly have nothing to do with navigating the *Jhuvel*. When I ask one of them, 'Are you a member of the crew?' she gives me a flash of dark eyes and a coquettish smile: 'Just travelling to Cebu and back for the ride.' She has a sister-in-law in London. 'So many Filipinos want to go there.' She winked. 'Me too.'

Last night in the canteen the Filipinos I was drinking beer with asked eagerly, 'Are there many Filipinos in England?' Some, I said, but probably more in Saudi Arabia and the Gulf. 'How can we get there?' they wanted to know. But I had no answer to that. The conversation reminds me of a smear campaign in Britain some years ago aimed against well-to-do British families hiring Filipinos as domestic servants, cooks or nannies. The employers were equated with slave drivers, the Filipinos with cringing slaves. But the jobs represented a scintillating leap for the Filipinos, far from slavery; the slavery they know and flee from is here in the Philippines and, for many of them, no work of any kind.

Coming into the tiny port of Dumaguete, Captain Max takes off the dressing gown and flower-patterned shirt he wears at sea and Chief Officer Eddie gets out of his tracksuit pants; they appear on the bridge in clean white bush jackets and big peaked caps loaded with yellow braid. We have thirty minutes in Negros.

There are two wharves, lined with ships, launches and outriggers. No sooner is the gangway down than a mob of howling food vendors charge up it like a medieval army storming a castle. Girls and women tote baskets of mangoes, cakes, lemons, wrapped biscuits, peanuts, Coca-Cola. Eager young porters tumble into my cabin like puppies, crying, 'Hey! Porter, surr?' I wish I had some luggage for them to play with. Instead I go ashore with the chief officer, who walks across the quay to visit a friend on the bridge of a steamer called *Don Joaquín*. I walk past cycle-rickshaws, past wooden offices, shops, and, in ten minutes, find a café advertising 'Shakes – mango, avocado, papaya', and drink a San Miguel beer in the shade. Returning to the ship – Dumaguete is hardly big enough for a long walk – I meet a huge woman with a basket on her head coming down the gangway, her T-shirt, stretched almost to snapping point, carrying in bold letters the challenge 'Hug Me!' She squeezes by me and says, 'Good morning,' with great dignity. Even as one calculates the chances of getting one's arms around her, her alderman's voice cancels the invitation that bombinates from her bosom.

The last building to fade from view as the *Jhuvel* steams away toward Cebu is Silliman University on the seafront. A magazine article ('From Football Player to Millionaire') in Frank Manching's office had told me that William Chiongbian, the shipping magnate, founder and chairman of the board of William Lines, had spent eight poverty-stricken years at Silliman as a football star. Mr Chiongbian's kicking prowess and agility were the mainstay of his team and the envy of their opponents. William Chiongbian's brothers, George and Peter, own the *Jhuvel*.

On the *Jhuvel* I can't pretend I didn't feel a letdown. She was a magnificent ship, but she wasn't a kumpit. I didn't like to be so high above the water, so cut off from the crew, and I was still unused to being so free from anxiety. I had only one worry at the back of my mind – that I might miss the Swire vessel from Manila to Hong Kong – but that was some way ahead. Oddly enough, the absence of immediate problems made me uneasy, as if I'd overlooked something of great importance.

We arrived at Cebu at five thirty in the evening, and at the offices of William Lines I found that most of the staff had gone home. A girl said, 'Victor Chiongbian? He's no longer working here.'

Had there been a coup d'état? Had the president of the company, the founder's son, been abruptly fired since I spoke to him from Zamboanga? No; with a brisk clack of heels, a more authoritative secretary appeared, said, 'I'm Gloria,' and got to work on the telephone.

I found Victor Chiongbian and his wife at an antique show at the New Plaza Hotel, a modern hotel built above the port apparently from the plans of Hitler's bunker. They were an attractive couple. Victor, a pleasant, friendly man with a fair skin and a decisive manner, drove me to the Magellan Hotel, quite grand and busy, with more plants and much less concrete than Hitler's bunker. 'You'll stay two or three days?' he asked. 'Our flagship, the *Doña Virginia*, sails to Manila on Monday. My father is very proud of her; we all are. You will have a stateroom, that's easy. We'll see our farm tomorrow, and we'll take you to where Magellan was killed in Lapu-Lapu. You might like to see a cockfight. You've never seen one? I will arrange it. And you'll meet my father. He is well over sixty, but spends his evenings in nightclubs.' He laughed and glanced at his wife. 'I like early nights. He has the energy.'

The security and hospitality of the Chiongbians and a ship waiting: the contrast with the past month was complete. I soon found that the flamboyance of the tropical islands of the south, where you can so easily imagine that men are leopards in human skins, was muted here. Compared with Manila or at least the southern Philippines, Cebu is a quiet, unhurried place that pillows its cheek against the soft folds of a mountain range and seems to doze.

Victor said, 'Anyone who says he's busy in Cebu is a liar. People work harder in Luzon [the northernmost of the Philippine Islands where Manila is], where life is more insecure. It is harder to find work there, and they are frequently visited by typhoons that sweep away hillsides, bridges, even dams. Cebu is a city of the semi-retired.'

'Yet from Cebu you and your father are running this great shipping line, which he built from nothing.'

'Oh, well . . .'

I liked Victor's gentle, firm style and modesty as much as I came to like his generous, hardfisted and boastful father, William. Victor's house in the Cebu equivalent of Beverly Hills looked down from green lawns on Magellan's landing place. Here the explorer's three ships, *Trinidad*, *Victoria* and *Concepcion*, arrived in April 1521, flying the flag of Spain. (He had found a sponsor in King Carlos after suffering poverty and scorn in the service of Portugal.) Here the noble and diplomatic Portuguese limped ashore – he had been badly wounded in a battle with the Moors – and made friends with Rajah Humabon, impressing him with the roar of his cannon and the thickness of his men's Spanish armour, receiving presents of gold, ginger, palm wine, fish and figs 'more than a foot long', according to his chronicler Antonio Pigafetta.

Victor could also look down on the little island of Mactan, where, three weeks later, Lapu-Lapu's warriors killed Magellan and his landing party with rocks and bamboo spears.

Magellan's peaceful wooing of the friendly rajahs lasted barely a month. Less than three weeks before the landing at Cebu, he and his dying crew had made their landfall at the uninhabited island of Homonhon at the mouth of the Leyte Gulf in the eastern Philippines. His men were sick and had been terribly weakened by the crossing of the Pacific. Pigafetta recounted:

We [were] three months and twenty days without taking on board provisions or any other refreshment, and we ate only old biscuit turned to powder, all full of worms and stinking of the urine that the rats had made on it, having eaten the food. And we drank water impure and yellow. We ate ox hides, which were very hard because of the sun, rain and wind.

On Homonhon, Magellan's polygot crew – Spaniards, Greeks, Germans, Italians, French, Flemings and Malays – found freshwater springs, and the coconut milk refreshed them. They wooed the Tagalog-speaking islanders like suitors and brought ashore presents – 'red caps, mirrors, combs, bells and other things'. Magellan himself gave the local rajah, Calambu, a robe of yellow and red cloth and a fine red cap, and then, to the rajah's delight, suggested that they become blood brothers. They embraced and cut their wrists, letting their blood mingle according to the Malay custom of *casicasi*.

A few days later, on Easter Sunday, Magellan invited the rajah and his brother to attend mass ashore. Kneeling in the sun, the rajahs copied the actions of the Portuguese captain and his crewmen, 'going on their knees with raised hands at the elevation of the Host'. As they did so, a salute from the guns of the three ships rolled across the bay.

Magellan had already refused to accept a 'bar of massy [heavy] gold' and, in other ways, had shown the Filipinos that he was not there to plunder or harm them. As the result of such modest behaviour, the rajah volunteered to guide the three ships to the larger islands to the west, only asking Magellan to wait two days while his people took in their rice harvest. Thus it was that the King of Spain's little fleet came to Cebu and astonished the eyes of Rajah Humabon. Introduced by the friendly rajah from the Gulf of Leyte, Magellan made a Christian of Humabon almost at once, christening him 'Don Carlos' after the Spanish king. Within ten days Cebu was a Christian island.

But the end of the idyll was not long in coming. A chief, a vassal of Humabon, arrived from the little island of Mactan, pleading for help against a rival chief named Lapu-Lapu. Magellan moved his ships across the narrow strait and disembarked a landing party in the shallow water of Mactan, Lapu-Lapu's capital. Tragedy followed because the guns of the ships were too distant to cover the landing. Lapu-Lapu's fifteen hundred warriors charged down to the shore hurling rocks, spears and arrows at Magellan's forty-nine men. Later, Pigafetta told the King of Spain that the captain 'ordered us to withdraw slowly, but the men fled while six or eight of us remained with him. As a good captain and a knight he still stood fast, fighting for more than an hour.' The end came when an islander jabbed at his face and Magellan thrust him through with his lance, leaving it in his body. He struggled to draw his sword, but a spear took him in the left leg and he fell face down. In the clear shallows, over sand as white as sugar, like the shallows I had waded through on the Sulu island, Lapu-Lapu's warriors finished him off. In crystal water Magellan died – 'Our mirror, our light, our comfort and our true guide.'

Standing beside Victor and looking down on the narrow strait between Mactan and Cebu and the modern steel bridge arching over it, Jalah's wobbly chant came back to me from the *Allimpaya*'s wheelhouse:

'Rajah Humabon make them veree happeè,
All people will baptize under the church of Christ . . .
But Lapu-Lapu is veree bad.
To drive Magellan to go back home . . .
O, Mother, Mother,
I am seek,
Call the doctor veree queek . . .'

My notes continue:

Victor is dynamic and restless. Perhaps he alone is a busy man in Cebu. On his farm on the western side of the island, he walks fast and determinedly through the acres of trees and cultivation. He has a ranch in Mindanao, he says, but doesn't go there now because of the violent deeds of the Moros. Instead, to get away from it all he goes fishing and shooting on Palawan Island. Here he has knobbly green hills to stride over that are cultivated with coconuts, mangoes, bananas and rice. Plans fill his head: for pigs and pig manure, the marketing of sweet lemons, a distillery.

Victor is not a particularly big man, but he orders huge meals – I suspect only for my benefit – and gulps them down. We drink at least two sorts – one sweeter than the other – of home-made *tuba*, the fermented sap of the coconut palm, coloured and slightly embittered by powdered tanbark, the mangrove husk that the *Allimpaya* carried from Sandakan. It's good the dry kind especially, and costs less than 25 pence a gallon.

In the market of Asturias there are slabs of dolphin meat, dark red like horse's liver, and manta-ray steaks. The local villages are of wood, houses bright with coconut shells suspended by thin chains from their gables holding sprays of orchids. Their plaster-fronted, ornate Spanish churches remind me of the flamboyant birthday-cake churches of Tuticorin in southern India. To reach Asturias we have to pass the Atlas copper mine – 'the biggest in all Asia,' says Victor. It is like a huge quarry, an ugly dried-up wound in the landscape. Foliage for acres around is grey with dust from it. It is the biggest man-made wound in Asia.

Chapter Thirty-Six

A SMALL WICKET gate leading to the cockpit announced that ringside seats cost twenty pesos and the balcony ten pesos, or rather more than fifty pence.

From the car park to the cockpit gate dozens of men and boys shifted from foot to foot, lovingly stroking the backs of roosters they held in the crooks of their arms like bagpipes. The bound legs of the roosters hung down, their long, glossy green-black or white tail feathers arching over their owners' elbows, and they glared about, beadily eyeing their rivals. Defiant cock-a-doodle-doos filled the air.

Near the gate, food vendors were roasting chicken on spits; some of the turning naked bodies on the spits were birds killed earlier in the ring. The smell of the flesh of their brethren did not appear to worry the living roosters.

We ducked through a wooden tunnel into the small pyramid-shaped building with a corrugated roof that housed the cockpit. Victor Chiongbian's brother led me to a tiny stall, like a box at a theatre, with three wooden seats in it. Metal rails separated us from the eight-sided ring. People stood ten deep in the balcony and around us, at the ringside, twelve to fifteen deep, shouting and sweating under overhead lamps.

Two handlers bring in their birds and squat with them between their knees, facing each other. Each handler grasps his bird's longest tail feather, curbing it as it strains forward, beak to beak with its opponent. The shouting grows. Men in the audience leap up to flourish fingers at men in the

arena, and exchange complicated hand signals like deaf and dumb language. The betting has begun.

A golden-maned bird is matched with a monster with a russet ruff. They are held up by their handlers, who thrust them forward so that each bird can get in a few pecks on its opponent's neck or breast; thus they further madden each other. Then the handlers fix a spur like a small scimitar to each of the birds' heels, unwind the threads that imprison their legs and then set them down, beady eye seeking beady eye, ruffs rising in a fury. Immediately they spring at each other, clash in mid-air with an explosion of feathers, drop, wings outspread, brushing the earth, fly up again, slashing, changing places as one cartwheels over the other. They teeter, recovering balance, then are up again, slashing. In a flash, one bird is capsized in the dust, tries to rise, sinks back twitching, dying and its handler snatches it up before it is pecked to pieces. Head down, inert, blood coming from its beak and nostrils, the dead bird is carried away, a lump with feathers, tonight's meal, legs dangling, beak ajar; it is hard to recognize it as the monster with the russet ruff.

The victor, still furious, is gathered up firmly and proudly by its owner. Its spur is carefully sheathed; and sheath and spur are untied. As it is borne out of the arena it shrieks one last triumphant crow to its applauding fans. The fight has taken ten or fifteen seconds. Now it is time for another, and without delay the next two birds are brought in.

Bout follows bout through the afternoon. White bird against red; greeny black against mottled white and black. Flutter, spring, roars from the crowd, flutter, spring, slash. The birds cartwheel about the ring like feathered squibs, and small feathers fly outwards, tickling nostrils at the ringside. Speed blurs the flurries, so that I find them impossible to follow. In next to no time, the winning birds are on tiptoe, crowing; the losers are tottering, falling, twitching, dying. The mayhem goes on and on in the heat of the overhead lamps and the noise of betting.

'A good cock imported from the United States can cost four thousand pesos,' a friend of Victor's brother shouts in my ear. 'Over five hundred dollars.'

'A lot of money to lose for twenty seconds in the ring.'

'Sure. A fight can take ten seconds, or it can last ten minutes with a good pair that last well. Ten minutes is the limit.' He peels off a handful of banknotes and hands them to a man in a sports shirt in the ring who leans over the metal rail.

A seated group of fat, elderly women munch scarlet half-moons of dripping watermelon. Bottles of Pepsi-Cola are passed down the rows of spectators, and a vendor holds up, fanlike, five roasted chickens on skewers.

My friend says, 'There are all walks of life here in the cockpit – hustlers, pickpockets. The important thing is to know and watch who you bet with; otherwise, if you win, you may find he's disappeared.'

'Would you like to see a slasher?' asks Victor's brother. 'That's what we call the spurs.'

He hands me a tiny scimitar two inches long, with a sheath to match. 'Be very careful with the slasher, eh? It is very sharp.' It was as keen as a razor blade.

'Sometimes, when the bird starts struggling, the handlers get cut themselves. The sheaths we call holsters. The vulnerable part of a bird is under the armpit, near to the heart, or the spinal column at the back of the neck. Not the head; the head can withstand.'

'It's all luck, isn't it?' I ask.

'Mostly luck, except that maybe a good imported chicken has better feeding and endurance to bear wounds and the heat. Of course, the slashers puncture the flesh going in and cut coming out, so they make a big wound. That's why they can reduce endurance to nothing. One cut and you're dead.'

As we watch it is explained to me that some fighting-cock owners keep stables of hundreds of birds. Win some, lose some. 'Look, that white one has turned chicken,' Victor's brother says with unconscious humour when a contestant loses interest in the fight and tries to run out of the cockpit.

The cockfights are on every Sunday, and on fiesta days and legal holidays, and sometimes are held to raise funds for a charity. There are two cockpits in Cebu City, always full.

'How long will the fights go on today?'

'As long as there are chickens outside. If there are plenty of chickens, they'll run until midnight. There'll be plenty of chicken dinners in Cebu tonight and tomorrow.'

We stayed about two hours, through countless fights, none lasting more than a minute. I wasn't sorry to leave the inferno of heat, noise, blood and feathers. When we left, men and boys were waiting outside in the sun, stroking the birds they held lovingly under their arms.

Sixty-six-year-old William Chiongbian, the multi-million-aire founder of the William Lines and the father of Victor, is a keen cockfighter like most Filipinos, and, from time to time, has kept expensive stables of fighting cocks. He told me a strange story.

Once, on his farm, a cobra swallowed a nestful of twelve hen's eggs – twelve potential fighting cocks. Soon the snake was discovered by William Chiongbian's cowboys, who killed it. The eggs were rescued from the stomach of the cobra, but only one hatched. This chick grew up to be an amazing fighting cock, and, of course, it was named Cobra.

'Yeah,' said William, 'Cobra survived eighteen fights. Imagine that. Eighteen. That's somethin'. Then I put it out to stud, and finally it died in its bed. Its progeny, though, were terrible cowards – one scratch and they ran away. I was a laughing-stock, so I gave up. A cock that runs away shames his owner dreadfully.

'You know, it's a cruel business. You tend a chicken, right? Stroke it, feed it like a child, give it the best vitamins, talk to it, name it. All this for two years. Then you lovingly carry it into the cockpit like your own baby and – phwit! – in five seconds it's a bundle of feathers, lifeless, gone. Pitiful.' I was glad he had said that.

I met William at an evening reception Victor and his wife had taken me to. He was shortish, broad, his slicked-

back hair black in spite of his age; his waist was slim and he looked quick on his feet like the boxer and footballer he'd been forty years before. He himself had the face of an ageing fighting cock, a lightweight-boxer face, with a square jaw and a pleasant grin.

Straight away William said, 'Let's beat it. I'll take you to a disco, what do you say?' He drove there fast. In a dark room, looking through a wide, high plate-glass window into a lighted room where twenty or thirty girls waited on benches like fish in a restaurant tank, he ordered two girls from the woman attendant – 'Numbers three and fifteen' – and we entered the disco. There he ordered whisky for me, Coca-Cola for himself and the girls. He shimmied around the floor and chatted to the girls for two hours, then, as abruptly as he had arrived, he handed out large tips, promised the girls he'd be back – their grateful eyes and his grin exchanged white signals in the gloom – and drove me home.

Twenty-five ships: six container vessels, twelve container–

passenger ships, six luxury liners and one luxury container–liner (my transport to Manila, the *Doña Virginia*, named after his wife) – a biggish fleet. 'I handed it all over to Victor in 1965 to let him learn. I've seen friends of mine who keep on controlling their businesses late in life. Why did they send their sons to school? You find these sons – middle-aged men – still like children.'

His office was on the first floor of the William Lines office building near the docks. The offices were not particularly grand, but the walls of William's room were lined with framed photographs of distinguished people: Nehru, Averell Harriman, Imelda Marcos, the president's wife. He sat before me at his desk, short sleeves revealing muscled arms, his face smooth, teeth perfect, wearing a silver Rolex and lightly tinted glasses, a former congressman, present shipping tycoon, grown from gangsterdom.

'I was nearly a gangster before I was engaged. I was a nobody, and I didn't like that. When I was courting my wife, her relatives tried to stop us, and I told her, 'I'll kill everyone in your house if you don't marry me.' I decided to turn over a new leaf when war began in 1941 and we ran into the hills in Leyte to join Marcos and the guerrillas fighting the Japs. Then I went into my first venture; war or not, I had to make money to feed my family. I bought a *banca* – a sailing boat with outriggers – and sailed it from Leyte to Mindanao. Halfway, near Bohol Island, I encountered a Jap navy patrol boat. Three of us jumped into the sea for our lives, and two remained in the boat. We swam eight to ten hours in waters full of sharks before we hit the beach. I thought God had saved my life. I felt, Something big will come in my life. I felt, I will survive! The two who stayed in the banca were killed by the Japs.'

William thumped the desk with his fist like a gospel preacher. 'I tell you, Gavin, it was the turning point in my life. Like you surviving the Sulu Sea and the Moros in the kumpit. I survived Japs and sharks. I was twenty-nine. After that, everything I touched turned to gold. I made profits of two hundred and three hundred per cent. I'll sum up my life: courage, my gambling spirit, imagination, hard work and, of course, luck given by God.

'Even now I go on board my ships – oh yes – without warning. Sometimes I have a tip; something is dirty, something is not correct on a ship, and I take the chief steward, or whoever is guilty, by the neck and bash him. I really slap him in front of the other officers and crew – goddamn it, I don't mind.

'Once I waited for a captain to return to his vessel. Two hours in the sun, waiting with the crew and officers. I said to them, "You wait here and see what I do to this captain who keeps the ship waiting two hours."

'When he comes he sees I am furious. I grab him by the throat. He's pleading: "Sir, the crew will see. I'll be humiliated." Well, he was a small man. I said, "In future I don't bother to hit you, I fire you away."'

It wasn't the sort of behaviour I associated with a ship-owner like John Swire, but it did sound very Filipino. William was genuinely concerned for the underdog. 'I go always to the crew's quarters first. I won't have my crew living like pigs. If a ship is late or dirty, who is to lose? The public. Who is to blame? I am. That's why I get mad. The public pays. It's rough-and-tumble, but those officers I slapped are still with me. Who's made their lives for them?'

Later, Victor, a man who would never hit anyone whatever his size, said his father had once found one of his foremen idling. The foreman was much bigger than William, but William had beaten him up, then handed the foreman an axe and said, 'Go on, hit me.'

'I suppose I've always been a playboy, too,' grinned William, walking me to his favourite coffee shop, the Red Carpet, his rendezvous every morning. At a table his friends – journalists, lawyers, company men – sat drinking coffee, and William introduced me, then pointed to them. 'All businessmen, pimps and hustlers,' he barked, and their hard masculine faces creased into affectionate smiles.

Next day, as I was talking to Victor in his office, Jan walked in, followed by other members of the crew of the *Allimpaya*. They had arrived that morning. Jan had shaved his little beard; moonfaced Jalah had cut his hair short; big Carlos had a sty on his mongoloid left eyelid and looked cast down by it. The captain, Amin, was there too, gold flashing in his mouth.

Kind Victor immediately led them into his office as if they were pirate princes. He was excited by their appearance, and plied them with questions about their voyage, kumpit, cargo and charter rates. He had sent his own car to pick them up when he heard that the *Allimpaya* had been sighted at Cebu's kumpit wharf, and now he ordered Coca-Cola all round. I realized then that the Chiongbians knew everything that went on in Cebu. The wild quartet had been driven to the office by a chauffeur with Muzak and the air conditioning going full blast, Jan reported across Victor's boardroom table, and the reception had deeply impressed them. Jan's ebullience was undiminished by the strange setting. He and the others looked very dark beside Victor.

When I gave Carlos a hundred pesos to buy a pair of jeans – he had told me he needed some – he cheered up and put an arm across my shoulder, saying, 'Zank you.' I said, 'Say hello to Small–But–Terrible.'

'Yeah, yah. Okay.'

Jalah said, 'Don't write your book until my letter comes. Eet weel be my life storee. Please put eet all in book.' (Alas, Jalah's letter has not arrived.)

The captain said, 'Thank you for coming with us.'

'No, no. I am grateful for the ride. I thought in Sandakan you would not take me, in case we were caught by the Filipino navy.'

Jan said, 'We will be lonelee on the kumpit now.'

They spoke in another language to Victor, who told me, 'They are saying in Cebu language, "We had good fun on the kumpit." '

'We did,' I said, and added, 'I'm coming back to Zamboanga. Wait and see.'

'We weel wait,' said Jan. 'We weel be lonelee.'

The captain and Jalah shook my hand. Carlos kissed my cheek, as did Jan, who, before I could draw it away, kissed my hand too. Then they left.

Victor drove me to the *Doña Virginia* on the evening she sailed for Manila. Her sides were immense and white, rows of portholes gleaming in them like golden studs. She could carry fifteen hundred passengers, and was eighty per cent full year round. Containerized too. On that warm night, with her lights blazing, she was like a luxury liner in a Hollywood film.

Victor moved casually about the ship like a prince, shaking clutching hands, hailed on all sides. He left me on the bridge, which was wider than anything I'd seen since *Patrick Vieljeux*. As we cast off I saw him on the quayside mouthing, 'See the boss.' Following his finger, I saw a darkened car with his father, William, in it, nearly out of sight behind a barrier. Unseen, he had come to watch his beautiful flagship, his pride, the prize at the end of his struggles, after all the rough-and-tumble since those many hours in shark-and-Jap-filled waters. Under his adoring eyes, the *Doña Virginia* slid off into the dark strait, agleam, white and gold, while passengers on other lines stared at us from their rails. I waved at the shore, where the kumpit wharf lay in shadow. They wouldn't see me from the *Allimpaya* even if they were looking my way, but that didn't matter. We moved up the strait, the forward mast and radar mast barely clearing the modern bridge that joins Cebu Island and Mactan Island, Cebu City and Lapu-Lapu. But the stern mast had to be lowered by motor, and small boys on the bridge cheered as our lights slipped past, almost scraping the soles of their feet.

Victor had given me a two-bed suite with a bath and shower attached. I had a sofa, two chairs, TV and – a godsend – good lights for reading in bed. I toured the ship. Passengers lay on two-tiered bunks on deck or wandered up and down bright neon-lit staircases and along the rails. Disco music throbbed until late at night. Before turning in, I shared a beer with a Filipino – the beer came in pitchers, not glasses, a gallon at a time, too much for one person – and he told me that yesterday three bombs had exploded in movie houses near Zamboanga. There were sixteen dead and many wounded. Moros? 'Maybe some Christian group of terrorists,' he said. He told me a story about an American and an Englishman who had sailed a yacht south a year or two before. Pirates had caught them, and the American escaped somehow, but the Briton was killed. 'Somewhere near Zamboanga, those islands.'

It was a luxury to have stewards again, and breakfast in the suite: fried egg, sausages, cheese, Nescafé, tomato ketchup and Red Devil Hot Sauce.

Sitting in the sun, I watched the islands go by. Panay, long and wooded; Sibuyan, a pinhead. Small steamers, blue and orange sails, a white lighthouse in the Sibuyan Sea.

A boy in deck class told me that he was heading for Saudi Arabia as an accountant. 'Eet weel be hard. No cheeks, no beer, sand. Hard life. But the money ees good, so what can I do?'

His friend said to me, 'You look like Robert Mitchum.' He had lively Oriental features and very short hair. 'You must be Yul Brynner,' I told him. General laughter.

From the passage of the gap between Mindoro Island and Batangas, the south-western tip of Luzon, I stay more or less constantly on the bridge. Despite its size, it is not a place for a sufferer from claustrophobia; officers, apprentices and wives surge about, and rock music pumps out of the loudspeakers. Even the master, Captain George Geraldez, snaps his fingers while moving rhythmically about in jeans and a white sports shirt with his name on the pocket. He is short and plump, twenty-nine years with William Lines, and was voted 'Outstanding Captain' in 1975 and 1976 while master of m.v. *Dumaguete City.*

The wheelhouse is white, with sea-green rails to the wings, sea-green metal decks, yellow masts and derricks. The big square containers on the foredeck are a brilliant orange. We pass smaller liners and freighters effortlessly. The *Doña* is queen of the seas; whatever vessel we pass, its crew and passengers stare at us and wave.

Luzon, blue and lazy in the 10.00 a.m. sun. On the windscreen of the bridge, a sign reads: SAFETY FIRST TAKE NO CHANCES. It is not easy sailing here. One night a tanker rammed the *Don Juan*, a luxury liner belonging to the Chiongbians' rival, and sank her, drowning hundreds of passengers. Approaching Manila Bay, Captain Geraldez came out on to the wing and pointed. 'Bataan. Where many Filipinos died during the Japanese occupation.'

To port, a great mountain ridge ran into the sea, forming a large wing to the bay, which is almost a sea of its own. Here the Americans sank the Spanish fleet before taking Manila and occupying the Philippine archipelago.

'Corregidor Island.' A crescent shape, a reminder of Second World War movies starring John Wayne. Just off our port bow, a round sea fortress stuck up out of the water: a concrete bunker island, rusted guns, a ruined bastion riddled with shell holes. Manila is a white cluster ahead, a few skyscraper shapes in haze, like the outline of Bombay, Karachi, Piraeus or almost any other big port.

I took pictures of the captain's niece and two elderly lady friends and, after the niece had photographed me and the others, we swapped snaps and names.

The odd thing about a modern wheelhouse is that it resembles a space-age dentist's surgery. The telegraph is something between an extremely sophisticated milk-shake dispenser and a giant pinball machine; you expect it to spew out either a banana split or a jackpot.

The second officer is barking like a dog and has the apprentices in fits. Now he is dancing around the helmsman hanging on to the little tassle attached to the brass bell on the ceiling. An apprentice with bushy hair under his cap is quietly jiving to 'Rock Around the Clock'.

'Two hours of manoeuvring to get alongside,' the captain says. The minuet begins.

Captain: 'Stop two engines.'

Helmsman: 'Stop two.'

'Course 057.'

'Dead slow ahead two.'

'065.'

'065, sir.'

We turn into the anchorage of Manila harbour.

'Starboard twenty.'

We are at 'Dead Slow', but still moving quite fast.

'Stop starb'd.'

'Stop two engines.'

There are eighteen ships in port, eight waiting at anchor.

'Midships.'

'Rudder midships, sir.'

'Hard to starb'd . . . Slow astern . . . Slow ahead port . . . Stop starb'd.'

We inch around a red buoy.

'Stop two engines.'

A handsome white William Lines ship, the *Cagayan de Oro*, eases out of her berth ahead, working her way out of the tangle of shipping, and we hail her with two hoots on our siren.

A pilot takes over the last part. He uses the bow thrusters

– the propellers under the bow – which makes manoeuvring easier.

'Thrust to port.'

'Let go one anchor.'

'Steady.'

A gentle bump. A cluttered wharf and godowns, orange containers waiting, huge fork-lift trucks pumping petrol fumes, barriers to protect passengers from descending containers. William and Victor Chiongbian's pride, the *Doña Virginia*, has docked in Manila.

Chapter Thirty-Seven

I HADN'T ESCAPED from the Tropic of Piracy by moving north. In Manila I read this story in a newspaper:

PIRATES BOARD CONTAINER SHIP AND KILL CAPTAIN
Barefoot pirates sneaked into a British container ship in Manila Bay today, shortly after midnight, grabbed two Chinese crewmen as hostages and then shot dead its captain after failing to rob the ship's money . . . The ship's chief mate, Sin Tiu Chiu, 35, said Capt. Dyason had apparently awakened when the pirates entered his cabin, poked the pistol at his neck and demanded: 'Money, money, where's the money?'

The captain never replied but tried to push the pistol away with his left hand but a man with a long gun fired at him with successive shots . . . After the captain was shot, the pirates ordered Mr Sin . . . to open the vault where the ship's money was kept, but were told only the captain knew the safe's combination.

As far as I know, those pirates have never been caught.

'Money, money, where's the money?' has a Conradian ring about it; it is something like a hiss in the dark from the villainous Ricardo in *Victory*. An ironic touch was that Captain Dyason's ship, the *Oriental Ambassador*, which had left Manila for Taiwan early in the morning, would not have been lying at anchor in Manila Bay that night at the mercy of the pirates but for his decision to shelter there from a typhoon. He wasn't one to take risks. I see him as a prudent man; he had sought a safe haven and, having found sanctuary from nature; had slept soundly until he heard that voice in his ear and felt cold metal on his neck.

I heard of another aspect of violence when I went to see a Filipino businessman, a friend of William Chiongbian. We had a drink at a table full of his cronies: journalists, an ex-congressman, a coconut baron, a lawyer and a judge. Conversation turned, as it tended to among such people, on the health of the president. Was Marcos dying of a kidney complaint? Recently he hadn't looked his usual healthy self on TV, someone said.

My friend talked of a recent epidemic of arson bombs in Manila, aimed primarily at Filipino businessmen of Chinese extraction. Some people thought that it was the work of hit men sent over by the powerful tongs, the Chinese secret societies of Hong Kong. At any rate, Hong Kong police experts had come to Manila to investigate explosions and certain kidnappings that seemed to point that way.

'Frankly, I want to get out of Manila and live in Cebu,' a lawyer admitted. 'See that?' He pointed to a newspaper. 'Two died here' was the caption for a photograph showing police officers examining a hole in a stretch of tarmac. Someone had bombed a technical institute near Manila.

'Most people carry guns now,' my new friend said. 'They cost three thousand to four thousand pesos' – that is, at least two hundred pounds.

The judge said, 'A police special, that's what we like here in Manila. A brand new .45.'

Violence and music, violent music. The garish jeepney buses thump and howl about the city like travelling juke-

boxes, with small statues of silver horses on their hoods and kids swinging and jiving on their tailboards. There is little beauty in this city. American and Japanese bombs razed its elegant Spanish past to charcoal. No beauty in Roxas Boulevard, or in the business ghetto, Makati – only muddle.

When I first came to Manila the year before, it was John Travolta time. The music of his film *Saturday Night Fever* bombarded me from taxis, buses, hotel elevators and shopping complexes; it was almost impossible to escape. When I went to interview President Marcos for the *Observer*, it even pursued me to his Malacanan Palace. In a waiting room there, small woolly mice scuttled about the floor and an old Bette Davis movie ranted and sobbed from a television set. The president was delayed, and after an hour's wait I was introduced by guards to the presidential library, a magnificent chamber with twelve-foot-high doors and twenty-foot ceilings. It was an august place, but Muzak reigned here, too; twanging gusts of music from *Saturday Night Fever* enveloped me and the two Filipino lady librarians who were making tea. They lightly swung their hips to the music under a shelf full of grandly leather-bound speeches of the president. It had been John Travolta in *Saturday Night Fever* then; it was John Travolta in *Grease* now, and soon it would be John Travolta in *Urban Cowboy*. Apparently, John Travolta could make a life's work out of making musicals for the delectation of Filipino youth. Year in, year out, these frisky Catholic youngsters with Jesus medals bouncing on their chests yearned for their next 'fix' of Travolta.

There was other music, of course. There is a saying in Manila: 'Filipinos have survived Spanish and American domination: four hundred years in a convent and fifty years in Hollywood.' Behind the broad sweep of Roxas Boulevard with its palm trees, skyscrapers, hotels and supper clubs, the Quick-Quack coffee lounge leaned against the Guernica restaurant. There the strolling guitarists, Filipinos of Basque origin, bawl out 'Arriba España' and 'Valencia' until you are tempted to cry 'Enough' or beg them to switch to the songs they keep up their broad gaucho sleeves for British visitors: 'Onder Neath Ze Arches' or 'Mi-bee it's bee-corz oi'm a Londoner'.

I liked the smiles and Spanish-American accents of Manila ('hot dogs' pronounced 'hut dugs', 'leisure' becoming 'lee-shure') and the sign my smiling taxi driver from the docks had pinned on his dashboard:

> Grant me, O Lord,
> A Steady Hand and a Watchful Eye
> That No one
> Shall be Hurt As I pass by.

It says something for the Filipinos that they affectionately bestow on their public-transport vehicles the name 'love buses', and paint large imprints of scarlet lips on their sides.

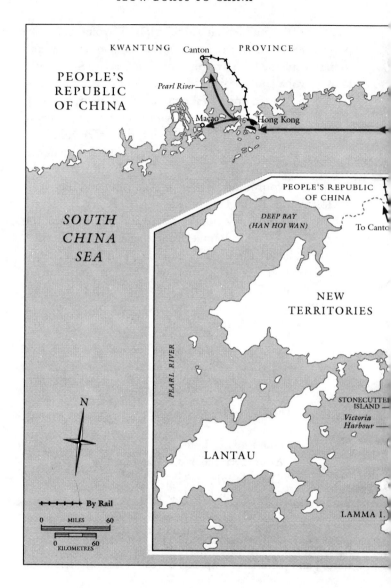

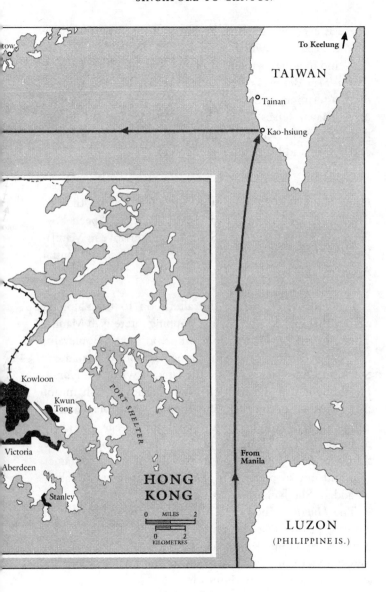

There is even an attractive liveliness to the American-style tabloid headlines, which refer to city councillors as 'city dads' and to congressmen as 'solons'. Two headlines I noted: 'Baron Slay Brains Tagged', which referred to the arrest of the mastermind in the case of a kidnapped foreign nobleman. 'Mayor Nixes Graft Charges, Blames Ex-dad' meant that the present mayor of Manila had denied accusations of corruption and blamed his predecessor.

Hong Kong was the next stop, and there was no time to dawdle. A well-named taxi driver, Ramon 'Speed-boy' Perez, drove me to see John Swire's representative in Manila, Duncan Pring, who had dug up ancient artifacts in Central America and won a Ph.D. in archaeology from London University before joining Swire's.

Pring delivered me in the afternoon to the shipping agency that looked after Swire's shipping interests in Manila. There, in a neon-lit first-floor office on Roxas Boulevard, Mr Xavier Pertierra, the general manager of the Soriamont Steamship Agencies, gave me the latest news of the *Hupeh*. He thought that she had left New Guinea, which meant that, weather permitting, she should reach Manila in a couple of days. Another Swire vessel, the *Poyang*, was likely to be delayed in Hong Kong, he said. Yet another Swire ship, the *Asian Jade*, was on its way, but it was a container ship and not so pretty. The *Hupeh* had an owner's cabin, he added. She had a nice name too.

The *Hupeh* seemed certain to stop a day and a night in Taiwan, probably at the port of Keelung (Chi-lung), on her way to Hong Kong. Mr Pertierra urged me to get myself a visa from the Taiwanese consul, for I wouldn't be allowed ashore there without one.

Manila is one of those capital cities – they are in the majority these days – in which the Taiwanese consulate must pretend to be something else. Marcos's government recognized mainland China; officially, therefore, the Philippines has no Taiwanese diplomatic connection at all.

Duncan Pring guided me to the right building, pointing out where the office sheltered coyly behind a notice – 'Pacific Economic and Cultural Centre' – that assumed a bland innocence. I took the lift. On the eighth floor a door faced me, with nothing but a sign that said OPEN. Beyond it, a second door said, AUTHORISED PERSON ONLY. Inside were counters, partitions and girls behind stacks of passports with application forms in them, like waitresses behind piles of cafeteria sandwiches.

When I reached the head of a queue a girl looked at me and said, severely, 'You'll need a certificate for your transit visa application.' I returned to Soriamont where the kindly Mr Pertierra dictated a certificate to his secretary:

This is to certify that Mr. Gavin David Young will board our M.S. HUPEH sailing Manila for Kaohsiung, Keelung and Hong Kong. Inasmuch as the M.S. HUPEH is not a passenger ship, sea fare tickets are not issued before arrival of the vessel; only the Master will do so on board.

Back at the eighth-floor office, this did the trick and my transit application was granted.

The next day Duncan Pring rang to say that the *Hupeh* had arrived, and was expected to sail in two days, some time in the evening. The next-to-last leg of my journey was secure.

Chapter Thirty-Eight

M ADANG, LAE, KIMBE, Rabaul, Kieta: these ports formed part of the ocean-girt island chain of calling places familiar to the crew of the China Navigation Company's *Hupeh*. How many geography teachers can name the islands on which these small and remote towns are situated?

The *Hupeh* had come to Manila direct from Port Moresby, the capital of Papua New Guinea. But these other names? The captain, Ralph Kennet, had to tell me that Madang and Lae are also ports of Papua, but on its northern coast; and that Kimbe and Rabaul, a day's steaming apart, are both on the island of New Britain, which divides the Bismarck Sea from the Solomon Sea, east of Papua. Good names; they seemed to me to speak of those 'tales, marvellous tales/Of ships and stars and isles where good men rest'.

Nylon fishing nets (for Rabaul), plastic combs (from Port Moresby), talcum powder and asphalt roofing (for Kimbe), sewing machines (from Kao-hsiung in Taiwan to Nouméa in New Caledonia), copra cakes, shells to make buttons, car parts and plywood are some of the general cargoes that the China Navigation Company – part of John Swire's Oriental dominion – carry through the area in the holds of the *Hupeh*.

Captain Kennet was in his early fifties, an old hand east of Suez, including all seas and most shorelines between Jedda in the Red Sea and the Fiji Islands in the Pacific, and between Vladivostok in eastern Russia and Perth in Western Australia. He was a man of medium height, slight, with grey eyes and a humorous mouth, which, after a glass or two of the rum and Coke to which he was partial off duty, took on the mobility of a comedian's hand puppet. He was a good man to sail with – warm-hearted, modest, a born talker, intelligent and funny. He had worked out East for half a lifetime, but for his retirement he had bought what he called 'my shed' in Gloucestershire. From his photographs, I could see that this was a fine country house in Cotswold stone. He was not a Gloucester man himself, but a York-shireman from Don-caster, which is how he pronounced it. This led to much good-natured badinage with the chief officer, a much younger Yorkshireman called Jimmy Granger, who came from Robin Hood's Bay.

Kennet had a fine way with words, and liked to employ unlikely ones that meant something nobody quite under-stood. 'You're a nutmeg, you are,' he said laughing over a drink in the ship's little bar after a sally by Granger, adding 'You're as daft as a brush.' ('God knows what "nutmeg" means,' Jimmy Granger said when I asked him later. 'No one knows. Maybe the Old Man doesn't either.')

Kennet had dipped into English literature too and quo-tations slipped out of him at the most unlikely moments. ' "Shall I com-pare thee to a soomer's day?" ' he murmured once to Granger on the bridge apropos of nothing at all, and then turned on his heel and disappeared down the companionway.

The *Hupeh* had more British officers than any ship I had travelled on so far. Apart from the captain and first officer, her officers included a Scots chief engineer named Jimmy Morrison, a second engineer with a beard, and a second and third officer, respectively a Londoner and a Pole who lived in Essex. The radio officer was a Pakistani, Sajid Ali, and the third and fourth engineers were Chinese and Burmese. There were also three cadets, two of them Hong Kong Chinese and one a long-haired boy from New Guinea called Samson.

Jim Morrison, the chief engineer, had been the first on the *Hupeh* to welcome me. Boarding a big ship for the first time is an uneasy experience, and each time I did so I remembered boarding the *Northgate* all those years ago, so I was grateful to him from that moment. He was standing in the doorway of his cabin as Mr Cheung, the steward, led the way to the owner's cabin next door. 'You could do with a beer, I've no doubt,' he said and, when I gratefully agreed, he handed me an opened, chilled can of Brisbane beer.

Morrison's cabin had a false fireplace of real stone and a mock fire that switched on and pretended to be real. He had a red face, a moustache and an arrangement of cheeks, jaw and teeth that reminded me of pictures of the middle-aged Arnold Bennett. On one wall a poster displayed 'The Game Birds of Scotland', and several knick-knacks and bits of tartan, as well as Morrison's accent, spoke of north Britain. Attached to the cabin was an equally large bedroom and a bathroom with a real bath.

'A bath! You could bring your wife with you.'

'Oh, I have in the past. Mr Cheung, the steward, calls her "My Missy".' He pointed to a framed photograph showing an attractive blonde woman. 'That's Betty. She's lived in Hong Kong for twenty years. Trouble is, rents are awful high there now, so we've bought a place in Scotland. That's the only place for me in the end.'

The Morrison I saw later in his engine room was a prince in his dominion. I would never have descended into that kingdom except by special invitation. Gleaming cliffs of metal towered up to the skylights far overhead like the walls of the Ice King's palace and, though the *Hupeh* was far from being a giant of the seas, the descent down those twisting, metal catwalks and companionways was a dizzying experience. As I descended towards Morrison's upturned face, the infernal racket of the engines seemed to engulf me.

'What's the matter?' Morrison shouted in my ear when I reached him. 'It's verra quiet down hee-er, isn't it?'

He wandered confidently about in oily white overalls turning wheels, tapping dials, and patted the shoulder of a young Chinese who stood, hands on hips, a torch in his hip pocket, a spanner in his breast pocket, watching the telegraph. On metal walks, other Chinese engineers peered at electrical switches and panels, padding like caged animals up and down shimmering catwalks between rods, pipes and tubes.

The *Hupeh*'s crew was Chinese to a man, all from Hong Kong. Most of them had worked on China Navigation Company vessels for years, even decades. Swire's, everyone said, was a good employer, and had been since John Samuel Swire started trading in the Far East in 1866.

Ralph Kennet liked Chinese – luckily, for he could hardly have worked on ships out East if he had been unable to get on with them. For one thing, he didn't underestimate them. 'The essential thing in coping with a Chinese crew', he explained, 'is to understand from the outset that *you can't win. They* are going to win any dispute. Now, when that piece of wisdom has settled into your brain, it's simply a question of hanging on as long as you can until the inevitable moment when you give up. Face. You save that, d'y'see? But then you give in. Got it?'

Kennet had had experience. He'd even had a mutiny. 'It

was in Brisbane, years ago – '67, '68. The crew began shouting and yelling and meeting and discussing. All about work shifts or pay. They'd come to me; I'd answer their complaints; they'd have another conference and start shouting again. So it went, back and forth. I'd start out patiently explaining, but at the end one of them would say that he couldn't understand my Cantonese dialect – could I speak Hakka? Another would shout he wanted everything explained in Swatownese, and another in Mandarin. On and on, just to foil me. I couldn't win. No one could.'

Kennet had a basic maxim: 'Watch your crew in fine weather. That's when there can be trouble. If it's rough, there are no problems; people feel they need each other, and close ranks. The complaining begins when it's calm.' I remembered the closeness Londoners felt in the aerial bombardment of the Second World War.

He swapped my tale of the Moros with one about Chinese pirates. Selwyn Jones was the name of the last captain to be pirated in the China Navigation Company – well, touch wood, Kennet added. In the Taiwan Strait, it was, about 1955. 'A junk came alongside old Selwyn's ship, the *Hupeh* – the old *Hupeh*, not this one. It had Oerlikon guns aboard, and it fired a few rounds, so Selwyn Jones prudently stopped.' Here Kennet stopped, too, remembering what a character Selwyn Jones had been.

'Well, he sent off a radio SOS and then went to his cabin and sat there, waiting for his visitors. The pirates burst in armed to the teeth, filling the cabin. At first, he said, he was nonplussed, and just looked at them through his misty glasses. They stared back. This wouldn't do. He pulled himself together and sent for his quartermaster, a Chinese, to translate. "Who is the Number One pirate?"

he asked of this wild crowd. One or two pointed to one of them, and he stared at the man for a minute, then suddenly yelled, "He's got a bloodshot eye. It's bloodshot. Send for the doctor." The pirates were thunderstruck.

'They laid the Number One pirate down and the chief officer poured eyedrops into his eyes. The pirates were bamboozled by this and, when their Number One had got up blinking and happy, they disappeared for some time, coming back eventually to hand Jones a handful of fountain pens. They were all filched from the passengers, of course, but it was the thought that counted and this was their way of thanking him.

'Now, what was admirable about all this, and showed there is trust and honour at sea even among pirates, was that, when a New Zealand frigate appeared at the top of the strait in response to the radio call, the pirates did not do Selwyn any mischief. Formerly, in like circumstances, a captain and his chief mate would have been taken ashore and marched all over China, sometimes shown to the public in cages, like strange animals. Now the pirates came to Selwyn and said, "Look at that frigate. We'll need hostages. You'll have to come ashore with us." Nasty.

'But Selwyn stood up slowly and majestically, like some sort of white god. "Go in peace," he said, like Jupiter addressing a few of his favourite mortals. "I will personally order that frigate to bugger off. You, pirate chappies one and all, are not to worry. Savee?"

'Perhaps he used the royal "we". At any rate, those murderous Chinese pirates trusted him, and off they went and the *Hupeh* sailed on. All because of those eyedrops in the Number One pirate's eye.'

'The captain of the New Zealand frigate must have been

mystified. One moment "Pirates aboard", the next "Bugger off".'

'I daresay old Selwyn Jones explained it all to him later over a gin. Bit of nutmeg, Selwyn Jones.'

A deck higher, in the ship's laundry, a dignified white-haired Chinese with the face of an elderly violinist worked among a garden of white cotton shirts on hangers. A huge pair of white bloomers three feet across, like a giant's shorts, was draped over a clothes horse.

The old laundryman saw me looking at them, and laughed. 'Those tlousa belong ladio offica. Indian style. Velly stlange tlousa. One day on ship I see many tlousa same this in laundly. All Indian. Velly funny.'

My cabin was straight out of Somerset Maugham. Bigger than that on the *Perak* and the *Straits Hope*, the owner's cabin consisted of a dayroom with simple panelling, a desk, a large table, a sofa and armchairs, and a quartz wall clock; a good-sized bedroom; and a shower room leading off a tiny entrance in which hung five lifejackets – made, a tag said, by Cheong Keo of Hong Kong, three for 'persons under 70 lbs.' and two for 'persons of 70 lbs. or more'. Every morning Mr Cheung, the motherly steward, a pale-skinned man with widely spaced eyes, knocked on the door and quietly entered in soft black Chinese slippers.

'Bling breakfast now, afta five minutes.'

'Thanks, Mr Cheung.'

'Okay same-same yestaday?'

'Yes, fine.'

'Egg, bacon, melon, two toast, mamalade, butta, okay?'

'Okay.'

The officers seldom used the dining room together.

According to their watches, they ate at staggered intervals, and wasted no time at the table. In the bar after dinner, the scene was livelier. Here Ralph Kennet's genial cries of 'You're a nutmeg, you are' could be heard while one officer or another served behind the little bar. Here, one evening, Jimmy Granger, the first officer, gave us the history of the Battle of Trafalgar as seen by a Yorkshire lad named Joe. In the quiet accent of Robin Hood's Bay, leaning on the bar, he recited:

> 'I'll tell you a seafarin' story
> Of a lad 'oo won 'onour and fame,
> Wi' Nelson at Battle Trafalgar.
> Joe Muggeridge, that were 'is name.
> ''Ee were one o' the crew o' the *Victory*
> An' 'is job when t' battle begun
> Were ta pick cannonballs out t' basket
> And shove 'em down front end o' t' gun.'

Many stanzas later Admiral Nelson was declaring that Joe deserved the VC.

'But findin' 'ee 'adn't none 'andy,
'Ee gave Joe an egg fer 'is tea.
An' when battle were over,
An' t' *Victory* were safely in dock,
Crew saved up all their coupons –
And bought Joe a nice marble clock.'

'Daft as a brush,' said Ralph Kennet, happily congratulating Granger for his recitation. On that warm note we sailed next day into the port of Kao-hsiung on the island of Taiwan, formerly known as Formosa.

A scattering of small explosions greeted us at the approach to Kao-hsiung harbour, and puffs of blue smoke from fire-crackers floated across the narrow entrance, where a cluster of fishing boats jostled each other. Ralph Kennet was already on the bridge, bareheaded, wearing half-moon glasses. 'How'd you feel this mornin', Gavin?'

'Not so good, thanks.'

'Ha! Nutmeg!'

'At 6.30 a.m. it was cold; the bronze sun glowed without warmth through a thick haze. Our wake trailed slowly behind us, luminously green like submerged coral, and lingered long after our passing in a level sea that looked oily and sluggish. A Liberian-registered tanker, the *Fortune*, lay hove to, a rusty Greek beyond her, and on our side a Panamanian ship called *Fiji*, well down in the water and her deck smothered in tree trunks.

The fishing boats danced impertinently around our bows, and men in windcheaters whistled and shouted, 'Go away,' at us from their sterns, as if they were legally blockading the harbour mouth, not simply obstructing it. Dead slow ahead. Kennet looked impatient, and the *Hupeh* hooted once like an exasperated whale.

Gun emplacements and blockhouses overlooked the narrow entrance to the harbour. Considering Taiwan's mistrust of China, I imagined anti-submarine devices on the seabed. A sentry in a steel helmet made no response when I waved to him. Past the entrance, the grey skyline of the city formed a backdrop to rows of ships under the nodding cranes at the wharves.

We edged stern first into a berth next to the *Vishva Amabar* of Bombay. 'Curry ship,' explained Sajid Ali, the Pakistani radio officer, who stood on the wing of the bridge with me, watching the third mate – the young Pole, Komorowski – shirtless, marshalling the Hong Kong apprentices in the stern. ('Curry ship' means any ship from India.)

The day before, I had noticed that Ralph Kennet, seeing one of his officers taking his watch naked to the waist, had not rebuked him, although many captains would have fulminated against such slovenly dress on the bridge. Later I mentioned this to him. 'No point in making a fuss on the bridge,' said Kennet. 'I had a quiet word later.'

Jimmy Granger murmured into his radio handset, 'Send the heaving line from the stern.'

In the stern, Komorowski's mouth moved, and his voice came out of Granger's handset. 'Come again?'

'The heaving line.'

A line flew from the stern on to the concrete wharf; the *Hupeh* slid alongside, a bump sent a shiver through her deck, and then she was motionless. Komorowski peered at the *Sovereign Ventura*, the freighter just astern of us, and reported, 'Fifty foot clear.'

'Finished with engines.'

The Chinese were eager to go ashore; there were cheap clothes and esoteric items of food they wanted to buy. Next day the old laundryman with the violinist's face said he had bought a lot of dried meat. 'Hong Kong has, but velly expensive, so I buy here for cousins, childlen.'

Captain Kennet knocked on my cabin door and said, 'The agent's asked me to dinner tonight. Like to come? About six o'clock. Good Chinese food, I dare say.'

On an earlier visit to Taiwan, a few years before, I had particularly liked the food of the indigenous Taiwanese, but now our gastronomic ambitions were thwarted. The agent, a pleasant young Chinese in a dark suit, came aboard and said to Kennet, 'I have a car waiting. What food do you like?'

'Chinese,' said Kennet. 'In Taiwan, what else, eh?'

'Certainly, Chinese, please,' I said.

We bundled into the car and the agent unhesitatingly drove us to a Japanese restaurant; waitresses brought us shashimi. 'Is this saké that I see before me?' said Ralph Kennet. 'Come, let me pour thee.'

At night Kao-hsiung had a gloomy, closed-down air; it seemed to consist of large grey warehouses. We were back on board by ten o'clock, the mystery of the Japanese food unsolved.

'I know you want to see one, but you shouldn't.' Over a late-night rum and Coke, Ralph Kennet was answering my question about the chances of running into a typhoon in the China Sea.

In *Typhoon*, Captain MacWhirr, the master of the steamer *Nanshan* heading to Foo-chow, thinks to himself, 'There's some dirty weather knocking about,' and soon that 'ordinary, irresponsive and unruffled' but experienced old salt is vouchsafed his first horrifying and unforgettable glimpse of the sea's 'immeasurable strength and immoderate wrath that passes exhausted but never appeased'. I wanted to see for myself what I had read about in Conrad: the swell increasing, the ship labouring extravagantly and taking water on her decks, the barometer inexorably falling; then, the great darkness lying upon a multitude of white flashes, the rain, the crushing weight of toppling waves, the howlings of the gale . . .

Kennet had seen typhoons, had seen ships anchored near the shore dragging their anchors. He'd known that uncontrolled yawing could wrench them out of the mud, turning them so that their teeth came upwards and couldn't grip, so once he had had two anchors out and had put the helm over to port to prevent the yawing. His ship had held firm while others broke loose.

'I wouldn't want to go through that again, not if you gave me the moon between two slices of bread. The other wretched ships were sliding back past me and were washed up on the beach. Oh, yes, washed *right* up. One of our captains had an engine that broke down. It could have been repaired if he'd gone down to the engine room and said, "Get that bloody engine going." But where was he? On the bridge, you'd think, right? But he was with the passengers conducting "Abide with Me".' He laughed. 'Of course the passengers loved it, but the poor bloody ship was dumped so far inland that they had to dig a canal to get her into the water again. "Abide with Me" indeed! The chief engineer and engine-room staff were fired. By rights, *he* should have been fired too. What a nutmeg.'

By now, the Land Above the Wind was well below us. This was Typhoon Alley, said Kennet, an area embracing Guam, northern Luzon, Taiwan and eastern Japan. From here rogue typhoons ran amok to Saigon and Hong Kong. But we didn't sail into one, and now I realize how lucky we were. A day or two ago, as I was writing this chapter, the radio reported that a 190,000-ton British tanker, the *Derbyshire*, foundered with all hands in a typhoon in that area. When her owners confirmed her loss, other ships gathered to strew wreaths over the spot where she went down without a trace.

Sajid Ali, the radio officer, walked with me towards his radio room. Ralph Kennet had allowed me to communicate with a friend in Hong Kong; we would be there next morning.

A smell of curry filled the corridor. 'Ah, ha. Now I see what you were up to in Kao-hsiung,' said Jimmy Granger, coming the other way and pointing to Sajid's hair, which had been blow-dried into a silky quiff. 'Very pretty, Sparky.'

Sajid sniffed the air. 'Umm, what a delicious smell. Curry.'

Granger grinned. 'Too bad for you, Sparky. It's pork.'

'Hell.'

On the ship's radio telephone I talked to Donald Wise in Hong Kong, who told me he would book me into the Luk Kwok Hotel in the Wanchai district of the island. 'It's the world-of-Suzie-Wong district. You should be happy there.' I could sense his leer across the airwaves.

Chapter Thirty-Nine

THERE ACTUALLY *WAS* a Suzie Wong Bar just behind the Luk Kwok Hotel, although I never passed through its doors. Nor did I visit the Pussy Cat topless nightclub announced by a tall neon sign next door, or a hotel that advertised 'Rooms Purely for Let' (I liked the 'purely'). The Luk Kwok Hotel was not that sort of place. It was a modest Chinese hotel, where I seemed constantly to be meeting in the corridors elderly and dignified lady servants shuffling about in black silk slippers and carrying bowls of cornflakes.

The Luk Kwok wasn't far from the offices of the China Navigation Company in the multi-storeyed Swire House, and I called in there to say thank you for their help,

although, of course, it was John and Glen Swire in London I had to be grateful to.

I missed the *Hupeh* as soon as I left her at anchor in the western roadstead near Stonecutters Island. I sat unhappily on the hard bench of the launch that carried me and smiling crew members to the landing stage under the new towers of Kowloon. Most of them clutched plastic bags of duty-free goods from Kao-hsiung. I had seen them on *Hupeh*'s deck only in oily shorts, T-shirts and heavy rust-stained gloves; now, their hair neatly oiled, their scrubbed bodies dressed in well-pressed blue serge, white shirts and sober ties, they waited in formal Chinese fashion to be reunited with their families. Suddenly I was conscious of my scruffy look, of uncombed hair, of the hole in my sports shirt and the oil and sweat stains that had become ineradically part of it since leaving Sandakan.

I missed the *Hupeh* partly because I was leaving the last big ship of my long odyssey. Captain Kennet would soon be leaving the *Hupeh* to take up command of China Navigation's *Coral Princess*, and would begin shuttling Japanese passengers between Korea, Japan and China. If I could have continued on the *Hupeh*, I would have been able to see Madang, Lae, Kimbe, Rabaul and Kieta from her decks. Once more I had to remind myself that a voyage is not a marriage.

'You took your time.' At the Luk Kwok I was reunited with Donald Wise, and with the unexorcisable ghosts of Vietnam.

I had first met Donald's tall, lean soldierly figure in the Congo (as Zaïre was called then) during the bloody upheavals that month after month in 1960 and 1961 replaced rejoicing for independence in Kinshasa (then called Leopoldville after Leopold II, the despotic, colonizing king of the Belgians) when we both were war correspondents. The massacres and horrors of the Congo in 1960 and 1961 had been mirrored to some degree in an uprising in 1961 in the neighbouring Portuguese colony of Angola, and Donald had written from its capital, Luanda, a story that began so vividly that I have never forgotten it:

> The first African to die before my eyes on this Black-and-White battleground nearly fell into my beer. A group of Whites had thrown him off the roof of a six-storey building, and he crashed to his death through the candy-striped umbrella of a main street café.

Thereafter we had run into each other on many battlefields, from Africa to Vietnam. In the days before the full-scale American military invasion of Vietnam, when the US involvement was still confined mainly to advisers, the marines and aerial bombardment, Donald had taken the trouble to look closely at a Vietcong guerrilla:

> He is lying dead at my feet, trussed hand and foot and hung on a long pole like a wild pig. His skin, showing through his rumpled black pyjamas, is parchment-coloured. In life, he was the colour of butterscotch.
>
> He was shot by US Marines . . . He is about 5 ft 2 in. tall, six inches shorter than model Jean Shrimpton, but weighing the same 120 lbs. He carries a week's rations of glutinous rice – flavoured with a sauce made of rotting fish and sea water – in a cloth bandolier around his

chest. He wears flip-flops on his feet – sandals made of worn rubber tyres.

Not only did Donald interest himself in communist (and other) Vietnamese, which most writers on Vietnam have failed to do even today (Graham Greene is one outstanding exception), but he also put, in that piece, a finger on a great truth about the Vietnam war, about the parochial psychology of America in the 1960s and about the unquenchable soul of Asia. In 1965 he wrote:

American planes will continue a fiery rain of napalm. But still the key to all this is the little man at my feet. Someone has to go into his shadowy country to convince him that he is *not* the world's greatest jungle fighter. The Americans can bomb North Vietnam until the cows come home, but they will never win the war without doing this.

And they never did.

I registered at the Luk Kwok and then took a taxi with Donald to the Foreign Correspondents Club.

On the staircase to the fifth-floor dining room were reminders in photographs greatly enlarged: a Vietnamese soldier in a desolation of the spirit, his head in his hands in an empty room; an American gunner in a helicopter screaming across the dead body of his comrade; a Vietnamese family – mother, baby and three small children – swimming for dear life. They had been taken by Larry Burrows, of *Life* magazine, born 1925, died 1971; and Kyochi Sawada, of United Press International, born 1936, died 1970. Both were friends of mine, Larry a close one.

People who saw it happen told me that, when a missile hit the helicopter Larry Burrows was riding in over Laos, it dropped into the jungle 'like an egg'.

Grim memories, not easy to put out of mind in Hong Kong. Suddenly Vietnam seemed very close again. In this city, which is still a great press centre, one was aware of the comings and goings of journalists; of men and women working for the Red Cross, Save the Children, Oxfam or Caritas in the camps in Thailand for starving Cambodian refugees; of fifty-five thousand Vietnamese boat people in camps in Hong Kong.

In the atmosphere of the Foreign Correspondents Club it was impossible to forget the reports and colour pictures from the camps in Thailand; the reports from journalists in the interior of Cambodia; the interviews with Khmer Rouge leaders, who served whisky and wine and asked to be excused for the premeditated killing of half a million or one million (or was it a million and a half?) of their own people; the descriptions of fields of human skulls; the accounts of exhausted boat people, after many days at sea, raped, robbed or killed by Thai fishermen at the very moment when they seemed to have found safety for themselves and their children on the islands and shores of the Gulf of Siam. But they were as hard to think about as they were to forget. One could only summon up a monstrous revulsion against the perpetrators of these immeasurable miseries, and at the same time feel an overwhelming tenderness towards South-east Asians. The little soldier from Nha Trang muttering, 'Hurt, me,' and dying in the rain across my knees had been a hundred times luckier than some. What had my Khmer friends who gave me the dancing dolls suffered before they died?

'Boys throw stones at frogs in sport,' wrote Plutarch. 'But frogs do not die in sport, they die in earnest.'

Were the politicians at their sport plotting similar horrors for Chandra, Sumar and Crazy Jan?

Donald Wise, now an editor on the *Far Eastern Economic Review,* loved Asia and wanted to stay in Hong Kong, perhaps for ever, but he hadn't reached this decision thoughtlessly. He had seen the war in Vietnam; he had also been a prisoner of the Japanese and, as such, had worked on the notorious railway over the bridge on the River Kwai. Fifty thousand prisoners died on that railway building a line two hundred and fifty miles long. Over a drink in the club bar we talked about an amazing event a year or two before, when survivors and Japanese guards had arranged – at the suggestion of a guilt-ridden Japanese liberal business-man – a reunion on that bridge in Thailand.

'I felt a twinge,' Donald said, 'when I saw those Japanese tumbling out of their airport bus in that follow-your-leader, don't-push-just-shove way of Japanese tourists.'

'Did they look like the brutal guards you remembered?'

'Mostly farmers. Brutal? No, you couldn't say that. Small and sunburned. In the old days, because of their size, they made all but the smallest prisoners kneel to be beaten.'

Up to then, the imperial Japanese army had used pris-oners for live bayonet practice, but now the generals in Japan had ordered the railway to be built at whatever cost in prisoners or Japanese soldiers.

'We'd seen Japanese officers kick and whip their own men, and at the reunion every ex-POW made a point of mentioning this. You see, it explained a lot, even though it didn't excuse a damned thing.'

Memories. The memory, for example, of the two-minute anaesthesia under Thai liquor or amateur hypnosis for an amputation; of someone running to the guardhouse to plead for the wood saw when the water for sterilizing it had come to a boil; of the Japanese guards ineptly shooting a young prisoner who had contracted cholera – so ineptly that he lay screaming on the ground and a British officer in tears had seized a guard's rifle and given him the *coup de grâce*.

'I didn't want to go berserk and assault anybody at that reunion. The Japanese who had organized the get-together told us how the British prisoners had buried cigarette tins with their dead mates, and in the tins were detailed reports on the behaviour of inhuman guards in the hope that eventually they would be punished. Which a lot of them were.'

When he wrote about the reunion for the *Far Eastern Economic Review,* Donald concluded: 'It seemed that by saying *sayonara* to the fallen together, we made some sort of step towards reality.'

Seen through the windows of the Foreign Correspondents Club, white multi-windowed buildings march like a forest of dragon's teeth up the slopes of the Mid-Levels district and down to Star Ferry. One of the most obtrusive buildings on the waterfront had rows of circular windows. The Chinese called it the House of a Thousand Arseholes.

Sitting at a table by a dining-room window, two journalist friends looked up from their aperitifs and beckoned us over. They were Marsh Clark, the head of the Hong Kong bureau of *Time,* a quiet American with the face of a sad young senator, and Dick Hughes, the dean of all journalists in the Far East, Australian, in his seventies, his figure that of an arthritic Buddha, his face the colour of a cardinal's robe, his hair the soft white fringe of a bishop. 'Welcome, your Grace,' Hughes boomed pontifically, raising a glass of vodka and ice in salute.

For years the Far East correspondent of the London *Sunday Times*, Hughes had written about his flamboyant life and times in a book called *Foreign Devil*. He had started out in Japan during the Second World War before Pearl Harbor, and since then few people or events of note had passed him by. In Tokyo, he had attended drinking sessions with Stalin's 'super-spy' Richard Sorge, who had saved him from a beating at the hands of a Nazi diplomat, and he had talked exclusively with Guy Burgess and Donald Maclean after they had defected to Moscow. He was a Sherlock Holmes addict and expert. Ian Fleming, author and creator of James Bond, had been his boss at the *Sunday Times* and a friend, and in Fleming's novel *You Only Live Twice* Hughes had appeared in the fictional guise of Australia's secret service boss in Tokyo. Later, John le Carré turned him into old Craw, a British agent, in *The Honourable Schoolboy*. I had seen Hughes easing his arthritic legs out of an American helicopter in the Central Highlands battle zone of Vietnam when he was well into his sixties. Now, ten years later, he showed few signs of wear.

'You've heard of Dick's burglary?' Donald Wise asked.

'I have been robbed four times in my thirty-five years of happy travail in the Orient as a resident barefoot reporter,' Hughes declaimed in the rolling tones of an Australian Mr Micawber. 'Twice in Tokyo between 1948 and 1950 by individual operators, once in Laos by a gang of two and now, with my wife in Hong Kong by a gang of three armed with a meat cleaver and heavy sticks. They were Cantonese thugs, evidently illegal immigrants from Canton, who threatened my dear Chinese wife with the cleaver and struck me with a stick, and then gagged and bound us in our humble Mid-Levels abode at 3.00 a.m.'

Dick stuck a fork into the boeuf Wellington on his plate. Marsh Clark poured more wine.

I said, 'Donald, did anyone whistle "Colonel Bogey" when you were building that railway line over the River Kwai as they did in the film?'

'I never heard it in Thailand. We hadn't much breath left for whistling. But in Bangkok I was told that David Lean, the film's director, became mad at the extras who played the prisoners – us – because they couldn't march in time. Lean shouted at them, "For God's sake, whistle a march to keep time to." And a bloke called George Siegatz—'

'George who, your Eminence?'

'George Siegatz – an expert whistler – began to whistle "Colonel Bogey", and a hit was born.'

Dick said, 'Donald's piece on the River Kwai was right. The past is passed. Think about the past, yes. Talk about it. But never worry about it.'

A photocopy of an old newspaper dated 19 February 1968, whose front-page headline read 'US Throws More Troops into Battle', hung in a frame on the wall opposite me. It was datelined Dong Ha, South Vietnam, the site of a mountain named Hamburger Hill because American generals fed their soldiers into the long battle to capture it as if they were stuffing meat into a sausage machine. Marsh's eye followed mine to the front page on the wall, and he said, 'I want to forget the whole goddamn thing.'

'You're not likely to,' Donald said.

Marsh had just returned, he explained, from Cambodia, where he had visited the hidden headquarters of what was left of the Khmer Rouge army of Pol Pot and interviewed Khieu Samphan, the Khmer Rouge 'prime minister'. Marsh was a member of an international committee of journalists who were attempting to trace Western reporters still missing in Cambodia. Over fifty of them had been killed in Vietnam and Cambodia – that was known – but these were missing. Now he took some sheets of paper from a briefcase. 'Take a look. This is a copy of what I asked Khieu Samphan.'

I read:

Q. One final matter I want to bring up. It is a matter which is profoundly disturbing to many people, and that is the disappearance in Kampuchea [Cambodia] of twenty-one Western journalists without trace. I am sure you are aware of them. I have a list of their names here. What happened to these journalists? Are any of them still alive? I would like to set this matter at historic rest. There are worried wives and parents and friends.

A. I would like to know the exact time this happened.

Q. Here are the dates.

A. I don't need the exact days, but a general idea.

Q. In 1970 and 1971 in Svay Rieng Province, and on various routes leading out to the countryside from Phnom Penh. Twenty-one journalists disappeared and have never been heard from again.

A. I can say to you that all the foreign journalists that were captured were released. We gave them all back.

Q. Is it possible that any journalists were alive in

Cambodia during your administration? You would surely have known about them?

A. I am sure that if there were any foreign journalists in our hands, I would have been aware of that.

Q. So you are not aware of any journalists alive?

A. No, none.

I ran my eye down the pages containing the names and a few details of the missing men:

Marc Filloux: French citizen working for Associated Press. Last seen April 12, 1974, in Sithandone Province in Laos near the Cambodian border.

Taizo Ichinosei: Japanese freelance photographer. Last seen November 22, 1972, near Angkor Wat, Cambodia.

Wells Hangen: American journalist with NBC. Last seen on May 31, 1970, on way from Phnom Penh to Takeo.

Kitomoharu Ishii: Japanese television photographer . . .

Kieter Bellindorf: German television cameraman . . .

Sean Flynn: American freelance working for *Time* as a photographer . . .

Dana Stone: American photographer . . .

The names went on and on. I had known Wells Hangen for years. Sean Flynn was the son of the film star Errol Flynn. Most journalists in Vietnam and Cambodia had known him and his friend, Dana Stone. They had vanished together.

'So they're all dead,' I said.

'They're dead,' Marsh said. 'Plus the fifty more who were verified. The wounded are extra.'

There was a pause. Then Dick swept up his glass. 'The wine that cheers, your Graces?' he cried. 'It's an evil world, and it's not going to get any better. Christ in hell, no.'

I had other, happier, if more trivial, matters to mention to Hughes. Dick was one of the founders in Tokyo in 1948 of the Baritsu Chapter of the Baker Street Irregulars, the worldwide fraternity of readers of Arthur Conan Doyle's stories who staunchly profess to believe that the great detective actually trod this earth. 'Holmes, of course, is alive and well and still living in Sussex, although by now, I'm afraid, he must be a hundred and twenty-six years old,' he said after our lunch.

I broke to him my disconcerting news from the Andamans that Watson had erred in his chronicle of the murder of Bartholomew Sholto at Pondicherry Lodge. Further, he had compounded the slip in his account of the subsequent capture of Jonathan Small and the little Andaman 'hellhound', Tonga, on the Thames between Barking Level and Plumstead Marshes.

Hughes took the news well, only asking mildly, 'Are you personally convinced that blowpipes and darts never existed in the Andaman forests? It was always spears, bows and arrows?'

Reluctantly I told him that I had been able to find no evidence of blowpipes and darts. He shook his head sadly. 'Watson's slip-up, I imagine. Certainly not Holmes's.'

But what about the presence of the white convict Small in the Andaman penal colony around the time of the Indian Mutiny? I had to inform Dick that there seemed to be no record establishing that a European convict had ever been sent there, much less one with a wooden leg. Again he shook his head dolefully. 'But the records on that score could be incomplete, don't you think?'

I had to admit that they could be. Though they would attract attention today, wooden legs would have been hardly worth mentioning in the aftermath of the Mutiny.

'And breakwaters? Small told Holmes that the convicts spent a lot of their time building breakwaters in the Andamans. Are there any there?'

I was glad to be able to assure him that there were several.

Dick Hughes had mentioned that he believed illegal immigrants from Canton had bound and robbed his wife and himself in the middle of the night. From time to time I had read newspaper stories about how Chinese men and women risked their lives in waters full of sharks in trying to swim to Hong Kong from the coast of the communist mainland.

Understandably, the Hong Kong newspapers were obsessed with the problem; five hundred Chinese were said to be infiltrating into the overcrowded little colony every day. 'Send Back All the I.I.s', a frontpage headline in the *Star* said on the day I arrived. A Chinese member of the Hong Kong Legislative Council proposed new laws to prevent employers from hiring illegal immigrants, to stop their obtaining identity cards, and to crack down on landlords renting any premises to them. 'News of these tough measures would soon spread across the border and should help reduce this unlawful exodus at its source,' he said. But clearly the bright lights of Hong Kong, reflecting off the clouds and easily visible from the mainland, would continue to tempt people into these dangerous waters.

Donald Wise knew an assistant commissioner of the Hong Kong police who was directly involved with the problem of illegal Chinese immigrants, and I made an appointment to see him.

About 178,000 immigrants crossed into Hong Kong every year, he said, and of these 110,000 came illegally. Another 90,000 were caught and promptly sent back to China. It was like the children's game of Grandmother's Footsteps, he explained. If an illegal entrant was clever enough to sneak past all the obstacles – sea searches, army and police patrols, barbed-wire fences, dogs, sharks, treacherous currents – and reach the sanctuary of the home of a relative already living in the colony, he was 'home'; he could apply for and would be granted an identity card, and henceforth could remain in Hong Kong legally. The pavement outside the immigration office was often blocked for a hundred yards or so with men and women who had made it 'home' lining up for their identity cards; they were the lucky ones who could smile and be patient now. But an average of 130 unlucky ones were caught every day.

'They swim over?'

'The swimmers are the young ones – fifteen to twenty-nine years old. Farmers or fishermen. The family groups come by sea in boats – men, women, small children. It's the swimmers, of course, who are taken by sharks, but that doesn't stop them trying. I don't think our job of trying to keep them out will be redundant for some time – perhaps not until conditions in China are the same as they are here.'

The assistant commissioner's walls displayed a rash of maps and charts. 'It's a three-hundred-sixty-degree problem. A hundred and twenty miles of sea and twenty miles of land to patrol.'

I pointed to the pimple labelled Macao, the Portuguese smaller Hong Kong a little further down the coast.

'Oh, Macao,' the policeman said sadly. 'Smuggling illegal immigrants from China to Macao to Hong Kong is big money there. The syndicates [the Chinese tongs] actually sell tickets for places in their launches, "snake boats" and speedboats. They are difficult to catch – faster than ours, sometimes.'

Last year the Hong Kong marine police had picked up 451 bodies out of Deep Bay at the mouth of the Pearl river, which runs up to the port of Canton. 'The Chinese are born gamblers,' the assistant commissioner said sadly.

Chapter Forty

A FEW NIGHTS later, when I reached the marine police's illegal immigrant patrol depot, the Chinese crew of the Special Boat Unit (SBU) I had been permitted to accompany were taking their evening meal of pork, fish, rice and beer. After eating, they pulled on camouflage jackets and army-style boots, and looped lanyards with whistles over their shaven necks and into their breast pockets.

Mark Jones, their commander, a blond British officer hardly more than a boy, said, 'Since we have Mr Young with us tonight, we want to catch as many I.I.s as possible, so he can see how active SBU is. Also, he's writing a book, so you may become famous as well.' At this the crew clapped and cheered.

'Another thing, there are more sampans around now carrying hidden I.I.s, so we want to look out for them, too.'

Near Queen Elizabeth's portrait, a notice on the wall

stated: 'From 3rd Nov. 1979 to 26th Nov. 1979, 1,000 I.I.s Arrested. Best total for a night – 80 I.I.s'.

A young Chinese sergeant tugged on a cap with a long peak, and called, 'Ready?'

I asked Jones, 'Do many journalists come out with you?'

'No, very few. Maybe they don't like the wet.'

'Oh, I don't think journalists are scared of water.'

The crew gathered up Sterling sub-machine-guns and gas grenades ('We don't use those,' said Jones) and riot batons ('They're handy sometimes').

Down at the pier a grey launch with 'Police 31' on her side was ready to put to sea, her radar arm already turning, the blue police light glowing at her masthead. The crew carried aboard chopsticks, rice, tea, a boathook, a Verey pistol, blankets, plastic pillows, and a spare Zodiac outboard engine. The big launch acted as the mother ship for four Zodiac motor dinghies, and their crews revved their engines, testing them.

Finally Mark Jones said, 'Cast off.' It was a dismal evening with a grey sea and sky. The islands of Lantau and Ma Wan were outlines of warship-grey in a deep haze. 'Not a bad night for I.I.s,' said Jones. 'They like a bit of mist.' He might have been talking of migrating geese or a rare species of owl.

Our little convoy began to make its way west. At the point of the New Territories we would swing north and head for the white beacon in Hau Hoi Wan, or Deep Bay, whose long northern Chinese shore swept around like the wing of a predatory bird. The mother launch would tie up at the beacon, and the little Zodiacs would start beating about in the darkness of the bay as eagerly as beagles casting for a scent.

Our armament, I noticed, included a .50 calibre Browning on the bows and at least two twelve-bore pump guns. I asked Mark Jones about the rules of the game on this sensitive edge of China. 'We have pistols galore,' he said. '.38s. We also have hand flares. You can tell a sampan, "Stop or we fire," but in no circumstances can you *really* fire – not unless they open fire first. We throw a flare or two at them, and they either stop or move faster to try to reach shore. Then it becomes a race.'

Swimmers who drowned imposed a grisly problem I hadn't considered, for the bodies had to be picked up. Mark Jones said, 'One in every hundred drowns, and the corpses lie around for months. They sink, you see, and surface again after two or three days. The stink is terrific. Of course, they attract sharks. But they might float around to the Hong Kong beaches, and people wouldn't want to see these hideous, bloated bodies, would they? So we have to haul them into our launch. It's not really our work, and the stink can take three or four days to get rid of, but someone has to do it. Unfortunately, we can't stuff them into plastic bags. Our police constables hate to touch a dead body. They're a very superstitious lot, you know – spirits and all that – so I have to disentangle the corpses or arrange them for their photographs to be taken. We get them out of the water by putting a sack and two slings under them and hauling them up, but sometimes an arm or leg slips out. It's really very hard on our boys because, whatever we do, sometimes it's impossible to get the bodies out of the water without touching them. Our crews are all volunteers, by the way.'

'I should think they must be.'

The night crept by. The mist cleared, but it became increasingly cold after midnight, and the policemen began rubbing their hands together. I went below and pulled on my anorak, the one Ali had demanded in very different circumstances. I hadn't worn it since, and when I put my hand in a pocket I found a piece of paper with crazy Jan's address on it. A Chinese corporal brought biscuits and a mug of coffee, and the shift drank it on deck as the generator thudded away. When the shifts changed, the men going off duty went below to the forward cabin, discarded their outer clothing and, in T-shirts and underpants, swung short, white, muscular legs into sleeping bags, zipped up the flaps and fell asleep at once.

I imagined the illegal immigrants paddling slowly across the bay, their hearts racing, chilled from head to foot, led on, like men in a dream, by the lights of Hong Kong reflected on the clouds and the hope of a better life. They had whispered their plans to each other night after night for months, waiting for the high tide, the low moon, the favourable horoscope; now they inched towards us where we waited under the flashing beacon and the crews in the Zodiacs raked the water with their night glasses.

A few minutes later one of the rubber Zodiacs put-putted up, and by the beacon's light I could see its crew of three policemen and five illegal immigrants crouching in the bottom of the Zodiac like the wise monkeys, their hands on their heads.

Hauled on board the gently rolling launch, the four men and one young woman squatted again, staring at the deck between their knees as if they'd lost something there. Expressionless and unresisting, one by one they were made

to stand, and the water of Deep Bay dripped from their dark-blue overall jackets and pants. A policeman removed their belts and handed them blankets; then they were guided below, the men to a shower room the size of a big cupboard, the girl to the toilet.

There was no rough stuff; no one even pushed them. When the questioning started, it was informal, a murmured conversation more than an interrogation. The oldest of the men became spokesman; the youngest listened and tried to smile; the other two, more rustic than their comrades, hung their heads. The single bulb shone on their spiky cropped hair, their high russet cheekbones and wide peasant hands.

Jones said to his Chinese sergeant, 'Okay, ask them,' then translated the Cantonese for me.

'Why do you want to come to Hong Kong?'

'To earn some money.'

'What are your jobs in China?'

'Small farmers. We are very poor.'

'How long have you been in the water?'

'Two hours. Since sunset.'

'Why did you come at this time?'

'It's high tide and there's a little mist.'

'Did they live in Po On district (the border district of Kwangtung, or Guandong, province)?'

No; they came from far away, from outside Kwangtung province even. A month's walk away.

How had they avoided arrest by Chinese soldiers on the way?

Many soldiers had gone to fight the Vietnamese, so there were far fewer to patrol this border now.

'Is this the first time you've tried to escape?'

'Yes.'

'Will you try again?'

'No.' But the sergeant grinned at me and said, 'I don't believe. I see one man come back seven times. Try and try again.'

I asked what would happen to them when they were sent back over the border to China the next morning. The sergeant translated this and their answer: 'A fine of two hundred Hong Kong dollars [twenty pounds] and, if we cannot pay, three months in detention.'

I peeped through a skylight at the girl in the lavatory. She looked cold and miserable; standing in a corner, she wrapped her arms around her body and looked close to weeping. The police crew of the Zodiac had dropped on the launch's deck the waterlogged mattress the five escapers had turned into a makeshift raft by draping it over a ring of small inflated plastic cushions. This had been their magic carpet to a new life. The sergeant noted the men's ages: fifty, thirty-one, thirty and twenty; the girl was twenty-three.

Jones looked at his watch. 'Only one hour gone and we've bagged five already,' he said with satisfaction. 'Give them some coffee.'

At two thirty we picked up two more men and two women. For all their desperate paddling, a current had carried them almost up to the mother launch. They floated on a similar sort of raft to the first group, but, before encountering the current, they had made good progress, propelling themselves with home-made wooden paddles like Ping-Pong bats. Dripping and shivering on the launch's deck, their adventure over, one of them blurted out bitterly that three months of planning and concealment had been wasted. A search of the pockets of their blue peasants' clothes turned up a piece of paper with the address and telephone number of one man's relatives in Hong Kong – this would have been 'home' in his game of Grandmother's Footsteps – a small jar of Tiger Balm balsam (rubbed into the skin, it produces a warm glow), two or three boiled sweets and a tiny penknife. One of the men had long delicate hands; the other and the two women were evidently farmers. The men's cheeks were reddish and weather-worn, with wisps of moustache at the corners of their mouths. They joined the four prisoners in the shower, and the two women were ushered into the toilet. They glanced impassively at the single girl already there, but didn't speak to her, just as the newly arrived men had said nothing to their countrymen in the shower. They all seemed stunned by their failure.

A policeman said to me, 'Please be seated, sir,' and handed me a bowl of cold noodles he had ladled from a saucepan. Other crew members handed bowls and chop-sticks to the prisoners, but after gingerly tasting the noodles they shyly poured them back into the saucepan.

'They don't like noodle,' a policeman explained. 'They like rice. Maybe eat before they start.' These peasants were relatively plump. The women, I saw, were even smiling, showing a lot of teeth as they poured the noodles back. Later, they drank the hot coffee eagerly. They needed something to warm them. I took a swig from my flask of whisky.

Mark Jones said, 'Like to come with me in a Zodiac? Just to take a scout round the bay?'

The water was a little choppy by now, but we set off at speed towards a dark shape like a camel's back on the skyline. 'That's China,' Jones said, opening the throttle. He pointed at a cluster of distant lights high in the sky. 'That's Chinese army headquarters there.'

'Don't go too near,' I said, and he laughed.

We circled the bay far from the beacon. The mother launch disappeared in the darkness behind us and, ahead, other lights appeared: ships at anchor, fishing boats, houses on the China shore. Rubbery and light, the Zodiac bounced and slapped on the surface of the water, and our engine's roar was so loud that it seemed they must hear us in Canton – not that it mattered, because the Chinese knew and approved of these patrols; otherwise they would hardly have been effective. The Chinese had no objection to the repatriation of their escaping compatriots. Still, Jones said, a Royal Navy hovercraft had shot around a headland and collided with a Chinese gunboat, and the Chinese had drawn guns and threatened to shoot the British crew. Apologies had had to be made swiftly and at high level ashore before they returned the hovercraft, its crew unharmed. 'But that doesn't happen more than once in a blue moon, if then.'

As Jones was saying this, the Zodiac's engine died. 'Soon get it going again,' he said, wrenching at it. But it refused to start, no matter how hard he tugged at the starting line and blew down the fuelpipes. We bobbed helplessly on the cold water under the eyes and ears of the Chinese army – we were a mile or two from the coast, according to Jones, but it seemed much nearer than that – and the tide and wind, now quite strong from the east, were edging us closer. With his blond head still bent over the useless engine, Jones muttered, 'Ironic if we have to go ashore on the Chinese mainland and ask them, "Please, can we go back through your territory?" I'm not at all sure they'd do that. They don't mind us fooling about out here in the bay, but anyone landing . . .'

I thought, My journey ends in Canton, but I hadn't thought of completing the final stage overland and in chains.

Jones had the radio going, and we could hear his sergeant's voice, as remote as Mars. The other Zodiacs would have a tough time finding us – we made a very low profile in the choppy sea – unless we could give them a fairly accurate idea of our position. We were about five miles from the beacon, too far to show up on the radar screen.

'Turn your searchlight and swing it about. When I say "Stop," that will mean it's pointing dead at us,' Jones said into the radio, enunciating every word with the exaggerated care of an elocution teacher. Then he would revert to Cantonese.

It took time for the sergeant to respond to Jones's cries of 'Left' or 'Right'. 'No, no, forty degrees *right*; that's left. Your army right, for heaven's sake.' Finally, when we seemed far too near the shore of Kwangtung province of the People's Republic of China, the searchlight's beam pointed directly at us, and two Zodiacs raced down its line while Jones stood up flashing his torch.

There was more coffee and an extra nip of whisky on the launch's deck, and a considerable feeling of relief.

During the hour and a half we had been away the operation had continued, and the total of captured I.I.s had risen to twelve. The constables were satisfied with their night's work.

When a cold, pale sun came up, I saw the camel's back from which lights had glowed down in the night like suspicious eyes. Now Chinese army headquarters showed nothing but wireless masts and a few white buildings in a cockscomb of trees. The shore of Kwangtung looked impassive and disdainful.

Casting off from the beacon, we moved westwards towards the higher, denser hills of Hong Kong's New Territories still veiled in mist. A junk dipped by, and a group of high-sterned Chinese trawlers stood motionless in the shallow, deep-brown water of the bay, awnings over their decks, anchors dangling from their bows and single masts pointing to the grey sky.

I couldn't resist a last look through the skylight at the drooping figures in the shower. They stood or crouched in silence; two or three leaned together, propping each other up with arms on each other's shoulders, their eyes closed. Two of the more recent arrivals, young men, were naked except for thin cotton undershorts, and the arched muscles of their bare backs trembled from nerves or the cold.

From the moment the launch reached its pier, these I.I.s would move on to the smooth, impersonal conveyor belt of official routine. Shore-based police would take charge of them; they would be linked to each other by simple plastic slip-catch loops, be taken to a police documentation centre, eat a hot meal and then be allowed a rest.

Soon trucks would carry them to the Man Kam To bridge, the only road crossing-point to China. One by one the trucks would be driven across the bridge, and near a roadside clump of trees the men and women in them would be told to get out. Still linked by the plastic thongs on their wrists, they would clamber awkwardly over the tailboards of the waiting vehicles of the Chinese government; sitting in these, they would stare at the empty trucks driving away back to Hong Kong. Would they be thinking of their ordeal in the cold waters of the bay, of the still unrung telephone number of the relatives in Hong Kong, of the eldorados of America and Europe? And how many under the burden of their despair would already be plotting their next attempt?

The assistant commissioner of police in Hong Kong had spoken about the money the Chinese syndicates – and even the Chinese communist officials on the mainland – made out of smuggling I.I.s across to Macao and then to Hong Kong.

I travelled to Macao with Donald Wise on the motor vessel *Nam Shan*, which shuttled daily back and forth through the western islands from the Hong Kong ferry wharf. We sat in a row of comfortable, adjustable seats in a wide cabin full of Chinese families eagerly watching the flickering images on a television set in the wall. Their bundles and baskets were stacked around their feet, and children ran up and down the aisles.

The *Nam Shan* had a mah-jongg room, as well as a cabin where Chinese youths in cardigans played the one-armed bandits. Further forward, there was a light, glass-sided dining room where polite Chinese waiters in black bow ties dispensed fish chowder and shrimps with oyster sauce under tasselled Chinese lanterns. There was also a bar, and in it I found one of the ship's engineers sucking up a pint of Guinness through toothless gums. Chinese singing mewed from a radio.

As we passed through the crowded western anchorage, hovercraft swished by between the two white fans of their bow waves. Chinese tourist ships lay at anchor. The steep bow of the *Hupeh* under Stone cutters Island immediately caught my eye – she was easy to recognize and I waved to her. And then we were moving between islands with such a close resemblance to Scotland and Wales that I expected to see sheep grazing on their slopes.

Nearer Macao, trawlers and junks recalled what Mark Jones had told me, 'The syndicates run I.I.s in by junks, a very good business. Twenty knots to our nine or ten.'

'What if you catch a sampan full of I.I.s?'

'There are pretty stiff penalties: fines, confiscation of boats, a seven-year jail sentence.'

Fourteen hundred Hong Kong policemen, twelve hundred British troops, forty-seven vessels supported by two hovercrafts and a squadron of helicopters – a lot of adults could play this game of Grandmother's Footsteps. Still, over one hundred thousand I.I.s sneaked 'home' – 'home' being a ramshackle, overcrowded tenement in Kowloon. I watched a sampan bustling by and wondered if her blank sides concealed cowering figures among the bales of dried fish in her hold.

Though it is a beautiful old city, with its location on the lip of China adding a pleasant extra touch of glamour, a night and a day in Macao were enough for me. After seven months I was impatient for Canton, the end of the line.

Also, the night outing with the marine police and the sight of those bedraggled fugitives had soured my attitude toward pleasure domes like the casino of the Lisboa Hotel.

The Lisboa was a very grand pleasure dome indeed, like a wedding cake baked by a chef with a penchant for kitsch. All that held me there was the sight of old Chinese men and women thrusting piles of banknotes on to the gaming tables. The men scuttled about on bowed legs, coughing angrily at one another, while the women's button eyes gleamed as they followed the motions of the wheels, the dice and the croupiers' hands over the green baize.

On the edge of China it was strange to see notices saying, PARQUE DE DIVERSÃO and CAFÉ NOITE E DIA and to read on restaurant menus dishes like *Loja de Sopa de Pata*, which simply means duck soup. A bonus was the Casalinho, a cool white wine with a slightly metallic taste, that we drank on the terrace of the Bela Vista Hotel overlooking the sea. And in a restaurant it was pleasant when I pointed to a fish floating motionless and upside down in a tank to hear a little waitress explain, 'He rest.'

'But why upside down?'

'When rest, cannot move.'

Over the wine on the terrace and afterwards in Henri's restaurant on the corniche Donald and I talked about the recent past. Over Calvados we recalled the shambles of wartime Saigon, the black market, the grubby urchin thieves who infested every side street and doorway, the bar girls and whorehouses.

'Were you ever really frightened?' Donald asked.

'One night I was so scared that to think about it still makes me sweat with shame to this day.'

'Let's hear about it.'

It had been in the time of the 1972 North Vietnamese army offensive into South Vietnam. The South Vietnamese army divisions in the north were in a state of rout, and unit after unit had fled back down the road to Hué, the former imperial capital of Annam. There were no American troops to help restore the situation; Richard Nixon and Henry Kissinger had disengaged them.

I, too, fled south to Hué down the crowded highway. By then my love affair with the seedy city on the Perfume river was seven years old. I had made close friends with a poor Vietnamese family there, and stayed with them every year since 1965, sometimes several times a year, and had come to see the war through their eyes. Like all Vietnamese families, they had suffered terribly from the war, which by then had lasted thirty years for them. Every time I visited Hué they told me of yet another brother, cousin or nephew killed in action. Sometimes I had attended their weddings; sometimes I was godfather. Each time a death was reported, the strong mother of the family – I thought of her as Mother Courage – travelled through the war-ravaged countryside to collect the pieces of her relative from the battlefield and bring them back to Hué in a plastic bag for burial in the family plot, among the family spirits.

This time I reached Hué after dark and found a horrifying state of anarchy and violence. Armed deserters milled about the streets, their uniforms discarded, looting shops and abandoned houses. They had broken into the liquor stores; drunken soldiers roamed about firing wildly into the air, and sometimes down the streets as well. Their dancing demonic figures were lit by the leaping flames of the market, which had been set on fire.

My family's house was empty. I was stunned. It was the

first time they had ever deserted it – even in 1968, when it had been occupied by the Vietcong, they had stayed on – so I knew that something truly horrible was in the offing. As I stood outside their barred door, a terrible disquiet flooding through me, a tangle of hostile cycle-rickshaw (cyclo) drivers seized my arm, shouting obscenities and smelling of cheap liquor.

I crossed the Perfume river in a daze and found the only hotel. It was empty of guests, and the lobby floor was littered with broken glass. The surly young men in charge gave me a key, and one of them said, 'Tonight VC come to Hué. Maybe VC think you American.' He drew his finger across his throat and leered. I felt he would enjoy seeing me disembowelled in the lobby.

I sat up all night, unable to sleep. It seemed endless. Scattered shots crackled frequently across the river, and long stammering bursts of fire under the hotel walls shattered my nerves. Once a woman's scream arched into the night and was suddenly cut off. Explosions that seemed to creep nearer all the time rattled the windows and door; they sounded like heavy mortars. Now and again, people ran down the corridor outside my room, and once someone stopped to rain thunderous blows and kicks on my flimsy door. I sat in breathless silence until whoever it was went away; I had thought it was the Vietcong.

I had a bottle of Johnnie Walker Red Label with me. There was not even a plastic cup in the room and the tap water looked poisonous, so I drank the whisky from the bottle, sitting in the dark fully clothed, listening to the terrifying sounds outside. With time to waste, I tried to decide what to do if the Vietcong did come. In Hué in 1968 they had forced some German doctors into the jungle at gunpoint; their bones were found some time later. I examined the cupboard; it was an impossible hiding place, and the room had no concealing corners. The only spot where I could possibly hide myself was on the top of the cupboard, right back against the angle of the wall. I put a couple of pillows up there to represent myself, and then bent my knees to lower my head to the height of a Vietcong soldier's head; a Vietnamese would probably be about nine inches shorter than I. At that level my eyes couldn't see the pillows, so there was at least a possibility of concealing myself, although I had a feeling that my ankles and feet would be visible.

But all the time – and time seemed infinite – I thought of my isolation; of my Vietnamese family's instinctive wisdom in fleeing (later they told me they'd been convinced the city would fall that night); of the imminence of torture and death (my imagination suppressed any hope that the Vietcong would simply take me prisoner). Altogether it was not my finest hour.

When dawn broke, I swayed down to the lobby exhausted, unshaven and quite drunk. The Vietnamese youth at the reception desk winked and said, 'VC no come?'

'Maybe you VC,' I said. He grinned. 'Yeah, maybe.'

On the peaceful hotel terrace in Macao eight years later, Donald Wise said, 'Why be ashamed? I'd have been scared to death too.'

'Let's have a lot more of that Calvados,' I said.

The next morning we took the ferry back to Hong Kong, but I still had traces of my Macao hangover a day later when, in mist and rain, I took the hydrofoil – my last vessel – from the Tai Kok Tsui pier in Kowloon up the Pearl river to Canton.

★ ★ ★

Mist and rain. August to April: the contrast could hardly have been greater. Seven months before, I had bathed in the sun and warmth of the Mediterranean at Piraeus, the blue of the sea and sky and the white of whitecaps and white ships. The colours of the Greek flag, I had thought then; now I was immersed in an all-pervading greyness of sea, sky, island and mainland, the pearl greyness of the Pearl river delta.

I was the only non-Chinese on a hydrofoil manufactured, according to the metal plaque, by Hovermarine Transport, Southampton. We sat as if in a small theatre in ten rows, seven seats to a row, arranged two, three and two, with two aisles. From time to time the people nearest the windows rubbed them with their sleeves in a vain effort to de-mist them or clear them of the rain and spray that almost totally obscured our view of the river, passing ships and the shore. Occasionally I caught a glimpse of the pale yellow funnel, with its golden stars and stylized waves on a red band, of a Chinese freighter coming down from Canton (or Guangzhou, as it was written on the blue and white baggage label presented to me by kind Mr Phelim Lo of the China Travel Agency's branch in Hong Kong).

With not much to look at and a young man in the next seat who was little disposed to chat – after telling me that the giant pandas in the Canton zoo were 'very interest', he had lapsed into silence – I had little to occupy myself with but my thoughts. To ease the softly nagging ache in my temples, I ordered a can of Pabst beer from the steward and let my mind wander back.

It had been more difficult to travel by sea from Europe to China than I had imagined. I recalled the moments of despair in Jedda, Dubai and Colombo when I had almost convinced myself that I was going to be stopped once and for all. I remembered the malevolent agent's representative in Jedda, who had forced me to leave the *Patrick Vieljeux*, and the tourist official in Bombay who had hung up on me when I mentioned a permit for the Andaman Islands.

But when I was halfway through my second beer and my headache had faded, I remembered the compensating angels. Tom Abraham had plucked my Andaman permit out of a sea of red tape; Captain Bill Nelson, who indirectly had found me the launch *Al Raza*, Chris Pooley, John Swire's man in the Gulf, and the helpful Pakistani consul general, between them, had launched me towards Karachi from Dubai. Captain Choudhuri and the ebullient Bala, who had introduced me to their old shipmate Dennis Beale in Port Blair, had become my friends; so had Tony Blatch, who saw me off from Singapore in the little *Perak*, and William and Victor Chiongbian, who watched their mighty *Doña Virginia* bear me away from Cebu. From Sandakan Captain Amin had provided me with one of the best adventures of my life, and at Port Said Captain Visbecq had saved me from the humiliation of having to negotiate the Isthmus of Suez by desert road.

And there had been others . . .

Now, as I type this, Walid writes from Dubai; to his extreme anguish, the doctor he consulted after severe stomach pains has diagnosed an ulcer. The doctor has told him to stop working, and he may have to go home to Pakistan. If so, he thinks he will lose his job and his foothold in Dubai, and be unable to leave Pakistan ever again. His letter is a cry of anguish from the ranks of hopefuls straining toward the West.

Francis, the teacher at the government college in Port Blair, has written from the shadow of the Cellular Jail to say that he has just married a Protestant girl from Madhya Pradesh, and that in time he hopes his Catholic parents will come to accept her Protestantism. Metin has written a letter from the ancient barracks of Scutari complaining about the humiliation of his shaven head. And Mr Missier, that noble old man who put me on board the *Herman Mary* to Tuticorin, has sent me a five-hundred-gram packet of Ceylon's finger tea and an invitation in silver lettering embossed on a white folding card. It reads:

The Bells of St Lucia's Cathedral Will Chime for
PUNEETHA
Daughter of Mr. and Mrs. R. Missier, and
BERNARD
Son of Mrs. Ignatiusammal and Late Mr. J. Leo Fernando
On Monday, 15th September at 10.00 a.m.
We cordially solicit the presence of Mr. Gavin Young
to share their happiness and ours
at the above solemnization

I am very sorry I won't be there, but I intend to see Mr Missier again one day.

Hentry has used the services of a professional letter-writer – to judge from the florid style – to announce the death of his baby sister, and to inform me that he has changed schooners; he is now beating up and down the Malabar coast of India and across to Colombo, in a three-master. Hentry, his friends and relatives have a hard, precarious life, no doubt, but at least no politician promising universal salvation has yet appeared to lead them to the madness, blood and destruction to which my two Cambodian dancing dolls stand memorial.

Higher up the Pearl river the water grew choppier, and the hydrofoil advanced between denser wings of spray. As the twin shorelines converged, the shipping thickened: freighters, trawlers, and junks with brown autumnal sails that had the brittle beauty of dead leaves. At one point a Chinese police launch came alongside, and three young Chinese with red stars on their uniforms glanced in as we sat staring in front of us like people in a cinema where the film had broken down. The launch soon sheered away, its engine fading, and we moved on through the rain and cloud of our own spray.

Seven months of travel, irritation, anxiety and near despair had got me here. Now, after only a few miles more, by the time the silent young man on my right finished the cigarette he had just lit, I would have arrived in Canton.

I stepped ashore at Zhoutouju Pier in Canton carrying the old zip-bag that now bore dark oil stains at each corner, red smears of Borneo tanbark and a sticky label, turned up at its edges like a piece of stale bacon, that said 'Sealord Hotel, Cochin'. A nondescript Chinese official of the China Travel Agency shook my hand ('So happy') and, leading me to a car where a driver waited, asked me what

I wanted to see in the city. The museum? Certainly. A tour of the city? Very good. The giant pandas in the zoo? Unquestionably. The people's supermarket? Well, umm . . .

In the pouring rain, Mr Chong led me about, but left me to eat my midday meal alone, although I asked him to accompany me, in the dining room of the Tung Fang Hotel, where all the tourists stayed and where there was television and Western Muzak in all the bedrooms. We saw everything he had proposed and, perhaps as a consolation for the fact that the city was not looking its best in the rain, he even added an evening at a school for acrobats. Luckily, the pandas ignored the rain, and lay on their backs in the open sucking long bamboo canes like fat men playing the recorder. In the cut-rate supermarket I bought two minia- ture bottles of whisky for the driver and a red umbrella for a delighted Mr Chong, who said that red was his wife's favourite colour.

Mr Chong seldom drew breath; as a guide he was expert and indefatigable, but I fear he may have found me inatten- tive. I was conscious of a light-headed feeling of end-of- term. I wanted to see China and would return, I hoped. For the moment I couldn't stop my mind from wandering back to the last thirty weeks of travel.

I walked the glum, wet streets of Canton, ate alone in the hotel dining room and gazed at the rare vultures and the tigers in the zoo while half my mind loitered in the immediate past. Stared at in the museum by brown-skinned Cantonese, I couldn't help imagining them dripping and shivering on the deck of a British launch in Hong Kong's Deep Bay. Whatever I did, images of Asia whirled about in my brain.

I wasn't going to stay in Canton more than one night

now that I had made it 'home' there in my private game of Grandmother's Footsteps. Next morning Mr Chong drove me to the railway station, and from the platform I watched him hurry away to meet the next incoming hydrofoil from Hong Kong.

The train wriggled its way across the border of China and into the green hills of Hong Kong's New Territories. An hour later I saw, between an escarpment and Kowloon's high-rise towers, a silver crescent of sea. It recalled the gleam of water I had first glimpsed as a boy across the rooftops of Bude, and the graveyards of drowned sailors and the battered cliffs of that coast halfway around the world where the dream of this journey had been born.